Music and Cosmopolitanism

Alejandro L. Madrid, Series Editor
Walter Aaron Clark, Founding Series Editor

Nor-tec Rifa!:
Electronic Dance Music from Tijuana to the World
Alejandro L. Madrid

From Serra to Sancho:
Music and Pageantry in the California Missions
Craig H. Russell

Colonial Counterpoint:
Music in Early Modern Manila
D. R. M. Irving

Embodying Mexico:
Tourism, Nationalism, & Performance
Ruth Hellier-Tinoco

Silent Music:
Medieval Song and the Construction of History in Eighteenth-Century Spain
Susan Boynton

Whose Spain?:
Negotiating "Spanish Music" in Paris, 1908–1929
Samuel Llano

Federico Moreno Torroba:
A Musical Life in Three Acts
Walter Aaron Clark and William Craig Krause

Representing the Good Neighbor:
Music, Difference, and the Pan American Dream
Carol A. Hess

Agustín Lara:
A Cultural Biography
Andrew G. Wood

Danzón:
Circum-Caribbean Dialogues in Music and Dance
Alejandro L. Madrid and Robin D. Moore

Music and Youth Culture in Latin America:
Identity Construction Processes from New York to Buenos Aires
Pablo Vila

In Search of Julián Carrillo and Sonido 13
Alejandro L. Madrid

Tracing Tangueros:
Argentine Tango Instrumental Music
Kacey Link and Kristin Wendland

Playing in the Cathedral:
Music, Race, and Status in New Spain
Jesús A. Ramos-Kittrell

Entertaining Lisbon:
Music, Theater, and Modern Life in the Late 19th Century
Joao Silva

Music Criticism and Music Critics in Early Francoist Spain
Eva Moreda Rodríguez

Carmen and the Staging of Spain:
Recasting Bizet's Opera in the Belle Epoque
Michael Christoforidis Elizabeth Kertesz

Rites, Rights and Rhythms:
A Genealogy of Musical Meaning in Colombia's Black Pacific
Michael Birenbaum Quintero

Discordant Notes:
Marginality and Social Control in Madrid, 1850–1930
Samuel Llano

Sonidos Negros:
On the Blackness of Flamenco
K. Meira Goldberg

Opera in the Tropics:
Music and Theater in Early
Modern Brazil
Rogerio Budasz

Sound-Politics in São Paulo
Leonardo Cardoso

Bossa Mundo:
Brazilian Music in Transnational
Media Industries
K. E. Goldschmitt

After the Dance, the Drums Are Heavy:
Carnival, Politics and Musical
Engagement in Haiti
Rebecca Dirksen

The Invention of Latin American Music:
A Transnational History
Pablo Palomino

Latin Jazz:
The Other Jazz
Christopher Washburne

Panpipes and Ponchos:
Musical Folklorization and the Rise of the
Andean Conjunto Tradition in La Paz,
Bolivia
Fernando Rios

Elite Art Worlds:
Philanthropy, Latin Americanism, and
Avant-Garde Music
Eduardo Herrera

The Sweet Penance of Music:
Musical Life in Colonial Santiago
de Chile
Alejandro Vera

Música Típica:
Cumbia and the Rise of Musical
Nationalism in Panama
Sean Bellaviti

Text, Liturgy, and Music in the
Hispanic Rite:
The Vespertinus Genre
Raquel Rojo Carrillo

Africanness in Action:
Essentialism and Musical Imaginations
of Africa in Brazil
Juan Diego Diaz

Inventing the Recording:
Phonographs in Spain, 1877–1914
Eva Moreda Rodríguez

Inca Music Reimagined:
Indigenist Discourses in Latin American
Art Music, 1910–1930
Vera Wolkowicz

Coros y Danzas:
Folk Music and Spanish Nationalism in
the Early Franco Regime (1939–1953)
Daniel David Jordan

Silvestre Revueltas:
Sounds of a Political Passion
Roberto Kolb-Neuhaus

Cuban Music Counterpoints:
The Vanguardia Music in Global
Networks
Marysol Quevedo

Mario Lavista: Mirrors of Sounds
Ana R. Alonso-Minutti

Immaculate Sounds: The Musical
Lives of Nuns in New Spain
Cesar D. Favila

Indigenous Audibilities: Music, Heritage,
and Collections in the Americas
Amanda Minks

Music and Cosmopolitanism:
Rio de Janeiro at the Turn of
the 20th Century
Cristina Magaldi

Music and Cosmopolitanism

Rio de Janeiro at the Turn of the 20th Century

CRISTINA MAGALDI

OXFORD
UNIVERSITY PRESS

Oxford University Press is a department of the University of Oxford. It furthers
the University's objective of excellence in research, scholarship, and education
by publishing worldwide. Oxford is a registered trade mark of Oxford University
Press in the UK and certain other countries.

Published in the United States of America by Oxford University Press
198 Madison Avenue, New York, NY 10016, United States of America.

© Oxford University Press 2024

All rights reserved. No part of this publication may be reproduced, stored in
a retrieval system, or transmitted, in any form or by any means, without the
prior permission in writing of Oxford University Press, or as expressly permitted
by law, by license, or under terms agreed with the appropriate reproduction
rights organization. Inquiries concerning reproduction outside the scope of the
above should be sent to the Rights Department, Oxford University Press, at the
address above.

You must not circulate this work in any other form
and you must impose this same condition on any acquirer.

Library of Congress Cataloging-in-Publication Data
Names: Magaldi, Cristina, author.
Title: Music and cosmopolitanism : Rio de Janeiro at the turn
of the 20th century / Cristina Magaldi.
Description: [First.] | New York : Oxford University Press, 2024. |
Series: Currents in Latin American and Iberian music |
Includes bibliographical references and index.
Identifiers: LCCN 2023046743 | ISBN 9780199744770 (hardback) |
ISBN 9780197646083 (epub) | ISBN 9780197646090 (ebook)
Subjects: LCSH: Music—Social aspects—Brazil—Rio de Janeiro—History—19th century. |
Music—Social aspects—Brazil—Rio de Janeiro—History—20th century. |
Cosmopolitanism—Brazil—Rio de Janeiro.
Classification: LCC ML3917.B6 M35 2024 |
DDC 306.4/842098153—dc23/eng/20231006
LC record available at https://lccn.loc.gov/2023046743

DOI: 10.1093/oso/9780199744770.001.0001

Printed by Integrated Books International, United States of America

Nothing here is foreign, because everything is.
—Paulo Emílio Sales Gomes, *Cinema: Trajetória no subdesenvolvimento* (São Paulo: Paz e Terra, 2001 [1996]), 90

Contents

List of Illustrations	xi
Acknowledgments	xiii
A Note on Translations and Spellings	xv
Introduction	1
1. Cosmopolitanism and the City	21
The Possibilities of Cosmopolitanism	21
Urban Networks	34
A Connected *Fin-de-Siècle*	39
2. A City to Be Seen and to Be Heard	46
3. A Tale of Three Anthems	57
Music and Republicanism	57
Songful and Memorable	68
4. Race in the Universal and Eternal Tradition	76
Forging a Local Tradition	76
European-ness	81
The Race of Music	88
5. At the Cabaret	100
Mlle. Ywonna	100
The Voice of Decadence	111
6. Diversifying	121
Café Concerts	121
Music Halls	135
Singing and Dancing	147
7. Local Cosmopolitanisms	167
Dandy and Quaintrelle	167
Singing Flâneurism	178
8. The Widows	193
Many Travels	193
Multilingualism	201
Intermedialism	211
At the Circus	222

X CONTENTS

9. Cosmopolitan Traditions	233
An Unexplainable Tradition	233
A Profusion of Melodies	249
The Guaranis	262
10. Sounds of Urban Worlds	295
Composing and Performing Places	295
Cake-Walking	307
11. A World of Many Musics	320
One Thread in the World of Musics	320
The Concert Hall and the Music Hall	332
No Extra-Lives	338
Assembling Music	342
Conclusion: Arriving at the Future	352
Bibliography	357
Index	395

Illustrations

Figures

2.1.	Artur Azevedo.	46
2.2.	Rio de Janeiro, Avenida Central, 1906.	49
2.3.	Inside a Favela, Rio de Janeiro, 1906.	51
3.1.	Proclamation of the Republic. Rio de Janeiro, *Correio do Povo*, November 1889.	59
4.1.	José Maurício Nunes Garcia.	77
5.1.	Advertisement for Ywonnas' cabaret in Rio de Janeiro.	101
5.2.	Mlle Ywonna.	101
5.3.	Gonzaga Duque.	103
5.4.	Olavo Bilac.	105
5.5.	João do Rio.	107
5.6.	Aristide Bruant, poster by Toulouse Lautrec.	109
6.1.	Moulin Rouge.	136
6.2.	Maison Moderne.	137
6.3.	Carmencita.	143
6.4.	Pepa Ruiz.	152
6.5.	Cover of "O mungunzá" with photo of Pepa Ruiz.	154
6.6.	Photo of Pepa Delgado in a Bahiana outfit.	156
7.1.	Geraldo Magalhães.	168
7.2.	Nina Teixeira. O Malho, 1909.	175
7.3.	Eduardo das Neves.	179
8.1.	Companhia de Operetas e Opera-Cômica Italiana Ernesto Lahoz, *Viúva alegre*, act III.	198
8.2 a–c.	Female singers as Hanna: Kate Hansen (a), Gisela Morosini (b), Cremilda de Oliveira (c).	200
8.3.	"A sad Japanese widow who wanted to see the German Merry Widow."	203
8.4.	*The Merry Widow* at the Cinema Rio Branco.	216
8.5.	Circo Spinelli, presenting *A viúva alegre* (1910).	222

xii ILLUSTRATIONS

8.6.	"The Merry Widow at the circus ring."	225
8.7.	Lili Cardona.	227
8.8.	Benjamin de Oliveira and his various theatrical characters.	229
9.1.	"The old *realejo* performer who only plays "Miserere" from Il *trovatore*."	262
9.2.	Carlos Gomes (photo ca. 1886–1991).	263
9.3.	Cover page of the Italian translation of *O Guarany*.	268
9.4.	Benjamin de Oliveira and Cruzet as Peri and Ceci.	290
10.1.	Aurélio Cavalcanti.	296
11.1.	Alberto Nepomuceno.	342
C.1.	Theatro Municipal, Rio de Janeiro.	353

Musical Examples

3.1.	Francisco Manuel da Silva, Brazilian National Anthem.	60
3.2.	Claude Joseph Rouget de Lisle, "La Marseillaise."	62
3.3.	Leopoldo Miguez, Anthem to the Proclamation of the Republic.	65
4.1.	José Maurício Nunes Garcia, Requiem.	86
5.1.	"Berceuse bleue," Gabriel Montoya.	116
6.1.	"A casa branca da serra."	132
6.2.	"O Mugunzá".	159
7.1.	"Vem cá mulata."	172
7.2.	"Oh! Minas Gerais!"	191
8.1.	"The Merry Widow Waltz."	195
8.2a.	*The Merry Widow*, act II, "*Wie di Weiber*"	208
8.2b.	*The Merry Widow, act III, "Grisetten- Lied."* Franz Lehàr	209
9.1a.	"Sento una forza indomita"	276
9.1b.	"Qualunque via dischiuderti"	277
9.2.	Il Guarany, "Senza tetto, senza cuna."	279
9.3.	Il Guarany, act III, "O Dio degli aimoré."	280
10.1.	Aurélioa Cavalcanti, "Bregeira."	299
10.2.	Cavalcanti, "Muchacha."	305
10.3.	Cavalcanti, "Cake-Walk."	314
11.1a.	Nepomuceno, "Variations sur un thème original."	347
11.1b.	Nepomuceno, "Variations sur un theme original," op. 29, final variation (XI).	348

Acknowledgments

The research for this book was supported by a summer grant and a fellowship from the National Endowment of the Humanities. I was also awarded a summer research grant and a sabbatical leave from Towson University to work on the project. Drafts of some chapters were presented at several conferences and lectures over the years, and I thank students and scholars who contributed with pertinent questions and suggestions.

A new generation of scholars focusing on Rio de Janeiro, on urban cultures, and on the globalization of past cultural production have contributed in recent years to sophisticated historical and cultural analyses of the period. Their work has served as an inspiration for this book. Thus, I made a conscious effort to include detailed notes to acknowledge their innovative work, which is sometimes taken for granted. I hope it will show that scholarship is a product of a cosmopolitan experience and a practice of knowledge sharing.

Over the many years I worked on this project I profited from the support of many friends and scholars. At Towson University, I thank Diane Luchese who was always available to assist with administrative matters and with her devoted friendship. I owe my deepest gratitude to Walter Clark, a colleague and friend since our days as graduate students at UCLA, who has supported my work over the years. Last, but not least, this work was only made possible because I was supported by the love of two very special guys: my husband Keith and our son Alex. This book is dedicated to them.

A Note on Translations and Spellings

All the translations from Portuguese in this book are my own, unless otherwise noted. Translations from other languages are taken from published sources and are cited accordingly. To avoid extending the citation section considerably, I opted not to reproduce original texts but rather to cite the sources in which they appear. Portuguese terms or idiomatic language are not translated directly into the text but are offered as a translation in parenthesis. Because some of the primary sources in Portuguese use foreign words, including English, when translating these passages into English, I italicized such foreign words to capture the local flavor for linguistic variety. Issues of language variety in titles of works made it challenging to keep a unified strategy for their translation. This will become evident as the book develops, as more titles of works appear in many languages. A case in point is Chapter 8, on the operetta *Die Lustige Witwe*. Since the operetta appears in Rio de Janeiro in many languages, I chose to introduce the work in the language in which it was advertised in its premiere and then to continue to refer to the work in English as *The Merry Widow*. Throughout the book I maintained the original time-specific spelling for theaters' names as they were used in the sources I used as reference. Finally, I use the word *mulatto/mulatta* to refer to mixed-race individuals as they appeared in the sources and avoid the term "Afro-Brazilian," since it was not used in turn-of-the-century Rio de Janeiro. Instead, I use Black for *preto*, which was the Portuguese racial term used during the period.

Introduction

This book is about the role of music in fostering cosmopolitanism at the turn of the 20th century. This broad topic intertwines the overarching concept of cultural cosmopolitanism—of shared cultural experiences and practices operating beyond locality—with two subtopics: on the one hand, musical works, musical practices (spaces, technologies, exchanges), and music-making (composing, performing, listening) as stimuli for expressive, intellectual, sociopolitical, and ideological projects; on the other hand, music-making as a tool for expressing and shaping the fragmented sociocultural experiences of *fin-de-siècle* urban modernity. The final result is an exploration of relationships, of complex and multilayered processes of individual and communal sociopolitical and cultural connections and disconnections, furthered by music.

The core of the book is geographically and historically specific, however: Rio de Janeiro, the capital of Brazil at the turn of the 20th century. I explore the aftermath of the 1888 abolition of slavery and the first two decades of the newly established republican government—roughly from 1889 to 1910. These years were marked by extreme sociopolitical instability in Brazil, since they saw the end of the centuries-long institution of slavery and almost seven decades of monarchical rule, which in turn had followed centuries of Portuguese colonial control. Considering the rapid and pervasive changes that swept the country during the short period of two decades, the turn of the century was inevitably a time when national ideals and political agendas emerged with relentless force in the form of governmental institutions, political directives, and laws. As a result, my explorations of music-making in the country's capital during this period led me unequivocally into issues of nation-building, which are incidentally embedded in the many stories I tell here. But my goal is not specifically to explore or critique music's role in such a process, nor to support claims that the turn of the century was a starting point in a teleological account of Brazilian cultural nationalism and exceptionalism through racial, cultural, and musical hybridity. The main thread of this study is not a nation, but a city. With a fast-growing, transient, and socially and racially heterogeneous population, Rio de Janeiro was also at a historical crossroads. As the capital of the country and the seat of the new regime, government actions were felt firsthand in the city and were often showcased in public displays meant to gather people's support, but which also fueled fervent opposition. Adding to a new set of sociopolitical dynamics, an urban

Music and Cosmopolitanism. Cristina Magaldi, Oxford University Press. © Oxford University Press 2024.
DOI: 10.1093/oso/9780199744770.003.0001

2 INTRODUCTION

metamorphosis in terms of architecture and overall landscape meant to "modernize" the city further changed daily social interactions. Of particular interest to this study are the musics performed in new venues that sprawled through the city center and its surroundings, and which added considerably to Rio de Janeiro's physical, social, and cultural transformations. These performing venues opened new spaces for artists, musicians, and audiences of many ilks who engaged with a variety of musics and performance practices to express, problematize, and ultimately help shape modernity in the *fin-de-siècle* city.

With one of the continent's largest ports, Rio de Janeiro was also a strong link in a web of external commercial and cultural connections fostered by technological advances and by globalizing processes led by European imperialism and rampant capitalism. While internal politics molded the city from within, viewed as a link in a web of external connections the city's physical and sociocultural fabric betrayed its many commonalities with other *fin-de-siècle* cities. Accordingly, Rio de Janeiro's residents shared with residents in many contemporary cities a sense of world connection and disconnection characteristic of their times: in the city they experienced a gamut of unsettling feelings caused by worldwide sociopolitical changes and uncertainties; in the city they were in close contact with migrating people of many backgrounds, provenances, social standing, race, and gender, a coexistence that generated a myriad of anxieties, while also fostering new sociocultural and political relations; in the city they confronted the compression of time and space brought about by new technology and media, and reveled in the new fashions and trends circulating among geographically unbounded crowds.[1] In fact, the more I delved into Rio de Janeiro's musical practices, the more it became clear to me that some of the stories I tell in the following chapters could perfectly well apply to Lisbon, Madrid, Florence, Rome, New York, London, Vienna, Paris, Mexico City, Havana, Buenos Aires, and many other contemporary cities. That realization brought into focus the fact that, although the historical period studied here has been scrutinized by scholars in various fields, and the cities mentioned above have each been studied in their individualized contexts, there is still much to explore in music scholarship in terms of the sociocultural interrelatedness provided by music and musicmaking. To understand music and performance as part of a larger system of human connections and disconnections that are always in motion, I offer a story of musical Rio de Janeiro that was built as much as, or perhaps more so, from the outside in than from within its sociohistorical and cultural contexts. Here, Rio de Janeiro is a capital city in republican Brazil, but also a city in the Americas, and a

---

[1] These aspects are explored by Stephen Kern in *The Culture of Time and Space: 1880–1918* (Cambridge, MA: Harvard University Press, 2nd ed. with new preface, 2003 [1983]); also David Harvey, *The Condition of Postmodernity: An Inquire into the Origins of Cultural Change* (Cambridge, MA: Blackwell, 1989).

INTRODUCTION 3

city deeply connected to Europe and to Africa by history, politics, and trade (including slavery), and to many other places where European imperialism and unbounded capitalism left their marks. Like other cities throughout the long 19th century, Rio de Janeiro grew to become one place containing many worlds: its streets were a Babylon, in the words of chronicler João do Rio, a referent that many before him had used to describe other growing cities.[2]

Regenia Gagnier has observed, "Historians of forests cannot do without historians of trees, but the reverse is also true. The unit of analysis is the functional relationship of part to whole, which is always changing and must always be specified."[3] Historians of forests deal with large compounding data and generalizing interpretations that sometimes can generate incomplete or misleading pictures.[4] But they also provide valuable multilayered explanations and interpretations, which can uncover historical connections or missing links that are crucial to the understanding of both localized contexts and to the building of a larger picture of cultural relationships. Grappling with large data as tools for historical analysis, scholars have approached them as networks that sometimes can be summarized in graphs and computational data analysis. When these data are applied to cultural history, they offer what Franco Moretti calls a "distant reading" of cultural texts, a reading that seeks to explain large sociopolitical and cultural-geographical patterns of movement by considering the "whole system of variables at play."[5] Some of Moretti's distant reading suggestions are intertwined in chapters of this book, but not as a framework or model to neatly align distant "readings" with distant "listenings," or to provide a definite sociopolitical and historical large system for a specific musical genre, as Moretti does with the 19th-century European novel. In fact, I admit at the start that I cannot offer statistically proven arguments based on select historical sources, nor do I believe it is viable to strictly correlate literary texts with the ephemeral and evanescent nature of music and performance through the stories I tell here. To avoid diluting the focus of my explorations amid a large array of relationships, I use case studies of musicians, works, performance practices, audience interaction, and new technologies to offer but a glimpse into a complex set of alliances, affinities, and struggles that helped characterize the sounding turn-of-the-century city. Nonetheless, the following chapters should point to the possibilities that a mix of

[2] João do Rio, *A alma encantadora das ruas* (Rio de Janeiro: Secretaria Municipal de Cultura, 1995 [1908]), 10; for London in the first half of the 19th century, see James Davis, "A Musical Souvenir: London in 1829" PhD dissertation, Cambridge University, 2005, especially the chapter "A Life of Babylon," 1–16.

[3] Regenia Gagnier, *Individualism, Decadence, and Globalization: On the Relationship of Part to Whole, 1859–1920* (New York: Palgrave Macmillan, 2010), 163–164.

[4] For a critical analysis of academic studies attending to large-scale processes in ahistorical and generalizing ways, see Fredrick Cooper, "What Is the Concept of Globalization Good for? An African Historian's Perspective," *African Affairs* 100, no. 399 (April 2001): 189–213.

[5] Franco Moretti, *Distant Reading* (London: Verso Books, 2013, Kindle).

4   INTRODUCTION

close and distant readings, or listenings, can help build a larger picture, or sound, for historical, cultural, and musical analysis, one that can place music and music-making at center stage, literally and metaphorically, during a period of extreme sociopolitical, economic, and cultural transformations.

The book is therefore not intended as a comprehensive or a linear history of music in Rio de Janeiro, and one should not expect to find in the following chapters discussions of all musicians and musical works that are now part of a musical canon in Brazil. My exploration is selective, even if it covers an array of different musics, performance practices, and varied spaces of music-making: from the concert hall to the theater and the music hall, from the movies and the circus to the streets. The social-racial-gender contexts, repertories, and practices of these many urban spaces have often been studied separately, and as such they have generated parallel and sometimes contradictory discourses anchored in different scholarly paradigms and methodologies.[6] In this book, I discuss them together as moving components within the varied and dynamic sociocultural contexts of the turn-of-the-century cosmopolitan city. The result is an account that may appear jumbled within its own heterogeneity, but one that I believe is necessary to address the complexity of the musical city. The select stories are also only loosely chronologically organized, going from the establishment of music institutions supporting the new republican government late in 1889 and the multiplication of private musical venues in the city, to roughly the end of first decade of the new century with the arrival of Franz Lehár's operetta *The Merry Widow*, the proliferation of movie theaters, and the inauguration of the Theatro Municipal in 1909. Examined together, the chapters should provide an overall sense of the city's sociocultural and historical changes across two decades.

Yet such a chronology is but a tool for the organization of miscellaneous case studies and should not be read as a linear historical narrative. In fact, sociohistorical change is less straightforward in the modern city than one would expect, especially in a period of striking local and world transformations. The "modern" in the city's modernity was lived and experienced through nonlinear, discontinuous, and fragmentary worlds, a characteristic that indeed defined Rio de Janeiro as well as Buenos Aires, Mexico City, Madrid, Paris, Lisbon, and many other cities.[7] Thus, social determinism and teleological accounts did not find in the city a clear-cut context to support their narratives. Instead, an endless flow of

---

[6] For a discussion on this topic, see Tim Carter, "The Sound of Silence: Models for an Urban Musicology," *Urban History* 29, no. 1 (May 2002): 8–18.

[7] David Frisby, *Cityscapes of Modernity: Critical Explorations* (London: Blackwell, 2001), 2. For a study of Buenos Aires at the beginning of the 20th century, see Adriana Bergero, *Intersecting Tango: Cultural Geographies of Buenos Aires*, trans. Richard Young (Pittsburgh, PA: University of Pittsburgh Press, 2008).

INTRODUCTION 5

passing fashions from a range of provenances connected "old" and "new" musics, which were somewhat blurred categories and sometimes distinguished, or disguised, by date of composition, frequency of presentation, or by idiosyncratic performances, rather than by specific musical characteristics. Several decades-old formulaic melodic and harmonic musical structures coexisted peacefully with varied harmonic experimentations, which were in reality also far from new; timbre explorations allowed by instrument technological developments helped music reach larger crowds, while also opening the path for a variety of ensemble combinations that were able to entice people to listen in various spaces and in new ways. Persistent efforts to make sounds visible, as suggestive of visual objects, people, nature, or feelings—through the overuse of specific musical techniques, timbres, performance gimmicks, and other tools—followed the period's growing penchant for imagery; and while new sound technologies led to experiments in musical expressions and ways of listening, and the music printing business solidified many trends, they did not lead to a divorce or a move away from oral and aural traditions, as live performances coexisted with medialized and virtual musical cultures. In a state of coexistence, the old and the new—still flexible and welcoming to endless reconfigurations—fostered a multitude of creative alternatives, rather than solutions, to established modes of music production and performance. It is within this transition that one can shed light on the many connections and relationships made possible by music and music-making and to start understanding their relevance to the complex and dynamic cultural processes that made (and makes) the modern city. Turn-of-the-century Rio de Janeiro exuded a modernity-in-the-making that could be defined in the Baudelairian sense as "the transitory, the fleeting, and the contingent" eventually meeting, and living with, its matching other half, "the eternal and [potentially] immovable."[8]

In addition, social disparities that segregated people in the city through housing, clothes, books, objects, art, and political power, did not appear to transfer easily to the consumption of music or musical tastes in general. As John Dizikes pointed out a while ago regarding New York, "Music, being intangible, was not easy to assimilate to materialist plutocratic culture."[9] Anselm Gehard also warned that the vagueness that terms like "bourgeoisification" in 19th-century Paris, associated with economic and social history, do not help to explain musical experiences and tastes of everyday life in the city,[10] while Jann

---

[8] Charles Baudelaire, "Modernity," in his *The Painter of Modern Life and Other Essays* (London: Phaidon Press, 1995 [1863]).

[9] John Dizikes, *Opera in America: A Cultural History* (New Haven, CT: Yale University Press, 1993), 290.

[10] Anselm Gerhard, *The Urbanization of Opera*, trans. Mary Whittall (Chicago: University of Chicago Press, 1998), 4–5.

6 INTRODUCTION

Pasler offered a range of data in the marketing of music in French magazines and newspapers showing many intersections of musical taste and repertory among different social classes.[11] In Rio de Janeiro, the stories of musicians, listeners, and the circulation of musical works also show that the porosity of the city's musical borders confronted its many social and racially segregated physical borders.

Each chapter in the book is organized around people, works, practices, and performance spaces, and each serves as a focal point from which I investigate political, aesthetic, sociocultural, race, and gender relationships that defined the period and shaped the city. In addition, several chapters offer insights on the processes of formation of urban traditions and of musical canons more generally. Altogether, the select stories explore how composers, performers, and audiences listened and performed *in* a thriving, growing city, as well as how they listened and performed *the* modern city. I bring into the discussions musicians and works that are now part of the local musical canon, as well as some that are often used as highlights in the general historiography of music in Western European cities. But I move beyond monolithic canonic positions to explore them alongside musicians, works, and performance practices that have for the most part been left outside historical narratives of music-making in Rio de Janeiro, and indeed of many other cities. There are discernible reasons why some musicians and works studied here are often sidelined in scholarship, in addition to the obvious impossibility of covering everybody and everything: first, because some artists and works explored in the following chapters are not originally from the city or the country and thus are considered "foreigners," they are usually not understood as part of the local culture and by extension not worthy of study. Second, some musical works lack local specificity and are thus not conducive to discussions of nation-building, nor are they effective in arguments supporting local agency against European hegemony. Third, some works and performances discussed do not support music analyses and value-led interpretations that rest on originality, authenticity, or aesthetic authority that form the core of music historical studies. Yet my final goal is not to merely document the lives of obscure protagonists, or rescue forgotten works to include them in the canon and inflate canonic narratives. Rather, the book aims to offer a critical understanding of how musical works, musicians, ideas about music, and musical practices connected the lives of large numbers of people in the turn-of-the-20th-century city; how musical works were brought to life or revived in different places; and how their sonic and musical contexts served to articulate and shape a myriad of

---

[11] Jann Pasler, "Musical Scores in French Magazines and Newspapers," in *The Idea of Art Music in a Commercial World, 1800–1930*, ed. Christina Bashford and Roberta Montemorra Marvin (Suffolk, UK: Boydell & Brewer, 2016), 297–325.

INTRODUCTION 7

sociopolitical positions, from the most individualist artistic experimentations to the expressions and aspirations of many.

The story of music-making in turn-of-the-century Rio de Janeiro is told here through snippets of the lives of businesspeople, composers, performers, and audiences (including music critics) who played roles in fostering the cultural connections that made up the turn-of-the-century city. Among the individuals who became a part of the cosmopolitan city narrated from within, I spotlight: the singer, actor, music director, and entrepreneur Mlle. Ywonna (Chapters 5 and 6); the educators, directors, and composers José Maurício Nunes Garcia (Chapter 4), Leopoldo Miguez, and Alberto Nepomuceno (Chapter 11); the businessmen, writers, composers, actors, and singers Geraldo Magalhães, Eduardo das Neves (Chapter 7), and Benjamin de Oliveira (Chapters 8 and 9); the composers Carlos Gomes (Chapter 9) and Aurélio Cavalcanti (Chapter 10). Their trajectories are intertwined with 19th-century canonic European composers such as Mozart (Chapter 4), Wagner (Chapter 11), and Verdi (Chapter 9), and with more contemporary composers, artists, and performers, such as Yvette Gilbert and Aristide Bruant (Chapter 5), Plaquette, Lecquoc, Varney, and Pepa Ruiz (Chapter 6), Franz Lehár, Ismênia Matheus, Giselda Morosini, Cremilda de Oliveira, and Lili Cardona (Chapter 8), among others. Together, these composers, performers, and businesspeople and their works provide a fledgling access into a larger set of musical practices and experiences that are connected in and through the city during a period of unprecedented global cultural exchanges. Most importantly, their stories are not merely sites where the lives, views, and music of White men converge in the cosmopolitan city, but they bring to the fore the subjectivities of women and non-White performers, composers, and audiences who were major agents in a complex, emergent globalizing world of sociocultural connections and disconnections. Their stories reveal that a large number of individuals with varied backgrounds became full participants in the building of Rio de Janeiro as a cosmopolitan city, that they did not do so uncritically,[12] and that they performed in the city and shaped the modern city in conjunction with musicians and audiences from a number of other contemporary cities both near and far. At the same time, their individual stories make it blatant that the very premise of "shared" experiences and practices needs to be decoupled and questioned, for while various individuals shared a musical practice, not everyone had the same experience with it, or from it. The sociopolitical contexts in which music traveled as cities grew into metropolises were permeable, but not harmoniously so. At the same time, while to narrate "an experience" other than our own is a daunting

---

[12] In this regard, see José Manuel Izquierdo König's argument about Latin American composers' cosmopolitanism early in the 19th century in "The Cosmopolitan Muse: Searching for a Musical Style in Early Nineteenth-Century Latin America," in *Music History and Cosmopolitanism*, ed. Anastasia Belina, Kaarina Kilpiö, and Derek Scott (New York: Routledge, 2019, Kindle), 58–72.

8   INTRODUCTION

endeavor, considerations about a "musical experience" and its association with the "experiences of everyday life" cannot be dismissed at the outset.[13] From a historical viewpoint, patterns of behaviors, tastes, and engagements with various musics can be observed and interpreted, compared and contrasted, and together they can provide a picture, or a soundscape, of cultural spaces in a specific point in time.

To tell the story of musicians, works, and audiences in turn-of-the-century Rio de Janeiro, I use as documental support archival materials, newspapers and periodicals, scores, recordings, as well as a vast array of current studies. And since the process of gathering documents and interpreting sources is selective and individual, the book has undoubtedly many vestiges of my own historical and cultural paths and individual positions. But I also had the assistance of turn-of-the-20th-century writers, poets, and critics who are here both informants and protagonists. Their "flanueristic" approach to the city involves a critical stance, while it reveals their own sociopolitical beliefs, racial profiles, and gender affiliations. Olavo Bilac (1865–1918), Luis Edmundo (1878–1961), João do Rio (pseudonym of Paulo Barreto) (1881–1921), Lima Barreto (1881–1922), Gonzaga Duque (1863–1911), and Artur Azevedo (1855–1908) are among several such individuals who assisted me in telling the story of musical Rio de Janeiro as a cosmopolitan city. They published profusely in contemporary newspapers and magazines, and wrote books and memoirs of their lives in the city. Their styles are individualistic, and each one offers varying and sometimes contradictory views of Rio de Janeiro and its sociocultural contexts. They serve as examples of a local *intelligentsia*, an undeniable elitist term used to refer to a few intellectuals and artists who offered a doubtless privileged take on a city with a preponderantly illiterate population. Yet the word "intellectual," used here to denote this small group, is a protean term, for these protagonists and informants were not all part of a social elite, only a few had political power, and not all of their works enjoyed some measure of cultural capital. In fact, some were inveterate bohemians who at some point in their lives had to struggle day-to-day to make a living, and indeed to survive; some were ignored during their lifetime or forgotten soon after their deaths. And notwithstanding the fact that these individuals are all male, their race, gender identification, and social backgrounds are varied, and their views and experiences of the city were multifaceted. João do Rio and Luis Barreto

---

[13] For considerations about music and experience, including the musical work, composer, critic, performers, and listeners, see Ruth Finnegan, "Music, Experience, and the Anthropology of Emotion," in *The Cultural Study of Music: A Critical Introduction*, ed. Martin Clayton et al. (London: Taylor & Francis Group, 2011), 352–353; see also David Hesmondhalgh, "Towards a Political Aesthetics of Music," in *The Cultural Study of Music: A Critical Introduction*, ed. Martin Clayton et al. (London: Taylor & Francis Group, 2011), 364–374. For considerations of consumer culture and the power of culture in everyday life, see Michael de Certeau, *The Practice of Everyday Life*, trans. Steven Randall (Berkley and Los Angeles: California University Press, 1984).

were both mulattos writing in and about a city where racial segregation was their living reality. João do Rio was a homosexual whose many intellectual and literary connections beyond the city betray his role of a nonchalant male *flâneur* who captured the city's most fleeting moments with finessed skill but also with complete detachment. Lima Barreto, a veteran bohemian who struggled with alcoholism throughout his life, narrated the city without subterfuges, offering realistic and critical views of its social and racial disparities, and unapologetically exposing the new republican government's many failures. Bilac, a journalist and poet, provided conflicting views of the city and its politicians, but managed to navigate swiftly the city's sociopolitical contexts and reach his career goals and upward social mobility by siding with, and eventually becoming, the status quo. The symbolist Gonzaga Duque provided a mostly top-down perspective of the city's *fin-de-siècle* complexity while, as a bohemian, he took apart the local bourgeoisie which he thought to be the root of the city's many problems, even if he was a typical bourgeois himself. The playwright Artur Azevedo's interest in all things related to the theater made him a useful insider to the city's artistic and musical milieu. At the same time, his many takes on the city's complex culture and social milieu are contradictory and often conflict with his own artistic production, as he ultimately became one of the most powerful intellectuals and artists in the city. These writers provided many narratives attempting to explain and codify the city's daily experiences; they became social actors in their own right, reflecting on commonplace events and on the "cultures in constant movement" that made up their city.[14] All in all, the stories and viewpoints of these many writers add to the stories of composers, performers, audiences, and businesspeople to provide both individual and communal takes on a multitude of cultural and musical connections and disconnections that allowed for a cosmopolitan modern city to be sounded, shaped, contested, and revealed.

A World of Terms

The concept of cosmopolitanism, revived and widely studied in the social sciences, seems to me not yet fully explored in music scholarship. That was the case over a decade ago when I started this study, and I believe it is still the case today as I prepare to send the manuscript to the publisher. As I detail in Chapter 1, rather than a normative term or a utopian ideal with elitist undertones, cosmopolitanism is used here to refer to an experience and a practice that emerged both as a symptom of and as a response to a connected and complex turn-of-the-century urban world; an experience and a practice that can be observed, sounded, and

---

[14] For a similar examination of Buenos Aires, see Bergero, *Intersecting Tango*, 89.

10 INTRODUCTION

heard through real-life stories and musical practices and that accommodates multiple and fluid expressions of belonging and detachment beyond the local. Thus, the use of the concept of cosmopolitanism for cultural and musical critique of a turn-of-the 20th-century Latin American city should not suggest a process in which musics and performances become hegemonic traveling paradigms, either by erasing difference or by highlighting idiosyncrasies, but rather it should point to how various musics and performance practices become tools for the exploration, reflection, and critique of connections and disconnections of an early globalizing moment.

Historians have long been toying with the narration of a "global history,"[15] while scholars in literary studies have explored the possibilities of a "world literature" in an attempt to grasp the implications for literary creation of a boundless world. Music scholarship followed with efforts to provide a "global music history."[16] But these attempts, as fitting as they are, have not yet fully invested in moving past the organizing logic and reification of nation-states and national subjects as objects of inquiry.[17] Whether or not it is possible to think beyond or through the nation remains a controversial topic among historians, but there seems to be a consensus that historical accounts of nation formation solely from within are no longer sustainable vis-à-vis recent scholarship. While the main goal of the new Brazilian government was to construct the nation according to new republican political ideals, Antoinette Burton reminds us that focusing on the nation by itself, in isolation, cannot account for the complex cultural connections that emerged during the period as results of various global processes, such as trade, diasporas, technological advances, and, of particular interest for this book, music distribution, performances, and audiences' engagements with a shared aural world. Burton also notes that each of these processes have their own structure, contradictions, and historicity, as people claimed their entitlement to participate in and to enact various ways of belonging to wider, alternative, and overlapping worldly contexts.[18]

---

[15] The literature on global history is long, rich, and challenging, and the topic has inspired numerous congresses for several decades, conspicuously in European cities. For a brief summary and a localized perspective, see Frederik Schulze and Georg Fischer, "Brazilian History as Global History," *Bulletin of Latin American Research* 38, no. 4 (2019): 408–422. For an extended discussion on methodology and historiography, see Matthias Middell and Katja Naumann, "The Writing of World History in Europe from the Middle of the Nineteenth Century to the Present: Conceptual Renewal and Challenge to National Histories," in *Transnational Challenges to National History Writing*, ed. Matthias Midddell and Lluis Roura (New York and London: Palgrave Macmillan, 2013), 54–139.

[16] See, for instance, the many articles compiled in Reinhard Strohm, *Studies on a Global History of Music: A Balzan Musicology Project* (New York: Routledge, 2018).

[17] Antoinette Burton, *After the Imperial Turn: Thinking with and through the Nation* (Durham, NC: Duke University Press, 2003, Kindle), 105–110.

[18] Burton, *After the Imperial Turn*, 105–106. For an excellent discussion of 20th-century historiographies conforming to national methodologies, see Matthias Middel and Lluís Roura, "The Various Forms of Transcending the Horizon of National History Writing," in *Transnational Chalenges*

INTRODUCTION 11

Exploring cosmopolitanism as a musical practice and experience cannot assist in building a "global music history," but it can offer parallel approaches or alternatives to it. Globalization enables larger sociopolitical, economic, and cultural processes, and cosmopolitanism is but one of its many outcomes: it is a fragment in the complex and multidimensional history of globalization.[19] Of course, while globalization is an observable process, "the global" is but a convenient imaginary construct within that process. In turn, as an experience and a practice, cosmopolitanism is located in time and space, even if one of its symptoms is the contemplation of and engagement with a world of possibilities beyond locality, including the conceiving of universals.[20] Moreover, in the context of a cosmopolitan cultural sphere, the boundaries of locality and the unboundedness of the imaginary global, or the utopian universal, are not stationary ideas, nor are they always antagonistic, but they morph into one another in many movements, opening and closing spaces for negotiations, engagements, and disengagements.

"Cosmopolitanism" is preferred here over the term "transnational," which has been in use for some time in scholarly literature also to denote a process resultant from globalizing forces. To be sure, several of the musical and performative connections that I explore in the chapters to follow are indeed parts of a process of transnational and transatlantic flows.[21] But while investigations on the transnational flux of people and things have in their premises the porosity

to National History Writing, ed. Matthias Middel and Lluís Roura (New York and London: Palgrave Macmillan, 2013), 1–35.

[19] Anna Tsing, Friction (Princeton, NJ: University Press, Kindle), 270–271. For a broad view of the many issues surrounding culture and globalization, see Paul Hopper, Understanding Cultural Globalization (Cambridge, UK: Polity, 2007). For a study of the complex cultural globalization processes in the 19th century, see the international cooperation project bringing together researchers from 23 research institutions and four countries (England, France, Portugal, and Brazil) at São Paulo School of Advanced Studies in Globalization of Culture in the Nineteenth Century, https://espca.fap esp.br/school/sao_paulo_school_of_advanced_studies_on_the_globalization_of_culture_in_the_nineteenth_century/42/

[20] Tsing notes the importance of considering universals for the understanding of processes of global connections; see Friction, 6–11. For a consideration of universals in music studies, see Olivia Bloechl, Melanie Lowe, and Jeffrey Kallberg, Rethinking Difference in Music Scholarship (Cambridge, UK: Cambridge University Press, 2015, Kindle), 4.

[21] For the studies on transnational history and globalization used in this book, see Pierre-Yves Saunier, Transnational History (New York and London: Palgrave Macmillan, 2013); Akira Iriye, Global and Transnational History: The Past, Present, and Future (New York and London: Palgrave Macmillan, 2013); and Axel Körner, "From Transnational History to Transnational Opera: Questioning National Categories of Analysis," University College, London, online publication, https://www.ucl.ac.uk/cen tre-transnational-history/sites/centre-transnational-history/files/from_transnational_history_to_transnational_opera_english_version.pdf>; Michael Mann, "Globalization, Macro-Regions and Nation-States," in Transnationale Geschichte: Themen, Tendenzen und Theorien, ed. Gunilla Budde, Sebastian Conrad, and Oliver Janz (Göttingen, Germany: Vanden-hoeck & Ruprecht, 2006), 28. See also Michael Geyer, "Review of Transnationale Geschichte. Themen, Tendenzen und Theorien, ed. Gunilla Budde, Sebastian Conrad, and Oliver Janz, (Göttingen, Germany: Vanden-hoeck & Ruprecht, 2006)," H-soz-kult (October 10, 2006), online publication www.hsozkult.de/publicatio nreview/id/reb-9016.

12 INTRODUCTION

of borders, they also presuppose the sociopolitical foundation of a nation as homogeneous, and with this come assumptions of authority of national origin and value-laden cultural ownership validated by citizenship. Transnational relations are usually explored within a passive or agent-less "one-way traffic,"[22] from either "inside-out" or "outside-in" perspectives that ultimately are limited by the borders of the nation. As an experience and a practice, cosmopolitanism underscores connections that are not solely the result of national impulses and that cannot always be revealed empirically. It highlights a complex set of unstable sociocultural interconnections and relationships not always supportive of the nation, while it points to the ones that emerge exactly when the idea of the nation loses its centrality. Most importantly, music and music-making become crucial in the process of forming cosmopolitan connections, for the atemporal, subjective, non-fixable aurality of music allows for the emergence of various collectivities that operate beyond the local and the nation in multiple flows, revealing the complex entanglements that the circulation of culture entails.

Terms like "trans-culturation" and "cross-culturation," or the process of "cultural transfer,"[23] have proved helpful in that they account for the cultural complexity generated by the circulation of theatrical and musical productions and performances beyond geographical borders. Still, they do not necessarily generate the cosmopolitan experiences and practices that I explore in the following chapters, for they underline connections between and among cultures, each understood as self-contained, unique, locally specific, and often tied to a nation, rather than experiences and practices that are shared in time and space regardless of provenance. Terms like hybridity and acculturation, which have been part of a long-standing narrative addressing the political, cultural, and racial negotiations in Latin America, are also sidelined here, for they bring to fore an exceptionalist local identity and suggest that a cultural experience or product resulting from a mix would eventually become "an Other" culture.[24] Even when the hybrid is evoked as a creative "alternative space," as Brigid Cohen suggests,

---

[22] For a critique of the one-way flow of transatlantic studies, see Benita Sampedro Vizcaya, "Engaging the Atlantic: New Routes, New Responsibilities," *Bulletin of Hispanic Studies* 89, no. 8 (December 2012): 906.

[23] For an overview of studies on cultural transfer, see Michel Espagne, "Comparison and Transfer: A Question of Method," in *Transnational Challenges to National History Writing*, ed. Matthias Midddell and Lluis Roura (New York and London: Palgrave Macmillan, 2013), 54–139; for cultural transfer in music, see Annegret Fauser and Mark Everist, "Introduction,: in *Music, Theater and Cultural Transfer: Paris, 1830–1914*, ed. Mark Everist and Annegret Fauser (Chicago: Chicago University Press, 2009), 1–8.

[24] Fernando Ortiz's 1930s term "transculturation" and the idea of hybridity as an intellectual and political tool for cultural interpretations in Latin America have been particularly celebrated, mostly as a result of uncritical readings of Nestor Garcia Canclini's *Culturas híbridas: Estrategias para entrar y salir de la modernidad* (México: Grijalbo, 1990); for a critique of these terms, see Alberto Moreiras, "Hybridity and Double Consciousness," in his *The Exhaustion of Difference: The Politics of Latin American Cultural Studies* (Durham, NC: Duke University Press, 2001), 199–267.

these approaches still shun reflections on the existence of "shared spaces" of collective creativity and political force, ones in which fluid and critical cosmopolitan experiences and practices can take place.[25]

The term "cosmopolitanism" has often been linked in literary studies to the concept of eclecticism in the creative, poetic, and textual domain, and understood generically as style mixing. Exploring Victorian literature, Christine Bolon-Reichert notes that eclecticism and the eclectic can become valuable as a critical and aesthetic category, since once writers saw their creations as falling within the eclectic, "the act of combination could be perceived" and thus "they neither asked for nor were offered the position of original and therefore were more predisposed to offer more creative solutions . . . becoming more cosmopolitan, sharing more." Eclecticism, she continues, is "a mode of critical engagement that ultimately could lead to a rethinking of the contrast between creation and criticism, and the very idea of the original."[26] As such, eclecticism as a creative process can be seen as a deliberate and critical engagement that allows for questioning the (assumed) models' uniqueness, originality, completeness, authority, and ultimately their aesthetic validation. According to Rebecca Walkowitz, the novelist Salman Rushdie (b. 1947) promotes eclecticism to showcase his "ability to take from the world what seems fitting and to leave the rest."[27] His strategy implies a "knowledge of the world" from which to select, while it defines and delimits that world and then uses a "mix-up" as a critical strategy that ultimately gives him subjectivity.[28] Walkowitz also notes that the writer Jorge Luis Borges (1899–1986) believed that there is a great deal of freedom when artists "cut, select and reorder foreign literatures without preconceptions,"[29] a freedom, I argue, that is bestowed mostly to those who are not constrained by authority or by slippery assumptions of cultural ownership.

This is the critical cosmopolitanism which Dana Gooley perceptively assigns to Meyerbeer's work by bringing to the fore the composer's "openly eclectic" compositional practice and that points to his lack of "commitment to a particular school, nation, or idea" as a critical stance, rather than merely as an opportunity

---

[25] Brigid Cohen, "Diasporic Dialogues in Mid-Century New York: Stefen Wolpe, George Russel, and Hannah Arendt, and the Historiography of Displacement," *Journal of the Society for American Music* 6, no. 2 (2012): 145. Homi Bhabha's postcolonial interpretation of the hybrid as a liminal "third space," is also not appropriate to address the circulation and sharing of musical practices that are explored in this book, for it still rests on the premise that cultures, as not static, change through mixing to produce differences; see *The Location of Culture* (London: Routledge, 1994).

[26] Christine Bolon-Reichert, *The Age of Eclecticism: Literature and Culture in Britain 1815–1885* (Columbus: Ohio State University Press, 2009), 3. The terms "collage," "bricolage," and "assemblage" have also been used in literary, music, and cultural studies to similar effects.

[27] Rebecca Walkowitz, *Cosmopolitan Style, Modernism Beyond the Nation* (New York: Columbia University Press, 2006), 67.

[28] Walkowitz, *Cosmopolitan Style*, 139.

[29] Walkowitz, *Cosmopolitan Style*, 139.

14 INTRODUCTION

for style selection.[30] Michael Tusa's appraisal of Weber's choices in *Der Freieshcultz* presents the opera as a patchwork of different styles, a "combination and synthesis" of "the best" foreign styles, namely the French and Italian.[31] Richard Taruskin depicts Glinka as a cosmopolitan composer because of his ability to "organically unit[e] the best of the West," understood as a mix of German, Italian, and French musics.[32] Camilla Fojas has expanded notions of eclecticism to the sociocultural, noting that for a *modernista* in Latin America it meant "adding new points of reference, new contexts, and understandings of social and cultural phenomena."[33] From these perspectives, eclecticism becomes a critical position that challenges the boundaries and limitations of the (supposed) models' authority and originality, offering extra perspectives and possibilities that could function as "disruptive aesthetics."[34] This issue is discussed in Chapter 11 with the work of Alberto Nepomuceno. Nonetheless, while cosmopolitan experiences and practices can generate and be generated by eclectic styles, in that capacity they can also become a starting point for "an Other" cultural product or experience. Investing in the ability of some writers and composers to navigate eclectic textual spaces, these studies have at their core the idea that one owns not merely a musical work, a performance, or a recording, but that one owns a culture or a musical style. There is also a problematic assumption that an artist's work or performance "represents" a culture by default, or that it defines his/her individual identity as a tidy unity, in an uncomplicated leap from the individual, to the sociopolitical, to the cultural, and eventually to the nation.

The stories I tell in the following chapters show that not all cosmopolitan experiences and practices are eclectic. The cosmopolitan urban network I explore here, and of which Rio de Janeiro is a part, infers shared understandings of cultural belonging and allows for the aesthetic validation of the replica. It places meaning in the copy without the need to reassemble new modes of expressions, cultural products, or practices. In the cosmopolitan urban network, cultural modes of expression come to belong to many, and in the process they lose their centrality and claims of ownership and originality. Nelly Richard notes, "To be at the peripheral extension of models centrally promoted by the metropolitan networks means to belong to a culture distinguished as secondary with respect to the anteriority and superiority of the model, but one that also demystifies the

---

[30] Dana Gooley, "Meyerbeer, Eclecticism, and Operatic Cosmopolitanism," *Musical Quarterly* (2017): 175 and 167–168.

[31] Michael Tusa, "Cosmopolitanism and the National Opera," *Journal of Interdisciplinary History* 36, no. 3 (2006): 498.

[32] Richard Taruskin, *Nineteenth-Century Music* (Oxford and New York: Oxford University Press, 2010), 239.

[33] Camilla Fojas, *Cosmopolitanism in the Americas* (West Lafayette, IN: Purdue University Press, 2005), 5.

[34] Fojas, *Cosmopolitanism in the Americas*, 103.

model by replicating it endlessly . . . and generating an image of an image of an image, reproduced until the very idea of an original is lost in the distance."[35] As the "idea" of the supposedly original and assumption of its aesthetic and political (and national) force are lost in the process of replication, it ultimately becomes irrelevant. Thus, while the processes of assemblage and re-assemblage of the eclectic make expressive works aesthetically meaningful, it is in the process of disassemblage that they acquire cultural and sociopolitical force, a topic that is discussed in Chapter 9.

Reception studies exploring the dissemination of musical works away from their places of origin have followed music's many "afterlives," starting from the assumption that audiences in specific places necessarily listen to various musics "with a *different* ear."[36] Simon Frith observes quite pointedly that "while music may be shaped by the people who first make and use it, as an experience it has a *life of its own* [my emphasis]."[37] This "life of its own" that Frith suggests implies that, as music travels, it allows for the musical experience to become different. And while this might be the case, one also needs to consider that the cultural flow of music can generate an outcome that does not have an immediate "life of its own." In the chapters that follow, the focus on cosmopolitan experience and practice allows for explorations beyond the "afterlife" of cultural practices and highlights instead the many "extra lives" of cultural products and practices, whether or not they acknowledge models or places of origin. Exploring the afterlife involves an emphasis on the original; the focus on the extra life allows for the scrutiny of its transcendence. It is these extra lives of musics that connected people through common experiences in the turn-of-the-century city. Music's subjectivity allows for this transcendence more so than other expressive media, Tusa notes, and as such it is "one of music's valuable aesthetic dimensions."[38] I would add that it is also through its subjectivity and ephemeral character that music evinces its most powerful sociopolitical and cultural dimension, one that is most discernible when it sounds through many borders to touch the lives of many.

---

[35] Fojas, *Cosmopolitanism in the Americas*, 8, quoting Nelly Richard, "Cultural Peripheries: Latin America and Postmodernist De-Centering," *Boundary* 20, no. 3 (1993): 156–161.

[36] Jim Samson, *The Cambridge History of Nineteenth-Century Music* (Cambridge, UK: Cambridge University Press, 2008), 9–10. The term "afterlife" of musical works, used by Walter Benjamin and Carl Dahlhaus in addressing reception, is discussed in Mark Everist's "Reception Theories: Canonic Discourses, and Musical Value," in *Rethinking Music*, ed. Nicholas Cook and Mark Everist (Oxford and New York: Oxford University Press, 1999), 378–402.

[37] Simon Frith, "Music and Identity," in *Questions of Cultural Identity*, ed. Stuart Hall and Paul Du Gay (London: Sage Publications, 1996), 108–127. Timothy Taylor makes a similar claim regarding the social nature of the production and distribution of technology vis-à-vis consumption (listening): "The social production of technology is quite different from its subsequent social uses"; see his *Strange Sounds: Music, Technology, and Culture* (New York: Routledge, 2001), 16.

[38] Tusa, "Cosmopolitanism and the National Opera," 499.

16 INTRODUCTION

Finally, as I reckoned with how cosmopolitan experiences and practices worked musically and in the past, I started from the assumption that musical works prompt knowledge production, and I suggest that the "music itself" was a catalyst to individual and communal cultural engagements.[39] I thus argue that one needs to fully explore the role of musical clichés, established musical structures, and specific musical elements, such as melody and rhythm, and the appeal of the musical familiar to start grappling with the social, political, and aesthetic relevance of music's travels during a period of early mass production of cultural forms. While music scholarship about the long 19th century, supported by deterministic notions of progress, tends to focus on works that are new and particular, one has yet to grasp why and how they could be separated from the old and the general, and why particularities matter, or not, for claims of historical relevance and the understanding of cultural change. In the following chapters, I highlight the force of the musically familiar and performance practices that helped shape the period.

At the same time, as I take experience and practice as guiding principles, I also assume that musical works by themselves are not sufficient to convey the complex cultural relationships that I consider here. The works explored in the following chapters are taken as agents in fostering cosmopolitanism through social practice insofar as they are enabled by composers, performers, listeners, critics, and various groups of individuals acting in a gamut of social, racial, gender, and political relationships. Furthermore, musical performances, both by individuals and groups, are considered in their widest sense and are taken both as modes of cognition and as ephemeral but conscious ways of experiencing music, individually and in groups.[40] At a time when a long tradition of live performances met the new media of recordings and film, the power of performance to convey meaning and as a vehicle for engagement with music turns particularly poignant, exactly so when it is (wrongly) forecasted to disappear. Thus, in the stories told in this book, the performing body and the music itself are intertwined as ways of rendering history, culture, and communal belonging in a time of extreme fragmentation of ideas and modes of individual and collective expressions.

---

[39] Tia DeNora, "Music as Cognition," in DeNora, *After Adorno: Rethinking Music Sociology* (Cambridge and New York: Cambridge University Press, 2003), 59–82, especially 63–65.
[40] Carolyn Abbate, "Preface," in Abbate, *In Search of Opera* (Princeton, NJ: Princeton University Press, 2001), vii–xvi. Also, Nicholas Cook, "Music as Performance," in *The Cultural Study of Music: A Critical Introduction*, ed. Martin Clayton et al. (London: Taylor & Francis Group, 2011), 184–194.

INTRODUCTION 17

An Outline

The book is divided into 12 chapters. In the first chapter, I summarize the scholarly framework that guided my explorations and that provided methodological tools for the conceptualization of turn-of-the-20th-century Rio de Janeiro as part of an interdependent cultural and musical urban network. I explore cosmopolitanism as an experience of cities and as part of an urban modernity that saw many variants. In Chapter 2, I introduce Rio de Janeiro as a cosmopolitan city and place its socio-political developments in a larger geographical-historical context, one that will frame the musics, people, and performances discussed in the following chapters. In Chapter 3, I discuss some ways in which music was used to invoke symbolic participation in the republican cause and posit that both an imperial anthem by Francisco Manuel da Silva and "La Marseillaise" served that purpose. The chapter considers the ramifications of political engagement through singing and listening across geographical distances before the advent of recordings, the radio, and the internet, and how songs that cross boundaries can foster both a sense of inclusion and exclusion. In Chapter 4, the focus is on the revival by the republican political and musical establishment of the work by a composer from colonial times, José Maurício Nunes Garcia (1767–1830), to forge a past that could represent the republican nation. I discuss the complexities and contradictions that emerged from the use of the music by a Black man who lived during the height of the country's profit from slavery as symbolic of an idealized national musical past centered on Austro-Germanic musics and at the service of Rio de Janeiro's White political, intellectual, and musical status quo.

In Chapter 5, I explore the activities and musical performances of the artist and entrepreneur Mlle. Ywonna in her short-lived, but influential, Rio de Janeiro cabaret. Mlle. Ywonna's venue became a gathering place as well as a refuge for young republican intellectuals, bohemians, and artists who questioned military republicanism and the country's new status quo. In the intimate cabaret, a select clientele engaged with Ywonna's voice, her performances, and her reconstructions of Montmartre chansons in Rio de Janeiro to experiment with alternative ways of imagining the city. Ywonna's renditions of chansons came to define an era of Rio de Janeiro's nightlife that shaped a generation.

Chapter 6 moves away from institutionalized contexts and politically inspired performance practices to focus on the many musical fashions that shaped the city's emergent music business. Here Mlle. Ywonna returns as a protagonist, as she ventures further into Rio de Janeiro's heterogeneous and cosmopolitan booming theatrical environment. The chapter follows several female performers and entrepreneurs who arrived from Europe and worked with Ywonna and shows how they contributed to the diversification and growth of the music business in the Brazilian capital. I discuss the use of "old fashioned" musics in

18 INTRODUCTION

Ywonna's café concerts and how they were presented as something already part of city culture. I also explore the disconnect between musical and performance styles with the citizenship of the artists and the language used in songs to (re) consider the relation between concepts of "national" and music-making during the period. I suggest that female performers of various provenances were instrumental to the solidification of the stereotypical "dancing mulatta" as a part of an urban theatrical and musical network that fed on the commodification of female Black bodies. In Chapter 7, the focus is on the roles played by Geraldo Magalhães and Eduardo das Neves in the building of the city's multifaceted and heterogeneous entertainment business. Magalhães used his skills as a performer and entrepreneur to venture across national borders. He mastered various languages, performances, and musical styles to overcome racial stereotypes and to bridge cultural differences and to eventually become a truly cosmopolitan artist. As a *flâneur* singer and performer, Neves's skills as a composer, performer, and businessman allowed him to build a successful career in Rio de Janeiro. As he reflected on the city's daily experiences, Neves became a key interpreter of the city's multicultural and cosmopolitan environment. The chapter also discusses the restricting contexts in which Black musicians and performers are usually featured in historical accounts of the cosmopolitan city.

Chapter 8 traces the many paths taken by Franz Lehár's operetta *The Merry Widow* in Rio de Janeiro as the work was fully embraced by the city's audiences. Staged in a variety of locales and performed in different contexts, the operetta's popularity fueled a local multilingualism and became central to the local explorations of music and sound through the mixing of new technologies and media. I discuss connections and disconnections about music and language in the city stages and their respective possibilities and limitations as referential for exploring issues of national belonging. *The Merry Widow* eventually branched off from main theaters of the city center to be welcomed in the circus, where it was reworked by Black composers and performers, and by Spanish performers who dominated the circus circuit. Here, issues of race are coupled with cosmopolitanism as a shared experience of a few, while questions of timbre and instrumental ensemble formations also illuminate a shared soundscape that evades many borders.

In Chapter 9, I turn to the spread of opera in the city, and Italian opera in particular, to consider the genre as an integral part of a turn-of-the-20th-century cosmopolitan urban tradition, and the implications of understanding operatic music as a local tradition. The chapter invites a shift from the focus on opera as a delimiter of social boundaries to operatic music as a border-crossing agent during an early period of globalization. It considers the process of opera's disassemblage as a counterweight to the idea of an organic "musical work." Within this context,

I explore the opera *Il Guarany* (1870) by Antônio Carlos Gomes (1836–1896) as crucial in the process of transforming a cosmopolitan tradition into a local tradition, and I address ways in which the selection of canons and the process of solidifying musical traditions intertwine.

The composer Aurélio Cavalcanti is the main protagonist of Chapter 10. A main figure in Rio de Janeiro's entertainment venues, he worked as a pianist in salons, dance halls, and movie theater waiting rooms, and as a musical director and conductor of one of the most prestigious movie theater orchestras. Cavalcanti had the experience and creativity to instantly adapt many musics to the fast-moving scenes of silent movies, a skill that he used to write music suggestive of many peoples and places, even if he had never met the people or had never been to the places that his works were set to portray. Cavalcanti wrote waltzes and polkas that became local staples during his time; they had suggestive titles that served to project imaginations of places beyond the city through music. The chapter also traces the arrival and dominance of the cake-walk in Rio de Janeiro and explores how the dance conflated Parisian fashionable trends with African-derived musics and dance within the cosmopolitan urban networks.

Chapter 11 focuses on the failed attempts to replicate in Rio de Janeiro the vogue for Wagner's music that had taken over several European music centers. I discuss the extent to which, at the turn of the 20th century, Wagner's music did in fact have a following outside large European centers and outside the domain of a few critics, intellectuals, and artists. I suggest that, in practice, Wagnerism reflected a look back to a stable, secure, and idealized past rather than offering a real, practical promise of musical renewal. I also consider the extent to which composers such as Leopoldo Miguez and his circle in Rio de Janeiro, the so-called Musical Republic, became attached to the idea of a "music of the future." I examine the repertory of a few concerts that the group organized during the period to show that they consistently offered a gamut of musics from various composers, provenances, styles, and languages as educational tools for the "general public." The chapter also examines works by Alberto Nepomuceno as examples of an eclectic approach to music composition that was quite common among many composers of his generation. I suggest that some of Nepomuceno's works can be described as assemblages of the many musical possibilities available to him, and that the connections the composer makes, how the many parts are put together, are more aesthetically significant than the final work. The chapter shows how, as an assemblage, the "musical work" is made up of many pieces, defying a precise, coherent musical style or practice and, as such, also resisting canonicity.

The concluding chapter, "Arriving at the Future" shows that the inauguration of the Theatro Municipal in 1909 was a crowning event at the closing of

20 INTRODUCTION

the first decade of the 20th century. The project took several years to come to fruition, but when the theater was finally opened, it represented the consolidation of an imagined future that was now concrete but already past. Like many similar buildings around the world, the theater's hermetically closed neoclassical walls were also soundproof to the city outside, which continued to echo an ever changing musical world soon to be dominated by the sounds of a world war.

1

Cosmopolitanism and the City

The Possibilities of Cosmopolitanism

As a theory of world politics and human rights, cosmopolitanism has a long history, going back to the Greek Stoics, who envisioned the cosmopolitan as a "citizen of the world," free to cross borders and with aspirations for shared morals and legal rights. This cosmopolitan ideal became crucial in the shaping of European Enlightenment thought during the 18th century, serving to support Immanuel Kant's call for free republics that together could sustain global peace, as well as Johann Gottfried Herder's acknowledgment of the world's cultural plurality.[1] But the protean nature of the term had already given itself to many different definitions, interpretations, and political uses in 1762, when the Académie Française defined the cosmopolitan as "the one who adopts no country at all."[2] Yet Enlightenment cosmopolitanism with its many definitions and utopian universal ideals endured and helped shape the long 19th century at the same time as it was put to the test, since the shaping of nation-states and the expanding forces of global capitalism led to new sociopolitical models and ideals. Gerard Delanty suggests that one should consider the political forces of both nationalism and cosmopolitanism as essential parts of "the paradox of modernity" taking shape during the long 19th century.[3]

In recent decades, the concept of cosmopolitanism has been revived and revised to become a promising tool in socioeconomic and political explorations of the late-20th- and early-21st-century globalized worlds. These studies have broadened and reappraised cosmopolitanism's associations with both utopian

---

[1] For a study on the various approaches to cosmopolitanism during the Enlightenment, see Pauline Kleingeld, "Six Varieties of Cosmopolitanism in Late Eighteenth-Century Germany," *Journal of the History of Ideas* 60, no. 3 (1999): 505–524. For an overview of Herder's notion of cultural relativism and universalism, see Sonia Sikka, *Herder on Humanity and Cultural Difference: Enlightened Relativism* (Cambridge, UK: Cambridge University Press, 2011); and Phillip Bohlman's "Prologue: Again Herder," in *Song Loves the Masses: Herder on Music and Nationalism*, trans. Phillip Bohlman (Berkeley: University of California Press, 2017), 1–20.

[2] Moretti, *Distant Reading*, 23–24.

[3] Gerard Delante, "Nationalism and Cosmopolitanism: The Paradox of Modernity," in *The SAGE Handbook of Nations and Nationalism*, ed. Gerard Delante and Krishan Kumar (London: Sage, 2006), 357. For the political uses of Enlightenment cosmopolitanism, see Pheng Cheah, "The Cosmopolitical—Today," in *Cosmopolitics: Thinking and Feeling Beyond the Nation*, ed. Pheng Cheah and Bruce Robbins (Minneapolis: University of Minnesota Press, 1998), 22–30.

Music and Cosmopolitanism. Cristina Magaldi, Oxford University Press. © Oxford University Press 2024.
DOI: 10.1093/oso/9780199744770.003.0002

22 MUSIC AND COSMOPOLITANISM

Enlightenment ideals and nationalist ideological precepts. Nevertheless, as a form of cultural connection and broadly defined as "an ability to navigate various cultural contexts,"[4] cosmopolitanism did not make a comeback without its share of criticisms. Scholars were quick to point out that broad definitions expose cosmopolitans' paradoxical inclination toward cultural difference and that they conceal, rather than critique or overcome, economic, political, and socio-cultural hierarchies propelled by capitalism and imperialism, and xenophobic nacionalisms.[5] Still, while defining cosmopolitanism continues to be a contested issue, the (re)embracing of the concept in the social sciences and humanities has also inspired studies that contemplate ideals of modernity during the long 19th century in a fresh light, studies that have assisted me in exploring the crucial role that music played in the process.[6]

The term *cosmopolitanism* is understood here within the experiential realm of shared cultural belongings allowed by music and music-making and within a community of artistic expressions that is larger than the local and that transcends the nation. As such, cosmopolitanism enables critical reflections that challenge views of culture as being constructed, historically and politically, in autonomous associations to localized communities and/or nation-states. As Jeremy Waldron points out, "one's culture should be considered as a negotiable process of interactions and engagement, and of disengagement, to one's community social structure; a process that is open to new modes of interactions and negotiations, individually and collectively," provided that we acknowledge a "community" as an open-ended and changing social structure. While an uncontaminated single culture is an anomaly, Waldron maintains that "one culture does not need to be clearly and importantly different from another, either in its appearance to an outsider or in the consciousness of its practitioners, in order to be the culture that it is." In particular, Waldron calls into question some self-conscious posturings often associated with nationhood and points instead to a cosmopolitan ideal in

---

[4] Ulf Hannerz, *Transnational Connections: Culture, People, Places* (London and New York: Routledge, 1999), 151.

[5] For James Clifford's insightful critique on cosmopolitanism, see *Routes: Travel and Translation in the Late Twentieth Century* (Cambridge, MA: Harvard University Press, 1997), 36. For a critique of Hannerz and an overview of the ways in which cosmopolitanism has been evoked in the social sciences, see Robert Holton, *Cosmopolitanisms: New Thinking and New Directions* (New York: Palgrave Macmillan, 2009), 18–19. For a critique of the revival of cosmopolitanism in the social sciences, see Craig J. Calhoun, "The Class Consciousness of Frequent Travelers: Towards a Critique of Actually Existing Cosmopolitanisms," *The South Atlantic Quarterly* 101, no. 4 (Fall 2002): 869–897.

[6] The following authors were seminal in the shaping of my ideas: Jeremy Waldron, "What Is Cosmopolitan?," *The Journal of Political Philosophy* 8, no. 2 (2000): 227–243; Gerard Delanty's "The Cosmopolitan Imagination: Critical Cosmopolitanism and Social Theory," *The British Journal of Sociology* 57, no. 1 (2006): 25–47; David T. Hansen, "Chasing Butterflies Without a Net: Interpreting Cosmopolitanism," *Studies in Philosophy and Education* 2, no. 2 (2010): 151–166; Bruce Robbins and Paulo Lemos Horta, "Introduction," in *Cosmopolitanisms*, ed. Bruce Robbins and Paulo Lemos Horta (New York: New York University Press, 2017), 1–17.

COSMOPOLITANISM AND THE CITY   23

which "shared ways of life do not need to be restricted to a geographical area (although they can be), but are shaped by social practices, feelings of exclusion and belonging developed over time, and many other feelings that pertain to human experiences and their understandings of the world."[7] The possibilities of engaging with cosmopolitanism as a sphere of shared cultural belonging in a macro context have led scholars to reframe established assumptions that favor nationally bound cultural identities and that focus solely on a group's cultural specificities and differences. Rather than rejecting core assumptions of anthropological understandings of culture and identity, recent scholarship on cosmopolitanism has engaged with it critically by offering tools to address "similarities and patterns of integration, historically constructed and shared among spaces."[8]

Conversely, the assumption that a nation, imagined or otherwise, unequivocally shares one culture that defines it, has had unexamined consequences in music scholarship. Hans Weisethaunet points out with keen attention that "the fatal junction of the concept of nationality with the concept of culture" has dominated music scholarship to the point that "for some music historians and ethnomusicologists, the 'nation' and its 'culture' seem almost a given ... an unambiguous relation that has shaped the ways we construct music historiographies, how we select and preserve canons, how our music history narratives are framed, whose voices are represented, and in what language they are allowed to speak." To the extent that music constructs place and "emplaces our images and sense of being in the world," Weisethaunet argues, "there is no reason to assume that these experiences and possibilities are delimited to the nation and its borders."[9]

Exploring the cosmopolitan dimension of cultural and musical experiences and practices as a historical project continues to pose challenges, however. The first lies in the focus on cosmopolitanism as a phenomenon derived from late-20th- and early-21st-century globalization, that is, the focus on "newness" as the main characteristic for cultural analysis.[10] Because scholars of popular music

---

[7] Waldron, "What Is Cosmopolitan?," 234 and 243.

[8] Waldron, "What Is Cosmopolitan?," 233. For studies on cosmopolitanism within the perspective of anthropology, see Pnina Werbner, "Introduction: Towards a New Cosmopolitan Anthropology," in *Anthropology and the New Cosmopolitanism: Rooted, Feminist, and Vernacular Perspectives*, ed. Pnina Werbner (London: Bloomsbury Academic, 2008), 1–30. For the roles of literature and music in this process, see Robert Fraser, *Literature, Music, and Cosmopolitanism* (London: Macmillan, 2018).

[9] Hans Weisethaunet, "Historiography and Complexities: Why is Music 'national'?" *Popular Music History* 2, no. 2 (2007): 170–171.

[10] Nayan Chanda notes that our understanding of the various implications of globalization, including cosmopolitanism, is predominantly ahistorical because it is linked too much to recent socioeconomic and cultural history; see his *Bound Together: How Traders, Preachers, Adventurers, and Warriors Shaped Globalization* (Yale University Press, 2007), 246–248, and 319. For a still relevant critique of sociohistorical accounts that overlook global connections see Eri Wolf's introduction in *Europe and the People Without History* (Los Angeles and Berkeley: California University Press, 1982), 3–23. For considerations of historical models that could offer alternatives for thinking past and beyond nation see Burton, *After the Imperial Turn*; and Stephen Greenblatt et al, *Cultural Mobility, A Manifesto* (Cambridge: Cambridge University Press, 2010).

24 MUSIC AND COSMOPOLITANISM

have dealt with the cultural ramifications of globalization, and with the political, cultural, and aesthetic implications of music as a commodity, they have provided most of the insights about music as a global phenomenon, even if still holding concepts of nation and empire at the core of their explorations. Jason Toynbee and Byron Dueck's collection of case studies about popular music provides flexible contexts of musical sharing with fruitful results.[11] Veit Erlmann has provided a valuable analysis of the historical process in South Africa,[12] while Steven Feld has offered insightful reflections about cosmopolitanism and music, some of which I have used as a basis for my own analysis.[13] However, often situating their object of study in the 20th and 21st centuries, there is the implication in these studies of a musical past that is filled with mythical associations of local authenticity, roots, and the consequent understanding of past cultures as static and pure. The concept of cosmopolitanism as a space of shared cultural expressions can prove fruitful here, for it offers tools for a more nuanced exploration of a context-based historical interpretation of large music repertories that flowed beyond their places of origin well before jazz, rock 'n' roll, bossa nova, hip-hop, K-pop, and various forms of electropop.[14]

---

[11] See Jason Toynbee and Byron Dueck, eds., *Migrating Music* (New York: Routledge, 2011). Motti Regev points to a shared cosmopolitan culture, but does not leave behind concepts of unique national cultures; see his "Cultural Uniqueness and Aesthetic Cosmopolitanism," *European Journal of Social Theory* 10, no. 1 (2007): 123–138. Thomas Turino, *Nationalists, Cosmopolitans, and Popular Music in Zimbabwe* (Chicago: University of Chicago Press, 2000) provides a nation-centric approach that differs from my own. Martin Stokes offers valuable insights on the topic, but also in keeping with the centrality of national cultures; see his "On Musical Cosmopolitanism," *Macalester International* 21 (2008): 3–26. There are several studies that pertain to globalization and popular music in Latin America; Alexandro Madrid and Robin Moore, *Danzón: Circum-Caribbean Dialogues in Music and Dance* (Oxford and New York: Oxford University Press, 2013), and Matthew Karush, *Musicians in Transit: Argentina and the Globalization of Popular Music* (Durham, NC: Duke University Press, 2017), are examples that also served as models for my work.

[12] Veit Erlmann, *Music, Modernity, and the Global Imagination: South Africa and the West* (New York: Oxford University Press, 1999).

[13] I was inspired, in particular, by Steven Feld's following self-critique: "I was knocked out . . . by the sensation that as complete strangers we could so instantly know each other, by the sensation that we might equally embody closely overlapping genealogies of listening. I was equally knocked out by the question of whether my amazement was itself the historical product of an unwitting racism. I mean, why should I be surprised that an African musician has spent equally many years listening to what I've been listening to? Why should I be surprised by Nii Noi's similar passion for linking music, culture, and politics, by his distinct knowledge of Pan-Africanism, and by the central position he locates there for the legacy of John Coltrane? . . . Was it that hard to imagine that an African musician could be as deeply into the same sonic way of knowing and being that first inspired me? What could it mean that Nii Noi's was a cosmopolitan that reached vastly beyond his modest and remote if not outright marginal location in the world of jazz?," in *Jazz Cosmopolitanisms in Accra: Five Musical Years in Accra* (Durham, NC: Duke University Press, 2012, Kindle), 32–33 and 153–160.

[14] Already in 1996, Veit Erlmann asked for an analysis of "the historical space between compact disc, MTV, *Graceland*, and everything that preceded them"; see his "The Aesthetics of the Global Imagination," *Public Culture* 8, no. 3 (1996): 476. But even though the literature on popular musics in the long 19th century is extensive, one still needs plenty of localized source studies that explore more than local and national characteristics before a clear picture of repertories and larger patterns of music circulation and consumption can emerge.

COSMOPOLITANISM AND THE CITY   25

The second challenge in exploring the cosmopolitan dimension of music-making as a historical project involves considering cosmopolitanism's various shifts and conflicting interpretations through the long 19th century. This is particularly difficult because the period is associated with Enlightenment cosmopolitan ideals and entangled with deterministic and teleological accounts of the emergence of nation-states and nationalism.[15] The task of contemplating cosmopolitanism amidst the usual nation-centric line of thought is heightened by the fact that music as a topic of scholarly interest, both in the musicological and ethnomusicological domains, emerged exactly as a result of political struggles to establish nation-states and the need for forging cultural roots to help define them. Consequently, music historiography still abounds with the period's own historical nation-centric filters, which privilege music's role to enforce, shape, and represent the local and the nation.

To be sure, the emergence of the political force of nation-states and ideologies of nationalism did leave a strong mark on discourses about music, as well as on the music production and practices in Europe and elsewhere, and Brazil was not an exception.[16] Furthermore, music certainly served (and continues to serve) as a sociopolitical force strengthening local and national communities worldwide. It is telling, however, that the association of music with the politics of nationalism and the construction of national cultural identity has taken precedence over a wider exploration of musical practices during the period. Carl Dahlhaus acknowledged that "[t]he notions of human commonality, cosmopolitanism, nationalism, and individualism all impinged on music aesthetics in the nineteenth century," but he avoided explorations that went much beyond the politics of nationalism, perhaps, as he contended, because "nineteenth-century thought went around and around these anthropological categories [and] the relations between [these categories] are so tangled."[17] Thus avoiding the entanglements of a past cosmopolitan musical context, discourses about music continued to approach cosmopolitanism as an opposite or a counterpart to nationalism, or as a

[15] See, for example, Friedrich Meinecke's *Cosmopolitanism and the Nation State*, trans. Robert B. Kimber (Princeton, NJ: Princeton University Press, 1970 [1907]), which has been widely quoted in musicological studies.

[16] The standard overview of music nationalism has been established by Richard Taruskin in "Nationalism," in *The Revised New Grove Dictionary of Music and Musicians*, ed. Stanley Sadie and John Tyrrel (Basingtoke, UK: Macmillan, 2001), 687–906. A critique of this study can be found in Daniel Grimley's "National Contexts: Grieg and Folklorism in Nineteenth-Century," in *Music, Landscape and Norwegia Identity* (Suffolk, UK, and New York: Boydell Press, 2006): 11–22; see also Celia Applegate, "How German Is It? Nationalism and the Idea of Serious Music in the Early Nineteenth Century," *19th-Century Music* 21, no. 3 (1998): 274–296. A summary of the main studies on nationalism in music in the 20th century can be found in Harry White and Michael Murphy, eds., "Introduction," in *Musical Constructions of Nationalism* (Cork, Ireland: Cork University Press, 2001), 1–15.

[17] Carl Dahlhaus, *Nineteenth-Century Music* (Berkeley and Los Angeles: California University Press, 1989), 37.

26   MUSIC AND COSMOPOLITANISM

stigmatized term with racial and gender undertones. Revising these approaches involves reconsidering the period not solely as the "age of nationalism" and opening our investigative eyes and ears to other sociopolitical and cultural contexts.[18] It requires a move from a "methodological nationalism" to a "methodological cosmopolitanism," an epistemological turn that offers alternatives to the nation-centered investigations about music during the period (and beyond).[19]

Discourses about music during the long 19th century show that the uncomplicated narrative about music and nation has been not only one-sided, but also, to an extent, contradictory. Georges Jean-Aubry, a critic preoccupied with establishing music's role in the politics of nationalism in early 20th-century France, for example, suggested that composers would be better off skipping 19th-century music altogether as a source of inspiration in the building of a French national musical language and focus instead on the remote past.[20] Jean-Aubry saw the 19th century as a period of "contamination," when the availability, need, and interests in engagements with the foreign was a reality that obfuscated the potential of music to build nationalisms. For Jean-Aubry, cosmopolitanism was not a utopian Enlightenment ideal of the past, but rather a significant experience of his present, one that problematized and questioned essentialized ideas of European-ness in music (and of German-ness, Italian-ness, French-ness, etc.). The degree to which these anxieties were intensified as the 19th century came to a close paralleled the pace at which cosmopolitanism as an experience and practice became more conspicuous. Jann Pasler contends that 20th-century musicologists, grounded in the aftermath of world wars, ignored the cultural entanglements of turn of the century to move beyond them.[21] Nonetheless, as the 21st-century sociopolitical order continues to bring to the fore complex cultural connections and disconnections, it has become more urgent for scholars

[18] Welcome studies by Dana Gooley and Ryan Minor have started to scrutinize the 19th century as a period of cosmopolitan engagements in music; see Dana Gooley, "Cosmopolitanism in the Age of Nationalism: 1848–1914," *Journal of the American Musicological Society* 66, no. 2 (2013): 523–549; see also Elaine Kelly, Markus Mantere, and Derek Scott, eds., *Confronting the National in the Musical Past* (London and New York; Routledge, 2018).

[19] Ulrich Beck, *Cosmopolitan Vision* (Cambridge, UK: Polity Press, 2006), 19 and 75–85. For a critique of Beck's historical understanding of cosmopolitanism, see Holton, *Cosmopolitanisms*, 64–72. The idea of a "methodological cosmopolitanism" can be a way of exploring a "relational musicology," which Georgina Born describes as a reflection on not only "what counts as music to be studied, but [also] how it should be studied"; see her "For a Relational Musicology: Music and Interdisciplinarity, Beyond the Practice Turn," *Journal of the Royal Music Association* 135, no. 2 (November, 2010): 205–242. Nicholas Cook makes a similar argument in "Anatomy of the Encounter: Intercultural Analysis as Relational Musicology," in *Critical Musicological Reflections: Essays in Honor of Derek B. Scott*, ed. Stan Hawkins (Aldershot, UK: Ashgate, 2012), 193–208.

[20] Georges Jean-Aubry, "La Musique française d'aujourd'hui," (1916) quoted in Carlo Caballero, "Patriotism or Nationalism? Fauré at the Great War," *Journal of the American Musicological Society* 52, no. 3 (1999): 604.

[21] Jann Pasler, *Composing the Citizen: Music as Public Utility in Third Republic France* (Berkeley and Los Angeles: University of California Press, 2009), 29.

to address not only music's historical role in constructing sociocultural relations within and among nations, but also music's historical roles in questioning and transcending them. Unlike the novel and written sources, which Benedict Anderson used to theorize the imagining of the nation, music did not give itself easily to such imaginations.[22] As Robert Fraser argued, "the permeability of music as an art form makes it exceptionally portable,"[23] and creates ephemeral and transitory communities seldom supported by clear-cut national alignments. The evanescent and ethereal nature of music and performance thus offered "different and alternative imagined communities, each configuration lying across many others, congeries of overlapping, intersecting circles."[24]

The focus on cosmopolitanism can help us to explore the long 19th century as a time when nations and empires, being developed, shaped, and constantly disputed, challenged forms of cultural belonging while spawning alternative cultural connections. One can say that by the turn of the 20th century, cosmopolitan experiences and practices helped individuals to understand, confront, and ultimately control new political, social, and cultural relations resulting from the dissolution of long-standing oligarchic systems of production, political power, and of religious conceptions of the world. The period can provide us with vivid examples of the challenges in comprehending the very notion of one's culture and one's identity, the struggles to grasp the force as well as the vulnerability of nations and their forged boundaries, and the possibilities and dilemmas presented by a world connected by rampant capitalism, imperialism, and technological advances. The case examples explored in the following chapters are thus illustrations of how music served to express, support, and confront these dilemmas and challenges.

Throughout the long 19th century, cosmopolitanism moved from a utopian ideal and a sociopolitical theory inherited from the Enlightenment thought to a daily reality that increasingly encompassed the lives of those living through the process of Europe's imperialism—the lives of those participating in the process from within and those connected to it from well beyond its borders. As such, cosmopolitanism gave "expression to a different dimension of belonging than that of nationalism," Delante notes, for it pointed to a shared "critical and reflexive consciousness" of the political, social, and cultural entanglements of modernity.[25] Therefore, rather than addressing cosmopolitanism as the result of connections that lead to cultural homogeneity, or as a way to navigate cultural differences, the term is used in this book to highlight an *experience*, a *practice*, and

---

[22] Benedict Anderson, *Imagined Communities: Reflections on the Origins and Spread of Nationalism*, rev. ed. (London and New York: Verso, 2006).
[23] Fraser, Literature, Music, and Cosmopolitanism, 195.
[24] Fraser, *Literature, Music, and Cosmopolitanism*, 148.
[25] Delante, "Nationalism and Cosmopolitanism," 357.

28   MUSIC AND COSMOPOLITANISM

a *reflective consciousness* of and about the modern city, where the sociocultural entanglements of a collective imagination of the global made itself utterly conspicuous.[26] And while such experiences and awareness are here linked mostly to an expanding European geopolitical and cultural "urbanscape,"[27] they were not Europe-specific and were more than counterparts to forces of nation-building. They entailed shared perceptions and imaginations of the world that exposed and challenged social, gender, and race differences, that questioned binary concepts such as old and new, unity and diversity, and that challenged the limits between the Self and the Other, the rational and the illusory, between the real and social versus the ideal and the reflective, between art and non-art, and ultimately between the original and the copy. This cosmopolitan consciousness was realized and recognized in a variety of ways and did not always point to a positive perspective or reveal an emancipatory practice. Acknowledging the confluence of forces that eluded local cultures, in 1890 François Mainguy wrote in *Le fin de siècle*: "No more rank, title, or race.... All is mixed, confused, blurred, reshuffled, in a kaleidoscopic vision."[28] In 1904 Rio de Janeiro, Bilac was concerned with the pace of transformations led by technology in the modern times: "The human activity has augmented in a staggering progression. The men today are forced to think and execute, in a minute, what their grandparents thought and executed in one hour. The modern life is made of thunderstorms inside our brains and fever in our blood."[29] For abolitionist, critic, and writer Joaquim Nabuco (1849–1910), globalization and new technologies allowed for more than worries about, transformation, heterogeneity, or homogenization, but led to a worldwide drama: "I am more a spectator of my century than of my country," he noted in 1900, "the drama, for me, is civilization, and it is being performed on all the states

---

[26] To be true, this consciousness of modernity and the imaginative nature of large cultural attachments delineated by Benedict Anderson goes beyond the association with the nation, although music scholars tend to focus on the latter aspect of Anderson's writings solely as "Imagined Nations." For an analysis of the full implications Anderson's thinking, see Pheng Cheah and Jonathan Culler, *Grounds of Comparison Around the Work of Benedict Anderson* (New York: Routledge, 2003). For an informed contestation of Anderson's ideas, see Fraser, *Literature, Music, and Cosmopolitanism*, in particular the chapter "Beyond the National Stereotype: Benedict Anderson and the Bengal Emergency of 1905–06," 125–160. The idea of a reflective consciousness is explored in Felix Guttari's *Chaosmosis: An Ethico-Aesthetic Paradigm*, trans. P. Bains and J. Pefanis (Sydney: Power, 1995), and is used by Nikos Papastergiadis to articulate the artistic sphere of cosmopolitanism; see his *Cosmopolitanism and Culture* (Cambridge, UK: Polity Press, 2013, Kindle).

[27] Arjun Appadurai's suggestions of the sociocultural implications of a global imagination propelled by media technology late in the 20th century have served as a background to my own explorations of a process that, I believe, was already in gear early in the century; see his *Modernity at Large: Cultural Dimensions of Globalization* (Minneapolis: University of Minnesota Press, 1996).

[28] Quoted in Noel Orillo Verzosa, *The Absolute Limits: Debussy, Satie, and the Culture of French Modernism*, PhD dissertation, University of California, Berkeley, 2008, 3; original text in Eugen Weber, *Fin de Siècle* (Cambridge, MA: Belknap Press, 1986), 10.

[29] Olavo Bilac, "Chronicas," *Kosmos* 1, no. 1 (January, 1904).

COSMOPOLITANISM AND THE CITY   29

of mankind, each one connected today by the telegraph."[30] The novelist Fyodor Dostoevsky (1821–1881) offered a more pessimist and skeptical view in 1880:

> The world has proclaimed freedom, especially of late, but what do we see in this freedom of theirs: only slavery and suicide! . . . We are assured that the world is becoming more and more united, is being formed into brotherly communion, by the shortening of distances, by the transmitting of thoughts through the air. Alas, do not believe in such a union of people.[31]

Also a pessimist about humanity, Rio de Janeiro novelist and critic Machado de Assis (1839–1908) shared in the misgivings of the times:

> Whoever puts their noses outside the door can see that the world is not well. . . when the newspapers bring the daily news, they afflict you profoundly, if they don't kill you . . . thus I tell you, the world is not well. . . . I guess that there is a divine plan inaccessible to human eyes. Maybe the planet is pregnant. [One would ask] Which animal moves inside the uterus of this earth and who destroys one another? I don't know; it may be [that the world is not well because of] a social war, national, political, or religious, a dislocation of classes or races, an array of new ideas, an invasion of barbarians, a new moral, the end of the fashion for suspenders, or maybe the arrival of the automobiles?[32]

Many writers and intellectuals could be added to this list, of course. But the point is that if one is to follow a narrative of music-making during the long 19th century, one needs to account for the relationship between musics and sociopolitical constructions of nations and nationality, for how they were (and continue to be) imagined.[33] But one also needs to address how music served to navigate, express, and confront the complex "kaleidoscopic vision," and the kaleidoscopic

---

[30] Joaquim Nabuco, *Minha Formação* (Rio de Janeiro: Garnier, 1900), 33–34; for a critique of Nabuco's publication, see Silviano Santiago, "Worldly Appeal," in *The Space In-Between: Essays on Latin American Culture* (Durham, NC: Duke University Press, 2001, Kindle).

[31] Fyodor Dostoevsky, *The Brothers Karamazov: A Novel in Four Parts with Epilogue*, trans. Richard Pevear and Larissa Volokbonsky (New York: Farrar, Straus, and Giroux, 2002 [1880]), 313.

[32] Quoted in Nicolau Sevcenko, "A capital irradiante: técnica, ritmos, e ritos do Rio," in *História da vida privada no Brasil República: Da Belle Époque à era do rádio*, ed. Fernando Novais and Nicolau Sevcenko (São Paulo: Companhia da Letras, 1998), 557–558.

[33] See Anderson, *Imagined Communities*, 1–7. For music as an instrument of national unity and political nationalism, see Pasler, *Composing the Citizen*; for ways in which musical difference has been used politically, see Georgina Born and David Hesmondhalgh, eds., *Western Music and Its Others: Difference, Representation, and Appropriation in Music* (Los Angeles: University of California Press, 2000); Timothy Taylor, *Beyond Exoticism: Western Music and the World* (Durham, NC: Duke University Press, 2007); Ralph Locke, *Musical Exoticism: Images and Reflections* (Cambridge, UK, and New York: Cambridge University Press, 2009); and Bloechl, Lowe, and Kallberg, *Rethinking Difference in Music Scholarship*.

30 MUSIC AND COSMOPOLITANISM

sounds, brought by modernity and a world being shaped and unified by technology, imperialism, and global markets. In sum, one needs to account for how music served to assert, challenge, and offer creative solutions to the context of a past globalized scenario and to express and shape a world that quickly became larger than one's locality.

The third challenge in approaching a culturally and musically connected past lies in confronting cosmopolitanism's uncosmopolitan roots, as a concept tied to Enlightenment Eurocentric ideals, European-led globalization, colonialism, and imperialism.[34] To be sure, cosmopolitan ideals are not, and never have been, a privilege or a curse of "Westerners," for concepts of cosmopolitan universalism traverse various geographical and cultural contexts.[35] But one also needs to acknowledge that when used in a political sense in the context of the European expansion at the turn of the 20th century, as is the case in this book, ideals of cosmopolitanism have indeed served to promote and justify the politics of the nation-state, imperialism, gendered hierarchies, and racism. Thus, addressing cosmopolitanism as an experience and a practice from the viewpoint of turn-of-the-century Rio de Janeiro, with its still latent colonial and imperial history and its relationship with Africa within a context of slavery, unavoidably leads to issues of imperialism, racism, and unequal power relationships.[36] Furthermore, historical perceptions of modernity, with which cosmopolitanism is here entangled, are clearly dependent on uneven economic and sociopolitical globalizing processes. It is thus necessary to emphasize that some of the cosmopolitan practices, experiences, and expressions explored in this book *were* driven by issues of economic, social, and political power, and some of the musical examples discussed in the following chapters were indeed rendering the

[34] For a discussion and critique about cosmopolitanism as Eurocentric, see Robert Holton, "Some Comments on Cosmopolitanism and Europe," in *European Cosmopolitanism in Question*, eds. Roland Robertson and Anne Sophie Krossa (London and New York: Palgrave MacMillan, 2012), 25–43. For a case study in the complexity of cosmopolitanism's association with Eurocentrism, see Ackbar Abbas, "Cosmopolitan De-scriptions: Shanghai and Hong Kong," in *Cosmopolitanism*, ed. Carol Brenckenridge et al. (Durham, NC, and London: Duke University Press, 2002): 209–228, especially 210–213.

[35] Holton, "Cosmopolitanisms," 5; also Hansen, "Chasing Butterflies," 153; Gerard Delanty and B. He, "Cosmopolitan Perspectives on European and Asian Transnationalism," *International Sociology* 23, no. 3 (2008): 323–344; and Myles Lavan, Richard E. Payne, and John Weisweiler, *Cosmopolitanism and Empire: Universal Rules, Local Elites, and Cultural Integration in the Ancient Near East and Mediterranean* (New York: Oxford University Press, 2016), 1–4. For cosmopolitanism before 1800s, see Margaret Jacob, *Strangers Nowhere in the World: The Rise of Cosmopolitanism in Early Modern Europe* (Philadelphia: University of Pennsylvania Press, 2006).

[36] For this aspect of cosmopolitanism, imperialism, and power, see María Fernández, *Cosmopolitanism in Mexican Visual Culture* (Austin: University of Texas Press, 2013, Kindle); Gerard Delanty, "Cosmopolitanism and Violence: The Limits of Global Civil Society," *European Journal of Social Theory* 4, no. 1 (2001): 41–52; and Robert Fine, "Cosmopolitanism and Violence: Difficulties of Judgment," *British Journal of Sociology* 57, no. 1 (2006): 49–67.

COSMOPOLITANISM AND THE CITY   31

views and experiences of an elite, White, male majority, whose subjectivity may be viewed within the larger framework of empire formation.

Yet the musical practices examined here also show that the cosmopolitan cultural connections that became evident in turn-of-the-20th-century Rio de Janeiro offer a more complex picture than the allegations of imperial power, utopian Enlightenment thought, and elite dominance can provide. One cannot ignore, for example, cosmopolitan networks that have celebrated women's subjectivity, abolitionist ideas, and socialist reforms. In fact, throughout the long 19th century, music served to create a gamut of political, social, and cultural bonds among people from distant places, fueling everything from bohemians and anarchist causes to anti-slavery and feminist movements, to literary movements whose participants were determined to detach themselves from the aesthetic grasp of nationalistic agendas.[37] Even when cosmopolitan experiences and practices were articulated by a powerful White bourgeoisie centered in large cities, the urban bourgeoisie was not a monolithic sociopolitical group, and their responses to globalization and the resulting cosmopolitan experiences were not ones of wholehearted engagement. They were threatened by the emergence of socialism on a global scale and felt vulnerable before ideals of progress that relegated the past to a mythical state and over-estimated the future in lieu of the present. In reality, the confrontation with the possibilities of cosmopolitanism led the urban bourgeoisie to a sense of historical unpredictability, to a gloomy presage about an uncertain future without ties to locality, and resulted in a general angst manifested by expressions of romantic detachment from a potentially larger world beyond oneself, by various levels of aestheticism that eschewed the social, and by disinterested positions revealed in characteristic bohemian escapisms.[38]

Furthermore, if the cosmopolitan dynamics of the modern era were ultimately an outgrowth, or ideological reflection, of global capitalism, it is also true that markets, capitalism, and imperialism have led to a level of consumption, and musical consumption, that permitted the emergence of cosmopolitans

[37] For the anarchist movements connecting people during the period, see Benedict Anderson, *The Age of Globalization: Anarchists and the Anticolonial Imagination* (London: Verso, 2005). For connected political movements in Latin America, see Ori Preuss, *Transnational South America: Experiences, Idea, and Identities, 1860s–1900s* (New York: Routledge, 2016); also his "Discovering "os ianques do sul:" Towards an Entangled Luso-Hispanic History of Latin America," *Revista Brasil Política Internacional* 56, no. 2 (2013): 157–176. For cosmopolitan literary connections, see Camilla Fojas, *Cosmopolitanism in the Americas* (West Lafayette, IN: Purdue University Press, 2005); Jaqueline Loss, *Cosmopolitanisms and Latin America: Against the Destiny of Place* (New York: Palgrave Macmillan, 2005); and Amanda Anderson, *The Powers of Distance: Cosmopolitanism and the Cultivation of Detachment* (Princeton, NJ, and Oxford: Princeton University Press, 2001).

[38] For an outlook of the various ways in which the bourgeoisie acted as a political group, see Peter Gay, *Schnitzler's Century: The Making of Middle-Class Culture 1815–1914* (New York: W. W. Norton, 2002), 3–34.

32 MUSIC AND COSMOPOLITANISM

who never left home, who were not part of a dominant bourgeoisie, and who unwillingly were displaced from their homes and did not fit the image of the "citizen of the world" who traveled by preference.[39] Like today, past cosmopolitan experiences and practices encompassed more than a privileged (White) elite and intellectual travelers attempting to make sense of their own identity politics. They became part of the experiences of a wide spectrum of individuals and groups that, willingly or not, became entangled in the various political agendas, commercial routes, and cultural fashions originating mostly in Europe and later in the United States. At the turn of the 20th century, a cosmopolitan experience was a part of a wide spectrum of social, gender, and racial contexts, and became, to a large extent, unavoidable. The narrative about music and cosmopolitanism explored in the following chapters is thus dependent on the understanding that a wide range of musical practices and experiences were produced and shared as commodities and understood as a result of capitalist practices. At the same time, musical works and performing and listening practices were stories of production and consumption that nonetheless intertwined the social, the aesthetic, and culture as capital.[40]

Yet to grasp all the aspects of the cosmopolitan musical practices and experiences that I explore here, one needs to go beyond the economics of cultural sharing. The growth of the music business and the emergence of the recording industry led to a new music professionalism that heightened composers' and performers' needs to negotiate, and thus to reflect on, their professional aspirations and needs for self-expression, and the needs of patrons and audiences who were not only near and familiar, but also of those who were far away and unknown to them—those who could only be imagined.[41] In addition, an unprecedented number of artists, performers, directors, teachers, composers, and arrangers took advantage of affordable and rapid transportation to travel in search of employment and to perform for new audiences and with musicians from all corners of the globe. These musicians were not nation-builders, although some capitalized on the appeal of local practices. They were also not

---

[39] Bruce Robbins, "Introduction Part I: Actually Existing Cosmopolitanism," in *Cosmopolitics: Thinking and Feeling beyond the Nation*, ed. Pheng Cheah and Bruce Robbins (Minneapolis: University of Minnesota Press, 1998), 8.

[40] For consumer culture, the morality of consumerism, and the need to understand global dynamics historically, see Frank Trentmann, "Crossing Divides: Consumption and Globalization in History," *Journal of Consumer Culture* 9, no. 2 (2009): 187–220. "Cultural capital" is a term coined by Pierre Bourdieu and Jean-Claude Passeron; see Pierre Bourdieu, "The Forms of Capital," in *Handbook of Theory and Research for the Sociology of Education*, ed. John Richardson (New York: Greenwood Press, 1986), 241–258. See also John Urry, *Consuming Places* (New York: Routledge, 1995), and Jeannie Germann Molz, "Cosmopolitanism and Consumption," in *The Ashgate Research Companion to Cosmopolitanism*, ed. Maria Rovisco and Magdalena Nowika (Surrey, UK: Ashgate, 2011).

[41] William Weber, "Introduction," in *The Musician as Entrepreneur, 1700–1914: Managers, Charlatans, and Idealists*, ed. William Weber (Bloomington: Indiana University Press, 2004), 15–17.

merely "cultural brokers" interested in building bridges between cultures, although they eventually did just that.[42] They navigated a subjective media to overcome physical borders by exploring shared modes of musical expressions that catered to people beyond the scope of their locality, and by providing musics that reflected on, constructed, and challenged the complexities of their modernity. To make themselves relevant and meaningful to large and varied audiences, and to make a living, musicians of all walks of life—those active in concert halls, theaters, music halls—provided their audiences with an expressive way to locate themselves at the cusp of an imagined modern world, which was often believed to lie both nearby and beyond the boundaries of their locality.

It can be said that by the turn of the 20th century, musical exchanges and sharing became not only necessary, but expected and, to some degree, coveted. The entertainment and music businesses, including the business of the operatic theater and, to some extent, the concert hall, were cosmopolitan at their inception and thus shaped and were shaped by the experiences and tastes of a growing and increasingly connected large middle-class strata often located in cities. Nineteenth-century music audiences were also cosmopolitan consumers who shared a sense of aural-historical position.[43] In fact, studies on music reception during the long 19th century have pointed out that urban audiences were rarely bound to musical markers of places, or requested to hear particular composers that are now understood as canonic figures representative of the nation, but rather they sought multiplicity in performance styles, media, instrumentation, and explorations of novel sounds. Within this context, some musical works and performances went viral—from "La Marseillaise" to cabaret songs, from dances like cake-walks, polkas, and *maxixes* to popular theater songs such as Lehár's "Merry Widow's Waltz;" from Mozart's Requiem and Wagner's *Tannhäuser* overture to excerpts from Verdi's *Il Trovatore* and Carlos Gome's *Il Guarany*. These and many other musical works pervaded in the most unexpected places, their appeal and cultural and musical relevance resting both on their musical qualities and on responses from diverse audiences in many sociocultural contexts. Thus, within a connected musical environment, the multiplicity and multidirectionality of specific works, and performers' and audiences' agencies, do not fit discourses of "universalism nostalgia,"[44] or narrations of "Othering" mostly supported by

---

[42] Martin Rempe and Claudius Torpe, "Cultural Brokers and the Making of Glocal Soundscapes," *Itinerario* 41, no. 2 (2017): 223–233; see also Rutger Helmers, "The Traveling Musician as Cosmopolitan: Western Performers and Composers in Mid-Nineteenth-Century St. Petersburg and Moscow," in *Confronting the National in the Musical Past*, ed. Kelly, Mantere, and Scott, 64–77.

[43] Hoganson explores this aspect of audiences in the U.S.; see her "Cosmopolitan Domesticity," 55–83.

[44] James Clifford, *The Predicament of Culture: Twentieth-Century Ethnography, Literature, and Art* (Cambridge, MA: Harvard University Press), 362; cited in Jacqueline Loss, *Cosmopolitanisms and Latin America: Against the Destiny of Place* (New York: Palgrave Macmillan, 2006), 12.

34 MUSIC AND COSMOPOLITANISM

Eurocentric perspectives. Their engagements with music and performances were explorations and critiques of expanding spaces of cultural belongings, a reflection of one's position in an interconnected and interdependent cosmopolitan urban network at a particular historical moment.

As Papastergiadis contends, the cosmopolitan dimension of artistic practices suggests a more ambiguous terrain and multidirectional flow than the usual focus on cosmopolitanism as a tool for moral, ethic, and political claims. For cosmopolitan experiences and practices ultimately come to exist beyond politics of the nation and the marketability of cultural capital, to shape musical tropes of time and space codified historically and transmitted to large numbers of people: a cosmopolitan expressive worldview that was produced through shared aesthetics.[45] In the selected examples in this book, I show how a cosmopolitan lens can interrogate music's role for both "imagining the world" and for "world making," adding aural and musical elements to visual experiences, oral expressions, and cultural literacy that have characterized the many layers of shared social experiences during the period. The explorations of the cosmopolitan realm of musical practices should lead to the rethinking of how music mattered then and ultimately also show that the full story of music-making during the period is yet to be told.[46]

Urban Networks

I do not want to suggest that cosmopolitanism is a practice or experience that is present everywhere, but rather that it surfaces in specific sociohistorical conditions and privileges particular places, times, and groups.[47] In the second half of the 19th century, the term became especially associated with the growth of cities, city life, and notions of urban modernity. Tanya Agathocleous argues that cosmopolitan experiences and practices thrived in cities exactly because they allowed for an aesthetic perception that linked world perspectives to a

---

[45] Papastergiadis, *Cosmopolitanism and Culture* (Kindle). Nicholas Cook suggests a similar approach to 21st-century musics, pointing to how electronic technologies have "opened up possibilities of composing, layering, and fusing global sounds on a purely aesthetic basis, without regard to their cultural or geographical origins"; see his "Western Music as World Music," in *The Cambridge History of World Music*, ed. Philip V. Bohlman (Cambridge, UK: Cambridge University Press, 2013), 91. Cook had explored this idea earlier in "Anatomy of the Encounter: Intercultural Analysis as Relational Musicology," in *Critical Musicological Reflections: Essays in Honor of Derek Scott*, ed. Stan Hawkins (Farnham, Surrey, UK: Ashgate, 2012), 193–208.

[46] I am paraphrasing Susan MacClary's analysis of 20th-century music studies; see her *Conventional Wisdom: The Content of Musical Form* (Berkeley: University of California Press, 2001), 196.

[47] Bruce Robbins and Paulo Lemos Horta, eds., *Cosmopolitanisms* (New York: New York University Press, 2017), 1–2.

COSMOPOLITANISM AND THE CITY   35

localized, urban experience claiming to be unbound by nation-state ties.[48] As cities were solidified into social and cultural "new organisms," to use Richard Sennett's term, their inner workings tended to follow urban networks marked by economic interdependency and migration, rather than by politics of nation-building.[49] Osterhammel suggests that these networks emerged either as a vertical organization—a multiplicity of villages at the bottom to a central location at the top—or they could be organized through horizontal relationships, depending on each city's function and role within a network. The horizontal network "may be seen in terms of interaction between an urban center and its peripheries, or with another urban center of a similar kind . . . depending on their control over distant markets or sources of supply." These horizontal urban networks, Osterhammel argues, are organized not only over commerce and markets, but also as sociocultural hubs characterized by an "openness . . . to the outside world" and are "the product of human action . . . [with] no objective existence"; and as such they "are sometimes not visible on maps."[50]

In both the theatrical and musical worlds, these horizontal urban cultural networks were often shaped by intercontinental and transcontinental trade routes that operated mostly outside national cultural policies and that generated complex and fluid patterns of commercial and cultural connections that are difficult to tackle as a large system, even if from the perspective of a select macro-region, as Mark Evarisk suggests.[51] Christopher Balme points out, for example, that "Even familiar transatlantic routes such as London–New York or Berlin–New York remain under or not at all researched in terms of the way they constructed and sustained a public sphere that appears to be coexistent

---

[48] Tanya Agathocleous, *Urban Realism and the Cosmopolitan Imagination in the Nineteenth Century: Visible City, Invisible World* (Cambridge, UK, and New York: Cambridge University Press, 2010), xiv and 118.

[49] For a connection between cities and globalization, see Richard Sennett, "Capitalism and the City: Globalization, Flexibility and Indifference," in *Cities of Europe: Changing Contexts, Local Arrangements, and the Challenge to Urban Cohesion* (New York: Blackwell, 2008), 109–121; Andreas Huyssen, "Introduction: World Cultures, World Cities," in *Other Cities, Other Worlds: Urban Imaginaries in a Globalizing Age*, ed. Andreas Huyssen (Durham, NC: Duke University Press, 2008), 1–23. For connection among cities in Latin America, Beatriz Helena Dominguez, "Cidades como pessoas: Uma genealogia das formulações de Richard Morse sobre as cidades na América Latina," *Intellèctus* 15, no. 2 (2016): 1–24; Beatriz Helena Dominguez, "Do Fausto de Goethe ao Fausto de Estanislao del Campo: Cidades e identidades em arenas 'periféricas' da Europa e da American Latina em fins do século XIX," in *História da América: historiografia e interpretacões*, ed. Luis Estevão de Oliveira Fernandes (Ouro Preto, MG: Universidade Federal de Ouro Preto, 2012), 306–319; and Camilla Fojas, *Cosmopolitanism in the Americas* (West Lafayette, IN: Purdue University Press, 2006), 1–25.

[50] Jürgen Osterhammel, *The Transformation of the World: A Global History of the Nineteenth Century*, trans. Patrick Camiller (Princeton, NJ: Princeton University Press, 2014 [2009]), 261–263.

[51] Mark Evarisk, "Cosmopolitanism and Music for the Theater: Europe and Beyond, 1800–1870," in *Music History and Cosmopolitanism*, ed. Anastasia Belina, Kaarina Kilpiö, and Derek Scott (New York: Routledge, 2017), 27.

36   MUSIC AND COSMOPOLITANISM

in two places at once." [52] Those transoceanic routes, he notes, could also include Madrid-Buenos Aires, London-Calcutta, Paris-Algiers, not to mention connections among many ports within Latin America, Asia, the Mediterranean, etc., Notwithstanding, Adam Krims argued that "the commercial life of music production and consumption . . . [occurs] often within a small number of specific cities."[53] Krims referred to the 20th-century music business, but his observation could easily refer to specific late-19th-century cities, such as Paris, London, or New York. By the beginning of the 20th century, these cities had grown into complex human conglomerates that centralized and crystallized the political, economic, and cultural expansion of Europe and the United States. While scholars have underscored them as "imperial cities," as places where imperial politics of nation-states were showcased in World Exhibitions, these metropolises also became sites for experiencing, critiquing, and imagining sociocultural, ethnic, racial, and gender encounters, and as spaces for awareness of and reflections on disconnections and exclusions (from nearby and faraway) brought about by urban modernity. And as these cities continued to grow and connect to other cities, they brought into question not only the concept of nation, but ultimately also the concept of Europe as a unified whole.[54] These cities solidified some of the period's most marked characteristics of Western urban expansion and became staples of a historical moment, encapsulating feelings of both the *belle époque*'s disinterestedness and the *fin-de-siècle*'s pessimist views of a world at the fringe of collapse. Agathocleous notes that Victorian realist writers unapologetically explored London as a prototype of a "world-city," as a "representative of mankind," a place with "universal resonances" where one would "apprehend global modernity," both in its utopian possibilities and failures.[55] Walter Benjamin described Paris not merely as the capital of France, but as the capital of the 19th century, as a place that encapsulated a temporal *geist* that exuded modernity while exposing capitalism's flaws.[56] Early in his career, Richard Wagner

---

[52] See Christopher Balme, "Theater and Globalization, the Cairo Opera House," in *Syncretic Arenas: Essays on Postcolonial African Drama and Theatre for Esiaba Irobi*, ed. Isidore Diala (Amsterdam: Brill, 2014), 145. See also, Christopher Balme and Nic Leonhardt, "Introduction: Theatrical Trader Routes," *Journal of Global Theatre History* 1, no. 1 (2016): 1–9.

[53] Adam Krims, *Music and Urban Geography* (New York: Routledge, 2007), xvii; see also Markian Prokopovych, "Introduction: Music, the City, and the Modern Experience," *Urban History* 40, no. 4 (November 2013): 597–605.

[54] Moretti, *Distant Reading*, 42–43.

[55] Agathocleous, *Urban Realism*, 117–119. See also Joseph Jeffrey De Sapio, *Modernity and Meaning in Victorian London: Tourist Views of the Imperial Capital* (New York: Palgrave Macmillan, 2014). For a focus on Paris, see David Harvey, *Paris, Capital of Modernity* (London: Routledge, 2003).

[56] Walter Benjamin, *The Arcades Project*, trans. Rolf Tiedemann, ed. Howard Eiland and Kevin McLaughlin (Cambridge, MA: Harvard University Press, 2002). Georg Simmel used Berlin as an example as he thought of the industrializing city as a state of mind; see *The Metropolis and Mental Life* [1903], cited in James Donald, *Imagining the Modern City* (Minneapolis: University of Minnesota Press, 1999), 8.

described Paris as "the center of the world, where the arts of every nation stream together to one focus,"[57] only to disparage Paris later for the city's capacity to embrace outsiders and minorities and enthrall a decadent bourgeoisie with no national commitments. Either way, Wagner and many other composers saw in the city more than its local context.

The cosmopolitan experiences and practices explored here are thus inextricably tied to these and other cities in Europe and later also in the United States. However, acknowledging the ubiquitous positions of these metropolises vis-à-vis a network of urban culture and the production, circulation, and sharing of musics does not grant them exclusivity, autonomy, or precedence in the experiences and artistic expressions of modernity and the imaginations of the world that I explore here. For cities were not complete sociocultural organisms, but rather depended on a world beyond themselves in which to build and establish and expand their own positions in an urban network of cultural practices. Thus, the turn-of-the-century cosmopolitan musical cultures that I consider here were a result of networks that included not only Paris, London, Milan, Berlin, or New York, but also Lisbon, Madrid, Buenos, Aires, Montevideo, Havana, Rio de Janeiro, and many other cities—and here I explore the Brazilian capital as a node in a complex cultural and musical network. This focus on horizontal and interdependent networks has the potential to disrupt familiar dichotomies of dominance/dependency and home/away that underwrite national narratives of music production and performance. It allows us to conjecture that the cosmopolitan experiences and practices that surfaced within and among cities were located in both material and imaginative spaces emerging either in a sequence or simultaneously. It was within this extended urban cultural network, I suggest, that a cosmopolitan experience and practice could be fully manifested, critiqued, mediated, amplified, and further multiplied. From this perspective, London, Paris, and other contemporary growing cities projected an imagined world that colored the imaginations and shaped the experiences of millions of individuals living in cities nearby and faraway.[58] These metropolises emerged as poetic sources for an urban collectivity situated well beyond their own geographies through literary works, the arts, architecture, and through music production, performance, and listening. These cities were, as James Donald suggests,

---

[57] Therese Dolan, *Manet, Wagner, and the Musical Culture of Their Time* (Surrey, UK: Ashgate, 2013), 23.

[58] For imaginaries of Paris in Latin America, see Marcy Schwartz, *Writing Paris: Urban Topographies of Desire in Contemporary Latin American Fiction* (Albany: State University of New York Press, 1999); and Fojas, *Cosmopolitanism in the Americas*, 1–25. For imaginaries of Paris in Northern Europe, see Elisabeth Oxfeldt, *Nordic Orientalism: Paris and the Cosmopolitan Imagination 1800–1900* (Copenhagen: Museum Tusculanum Press, 2005). For the cultural dimensions and the ecological scope of *fin-de-siècle* urban cosmopolitics, see Henk Driessen, "Mediterranean Port Cities: Cosmopolitanism Reconsidered," *History and Anthropology* 16, no. 1 (2005): 136–137.

"laboratories and archives of experiences, a conceptual location and an embodiment of modernity."[59] Paris in particular, Marcy Schwartz points out, turned into a form of agency in Latin America, "a metaphor for a broad spectrum of culturally bound desires."[60]

Ultimately, the study of a cosmopolitan urban network in the context of cities, and of Rio de Janeiro in particular, allows us to put the idea of musical Europeanness to the test. While scholars have critiqued how the building of music canons has elevated and prioritized a hegemonic West-Eurocentric music culture, they have also essentialized an imagined European musical language and its forged canons, which are often seen as unique, static, and complete social and cultural systems, as both the source and the final product. Exploring the many paths taken by the novel in the 19th century, Moretti claims that for the understanding of the novel "[h]egemony does not belong to those that produce exiles, but to those that welcome them."[61] Exploring a network of shared music cultural relationships among cities can thus allow the burden of national cultural ownership to lessen and erode assumptions of authenticity, originality, and ultimately of hegemonic force, as one follows music flowing through the fragility and porosity of borders. Rather than a perceived center, one can thus observe "Europe breaking away" as an archipelago of cities, Moretti suggests, a discontinuous space that finds force through widely different paths outside itself.[62] Considering musical practices in Rio de Janeiro as part of such a cosmopolitan network allows us to explore music's openness to unbounded transformations, collective creativity, and shared aesthetic experiences as they were fostered by a turn-of-the-century multilayered urban imaginary.

Such an exploration will also lay bare the cultural complexities of a rapidly changing historical period: a temporal/geographical position that places Rio de Janeiro on the periphery of the global capitalist market, but no less a participant in a cosmopolitan circuit of urban culture. The urban network in which Rio de Janeiro's composers, performers, and audiences operated did not lead to a lack of subjectivity or creativity, but it often reveals a lack of power to have a role beyond their locality. In the end, that realization highlights the fact that Rio de Janeiro musicians and audiences were not cultural outsiders, nor did they lack agency in the process, but they were often political outsiders. Still, Walter Mignolo suggests that today people are bringing themselves into the conversation of cosmopolitan

---

[59] Donald, *Imagining the Modern City*, 8–10; also Sennett, "Cosmopolitanism and the Social Experience of Cities," 42–47.

[60] Schwartz, *Writing Paris*, 1. For the influence of Paris on Latin American modernist writers, see Mariano Siskind, *Cosmopolitan Desires: Global Modernity and World Literature in Latin America* (Evanston, IL: Northwestern University Press, 2014); and Fojas, *Cosmopolitanism in the Americas*, 43–60.

[61] Moretti, *Distant Reading*, 44–45.

[62] Moretti, *Distant Reading*, 27.

COSMOPOLITANISM AND THE CITY   39

projects, rather than waiting to be included.[63] Similarly, I suggest that before Brazil became engulfed in the political and intellectual currents of nationalism in the second and third decades of the 20th century, individuals living in Rio de Janeiro were also bringing themselves into the cosmopolitan conversation, willing to express themselves in many musical and cultural languages, to pose ideas, and to offer critiques of their own positions within their imagined modern city.

A Connected *Fin-de-Siècle*

Timing was critical in creating the conditions for Rio de Janeiro to partake in this urban cosmopolitanism. At the turn of the 20th century, the strengthening of European imperial forces, the emerging power of the United States, and the expansion of global markets led to an unprecedented growth of direct and indirect connections among peoples and places across borders. Jürgen Osterhammel argues that "[t]he *fin-de-siècle* would be the most intense period of migration in world history," leading to "a surge in globalization that for the first time linked all continents into economic and communications networks."[64] This "first wave of globalization" is often described as the period that runs roughly between 1870 and 1914, from the aftermath of the Franco-Prussian War to World War I, although some indications had been in place much earlier.[65] This condition would change dramatically after the Great War, when high transportation costs and nationalizing policies caused the fragmentation of world commodity markets and the disruption of global trade.[66] The "first wave of globalization" was no doubt intensified by an unprecedented growth of technological advances. According to Vaclav Smil, the turn of the 20th century was, in the technological sense, "when the modern world was created."[67] Advances in navigation, the steam engine, and

---

[63] Walter Mignolo, "The Many Faces of Cosmo-polis: Border Thinking and Critical Cosmopolitanism," *Public Culture* 12, no. 3 (2000): 736–737.

[64] Osterhammel, *The Transformation of the World*, 64 and 910; see also Christopher Bayly, *The Birth of the Modern World* (Oxford: Blackwell, 2004), 458.

[65] For explorations of cosmopolitanism in early 19th-century Britain, see Esther Wohlgemut, *Romantic Cosmopolitanism* (New York: Palgrave Macmillan, 2009). For the economic outlook that characterizes this early globalization, see Frederic S. Mishkin, *The Next Great Globalization: How Disadvantaged Nations Can Harness Their Financial Systems to Get Rich* (Princeton, NJ: Princeton University Press, 2006), 2–3. For the growing pace of the economic interaction within the continents, see Bayly, *The Birth of the Modern World*, 451–487; Michael Howard, "The Down of the Century," in *The Oxford History of the Twentieth Century,* ed. Michael Howard and Wm Roger Louis (Oxford: Oxford University Press, 2000), 3–9; and Michael Geyer and Charles Bright, "World History in a Global Age," *American Historical Review* 100, no. 4 (1995): 1034–1060.

[66] Stephen Broadberry and Kevin O'Rourke, *The Cambridge Economic History of Modern Europe*, Vol. 2: *1870 to the Present* (Cambridge, UK: Cambridge University Press, 2010), 1–2.

[67] Vaclav Smil, *Creating the Twentieth Century: Technical Innovations of 1867–1914 and Their Lasting Impact* (New York: Oxford University Press, 2005), 4.

railway systems made transportation considerably cheaper and shortened geographic distances; the telegraph, the mail, and the telephone sped up old and sustained new modes of communication;[68] further developments in printing technology, photography, the phonograph, and the movies accelerated and helped broaden the circulation of news, images, and sounds from and within places in Europe, its colonies, the Americas, and elsewhere. In the end, one can say that few escaped the tentacles of this early globalization, if at different paces and in different ways.[69]

As a result, the turn of the 20th century was also a period of exceptional levels of cultural sharing that spawned multifaceted imaginations of a world beyond one's locality. The period encapsulates contrasting but intertwined ideals of modernity and expressions of an unbounded world. On the one hand, the so-called *fin-de-siècle* was characterized by sociopolitical concerns, confrontations with the forces of imperialism and capitalism, feelings of decadence and moral decay, and overall pessimism about the future. On the other hand, the *belle époque* displayed bourgeois sociopolitical naïveté, a faith in order and progress, belief in the superior powers of the Western world, and detachment from the social, racial, and gender consequences of imperialism.[70] With its promises and disappointments, interconnections and discontinuities, the turn of the 20th century recalls our own contemporary world, and as such it has cultural and historical implications that go beyond its own time: as Dariusz Gafijczuk eloquently put it, the period is "the closest we have come to something like the founding mythology of the present time."[71]

Expectedly, Rio de Janeiro chroniclers were in sync with the larger trends that characterized their time. Yet the urgency with which they describe the changes around them and their city's worldly connections points to idiosyncrasies of a local context: a time when many Latin American countries, having consolidated their links to North Atlantic centers, were attempting to participate in the capitalist system centered in Europe and the United States. The entrance and

---

[68] David Henkin, *The Postal Age: The Emergence of Modern Communications in Nineteenth Century America* (Chicago: University of Chicago Press, 2007).

[69] Kevin O'Rourke and Jeffrey Williamson suggest that during this period Asia, Africa, the Middle East, and Eastern Europe failed to catch up with the growing Atlantic economy; see their *Globalization and History: The Evolution of a Nineteenth Century Atlantic Economy* (Boston, MA: MIT Press, 2001), 5.

[70] For these and other readings of the period, see Barbara Tuchman, *The Proud Tower: A Portrait of the World before the War, 1890–1914* (New York: Ballantine Books, 2011 [1963]); and Michael Heffernan, "Fin de Siècle, Fin du Monde? On the Origins of European Geopolitics: 1890–1920," in *Geopolitical Traditions: A Century of Geopolitical Thought*, ed. Klaus Dodds and David Atkinson (London and New York: Routledge, 2000), 28–31.

[71] Dariusz Gafijczuk, *Identity, Aesthetics and Sound in the Fin de Siècle: Redesigning Perception* (New York: Routledge, 2014), 2. See also Keith Hanley and Greg Kucich, "Introduction: Global Formations and Recalcitrances," in *Nineteenth-Century Worlds: Global Formations Past and Present*, ed. Hanley and Kucich (New York: Routledge, 2013), 1–8.

COSMOPOLITANISM AND THE CITY   41

participation of Latin American countries in the "Atlantic economy" was unequivocally European centered, a process in which dependency and prosperity
conspired with one another.[72] Unlike places where globalization and dependency were strengthened by colonial rule, in Latin American independent nations the process was one of opportunity and, to a degree, self-driven, mostly by
a White political and intellectual elite whose ties to Europe continued from the
early days of colonization.[73] These ties were ultimately furthered by the middle
section of the social strata living in large cities, who saw themselves as a part of
the European sociohistorical and cultural nexus and whose subjectivity could
not be extricated from a European political, economic, and cultural network.[74]

Capital and port cities like Rio de Janeiro became important hubs in the ex-
port/import circuit of commercial and cultural goods and, as such, they came
to exhibit a homogenous pattern of economic growth and cultural sharing.[75]
With similar forms of urban development and growth resulting from similar
aspirations of the emergent middle class, port cities became part of a larger cultural nexus, one that helped define Latin American cities through their historical,
political, economic, and cultural links to Europe and its colonies and that also
became a common thread connecting cities in the Americas to one another.[76] At
the end of the 19th century, Rio de Janeiro held the second-largest influx of foreign commerce in the Americas, behind only New York City.[77] By the beginning
of the 20th century, Rio de Janeiro's port was the third-largest commercial hub
in the Americas, after New York City and the emerging Buenos Aires. Together,
Rio de Janeiro, Buenos Aires, and Montevideo formed the fourth-largest international commercial circuit in maritime trade in the world.[78] As such, they became strong links in a network of migration from North to South of the equator

[72] O'Rourke and Williamson, *Globalization and History*, 9; Leslie Bethell, *Brazil: Empire and Republic, 1822-1930* (Cambridge, UK: Cambridge University Press, 1989), 7-8 and 44.

[73] For a study of the continuing connections between Latin American countries and Europe after independence, see Matthew Brown and Gabriel Paquette, "Between the Age of Atlantic Revolutions and the Age of Empire: Europe and Latin America in the Axial Decade of the 1820s," in *Connections after Colonialism: Europe and Latin America in the 1820s*, ed. Matthew Brown and Gabriel Paquette (Tuscaloosa: University of Alabama Press, 2013), 1-28.

[74] Frank Zephyr goes as far as to say that in Brazil, "there were no ideas other than European ideas"; he means, of course, from the perspective of the White, literate ruling classes; see his *Reading Rio de Janeiro: Literature and Society in the Nineteenth-Century* (Stanford, CA: Stanford University Press, 2016), 18. For a similar connection in the United States, see Kristin Hoganson, "Cosmopolitan Domesticity: Importing the American Dream, 1865-1920," *The American Historical Review* 107 (2002): 55-83.

[75] Osterhammel, *The Transformation of the World*, 275-282.

[76] Preuss notes the connections and disconnections between the Latin American countries and Brazil during this period; see his *Transnational South America*, 5.

[77] Fernando Mencarelli, "A voz e a partitura: Teatro musical, indústria e diversidade cultural no Rio de Janeiro (1868-1908)," PhD dissertation, Universidade Estadual de Campinas, S.P., 2003, 29.

[78] Osterhammel, *The Transformation of the World*, 714; see also Mark Frost, "Maritime Networks and the Colonial Public Sphere, 1840-1920," *New Zealand Journal of Asian Studies* 6, no. 2 (2004): 63-94.

42   MUSIC AND COSMOPOLITANISM

and a significant link in the transatlantic cultural flows that fueled the careers of performers, composers, theater managers, and that sustained the music printing and early movie businesses.

In the two decades studied here, Rio de Janeiro's population doubled, growing from 500,000 in 1890, to 800,000 in 1901, and to about one million at the end of the first decade of the century. By 1910, Rio de Janeiro became an urban conglomerate comparable to several contemporary cities, like Madrid, Philadelphia, and Buenos Aires. Yet Rio de Janeiro's dimensions could not compare with much more densely populated Paris, London, New York, or Berlin,[79] and its population had a much more diversified social, racial, and ethnic fabric than most contemporary European cities. By the early 1900s, more than a quarter of Rio de Janeiro's population was made up of European immigrants, mostly Portuguese, Spanish, Italians, French, and Germans.[80] Second only to the United States by the early 20th century, Brazil and Argentina—and mostly Rio de Janeiro and Buenos Aires—had received the largest numbers of European immigrants in the world. Furthermore, at the turn of the 20th century the city's Black population was the largest in the Americas; half of Rio de Janeiro's population was of African descent, their life experiences linked to both a very recent past of slavery and a present defined by lack of opportunities and exclusion.[81] If, for some, the city's worldly connections suggested a bright future for development and growth, its streets were marked by intense competition, segregation, and constant urban sociopolitical and racial tensions.

These tensions were further exacerbated by the rapidly changing sociopolitical order inside Brazil. In 1888, after external political and economic pressures and much controversial internal political debate, slavery was abolished, officially ending a long history of human subjugation, although the rights to citizenship and political participation of Blacks remained an unfulfilled dream for most. For the White, Eurocentric population of the city, the presence of large numbers of

---

[79] Bruno Carvalho, *Porous City: A Cultural History of Rio de Janeiro* (Liverpool, UK: Liverpool University Press, 2013), 48–49. For a broader comparison of urban populations around the world, see Bayly, *The Birth of the Modern World*, 189; Osterhammel, *The Transformation of the World*, 953; and Jean-Pierre Bardet and Jacques Dupâquier, *Histoire des populations de l'Europe* (Paris: Fayard, 1997), 227.

[80] Leslie Bethell, *Brazil: Empire and Republic, 1822–1930* (Cambridge: Cambridge University Press, 1989), 19.

[81] Jeffrey Needell, A *Tropical Belle Époque: The Elite Culture of Turn-of-the-Twentieth-Century Rio de Janeiro* (New York: Cambridge University Press, 1987), 49. For how African practices were targeted during this period, see Thomas Holloway, *Policing Rio de Janeiro: Repression and Resistance in a Nineteenth-Century City* (Stanford, CA: Stanford University Press, 1993); Benchimol, *Pereira Passos*, 277– 285; Nicolau Sevcenko, *Literatura como missão: Tensões sociais e criação cultural na Primeira República* (Companhia das Letras, 2003), 49; and Carvalho, *Porous City*, 1–10. For the resulting "structural racism" in today's society, see Jennifer Roth-Gordon, *Race and the Brazilian Body: Blackness, Whiteness, and Everyday Language* (Oakland: University of California Press, 2017, Kindle).

Blacks was viewed with much caution, since they understood the Black population, now free, to be a threat to their property and personal safety. As a result, laws, social institutions, and social relations post-abolition were carefully shaped as to racially segregate more, rather than less.[82] At the same time, the government started to promote European immigration in a deliberate attempt to "whiten" the local population that had become inescapably dominated by Blacks and mixed-race individuals, a strategy that was mirrored in many Latin American cities with high European immigration like Havana, Montevideo, and Buenos Aires.[83]

One year after the abolition of slavery in 1889, Brazil's nearly 60-year-old monarchy was overturned in favor of republicanism, a move that had been in the works for decades and that launched the country into a new political and economic era under the positivistic motto "Order and Progress." The new government immediately put in place measures that further opened Brazilian markets to foreign investments, and a new republican constitution endowed citizenship to immigrants living in the country, while restricting the rights of the Black and Indigenous populations. While during the nineteenth century the monarchical regime had sustained old political systems and cultural connections across the Atlantic, during the first two decades of the Republic, in rapid succession the country saw the construction of new social institutions and the establishment of a new set of social, racial, and cultural relations that were dependent on intense external political, commercial, intellectual, and cultural connections with Europe. The decades from the late 1890s to 1914 became major historic catalysts that propelled Brazil into the twentieth century, a time that historian Lilia Schwarcz has defined as the country's "opening to the world," having Rio de Janeiro as the main gateway.[84]

---

[82] Marc Hertzman, *Making Samba: A New History of Race and Music in Brazil* (Durham, NC: Duke University Press), 37. See also Lilia Schwarcz, *O espetáculo das raças: Cientistas, instituições e questão racial no Brasil, 1870–1930* (São Paulo: Companhia das Letras, 1993). It was not until 1916, when Brazil finally adopted a Civil Code, that the last legal traces of slavery were wiped away; see Keila Grinberg, "Slavery, Liberalism, and Civil Law: Definitions of Status and Citizenship in the Elaboration of the Brazilian Civil Code (1855–1916)," in *Honor, Status, and Law in Modern Latin America*, ed. Sueann Caulfield, Sarah C. Chambers, and Lara Putnam (Durham, NC: Duke University Press, 2005), 109–127.

[83] For studies about race in general, and in association with theater and music, see Jill Lane, *Blackface Cuba: 1840–1895* (Philadelphia: University of Pennsylvania Press, 2005); and Susan Thomas, *Performing Race and Gender Havana's Lyric Stage* (Urbana and Chicago: University of Illinois Press, 2009). For Argentina and Uruguay, see Lea Geler, *Andares negros, caminos blancos: Afroporteños, estado y nación Argentina a fines del siglo XIX* (Rosario, Argentina: Prohistoria Ediciones; Universidad de Barcelona, 2010); George Reid Andrews, *Blackness in the White Nation: A History of Afro-Uruguay* (Chapel Hill: University of North Carolina Press, 2010); and Alex Borucki, *From Shipmates to Soldiers: Emerging Black Identities in the Río de la Plata* (Albuquerque: University of New Mexico Press, 2015).

[84] Lilia Schwarcz uses the expression as a title to her edited book *A abertura para o mundo, 1889–1930* (Rio de Janeiro: Objetiva, 2012); see also Joseph Love, "The Brazilian Federal State in the Old Republic: Did Regime Change Make a Difference?," in *State and Nation Making in Latin America and Spain: Republics of the Possible*, ed. Miguel Centeno and Agustin Ferrano (Cambridge, UK,

44 MUSIC AND COSMOPOLITANISM

The almost concomitant abolition of slavery, the end of the long years of monarchy, the launching of a republican government, and the need to incorporate the new nation as part of a larger global whole gave rise to conflicting political and intellectual discourses of Enlightenment, universalism, and human freedom. These were entangled with an uncritical adherence to Comte's positivism, social Darwinism, and various strains of 19th-century anthropological and scientific understandings of race, culture, and nationality, which had already brought about full-fledged racist and nationalist ideologies in Europe. Local writers, artists, musicians, and critics provided their own accounts of the country's sociopolitical and cultural moment. Theirs were doubtless privileged accounts in a country with a predominantly illiterate population, but ones that nonetheless laid bare the political, cultural, and aesthetic differences between official government narratives and many parallel and contradictory contemporary ideas of how to understand and forge the new nation and to locate the modern city within a world believed to be larger than its surroundings. In Rio de Janeiro, romantics, Parnassians, realists, and symbolists coexisted and competed among one another, providing views of the city that were either preponderantly pessimist or deliberately escapist. Narrated from within the city, the new nation was above all irreconcilable and excluding; "The nation is repugnant to me," Lima Barreto declared. Writing from a privileged position in the city, as a mulatto he still pointed to a nation from which he felt left out.[85]

These complex experiences and sociopolitical modes of thought underlined an acute sense not only of geographical spaces, but also of time. On the one hand, the new Brazilian political system began to take shape and the country started to offer a market for North Atlantic investments and trade, fueling local aspirations for an equal partnership. On the other hand, the international globalization process propelled by European imperialism and the expansion of capitalist markets started to show its maturation and was, in fact, about to decline. While those in some European countries were engaging with definitions of physical and cultural borders, looking inward to shape their own cultural histories in support of ideologies of nationalism, in the Brazilian capital, intellectuals, politicians, and artists were imagining a local context that mingled various possibilities to define their past, to understand their present, and to shape their future, harvesting ideals of modernity for a society plagued by the socio-racial consequences of colonialism, a monarchical system, and a long-held institution of slavery. Within a turn-of-the-century cosmopolitan sociocultural urban network, Rio de Janeiro

and New York: Cambridge University Press, 2013), 108; and Angela Marques da Costa and Lilia Schwarcz, *1890–1914: No tempo das certezas* (São Paulo: Companhia das Letras, 2007).

[85] Cited in, Maurício Silva, *A hélade e o subúrbio: Confrontos literários na belle époque carioca* (São Paulo: Editora Universidade de São Paulo, 2006), 24.

was at the beginning of its ascendancy as a participating player at a historical point of global downturn. And yet, in the context of such fast-paced changes, Rio de Janeiro's political and sociohistorical position allowed for the rise of a fecund, though ephemeral, moment of artistic and musical expressions in which the old and the new, the local and the worldly, the visual and the sonic met in complex ways to forge a sense of both historic continuity and discontinuity, community and segregation, in tandem with aspirations for participation in a modernizing and globalized world with all its possibilities and disappointments.

2
A City to Be Seen and to Be Heard

On December 7, 1904, the Theatro Apollo in Rio de Janeiro presented the musical comedy *O Mambembe*, with text by Artur Azevedo (Figure 2.1) and music by Assis Pacheco (1865–1937). The plot, about the inner workings of a traveling theater troupe, was also a critique of the government's lack of support for the arts, a preferred topic of Azevedo's satirical plays. One of the characters is a government worker called Pantaleão, who aspires to become a playwright and uses his position to spotlight his new play titled *A passagem do mar amarelo* (The Passage of the Yellow Sea). Pantaleão's work is supposed to focus on Moses, but when questioned with suspicion about how the title could fit Moses's story, Pantaleão offers the following rationale:

> The topic of the drama is, in reality, the passage of Moses and his people to the promised land, but if [in my story] I had made him take the people through Egypt and the Red Sea it would be too easy! I wanted [Moses] to go through a longer route. So, in my story I take him to Siberia, so that I can have some scenes with ice; from there [Moses] goes south to Manchuria, Korea, Japan, and then cross the Yellow Sea. . . . On the next day—and the play will be presented over

Figure 2.1. Artur Azevedo.

two days—Moses goes through China, Hindustan, Afghanistan, Balochistan, Arabia, and then passes through the Red Sea.[1]

While Azevedo's play reveals his attempts to develop a theatrical language based on sociopolitical satire, the work also exemplifies his skill in capturing the audience's attention by leading them to imagine a world geographically bigger than it needed to be to convey Moses's story. Azevedo knew well that his audiences could be entertained by and engaged with such a plot, for the sociocultural context of the turn-of-the-20th-century Brazilian capital allowed for such imaginary travels and associations with a world larger than the local.

Rio de Janeiro itself was repeatedly depicted in the theater, newspapers, and magazines as a world in miniature: one need not travel far away, for the world was right there. Already in 1886, the actor and playwright Francisco Correia Vasques (1839–1893) saw the city as an ideal site where imaginary travels could be enacted locally. In his *A volta ao mundo in 80 days, a pé* (A trip around the world in 80 days, on foot), a parody of Jules Verne's *Le tour du monde en quatre-vingts jours* (1872), the main character claims that he could experience the world just by walking from one Rio de Janeiro street to another. "To go around the world," he affirms, "I don't need locomotives, steamboats, or elephants. I go in a more economical way: on foot." Then Vasques describes the city's streets as part of an imaginary world, referring to local restaurants and cafés with names linked to various European cities:

> Electric nation! City of great magicians! [Here] there are no foreigners, everybody is cosmopolitan, everybody is naturalized! . . . To make a trip around the world, it is sufficient to drink chocolate at the "Rio de Janeiro" [café], have lunch at the "Four Nations" [restaurant], have a snack at the "Portugal" [café], have dinner at the "Europa" [restaurant], have coffee at the "América" [café], a late dinner at the "Paris" [restaurant], and sleep at the "Universo" [hotel].[2]

To better convey the experience of long-distance travel within the city, Vasquez then uses music and dance as ways of being elsewhere while staying in place:

> Ah, compadre, let's cross the Ocean. There is France . . . one, two, three! We are in Paris (sing "Soir de Carnaval"); there is England . . . one, two, three, ready, we are in London (dance the *solo Ingles*);[3] let's go to Italy . . . one, two, three, here

---

[1] Artur Azevedo, "O Mambembe," in *Artur Azevedo: Obras* (Rio de Janeiro: Biblioteca Digital, 2013 [1904], Kindle).

[2] This excerpt of Vasques's play is cited in Silvia Cristina Martins de Souza, "Dos jornais ao palco: romances, folhetins, e textos teatrais no Rio de Janeiro da segunda metade do século XIX," *Tempo* 18, no. 32 (2012): 211–212.

[3] A jig or reel, a step dance.

48 MUSIC AND COSMOPOLITANISM

I am at La Scala (sing in Italian); now let's go to Germany (imitation of German [singing]); old Portugal too, I had forgotten ... one, two, three, here I am in Lisbon (sing a *fado*); and to finish the trip, let's go to Brazil; here I am in Rio de Janeiro, at the Beco da Boa Morte [street] (sing and dance [unspecified]).[4]

By the beginning of the 20th century, Vasques's imaginary ventures had become commonplace, and the idea that Rio de Janeiro was a multitude of places within one city, if a mostly Eurocentric multitude, became a recurring topic for the city's chroniclers. The poet, journalist, and critic Olavo Bilac reported in 1907, for example, that while walking from one Rio de Janeiro neighborhood to the next, and from one movie theater to the next, he could easily and quickly travel "to Paris, Rome, New York, and Milan."[5] The poet, journalist, and critic Luis Edmundo made similar observations, noting that "[Rio de Janeiro has] the highest number and the best [music halls] available on the face of the earth . . . we have here the companies and artists that perform in the most famous music halls in Europe and North America, [such as] the Alhambra in London, the Moulin Rouge in Paris, and the Winter Garden in Berlin."[6] Local *revistas* (magazines) filled with images and descriptions of places near and far corroborated the idea, allowing readers to view and wander through many cities, countries, and continents without leaving the confines of their city. According to Vera Lins, in the pages of the *revistas* one could live and experience at the same time a "picturesque farm in the countryside of the State of Goiás [Brazil], the architectural splendidness of New York City, and the eccentricity of the Arabian Peninsula."[7] Unmistakably, Rio de Janeiro started to grow into a large urban conglomerate and to boast an emerging cosmopolitan environment characterized by a connection to a world larger than itself.

Copious reports about Rio de Janeiro's daily life as the 19th century came to a close also refer to the allure of technological novelties altering the city's landscape—such as electricity, cable cars, phonographs, telephones, and the movies—and that replicated the marvels of contemporary growing cities in the Americas, across the Atlantic, and elsewhere, while helping those in Rio de Janeiro diminish geographical distances in their imaginations.[8] Vasques's

---

[4] Souza, "Dos jornais ao palco," 211–212.

[5] Olavo Bilac, "Chronica," *Gazeta de Notícias*, November 3, 1907.

[6] Luis Edmundo, *O Rio de Janeiro do meu tempo*, vol. 1 (Brasília: Edições do Senado Federal, 2003 [1938]), 285–286.

[7] Vera Lins, "O moderno em revista," in *O moderno em revista: Representações do Rio de Janeiro de 1890 a 1930*, ed. Monica Pimenta, Vera Lins, and Cláudia de Oliveira (Rio de Janeiro: Garamond, 2010), 14.

[8] For a summary of the major technological changes in Rio de Janeiro, see Nicolau Sevcenko, "A capital irradiante: Técnica, ritmos, e ritos do Rio," in *História da vida privada no Brasil República: da Belle Époque à era do rádio*, ed. Fernando Novais and Nicolau Sevcenko (São Paulo: Companhia da Letras, 1998), 513–580.

play made this clear. While he jokes that in the city one could find "[t]he last word in telephones" to overcome distance and longing, one could also "with a little push soon be able to marry while the husband stays in Paris, the wife in the United States, the cousins in Russia, and the in-laws in Turkey."[9] Rio de Janeiro's transformations became more intense, and decidedly visible, with the renovation of the old city center in the first years of the 20th century, a project planned by the Paris-trained architect Francisco Pereira Passos (1836–1913) and modeled on Haussman's Second Empire Paris urban renovations. As in Paris and many other cities that also followed the Haussman model,[10] Passos's project for Rio de Janeiro involved the demolition of the city's central areas, with their narrow streets and colonial buildings, to make space for the construction of open squares, neoclassical buildings, and large boulevards (Figure 2.2). The

Figure 2.2. Rio de Janeiro, Avenida Central, 1906.
Photo by Augusto Malta.
Source: Instituto Moreira Salles, Rio de Janeiro.

---

[9] Souza, "Dos jornais ao palco," 176.
[10] For Paris, see Stephanie Kirkland, *Paris Reborn: Napoléon III, Baron Haussmann, and the Quest to Build a Modern City* (New York: St: Martin's Press, 2013). For an overview of urban reforms in Latin American cities modeled on Haussmann, see Arturo Almandoz, "Introduction," in *Planning Latin*

50 MUSIC AND COSMOPOLITANISM

project provided much-needed infrastructure to parts of the city that had grown relentlessly throughout the previous decades. It also symbolized the dream of a growing urban bourgeoisie, as the architectural façades, large avenues, and public spaces with electric lighting encapsulated the image of contemporary, modern life with new dynamism, fashions, and behavioral patterns, giving some residents the feeling of being both at the center of their country and in an imagined modern world larger than their surroundings.[11] Rio de Janeiro's fast urban transformations also brought to its residents an unprecedented sense of time, and a sense of time lost, a feeling that someone living in other turn-of-the-century cities could empathize with. The destruction of old buildings invoked a nostalgia for a past that, now disappearing, became conspicuously present. As the possibilities of photography allowed for the documentation of the decaying present, *revistas* were inundated with pictures of what the city used to be, which appeared alongside photographs of a romanticized countryside untarnished by urban modernity. Mônica Velloso has argued that through the *revistas*' copious images there is a suggestion that one could be placed, at the same time, "in permanent contact with past revolutions [and] with forbidden worlds." In the pages of these magazines, one could not only simultaneously visit a variety of

Ameria's Capital Cities 1850–1950, ed. Arturo Almandoz (London and New York: Routledge, 2002), 1–12; Fania Fridman and Mauricio Abreu, *Cidades latino-americanas: Um debate sobre a formação de núcleos urbanos* (Rio de Janeiro: Casa da Palavra, 2010); and José Luis Romero, *Latinoamérica: Las Ciudades y las ideas*, 2nd ed. (Buenos Aires: Siglo XXI Editores, 2007), 247–318. For Buenos Aires, see Bergero, *Intersecting Tango*. For an analysis of the reforms in Mexico City, see Mauricio Tenorio-Trillos, *I Speak of the City: Mexico City at the Turn of the Twentieth Century* (Chicago: University of Chicago Press, 2012), in particular 8–18. For the influence of Haussmann in the renovations of Rome, see Geza Zur Nieden, "The Internationalization of Musical Life at the End of the Nineteenth Century in Modernized Paris and Rome," *Urban History* 40, no. 4 (November 2013): 663–680. For Lisbon, see João Silva, *Entertaining Lisbon: Music, Theater, and Modern Life in the Late 19th Century* (Oxford and New York: Oxford University Press, 2016), especially 51–60; for Madrid, see Deborah Parsons, *A Cultural History of Madrid: Modernity and the Urban Spectacle* (New York: Berg, 2003), especially 81–82; and Borja Carballo, Fernando Vicente, and Rubén Pallol, *El ensanche de Madrid: historia de una capital* (Madrid: Catarata, 2013). São Paulo, although smaller in size, would overtake Rio de Janeiro in the second decade of the 20th century and follow some of Haussmann's urban reforms; see Heloísa Barbuy, *A cidade-exposição: Comércio e cosmopolitismo em São Paulo, 1860–1914* (São Paulo: Edusp, 2006). Like other 19th-century growing cities, Vienna's urban transformation captured not only the eyes but also the ears of those living through demolitions on a daily basis, as it was recorded in Strauss Jr.'s *Demolier-Polka* (1862).

[11] For the sociopolitical dynamics during the urban renovations in Rio de Janeiro, see Andre Nunes de Azevedo, *A Grande reforma urbana do Rio de Janeiro: Pereira Passos, Rodrigues Alves e as ideias de civilização* (Rio de Janeiro: PUC, 2016); Lilian Schwarz, *1890–1914: No tempo das certezas* (São Paulo: Companhia das Letras, 2007); Cláudia Oliveira, "A representação da grande Avenida e o sublime dos 'melhoramentos urbanos' nas ilustradas *Fon-Fon! e Para Todos*," in *Escritos: Revista da Casa Rui Barbosa* 1, no. 1 (2007): 93–109; Glória Kok, *Rio de Janeiro na época da Av. Central* (São Paulo: Bei Comunicação, 2005); Osvaldo Rocha, *A era das demolições: Cidade do Rio de Janeiro, 1870–1920* (Rio de Janeiro: Prefeitura do Rio de Janeiro, 1995); Jaime Benchimol, *Pereira Passos: Um Haussmann tropical: A renovacão urbana do Rio de Janeiro no início do século XX* (Rio de Janeiro: Prefeitura do Rio de Janeiro, 1990); and Jeffrey Needell, *A Tropical Belle Epoque: Elite Culture and Society in Turn-of-the-Century Rio de Janeiro* (New York: Cambridge University Press, 1987).

Figure 2.3. Favela, Rio de Janeiro, 1906.
Photo by Augusto Malta, 1906.
Source: **Viviane da Silva** Araujo, «Cidades fotografadas: Rio de Janeiro e Buenos Aires sob as lentes de Augusto Malta e Harry Olds, 1900–1936», *Nuevo Mundo Mundos Nuevos*, January 17, 2009. Online source: https://journals.openedition.org/nuevomundo/docannexe/image/50103/img-4.jpg

places, but also experience the coexistence of different temporalities in a kind of imagined atemporal omnipresence.[12]

But while Rio de Janeiro's fast-changing urban landscape enchanted and amazed some, it also disappointed, dislocated, and segregated many others. The urbanization projects emptied the public coffers and forced thousands of residents to relocate to nearby areas in poor conditions, initiating a pattern of urban social and racial displacement and segregation that also afflicted many contemporary cities, but became a chronic factor in Rio de Janeiro's growth, a pattern that can be seen to this day in the city's urban *favelas* (Figure 2.3).[13] Contemporary chroniclers

---

[12] Mônica Velloso, *Modernismo no Rio de Janeiro: Turunas e Quixotes* (Petrópolis, RJ: KBR, 2015), 52; see also Cláudia Oliveira, "Arqueologia: viagens ao passado da cidade," in *Fon-Fon: Buzinando a modernidade*, Cadernos de Comunicação, Série Memória 22 (Rio de Janeiro: Secretaria Especial de Comunicação Social, 2008), 45–58. For images of the changing landscape of the city from 1903 to 1906 captured by photographer Marc Ferrez see *A Avenida Central* [1907] available in digital format at Rio de Janeiro Biblioteca National, at https://objdigital.bn.br/objdigital2/acervo_digital/div_icon ografia/icon1387674/icon1387674.htm

The Instituto Moreira Salles in Rio de Janeiro also has an extended collection of Augusto Malta's photographs of the city's changing landscape available digitally at https://acervos.ims.com.br/port als/#/search/Fotografia?collection=Augusto_Malta%3Fpage%3D2.

[13] Lilia Schwarcz shows how the expectation of modernization in Rio de Janeiro was counteracted by social segregation; see her *A abertura para o mundo 1889-1930* (Rio de Janeiro: Objetiva,

52   MUSIC AND COSMOPOLITANISM

were quick to expose Rio de Janeiro's many shortcomings. João do Rio, for example, was bleak in his portrayal of the city's busy port region. For him, the place was a constant reminder of Rio de Janeiro's worldly connection and epitomized the somber side of a daunting globalized scenario. The old Misericordia Street, for example, reminded him of "the somber Amsterdam of Rembrandt," and the Beco da Fidalga (street) recalled "the soul of the streets of Naples, of Florence, the old streets of Portugal, and of the streets of Africa." In João do Rio's reckoning, Rio de Janeiro's streets recalled streets elsewhere because "these streets are near the ocean, streets of travelers with visions of other horizons . . . these alleys share the treason of the oceans, the misery of the immigrants, the great vice of the ocean and of the colonies."[14] João do Rio's observations about Rio de Janeiro's links to Europe and Africa's old and hostile places highlight the dark side of his city's worldly connections. At the same time, they contextualize the core of his experiences: a skepticism and pessimism that were part of his own urban context, but which were also conspicuously linked to imaginaries of places far away.

João do Rio was one of several Rio de Janeiro *flâneurs* whose writings provide a bird's-eye view of the city's physical metamorphosis and its multi-city sociocultural contexts. Unequivocally joining *flâneurs* from other contemporary cities in the midst of similar urban changes, he was one among many writers who used their chronicles as a way of engaging with the many facets of their urban modernity through "literary and political seeing."[15] Maite Conde suggests that their chronicles became a literary form akin to that of moving images in early films, as they offered readers short vignettes of urban geographies and experiences from nearby and far away, and which helped the city's residents to re-situate and expand their spatial senses.[16] As such, the work of these chroniclers added to the many contemporary modes of visual expressions, such as photography and the movies, and contributed to a visual culture that helped shape the period's urban experiences.[17]

2012), 35–83. For the history of Rio de Janeiro's favelas, see Rafael Gonçalves, *Favelas do Rio de Janeiro: História e direito* (Rio de Janeiro: PUC, 2013); Carvalho, *Porous City*; Sidney Chalhoub, *Cidade febril: Cortiços e epidemias na corte imperial* (São Paulo: Cia. das Letras, 1999); and Lia de Aquino Carvalho, *Habitações populares: Rio de Janeiro 1866–1906* (Rio de Janeiro: Secretaria Municipal de Cultura, 1995).

[14] João do Rio, *A alma encantadora das ruas* (Rio de Janeiro: Secretaria Municipal de Cultura, 1995 [1908]), 10.

[15] Rebecca Walkowitz, *Cosmopolitan Style: Modernism beyond the Nation* (New York: Columbia University Press, 2006), 18. For an analysis of the *flâneurs'* sociopolitical role in turn-of-the-century Rio de Janeiro, see Patricia Acerbi, "A Long Poem of Walking: Flâneurs, Vendors, and Chronicles of Post-abolition Rio de Janeiro," *Journal of Urban History* 40, no. 1 (2014): 97–115.

[16] Maite Conde, *Consuming Visions: Cinema, Writing, and Modernity in Rio de Janeiro* (Charlottesville: University of Virginia Press, 2012, Kindle).

[17] For the preponderance of visual cultures, see Vanessa Schwartz and Jeannene Przyblyski, "Introduction," in *The Nineteenth-Century Visual Culture Reader*, ed. Vanessa Schwartz and Jeannene Przyblyski (New York: Routledge, 2004), 3–12.

A CITY TO BE SEEN AND TO BE HEARD   53

But the ethos of the visual did not sum up the sociocultural complexity of late-19th-century Rio de Janeiro and its connections to a world beyond itself, for the city was not only to be seen, but also to be heard. As Jonathan Stern pointed out, during the 19th century sound was "re-conceptualized, objectified, imitated, transformed, reproduced, commodified, mass-produced, and industrialized," and in new formats sound "rendered the world audible in new ways."[18] This new "audible world" became a conspicuous part of the city experiences and was characterized by a gamut of new sounds from a myriad of sources, from typewriters, cable and motor cars, to miscellaneous musics coming from mechanical pianos, street barrel organs, gramophones, or by "noises," musical or otherwise, audible among closely situated houses and packed residential buildings. This "audible world" provided an extra dimension to narratives and expressions of the new and the modern as they were rendered in the turn-of-the-century city. As an expressive media and a cultural parameter that is not crystallized in images, writing, or architecture, the abstract aural and temporal fluidity of sound and music shaped an important part of the turn-of-the-century urban experiences. More so than the period's visual culture, and more significant than the written texts that also helped shape the Latin American city—as in Angel Ramas's concept of the Lettered City—the sonic, musical, and performative realms prompted and assisted those living in cities to interact with people nearby and faraway, imaginatively and objectively, to partake in the period's most dramatic sociopolitical and cultural changes, and share the multifaceted experiences of urban modernity.[19]

Expectedly, the sonic ethos of the modern city did not escape the scrutiny of Rio de Janeiro's chroniclers, as they engaged in listening as a mode of being in and experiencing the city. As "aural *flâneurs*" and "attuned" to their urban surroundings,[20] they walked through the city's streets listening to and reporting on its eclectic and fragmented sounds, where noises of automobiles, cable cars, and the rhythmic clicks of typewriters overlapped with the sounds of street cleaners with their straw brooms, and the parroting sounds of barrel organs and

---

[18] Jonathan Sterne, *Audible Past* (Durham, NC, and London: Duke University Press, 2003), 2–4.

[19] For the concept of a Lettered City as a major force in shaping politics in Latin America, see Angel Rama, *La ciudad letrada* (Hanover, NH: Ediciones del Norte Hanover, 1984; University Press, 1996). For the idea that it was a performance tradition, rather than a literary tradition, that shaped Havana's public spaces, see Jill Lane, *Blackface Cuba, 1840–1895* (Philadelphia: University of Pennsylvania Press, 2005), 146.

[20] The expression "aural *flâneurs*" is used by Aimée Boutin in *City of Noise: Sound and Nineteenth-Century Paris* (Urbana and Chicago: University of Illinois Press, 2015, Kindle). For the sonic dimension of Edwardian London as transpired in contemporary literature, see Patricia Pye, *Sound and Modernity in the Literature of London, 1880–1918* (New York and London: Palgrave Macmillan, 2017). The word "attunement" is suggested by Daniel Grimley as a way of grasping our relationship with the auditory world around us; see Daniel Grimley, "Music, Landscape, Attunement: Listening to Sibelius's *Tapiola*," *Journal of the American Musicological Society* 64, no. 2 (2011): 397–398; also Grimley, "Hearing Landscape Critically: Prospects and Reflections," in *Studien Zur Wertungsforschung* (Vienna: Universal Edition, 2019), 94.

54 MUSIC AND COSMOPOLITANISM .

gramophones, which gradually replaced the harmonicas and rattles of street vendors. Aural *flâneurs* recounted the sounds of peddlers' cries, the blind violin performer at the street corner, the pervading sounds of wind bands dispersed throughout the city, the drumming gatherings of blacks and mulatto groups alongside street whistling of Verdi's many melodies and Puccini's *Tosca*, and the unstoppable whistling of Franz Lehár's "Merry Widow's Waltz," from which few could escape. Bilac was not altogether pleased with the new sounds around him, noting in perplexity the dominance of the phonograph at the fashionable Rua do Ouvidor (street) in 1907:

> From every door one could hear the shrieks coming from the speaking or singing boxes: shouts, screams, frantic squeals, moaning, bellows, howls, barks, mews, moos, squeaks! And the desolate Rua do Ouvidor felt like a sound gallery of hell filled with screams [that sounded like] condemned marginals and prisoners being thrown into boiling water, vociferously asking for mercy![21]

Luis Edmundo remembered well the many sounds of the streets around the old port, where "the sounds of a *realejo* (a small barrel organ) alternated with the voice of a mulatto singing and entertaining the pedestrians with *modinhas* (songs in Portuguese), [while] . . . the seven-instrument man with drums and horns attached to his body managed to play them all together, while dancing and multiplying by seven the act of music performance." The seven-instrument man then competed with the phonograph salesman, "who usually set up his equipment on a bench, surrounded by children, who sang along happily to the dragging, squeaky sounds of the modern instrument."[22] João do Rio also left several accounts of the heterogenous sonic experiences of the city, noting that "[d]espite the gramophones in hotels, bars, and shops and the multiplication of pianos, the city was also filled with musicians of all kinds who would perform in the streets and cafés, singing songs from popular operas, *cançonetas* (songs in Portuguese) and *modinhas* (songs in Portuguese) accompanied by violins and guitars, [while a] German band with their stands and out-of-tune wind instruments would torment [the people] in the squares."[23] Reflecting on the need for a change of pace in the city right after the busy 1910 outdoor carnival celebrations, the chronicler of the magazine *Fon-Fon* described his unsuccessful

---

[21] Bilac, *Kosmos* 4, no. 9 (September 1907).

[22] Edmundo, *O Rio de Janeiro do meu tempo*, 110. For the dominance of street organs in Parisian public spaces, see Karolina Doughty, "Rethinking Musical Cosmopolitanism as a Visceral Politics of Sound," in *Sounding Places, More-Than-Representational Geographies of Sound and Music*, ed. Karolina Doughty, Michelle Duffy, and Theresa Harada (Northamptom, UK: Edgar Elgar, 2019), 192. For Madrid, see Samuel Llano, "Street Music, Honour and Degeneration: The Case of Organilleros," in *Writing Wrongdoing in Spain, 1800–1936: Realities, Representations, Reactions*, ed. Alison Sinclair and Samuel Llano (Martlesham, UK: Boydell & Brewer, 2017), 197–215.

[23] João do Rio, *A alma encantadora das ruas*, 65. For João do Rio's use of sound to describe Rio de Janeiro's streets, see Julia O'Donnell, *De olho na rua: A cidade de João do Rio* (Rio de

A CITY TO BE SEEN AND TO BE HEARD   55

attempts to retreat to his home in silence and solitude, since when he opened the window leading to a public square he could not escape from

> five vigorous pianos entertaining the neighbors with Grieg's "Au Printemps," which appears in a strange harmonious happiness with [the *lundu*] "Yayá me deixa subir nesta ladeira,"[24] the "Sonho de valsa" (Waltzertraum), the "Merry Widow waltz," and a Beethoven sonata, not to mention a flute that dignifies the neighborhood with squeaky polkas and tangos. This was one of the most rigorous penitences [for Lent] that I had to endure. I then close the window, recluse myself to my dinner table, and crank my phonograph, which then hurries to its eclectic repertory, including *modinhas* by Bahiano [singer] from Casa Edison [store] and Caruso's melancholic [songs] in Odeon and Victor recordings.[25]

As the new sounds in the city's streets became inescapable to most and unbearable for some, the heterogeneous context of the *fin-de-siècle* city's sonic realm was also experienced in more formal musical settings. In concert halls, theaters, cabarets, music halls, circuses, and in the music publishing business, a gamut of "modern" musics arriving from abroad and produced locally seemed to have enough sonic attractiveness to coexist with the popularity of the beloved operatic repertory, which had a local stronghold since the early 19th-century. As managers, performers, composers, and audiences worked to assemble a repertory with which they could partake in an urban sonic modernity within their local context, they summoned works by past and contemporary champions of the European concert and opera hall, such as Mozart, Berlioz, Meyerbeer, Massenet, Wagner, Verdi, Saint-Saëns, Massenet, and Puccini, among many others. But works by these composers were not the only ones that marked their presence in Rio de Janeiro, nor did they occupy an exclusive canonic space disconnected from everything else. The available repertory included works by many lesser known (by today's historiography standards) composers of "art" music, in addition to composers of trendy songs, *chansons* (in French), *canzonettas* (in Italian), *cançonetas* and *modinhas* (in Portuguese), fashionable dances by Johann Strauss Jr., Cécile Chaminade, and Emil Waldtaufel, and catchy song/dances by champions of the musical theater, such as Plaquette, Lecocq, Varney, Lehár, and Straus and a myriad of others who have today faded into obscurity. Local composers strove to keep up with the demand by providing works for the

---

Janeiro: Zahar, 2008), 149–152. German bands were a street attraction in Rio de Janeiro already in late 1870 and continued through the early 20th century. Derek Scott describes a similar sonic context in London's streets, in particular the presence of German bands and the barrel organ; see his *The Singing Bourgeois: Songs of the Victorian of the Victorian Drawing Room and Parlor*, 2nd ed. (New York: Routledge, 2001 [1989]), 184.

[24] *lundu*, a stylized urban dance of Afro-Brazilian derivation.
[25] "Flavio," *Fon-Fon* 4, no. 8 (February 19, 1910).

56 MUSIC AND COSMOPOLITANISM

growing needs of the emergent music business in a similar vein to the musics arriving uninterruptedly from overseas. An array of orchestrators and arrangers thrived in this rich cosmopolitan sonic environment as hidden but creative figures who transformed all kinds of musics, whether they were written for the parlor, concert hall, or theatrical venues, partaking in a compositional process that expanded our understanding of music authorship. They made music into malleable, traveling cultural and commercial products ideal to be performed in many settings and social contexts.

Some of the works within this rich urban soundscape were not new, some became musical tropes of a period, even if their transitory nature allowed them to be forgotten and left aside as ghosts in the history of music. Still, they pervaded in Rio de Janeiro and many other contemporary cities and are testaments to the sonic and musical ethos of the turn-of-the-20th-century urban modernity. It is difficult to grasp the full scope and the nature of all the musics available, for the sheer number and variety preclude a clear characterization of a preponderant musical style, fashion, or practice.[26] However, a review of chronicles in *revistas* and newspapers, programs of concerts, theaters, *saraus* (*soirees*), café-concerts, and cabarets, and lists of publishing houses and recordings show that Rio de Janeiro started not only to feel and look, but also to sound like a typical turn-of-the-century city with an emerging complex urban environment filled with sonic and musical modernities. Like the city's visual ethos, Rio de Janeiro's soundscape fed from and fed into a cosmopolitan urban cultural network that connected its residents to people living in other cities through an eclectic mix of shared urban experiences.

This urban sonic cosmopolitanism became an aural conscience and experience, as well as a "creative force" that opened up new possibilities of expressions.[27] It sparked the imaginations of composers and performers and shaped the expectations of audiences. It was skillfully explored and exploited by the emerging music industry and was both forcefully regimented and challenged by the political and intellectual status quo. At the beginning of the 20th century, a gamut of sounds and musics unveiled a sense of aural global connection that became ubiquitous in Rio de Janeiro, as writers, musicians, performers, and audiences saw themselves as cosmopolitans with a perspicacity to both see and listen to an urban context connected to other contexts, as cosmopolitans displaying a desire to create, to share, and to belong to a world that was perceived to be larger than their immediate geographical surroundings. Most importantly, the complex sonic realm of the turn-of-the-century city became a significant gateway into the period's spirit of critique, one that was dependent on collective and shared understandings, engagements, and disengagements with fragmentary, uneven, and fleeting musical experiences of *fin-de-siècle* urban modernity.[28]

---

[26] For a summary of the many musical spaces in the city, see Martha Abreu "Histórias musicais na Primeira República," *ArtCultura* 13, no. 22 (2011): 71–83; see also Mônica Vermes, "A Cena Musical no Rio de Janeiro: 1890–1920," *Annals of the XXVI Simpósio Nacional de História* (São Paulo, 2011), 1–12.

[27] Jonathan Sterne, "Sonic Imaginations," in *The Sound Studies Reader* (New York: Routledge, 2012), 6.

[28] Beatriz Jaguaribe, *Rio de Janeiro* (New York: Routledge, 2014), 8–9.

3

A Tale of Three Anthems

Music and Republicanism

The early seeds of republicanism were planted in Brazil in the late 18th century through the influence of French revolutionaries and the U.S. founding fathers. In 1789, Joaquim José da Silva Xavier (1746–1792), known locally as Tiradentes, organized an insurrection against the Portuguese colonial power, but failed and was condemned as a traitor. His fate became a major source for political representations of martyrdom, and his fight for freedom was used during the 19th century to advance the republican cause locally.[1] In 1822, Brazilian independence from Portugal did not yield a move away from monarchy, but republican ideologies continued to be part of the rhetoric of local intellectuals and politicians, resurfacing more forcefully in the second half of the century. In 1870, republican intellectuals made headway toward legitimizing their movement by issuing a manifesto that espoused Enlightenment cosmopolitan ideals of universalism, claiming to speak for "the human race" and for "the rights of man," and suggesting that their revolutionary ideals would bring moral transformation and liberty to the entire globe.[2]

Brazilian republicans aligned themselves with French revolutionaries of the late 18th century and the Third Republic, anchoring their manifesto on equivalences between the fall of France's monarchy and the need to end Pedro

---

[1] For the use of Tiradentes in the rhetoric of republican politicians and intellectuals, see Carlos Roberto Ballarotti, "A Construção do mito de Tiradentes: De mártir republicano a herói cívico na atualidade," *Antíteses* 2, no. 3 (2009): 201–225; Cláudia Regina Callari, "Os Institutos Históricos: Do patronato de D. Pedro II à construção do Tiradentes," *Revista Brasileira de História* 21, no. 40 (2001): 59–83; Thais Nívia de Lima Fonseca, "Da infâmia ao altar da pátria: memória e representações da inconfidência mineira e de Tiradentes," PhD dissertation, Universidade de São Paulo, 2001. For the ambiguous narrative of Tiradentes in the arts, see Maraliz de Castro Vieira Christo, "Pintura, história e heróis no século XIX: Pedro Américo e 'Tiradentes Esquartejado,'" PhD dissertation, Universidade Estadual de Campinas, 2005.

[2] The Republican manifesto, written by Quintino Bocaiuva (1836–1912), is available at https://edisciplinas.usp.br/pluginfile.php/4360902/mod_resource/content/2/manifesto%20republicano%201870.pdf. For interpretations of the manifesto, see George Boehrer, *Da monarquia à república: História do partido republicano no Brasil* (Belo Horizonte: Editora Itatiaia, 2000); see also José Murilo de Carvalho, "República, democracia, e federalismo no Brasil, 1870–1991," *Vária História* 27, no. 45 (January–June, 2011): 141–157; and his "Radicalismo e republicanismo," in *Repensando o Brasil do Oitocentos: Cidadania, política e liberdade*, ed. José Murilo de Carvalho and Lúcia Maria Bastos Pereira das Neves (Rio de Janeiro: Civilização Brasileira, 2009), 19–48.

Music and Cosmopolitanism. Cristina Magaldi, Oxford University Press. © Oxford University Press 2024.
DOI: 10.1093/oso/9780199744770.003.0004

58   MUSIC AND COSMOPOLITANISM

II's monarchical rule in Brazil. Claiming Brazil as a participant in the West's political agenda, the manifesto points out the damaging effects that the monarchy had on the country's global connections: "Before Europe, we are seen as a democratic monarchy that does not inspire sympathy or adherence . . . [and] where the power and free will of the people cannot emerge . . . [monarchical] Brazil is an isolated country, not only in America but in the world. Our effort is aimed at changing this state of things, connecting us in fraternal and democratic solidarity with all peoples." Such passionate claims did not yield immediate results, however. Deeply rooted monarchical institutions, the power of a beloved monarch, and a large reactionary landed elite dependent on slave labor delayed the regime change. Finally, on November 15, 1889, Marechal Deodoro da Fonseca (1827–1892) led a military coup that precipitated the end of the monarchy and declared a republican government.

The arrival of republicanism through a military coup cast doubt on the legitimacy of the new government and complicated the establishment of new leadership. Deodoro da Fonseca, himself sympathetic to the monarchy, changed his position at the last minute to lead the military, while the head of the abolition movement, José do Patrocínio (1854–1905), loyal to Princess Isabel's effort to end slavery in Brazil the year before, remained a monarchist and organized a Black militia to create disruptions in republican rallies. Not unlike French and other revolutions, republican Brazil started as a complex compromise of factions and ideologies. Dependent on the support of hesitant monarchists, radical Jacobines, intellectuals inspired by the U.S. federalist model, and military liberals, the arrival of the Republic was an arrangement bound to be followed by political instability and protests that limited immediate political measures attempting meaningful changes. Furthermore, amid an international monetary crisis and internal predatory capitalism, Brazilian intellectuals cited Rousseau and Voltaire on one end, and Comte, Spencer, and social Darwinism on the other, moving swiftly from humanist to evolutionist and positivist ideas to anchor their lines of thought. But within the various and contradictory political positions, there was a common thread grounded in the belief of building a new nation that could stand on equal footing with a new world order centered on Western Europe: a republican nation should be a modern nation. Intertwined in the various interpretations of republicanism was thus the concept of linear time, a determinist view that followed a clear path toward republicanism as a way to reach an imagined modernity. To Maria Teresa de Mello, "Republic was the Brazilian name for modernity."[3]

According to multiple chroniclers of the November 15 event in Rio de Janeiro, some residents were baffled by the military parades staged by new republican leaders in Rio de Janeiro's central areas, as Deodoro da Fonseca overthrew the

---

[3] Maria Teresa de Mello, "A modernidade republicana," *Tempo* 13, no. 26 (2009): 31.

Figure 3.1. Proclamation of the Republic. Rio de Janeiro, *Correio do Povo*, November 16, 1889.
Source: Biblioteca Nacional, Rio de Janeiro, Hemeroteca Digital

beloved monarch and sent the imperial family into exile. Others offered jubilant support to a republican cause that was largely anticipated and that promised possibilities of a brighter future. Eventually, among feelings of surprise, excitement, and indecision, the moment summoned a commitment to a cause deemed inevitable.[4] Then, after exaltations of *Viva a República! Viva as Forças Amadas!* (Hurray for the Republic and the military forces) (Figure 3.1), people gathered around military leaders through the streets, accompanied by military bands, which gave a sonic character to the pivotal moment of transition by performing an old-time favorite: an anthem by Francisco Manuel da Silva (1795–1865) (Musical Example 3.1).

Written to celebrate the abdication of Pedro I in 1831, Silva's music was set to lyrics twice, the latter version written for the coronation of Pedro II in 1841 and continued as a monarchical anthem throughout his reign, mostly performed without lyrics.[5] Ironically, it was Silva's music that filled the streets

---

[4] For accounts of the process leading to the proclamation, see José Murilo de Carvalho, *Os bestializados* (São Paulo: Companhia das Letras, 1987); see also Maria Efigênia Lage de Resende, "O processo político na Primeira República e o liberalismo oligárquico," in *O Brasil republicano: O tempo do liberalismo excludente*, ed. Jorge Luis Ferreira and Lucília de Almeida Delgado (Rio de Janeiro: Civilização Brasileira, 2003), 91–120. For a different interpretation, see Maria Teresa de Mello, *A república consentida: Cultura democrática e científica do final do Império* (Rio de Janeiro: Editora Fundação Getúlio Vargas, 2011); and her "A república e o sonho," *Vária História* 27, no. 45 (January–June 2011): 121–139.

[5] For a history of Silva's anthem, see Avelino Pereira, "Hino nacional brasileiro: Que história é esta?," *Revista do Instituto de Estudos Brasileiros* 38 (1995): 21–42. For Silva and other anthem in the context of monarchy and Republic, see Analía Chernavsky, *A construção dos mitos e heróis do Brasil nos hinos esquecidos da Biblioteca Nacional* (Rio de Janeiro: Fundação Biblioteca Nacional, 2009).

60 MUSIC AND COSMOPOLITANISM

Musical Example 3.1. Francisco Manuel da Silva, Brazilian National Anthem.
Source: Acervo Musicabrasilis, www.musicabrasilis.org.br

with sounds to celebrate the regime change to republicanism. In the absence of sonic symbols of their own, republicans used Silva's music as a tool to unify the people toward their cause. Amidst a population that was largely illiterate, the instrumental performance conveniently bypassed the lyrics, and the monarchy with it, and was powered instead by the "aural recognition of the familiar," a tactical move that entailed a "phonocentric response," to use Peter Modelli's

A TALE OF THREE ANTHEMS   61

term.[6] It was a collective performance of the familiar, as sounds fueled the moment's need to unite the people by capitalizing on the music's long-time association with public and civic events.[7]

But Silva's anthem did not summon the musical nature of the celebrations for the new regime. As the parade progressed, the work was followed by another very familiar song, an old-time popular tune of revolution: "La Marseillaise" (1792) by Claude Joseph Rouget de Lisle (Musical Example 3.2). At the time of the proclamation of the Republic in Brazil, the performance of "La Marseillaise" was far from an uncritical adherence to a foreign sonic symbol. As ideals of republicanism had grown steadily in the country, so did the popularity of "La Marseillaise," which traveled as the sound of republicanism and revolution. Accounts of "La Marseillaise" performances prior to the proclamation abound, especially after the 1870 republican manifesto; the music helped bring steadfast attention to the republican cause as it was performed in a variety of formats and settings, from military bands performing at official events and outdoor celebrations, to performances in popular theaters, in small ensembles in vaudeville shows, and in the circus.[8] On July 14, 1889, a few months before the proclamation, in a concert celebrating the fall of the Bastille in Rio de Janeiro, for example, the composer Alexandre Levy included his own "Hymne à 14 juillet" for orchestra and fanfare, in which he combined "the [orchestral] effects with 'Chant du Départ' (1794, Etienne Méhul and Marie-Josseeph Chénier) and 'La Marseillaise,' with brilliant [instrumental] effects that caused ovation."[9] Republican abolitionists invariably included "La Marseillaise" in rallies for the abolition of slavery and in that capacity the work inspired a whole set of local variants.[10] On May 13, 1888,

[6] Peter Mondelli, "Phonocentric Revolution," *Acta Musicologica* 88, no. 2 (2016): 146, 149, and 154. The argument toward the phonocentric response serves to dislocate the interpretation of the anthem from its lyrics. This interpretation differs from Pereira's argument on the importance of the lyrics; see his "Hino nacional brasileiro: Que história é esta?," 33–34.

[7] Brazil's 1870 victory in the war with Paraguay is among the political events that served to unify the country and helped propel the republican cause, and in which music played a key role. See Luciana Pessanha Fagundes, "Música e guerra: Impactos da Primeira Guerra Mundial no cenário musical carioca," *Revista brasileira de história* 37, no. 76 (2017): 24.

[8] Carvalho affirms that "La Marseillaise" was sung in all republican manifestations and meetings; see *A formação das almas* (São Paulo: Companhia das Letras, 2009, [1990]), 122; also Camila Pereira Martins, "Republicanismo no Rio de Janeiro e em Lisboa: 1870–1891," PhD dissertation, Universidade de Juiz de Fora, 2015, 13. For "La Marseillaise" as a republican symbol in France, see Maurice Agulhon, *Marianne Au pouvoir: L'imagerie et la symbolique républicaines de 1880 à 1914* (Paris: Flammarion, 1989); Laura Mason, *Singing the French Revolution: Popular Culture and Politics, 1787–1799* (Ithaca, NY: Cornell University Press, 1996), 143–147; and Eric John Hobsbawm, *Echoes of the Marseillaise: Two Centuries Look Back on the French Revolution* (London: Verso, 1990). For interpretations of "La Marseillaise" today, see Alex Marshall, "The Twists and Turns of 'La Marseillaise,'" *New York Times*, December 13, 2016 https://www.nytimes.com/2016/12/13/arts/music/the-twists-and-turns-of-la-marseillaise.html.

[9] Clarissa Lapolla Bomfim de Andrade, *A Gazeta Musical: Positivismo e missão civilizadora nos primeiros anos da república no Brasil* (São Paulo: Editora Unesp, 2013), 180.

[10] Ângela Alonso has noted that, in contrast to anglican North America, rather than religious songs it was "La Marseillaise" that concluded all the meeting and rallies for the abolitionist cause;

Musical Example 3.2. Claude Joseph Rouget de Lisle, "La Marseillaise."
Source: Biblioteque Nacional de France, https://gallica.bnf.fr/

see her "A teatralização da política: a propaganda abolicionistta," *Tempo Social* 24, no. 2 (2012): 107. Flávia da Silva Braga notes that even the monarchist newspaper *Tribuna Liberal* of November 17 included a note about performances of "La Marseillaise" by wind bands; see Flávia da Silva Braga, "Para além do bestializado: Diferentes interpretações da (não) participação popular," *Revista Hydra* 1, no. 1 (2019): 186.

Valentim de Mello wrote lyrics to the tune as *Hino da 'Marselhesa' ou A pátria livre* (anthem of the Marseillaise, or The Free Homeland) to celebrate not republicanism, but the abolition of slavery by Princess Isabel.[11] Also in homage to the abolition, the composer Cardoso de Menezes (1848–1915) wrote a symphonic march, "Marseillaise of the Slaves," based on motives from the French tune, although the work seems to have been lost.[12] Attempts to translate the original French lyrics into Portuguese or add new lyrics to the tune—a common practice elsewhere—did not prove very successful in Brazil, however. Medeiros de Albuquerque wrote Portuguese lyrics to "La Marseillaise," but his lyrics ended up being used with new music by Ernesto de Sousa with the (unsuccessful) goal of becoming an anthem for the new Brazilian Republic.[13]

While the military band's memorable performance of "La Marseillaise" on November 15, 1889, could be sung with the original lyrics by those few to whom French was second nature, for most of the people in the streets of Rio de Janeiro, whose literacy in both Portuguese and French was a factor, the sound of "La Marseillaise" was familiar enough to be sung or heard as their own, and they provided a phonocentric response to the familiar, similar to the one accomplished by Silva's music. Silva's monarchical anthem and "La Marseillaise" allowed for a flawless continuity from monarchy to republicanism: together, both anthems enabled local political engagement and helped construct and fuel the present political moment, as they became sonic symbols embodied in historical familiarity and past communal performances; together, they came to signify "the collective identity of the voices that sang [them]," regardless of the words being sung or whether or not they were actually sung, for the familiar tunes evoked a collectivity that could modify "the semiotic content of things said and sung";[14] together, both anthems served the collective's attachments to the past and its hopes for a promising future. It was a combined sonic performance of the familiar that also connected those participating to distant peoples fighting for similar causes. Performed together, the two tunes led to the emergence of what Benedict Anderson called a "unisonance," as singing and listening enabled the physical

---

[11] *Gazeta da Tarde*, May 13, 1889; cited in Chernavsky, *A construção dos mitos e heróis do Brasil*, 40.

[12] Artur de Azevedo mentions the "Marseillaise of the Slaves" as being written in 1884 with the title "Grande marcha symphonica para orchestra e banda militar—written to celebrate the abolition in the state of Ceará"; see his article in *O Album* 1, no. 29 (1893): 225.

[13] Carvalho, *A formação das almas*, 124. Ernesto de Sousa's music written for piano is housed at the music section of the National library at Rio de Janeiro, as *Primeiro "Hino republicano*; cited in Chernavsky, *A construção dos mitos e heróis do Brasil*, 43–44.

[14] Mondelli, "Phonocentric Revolution," 146 and 149.

64 MUSIC AND COSMOPOLITANISM

realization of an imagined community, one that in this case was both local and cosmopolitan.[15]

Although accounts of performances of both anthems in newspapers and magazines emphasized their force at the pivotal moment in Brazil's history, the performance of "La Marseillaise" during the celebrations has been eclipsed by scholars' interest in the peculiar fate of Silva's anthem, a story that has been told several times and can be summarized here. After the proclamation, the new government subsidized a competition to lure composers to write a new anthem which could substitute for Silva's monarchical work and serve as a new musical symbol for the new regime. The competition took place on January 1890 at the Theatro Lyrico and had the participation of 20 composers allied to the republican cause. The winner was Leopoldo Miguez (1850–1902), a well-known composer and conductor, who had received a subsidy from the monarchical government to study abroad, but who nevertheless supported republican causes and quickly asserted his strong commitment to the new regime.

Miguez's anthem (Musical Example 3.3), set to lyrics by positivist Medeiros e Albuquerque, did not end up as the national anthem of Brazil, however. Those in the jury confessed their general dissatisfaction with the outcome of the competition, mostly because they were uncomfortable with the idea of letting go of Silva's familiar and popular music. Critics and readers of daily newspapers kept the controversy alive by reminding the new government that Silva's music had already been accepted among the people and urged for the old monarchical work to continue as the national anthem of the republican government. In the end, Deodoro da Fonseca decided to keep the old, familiar work as the Brazilian national anthem, arguing that Silva's music had been sanctioned by the people as their own through collective performances that were retained in their memories, although government officials made sure that new lyrics were added later.[16] Meanwhile, Miguez kept the prize for his victorious anthem and his work was declared the official anthem of the Brazilian Republic, a consolation honor that nonetheless boosted his status as a main player in the local musical establishment, usually referred to in scholarly writing as República Musical, or "Republic of Music," in a parallel to the "Republic of Letters."[17]

---

[15] Anderson's *Imagined Communities*, 167. For the relation of Silva's anthem and the historical contexts of its use, see Ricardo Marques de Mello, "Hino Nacional Brasileiro: Entre espaços de experiências e horizontes de expectativas," *Revista Múltipla* 18, no. 24 (June 2008): 77–93; and Rafael Rosa Hagemeyer, "Levando ao longe o canto da pátria: Gravações em disco e difusões no rádio do Hino Nacional (1900–1945)," *Revista de História e Estudos Culturais* 8, no. 3 (September–December, 2008): 1–22.

[16] Osorio Duque Estrada (1870–1927) provided new lyrics in 1909; the final version of lyrics and music was formalized in 1922 during the centenary anniversary of Brazilian independence from Portugal.

[17] The term "Musical Republic" was coined by Avelino Pereira in *Música, sociedade e política: Alberto Nepomuceno e a República Musical* (Rio de Janeiro: Ed. Universidade Federal do Rio de Janeiro, 2007).

Musical Example 3.3. Leopoldo Miguez, Anthem to the Proclamation of the Republic.

Source: Fundação Nacional de Arte, Brazil

66   MUSIC AND COSMOPOLITANISM

Government officials were thus struck by an unexpected problem: how to make something without a local history be embraced by large numbers of people, enough so to become a symbol of a new nation. Miguez's anthem suffered from a lack of historical baggage; his work had little time to prove its suitability to inspire "the people" and catch on at a moment that required immediate popular engagement. Still, those close to Miguez and supportive of his role within the musical status quo continued to promote the composer's work. The critic Eduardo de Borja Reis (1859–1896), for example, complained that Miguez's anthem had not received the importance it deserved. In his opinion, the work not only had great artistic value, but also "the music represents the conquest of our ideal of liberty."[18] In Reis's attempt to rescue Miguez's anthem from neglect, he pointed to the musical similarities between Miguez's work and "La Marseillaise," especially in the chorus "Liberdade, liberdade" (Freedom, freedom): marching patterns and dotted rhythms with similar ascending melodic lines working as a climax suitable for group singing, a musical cliché and a compositional strategy with parallels in many contemporary patriotic and civic musics, and popular songs worldwide.[19] But similarities, Reis observed, were not only easily noticeable, they were also not accidental, for the printed score included the first bars of "La Marseillaise" as an epigraph. Miguez's anthem was in fact a paraphrase of "La Marseillaise," which Reis defines as "a call to support ideals of the Republic . . . a cosmopolitan work [that] is and will always be the most important interpreter of the people's feelings . . . a cry of indignation of all oppressed peoples, a chant that strives for liberty."[20] Rather than seeing the musical similarities between the two anthems as a deterrent, Reis claims they were assets, as if Miguez's recognition of "La Marseillaise" in his own work would add political power to his music. Reis was probably correct. In a short unsigned note published in the newspaper *O Paiz* a few weeks after the competition that made Miguez's anthem victorious, the critic points to the composer's intentional paraphrase of "La Marseillaise" and explains:

> As [Miguez's] work is a revolutionary anthem, and since our Republic is a historical consequence of the French Revolution, which is symbolized in "La Marseillaise," the composer [Miguez] understood that the patriotic song [La Marseillaise] should also be the origin of the [Brazilian] republican anthem,

[18] Borja Reis, "Ao governo," *Gazeta Musical* 11 (1891), 2–6.

[19] Regina Sweeney, *Singing Our Way to Victory: French Cultural Politics and Music during the Great War* (Middletown, CT: Wesleyan University Press, 2001), 21. Derek Scott has noted similar songs published in England as English's "national songs"; see *The Singing Bourgeois: Songs of the Victorian Drawing Room and Parlor*, 2nd ed. (New York and London: Ashgate, 2001), 179.

[20] *Gazeta Musical* 11, 1891. See also Avelino Pereira, "Uma República Musical: Música, política e sociabilidade no Rio de Janeiro oitocentista (1882–1899)," XXVII Simpósio Nacional de História, July 22–26, 2013, 7.

and as such, he repeatedly shaped his melodic lines according to the work by Rouger de Lisle, but also he left [the model] and worked with his own noble and elevated style.[21]

One wonders, nonetheless, if Miguez's anthem failed to reach the expected public acclaim exactly because of its similarity to "La Marseillaise." Not because the paraphrasing itself was a feature worth condemning, as one can see from Reis's critique, but because a new anthem was not necessary after all: "La Marseillaise" was a cosmopolitan work that had already fulfilled the role of "interpreter of people's feelings" and "the conquest of *our* [my emphasis] ideal of liberty," aligning song and communal performance with "people" and "liberty." Within this scenario of utopian musical universalism, Miguez's anthem became superfluous. Not coincidentally, Silva's anthem also had plenty of musical similarities to "La Marseillaise," in addition to its Rossinian flare. The reception story of these three anthems reveals an intertwined textual narrative that helps us to change the focus from the use of music and songs for political engagement as dictated by the official establishment, to the people's power to choose and use established cultural and musical tropes for communal political participation and action.

Is it possible to understand the emergence of republicanism and its sonic symbolisms in Brazil without considering the various performances of "La Marseillaise" in the process? No doubt, the undermining of performances of "La Marseillaise" in historical narratives of music-making in Rio de Janeiro highlights a bias in telling local histories isolated from their larger cultural networks. This tale of three anthems compels us to revisit larger questions of music, representation, and identity formation that are recurring in scholarship, namely the assumption that local traditions or local music production alone can serve to articulate collective identities in the name of nation-building, or in the name of any other local collective cause. In a time of expanding global commerce and circulation of cultural goods, collectivity could be achieved using a variety of sources, and most likely something with a cosmopolitan history would already arrive with a story of its own to be shared. And since the performances of "La Marseillaise" in Rio de Janeiro were not unique events, but part of a larger, contemporary global trend, the story of the song in the Brazilian capital shows that, in a time of song proliferation and growing circulation, even patriotic songs could be shared as part of borderless cosmopolitan experiences.

---

[21] *O Paiz*, March 6, 1890.

68 MUSIC AND COSMOPOLITANISM

Songful and Memorable

Early in the 19th century, the composer André Grétry (1741–1813) was already reflecting on the wide dissemination of "La Marseillaise." He pointed to the song's musical characteristics, not its political use, as the reason why the work was repeated over and over beyond its place of origin:

> One can see, I say, that the air "Des Marseillois," composed by an amateur who had only his good taste and ignored harmonic progressions, that "Ça ira" and "La Carmignole," which come to us from the port of Marseille, have refreshed the music of our revolution. Why? Because these airs are songful and, without songfulness, no music could be remembered. And all music that is not memorable . . . is nothing but an unexplained enigma.[22]

Grétry did not provide an explanation of what he meant by "songfulness," but for "La Marseillaise" to be easily recognized and remembered by large numbers of people living far apart, geographically and historically, its artistry may have relied on a straightforward musical construction, repetitive rhythmic and short, stepwise melodic patterns suitable for syllabic text setting. Being memorable and songful surely are elements that could not be dismissed, as "La Marseillaise" became in itself a living example of what songful and memorable meant.

However, being songful and memorable may be seen as abstract qualities for a song. In fact, Grétry's opinion was not shared by all, and one could argue that "La Marseillaise" is actually difficult to sing. That was apparently the case of Silva's anthem, which needed to be simplified by the composer Alberto Nepomuceno (1864–1920) to better accommodate new lyrics before it was officially sanctioned as Brazil's national anthem in 1922.[23] Sweeney has argued that it was not merely a song's straightforwardness or its memorability that made for its dissemination and wide appeal, but the nature of the tune which, even if long and difficult to be repeated, was nonetheless easily susceptible to changes, adaptations, and varied modes of performances, without losing its initial allure.[24] Musical recipes for how to write a song that could achieve wide popularity are in fact conspicuously unusual through the 19th century, especially when at stake was not only the symbolism of a nation, but the more concrete worlds of markets and profits. That, of course, underlines the complex and speculative process of linking music production and reception. Nonetheless, a century after Grétry's comments, songwriters

---

[22] André-Ernest-Modeste, Grétry, *Mémoires, ou Essais sur la musique* (Paris, 1797) vol. 3, 203–204, cited in Mondelli, "Phonocentric Revolution," 158–159.

[23] For Nepomuceno's changes to Silva's original music, see Hagemeyer, "Levando ao longe o canto da pátria," 8–10.

[24] Sweeney, *Singing Our Way to Victory*, 21.

enmeshed in a wholesome international business of songwriting knew exactly what wide audiences would like, respond to, and, of course, spend their money on. If, by the beginning of the 20th century, there was already an "international tradition of song" and "a global conception of popular music practice," as Nicholas Gebhardt claims, the writing of new, or the rewriting of old tunes in new ways, with recognizable and short choruses that invited and allowed for communal performances, were already well-known recipes that integrated the familiar and the new in seamless fashion.[25]

Lawrence Kramer claims that songfulness maybe connected to "a fusion of vocal and musical utterance judged to be both pleasurable and suitably independent of verbal content," since the direct connection with the body in performance gives it more force than the meaning of the lyrics. Kramer does not elaborate on what kind of "musical utterance" is associated with songfulness, but he also admits that

> songfulness is one of those aesthetic qualities that seem to invite immediate recognition even while they elude definition. . . . The one who hears it may not be able to say for sure whether it is more an attribute of the music (which seems made for the voice) or of the performance (which saturates the music with voice), or even of the ear that hears it, but the quality nonetheless seems utterly unmistakable.[26]

It seems that it is the bodily connection with the sound in song, brought about after the moment of creation, that defines songfulness, Kramer concludes, a process that can be observed and interpreted at the time of performance and reception. Still, both the performative and the elusive musical qualities do not help us to understand why songs like "La Marseillaise" circulated so widely, while Miguez's anthem did not, both with similar musical characteristics and performed in similar social contexts. In this regard, I may propose that the songfulness attributed to works like "La Marseillaise" was marked by a specific and unmistakable communal recognition that could only be fully realized through collective performances able to elude time and space.

Thus, even if being songful and memorable helped in the case of "La Marseillaise," it did not hurt that the tune was performed and heard during the historical events that marked one of the greatest sociopolitical changes in

---

[25] Nicholas Gebhardt focuses on Irving Berlin and his "recipe" for song writing; see *Vaudeville Melodies: Popular Musicians and Mass Entertainment in American Culture, 1870–1929* (Chicago: Chicago University Press, 2017), 178 and 183.
[26] Lawrence Kramer, *Musical Meaning: Toward a Critical History* (Los Angeles: University of California Press, 2001), 53.

70   MUSIC AND COSMOPOLITANISM

the Western World: the French revolution.[27] One should not be surprised that the tune spread throughout France, Europe, and the Americas specifically as a song of revolution and of "the people" and that, as such, it inspired composers and performers from all walks of life. François-Joseph Gossec's (1734–1829) *Offerande à la Liberté* (1792) dramatized "La Marseillaise" on the stage,[28] and composers from Beethoven, Rossini, and Offenbach to Berlioz and Debussy paid homage to republican ideals by working on the tune. Revolutionaries from Russia to Latin American countries used the song for political purposes in performances at institutionalized venues and celebratory communal events. The zarzuela composer Manuel Fernández Caballero (1835–1906) left "La Marsellesa" (1876) for the popular theater, while composers of band and choir music had the tune up their sleeves, and so did arrangers, cabaret and music hall singers, and circus performers looking for familiar tunes to improvise upon and expect immediate audience response. The song also made it to the Italian countryside as a folk tune without connections to any revolutionary ideals.[29]

Rather than focusing on the song's revolutionary suggestion of "freedom of the people," one could choose instead to point out the imperial residues in performances of "La Marseillaise"; one could interpret it, for example, as a work that evoked the cleansing of "impure blood," as a song of the guillotine performed by Jacobins late in the 18th century; or as a song that early in the 19th century was sung to the flag of nationalist militarism.[30] From the perspective of Rio de Janeiro, we can point to its association with utopian ideals of Enlightenment universalism, as the Brazilian White elite chose to perform the work of revolution and liberty while they continued to invoke "the people" that did not include the country's large Black population, women, or the thousands of Indigenous groups who had become objects of anthropological, scientific, and political interests, rather than citizens.

But republicanism, French revolution, France, empire, and the politics of nationalism are intertwined enough to mask the cultural complexities that popular songs like "La Marseillaise" generated in the early days of European-led globalization. For in addition to its resilience as a songful and memorable tune of revolution and militarism, it traveled with many other flags, traversed opposing

---

[27] For the global role of the French revolution, see Suzanne Desan, Lynn Hunt, and William Nelson, eds. *French Revolution in a Global Perspective* (Ithaca, NY: Cornell University Press, 2013); see also Hobsbawm, *Echoes of the Marseillaise*, especially 34–37.

[28] Annegret Fauser, *Musical Encounters at the 1889 Paris World's Fair* (Rochester, NY: University of Rochester Press, 2005), 122–126.

[29] Roberto Leydi, "The Dissemination and Popularization of Opera in," *Opera in Theory and Practice, Image and Myth*, ed. Lorenzo Bianconi and Giorgio Pestelli (Chicago: University of Chicago Press), 321.

[30] Owen Connelly, *Blundering to Glory: Napoleon's Military Campaigns*, 3rd ed. (Lanham, MD: Rowan and Littlefield, 2006), 52, and Jennifer Wise, quoting Laura Mason, in "L'Enfant et le tyran: 'La Marseillaise' and the Birth of Melodrama," *Theatre Survey* 53, no. 1 (April 2012), 29.

movements and ideas, and meandered flagrantly through many borders—despite them and because of them. One will find, for instance, "La Marseillaise" as a key song early in the 19th century during the Haitian revolutionary movement for independence, performed both by the French troops and the enslaved Blacks fighting them, a case where "the bond association with revolution does not coincide with the nation boundaries," as Sujaya Dhanvantari notes. In this case, "La Marseillaise" provided "narratives of both rule and resistance, occupying a contested site of ideas concerning rights and freedoms."[31] Dhanvantari argues that the widespread use of songs like "La Marseillaise" require that we rethink established understandings of geographic boundary representations through sound to "account for the circular movement of ideas and images in a transnational and transcultural system of communication."[32] Music, and songs specifically, shared through flexible and instable cultural networks, enables bonds that are not immediately visible on physical maps. In the case of Haiti, Dhanvantari continues, performances of the tune make us rethink common classifications of colonial and colonized territories, which are often "viewed apart from one another in order to create the illusion of mono-ethnic [and racially homogeneous] identities," and that characterize "the colonized as silent figures of discourse."[33] While the experience of slavery powerfully oriented the enslaved people to the discourses of liberation offered by the lyrics of "La Marseillaise," as an oral musical expression of community bonding, performances of the song became a "concept-metaphor" that enabled them to redirect their experience of slavery to the struggles for freedom and justice articulated in the communal performance of the song. As Dhanvantari suggests, performances of "La Marseillaise" "help us to re-think the role of [European] colonization with respect to the Western values of liberty and equality,"[34] as both enslaved people and the French army were equally "predisposed to a discourse that would provide them with a way of striving for social transformation."[35]

The case of "La Marseillaise" also reveals a heterogeneous and flexible notion of cultural identity through a historical process in which cultural networks, ideas, and their ideologies spanned the Atlantic and beyond. At the turn of the 20th century, "La Marseillaise" served as propaganda for anarchists throughout Europe, who embraced the work as a form of subversion of the republican

---

[31] Sujaya Dhanvantari, "French Revolutionary Song in the Haitian Revolution 1789–1804," in *African Diasporas in the New and Old Worlds: Consciousness and Imagination*, ed. Geneviève Fabre and Klaus Benesch (Amsterdam and New York: Rodopi, 2004), 101–119.

[32] Dhanvantari, "French Revolutionary Song," 101. For the influence of French revolutionary ideas and the participation of Blacks as political actors in the spread of revolutionary ideas in Latin America, see Jane Landers, *Atlantic Creoles in the Age of Revolutions* (Cambridge, MA: Harvard University Press, 2011).

[33] Dhanvantari, "French Revolutionary Song," 101–102.

[34] Dhanvantari, "French Revolutionary Song," 112.

[35] Dhanvantari, "French Revolutionary Song," 114–115.

72 MUSIC AND COSMOPOLITANISM

establishment.[36] The song also appears, translated or with new lyrics, in numerous socialist songsters designed for performances at workers' movements, which were published not only in France, but also in England, Germany, Switzerland, and Austria. The inclusion of "La Marseillaise" in these songsters, Alexander McKinley suggests, "betrays a conscious effort to connect the socialist struggles with past revolutionary movements," and it also shows that the tune became key at a particular moment when people from all over Europe "embraced internationalism as a key ingredient of socialism,"[37] outlining both the cosmopolitan outlook of socialism and the role of songs to create communal bonds beyond the nation.

"La Marseillaise" was also used as a form of detachment from the establishment to serve the causes of rebellious bohemians at the close of the 19th century in large cities in Europe and across the Atlantic, including Rio de Janeiro. Rather than revolutionary political ideals, performances of "La Marseillaise" in café-concerts and cabarets enabled a bohemian generation to express feelings of both belonging and "outsideness," while pointing to the lack of borders between old and new. It was sung, for example, by bohemians through the streets of Montmartre when Rodolphe Salis (1851–1897) moved his Chat Noir to a new venue in 1885.[38] At the turn of the 20th century, "La Marseillaise" also became part of the heterogeneous repertory of music halls, early movies, and circuses in Rio de Janeiro; the cabaret singer Ywonna, for example, sung it for the July 14 celebrations in the Brazilian capital (see Chapter 5), and the Italian Antonio Cataldi sung it as a *filme cantante* as an early movie production in Rio de Janeiro (see Chapter 8). Their performances show that the song was an important part of a diverse popular discourse, and that it provided sonic background for contested sites of social and political practices and ideas. These multiple performances of "La Marseillaise" exemplify the idea of a "song network" suggested by Keir Keightley, one that was enabled by communal performances always moving in outward motion and in multiple flows.[39]

---

[36] Alexander McKinley, "Anarchists and the Music of the French Revolution," *Journal for the Study of Radicalism* 1, no. 2 (2007), 5–6; see also Gaetano Manfredonia, "De l'usage de la chanson politique: La production anarchiste d'avant 1914," *Cités* 19 (Paris, PUF, 2004): 43–53; and Hobsbawm, *Echoes of the Marseillaise*, 35–37.

[37] McKinley, "Anarchists and the Music of the French Revolution," 5–6; and Kate Bowan, "Friendship, Cosmopolitan Connections and Late Victorian Socialist Songbook Culture," in *Cheap Print and Popular Song in the Nineteenth Century: A Cultural History of the Songster*, ed. Paul Watt, Derek Scott, and Patrick Spedding (Cambridge and New York: Cambridge University Press, 2017), 93.

[38] Lisa Appignanesi, *The Cabaret* (New York: Universe Books, 1976), 16.

[39] Keightley, "Un voyage via barquinho . . . : Global circulation, musical hybridization, and adult modernity, 1961–9," in *Migrating Music*, ed. Jason Toynbee and Byron Dueck (New York: Routledge, 2011), 113–114. For the idea of cultural flows, see Arjun Appadurai's, *Modernity at Large: Cultural Dimensions of Globalization* (Minneapolis: University of Minnesota Press, 1996).

If the dissemination of "La Marseillaise" provides new insights into the complexities of an emergent global culture and its mass dissemination, it also highlights the need to account for the overlaps and similarities among many groups' engagements with cultural forms. Over time, "La Marseillaise" could evoke a collective memory that was not limited to the boundaries of the French nation, or any nation, nor to the boundaries of the republican cause, nor to the boundaries of imperialism, nor of slavery, nor to the boundaries of anarchists, socialists, or rebellious bohemians. "La Marseillaise" also exemplifies the fluidity and the wide-ranging cosmopolitan sphere of music performance and listening and their power to conjure up collectivity. It also provides an example of how during the long 19th century singing and hearing, music and sound, allowed for cultural sharing as an experience of collective belonging through a process of communication that was more effective than the one provided by literary works or visual imagery. Walter Wong has noted that in the 19th century written, visual, and oral cultural practices were rather intertwined,[40] but music-making could add layers of force to these practices. While literary production scattered information in all directions and crossed various national and cultural borders, song was more easily understood. It served especially illiterate and semi-illiterate audiences to whom tunes carried more meaning than written messages, since music subjectivity lends itself directly to the imagination, individual and collective. Songs were thus "sounding messages," Mondelli suggests, traveling beyond the strict meaning of words. They were accessible to all those who engaged with them in "collective performance and collective hearing,"[41] and allowed a privileged insight into "those who may otherwise not be immediately visible."[42]

This process may be more evident when local songs are used politically to articulate local identity or nationhood. Nonetheless, the case of "La Marseillaise" brings to the fore a more complex scenario, one that not only challenges established ideas about music and nation-building, but also questions the political power associated with cultural ownership. For when "La Marseillaise," once rooted in Marseille, then in revolutionary ideals, then in France, and then in republicanism, is disseminated over long distances and through long periods of time, the song and its many performances become an image of an image of an image, until its origins are lost in a network of elusive cultural connections. "La Marseillaise" then becomes a concept-metaphor, as Dhanvantari claims.[43] In fact, while it was the power of the French revolution and republicanism that set in motion "La Marseillaise" as a cosmopolitan song, it was through a

---

[40] Walter Wong's *Orality and Literacy: The Technologizing of the Word* (New York: Methuen, 1982), cited in Sweeney, *Singing Our Way to Victory*, 6–8.
[41] Mondelli, "Phonocentric Revolution,"164.
[42] Mckinley, "Anarchists and the Music of the French Revolution," 2–3.
[43] Dhanvantari, "French Revolutionary Song,"

74   MUSIC AND COSMOPOLITANISM

heterogeneous and complex set of sociohistorical references that its cosmopolitan strength and sociopolitical power could be fully exposed. For, ultimately, the music encompassed a cosmopolitan historical trajectory of cultural negotiations and imaginaries that came to signify far more than republicanism in its historical momentum in France, in Rio de Janeiro, or elsewhere, as the song continued throughout the 20th century to play a role in events demanding the solidarity of large groups across long distances.[44] Most importantly, if performances of "La Marseillaise" point to the pitfalls of Kantian universalism, it surely enabled Enlightenment utopianism to become global.

From the perspective of the development of sonic symbols of republicanism in Brazil, "La Marseillaise" and Silva's anthem fulfilled the need to find a balance between the old and the new, as both songs complemented each other through their familiar tunes and power to instigate group performances and participation. Not surprisingly, before the proclamation of the Republic, Silva's music, written for a monarch, was considered "La Marseillaise" of Brazil and equally sung indiscriminately during moments of political importance and events of national significance throughout the 19th century.[45] One can say with certainty that, alongside Silva's anthem, "La Marseillaise" became a deep and enduring sonic symbol in Brazil and, as such, it continues to this day to be brought up as a major force within Brazil's historical political imaginary.[46]

Yet if "La Marseillaise" was (and is) a song of an imaginary "many," contradictorily it was (and is) also a song of a very few. One can easily be distracted by descriptions of military parades in Rio de Janeiro and the political use of music in the city to unify what could not be unified solely through utopian ideals of universal republicanism. If some listening to "La Marseillaise" performed by military bands in the streets of Rio de Janeiro could claim to belong to a unified, cosmopolitan moment of political participation, the story of those performing in such military bands exposed the pitfalls of such a forged unified political moment. Lima Barreto, for example, reporting on his arrival in the cosmopolitan city as a mulatto trying to find work, described his first encounter with military displays in Rio de Janeiro and offered a rather bleak picture of those moments of pseudo-participation of the people. The military ranks were clearly defined by

[44] It was "La Marseillaise" that was heard during a Henri Lavendan's play in Rio de Janeiro at the cusp of World War I, in a performance by both the actors and the audience, who applauded frantically to support the country's entrance into the worldwide conflict; see Fagundes, "Música e guerra," 24.
[45] Mello, "Hino Nacional Brasileiro," 78–79.
[46] In Brazil, performances of "La Marseillaise" parallel the figure of La Marienne which, like in France, was used to represent revolutionary ideals. The painting A Marienne by Décio Villares remains to this day the symbol of the Brazilian republic, often appearing side by side with the image of Tiradentes. The image of La Marienne is displayed inconspicuously to this day on the Brazilian currency. In addition, until the first decade of the 20th century, the local establishment commemorated July 14 as a part of Brazilian history; see Reis Carvalho, "O Feriado Brasileiro de 14 de Julho," Kosmos, 5 no. 7 (July 1908).

the race of its members: Blacks, recruited to the fronts as the only option of work after the abolition of slavery, made the majority for the lower ranks, while Whites filled the upper echelons. To Barreto, this was a disturbing element of the patriotic display:

> The sound of a military fanfare, filling the street, came to agitate the multitude . . . they are the soldiers, someone pointed out. The battalion started to pass: the musicians blasted their lungs in an imbecile march. First came the commander, hardly hiding the displeasure that such an innocent military exhibition caused him. Then the officials, arrogant and proud of themselves, showing their military elegance. They were followed by the privates, who in a slow and stumbling march dragged the step without love, without conviction, indifferent, carrying deadly rifles and bayonets over their shoulders as if they were instruments of punishment. The officials seemed to me from one country and the privates from another. It was like a battalion of Sipals[47] or Senegalese shooters. . . . The battalion passed, and the flag passed, leaving me totally indifferent.[48]

The songfulness attributed to "La Marseillaise" did not affect Barreto, who did not see himself as a part of such collective performance; its sounding force was not enough to lure him in. As a mulatto, Barreto's voice was not part of such a cosmopolitan experience, and his personal story, like many others in the cosmopolitan city, was instead marked by the power of music to segregate.

---

[47] Indian soldiers serving the British army.
[48] Lima Barreto, *Recordações do escrivão Isaías Caminha* (Rio de Janeiro: Obliq, 2018 [1909], Kindle). For an analysis of Barretos's *Recordações*, see Alfredo Bosi, *Literattura e Resistência* (São Paulo: Companhia das Letras, 2002), 186–208.

4

Race in the Universal and Eternal Tradition

Forging a Local Tradition

On July 6, 1895, there was a massive outdoor public ceremony in Rio de Janeiro for the observance of the death of Marechal Floriano Peixoto (1839–1895). Peixoto was minister of war for Marechal Deodoro da Fonseca and was appointed vice president in February 1891; later in 1891, when Fonseca resigned, Peixoto assumed the presidency amid great political turmoil. He became known as the "iron fist" president because his tenure was characterized by a centralized government, the use of military force to control clashes among various sociopolitical sectors, and the nurturing of nationalistic sentiments. By the time of his death, Peixoto had gathered a fair number of enemies, but also some heartfelt supporters. In a posthumous eulogy, Candido Costa wrote that Peixoto was "the Brazilian Washington; he planted in the hearts of Brazilians the patriotic sentiment and the love for the Republic."[1]

The observance of Peixoto's passing was thus a moment of national significance and the religious service was attended by politicians, cabinet members, and diplomatic emissaries. Held at Igreja Irmandade da Santa Cruz dos Militares, the ceremony included an orchestra of 73 musicians which performed the Requiem (1816) by José Maurício Nunes Garcia (Figure 4.1) under the conductor Norberto Amancio de Carvalho, the music director and teacher at the military school.[2] Carvalho's musical choice for the event was not unusual, since Nunes Garcia's Requiem had been performed several times on past occasions mourning national figures. Originally composed in 1816 for the observance of the death of Queen Maria I of Portugal, the Requiem was also performed on March 19, 1830, in observance of the death of D. Carlota Joaquina, mother of D. Pedro I, a performance that Nunes Garcia conducted himself.[3] The work continued in the same trajectory, being performed in 1835 in observance of the death of D. Pedro I,[4] in the funeral of Princess D. Maria Amelia on April 13, 1853,[5] and at the mass

---

[1] *Jornal do Commercio*, July 14, 1895.
[2] *Gazeta de Noticias*, July 7, 1895.
[3] *Imperio do Brasil: Diário Fluminense*, March 23, 1830. D. Carlota Joaquina died on January 7, 1830.
[4] *Jornal do Commercio*, January 5, 1835.
[5] *Correio Mercantil*, April 13, 1853. D. Maria Amelia died on April 12, 1853.

Music and Cosmopolitanism. Cristina Magaldi, Oxford University Press. © Oxford University Press 2024.
DOI: 10.1093/oso/9780199744770.003.0005

RACE IN THE UNIVERSAL AND ETERNAL TRADITION   77

Figure 4.1. José Maurício Nunes Garcia.

in observance of the passing of the king of Naples, Pedro II's brother-in-law, in August 1859.⁶ The Requiem continued to be performed after the proclamation of the Republic on similar occasions; for example, during the ceremonies observing the deaths of Empress D. Thereza Christina Maria in 1890 and of D. Pedro II in 1891.⁷ Although both the empress and the monarch died in exile, and despite the republican government's attempts to ignore their passing, they were both beloved public figures who still evoked widespread public emotion. As such, they were remembered in small but elaborate religious ceremonies that included the performance of Nunes Garcia's work.

It is noteworthy, however, that while the various performances of the Requiem earlier in the century did not arouse any scrutiny by music critics, the performance during Peixoto's funeral mass was fiercely debated in daily newspapers and incited a series of discussions about Nunes Garcia and his work. The criticism did not target the musical choice for the ceremony, but rather the performance

⁶ *Jornal do Commercio*, August 23, 1859.
⁷ D. Tereza Cristina Maria died on December 28, 1889, in Oporto, Portugal; the mass in Rio de Janeiro was announced in *Jornal do Commercio*, January 29, 1890. Pedro II died in Paris on December 5, 1891, and the mass in Rio de Janeiro was announced in *Jornal do Commercio*, December 23, 1891.

78 MUSIC AND COSMOPOLITANISM

decisions and the arrangement of the Requiem which, in the view of the republican critic José Rodrigues Barbosa (1857–1939), "desecrated the work of the *Master* [my emphasis] . . . a work that every musician in the country has the obligation to safeguard and respect." The arranger, most likely the conductor, was criticized for not being a "serious musician," because he altered the Requiem's original instrumentation and therefore "[was not] faithful to *his traditions* [my emphasis]." The critic condemned the performance as a "crime of disrespect and a sacrilege [of a] Masterwork . . . a beautiful and inspired composition of a notable Brazilian musician." He further noted that such an altered instrumentation destroyed the "simplicity of the original orchestration of string quartet, two clarinets, two horns, and one bassoon *ad libitum*;"[8] instead, the critic heard, with dismay, cornets and trombones, even though such choices would have been obvious ones for a director of a wind military ensemble.

The discussion about the work's performance during Peixoto's funeral continued the next day with a newspaper article written by Visconde Alfredo d'Escragnolle Taunay (1843–1899), a prominent politician, intellectual, music devotee, and a heartfelt monarchist. Taunay refers to Nunes Garcia as "one of the greatest and *purest* [my emphasis] Brazilian glories," praising the conductor's musical choice during Peixoto's funeral, but adding his disgust of the republican authorities' neglect of a composer who "would be honored in the most advanced European nations." Taunay, who had asked the Senate for money to restore and publish Nunes Garcia's works "here or in Germany," had not been successful in his efforts and blamed the new government for a lack of support for the arts. "What a forgotten glory; what a disregard for an invaluable treasure . . . being damaged in the cathedral's archives or in the hand of some individuals," he lamented, a work "'[which] Neukomm, Haydn's disciple, believed to be on par with Mozart's Requiem." Nunes Garcia's works, he continued:

> are not only universal but eternal . . . a work of a true giant, [a work which] does not age, [because] it is the result of profound studies, not only of counterpoint and Gregorian chant, but also of the works by the German Masters, Bach, Haydn, Beethoven, from which stem the works of Wagner and Berlioz.

Taunay finishes by pleading for the new directorship of the music conservatory to acquire Nunes Garcia's manuscripts, because "they are national treasures."[9]

---

[8] *Jornal do Commercio*, July 9, 1895. For a compilation of Rodrigues Barbosa's chronicles, see Paulo Castagna, "Um século de música brasileira, de José Rodrigues Barbosa" (Instituto de Artes da Unesp, 2007), 39–40, online publication, https://archive.org/details/umSeculoDeMusicaBrasileir aDeJoseRodriguesBarbosa.

[9] *Jornal do Commercio*, July 10, 1895. Taunay's writings were later compiled by his son, Alfonse Taunay, as *Uma grande gloria brasileira: José Maurício Nunes Garcia, 1767–1830* (São

RACE IN THE UNIVERSAL AND ETERNAL TRADITION   79

Although described from different political viewpoints, these critics' reactions to the performance of Nunes Garcia's Requiem during Peixoto's funeral can shed light on the complexity of the negotiations taking place in the first decades of the new regime, in particular about the sanctioning of a local musical past that could represent the new Republic's principles and ideals. Because the forging of past traditions is in reality about the present and preparing for the future, a "task of mixing memory and desire,"[10] at the close of the century, constructing and safeguarding a past that could be claimed to have national significance became a main goal of republican intellectuals and politicians. It became an "obsessive idea," Diogo de Castro Oliveira claims, a belief that "a tradition could be created not by time, but by man's decisions."[11] Still, discussions and disagreements about a local musical past that could represent the new nation were largely expected, especially considering the volatile political and cultural contexts of the new Republic's early years. On the one hand, monarchists denounced the erasure of history by radical republicans attempting to obliterate the monarchical past. On the other, those speaking for the new regime clung to Tiradentes's mythicized image as a martyr who could bypass monarchical icons and provide continuity to the idea of the pursuit of liberty in accordance with republican ideals.

It is intriguing, nonetheless, that the republican narrative of a local musical tradition, as contested as it was, became intertwined with Nunes Garcia and his Requiem, a work originally written for a monarch, by an employee of the Portuguese court, during the height of the Portuguese colonial and imperial power in Rio de Janeiro. Having worked for the Portuguese court most of his life, and with a body of work consisting primarily of religious works and of musics catering to courtly events that usually did not welcome the general public, Nunes Garcia's music should have had little chances of surviving the scrutiny of republican politicians, intellectuals, and musical establishment. One would expect, especially, that supporters of the republican regime would object to the performance of such a work during a ceremony of remembrance of a republican military president. And yet the critics were not the least concerned with the choice of

---

Paulo: Melhoramentos, 1930) and *Duas grandes glórias brasileiras: José Maurício e Carlos Gomes* (São Paulo: Melhoramentos, 1930).

[10] John Storey, *Culture and Power in Cultural Studies: The Politics of Signification* (Edinburgh: Edinburgh University Press, 2010), 72–73 Storey's term echoes T. S. Eliot in The Waste Land. Ryan Weber has also noted that "to control the past means controlling the future"; see his *Cosmopolitanism and Transatlantic Circles in Music and Literature* (London: Palgrave Macmillan, 2018), 296.

[11] Diogo de Castro Oliveira, *Onosarquistas e patafísicos: A boemia literária no Rio de Janeiro fin-de-siècle* (Rio de Janeiro: Letras, 2008), 17 and 45. See also Angela Alonso, "Arrivistas e decadentes: o debate político-intelectual Brasileiro na primeira década republicana," *Novos Estudos* 85 (2009): 131–148, online publication; Carvalho has argued that never before had historical constructions been so relevant in Brazil as in the transition from monarchy to republic; see his *A formação das almas*, 125.

80 MUSIC AND COSMOPOLITANISM

the work and its monarchical connections. Rather, chroniclers suggested that the work needed to be safeguarded as part of a local, national, universal, and eternal canon in terms of both its physical symbolism (publication of the score) and its sonic reception (performance). Ultimately, in the context of the convoluted early years of republicanism, the Requiem became a tool onto which ideological, political, aesthetic, and racial projections would converge to forge a desired sonic symbol of a national past suited to the republican status quo and its positivistic motto, "Order and Progress."

As is often the case in times of regime change, in the early days of the Republic there were several forces at play during the process of forging the past and in defining a local tradition for the purpose of nation-building. The edifying characteristics of the "native," the "primitive," and of "nature" symbolizing a "pure nation" that had fed the imagination of romantic writers and artists during the monarchical years were now competing with new ideas from politicians and intellectuals who turned their attention to the rescue of the "folk" and the "popular." By harvesting associations between nation and "the people" derived from German intellectuals of the early 19th century, they followed notions of culture that had become widespread among European thinkers. At the same time, grounded in contemporary views of racial determinism, social Darwinism, and sociocultural evolutionism, Brazilian intellectuals and politicians set forth racial theories to justify rather than to confront the country's long history of slavery, its large number of Black Brazilians, and its racially and culturally diverse population. The social scientist and literary critic Sílvio Romero (1851–1914), for example, argued that the Brazilian "people" and the "folk" were made up by *mestiços*, a racialized ideal shaping, and ultimately dividing, the nation. Thus, Romero characterized the *mestiço* nation as a middle stage toward sociocultural-racial progress, having (White) European culture as the ultimate goal.[12] Romero praised the country's mixed-race population while supporting the government's push for a higher influx of European immigration, with the goal to "whiten" the population over time by racial mixing in an attempt to secure a preponderance of White Brazilians and effectively alienating Black Brazilians culturally, socially, and politically.[13]

---

[12] For analyses of Romero's thinking and his influence, see Alberto Luis Schneider, *Silvio Romero: Hermeneuta do Brasil* (São Paulo: Annablume, 2005); Antonio Candido, *O método crítico de Silvio Romero* (São Paulo: Universidade the São Paulo, 1988); and Eduardo da Silva Freitas, "A ideologia nacionalista republicana na história da literatura brasileira de Silvio Romero," *Matraga* 24, no. 40 (2017): 207–224. See also Renato Ortiz, *Cultura brasileira e identidade nacional*, 2nd. ed. (São Paulo: Brasiliense, 1986); and Mariza Corrêa, *As ilusões da liberdade: A escola Nina Rodrigues e a antropologia no Brasil*, 2nd ed. (Bragança Paulista: Editora da Universidade de São Francisco, 2001, Kindle).

[13] Paulina Alberto, *Terms of Inclusion: Black Intellectuals in 20th-Century Brazil* (Chapel Hill: University of North Carolina Press, 2011), 10; see also Schwartz, *O espetáculo das raças*.

Romero collected song lyrics from several regions of Brazil and built a cultural map of the country's traditions, using a racialized cultural geographic matrix to explain and justify the nation's "folk" traditions.[14] Nonetheless, the degree to which his explorations and conclusions impacted the musical life in Rio de Janeiro in the early years of the Republic remains elusive, be that in the politics and ideals of the musical status quo, in the musical choices of composers and performers, in the emergence of the local music industry, or in the preference of Rio de Janeiro's audiences. In fact, it took until in the second decade of the 20th century, in the midst of the unfolding nationalist politics, for intellectuals, critics, and musicians to clearly articulate the tenets of what should be considered a "distinctively Brazilian musical tradition," one that included the precepts of racial-cultural mixture in the understanding of the nation.[15] And it took until the golden age of radio during the 1930s and 1940s for these intellectual, racially motivated political ideas to have a direct and lasting impact on the local musical business and on the choices of audiences.[16] In the first decades of the Republican government, music critics and intellectuals in Rio de Janeiro were concerned with the forging of another kind of local musical past, one in which European-ness, more so than Brazilian-ness, became a contested terrain among intellectuals, music critics, and composers, a referent that also implicitly included a racialized notion of nation and culture.

European-ness

At the forefront of the discussion was the paradigmatic trinity of European concert and operatic musics from Italy, Germany, and France. Italian music was defined as opera and was represented mostly through the names of 19th-century composers, such as Rossini and Verdi; German music was defined as 18th- and early 19th-century orchestral works by Haydn, Mozart, and Beethoven, a lineage that also supported arguments toward Wagner's operas; and French music, hardly definable and thus more malleable, could be characterized by *opera-comique* and operettas by composers such Auber and Offenbach, as well as by programmatic instrumental music, such as Berlioz's orchestral pieces and later

---

[14] For a discussion of Romero's influence in music scholarship in Brazil, see Maria Alice Volpe, "Traços Romerianos no mapa musical do Brasil," in *Música e história no longo século XIX*, ed. Antônio Herculano Lopes (Rio de Janeiro: Casa Rui Barbosa, 2011), 15–35.

[15] Volpe, "Traços romerianos," 16. For a critic of the Brazilian music historiography on this aspect, see Juliane Cristina Larsen, "Republicana, moderna, e cosmopolita: A música de concerto no Rio de Janeiro entre 1889 e 1914," PhD dissertation, Universidade de São Paulo, 2018.

[16] For the narrative of national identity in music and the development radio broadcasts, see Bryan McCann, *Hello, Hello Brazil: Popular Music in the Making of Modern Brazil* (Durham, NC: Duke University Press, 20014).

82   MUSIC AND COSMOPOLITANISM

Saint-Saëns's works. These models of European-ness were (and are) in themselves essentialized and politicized constructions that reflected negotiations of power and cultural and musical prestige taking shape in European music criticism, negotiations that were undoubtedly fueled by the politics of nation-building in Europe. Furthermore, the understandings of French-ness, German-ness, and Italian-ness were about vague, though clearly imperialistic, assumptions that specific (European) musics—and mostly German—were aesthetically superior and morally anchored in Enlightenment universal beliefs and ideals also well suited for republicans across the Atlantic. For Rio de Janeiro's critics, European-ness endured time and transcended locality.

One could argue that the forging of a local musical past at the onset of the republican government was a task of picking and choosing from a cosmopolitan musical network delimited by imagined ideals of Italian, German, and French musics. In a simplified version the process could be seen as an example of "choosing the best colonizer."[17] In truth, however, the choices and arguments made by local critics followed a recognizable pattern of musical, political, and aesthetic narratives that mirrored contemporary discussions in various places in Europe and the Americas about music's moral, aesthetic, educational, and civic functions in society, and ultimately its role in forging national cultural identities. At the core of these discussions there was a motto about the damaging powers of capitalism and the destructive moral elements of music as it was embraced by the emerging entertainment business—the well-known dualisms about music as art versus commerce and entertainment, rather than the national versus foreign dilemma—and the belief in music as a contemplative art disassociated from body and the sociopolitical, even if in reality such a motto was politically, socially, and racially anchored in specific ideologies. Rio de Janeiro's critics thus joined critics from other contemporary cities, all of whom agreed on one thing: that the wide range of musics stemming from the theater, opera included, were controlled by the rule of markets and the demands of the public and, as such, they could escape the cultural and political control of the establishment and therefore should be repudiated. To that end, Rio de Janeiro's intellectuals again joined intellectuals and critics from Europe and the Americas to find rescue in a repertory of Austro-German derivation. In Brazil, the forging of a musical past based on German music was thus a narrative built alongside similar narratives that took shape in 19th-century European music criticism, of which Rio de Janeiro's critics were a part. Describing a similar tendency in Lisbon, Silva notes that this Germanism became a 19th-century trope that ended up permeating the most

---

[17] Gentil de Faria, "Comparative Literature below the Equator: The Dilemma of Choosing the Best Colonizer," in *Colonizer and Colonized*, ed. Theo D'haen and Patricia Krüs (Rodopi: Amsterdan and Atlanta, 2000), 259–268.

unexpected critical circles.[18] The trope was further cemented in 20th-century musicological writings in Europe and the Americas and resulted in what Mark Everist describes as the widespread endorsement of a "Teutonic universalism."[19]

Actually, such ideals of a musical past, as convincing as they may have looked and sounded, constituted the views of a select group of mostly White males who aligned themselves politically with specific strains of republicanism and positivism, and racialized understandings of culture. Unlike discussions in literary circles about the artistic moment and its relation to the past and the future, which filled the pages of Rio de Janeiro's journals and magazines with varied arguments challenging the status quo,[20] discussions about a musical past were less multifaceted. They were built on the opinions of a few critics and musicians whose experiences with and views of the musical world, if seemingly antagonistic on the surface, did not vary in their essence. These critics and musicians fought for and with the status quo, rather than challenging or offering alternatives to it. Liliane Carneiro dos Santos Ferreira calls attention to the small number of individuals involved in music criticism during this period and concludes that music critics in Rio de Janeiro were in fact talking to one another.[21] In the Brazilian capital, the Republic of Letters and its literary, aesthetic, and ideological confrontations differed greatly from the unified, restricted, and, I would argue, backward-looking "República Musical" (Musical Republic).[22] What defined the so-called República Musical was a small group (no more than 10 individuals): composers and conductors in charge of the educational projects of the new republican regime at the National Institute of Music, like Miguez and Alberto Nepomuceno, who operated alongside a few performers, dilettanti, and powerful critics, such as Rodrigues Barbosa and Luis de Castro (1862–1920), Vincenzo Cernicchiaro (1858–1928), as well as the more independent and sometimes confrontational Oscar Guanabarino (1841–1937).[23] João do Rio put it simply: "Who led the triumphs in the ancient era? the flute performer. Who leads the musical armies

---

[18] Silva, "Entertaining Lisbon," 91.

[19] Mark Everist, "Cosmopolitanism and Music for the Theater: Europe and Beyond, 1800–1870," in *Music and Cosmopolitanism*, ed. Anastasia Belinda, Kaarina Kilpiö, and Derek Scott (New York: Routledge, 2019), 12–13.

[20] Silva, *A hélade e o subúrbio*, 25–41.

[21] Liliane Carneiro dos Santos Ferreira, "Cenários da ópera na imprensa carioca: Cultura, processo civilizador e sociedade na belle époque (1889–1914)," PhD dissertation, Universidade de Brasília, 2017, 48.

[22] For the term "Republica Musical" see Pereira, *Música, Sociedade e Política*.

[23] Guanabarino was a powerful music critic who often confronted the Musical Republic. He believed one should not disregard the local operatic past, but argued that other musical styles should be used to educate and morally elevate the population. For a compilation of Guanabarino's writings, see Guilherme Goldberg, Amanda Oliveira, and Patrick Menuzzi, eds., *Transcrições Guanabarinas: Antologia crítica*, vols. 1–4 (Porto Alegre: LiquidBook, 2019), online publication, https://wp.ufpel.edu.br/criticamusical/oscar-guanabarino/antologia-o-paiz/.

84 MUSIC AND COSMOPOLITANISM

in Rio? Oscar Guarabarino."[24] By endorsing an imagined Austro-German musical culture, these individuals attempted to bypass a monarchical past in which opera, operetta, and an array of musical styles derived from the stage had prevailed in the Brazilian capital. In their aesthetic and political positions, they engaged with familiar narratives also at play elsewhere that disparaged musical theater abiding to the senses, its unrestrained effect on individual and collective emotions, its association with and dependency on the drama, and its appeal to the visual in sound and performance. They dismissed operettas and opera, and mostly Italian opera, as passé, melody-centered, frivolous, and lacking in harmonic development and structural organicism—qualities attributed to Austro-Germanic instrumental styles—arguments that are still dominant in today's teaching and scholarly endeavors.[25] The revival of Nunes Garcia's music as part of a local tradition during the early republican government was thus shaped by a familiar path of canon-building, whereby governmental institutions, powerful individuals, and music critics select and privilege specific genres, styles, works, and composers believed to be unconstrained by social class, race, fashion, and markets, and musics that are believed to endure time and that have the potential to be universal.

Taunay's claimed historical links between Nunes Garcia and Austro-German classical music are not difficult to trace, however. The family ties between the Portuguese monarchs and the Hapsburgs early in the 19th century had led to performances of musics by Haydn and Mozart at the court in Rio de Janeiro, where Nunes Garcia worked. And those willing to disregard Nunes Garcia's ties to the monarchy could alternatively claim that his music reinforced the ideals preached by republican advocates, who were attracted to German literary and intellectual thought during the 1870s and 1880s, the two decades when republicanism grew considerably as a political force in Brazil. For these republicans, Austro-German musics were not tied to a monarchical rule, either in Rio de Janeiro or in the Austro-German context, but to Enlightenment universal beliefs and republican positivistic aesthetic ideals of clarity, and scientific and cerebral musical construction that supported the republican government's positivistic motto of "Order and Progress." It was a supposedly morally elevated music of the mind and the spirit, rather than of the body and the senses. Not coincidentally, the 1880 Rio de Janeiro performance of Mozart's *Don Giovanni* became a major event highly praised by critics, although some lamented that those in attendance did not applaud with the enthusiasm that the work deserved. Taunay used the familiar claim that the work was not "easily understood" and, unintentionally admitting that Mozart's music was not eternal after all, he ended by apologizing

---

[24] João do Rio (under the pseudonym "Joe"), "Cinematoprapho," *Gazeta de Notícias*, July 3, 1910.
[25] See the discussion about music theorists' approach to opera in William Rothstein, "Common-Tone Tonality in Italian Romantic Opera: An Introduction," *Music Theory Online* 14, no. 1 (March 2008), 1–16, online publication.

for the composer for not yet having at his disposal during his time "the modern instruments that give the modern orchestra a new color."[26]

But the process of bringing Nunes Garcia's works into this picture needed more than apologies for their old-fashioned instrumentation. The "Italianate" and eclectic style of Nunes Garcia's music—some of which recall works by Niccolò Jommelli and Davide Perez, the two most well-known composers in Rio de Janeiro before the transfer of the court in 1808—and the Rossinian flare of his later works should also have been deterrents to the use of his music as part of a discourse forging a local tradition aligned with Austro-German musics.[27] And considering that early in the 19th century the music written for religious settings and the music composed for the theater were rather intertwined, one should not be surprised that Nunes Garcia was attuned to musical fashions of the theater. He wrote an opera and a few works not tied to the religious or court ceremonies and attempted to sell his music in the incipient music market. After his death, his song "Beijo a mão que me condena" was sold as a "beautiful Brazilian *modinha*" in a local music store alongside hymns, "new" *modinhas*, and "modern waltzes for piano."[28] Like the music of any composer, Nunes Garcia's output could not be disassociated from contemporary tastes. His musical affinities were ample and also included his knowledge of and appreciation for the music of Haydn and Mozart. Nunes Garcia alluded to Haydn's work and his interest in Mozart's Requiem are easily evinced in musical comparisons with the opening of the Kyrie (Musical Example 4.1).[29]

[26] André Rebouças, "O D. João de Mozart no Rio de Janeiro," *Revista musical e de bellas artes* (July 1880): 121; Alfredo d'Escragnolle Taunay, "D. Juan de Mozart no Rio de Janeiro," *Revista musical e de bellas artes* (July 1880): 122. Don Giovanni premiered in the Brazilian capital during Pedro I's reign; see my ."Sonatas, Kyries, and Arias: Reassessing the Reception of European Music in Imperial Rio de Janeiro," *Music and Culture in Imperial Rio de Janeiro,* Symposium organized by the Teresa Lozano Long Institute of Latin American Studies and the UT School of Music, March 7–8, 2005, online publication available at http://www.lanic.utexas.edu/project/etext/llilas/cpa/spring05/missa/magaldi-1.pdf.

[27] Mauricio Dottori, *The Church Music of Davide Perez and Niccolò Jommelli with Special Emphasis on Funeral Music* (Curitiba, Brazil: Federal University of Paraná Press, 2008), 1; see also Rogério Budasz, "New Sources for the Study of Early Opera and Musical Theater in Brazil," (Austin: University of Texas, 2005), online publication; Budasz, *Teatro e música na América Portuguesa, conversões, repertório, raça, gênero* (Curitiba, Brazil: DeArtes, 2008); Mítia Ganade D'Acol, "Decoro musical e esquemas galantes: Um estudo de caso das seções de canto solo das Missas de Requiem de José Maurício Nunes Garcia e Marcos Portugal," Masters' thesis, Universidade de São Paulo, 2015; and Renato Aurélio Mainente, "O período joanino e as transformações no cenário musical no Rio de Janeiro," *Revista história e cultura* 2, no. 1 (2013): 132–145. Antonio Campos Monteiro, "Marcos Portugal x José Maurício: O autodidata, o clássico alemão," online publication.

[28] Nunes Garcia's *modinha* was announced in *Jornal do Commercio*, August 30, 1837. For a discussion about the parallel between Nunes Garcia and Mozart, see Guilherme Goldberg, "Alberto Nepomuceno e a Missa de Santa Cecília de José Maurício," *Annals of the VI Meeting of Historical Musicology* (Juiz de Fora, MG, Brazil: Centro Cultural Pró-Música), 2006, 138–172. For Nunes Garcia's *modinhas*, see Alberto Pacheco, "As *modinhas* do Padre José Maurício Nunes Garcia: Fontes, edição e prática," *Per Musi* 39 (2019): 1–5.

[29] Ricardo Tacucchian, "O Réquiem Mozartiano de José Maurício," *Revista brasileira de música* 19 (1991): 33–52. See also Jetro Meira de Oliveira, "Structural Issues in the Three Requiem Masses of

86 MUSIC AND COSMOPOLITANISM

Musical Example 4.1. José Maurício Nunes Garcia, Requiem, CPM 185. Requiem in D minor, edited by Cleofe Person de Mattos.
Source: Acervo Musicabrasilis, "http://www.musicabrasilis.org.br"

If the republican account of Nunes Garcia's work did attempt to ignore any vestige of an Italianate style in the composer's music, it also overlooked the 19th-century context in which it was transmitted through performance. The most active composer and conductor at mid-century, Francisco Manuel da Silva (1795–1865), for instance, was not concerned with Nunes Garcia's works as a national treasure and performed them according to the tastes and practices of his day, adding parts, new arias, modernizing the instrumentation, and arranging them for the instrumental groups available. These flexible performances were clearly still the norm during the Requiem's performance during Peixoto's funeral, but they started to receive stark condemnation soon after, as the narrative of a pure and eternal past started to take shape.[30] Taunay's campaign to safeguard and revive Nunes Garcia's music as part of a local tradition gained momentum when he joined forces with the directors of the Instituto Nacional de Música to explore archives, recover, publish, and perform Nunes Garcia's music. Already in April 1892, the critic and educator Guanabarino gave a talk about the composer to musicians gathered for an orchestral rehearsal. Digressing over the "the forgotten musician of colonial times," he asked that all musicians in the orchestra participate in a concert planned for September 22 of that year [1892] to celebrate for the first time "the birth of the composer of the Requiem, [who was] applauded by Neukomm. . . . During the celebration Miguez will conduct the Masterwork [Requiem] of the Brazilian Master with great chorus and orchestra."[31] Attuned to the French Société Nationale de Musique directed by Saint-Saëns in Paris, Nepomuceno also became imbued with the idea of preserving the local musical patrimony focusing on Nunes Garcia's music. He worked toward completing orchestrations, making orchestral scores, fixing some "mistakes" needed to make some works follow the appropriate compositional rules, and, finally, organizing performances of the works.[32] The movement of musical rescue was strong in

---

Padre José Maurício Nunes Garcia (1767–1830), and the Requiem Mass CT 190 by Damião Barbosa de Araújo, with editions of CT 182 and CT 184," PhD dissertation, University of Illinois at Urbana-Champaign, 2002; and Maria Aida Barroso, "Ornamentação e improvisação no método de pianoforte de José Maurício Nunes Garcia," Master's thesis, Universidade Federal do Rio de Janeiro, 2005.

[30] Criticizing Silva's rendition of Nunes Garcia's music, for example, D. Cleofe Person de Mattos noted that Silva, "moved by the spirit of innovation and renovation . . . substituted the original arias with new ones, changed and reducing the instrumentations," and characterized Silva's performances of Nunes Garcia's music as "spurious performances lacking integrity." Cleofe Person de Mattos, *José Maurício Nunes Garcia: Biografia* (Rio de Janeiro: Ministério da Cultura, 1997), 188–189.

[31] *O Paiz*, "Artes & artistas," April 29, 1892.

[32] For the issues arising from the edition of Nunes Garcia works, see Carlos Alberto Figueiredo, "Análise da edição de Luiz Heitor Correia de Azevedo da Missa de Defuntos (CPM 184), de José

88   MUSIC AND COSMOPOLITANISM

1898, when Nepomuceno organized a solemn event to dignify Nunes Garcia's work during the inauguration of the sumptuous Igreja da Candelária in Rio de Janeiro.[33]

In the first part of the 20th century, music scholarship followed Taunay's and Nepomuceno's path to preserve Nunes Garcia in the local canon. Guided by the writings of the composer's early biographers, like Manuel de Araújo Porto-Alegre (1806–1879) and Taunay, Guilherme de Mello was careful to separate Nunes Garcia's music from any operatic tradition and stressed instead the composer's inheritance of "the teachings of the *pure* [my emphasis] Germanic school . . . a solemn school, which planted in the hard climate of the north a scientific art holder of infinite beauty."[34] Renato de Almeida (1926) goes a step further: characterizing Nunes Garcia not only as "an exiled son of the German classical music," but also claiming that Nunes Garcia's supposedly Germanic music was "a powerful affirmation of the Brazilian spirit."[35] The idea was passed on through Luis Heitor Correa de Azevedo in 1950, who described Nunes Garcia's music as a "Brazilian treasure."[36] Fortunately, this line of thought has been broken in recent years, as scholars started to revisit such narratives and to look at the composer's production with critical eyes, opening up new avenues for exploring Nunes Garcia's music.[37]

The Race of Music

But the evocation of Nunes Garcia's music as part of a universal and eternal local past took on a more convoluted path than the sidestepping of his association with the monarchy and the forged European-ness of his music. For Nunes Garcia was Black; he grew up and was employed at the Portuguese court during slavery and at the height of the monarchy's commercial gains from the slave trade. Although Nunes Garcia was born free, he had enslaved grandparents; as freed

---

Maurício Nunes Garcia (1767–1830)," in *Patrimônio musical na atualidade: Tradicão, memória, discurso, e poder*, ed. Maria Alice Volpi (Rio de Janeiro: University of Rio de Janeiro Press, 2013), 83–96.

[33] Luiz Guilherme Goldberg, "José Maurício Nunes Garcia: Um mulato civilizado na Primeira República," *Per Musi* 39 (2019), 9, n 5.

[34] Guilherme de Mello, *A música no Brasil* (Rio de Janeiro: Imprensa Nacional [1908], 1947), 162–163 and 166–167.

[35] *Historia de Musica Brasileira* (Rio de Janeiro: F. Briguiet, 1942 [1926]), 68.

[36] Luis Heitor Correa de Azevedo, *100 anos de music no Brasil* (Rio de Janeiro: José Olímpio, 1956), 40.

[37] An extended and updated bibliographical review of Nunes Garcia's historiography, see Irineu Franco Perpetuo, *João e José: Visões de um monarca e seu mestre de capela* (Austin, TX: University of Texas, 2005), online publication.

Blacks, his mother and father had few rights: they had no right to vote or to acquire government posts, for example.[38] As a freed person, Nunes Garcia's father lived in constant insecurity, since there was a possibility according to the law that he could lose his freedom and be returned to enslavement at the slightest sign of ingratitude to the "master" who freed him, or to any other authority. The result was, in Anderson de Oliveira's words, a system of "voluntary servitude."[39] Moreover, the high number of freed Blacks in the colony and after independence required a careful structuring of social hierarchies that could separate the freed Black person from the enslaved and from the European White. This structuring was based on the protectorate system driven by White individuals in posts of authority who functioned as the freed Black man's controller and beneficiary. The composer father's last name, Nunes Garcia, for instance, was the last name of his ex-"master" at the time of his manumission, a last name that the composer kept and passed on to his son, since it helped them within the tiered social-racial caste system. Furthermore, his father's ex-"master" was a priest; thus the composer Nunes Garcia's religious background, general and musical education, musical career within the church, and his eventual social mobility within the court were directly linked to a system of Black-White protectorate and social relationships that tied back to his father's condition as an emancipated Black man. According to Oliveira, Nunes Garcia's ordination to the priesthood, which eventually allowed him to become chapel master of the court, was also directly linked to such a system. To be ordained as a priest, the composer had to initiate an unusual legal process with church officials for "dispensation of color petition" to "excuse" his "defect of color," since Black individuals were not allowed in the ecclesiastic order. Nunes Garcia was eventually successful, but Oliveira observes that the composer's ordination process was atypical and suggests that the support that Nunes Garcia received to secure his "color dispensation" may be tied to the role of his father's ex-"master" within the religious hierarchy and the composer's last name being connected with the church.[40]

Within that grim scenario, Nunes Garcia's refined education, career path, and social achievements were more than remarkable.[41] This is especially true if

---

[38] André Emmanuel Campello, *A escravidão no Império do Brasil: Perspectives jurídicas* (Brazil: Sindicato nacional dos procuradores da fazenda nacional, Sinprofaz, 2013), online publication, https://www.sinprofaz.org.br/artigos/a-escravidao-no-imperio-do-brasil-perspectivas-juridicas/.

[39] Anderson de Oliveira, "Padre José Maurício: 'Dispensa da cor,' mobilidade social e recriação de hierarquias na América Portuguesa," in *Dinâmica imperial no antigo regime Português: escravidão, governos, fronteiras, poderes, legados, séc, XVII a XIX*, ed. Roberto Guedes (Rio de Janeiro: Mauad, 2012), 56–57.

[40] Oliveira, "Padre José Maurício," 56–57.

[41] For the education of enslaved and freed Blacks during colonial times and monarchy, see Maria Helena Camara de Bastos, "A educação dos escravos e libertos no Brasil: Vestígios esparsos do domínio do ler, escrever e contar (Séculos XVI a XIX)," *Cadernos de História da Educação* 15, no. 2 (May–August 2016): 743–768.

90 MUSIC AND COSMOPOLITANISM

one considers that, within the colonial and monarchical context of slavery, the musical profession was one of the few alternatives for financial gains and social mobility for freed Blacks, although most Black musicians still remained sub-employed.[42] Nunes Garcia was the exception. He was a choir boy and continued to secure relations within the church for social protection, career improvement, and education, which included studies in philosophy, theology, history, rhetoric, and oration (he was an accomplished speaker of sermons), and languages (he was knowledgeable in Latin, French, Italian, and some Greek and English). Nunes Garcia became an accomplished keyboard performer, composer, teacher, and music director of Rio de Janeiro's cathedral, a position of high distinction. Relying on his many musical skills, he managed to be visible enough within the local social-racial context to catch the eyes and ears of the Portuguese monarch in 1808, when Rio de Janeiro became the seat of the Portuguese monarchy. Nunes Garcia came to occupy a prominent position as chapel master of the Portuguese court installed in the city, in charge of one of the most important musical centers in the Americas during his time, a feat accomplished by very few, regardless of race.[43] At the same time, Black individuals continued to be antagonized and subjugated in the city's streets, an inescapable somber reality from which Nunes Garcia was hardly exempt, including within the professional context in which he functioned. The composer's early biographer, Manuel de Araújo Porto Alegre, noted that Nunes Garcia "was *tolerated* [my emphasis] at the court . . . where one's birth fated the men's worth and gave him all the rights, and where to be a mulatto was enough to distance from one's path all the favors and many rights."[44] The ostracizing of Nunes Garcia by the Portuguese musicians at the chapel was also linked to his race, which they considered to be inferior to theirs.[45] Race is also said to be central to the competition between Nunes Garcia and the Portuguese composer Marcos Portugal (1762–1830), who came to Rio de Janeiro to attend to the musics at the court.[46]

---

[42] For the musical career as a strategy of social uplifting, see Fernando de Souza and Priscila de Lima, "Músicos negros no Brasil colonial: Trajetórias individuais e ascensão social (segunda metade do século VIII e início do XIX)," *Revista Vernáculo*, 19–20 (2007): 30–66.

[43] For a summary of Nunes Garcia's achievements music within the colonial Brazil, see Paulo Castagna, "A produção musical carioca entre c. 1780–1831," *Apostila do curso de História da Música Brasileira* 8 (São Paulo: Instituto de Artes da Unespe, 2003). Lino de Almeida Cardoso, "O som e o soberano: uma história da depressão musical carioca pós-Abdicação (1831–1843) e de seus antecedents," PhD dissertation, Universidade de São Paulo, 2006.

[44] Manuel de Araújo Porto Alegre, "Apontamentos sobre a vida e as obras do Padre José Maurício Nunes Garcia," *Revista do Instituto Histórico e Geográfico Brasileiro* 19, no. 3 (1856): 359; see also his "Iconographia brazileira," *Revista do Instituto Historico e Geographico do Brazil* 19, no. 34 (1856): 349–378.

[45] Perpétuo, "João e José," 16.

[46] Luis Guilherme Goldberg, "José Maurício Nunes Garcia: Um mulato civilizado na Primeira República," *Per Musi* 39 (2019): 1–18.

RACE IN THE UNIVERSAL AND ETERNAL TRADITION   91

It might seem ironic or even contradictory that the music composed by a Black man within a monarchical political system that supported and profited from slavery was to be revived and praised in the early days of the Republic as part of a mythical eternal and universal Austro-Germanic tradition imagined by a group of White intellectuals in Rio de Janeiro who supported racist ideologies of whitening. How could a group who viewed Black persons as inferior and mixed-raced as midway toward a desired whiteness, see and hear Nunes Garcia as a "Master" with a "pure (Austro-Germanic) lineage" and embrace his works as universal, eternal, and worthy of national rescue? Marcelo Hazan argues that Taunay and others often referred to Nunes Garcia as a mulatto to obliterate his Black skin in favor of a local narrative of the *mestiço* taking shape during the last decades of the century, a political strategy also used in the process of canonization of other Brazilian Black intellectuals at the turn of the 20th century.[47] In the same vein, Goldberg suggests that remembering Nunes Garcia as a mulatto rather than as Black was a political maneuver to "wed the Germanic scientificism and the mulatto race."[48] During the first years of the Republic, however, racialized discourses used no subterfuges, and mulatto individuals were not rescued for having "lighter skin." In fact, clear-cut racial distinctions became all but more necessary, since the recent abolition of slavery in 1888 led to the need for the government to create a clear racial demarcation of political hierarchies, in addition to citizenship laws that could socially and lawfully segregate Black and mixed-race individuals.[49] Accordingly, racialized narratives about Nunes Garcia's music and his role in the nation's past had to thread carefully within republican racially unmarked Germanic musical ideals on the one hand, and the social, racial, and political reality of the composer on the other.

Nonetheless, Nunes Garcia's race was certainly not an issue brought to the fore in Januário da Cunha Barbosa's obituary, published immediately after the composer's death in 1830. A close friend who knew Nunes Garcia well and the environment in which he functioned, Barbosa points to the composer's refined

---

[47] Marcelo Campos Hazan, "Raça, Nação e José Maurício Nunes Garcia," *Resonancias* 13, no. 24 (2009): 24 and 38; and his "José Maurício, Marcos Portugal e a sonata de Haydn: Desconstruindo of mito," *Brasiliana* 28 (December 2008): 2–11. See also Pedro Razzante Vaccari, "O Padre José Maurício Nunes Garcia e o mulatismo musical: Embranquecimento histórico?" *Revista Música* 18, no. 1 (2018): 179 and 171.

[48] Goldberg, "José Maurício Nunes Garcia," 3.

[49] Scholars have shown that that were more prominent men of color in Brazil during the Empire than the first decades of the Republic; see Wlamyra Albuquerque, "A vala comum da 'raça emancipada': Abolição e racialização no Brasil, breve comentário," *História Social* 19 (2010): 100; see also Lilia Schwarcz, "Dos males da dádiva: Sobre as ambigüidades no processo da abolição brasileira," in *Quase cidadão: histórias e antropologias da pós emancipação no Brasil*, ed. Flavio Gomes and Olívia M. G. Cunha (Rio de Janeiro: Função Getúlio Vargas, 2007); and Sidney Chaloub, "The Politics of Silence: Race and Citizenship in Nineteenth-Century Brazil," *Slavery & Abolition* 27, no.1 (2006): 73–87.

92 MUSIC AND COSMOPOLITANISM

education, his musical skills, his moral qualities, and religious devotion, as follows:

> a fellow countryman who much honored us for his professional excellence ... a Chapel Master of the Imperial chapel of this court. .... He considered many spheres of music, without fixing a taste for the music schools from Italy, France, or Portugal; Nunes Garcia was the proof of what a man can accomplish when he studies and perfects himself. ... This luminary among Brazilian musicians, this respectable ecclesiastic and honorable citizen ... was recognized by teachers from both worlds and [has] honored our country.[50]

In 1836, Porto Alegre published in Paris an article about music in Brazil, which included his views on Nunes Garcia's music, a text that still features prominently in the historiography about the composer.[51] Driven by contemporary theories about nation, race, culture, and geography, Porto Alegre already outlines a cultural and aesthetic hierarchy in which the German music is at the top and the music produced by Black individuals is at the bottom as "savage and primitive." Nonetheless, having met the composer and heard his music firsthand, Porto Alegre obviously knew that Nunes Garcia was Black, but still suggests that he was a "Mozart Fluminense" (Mozart from Rio de Janeiro).[52] As a confirmation of support for the composer, Porto Alegre recalls the Austrian composer Sigismund Neukomm's appreciation for Nunes Garcia. Neukomm, a disciple of Haydn, was at the Rio de Janeiro court in 1816 and heard Nunes Garcia perform. Rather than "savage and primitive," Porto Alegre suggests that one should listen to Nunes Garcia's music as one would listen to Mozart's. The reference to the composer's race appears in Porto Alegre's 1856 text, when he describes Nunes Garcia's facial characteristics in detail, his "lips and his nose, and a salience of the cheeks that showed the characteristics of the mixed race." Rather than openly deprecating the composer, however, Porto Alegre notes that Nunes Garcia was

---

[50] Nunes Garcia's necrology was first published in *Imperio do Brazil, Diario Fluminense*, Friday, May 7, 1830 (101, vol. 15) and reprinted in *Estudos Mauricianos*; for the misguided historical interpretation of Nunes Garcia, see Antonio Monteiro, "Marcos Portugal x Padre José Maurício: A rivalidade cordial," online publication, https://padrejosemauricio.wordpress.com/author/monteirocampos antonio/.

[51] Manuel de Araújo Porto Alegre, "Sobre a música no Brasil," in *Nitheroy, Revista brasiliense*, vol. 1, ed. by Domingos José de Magalhães, Francisco de Sales Torres Homem, and Manuel de Araújo Porto Alegre (Paris, Dauvin et Fontaine Libraries, 1836), 177, available online at https://digital.bbm. usp.br/handle/bbm-ext/1272. For the influence of Porto Alegre's writings on musicology in Brazil, see Aldo Luis Leoni, "Historiografia musical e hibridação racial," *Revistta Brasileira dew Música* 23, no. 2 (April 2010): 95–119.

[52] Porto Alegre, "Sobre a música no Brasil," 182. Porto Alegre apparently met Nunes Garcia in his later years, when the former joined the Sociedade de Beneficência Musical; see Debora Andrade, "A Arvore e o fruto: a promoção dos intelectuais no século XIX," PhD dissertation, Universidade Federal Fluminense, 2008, 69.

a proof that Franz Gall's (1758–1828) phrenology theory of cranium sizes and race (European as the most developed) was actually false, since "it was the brain mass, not the outside features that one determines the individuals' value and his achievements."[53] In the 1880s and 1890s, Taunay's tone was markedly clearer in regard to Nunes Garcia's race. A defender of the current ideologies of race and culture, having European nations, and Germany in particular, as the most developed, it is apparent in Taunay's writings that he believed a Black person had inferior intellect. He used no pretext to describe Nunes Garcia as a "mulatto priest" and considered his musical skills and his connection to the German canon as an exception to the rule. Again, contradictorily, at the beginning of the republican government, a racist intellectual such as Taunay had no problems characterizing Nunes Garcia as "a genius" with "pure Germanic lineage" and suggesting that his music was "a national treasure." Rather than disparaging the composer, Taunay became the composer's most enthusiastic devotee.

The reviving, remembering, and listening to a Black composer as the "Mozart from Rio de Janeiro" during the early days of the republican government highlights complex political and cultural issues that go against and beyond both the narrative of Teutonic universalism on the aesthetic realm, the narrative of *mulatismo* as a racial subterfuge to justify the *mestiço* nation on its way to whiteness, and uncritical associations of race and culture, a link used at the service of the nation. For when those narratives are used in connection to a Black composer glorified exactly because he is believed to be a local equivalent to Mozart, it disrupts both assumptions of the superiority of Austro-German forged culture as White and the twisted politics of race used by republican intellectuals to reify the *mestiço* nation. Therefore, within a discourse that intertwines race, culture, and nation-building, Nunes Garcia's music is an idiosyncratic example. The revival of his music during the early Republic points to the many racial subterfuges used in the politics of musical aesthetic, and ultimately shows that, at the turn of the 20th century, a Black composer of European style musics still needed to have his race "excused" in order for his work to be considered and ultimately justified as a part of a musical canon worth of the nation.

Nunes Garcia was not the only Black musician to have had some prestige in European elite musical circles during his lifetime. The composer, conductor, and performer Chevalier de Saint-George (1745–1799) and the violinist George Bridgetower (1778–1860) are well-known examples, and there are many others who shared a common experience of social exclusion within the European elite circles in which they operated, but disappeared in racialized discourses of Western European music as White. Furthermore, as in the case of Nunes Garcia,

---

[53] Porto Alegre, "Apontamentos sobre a vida e as obras do Padre José Maurício Nunes Garcia," *Revista do Instituto Histórico e Geográfico Brasileiro* 19, no. 3 (1856): 369.

94 MUSIC AND COSMOPOLITANISM

the remembering of both Chevalier de Saint-George and Bridgetower has been intertwined with the names and works of the two most prominent canonic musicians in the literature of music of the "Western" concert music: Mozart and Beethoven. While Nunes Garcia became the "Mozart Fluminense," Chevalier de Saint-George became known as the "Black Mozart" and Bridgetower as the "Black Beethoven." And while the association with the names of Mozart and Beethoven had turned into a matter of acquiring prestige, for both White and Black musicians,[54] for Nunes Garcia, Chevalier de Saint-George, and Bridgetower the parallels invited a host of other issues. As Rinehart notes, these musicians were remembered as Black versions of White men, as "trivia and esoterica . . . at the expense of the squeaky clean whiteness of the canon."[55] Examining the historical narrative about Chevalier de Saint-George, Julian Ledford argues that such an understanding of Black composers' roles within the Western European canon "recalls the conflictual past of the critical approach to the black subject . . . for they were remembered not as black musicians, or a black composers . . . but as black Mozart."[56] While one should conjecture why "Black composer" and not "composer," Ledford further explains that the term Black Mozart "subsumes the musical output and lived experiences of Chevalier Saint-George into the Eurocentric gaze and perpetuates an epistemology and ontology of blackness that race theorists have tried to undo."[57] Ultimately, these musicians disrupt the "whiteness of the canon" and unsettle dualities such as Black music/performance/body/popular/ephemeral/commercial versus European (German) music/instrumental/mind/spirit/art/eternal. Since these composers were not creating and performing a supposed "Black music," defined in the contemporary narrative as sounds and rhythms believed to be "primitive," but rather were producing "elevated European/White sounds," understood as organically constructed music supported by harmony/melody structures, they were caught in both sides of essentialist assumptions that intertwine contexts of music production, performance, and aesthetics, with race and culture. The music of these composers did not fit notions of musical sounds/racial essence, neither Black nor White.

But the issue of race and Austro-German music canon-building is more complex in the case of Nunes Garcia. His life trajectory, the telling of his story, and the canonizing of his music during the early days of the Brazilian republican

[54] Mark Evarist, *Mozart's Ghosts: Haunting the Halls of Musical Culture* (New York: Oxford University Press, 2012); and Simon Keefe, *Mozart's Requiem: Reception, Work, Completion* (Cambridge, UK: Cambridge University Press, 2012).

[55] Nicholas Rinehart, "Black Beethoven and the Racial Politics of Music History." *Transition* 112 (2013): 128–129.

[56] Julian Ledford, "Joseph Boulogne, the Chevalier de Saint-George and the Problem with Black Mozart," *Journal of Black Studies* 51, no. 1 (2020): 63

[57] Ledford, "Joseph Boulogne" 63.

government are unique cases within the European-led musicological narratives of music and race, shaped and sanctioned in the long 19th and 20th centuries. Unlike Chevalier de Saint-George and Bridgetower, Nunes Garcia and his music became vital in the process of nation-building at the turn of the 20th century to the point of being considered "a national treasure" by Rio de Janeiro's critics. Like Chevalier Saint-George and Bridgetower, Nunes Garcia's name and work were tied to Austro-Germanic canonic composers, but in Nunes Garcia's case, rather than being remembered as a "Black Mozart," he was evoked as a "Mozart from Rio de Janeiro," without a reference to race, or as the "mulatto priest," without a direct connecting reference to his music. In the process of forging a national musical canon, Nunes Garcia's Black body needed not only to be erased, but to be imagined and heard as White within the essentialized understandings of race and culture. It was not simply that his music was "like Mozart's" or "as good as Mozart's": he needed to be heard as Mozart. Hearing Nunes Garcia as Mozart would then support a racially unmarked imagined sound which is always nonetheless assumed to be produced by a White individual. In the imaginative state allowed by the evanescent nature of music as sound, body and sound should match so that they enforce, rather than disrupt, forged associations of race, culture, music-making, and nation-building.

Suggestions that republican intellectuals and music critics could see in Nunes Garcia the equivalent of Tiradentes in the musical realm—as the White hero of the Republic's earlier days—were quite equivocal. While Tiradentes's insurgency co-opted by White individuals linked him with ideals of liberty and pointed to the end of colonialism, Nunes Garcia's body was a product of, and therefore a reminder of, both slavery and colonialism. By suppressing the materiality of the Black body and its experience of subservience, Rio de Janeiro intellectuals were thus free to focus on his music's aesthetic realm and its connection to a supposedly superior, racially unmarked Austro-German heritage. In this case, rather than a rebel with a cause on one hand, or an embodiment of colonialism and slavery on the other, Nunes Garcia was to be heard as a Master in a mostly White and Eurocentric way, with the assumption that music and race are not inextricable from one another. As such, his music became a part of a "pure [White] lineage," the republican critics explicitly noted, so that it could be touted as universal and eternal, and eventually national.

The many complexities that Nunes Garcia's music, personal history, and social-racial context entailed furthered disjunctions between music and race as they became part of narratives of nation-building at the turn of the 20th century. As Daphne Brooks argued, it was so "for the purposes of fortifying the myth of communal nation homogeneity . . . of 'Pure' whiteness,"[58] which in the case of Nunes Garcia was channeled into the aural. If the place of his music in the

---

[58] Daphne Brooks, *Bodies in Dissent: Spectacular Performances of Race and Freedom.* (Durham, NC: Duke University Press, 2006), 136.

96 MUSIC AND COSMOPOLITANISM

nation's pantheon was to be seemingly conciliatory through a focus on music, sound, and listening, rather than on his body, the result actually caused another deep contradiction in historical narratives of the nation. For the music Nunes Garcia produced was the same which one understands, complacently, as a part of a historically and politically powerful narrative of imperialism, Eurocentrism, Orientalism, racism, sexism, and elitism. This brings to the fore the unavoidable question: Does Nunes Garcia's position as a Black composer of Austro-German style music in a slavery society make him and his music complicit with these ideologies? Because the music Nunes Garcia created did not have an assumed "essence of blackness," or suggested an alternative musical experience or a resistance to the European, his life and work have no place in the established narratives of music, race, and culture. Is there a place for the music and for the artistic subjectivity of Nunes Garcia within the purportedly uncomplicated assumptions of colonizer and colonized, race and culture, when it is used to define an individual's expression and individual identity? Did his music suggest a separation of sound from the body that erased the social-racial reality of his experience of racial segregation? Derek Scott claims that "people make cultural and not racial choices."[59] Thus we may ask: Did Nunes Garcia have a cultural choice? If so, did he choose to be complicit with the "master" to become a music Master? We can then extrapolate this further and ask: to what extent does anyone have a cultural choice?

The writer, sociologist, and musicologist Mario de Andrade (1893–1945) had a stark answer. Early in his writings Andrade followed the republican critics and praised Nunes Garcia, his music, and their role in the history of the nation. Later in his life, however, when Andrade became fully enmeshed in the nationalistic rhetoric, he saw the issue quite differently. Rather than a national genius or a Master, to Andrade:

> There is no creativity in the composer . . . who stayed committed to his time and to himself . . . a composer without individualism. . . . A composer, who although mulato of the best "*mulataria*" ("mulatism"), dark and with curly hair, represented nothing, or very little, of the value of the free black and of *our* [my emphasis] racial idiosyncrasies; José Maurício was a mulato without the problems of *mulataria*, neither external nor internal, and so does his music. José Maurício does not represent the problems of Brazil, only of the colonizer. Sociologically he was not a Brazilian nor a voice for Africa. [A person] without courage, a musician without creativity . . . whose music was paid for by a monarch . . . and who did not provide music of the colonized, but of the colonizer; a composer whose nation lay on the other side of the Atlantic; . . . a typical

---

[59] Derek Scott, "In Search of Genetically Modified Music: Race and Musical Style in the Nineteenth Century," in *Musical Style and Social Meaning* (New York: Routledge, 2016, Kindle).

anti-revolutionary; a composer whose promised heaven does not include the delicious *batuques* [percussion of black Brazilians], but clarinets, flutes, cellos, violins, organs, bassoons, oboes, and everything else.

To Andrade, who avoided positioning his own race and gender identities during his life,[60] the nation's *mestiço* culture was his to shape and inherit, and the Black composer did not deserve it. To Andrade's forged nation, Nunes Garcia's blackness was a fraud, and his eternal and universal White music had no social or national purpose.[61]

These issues were interpreted differently by several scholars over the years, confirming or denying Andrade's positions, but the many contradictions that the associations between music, culture, and race, and their place within the understanding of individual and collective identity, uncover has persevered in the background to this day. As a Black individual subservient to a White monarch governing a slavery empire, Nunes Garcia supposedly did not have a double consciousness, the cultural strategy necessary for Blacks' survival in the New World which, according to Paul Gilroy and W. E. B. Du Bois before him, was a strategy needed for Blacks to have subjectivity within the domain of hegemonic White Europe, and eventually to become "emancipated as a black subject."[62] Nunes Garcia apparently did not claim to have had such a consciousness: his culture was European culture, which although varied in the composer's output did not strive to show any sonic "essence of blackness," or Otherness, or to express an experience sonically different from the European composers from whom he learned music. That is to say that if one takes away Nunes Garcia's claim to European culture, there should be nothing left of his artistic subjectivity and musical expression. He was a composer writing music in the classical tradition associated with, but not solely from, Austria and Germany, and creating works in operatic

---

[60] On the issue of Mário de Andrade's race see, André Valério Sales, "A desconhecida cor mulata e o obscurecimento 'forçado' deste assunto: Uma FotoBiografia," in *Mário de Andrade (1893–1945), um gigante das Letras brasileiras* (João Pessoa: Editora Mídia, 2023), full text online at https://www.researchgate.net/publication/368387613_Mario_de_Andrade_1893-1945_um_gigante_das_Letras_brasileiras_sua_desconhecida_cor_mulata_e_o_obscurecimento_%27forcado%27_dest e_assunto_Uma_FotoBiografia#fullTextFileContent. For Mario de Andrade's homosexuality, see Marcelo Bortoli, "A correspondência secreta de Mário de Andrade," *Época*, June 26, 2015, available at https://epoca.oglobo.globo.com/vida/noticia/2015/06/correspondencia-secreta-de-mario-de-andrade.html.

[61] Mario de Andrade, "José Maurício," *Mundo Musical*, April 20, 1944; published in Jorge Coli, *Música Final: Mário de Andrade e sua coluna jornalística mundo musical* (Campinas, Editora da Unicamp, 1998), 142–146.

[62] Paul Gilroy, *The Black Atlantic: Modernity and Double Consciousness* (London: Verso Books, 1993), 2. Gilroy also reflects on the suspicious associations between race and culture that have supported facism and more recent nationalistic politics in *Against Race: Imagining Political Culture beyond the Color Line* (Cambridge, MA: Harvard University Press, 2000), 32–34 and 279–326. For a critical assessment of Gilroy's main tenets, see Ronald Radano, *Lying Up a Nation: Race and Black Music* (Chicago: Chicago University Press, 2003), 39–44.

98   MUSIC AND COSMOPOLITANISM

styles associated with Italy and Portugal, but also not solely from there. These musics are not understood as organized sounds at the service of artistic expression of many, but are assumed to be institutionalized properties of specific nations, which in turn are defined through associations of race and culture. Nunes Garcia was one among several composers who were part of the cosmopolitan music context in the Americas early in the 19th century, and who were agents in and ultimately helped shape the imagined universality of such musics.[63]

At the same time, Nunes Garcia's musical expressions were tied to a narrow world in which religious devotion and loyalty to a monarch were at center, not nation-building or racial identification, and he strived to use the musical tools available to him to accomplish his individual subjectivity as such. If, as a Black man in a racially segregated society, the expressive power of Nunes Garcia's work had multiple "resonances,"[64] they were tied to his experience of servitude to both the monarch and the church, without which his subjectivity was set in a vacuum. Nunes Garcia's remembering and canonizing both obliterates and unsettles the racial imaginary and essentialism of music criticism of both whiteness and blackness. Radano has noted that we cannot assume that music has a consistent ontology somehow detached from the social forces that shaped it, while adding, quite appropriately, that one also cannot "have a specific musical determination of a social experience."[65] In the case of Nunes Garcia, both of these assertions prove appropriate, for his music both disrupts and supports music as an abstract art; at the same time, it both disrupts and supports homologies of music and sociocultural and racial contexts. Touted as a national treasure, Nunes Garcia's music also exposes "the tenuousness of nationalism and its fictions,"[66] for, in the case of Brazil, it unsettles the role of cultural practices and race associations at the service of nation-building.

Ultimately, Nunes Garcia and his music lead us to the question of who has, or should have, the claim on European classical music, or any music for that matter,

---

[63] Izquierdo König, "The Cosmopolitan Muse," 69. José Manuel Izquierdo König shows that José Bernardo Alzedo, a mulatto and the son of a freed slave, regarded Rossini as a symbol of both his private creative independence and the political independence of his nation. In "Rossini's Reception in Latin America: Scarcity and Imagination in Two Early Chilean Sources," in *Gioachino Rossini 1868– 2018: La musica e il mondo*, ed. Ilaria Narici, Emilio Sala, and Emanuele Senici (Pesaro, Italy: Fondazione Rossini Pesaro, 2018), 413–436. The participation of Black musicians in the building of an imagined universality of German music is also explored recently by Kira Thurman in *Singing like Germans: Black Musicians in the Land of Bach, Beethoven, and Brahms* (Ithaca, NY: Cornell University Press, 2021); see also Arne Spohr, "'Mohr und Trompeter': Blackness and Social Status in Early Modern Germany," *Journal of the American Musicological Society* 72, no. 3 (2019): 613–663. See also James Deaville, "Music and Cultures of Racial Representation in the Nineteenth Century," *Nineteenth-Century Music Review* 3, no. 1 (2006): ix–xiii.

[64] Radano, *Lying Up a Nation*, 53.

[65] Radano, *Lying Up a Nation*, 40–41.

[66] Brooks, *Bodies in Dissent*, 29.

at a time when a connected world started to complicate claims of cultural ownership. This is particularly relevant in the case of Brazil, where its large population of Black Brazilians, directly or indirectly, willing or not, engaged with many musics of European derivation without questioning whether or not that was part of their culture. As Brooke noted, it is at the point where difference is indiscernible that problems occur, and, I add, it is where politics of belonging become more vile.[67] That realization unveils issues of not only race, difference, and music-making at the local sociopolitical level, but of larger issues that music scholarship is yet to engage with, that is, the need to consider the multidirectional—temporally and geographically—sociocultural and aesthetic perspectives that music-making entails and to eventually open up to the possibility of considering universals.[68] In this regard, Ledford suggests that "though lived experiences and musical instruction eventually intervene to shape the type of musical expression produced, music still remains tethered to its human foundation."[69] That is the case, but there is more. The question is, who has the right to, or can, or should, be encompassed by musical greatness, a mythical greatness regardless, to claim his or her historical subjectivity. For if greatness is not a possibility for everyone, it loses its charisma as a possibility for an individual to mark his or her presence and indeed their existence in history and their place in the world.

[67] Brooke, *Bodies in Dissent*, 19.
[68] The many possibilities of "universals" implicit here and throughout this book align with the ones outlined in Tsing, *Friction*, 6–11.
[69] Ledford, "Joseph Boulogne," 74.

5

At the Cabaret

Mlle. Ywonna

On June 26, 1896, a new entertaining venue opened in Rio de Janeiro: Ywonna's cabaret.[1] Announced as a cabaret in the style of "Chat Noir, à Bruant," the venue was set up in a small room capable of holding about 100 people in an old building on the Lavradio street 15, but well situated nearby several theaters around the central Praça Tiradentes (Figure 5.1).[2] The idea of opening a venue in the style of the Montmartre's Chat Noir had been conjectured in Rio de Janeiro as early as 1891, when local writers envisioned a "Café Balzac," described as a place "like the Chat Noir, where literati and artists who like to drink get together and talk about similar subjects."[3] Nothing came out of idea, however. It took an entrepreneur like Ywonna (Figure 5.2) to open a successful enterprise offering poetry declamation, singing, and performances in the manner of contemporary Montmartrean cabarets, catering to local writers, young artists, and bohemians. On its opening night, one chronicler noted that Ywonna's cabaret was received with enthusiasm and that those in attendance behaved "as if they were very acquainted with this type of venue."[4] But some expressed doubts about the viability of the enterprise. One commentator observed with relief that in the new cabaret "there was less irreverence than the [similar] French establishments,"[5]

---

[1] Ywonna's name appears in the newspapers and chronicles with various spellings—Ivonna, Yvonne, Yvonna—but Ywonna is the dominant. Her last name is never cited in any Brazilian publication, and I found just one Parisian publication, the cover of a song, in which her name is spelled as Ywonna. Her business letterhead also only includes Mlle. Ywonna, without a last name. A note she wrote on her letterhead is held in the Biblioteca Digital AECID, Agencia Española de Cooperación Internacional para el Desarrollo, Spain.

[2] *O Paiz*, June 27, 1896. This apparently precedes by one year the cabaret Els Quatre Gats which opened in Barcelona in June 1897, and was one year behind an equivalent to the Parisian Chat Noir in Amsterdam, which also used Bruant as a model; see Willem Frijhoff, Yann Bank, and Maarteen van Buuren, *Dutch Culture in a European Perspective: 1900: The Age of Bourgeoisie Culture* (London: Palgrave Macmillan, 2004), 507.

[3] *Jornal do Commercio*, May 11, 1891.

[4] *O Paiz*, June 27, 1896. On July 11, 1896, the *Jornal do Commercio* published an article about Parisian cabarets, "A Journey through the eccentric cabarets of Montmartre," including detailed descriptions of Rodolphe Salis and Aristide Bruant, but does not refer to the local Chat Noir.

[5] *O Paiz*, June 27, 1896.

Music and Cosmopolitanism. Cristina Magaldi, Oxford University Press. © Oxford University Press 2024.
DOI: 10.1093/oso/9780199744770.003.0006

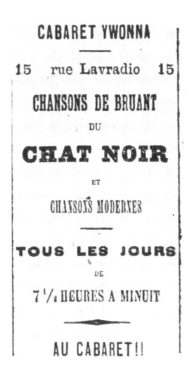

Figure 5.1. Advertisement for Ywonnas' cabaret in Rio de Janeiro. *Jornal do Commercio*, July 17, 1896.
Source: Biblioteca Nacional, Rio de Janeiro, Hemeroteca Digital

Figure 5.2. Mlle Ywonna.
Kosmos 11, November 1908.
Source: Biblioteca Nacional, Rio de Janeiro, Hemeroteca Digital

102 MUSIC AND COSMOPOLITANISM

while another noted cynically, and in rhymed poetry, that in Rio de Janeiro "we can have but a *petit-chat*."[6] Bilac was more sanguine, putting down Ywonna's cabaret and ultimately dismissing the enterprise altogether: "The idea of the Chat Noir by Mlle Ywonna . . . is so absurd, so comic, so ridiculous, that it is not worth the cost of a drop of ink."[7]

Such sundry reception points to the nature of Ywonna's clientele. Comprising mostly the city's White intellectual elite, a young generation of aspiring male writers and artists, and a group of outspoken and outcast bohemians, Ywonna's patrons were, at the surface, the face of the newly established republican government. In his recollection of the cabaret 12 years later (in 1908), the writer and critic Gonzaga Duque (Figure 5.3) pointed out that the literati and artists met in the cabaret without political concerns, since "we only accepted one principle or credo—the republican—and we excluded from our mental work any other ideal . . . partisan strife did not interest us."[8] Duque's recollections were correct in that Ywonna's clientele was probably made up of nothing but republicans. Ywonna herself did not hide her political convictions. A republican advocate like her clientele, she appeared at Rio de Janeiro's July 14, 1896, celebrations singing "La Marseillaise" for French expats, diplomats, and local government officials.[9] In her cabaret she regularly performed patriotic songs and made the chanson "La Gueuse" a local success, advertising it as a song of the republican war, which a local reviewer noted was "a beautiful song, applauded by audience with enthusiasm."[10] Ywonna also openly supported the republican government in the controversial military conflict in Canudos (state of Bahia), performing the song "A volta de Canudos" (The Return from Canudos). The song's Portuguese lyrics by the playwright and bohemian Demetrio de Toledo were set to the French march/chanson, "Le Retour du Dahomey, chanson patriotique" (The Return from Dahomey, patriotic chanson, 1895), music by Auguste Bosc and lyrics by Eugene Blairat, written for the victory of the French colonial army in Dahomey, Africa.[11]

---

[6] *O Paiz*, June 8, 1896.
[7] Olavo Bilac (under the pseudonym Fantasio), "O gato Preto," *Gazeta de Notícias*, June 7, 1896.
[8] Gonzaga Duque, "O cabaret da Yvonne," *Kosmos* 11, November 1908.
[9] *O Paiz*, July 12, 1896.
[10] *O Paiz*, July 18, 1896.
[11] *O Paiz*, March, 1898.

Figure 5.3. Gonzaga Duque.

But Duque's recollections miss the nuances of the cabaret crowd whose concerns were not merely the overthrown monarchists still trying to hang on to power, but the clash of ideas among the republicans themselves. Confronted with the political volatility in the years that followed the regime change in 1889, those attending the cabaret in 1896 had different perspectives on republicanism. In fact, they were unified only in their disillusionment with what the republican government had become, in their opposition to the hardline military officials who continued to cling to power, and in their distrust of Prudente de Morais (1841–1902), the first civilian president who seized the opportunity to channel power into the hands of landowners and oligarchs. The republican ideals that Ywonna's clientele celebrated in 1889 had been replaced by large-scale corruption and by recurring sociopolitical uprisings, countered by military displays around the city. In this regard, those in attendance in the cabaret were not different from those in Montmartre: they were a crowd with a range of political and ideological affiliations, republican progressives and reactionaries coexisting with would-be socialists and anarchists, and with those who tended to resort to unconventional patriotic displays in lieu of clear-cut political partisanship. If Montmartre in the 1870s and 1880s served as a space for contesting the power and limits of the new Republic's values, Ywonna's cabaret in Rio de Janeiro assembled the local

104　MUSIC AND COSMOPOLITANISM

intelligentsia, both those supporting and questioning the viability and realization of republicanism in the new nation.[12]

Yet all those in attendance at Ywonna's venue were engaged in reflections of and discussions about their growing and complex city. As the capital, Rio de Janeiro was supposed to display the promise of a bright future for the new republican nation; instead, the city showcased its most adverse downturns, a city plagued with social unrest and racial segregation and political upheavals regularly confronted by police force.[13] The situation was complicated by a shortage of housing and a lack of basic urban infrastructure. Complaints about dirty streets and lack of sanitation were compounded by the constant threat of epidemics. Rather than a celebrated façade of a modern city, Ywonna's clientele operated within a Rio de Janeiro that decayed. In their city, modernity was born out of gloom and fell quickly into decadence; in their city, they threaded between nostalgia and modernity, between an imagined lost past and a pessimist stance toward the future. In their city, modernity and decadence were two sides of the same turn-of-the-century symptom: an anxious presage about inevitable radical changes to come.

All in all, artists, intellectuals and bohemians who became habitués at the cabaret offered contradictory responses to the promises made by the new republican regime and reacted with cynicism toward the reality of their growing, modern, and decaying city; "Amigos, plus ça change, plus c'est la même chose," wrote Bilac in disillusionment, quoting the writer and critic Alphonse Karr in a mix of Portuguese and French (Figure 5.4).[14] Some cabaret patrons saw the government's plans about modernizing the city according to the Haussmann's model as being uncritical of and complacent with the bourgeoning of urban life. In an environment of constant political and ideological clashes, where modernity was in the making and up for discussion and negotiation, Ywonna's clientele included romantics, naturalists, realists, symbolists, and decadents alike.[15]

---

[12] John Kim Munholland, "Republican Order and Republican Tolerance in Fin-de-Siècle France: Montmartre as a Delinquent Community," in *Montmartre and the Making of Mass Culture*, ed. Gabriel Welsberg (New Brunswick, NJ: Rutgers University Press, 2001), 15–36. For the various conflicting ideas among intellectuals in Rio de Janeiro, see Maurício Silva, *A hélaide e o subúrbio: Confrontos literários na belle époque carioca* (São Paulo: Editora da Universidade de São Paulo, 2006), 22–41.

[13] Teresa Meade, "Living Worse and Costing More: Resistance and Riot in Rio de Janeiro, 1890–1917," *Journal of Latin American Studies* 21, no. 2 (May, 1989): 241–266 and *Civilizing Rio: Reform and Resistance in a Brazilian City, 1889–1930* (University Park: Pennsylvania State University Press, 1997). For a study of the many confrontations between the police, new immigrants, and Blacks, see Kit McPhee, "Immigrants with Money Are No Use to Us": Race and Ethnicity in the Zona Portuária of Rio de Janeiro, 1903–1912," *The Americas* 62, no. 4 (April 2006): 623–650.

[14] *Gazeta de Noticias*, February 1, 1897.

[15] The group included Guimarães Passos, Gonzaga Duque, Raul Pederneiras, Luis Edmundo, Paulo Mallet, and Olavo Bilac, among others; see Alvaro Santos Simões Junior, *A sátira do Parnaso* (São Paulo: Editora UNESP, 2006), 174, and 260–261; see also Ana Maria Tavares Cavalcanti, "Os embates no meio artístico carioca em 1890: Antecedentes da Reforma da Academia das Belas Artes," *19&20* 2, no. 2 (2007), online publication, available at http://www.dezenovevinte.net/criticas/emba

Figure 5.4. Olavo Bilac.

They engaged with contemporaries like Paul Verlaine (1844–1896), Stéphane Mallarmé (1842–1898), Émile Zola (1840–1902), Oscar Wilde (1854–1900), and many others to critique their city and their collectives, to understand their here and now, and to look with stark suspicion to the government's positivistic ideology of progress. Rather than supporting the Haussmann model, for example, Duque favored the ideas of Camillo Sitte (1843–1903), John Ruskin (1819–1900), and William Morris (1834–1896), who argued that cities should bring communities together through common experiences.

Yvonne's cabaret thus provided both an escape and an alternative space for those trying to find their way through the discontinuous parts of their own local context, which was unmistakably set up within the larger complex of *fin-de-siècle* cities. In the cabaret, intellectuals and artists reckoned with the human condition in an early globalized moment and with art's role in a society under capitalism. They attended the cabaret as if it were made especially for them, a space where individuality trumped impositions of collective identity. In the cabaret's intimate space, bohemians questioned the status quo while imposing their own authority

te_1890.htm; and Arthur Valle, "Sociabilidade, boêmia e carnaval em ateliês de artistas brasileiros em fins do século XIX e início do XX," in *Oitocento* 4 (Rio de Janeiro, 2017): 50. Bilac even wrote satirical verses specifically to be performed by Ywonna. For the group of symbolists during the first decades of the Republic, see Vera Lins, "Em revistas, o simbolismo e a virada de século," in *O moderno em revistas: representações do Rio de Janeiro de 1890-1930*, ed. Mônica Pimenta, Vera Lins, and Cláudia de Oliveira (Rio de Janeiro: Garamon, 2010), 38–40.

106   MUSIC AND COSMOPOLITANISM

through a mix of satire, humor, and artistic performative expressions. In the cabaret they found a place to entertain and be entertained, but also a venue to interrogate the modern urban ethos and to experience and experiment with the *fin-de-siècle* as a period of both extreme loss and open possibilities. As part of the city's privileged White, male, intellectual elite, in the cabaret Ywonna's clientele contradictorily allowed themselves to contest modernization and its excluding social reality. In the cabaret they metaphorically sided with the city's populace and ventured into its underworld to experiment with alternative social and political engagements not offered by the status quo. For them, Ywonna's cabaret became both a stage and a laboratory, a space where they could "problematize the city."[16]

Most importantly, in Ywonna's cabaret, artists and intellectuals could join other like-minded bohemians from elsewhere. Elizabeth Wilson has argued that despite bohemians' individualism, bohemia was a collective enterprise.[17] In the cabaret, no matter where it was located, bohemians gathered forces through a collective confrontation that was disruptive, but neither conventionally political nor apolitical. In the cabaret, they escaped from the sociopolitical order of the modern city, while joining in a larger collective quest for ideas that challenged the establishment. Ywonna's cabaret in Rio de Janeiro was thus both dependent on and a strong part of such a collective that had sprung up in many contemporary growing *fin-de-siècle* cities.

For Bilac, Ywonna's cabaret was not merely an eccentricity of yet another newly arrived artist in Rio de Janeiro, but a space with the potential to destabilize and challenge. Accordingly, he responded to the venue with skepticism. A few days before opening night, he questioned the local press who supported Ywonna's enterprise:

> [Ywonna] wants to gather our poets, our chroniclers, our composers around her skirts of *cabotine*. . . . What surprises me mostly is the seriousness with which the newspapers celebrate her initiative, viewing her as the one who is going to regenerate the national art, as a female Maecenas of our literature, and as a Mathilda princess of the new Brazilian generation.[18]

Bilac could be linking Ywonna to Princess Mathilde Bonaparte (1820–1904), who was known for regularly welcoming artists and writers in her Parisian salon,

---

[16] Julian Brigstocke, *The Life of the City: Space, Humour, and the Experience of Truth in Fin-de-Siècle Montmartre* (New York: Routledge, 2014), ix. For intellectuals in Rio de Janeiro and their attempts to mingle with the lower social classes, see Velloso, *Modernismo no Rio de Janeiro*, 18 and 45.

[17] Elizabeth Wilson, *Bohemians: The Glamorous Outcasts* (New Brunswick, NJ: Rutgers University Press, 2000), 2.

[18] Bilac, "O gato preto," *Gazeta de Notícias*, June 7, 1896.

but Edmundo saw in Ywonna's attributes similarities to Madame de Thèbes (1845–1916), a well-known French palm reader. Both writers connected Ywonna to a local Rio de Janeiro card and palm reader named Mathilda, whose house had become a popular gathering place for the literati in the previous decade. Edmundo recalls that local bohemians would meet at Mathilda's place to discuss a wide range of esoteric and mystic topics: from Indian ancient literature and religion—the Ramayana, Mahabarata, and Vedha—to the Jewish Kabbalah; from the mystic writings of the 18th-century Swede Emanuel Swedenborg (1688–1772) to the 19th-century Christian mysticism of the French Sar Peladan (1858–1918); from the French Allan Kardec's (1804–1869) spiritism to secularist religion advocated by Comte's positivism (1798–1857).[19] Comparing Ywonna's cabaret to Mathilda's meeting place, Bilac and Edmundo understood the cabaret as a mystic space that transcended the here and now. João do Rio remembered Ywonna's place as a "satanic cabaret... with the taste of the Parisian vice, all that is *rive-gauche* and *butte-sacrée*."[20] In the end, these chroniclers were not altogether wrong about the effect that the venue eventually had on an entire generation, for Ywonna's cabaret became an influential, if ephemeral, venue in the cultural life of late 19th-century Rio de Janeiro and, as such, it was remembered by writers well over a decade after it was closed. Writing about the cabaret more than 10 years later, for instance, João do Rio (Figure 5.5) claimed that Ywonna's cabaret created

Figure 5.5. João do Rio.

[19] Edmundo, *O Rio de Janeiro do meu tempo*, 113.
[20] João do Rio, "A decadência dos Chopps," in *Cinematógrafo, crônicas cariocas* (Rio de Janeiro: ABL, 2009 [1909]), 92.

108   MUSIC AND COSMOPOLITANISM

a tradition that stayed with Rio de Janeiro over the years and that it became in-grained locally in many forms, inspiring and shaping the local *botequim*.[21]

Ywonna's nationality, upbringing, and details about her early career are un-clear. Duque believed that she had come from "the south," that is, from Buenos Aires and Montevideo, cities within a South American commercial and entertain-ment circuit that became a magnet for large numbers of performers and directors from Spain, Portugal, Germany, France, and Italy, who traveled long distances in search of employment. Duque's guess probably reflects the fact that Ywonna had first performed in Rio de Janeiro at the Theatro Recreio Dramatico alongside several artists who traveled the circuit of Buenos Aires and Montevideo, such as the Spanish Pepa Ruiz (1859–1923) and Portuguese Amelia Barros (1842–?), both of whom also performed at Yvonna's venues (see Chapter 6).[22] But the an-nouncement for Ywonna's performance at the Recreio Dramático refers to her as a "Parisian celebrity" and a performer from the Eldorado in Paris, which points to her Parisian provenance.[23] Ywonna's updated knowledge of the contemporary Montmartre chanson repertory, which in 1896 had not yet circulated widely out-side Paris and a Parisian published song with her photo on the cover also point to her Parisian connections. One knows for sure that Ywonna was not a dilettante, but a skilled artist and an astute entrepreneur with profound knowledge of what worked in Montmartre and who saw in the Brazilian capital a fertile space for a similar enterprise. She socialized within the city's intricate sociocultural sphere and got to know local intellectuals, artists, and bohemians who meandered through the city until late at night.

Announcing her cabaret as Chat Noir, Ywonna decorated the venue with posters of Parisian artists, from Jules Cheret's (1836–1932) *maitres d'affiches* collection[24] to posters by Adolphe Willette (1857–1926) and Théophile Steilen (1859–1923), reserving a prominent spot for Henri de Toulouse-Lautrec's (1864–1901) famous il-lustration of Aristide Bruant (1851–1925), the poet and realist singer, who became a star at the cabarets Chat Noir and Mirliton in Montmartre (Figure 5.6). Appropriately,

---

[21] "A decadência dos Chopps," 93. A *botequim* is a small bar that usually serves food and drinks over the counter, and where people gather to socialize and talk about daily events.

[22] *Jornal do Commercio*, June 23, 1896. Both Pepa Ruiz and Amelia Barros were active in Lisbon at the Teatro Trindade under the director Sousa Bastos. Barros, already in her fifties when touring with Ywonna, had first performed in Rio de Janeiro 20 years earlier in 1876; a Spanish-born ac-tress raised in Lisbon, Pepa Ruiz became an influential performer and theater director both in Rio de Janeiro and in Lisbon. For information on these actresses, see Flávia Ferreira de Almeida, "O mercado de trabalho dos espetáculos: atrizes das companhias Portuguesas nos palcos do teatro musicado Carioca," *Transversos: Revista de história* 9 (2017): 222–246; Vanda Freire, "As mágicas e a circularidade de gêneros musicais no século XIX," in *Música e história no longo século XIX*, ed. Herculano Lopes, Martha Abreu, and Martha Ulhôa (Rio de Janeiro: Fundação Casa de Rui Barbosa, 2011), 209–235; see also Mencarelli, "A voz e a partitura," 180–190.

[23] The *Jornal do Brasil*, July 9, 1896.

[24] Duque mentions Cheret in his 1908 article, "O cabaret da Yvonne," Jules Chéret's *Maîtres d l'Afiche* (1895) was a publication of posters reproducing works by 97 Parisian artists.

AT THE CABARET 109

Figure 5.6. Aristide Bruant, poster by Toulouse Lautrec.

Ywonna placed the flags of France and Brazil as a background to the small area that served as a stage and where an upright piano complemented the decor. She then attended to her clientele as a master of ceremonies, using contemporary French slang in the style of Rodolphe Salis (1851–1897) at the Parisian Chat Noir, and appeared dressed à la Bruant, with the unmistakable large pantaloons, black cape, and falling hat, as in the image immortalized by Toulouse-Lautrec and Steilen.[25]

Ywonna thus created her stage persona following Bruant's, a double character that became an essential part of her cabaret performances. Still, her cross-dressing did not challenge, but contradictorily ratified the cabaret's gendered space as distinctively male.[26] A male observer noted that Ywonna's figure showed

---

[25] Bilac, "O gato preto," *Gazeta de Notícias*, June 7, 1896.
[26] For the role of female artists' cross-dressing in U.S. variety shows during this period, and for a similar point regarding Ywonna's cross-dressing, see Gillian Rodger, "Female Hamlets and Romeos: Cross-Dressing Actresses in Nineteenth-Century," in *Just One of the Boys: Female-to-Male Cross-Dressing on American Variety Stage* (Urbana: University of Illinois Press, 2018), 17–27.

the "best graces of her gender,"[27] which, if it departed from contemporary codes of female beauty, also played a part in her carefully built ambiguous stage persona. Bilac described her movements as indispensable to the ambience: "the fat Ywonna [moves] back and forth between the tables ... with her clever, large open eyes trickling with malice, and the distinctive mark on her chin accentuates her mouth always filled with kind laughs."[28] Similarly, in Duque's 1908 recollections, he claims that Ywonna's persona was central to the cabaret's setting: "[Despite the] tanned complex of her face, ornate with dark and abundant artificial hair cut to shoulder length, under the large hat in black felt with narrow crown and hard brim, as in the format of the bullfighters from Lisbon, one could notice her paleness, which was penetrated by the singular and diabolic tone of the supreme vices, and her alive nocturnal eyes suggesting the criminal temptation of her sadism."[29] While Bilac highlighted the mysterious aspect of Ywonna's persona as a trickster, Duque saw Yvonne as a Portuguese *matador*, a sadist bullfighter. For these observers, Ywonna was not merely a male-impersonator, which was common in contemporary pantomimes, in the comic theater, and in variety shows, but a successful impersonator of Bruant, whose mystery and alternative male performative abilities had become an essential part of the Parisian cabaret culture.

Bilac continued to attend the cabaret, despite his criticisms. Less than a month after the opening, he wrote a more detailed account of the venue, but now acknowledging the cabaret as an inexorable space of experimentation within the *fin-de-siècle* city:

The air is impure, the beer is bad, and the chairs are uncomfortable. . . . On the walls, macabre drawings, largely smudged with red paint; a skeleton falling apart drags a pale man; the Roquette's guillotine[30] opens its hard arms; a black cat flies through a sky of blood; a tragic figure contorts a hungry mouth. And in between all these representations of death and horrors, a French poster tells the public that *"la gaité, e l'harmonie sont de riguer."*

Bilac then continues to describe the sonic ambience and details of Ywonna's performance:

"Suddenly a hoarse and sinister bell (everything is sinister in that temple of happiness!) imposes silence among the drinkers. The singer climbs the small stage, puts

[27] *O Paiz*, June 27, 1896.
[28] Bilac, "O gato preto."
[29] Duque, "O cabaret da Ivonne."
[30] A reference to Bruant's poem and illustration in *Dans la Rue: Chansons et monologues* (Paris, 1889–1895).

her hands in her pockets in a boyish manner and starts to recite [Bruant's] poems *La Morgue, À Saint-Lazare, [A] la Roquette, [V'là] l'cholera [qu'arrive].* And then morgue, execution, cholera, hunger, assassins, and suicide, all that is tragic in life, everything that is horrifying about misery, everything that is dreadful in death, all that is presented there, glorified and enlivened by the joviality of the *diseuse,* is applauded with the laughter of those who drink.... Alas, God! We already have in Rio de Janeiro a place where we can laugh about death".[31]

As Bilac points to Ywonna's performance of Bruant's poems published in Paris as *Dans la Rue* (1889–1895), he suggests that one should learn from the Montmartre artist, because "all of us have a ridiculous and irrational fear of the death; *"vivre c'est apprendre a mourir"* (to live is to learn to die), and he further argues that "if happiness is the best way to counteract the fear of death, then one should enter death with a bang and with the sounds of carnival bells."[32] The parallel between the cabaret and a carnivalesque environment of Rio de Janeiro's streets in February and early March was also not lost in Duque, who evokes parallel images of carnival and the cabaret's environment, referring to Willett's Pierrot drawings as a "bohemian Pierrot."[33] The cabaret was thus a space for illusion, mask, and for escape from reality of life through imaginations of death, chaos, and darkness, "all beyond safe, known, and the 'normal.'"[34] In addition, while portraying Bruant's masculinity, Ywonna's body set forth physical movements that spotlighted her female performative style filled with mystery, illusion, and allusion. Her performance, encapsulating the temptations of the female fatale, was saturated with female eroticism and gender ambiguity. To the cabaret's male clientele, her female body and performative abilities highlighted Rio de Janeiro's *fin-de-siècle* gloom; to them, Ywonna was the embodiment of decadence.[35]

The Voice of Decadence

Bilac describes Ywonna as "an eccentric singer," a common designation for comedy singers in revues, vaudevilles, and music halls. He also stresses Ywonna's

---

[31] Bilac (Fantasio), "No Cabaré," *Gazeta de Notícias,* July 3, 1896.

[32] Bilac (Fantasio), "No Cabaré."

[33] Gonzaga Duque, "Princezes e Pierrots," in *Graves & Frivolos* (Lisbon: Livraria Classica editora, 1910), 122–123 and 192–193.

[34] Helen Hanson and Catherine O'Rawe, "Introduction: Cherchez la femme," in *The Femme Fatale: Images, Histories, Contexts,* ed. Helen Hanson and Catherine O'Rawe (London: Palgrave Macmillan, 2010), 4.

[35] In this regard, see the chapter "'All the Noblest Arts ... Expressed in the Measured Movements of a Perfectly Shaped Body': Embodiment and Spectacular Performances of Gender," in Catherine Hindson, *Female Performance Practice on the Fin-de-Siècle Popular Stage of London and Paris* (Manchester, UK: Manchester University Press, 2007), 35–54.

"triple voice" and characterizes her as a "Frègoli in skirts."[36] Leopoldo Frègoli (1867–1936) was an Italian comic artist with a wide vocal range, which he used to impersonate both males and females in comic acts of quick changing characters. He was known as a *transformista* artist because he could quickly transform himself from one character to another, creating the sensation of an illusion. Frègoli worked for the Italian army entertaining soldiers and was later stationed with the troops in Ethiopia. In the 1890s, his career took off as he became very popular in London. Frègoli visited Rio de Janeiro in July 1895, one year before the opening of Ywonna's cabaret, and performed at the large Theatro Lyrico with great success, being referred to as "a musical and dramatic phenomenon."[37] Therefore, Bilac compared Ywonna with Frègoli primarily because she, too, transformed herself into many personas, from a mystic Princess Mathilda, to a Portuguese matador, to Bruant's masculinity, to Fregoli's gender bending, and to many other characters, appearing on one occasion as Mary Stuart.[38]

Bilac also refers to Ywonna as a *diseuse*, that is, a female performer with a crafted mode of vocal delivery, weaving speech and singing to deliver poetry spattered with short piano accompaniments. More so than any other element in carefully crafted cabaret scenes, *diseuses* were able to embody the pain of unattainable love in a vocal and performative approach described by Parisian critics as "véritable, naturale, e brutale."[39] Kelley Conway observes that *dieuses* "were not the pretty, trained voices capable of glorious coloraturas . . . but, instead, [they had] rather nasal voices, which frequently ventured into the deeper chest tones and often broke, to great tragic effect, in the middle of a song."[40] The *diseuses'* vocal abilities and timbre broke not only with gender dualities, but also with the traditional separation between singing and declamation, a sound that Jennifer Goltz believes led to further musical and vocal experiments like *sprechstimme* used later by Arnold Schoenberg (1874–1951).[41]

But it was the low timbre of Ywonna's voice that became the staple of her performances in Rio de Janeiro. Known as a "chanteuse-barytone" (or in Portuguese as *cantora barítono*), she adopted the term professionally and used

---

[36] Bilac (Fantasio), "No Cabaré."

[37] *O Paiz*, July 23, 1895. Early in the 20th century, Frègoli traveled throughout Europe and then to the United States, where he worked in early movies, reaching unprecedented popularity on both sides of the Atlantic. In 1908, he returned to Brazil for presentations in Rio de Janeiro and São Paulo.

[38] *O Paiz*, October 25, 1896. For a discussion of Bruant's masculinity and the chanson genre, see Peter Hawkins, *Chanson: The French Singer-Songwriter from Aristide Bruant to the Present Day* (New York: Ashgate, 2000), 17–18 and 35–38.

[39] Kelley Conway, *Chanteuse in the City: The Realist Singer in French Film* (Berkeley and Los Angeles: University of California Press, 2004), 5–6.

[40] Conway, *Chanteuse in the City*, 6.

[41] Jennifer Goltz, "Pierrot le diseur," *Musical Times* 147, no. 1894 (2006): 67–70; see also Jacqueline Waeber, "Yvette Guilbert and the Reevaluation of the Chanson Populaire and Chanson Ancienne during the Third Republic, 1889–1914," in *The Oxford Handbook of the New Cultural History of Music*, ed. Jane F. Fulcher (London and New York: Oxford University Press, 2011), 264–306.

it in her business letterhead.[42] She deliberately explored her unique vocal timbre to create mysterious and dark sonic effects, which became another important tool in her male/female transformations, adding a particular aural aspect to her performances. João do Rio recalls Ywonna's voice as one of the reasons why the local bohemia attended the cabaret: "One would go to Ywonna's for the pleasure of her art, for her voice of the Pythia sacerdotal of Delos, an extravagant pleasure [as she] would recite sonically the "Nevroses" by [Maurice] Rollinat (1846–1903) and the most profound texts of [Charles] Baudelaire (1821–1867) and Bruant."[43] Ultimately, Ywonna's multi-range and varied vocal timbre added sonic elements to her performances, enabling her to create singlehandedly small-scale melodramas, minimalist total artworks, with lyrics, performance, and vocal sounds intertwining within the ambience of the small venue. In the form of sonic alternatives to theatrical prima donnas, and to women's position as objectified celebrities, Ywonna's low female voice, understood as anti-natural, added to her subjectivity as a performer, opening up imaginary spaces for local male symbolists and decadents alike, who went to her cabaret to inhabit decadence through sounds. All in all, Ywonna's female body, her performative gender bending, and the timbre of her voice allowed the cabaret's clientele to explore sexuality as abnormal, and to engage with the mystic as defiance of and alternatives to the conventional morality of their bourgeoisie society.

Ywonna's performances connect her most directly with one of the most famous contemporary Montmartre cabaret performers, Yvette Gilbert (1865–1944). Raised to popularity in the late 1880s and early 1890s in Montmartre's cabaret scene, Gilbert performed at the Divan Japonaise, the Parisian Chat Noir, and the Eldorado—where she most probably met Ywonna. Gilbert eventually made her mark internationally in Germany, England, and across the Atlantic in the United States.[44] Like Ywonna, Gilbert was a *diseuse* and also departed from contemporary codes of femininity; she explored a characteristic dress code to typify her performative persona, one that was also captured in drawings by Toulouse-Lautrec and Steilen. Her female subjectivity was not lost in the literary and musical world around her; the playwright and songwriter Maurice Lefèvre, for example, described Gilbert's performance in Paris as follows:

[42] The *Jornal do Commercio*, June 23, 1896, announces Ywonna as a "Parisian celebrity Ywonna, the woman barytone!" In a manuscript note to Ruben Dario, Ywonna used the description "chanteusebarytone d' Eldorado de Paris" in her business letterhead; the manuscript is available in the Biblioteca Digital AECID, Agencia Española de Cooperación Internacional para el Desarrollo, Spain. Rubén Darío (1867–1916) was a renowned writer and part of the Spanish-Latin American *modernistas*; he traveled extensively in Latin America and Europe, establishing residency in Santiago de Chile, Paris, and Buenos Aires where, according to the note, he met Ywonna.

[43] João do Rio, "A decadência dos Chopps," 92.

[44] Conway, *Chanteuse in the City*, 3.

114 MUSIC AND COSMOPOLITANISM

There she is! Long leech, sexless! She crawls, creeps with hissings, leaving behind the moiré trail of her drool. . . . On both sides of the boneless body hang, like pitiful wrecks, tentacles in funeral gloves. For she will, indeed, lead the burial of our Latin race. Complete negation of our genius. . . . Poor little Chanson, faithful mirror in which men reflect themselves, are you responsible for their hideousness?[45]

Gilbert's performative act, like Ywonna's, managed to evoke contempt for her artistic persona within the male-dominated cabaret, while at the same time offering her audiences performative experimentations framed within the familiar domain of the popular stage.[46] When Gilbert's career took off, she started to choose her repertory intentionally to exploit her abilities as a *diseuse* and her performance creativity, focusing on specific composers and poets, such as Bruant, Lèopold Gangloff (1856–1898), Léon Xanrof (1867–1953), and Gabriel Montoya (1868–1914). Gilbert worked directly with Xanrof, becoming the main performer of his songs in the 1890s; in 1902, she traveled with Montoya to Berlin, making quite an impression on the local cabaret scene. And like Frègoli, Gilbert's career continued as an actress in the movies, as she became an international phenomenon that marked the beginning of 20th-century celebrity culture.

It is therefore not a coincidence that Ywonna's choice of repertory for her Rio de Janeiro cabaret parallels Gilbert's. Bruant's realist chansons were performed daily at Ywonna's cabaret and made quite an impression among Rio de Janeiro's bohemia. "Ah! la Batignolles," Duque recalled 10 years later with nostalgia, as if he were talking about a lyrical love song.[47] But "La Battingnolle" was a Bruant love story, a chanson in which he narrates the story of his love for a prostitute and her tragic death of smallpox. The song was a typical Bruant *chanson realistique*, which was presented in the enclosed cabaret but which rendered the Parisian underworld, the poor and disenfranchised, while satirizing the morbid side of life in the age of a capitalist and bourgeoning modern city. These chansons' concocted populism laid bare their many social contradictions, but they served perfectly as an expressive, and experimental, voyeuristic scene, as a lyrical and sonic glance— as a sonic *flânerie*—through the topography and social hierarchies of the city affected by an unscrupulous modernity. Thus, as Ywonna could find a resonance for Bruant's realistic chansons in Rio de Janeiro's decaying, disease-infected, and social and racially segregated streets, she also took the role of the female sonic *flâneuse*,[48] chronicling through songs the lives and experiences of the city.

---

[45] Maurice Lefèvre quote appears in Waeber, "Yvette Guilbert," 272.
[46] Hindson, *Female Performance Practice on the Fin-de-Siècle*, 40.
[47] Duque, "O cabaret da Yvonne."
[48] Conway has suggested this idea, in *Chanteuse in the City*, 18–20.

But while some cabaret chansons chronicled the gloomy life of the city's streets, others reflected on a nostalgic rural space that would never return, and others fueled longing for distant lovers that could only be reached in the bohemian imagination. Ywonna thus often left her Bruant character to perform other chanson styles in a complex eclectic mix that was also characteristic of the *fin-de-siècle* cabaret. Her *chansons du jour*, announced daily in the newspapers as if it were a surprise, included: "La grande faucheuse," by Gangloff, a composer and *chef d'orchestre* at the Chat Noir; "Petit chagrin" (1891) a successful romantic chanson with music by Paul Delmet (1862–1904) and poem by Maurice Vaucaire (1863–1918); and the waltz-song "Titania, ronde enfernalle," with music by Xavier Le Mareille (18?–1937) and lyrics by L. Roydel (188?–1928). Ywonna also regularly performed her "signature song," "Berceuse bleue" (1894), which Duque remembered because of the song's "seduction that softens and delights."[49] With lyrics by Montoya and music by Yann-Nibor (1857–1947), both part of the Parisian Chat Noir line-up of artists, "Berceuse bleue" became very popular in Paris around the same time it was introduced to Rio de Janeiro's bohemians in Ywonna's cabaret. The song was published in 1895 in the influential Parisian magazine *Gil Blas Illustré* with illustration by Steilen and continued to be performed and included in chanson compilations well into the 20th century (Musical Example 5.1). The chanson inspired the popular "Berceuse vert," which reappeared in Rio de Janeiro as a short movie, as *chanson-filmée*, in the first decade of the 20th century, and sung by Gilbert (see Chapter 8).

Yet when Ywonna made her signature song "Berceuse bleue" popular in Rio de Janeiro, Montoya and Nibor were not yet the Montmartre veterans that they would eventually become. In his early career, Montoya was a pharmacist who arrived in Paris in 1893 after a sojourn in the West Indies on a medical ship. Nibor had worked in ships for decades before he established himself in Montmartre, a past that gave him the nickname the "Sailor Poet" of Parisian cabarets. Accordingly, unlike Bruant's *chanson realistique*, "Berceuse bleue" was a love song more in line with symbolism, as the music is set to assist the lyrics' depiction of elusive distances among oceans to equal the distance between lovers. Ywonna's choice of "Berceuse bleue" as her signature song was thus not based merely on the song's popularity in Paris, but on her (correct) assumption that such a song could reverberate beyond its place of origin and that it had the potential to reach a bohemian collectivity longing for an imaginary distant love. Ywonna's performances in Rio de Janeiro thus furthered the song's popularity beyond Paris and multiplied the song's cosmopolitan force, depicting a sailors' longing for an unreachable love, while her experimental performance allowed

---

[49] Duque, "O cabaret da Yvonne."

116 MUSIC AND COSMOPOLITANISM

Musical Example 5.1. "Berceuse bleue," Gabriel Montoya, in *Gill Blas Illustré*
Source: Gil Blas Illustré vol. 5, University of Michigan Library, Google books

for ample imagination among a network of disillusioned urban bohemians living in alternative worlds beyond the local.

Both "La Batingonles" and "Berceuse bleue" were recorded in the early 1900s by Bruant and Gilbert as the emergent recording businesses invested in the songs' potential to transcend the intimate cabaret scene and circulate further in the sonic-frozen context provided by the new technology. These recordings provide a glimpse of what these songs could have sounded like, although Ywonna's performance was retained only in Rio de Janeiro chroniclers' memories. Still, recordings of these chansons do not help us grasp the sonic cultural implications and the socio-gender-political roles in Yvonna's cabaret performances that I explore here. Contemporary critics note that musically chansons were "simple" by default, but that their simplicity was not a detriment to the works' appreciation since chansons needed to be brought to life through performance. Their effect, woven through their lyrics and minimalistic melodic lines, was dependent on the performers' privileged role, on their bodies, dress codes, attitudes, declamation, acting abilities, and use of their vocal qualities. Mary Poole notes that chansons were to be "presented almost as an improvisation"[50] and thus were expected to be gone after the moment passed. Repeated renditions of a song by a chansonnier or interpreter were sufficiently idiosyncratic in their performance to captivate the public before the affordability of recordings and the mainstreaming of radio.[51] The production of songs that were very similar to one another and to be repeated ad libitum depended on the premise that the works would be created in performance and that they were accepted by the audience as given by the artist's individual performance. And it actually needed to be so in order to set forth the process of circulation and sharing: performance singularity, rather than homogeneity, allowed the chanson to circulate. The small-scale, performance-oriented chansons were not conducive to mass production in the same way as other contemporary songs and dances, which were printed in large numbers and distributed internationally to be performed by professionals and amateurs alike. Cabaret chansons were dependent on live performances in the intimate atmosphere of the cabaret, which also encouraged and counted on audience participation, in an ambience that *chansonnier* Xanrof described as a "communal experience."[52]

---

[50] Mary Ellen Poole, "Chansonnier and Chanson in Parisian 'Cabarets Artistiques,' 1881–1914," PhD dissertation, University of Illinois at Urbana-Champaign, 1994, 103–104.

[51] For the idiosyncratic use of the body, acting/singing, and performative importance of contemporary singers, see Karen Henson, "Introduction: On Not Singing and Singing Physiognomically," in *Opera Acts: Singers and Performance in the Late Nineteenth Century* (Cambridge, UK: Cambridge University Press, 2015), 1–16.

[52] Poole, "Chansonnier and Chanson," 56.

118 MUSIC AND COSMOPOLITANISM

The popularity and effect of the cabaret's chanson was thus intertwined with the performer's expression and performative authority, an alternative authority that defied clear-cut and direct political engagements and that offered instead embodied experimentation through sounds and performance. The melody of Bruant's "La Batingnolles," for example, a repeating, descending line suiting the text's repetitive strophic setting, was straightforward enough to be used in disguise in other chansons.[53] Nonetheless, Rio de Janeiro male chroniclers recalled "La Batingnolle" clearly with association to Ywonna. Guided by the subject matter and assisted by the inevitability of the minimalistic melodic line, the chanson was nonetheless Ywonna's own creation. Similarly, the symbolist text/ sound combination of "Berceuse bleue," used to emulate the waves moving and to create the impression of the lover's distance, was also brought to life by Ywonna's performance in a cinematic fashion: image and sound depending on one another and encompassed in the body of the female *diseuse*, a reliance that contested and offered alternatives to the supposed inevitability of the new technologies threatening to commodify sonic and life performances.

Ywonna's use of her wide range and dark vocal timbre, her vocal delivery oscillating between singing and speaking, and her embodied male/female performances were also dependent on the specificity of the cabaret's ambience, its audience, and its urban context. It was an interactive performance intertwined within a *fin-de-siècle* cosmopolitan city, a place not specifically here nor there. Thus, bohemians experiencing Ywonna's performances in her Rio de Janeiro cabaret were not merely in an entertainment space disconnected from a larger social-cultural context, but were participants in an imagined shared geographical and sociocultural historical moment: the *diseuse* embodied the bohemian escapism, the cabaret sheltered their collective enterprise, and the city harbored their cabaret. In Ywonna's cabaret, the original and the copy, here and there, male and female, love and sadness, gaiety and despair, life and death, intermingled and depended on each other to shape the imaginary modern city. Looking at the turn-of-the-century urban culture, Peter Frietze noted that every city would eventually have cable cars and bicycles.[54] One can say that most cities would also have cabarets and that they would eventually become, as Julian Brigstocke claims, "one of the markers of urban vitality and dynamism."[55] And when that happened, Paris was no longer a specific place, but one among many cosmopolitan *fin-de-siècle* cities growing within the unfamiliar world of their modernity.

What Ywonna saw in Rio de Janeiro and its audiences that allowed her to succeed across the Atlantic was this shared urban experience—a

[53] See, for example, Bruant's song "La Vilette."
[54] Peter Fritzsche, "The City and Urban Life," in *The Fin-de-Siècle World*, ed. Michael Saler (New York: Routledge, 2015), 29 and 43.
[55] Brigstocke, *The Life of the City*, ix and 101.

cosmopolitan experience, in which geographies melded, distances became irrelevant, and the lives and experiences of people from nearby and far away became intertwined. Her success was dependent on the assumption that cabaret chansons would reverberate beyond their places of origin: not by printed publications in massive numbers or recordings, but by live, improvisatory, and collective performances that germinated and grew in a shared urban sonic space. This story is thus not solely about Rio de Janeiro or about Ywonna—as interesting as her individual history may be—but an exploration of a shared sonic, sociohistorical, aesthetic, and cultural context that shaped an urban generation. Ywonna's cabaret both taps into and shapes a musical collective and a shared experience of an urban geography with elusive borders, one that cannot be seen on maps, nor can it be reduced to visual representations. It was an ephemeral experience fostered uniquely by sound, music, and embodied improvisatory performances, which although elusive had aesthetic, musical, political, and cultural relevance.

In the end, however, Duque dismisses the political and artistic aspects of Ywonna's cabaret as merely constructs of his youthful male imagination:

> To recall the true without shame, I clarify that the fine spiritual flower of Montmartre that we forged was one of our frequent and flourished fantasies and imaginations. . . . But this did not stop us from bringing up the high spirituality of these [French] intellectuals every time we spoke. . . . And in this decanted spirituality, supposedly very refined, the cabaret seemed to us the most complete realization of the Parisian modes in which the race and intelligence contributed to the nature of the superiority that is inaccessible to common mortals.[56]

Truly so, such a cabaret scene framed the memories and experiences of a community made up of just a few males. Nonetheless, their collective memories were created and shaped by the authority and subjectivity of the *diseuse*. Ywonna was an example of the *fin-de-siècle* New Woman, one not independent from the sociopolitical and gendered urban space in which she acted, but one with autonomy to navigate a complex *fin-de-siècle* context in its experimental and aesthetic possibilities. Like many women performers during her time, Ywonna's female body and voice became a place in which to locate an experience, a "crossroads where all the transitional features of modernity converged."[57] Her vocal performances were individualist alternatives to deterministic views of progress

---

[56] Duque, "O cabaret da Yvonne."
[57] Bergero, *Intersecting Tango*, 197.

120   MUSIC AND COSMOPOLITANISM

of the new republican government, a sonic and embodied stance on cultural norms that she inhabited, but most possibly did not subscribe to.[58]

Expectedly, the cabaret's ephemeral ambience was eventually infiltrated by the forces of an emergent music business which required a less exclusive collectivity, as Ywonna herself would eventually find out (see Chapter 6). Yet assuming that capitalism alone cannot propel the sharing of cultural expressions and that people have a role in both creating and engaging with cultural expressions, Ywonna's enterprise and her individual use of the minimalist cabaret chanson had a ubiquitous force in shaping and propelling a cosmopolitan urban culture in Rio de Janeiro and beyond.

---

[58] For this take on feminism during the period as a form of autonomy but not of independence, and for the concept of the New Women, see Gagnier, *Individualism, Decadence, and Globalization*, 17 and 75.

6

Diversifying

Café Concerts

Capitalizing on her initial success in the Brazilian capital, three months after opening her cabaret Ywonna moved to a larger venue with a proper stage. The upgrade was subsidized by Luis Gaston, a bohemian among Ywonna's cabaret clientele who saw the potential for her business to attract larger crowds.[1] Located in the old Eldorado theater on the Beco do Imperio (Theotonio Regadas street), the new venue was central to Rio de Janeiro's theatrical and entertainment scene around Praça Tiradentes. To be competitive in the already crowded area, Ywonna again followed the trends in the 1880s and 1890s in Paris, when cabarets were restructured, broadening their repertories and performance formats to rival popular café-concerts like the Alcazar d'Éte and the (Parisian) Eldorado. Montmartre's Chat Noir did not escape the trend. Only three and a half years after its opening, it was remodeled and enlarged to host a larger stage that separated performers from the audience, and included added rooms dedicated to musical performances with small ensembles. It continued to feature the cabaret chanson repertory, but added extras such as dances, shadow shows, pantomimes, and excerpts or parodies of operas, operettas, reviews, and comic operas. The exclusive, intimate cabaret started to succumb to the entertainment business world, dispensing with the exclusive clientele and well-defined repertory in favor of a heterogeneous mix of performances and musical styles.[2]

Ywonna's path was thus predictable. The artist understood that the Brazilian capital followed the urbanization patterns of several contemporary cities, where the growth of urban audiences led to the multiplication of entertainment venues, an unprecedented fragmentation, and overlap of repertories and performing practices. Usually conglomerated in specific urban spaces, these venues became glaring visual and sonic symbols of the turn-of-the-century city and definers of city-life experiences. Parisian urban life was also in constant movement,

---

[1] Duque, "O cabaret da Yvonne." Advertisement for the new venue appears in *Gazeta de Notícias*, October 12, 1896.

[2] Poole, "Chansonnier and Chanson," 78–81 and 42–43. For the changes in the structure and repertory of late 19th-century Parisian cabaret, see Steven Whiting, *Satie the Bohemian: From Cabaret to Concert Hall* (New York: Oxford University Press, 1999), 34–72. See also Hindson, *Female Performance Practices on the Fin-de-Siècle Popular Stage*, 26–30.

Music and Cosmopolitanism. Cristina Magaldi, Oxford University Press. © Oxford University Press 2024.
DOI: 10.1093/oso/9780199744770.003.0007

122 MUSIC AND COSMOPOLITANISM

driven by its growing entertainment venues. While in 1869, café-concerts accommodated 3,000 to 4,000 people a night, and larger theaters had a total capacity for 40,000, by 1899, the growing number of new café-concerts in the city accommodated from 25,000 to 30,000 people, a number close to the theatrical attendance.[3] In 1865, London had 23 theaters accommodating altogether roughly 33,000 people and about 32 music halls seating between 500 and 5,000 each, but later in the century, with the number of music halls growing to about 80, the city's entertainment venues could hold double that number.[4] The theatrical glamor of New York City, with its lights and non-stop stages, emerged around that same period, and in many mid-sized cities like Rome, Madrid, Barcelona, and Lisbon the overall pattern was the same.[5] Balme maintains that in 1899 there were 302 permanent theaters in Germany, England, France, Austria-Hungary, and the United States together; by 1914, that number had grown to some 2,000 in Europe alone, a trend that was also evident in former and existing colonies in Southeast Asia and Latin America.[6] That was the case, for instance, in turn-of-the-20th-century Buenos Aires, when the concentration of new theaters and café-concerts in the area around Corrientes street, which, Bergero notes, "studded with lights and illuminated signs, stood for the city as a whole."[7] Nearby Havana's Paseo del Prado and old Havana, the Tacón theater, Irijoa theater (later Martí), and the Theatro Alhambra were joined by several smaller venues that served well to entertain a most vibrant city as the 19th century came to a close.[8] In Rio de Janeiro, performing venues formed a cluster around the city's center at the Praça da República and its surroundings and numbered around 10–12 theaters and music halls, with small to large dimensions, holding approximately 900 to 2,500 spectators apiece.[9] With the opening of the Avenida Central in 1905, the

[3] Christophe Charle, *Théâtres en capitales: Naissance de la société du spetacle à Paris, Berlin, Londres, et Vienne* (Paris: Albin Michael, 2008), 49–52. Matthew Jordan estimated that at the beginning of the 20th century Paris has 264 café concerts; see his *Le Jazz: Jazz and the French Cultural Identity* (Urbana: University of Illinois Press, 2010), 19.

[4] Lee Jackson, *Palaces of Pleasure: From Music Halls to the Seaside to Football, How the Victorians Invented Mass Entertainment* (New Haven, CT: Yale University Press, 2019), 68; see also Jerry White, *London in the Nineteenth Century: 'A Human Awful Wonder of God'* (London: Vintage, 2011, Kindle).

[5] For cities in the United States, like New York and Chicago, see David Nasaw, *Going out: The Rise and Fall of Public Amusements* (Cambridge, MA: Harvard University Press, 1993). For London, Judith Walkowitz, *Night Out: Life in Cosmopolitan London* (New Haven, CT: Yale University Press, 2012). For the building of popular theaters where international casts would perform to a middle strata of the population in Paris and Rome, see Gesa Zur Nieden, "The Internationalization of Musical Life at the end of the Nineteenth Century in Modernized Paris and Rome," *Urban History* 40, no. 4 (November 2013): 669–673. For theaters in Madrid and Barcelona, see Jeanne Moisand, *Scènes capitales: Madrid, Barcelona et le monde théâtral fin de siècle* (Madrid: Casa de Velázqvez, 2013). For the growing number of theaters and other entertaining venues in Lisbon during the period, see Silva, *Entertaining Lisbon*, 67–74. For Buenos Aires, see Bergero, *Intersecting Tango*, 77–89.

[6] Balme, "Theater and Globalization," 146.

[7] Bergero, *Intersecting Tango*, 77.

[8] Lane, *Blackface Cuba*, 109–110.

[9] The first theatrical boom was in the 1860s, when the number of theaters in Rio de Janeiro grew from three to eight; see Silvia Cristina Martins de Souza, *Carpinteiros teatrais: Cenas cômicas*

entertainment area was expanded further to reach the new Avenida Rio Branco, where new movie theaters would eventually also congregate. If in 1890 nine theaters could hold around 13,000 people, at the beginning of the 20th century João do Rio estimated that 25,000 people were in and around Praça da Republica and Avenida Central areas on a given night, a considerable number in a city with a population ranging around 900,000. Adding to the already busy scene, smaller theaters and improvised stages, beer houses, seasonal outdoor performances, and circuses catering to a larger spectrum of the city's residents sprawled well beyond the city center, as new transportation systems connected Rio de Janeiro's growing neighborhoods. All in all, the cities' transformations were fast and widespread, and considering that music was an essential part of theatrical life, the opportunities for growth, diversification, and circulation of similar repertories across countries and continents grew exponentially.[10]

With an eye on the competition, Ywonna understood that the dynamics of the markets dictated that she should begin to offer diverse musical styles from a gamut of provenances and performances by artists with multiple skills. She hired the music director Adolpho Lindner (1858–1897) to organize a typical medium-sized musical ensemble of 6–10 performers, which most probably included violin, flute, piano, double bass, clarinet, cornet, and guitar, and added excerpts from musical reviews, operettas, and zarzuelas to the show, while maintaining her established chanson repertory.[11] The hiring of Lindner, an established music director from the Theatro Variedades who worked with Artur Azevedo, shows that Ywonna was selective in her artistic pursuits. She followed other theater directors and traveled to Montevideo and Buenos Aires to hire performers with a broader range of experiences and expertise. As an entrepreneur, she became

---

e diversidade cultural no Rio de Janeiro oitocentista (Londrina, Brazil: Eduel, 2017), 13. At the beginning of the 20th century, the largest theaters were: Theatro Recreio Dramatico, Theatro São José, Theatro Lucinda, Theatro Carlos Gomes, and Theatro Variedades, in addition to the larger Theatro Lyrico, which presented both operas and variety shows; see José Dias, *Teatros do Rio: do século XVIII ao século XX* (Rio de Janeiro: FUNARTE, 2012); and Evelyn Lima, *Arquitetura do espetáculo: Teatros e cinemas na formação da Praça Tiradentes* (Rio de Janeiro, Ed. UFRJ, 2000).

[10] For a study connecting Berlin and London, see Len Platt and Tobias Becker, "Berlin/London; London/Berlin; Cultural Transfer, Musical Theater and 'the Cosmopolitan' 1870–1914," *Nineteenth-Century Theater and Film* 40, no.1 (2013): 1–14.

[11] *Gazeta de Notícias*, October 16, 1896. The number of musicians in orchestras for these shows varied and included a variety of formats: single songs interspersed with dances and dialogues usually had small ensembles with an assortment of instrument combinations; see Silva, *Entertaining Lisbon*, 138. Derek Scott claims that in variety theaters the number of musicians was around seven: clarinet, cornet, trombone, violin, piano, double-bass, and drums; see his *Sounds of the Metropolis: The 19th Century Popular Music Revolution in London, New York, Paris and Vienna* (New York and Oxford: Oxford University Press, 2008), 54. In larger venues such as prestigious music halls, the number of musicians was usually around 20–25, including the traditional string section, two flues, two horns, two oboes, two clarinets, bassoon, three trumpets, three trombones, and basic percussion. See Sarah Gutsche-Miller, "Pantomime-Ballet on the Music-Hall Stage: The Popularisation of Classical Ballet in Fin-de-Siècle Paris," PhD dissertation, McGill University, 2010, 340.

124   MUSIC AND COSMOPOLITANISM

a link in the circuit of artists who followed the North-South network, the loop Paris–Madrid–Lisbon–Buenos Aires–Montevideo–São Paulo–Rio de Janeiro–Lisbon–Paris, a route that had many tributaries which also was traveled by artists from a range of countries such as Italy, Germany, Russia, Cuba, England, and the United States. Ywonna's venue thus counted on a diverse cast of artists, some of whom she had met at her first appearances in the Theatro Recreio Dramatico and who had performed in her cabaret (see Chapter 5), including: Maria Lino (ca. 1876–1940), daughter of Italian immigrants who later became very popular in Paris; the French soprano, actress, and poet Rose Méryss (Rose Marie Baudon, ca. 1850–1929), who was in Rio de Janeiro since 1870 and who had a well-established local career;[12] the French performer Eugènie Chauvim, who had performed at the Parisian Alcazar before her appearance in Rio de Janeiro; the singer/actress Aurélia Delorme (Cândida Cardoso Sanchez, 1866–1921); the Spanish dancer M. del Valle, who performed with a zarzuelas company; the Portuguese actress and singer Amelia Barros (1842–?); and the Spanish-Portuguese actress, singer, and director Pepa Ruiz.[13] Many of these women had worked in Rio de Janeiro's theaters for over a decade and in many theaters concomitantly, while moving back and forth from Latin America to Europe.[14] They reveal a close-knit group of women performers and directors that traversed the Paris–Madrid–Lisbon–Rio de Janeiro–Montevideo–Buenos Aires circuit. Some, like Rose Méryss, became prominent figures in local intellectual circles and in politics; others became powerful directors and managers of their own companies. Ruiz, for example, who had already established herself as one of the most successful artists in Rio de Janeiro when she met Ywonna, became so influential that she alone challenged in a lawsuit the monopoly of White male theater directors in Rio de Janeiro, who usually made decisions in hiring casts and changing storylines in recurring plays.[15]

Gradually transforming her exclusive cabaret into a café-concert and welcoming a larger cast and a larger audience, on October 15, 1896, Ywonna offered a "*fin-de-siècle* repertory," starting with the chanson "Echo du cabaré,"

---

[12] For a full account of Mérys's activities in Rio de Janeiro and Paris, see Daniela Mantarro Callipo, "De vedette a poeta: A trajetória de Rose Mérys," *Miscelânea* 24 (July/December 2018), 145–163.

[13] Advertisements for performances at Ywonna's venue including these artists appear in *Gazeta de Notícias*, November 7, 1896, *Gazeta de Notícias*, November 26, 1896, and *O Paiz*, October 22, 1896.

[14] For the foreign actors, and French actresses in particular, in Brazilian theaters at mid-century, see Lená Medeiros de Menezes, "Ventos Franceses nas noites cariocas: A 'cocotte comedienne' e o Alcazar Lyrique no Rio de Janeiro Imperial," *Revista do Instituto Histórico e Geográfico do Rio de Janeiro* 24, no. 24 (2017): 99–120; and Orna Messer Levin, "Theatrical Culture and Global Audience: French Repertory in Rio de Janeiro," in *The Cultural Revolution of the Nineteenth-Century: Theater, the Book-Trade, and Reading in the Transatlantic World*, ed. Márcia Abreu and Ana Cláudia Suriani da Silva (London: Bloomsbury, 2016), 234–251.

[15] Almeida, "O mercado de trabalho dos espetáculos; see also Mencarelli, "A voz e a partitura," 180–190.

with Portuguese lyrics by Méryss, now starting her career as a poet, and set to the music of the already local favorite chanson "Berceuse bleue."[16] Thus, diversification did not only mean new musical material, but also included a wider range of familiar musical offerings performed in new ways. To that end, the *fin-de-siècle* repertory at Ywonna's café-concert also included Robert Plaquette's (1848–1903) opera-comique *Les cloches de Corneville* (1877), libretto by Louis Clairville and Charles Gabet, which had opened in Paris in 1877. Translated into Portuguese as *Os sinos de Corneville*, it was presented by Ywonna as part of a vaudeville act in an abridged version.[17] Already a major hit in various European cities in the previous decade, *Les cloches de Corneville* continued to circulate in English as *The Chimes of Normandy* and *The Bells of Corneville* to become a success in theaters in London, New York, Berlin, and Vienna.[18] "The Chimes," as the work was referred to in New York, remained in the repertory for 20 years and for over 40 years in other parts of the United States, where "[i]t is doubtful if there was a town of over five hundred people in the entire United States which was not visited between 1880 and 1890 by a touring troupe playing this opera."[19] As late as 1907, the Italian director and dancer Giovanni Vittorio Rosi, working at London's Alhambra, relied on the operetta's popularity to make it into a "dancing opera."[20] Despite the fact that critics discredited the work as derivative and repetitive, *Les cloches de Corneville* set records for performances and remained in the repertory of theaters and music halls on both sides of the Atlantic and beyond for several decades. Excerpts from the work further circulated in a range of arrangements, finding similar competition only a few years later in excerpts from Lehár's *The Merry Widow* (1905) (see Chapter 9). The most popular were the waltz-song "Rondeau valse" in the first act, "Chanson de Mousse," and the waltz-song not coincidentally titled "J'ai fait trois fois le tour du monde" (I have traveled around the world three times), recorded by the Pathés Frère orchestra in 1910 as "French Waltz, Valse des cloches de Corneville," and which survived over three decades in the repertory of a wide range performers, venues, and media.[21]

In Rio de Janeiro, a French lyric company had offered *Les cloches de Corneville* in French in 1881 at the Theatro Sant'Anna, while the Portuguese translation by

[16] *O Paiz*, October 17, 1896.

[17] *Gazeta de Notícias*, October 16 and 21, 1896.

[18] Marion Linhardt, "Local Contexts and Genre Construction in Early Continental Musical Theater," in *Popular Musical Theater in London and Berlin*, ed. Len Platt, Tobias Becker, and David Linton (Cambridge, UK: Cambridge University Press, 2014), 62.

[19] James Morgan, "French Comic Opera in New York, 1855–1890," PhD dissertation, University of Illinois, 1959, cited in Dizikes, *Opera in America*, 199.

[20] In 1917, while in Japan, Rossi directed *Les cloches de Corneville* as an operetta with a Japanese cast; see Naomi Matsumoto, "Giovanni Vittorio Rosi's Musical Theater: Opera, Operetta and the Westernisation of Modern Japan," in *Musical Theater in Europe, 1830–1934*, ed. Michela Niccolai and Clair Rowden (Lucca, Italy: Brepolss, 2017), 351–385, in particular 360 and 374.

[21] The Pathé recording (7258) is available at https://www.youtube.com/watch?v=LpbXlYH54zo.

126   MUSIC AND COSMOPOLITANISM

Eduardo Garrido (1842–1912) as *Os sinos de Corneville* was presented simultaneously at Phênix Dramática, so that audiences had the opportunity to attend performances of the same work in different languages, a practice that would become a trend in the city (see Chapter 9). By December 1882, the work was already in its 200th presentation in the Brazilian capital, and excerpts were performed several times in Artur Azevedo's popular musical reviews throughout the decade.[22] *Os sinos de Corneville* was a staple in Pepa Ruiz's repertory from 1887 through the 1890s, when Ruiz and Ywonna connected while working at the Theatro Recreio Dramatico. In 1892, a critic of the republican-inclined *Revista Musical* noted in discontent that the popularity in Rio de Janeiro of songs from the operetta was such that they were regularly sung as a potpourri by local schoolchildren.[23] In November 1896, almost two decades after the work's Parisian premiere, a Portuguese company offered the full operetta at the Theatro Apollo, announced as "the *legendary* [my emphasis] operetta by Plaquette, which last month commemorated its 1,650th presentation at the Parisian Gaité, and that has already had about 400 presentations in this capital; all that is needed here [in Rio de Janeiro] is one announcement of the happy work and the theater will fill."[24]

In that same year, when Ywonna presented the work at her café-concert, she thus relied on the operetta's place in an already established repertory, in Rio de Janeiro and elsewhere, as her choice of musical offerings clearly overlapped with the one presented in theaters in various cities. Ywonna's musical choices thus helped popularize and solidify a musical repertory that eventually came to shape the city's sonic ambience through music. Excerpts from Plaquette's operetta were still among the works most performed in Rio de Janeiro at the beginning of the new century in intermissions and waiting rooms at movie theaters. The famous waltz was recorded in Rio de Janeiro as early as in 1903 by the singer Bahiano as "Valsa dos sinos de Corneville" (Zon-O-Phone X-700), and later in 1910 by Mário Pinheiro (1880–1923) as "Sinos de Corneville" (Columbia, 11.738) for Casa Edison, the local recording studio (see Chapter 9).[25] But one needed not buy a record of the song, for João do Rio reported that Rio de Janeiro's street

---

[22] *Gazeta de Notícias*, December 28, 1882; cited in Aléxia Lorrana Silva Ferreira, "Jacinto Heller: Repertório de um empresário teatral (1875–1885)," *Cadernos Letra e Ato* 6, no. 6 (2016): 37.

[23] Critical debasement of the operetta's tunes was articulated in B. R., "O Canto-Choral," *Gazetta Musical* 11 (July 1892): 162; Mencarelli, "A voz e a partitura," 217.

[24] *Gazeta de Notícias*, November 26, 1896.

[25] A printed program for the music performed in the waiting room of the Cine Avenida in 1910, for example, lists the operetta alongside newer works, such as Lehár's "The Merry Widow Waltz"; cited in Carlos Eduardo Pereira, *A música no cinema silencioso no Brasil* (Rio de Janeiro: Museu de Arte Moderna, 2014), 38. For a list of early recordings by Baiano and Mário Pinheiro, see Martha Ulhôa, "Discografia de Mário Pinheiro, 1904–1013," and "Discografia do Bahiano, 1902–1915," online publication (2010).

DIVERSIFYING   127

performers with barrel organs got rich by repeating the famous waltz "Sinos de Cornerville" through the city's streets.[26]

Another hit in Ywonna's café-concert was Louis Varney's operetta *L'amor mouillé* (1887), lyrics by J. Prevel and A. Liorat, which also circulated concurrently in many cities. The English translation by William Yardley and Henry Bayatt enjoyed large success in London's Lyric Theater, fulfilling the English critic's forecast that the work would enjoy "long prosperity" in the competing market for operettas, for it had just "the perfect combination of sentiment and silliness."[27] *L'amor mouillé* opened with great success in Rio de Janeiro's Theatro San'Anna on November 11, 1887, only a few months after the Parisian premiere. Unlike Plaquette's work, Varney's operetta continued to be highly praised in the 1890s by local critics because of its "spontaneity of inspiration, with the dexterity of a scientific musician . . . several parts with such distinct and fresh melodies that some could argue for its entrance in a more serious repertory."[28] Performed in Rio de Janeiro in both its original French and in a Portuguese translation and in adaptation/parody by Moreira Sampaio as *O amor molhado*, the work offered plenty of songful and memorable tunes to entice local audiences, in particular the waltz-song "Valse d'oiseau," or in the Portuguese translation as "Valsa do beija flor." In 1892, a critic noted that it was "a delicate waltz," despite the vocal and performing challenges the piece presented for the female vocalist.[29] Continuing to circulate in Europe and the Americas in arrangements for a variety of instrumentations, the waltz-song was included in both early Edison and Victor catalogs, distributed wherever those early entrepreneurs managed to reach, and its popularity continued as famous singers retained the work in their repertories.

And, of course, "Valse des cloches de Corneville," and "Valse d'oiseau" are but a few examples of works that traveled around the world several times and made an appearance in Ywonna's café concert, and not all of them had Parisian provenance. Frederico Chueca's (1846–1908) one-act zarzuela/review *La Gran Via* (1886), for instance, also had similar widespread success. Premiered in Rio de Janeiro in 1888, excerpts from the work, mostly dances, were inserted in an infinite number of theatrical genres written in Rio de Janeiro; it was performed at Ywonna's venue, and remained in the repertory well into the first decades of the 20th century. At the beginning of the 1890s, there were few in the Brazilian capital who did not know the work's most notable dances; the lyrics of another comedy performed in the late 1880s, for example, made explicit references to

---

[26] João do Rio, *A alma encantadora das ruas*, 67.

[27] *The Speaker* 19, April 8, 1899.

[28] The operetta was first performed November 11, 1887, at the Theatro Sant'Anna, and a review was published in *Jornal do Commercio*, November 13, 1887.

[29] *Diario de Notícias*, January 27, 1892.

128 MUSIC AND COSMOPOLITANISM

the popularity of zarzuela as follows:[30] "In the city and in the suburbs, there is an epidemic, [here] violins, pianos, harmonicas, only play *Gran Via*."[31] Early in the 20th century, João do Rio again noted the dominance of the waltz "Caballero de Gracia" from *Gran Via* in the barrel organs playing intermittently through the streets. If in Rio de Janeiro dances from the review were an epidemic, in Madrid they were taken as sonic torture:

> There is no piano in cafés, no cornet in street bands, no barrel organ, no voice of workers, no blindman's flute that do not repeat at all times the chorus, the waltz, or the duet. . . . [After *Gran via*] Chueca lives inside his work. [His] world may sound like a barrel organ, which plays incessantly the music of *Gran Via*.[32]

Each dance of the work had multiple extra lives as they came to live on both sides of the Atlantic. As Sanchez observes, these were pieces that, organized structurally to shape a theatrical work, helped dramatize the satire and conflicts of text, and as such the music becomes self-explanatory as our ears are directed by the visual. But the succession of pieces was carefully crafted musically, as specific rhythmic patterns (waltz, polkas, jotas, habaneras), melodic shapes (step-wise, ornaments over one note connected to intervals of a sixth or octave, tresillos, etc.), and modes of performances (*legatos, rubatos, staccatos, accentuation*), in combination or separately, offered musical meaning to the theatrically dramatized social interactions and conflicts that defined the turn-of-the-century transforming city.

These songs and dances were not passing fads, a temporary state of being often understood in connection with the "light" side of musics with popular appeal, characterizations that more often than not come with a dismissive aesthetic judgment that drives them to the fringes of history. Their combination of rhythmic and melodic drive nonetheless captivated multitudes of listeners and offered a myriad of musical tools for performers' self-expression, who offered collective and individual responses to their aesthetic musical world. These songs, with their combination of songful and memorable tunes and rhythms, stayed in the repertory for several years, and indeed for several decades, and came to characterize the aesthetic of an epoch shaped by the transformation of cities into an experience of many: they were the musical equivalent to the flashing lights, the fast-moving crowds, and the cacophonous street ambience of the turn-of-the-century modernizing city.

---

[30] Victor Sanchez Sanchez, "La revista *La Gran Via*: Representaciones Sociales en a través de la música en el género chico," in *La zarzuela e sus caminos: Del siglo VII a la actualidad*, ed. Tobias Brandenberger and Antje Dreyer (Berlin: Lit Verlag, 2016), 137–159.
[31] Souza, *Carpinteiros teatrais*, 130–131.
[32] Sanchez Sanchez, "La revista *La Gran Via*," 143.

By the beginning of the 20th century, however, Artur Azevedo noted that the music presented in café-concerts had passed its prime: "Where does this old stuff come from?" he asked condescendingly in his weekly theatrical column.[33] However, where they came from was not the pertinent question but, as Moretti reminds us, where they managed "to survive and grow, [that] is relevant."[34] Already well-known when these works were performed at Ywonna's café-concert, excerpts from Plaquette's and Varney's operettas and Chuenca's zarzuela were but a part of an extended group of familiar works that survived and grew. One can easily follow, through theatrical presentations, catalogs of publishers, and recordings, the pace and extent to which these works were popular enough to be understood generically as "a classic," or "legendary," to use the words of the Rio de Janeiro critic. Works like these, when tracked through their complex net of geographical and historical paths through publication, performance, and recording, can eventually make salient larger patterns of musical trends that came to characterize the soundscape of the turn-of-the-20th-century city well before songs by The Beatles and their contemporaries began their global trajectories. As a group, these works can make audible the period's cultural connections which, as Osterhammel reminds us, were not immediately visible on maps.[35]

Studying musical comedies in 19th-century England, Len Platt observed that there was a musical mainstream in the culture of the 1890s, and we can also say that such a mainstream was not geographically restricted to England, Europe, or the Americas. Waltz-songs from French operettas, performed in upper-class social situations within plots, for instance, were guaranteed hits in a number of cities, becoming one of the predominant rhythmic accompaniments for songs, having musical and gestural implications that served well in operas, ballets, pantomimes, and operettas, zarzuelas, and reviews alike.[36] Undoubtedly, at the turn of the 20th century love was mostly sung in waltz time, following the style of waltz-songs from works like Plaquette and Varney, and later also from Lehár and Straus and their contemporaries: a stressed down-beat, contrasted by a supporting upward melodic movement suggesting sonic waves not essentially different from "Berceuse bleue" but in triple meter, melodic constructions that mimicked sonically the round movements of embraced couples dancing, while also allowing for extended, forced, suspended *rubatos* in the upper beats as a way of excitement and suspense. In this overall format, the right melody, songful and memorable, could then make lyrics in various languages intelligible to many.

---

[33] Artur Azevedo, "Chronica theatral," *Diario de Notícias*, November 12, 1901.

[34] Moretti, *Distant Reading*, 27.

[35] Osterhammel, *The Transformation of the World*, 262–263.

[36] For a discussion of the use of waltz in the theater in an earlier period, see Marion Smith, *Ballet and Opera in the Age of "Giselle"* (Princeton, NJ: Princeton University Press, 2000).

130   MUSIC AND COSMOPOLITANISM

The repertory being presented in venues like Ywonna's had a specific history, geographically and historically, but one which nonetheless became part of shared practices and experiences of the urban aural present and which was constructed within complex and powerful interdependent artistic and audience networks. And here it becomes clear, as Derek Scott has contended, that the musical repertory of the cosmopolitan city, if perceived and consumed as modern, was not necessarily modern timewise, and certainly not modernistic in a sense of breaking with the past.[37] In these venues, chronological time did not necessarily lead to a path toward the modern, for the modernity of the present remained a fluid concept. If one follows specific works over time and space, one also needs to come to terms with the random fate that accorded them popular status and aesthetic relevance in the multiple places and the discontinuous timelines of their dissemination across oceans and continents. Musical gestures aside, economics and markets were surely factors, but these urban musical fashions were ultimately shaped by human engagements and disengagements, by performers, directors, and audiences, who were the social actors holding together the sonic miscellanea of the turn-of-the-century city.

In that regard, the story of Ywonna's transformation of her cabaret into a café-concert in Rio de Janeiro does not end with a hit parade of the songs that were simultaneously popular in many contemporary cities. On August 2, 1896, while still in her old cabaret, she announced the performance of a *cançoneta* (song in Portuguese) with verses alluding to Brazil that she had written herself and that was set to music excerpted from a contemporary musical review called *Pão, pão, queijo, queijo* (1896). The review was written by Orlando Teixeira and had music by Demetrio de Toledo, two local artists and bohemians who wrote several musical reviews presented in 1896 and 1897.[38] Local critics disparaged the review for being nothing but an audience pleaser, a work "filled with fandangos and *maxixes*,"[39] a moralizing rhetoric aimed to dismiss a gamut of songs and dances constructed over marked rhythms, off-beat accentuations, and syncopations and that enticed *risqué* performances driven by a male gaze over sexualized female bodies, and mostly Black female bodies. Ywonna's decision to please her audiences in this way reveals her attempt to form close relationships with honorable members of the local, White male bohemia and to belong to, and eventually

---

[37] Derek Scott, "British Musical Comedy in the 1890s: Modernity without Modernism," Keynote paper presented at the biennial Music in Nineteenth-Century Britain conference, University of Birmingham, June 28–30, 2017; online publication, 30.

[38] Artur Azevedo, "Chonical Theatral," in *Diário de Notícia*, October 29, 1896, July 29, 1907, August 5 and 12, 1897, November 12, 1897, and November 10, 1904. For information on the authors of the review, see Antonio Sousa Bastos, *Carteira do artista: Apontamentos para a história do theatro portuguez* (Lisbon: J. Bastos, 1899), 596. The announcement for performance appears in *O Paiz*, August 2, 1896.

[39] A review of the work appeared in *Correio Paulistano*, September 11, 1897.

have a voice in, the local sociocultural milieu. Ywonna and many artists like her played a cunning role in the shaping of Rio de Janeiro's urban musical fashions, and it was in performing venues like hers that one can observe the intersections between a city with external cultural connections and a city with an internal cultural network of its own. By observing and listening to musics performed at her venue, we can refine our understanding of Rio de Janeiro's urban musics and identify which cultural contexts embedded them with social relevance and aesthetic meaning. We can also reconsider the contextualization of a local repertory as unique and suitable for nation-building and, instead, start reckoning with a musical repertory that was contingent on and a part of an already successful formula being built, concomitantly, elsewhere.

Duque recalls, for example, that in addition to her beloved cabaret chansons, Ywonna regularly performed the *cançoneta* "A casa branca da serra," which she sang in Portuguese and by heart, with a poem by the bohemian Guimarães Passos (1867–1909) and music by J. C. de Oliveira (Musical Example 6.1).[40] Passos had come to Rio de Janeiro from the northeastern state of Alagoas, making it into the capital's literary circles alongside other self-declared bohemians, including Bilac, Paula Ney, Coelho Neto, José do Patrocínio, and Luis Murat. A political activist, Passos participated in the insurgency against military President Floriano Feixoto and had to self-exile in Buenos Aires in 1894 in fear of political persecution. When he returned to Rio de Janeiro in 1896, he found some of his old-time bohemian friends conniving with the status quo in cushy government jobs. Deceived and out of place, he found rescue in Ywonna's cabaret and began a connection to the singer that continued well after the venue was closed.[41] Passos became a regular at Ywonna's venues, where his song "A casa branca da serra" was consistently performed alongside Bruant's chansons and excerpts from Paquette's and Varney's operettas.

Written while in exile, the lyrics of "A casa branca da serra" show Passos longing for a place away from the city, a refuge in the countryside on a *serra* (hill), where he could avoid governmental forces. Away from his country and disappointed by the path taken by republican politicians, Passos's white house on the hill became his imagined romanticized idyllic nation, as his pessimistic political views also reverted into nostalgia for a lost city. Like many contemporary *cançonetas* written by local authors, the music of "A casa branca da serra" was similar to chansons in their declamatory lyrics and subject matter, which

---

[40] Edmundo, *O Rio de Janeiro do meu tempo*, 169. Duque notes that Ywonna and Passos later traveled together to São Paulo. Although a few sources assign authorship of the music to Miguel Pestana, it is unlikely that Pestana was alive in 1896, when the work was sung in Ywonna's café-concert. For recordings of the song, see Marcelo Bonavides, "Estrelas que nunca se apagam" (online publication) https://www.marcelobonavides.com/2013/03/o-poeta-guimaraes-passos.html.

[41] Gonzaga Duque notes that Ywonna continued in contact with him after the cabaret in Rio de Janeiro was closed.

132 MUSIC AND COSMOPOLITANISM

Musical Example 6.1 "A casa branca da serra."
Source: Júlia de Brito Mendes, *Canções Populares do Brasil* (Rio de Janeiro: Livraria Cruz Coutinho, 1911)
Source: Universidade Federal de Santa Catarina, digital library

DIVERSIFYING 133

sometimes recreated dream-like places beyond the city.[42] Passos called his poem a *barcarolle* and Oliveira set the lyrics as an urban waltz-song. The melody, no less lyric than Plaquette's waltz-songs, worked in a typical 32-bar song structure and was more elaborate than the short two-melodic lines of Bruant's chansons that Ywonna had made popular in her cabaret. To perform "A casa branca da serra," she most likely had to leave her comfort zone not only in terms of language, but also in singing style, and venture into a lyrical waltz-song while using her female-baritone voice. Still, the melody of "A casa branca da serra" moved in conjunct motion and was shaped in the typical slowed-down version of a vocal ornament over one note, a familiar melodic device in many operatic arias and songs, first around G and then in similar melodic sequences, a format that helped the recitation of the lyrics and that propelled the strophic text setting of the long verses. The song could be managed without much vocal training if convincingly brought to life by a performance emphasizing the round movement of the waltz-song, a theatrical and cinematographic performance not dissimilar from Ywonna's version of "Berceuse bleue." Just like in the cabaret chanson, with the short tunes and strophic text settings, in the waltz-song "A casa branca da serra" Ywonna could bring Passos's verses to life by sounding them out in familiar ways. These general characteristics of lyrics, music, and performance do not bring to the fore any local specificity of works such as "A casa branca da serra." Apart from the Portuguese lyrics, not a single touch of so-called local color singles out the song from many others that circulated in Rio de Janeiro or in cities elsewhere. Passos's work was one among many contemporary songs that were published locally under the heading *cançoneta* and *modinha* and that were first transmitted orally through performance in entertainment venues such as Ywonna's before they eventually were published or recorded.

But "A casa branca da serra" did not immediately disappear amid a torrent of other contemporary songs, local or not, that came and went without leaving any vestige. It continued in the repertory for decades. In 1901, the lyrics were published in a compilation of Guimarães Passos's poems, *Horas Mortas*, and, in 1904, it was included in the songster *Trovador Brasileiro* by the publishing business Editora Quaresma, a company devoted to the publication of popular short stories, poems, and songsters in cheap formats to reach a wide range of readers.[43] A thriving business, the Editora Quaresma made the written discourse available to a wider

---

[42] For a 1907 recording of "A casa branca da serra" performed by João Barros (ca. 1888–?), see https://www.youtube.com/watch?v=-BD1d5bKH8A.

[43] The publication is mentioned by Luiz Edmundo in *O Rio de Janeiro do meu tempo*, 734–735. For an analysis of the compilations of songs of the period see Monica Leme, "Cancioneiros populares para Ioiôs e Iaiás: o mercado editorial para a 'música ligeira' no Rio de Janeiro (1870–1920), in *Vida divertida; histórias do lazer no Rio de Janeiro (1830–1930)* ed. Andrea Marzano and Victor Andrade de Melo (Rio de Janeiro: Apicuri, 2010), 179–209.

134 MUSIC AND COSMOPOLITANISM

population, also allowing leading narratives to be shaped by those outside elite circles, an endeavor that was made more successful when stories and poems were learned through and disseminated alongside songful and memorable melodies. "A casa branca da serra" was recorded in Rio de Janeiro several times, the earliest recording done in 1907 by João Barros and the latest in 1970 by singer Inezita Barroso. The song contextualizes the blurred borders and complex social dialogues taking place in the modern city in the first decade of the new century. For while some of these local songs are characterized as music of "the people," a general attribute that infers national ideologies, in reality they emerged in very flexible settings dominated by artists of many types and from many places. "A casa branca da serra" is a testament to the larger net of sociocultural connections that characterizes local songs, an example of the confluence and fluidity of written, oral, and aural traditions at the time when recordings started to become a part of music-making.[44]

Ywonna's enterprises in Rio de Janeiro were successful but short-lived. By December 1896, advertisements for her venue were no longer found in local newspapers. In March 1897, an unsigned short article announced that the Chat Noir would reopen in April, but that did not materialize.[45] Ywonna moved on with her career, traveling to the northern state of Pará, where she continued to perform with Amelia Barros, singing the chansons and *modinhas* that had made them popular in Rio de Janeiro. In 1897, local newspapers reported that Ywonna traveled to Paris to perform at the (Parisian) Eldorado and that she toured in Europe, Latin America, and the United States.[46] In January 1898, she was back in the Brazilian capital as part of the cast at the Theatro Lucinda, singing her already popular signature song "Ronda Infernale, Titania," and the *romanza* "Manon," advertised as being written specifically for her in Paris.[47] At the Theatro Lucinda, now directed by her long-time colleague Pepa Ruiz, Ywonna performed under the conductor Cavalier Darbilly (1846–1914), a composer, conductor, and music teacher at the Instituto Nacional de Música. On November 8, 1898, Ywonna appeared again in the capital with her own "company of *cançonetas*," which she presented at the Theatro Eudorado for a few nights.[48] There is no information about her whereabouts after that. Nonetheless, at the end of her venues' run, Ywonna had experimented with various formats of popular entertainment and had contributed to the shaping of Rio de Janeiro's turn-of-the-20th-century soundscape. Music venues like hers offer an alternative and dynamic way of understanding locality at an early globalizing moment and show how,

---

[44] The research of Martha Ulhôa in this regard is essential to the understanding of song and musical familiarity in the 19th century; see, in particular, her "'Perdão Emília! Transmissão oral e aural na canção popular," in *Palavra cantada: Ensaios sobre poesia, música, e voz*, ed. Cláudia Matos, Elizabeth Travassos, and Fernande de Medeiros (Rio de Janeiro: 7Letras, 2008), 249–267)

[45] *O Paiz*, March 18, 1897.

[46] *O Paiz*, November 11, 1897.

[47] *Gazeta de Notícias*, January 16 and 19, 1898.

[48] *O Paiz*, November 8, 1898.

DIVERSIFYING   135

in the growing turn-of-the-century city, local culture emerged from the lived experiences of many.

Music Halls

A few years after Ywonna disappeared from the local news, several enterprises followed in her footsteps. The Italian entrepreneur Paschoal Segreto (1868–1920) was the most successful, resourceful, and innovative.[49] With greater financial resources, he opened many theaters and *café-cantantes* (vaudevilles or music halls), although few survived more than two years without remodeling and restructuring. In December 1900, he announced the opening of a new and exuberant venue, the Moulin Rouge (Figure 6.1).[50] The critic of *O Paiz* reported on the new venue as follows:

> [with] [t]he opening of the Moulin Rouge in Rio de Janeiro one does not need to envy Paris in terms of café-concerts. The establishment by Paschoal Segretto includes all the modern amenities, it is elegant and comfortable, on par with the Parisian L' Ambassadeurs, La cigale, and Alcazar d'eté. The artists, constantly renewed, easily rival the cast at the Folies-Marigny and the Jardin de Paris, well-known establishments of Brazilians who visit the French capital. What else can the public expect while spending two or three pleasurable and leisurely hours, without the stresses of life? [at the Moulin Rouge] they [the public] have at their disposal a room with spectacles perfectly illuminated with electric light, a high number of ventilators which make amenable the high temperatures, a buffet with the drinks and snacks at modest prices and affordable to all, and a company of the first order which is renewed every day [and offer] the most celebrated novel artists? . . . In the coming days there will be important premieres at the Moulin Rouge of artists arriving directly from Europe and who already have an established career at the most important café-concertos in Paris.[51]

One of the most successful entertainment venues in the Brazilian capital at the beginning of the century, the Moulin Rouge was located at the old Theatro Variedades at the center of the city's bustling entertainment area. Segreto modernized the theater with electric lighting, luxurious boxes and stage props, ventilators to minimize heat, and a large section with tables where waiters would

---

[49] Segreto also had many theaters and music halls in São Paulo. For information on Segreto's activities in the Brazilian capital, see William de Souza Nunes Martins, "Paschoal Segreto: 'Ministro das diversões' do Rio de Janeiro (1883–1920)," PhD dissertation, Universidade Federal do Rio de Janeiro, 2004.

[50] *Jornal do Commercio*, December 22, 1900.

[51] *O Paiz*, February 4, 1901.

136 MUSIC AND COSMOPOLITANISM

Figure 6.1. Moulin Rouge.
O Paiz, July 25, 1901.
Source: Biblioteca Nacional, Rio de Janeiro, Hemeroteca Digital

bring food and drinks. He also added a terrace, a ferris wheel to entertain families, and a giant mill at the entrance to emphasize the venue's Parisian inspiration. At times advertised as a *café-cantante* and sometimes as a music hall, in addition to music numbers it included jugglers, contortionists, pantomimes, magicians, and animal shows. The Moulin Rouge closed in November 1901 and was reopened in a new format in 1907, but on March 19, 1903, Segreto opened a larger and more stable venue, the Maison Moderne, which followed a similar format to the Moulin Rouge with a mix of theater, circus, an entertainment park, and the showing of short movie scenes (Figure 6.2). These venues and others like them came to have a prominent role in the musical and cultural shaping of the Brazilian capital.

Figure 6.2. Maison Moderne.
O Malho 2, no. 53, September 19, 1903.
Source: Biblioteca Nacional, Rio de Janeiro, Hemeroteca Digital

In his regular chronicle about the city's theatrical life, Artur Azevedo reported in January 1907:

> In 1906, 2,242 theatrical performances took place in Rio de Janeiro, 420 at the Maison Moderne (music hall), 414 at the Palace Théatre (music hall), 336 at the Theatro Carlos Gomes/Moulin Rouge (theater/music hall), 313 at the Recreio Dramatico, 224 at the Theatro Apollo, 203 at the Theatro Lucinda, 150 at the Theatro São José, 129 at the São Pedro de Alcantara, and 52 at the Theatro Lyrico.

Azevedo's statistics end with a somewhat somber tone, "The music hall always winning."[52] The number of presentations had not changed much from two years earlier in 1904, when the two large music halls in the city, Maison Moderne and Casino Nacional, had offered 417 and 405 presentations, respectively, way more than the average presentations at theaters, which ranged less than 200 a year each. One year before, in 1903, when Azevedo started counting music halls

---

[52] Artur Azevedo, "Chrônicas," *A Notícia*, January 10, 1907.

138 MUSIC AND COSMOPOLITANISM

presentations, he justified the decision because "they [music halls] are so deeply entrenched in the daily customs of *cariocas* that it is becoming impossible to separate *them* from *our* theaters [my italics]."[53] Azevedo thought that the city was not well endowed in terms of theaters proportionally to its population, which had grown considerably, while the number of theatrical presentations had declined from around 1,800 in 1895 to around 1,000 in 1904. In the meantime, venues like music halls had become more attractive, for they produced new shows almost every day and offered matinées, while in theaters a play, operetta, musical review, or opera would be repeated several times.[54] According to Azevedo, music hall managers better understood the local public, for they offered varied programs, a practice that came with physical and financial challenges but that paid off in the end, for music halls continued to attract a growing clientele in the city.[55]

Heterogeneous entertainment took an even more fluid path at these music halls. Since they offered food and drinks to accompany an expansive list of performative acts, they emphasized leisure more than active listening. Larger than middle-sized theaters and with a varied and expensive line-up of artists, announcements for the Moulin Rouge claimed to appeal to the city's "larger audiences," again a general term that nonetheless hinted at a socially inclusive crowd. But while venues like the Moulin Rouge and Maison Moderne actually displayed the heterogeneous social outlook that comprised the city's growing working and middle classes, their seating accommodations veered toward social stratification.[56] As in the city's theaters, there were different ticket prices for different seating areas in these halls, ranging from expensive boxes at the top end to open galleries for cheap tickets. Music halls guaranteed a place for all—socially, and ultimately also racially, segregated nonetheless.[57] Therefore, in these music halls the musical offerings were set for mass appeal, to attract a wide spectrum of the local population and to offer something for everyone, although some were more welcoming to women than others, regardless of the internal social stratification or musical offerings.[58] In the end, while social distinction in the operatic

[53] Artur Azevedo, "Chrônicas," *A Notícia*, January 7, 1904.
[54] Artur Azevedo, "Chrônicas," *A Notícia*, January 14, 1901.
[55] Artur Azevedo, "Chrônicas," *A Notícia*, January 14, 1904.
[56] Martins suggests that the Maison Moderne was geared toward a lower social scale; see his "Paschoal Segreto," 56.
[57] For the overall social inclusiveness and segregation in Parisian café concerts, see Charles Rearick, *The Pleasures of the Belle Èpoque: Entertainment and Festive in Turn-of-the-Century France* (New Haven, CT: Yale University Press, 1985), 83–115, and 264. For Mexico, see Maya Ramos Smith, *Teatro Musical y Danza en el México de la Belle Epoque (1867–1910)* (Mexico City: Universidad Autónoma Metropolitana y Grupo Editorial Gaceta, 1995). In London, the high number of music halls circa 1900, around 100 with one million tickets sold a week, could not compare with Rio de Janeiro; nonetheless, in the Brazilian capital, musical variety, language variety, and performance variety characterized the more cosmopolitan environment. See, for example, John Mullen, "Patriotic Palaces of Pleasure? The Popular Music Industry in 1900," *Civilisations* 13 (2014): 179.
[58] Mencarelli, "A voz e a partitura," 38. See also Olivier Bara, "Vedettes de la scène en tournée: Première mondialisation culturelle au XIXe siècle?," *Romantisme*, 163, no. 1 (2014): 41–52.

theater or the concert hall could be associated with a specific musical repertory, in these venues musical repertories were not an exclusive domain of a specific social group, even if they enjoyed the presentations from different locations in the hall. Moreover, the fluidity of genres, music styles, and performances marked the music at the music hall as fitting to a conception of spectacle that was perpetually in motion; while people moved freely within different sections of a large hall, each offering various entertainments concomitantly, the "music" of the music hall was far more varied than the static, well-defined "music-hall song." Like the café concerts, the sonic ambiance and musical styles offered here were set to accompany songs of many kinds, to appeal to many political factions, to be complicit with as well as challenging them, to be open to satire of many social norms, or to capture love in various ways. They were nonetheless devoted to a present in the making, one in which composers and performers, as well as audiences, conspired to shape the sonic knowingness of the city at a specific historic moment, and one in which a connection with places and peoples beyond the city became a defining characteristic of the sounding city. As Peter Bailey put it, the music hall offered "a sense of identity as a recognition of an earned return on experience, with a potency to both universalize and select out a common popular *cognoscenti* in a fluid and variously collective drama of self-affirmation that punctured official knowledge and preserved an independent popular voice."[59] Bailey explores the song as group experience in terms of lyrical content, rather than its musical characteristics, and refers to music halls in a specific city, London. But his suggestions of music halls as both shaping and emanating a "shared experience of an urbanized world" that needed to be "ignited anew at every performance"[60] can be useful here. The question remains: Which musics and whose performances served that purpose?

To offer music with wide appeal, the Moulin Rouge had an "orchestra of 15 musicians," a size on par with similar-size halls in other cities and which most probably included strings, flutes, horn, oboe, clarinet, trumpet, trombones, and percussion.[61] After the passing of Lindner, Segreto hired the composer and conductor Luis Moreira (1872–1920) to direct the ensemble,[62] a well-established composer and conductor who had worked on several of Artur Azevedo's most popular plays. Throughout the first decade of the new century, Moreira wrote

[59] Peter Bailey, "Conspiracies of Meaning: Music-Hall and the Knowningness of Popular Culture," *Past & Present* 144, no. 1 (1994): 144.

[60] Bailey, "Conspiracies of Meaning," 145.

[61] *O Paiz*, December 22, 1900. Usually, in larger, prestigious music halls the number of musicians were usually around 20–25, including the traditional string section, two flues, two horns, two oboes, two clarinets, bassoon, three trumpets, three trombones, and basic percussion. See Gutsche-Miller, "Pantomime-Ballet on the Music-Hall Stage," 340.

[62] *O Paiz*, February 8, 1901. For information on Luiz Moreira, see Arquivo Marcelo Benavides, online publication, https://www.marcelobonavides.com/2020/05/maestro-luiz-moreira-100-anos-de-saudade.html.

140 MUSIC AND COSMOPOLITANISM

music and collaborated with lyricists and performers in a variety of settings, from comic theater and café-concertos to early movies, and was responsible for assembling a musical repertory for these venues that could attract the expected large crowds. To that end, Moreira took advantage of the format of the music hall and vaudeville, with numbers loosely organized, without a connecting plot and, like in Ywonna's café-concert, he offered music and performances in a mélange of styles, including old and newer pieces by local and foreign authors, performed by local and foreign artists, a variety in tandem with similar venues in other growing cities.[63] The resulting musical heterogeneity was such that it precludes a clear-cut characterization of musical trends, although the music originating in the musical theater continued to have a marked presence in these halls. Live performance and listening continued as essential parts of the understanding of a musical work, but in the music hall a modernity in the making also allowed for interactions with many other modes of performances and listenings in a seamless connivance and eventual transition to new media, recording, and film.

What we understand today as "fashion," as something that is transient but clear-cut enough to be recognizable as such at a given time, did not apply to the music repertory presented in these venues. While some of the works performed here can be tracked down to their first presentations on European stages, in the Americas, or in Rio de Janeiro, others came and went without a clear path of their origins or trajectories; they did not form or rely on a "mainstream" and, as such, they offer another facet of the sounding city. Although clearly disguised within the familiar and relying on well-known musical formulas and musical gestures already tested in the comic theater and operettas, the musical offerings of the music hall did not seem to be, at first sight and hearing, disruptive or transgressive. Nonetheless, the choice of musical numbers reveals a conscious avoidance of musical consistency, uniformity, and ultimately sonic and performative coherence. As such, the fragmentary nature of repertories and musical performances in these venues became in themselves musical practices of social disruption through their "aesthetic of discontinuity," which Altman defines as a practice "whereby divergent sound experiences alternated within a single program."[64]

If in the city's music halls, sundry sonic and performative spectacles could be viewed as examples of the blatant connivence of music-making with commercialism and appeals to artificial visual spectacles, they were at the same time venues that challenged any attempt to evoke or establish a stable musical

---

[63] Conway notes this characteristic in early 20th-century Parisian café concerts and music halls, where "one could experience in a revue the tango, flamenco, Russian music, Neapolitan music, Hawaiian dancers, Spanish dancers and singers," see her, "Chanteuse in the city," 60.

[64] Rick Altman, *Silent Film Sound* (New York: Columbia University Press, 2004), 51. See also Georgina Born, "The Social and the Aesthetic," in *Improvisation and Social Aesthetics*, ed. Georgina Born, Eric Lewis, and Will Straw (Durham, NC: Duke University Press, 2017), 33–58.

canon precisely when such a canon was vital as an indication of potential profit, or as a precondition to the cultural politics of nation-building. Undoubtedly, the musical nation was not expected to be forged or to naturally emerge in these halls and, as such, their offerings incongruently netted patriotic displays and moralizing discourses with satire, social critique, and sexually risqué performances. In practice, their musical offerings managed to exist and grow beyond politics of music aesthetics, even if they were viewed with contempt by the contemporary status quo and by historians afterward. Furthermore, here a myriad of musics arriving from various cities in Europe and the Americas comfortably alternated with music produced in Rio de Janeiro, and the differences among them were hardly identifiable or relevant. The music hall was a Babel of musics and performances, where claims of a unified musical nation, or a definable Europe or America (North and South), were defeated at all levels, while the ideas of progress, musically and politically, were set aside in favor of a fleeting practice of presentness. In Rio de Janeiro's music halls, "Europe breaks out of Europe"[65] to become a multitude of places shared among a growing urban audience not enticed by homogeneity.

Advertisements for music halls offered "new artists every day"; thus there was a clear focus on the performer. The repertory was most likely the artists' choices, who performed by memory works transmitted orally without the guidance of a specific score: here Angel Rama's idea of the "Lettered City" was transformed into a performing city.[66] Moreover, a flowing unconnected sequence of songs and dances were only loosely associated, if at all, with a composer or an "original" musical work. Rather, they were the performers' domain and were sometimes nothing but a conduit for the display of their individual artistic creativity in performances. In the years before recordings became commonplace, performers had a pivotal role in the making of musical fashions and ultimately mediating the circulation of musics; their success on stage was the precondition for the sale of printed scores. Singers were also actors and actresses, and vice versa, their body language, vocal abilities, and vocal delivery underlined their musical presentness, as they worked with viewers and listeners to experiment with and eventually codify the urban musical modernity of the moment. Unapologetically tied to commercialism and artificial spectacularism, and betraying their bourgeoning context, performers in Rio de Janeiro's music halls were mostly free from the demands of the political status quo, while also enjoying a degree of autonomy from social constraints.

With an eclectic mix of musical options, in these venues *cançonetistas* (performers who sung in Portuguese) easily mingled with *chanteuses*

---

[65] Moretti, *Distant Reading*, 46.
[66] Rama, *The Lettered City*.

142 MUSIC AND COSMOPOLITANISM

(performers who sung in French), with lyric singers (performers devoted to operatic numbers, usually in Italian), eccentric singers (comic performers of many provenances), and Spanish singers and dancers. With the constant need to hire new performers, Rio de Janeiro's music halls were seminal in the continuation and strengthening of the North-South transatlantic artistic connection and, at the turn of the century, there was a distinct group of artists who traveled regularly in the circuit Paris–Madrid–Lisbon–Rio de Janeiro (and later also São Paulo)–Montevideo–Buenos Aires. Italian artists, already spread over many opera halls wherever work was available, were also regularly featured. A few performers from Germany and Eastern European countries mingled with Spanish, Portuguese, and French artists, but it is difficult to track their origins and whereabouts, while artists active in the United Kingdom and the United States started to become more visible in the first decade of the new century. In December 1900, the *café-cantante* Alcazar Parque advertised the hiring of "the Franco-Spanish singer Bleuette, who has great fame in Buenos-Aires and Montevideo; the illustrious chanteuse pleased in all spheres; one does not know what to applaud more, her eccentric *cançonetas* or the way in which she presents the Spanish repertory."[67] As was customary, the artist's actual nationality was not disclosed. On March 19, 1905, the Parque Fluminense advertised "French *chansonnier*, Spanish singers and dancers, a cosmopolitan tenor (singer who performed in several languages and styles)," who appeared alongside "Brazilian *cançonetistas*."[68] To offer the best performances at his Moulin Rouge, Segreto claimed to have signed artists directly from the L'Ambassadeur in Paris, the Casino theater in Buenos Aires, and the Oriental in Montevideo. In the first months of the Moulin Rouge in 1901, the main success was the singer and dancer Carmencita (Carmen Dauset Moreno, 1868–1910?) (Figure 6.3), who started her career in Spain, performed her staged Spanish-ness in Paris, before moving to the United States to become a sensation in the vaudeville circuit and then appearing on the stages of Rio de Janeiro.[69]

The heterogeneous nature of offerings in Rio de Janeiro's music halls also shows that, alongside the varied provenance of artists, language variety in songs was more the rule than the exception; songs in Portuguese competed for space and audiences' interest on equal grounds with songs in French, Italian, Spanish, and English. The music hall was a Babel of languages as well as a Babel

---

[67] *Jornal do Commercio*, December 5, 1900.
[68] *Jornal do Commercio*, March 19, 1905.
[69] For information on Carmencita's career, see Michael Christoforidis and Elizabeth Kertesz, *Carmen and the Staging of Spain: Recasting Bizet's Opera in the Belle Epoque* (Oxford and New York: Oxford University Press, 2019, Kindle), in particular see chapter 6, "Transatlantic Carmens in Dance and Drama"; see also Kiko Mora, "Carmencita on the Road: Baile español y vaudeville en los Estados Unidos de América (1889–1895)," *Lumière* (2011), online publication, available at https://www.academia.edu/2452568/Carmencita_on_the_Road_Baile_espa%C3%B1ol_y_vaudeville_en_los_Estados_Unidos_de_Am%C3%A9rica_1889_1895.

DIVERSIFYING 143

Figure 6.3. Carmencita.
Source: New York Public Library.

of musics: the music-hall performer belonged to Rio de Janeiro, but could as well belong to Buenos Aires, Montevideo, Madrid, Paris, Lisbon, and so on, as similar venues in many contemporary cities also featured such a miscellaneous of musics, languages, and performance styles. In that regard, the song offerings in the music halls did not stray from the tendencies in Rio de Janeiro upscale concert halls or opera houses, as composers like Miguez and Nepomuceno were among several who wrote and performed both songs and larger works in several languages (see Chapter 11). That was also the case in other theaters where plays, operettas, reviews, and comic acts were regularly presented. According

144   MUSIC AND COSMOPOLITANISM

to an article in the magazine *Fon-Fon*, the major attraction in Rio de Janeiro's music halls in 1907 was the singer/performer Juanita Many, who "sang in many languages, Italian, Spanish, French, and Portuguese."[70] On December 7, 1908, she appeared at the Theatro Recreio Dramático show in benefit of comic actor Brandão, performing "beautiful *cançonetas* em Portuguese, Spanish, French, Italian, German, and English."[71] Like in the concert hall and operatic theaters, in the music hall setting the performer's nationality did not necessarily mean that they would be singing in their country's "natural" language. In fact, Spanish had become so commonplace in some stages in Rio de Janeiro that actors sometimes stressed, apparently to their advantage, that they could "speak Spanish perfectly . . . the language most akin to Portuguese,"[72] even though it is not clear that such a claim revealed the performer's nationality. Studying the circulation of Gran Opera in Europe, Jens Hesselager has suggested that one should question "the idea that the choice of vernacular language would always present itself as self-evident. . . . The preferred language for opera was not necessarily the first language of the majority of the audience."[73] In theaters in Madrid, Paris, Lisbon, and elsewhere, it was common practice for singers and dancers to "Frenchify," or "Spanishfy" their names depending on the targeted performance style and audience expectations, a practice also common with opera singers who would change their names to look and sound like Italian names and thus appear to be more "authentic."[74] In several cases, Spanish, French, Italian, and Brazilian artists wrote and performed songs in many languages, or in a mix of languages.[75] João do Rio best describes satirically this aspect of the music hall in his chronicle "Gente de Music Hall" (People of Music Hall) where he tells a fictitious story about a Count Sabiani and a Baron Belford who fell in love with a Black "oriental" dancer called Princess Verônica:

> "'Per Dio! Quelle femme, mon petit!' exclaimed the Baron . . . but she is black, shouted the Count, [but] from Jamaica, daughter of an Indian King. . . . After

---

[70] *Fon-Fon* 1, no. 14, July 13, 1907.

[71] *O Paiz*, December 7, 1908. Juanita Many was most probably from Spain, as she played a role in the Spanish version of *The Merry Widow* in Rio de Janeiro (see Chapter 8).

[72] Erminia Silva cites this trend in relation to performances at the circus, but considering that circus acts were also a part of the music hall, one can expect the same practice in the Moulin Rouge; see her *Circo-Teatro: Benjamin de Oliveira e a teatralidade circence no Brasil* (São Paulo: Altana, 2007), 212.

[73] Jens Hesselager, "Introduction," in *Grand Opera Outside Paris: Opera on the Move in Nineteenth-Century Europe*, ed. Jens Hesselager (New York and London: Routledge, 2018), 6. Also in the same volume, Laura Moechli, "Parisian Grand Opera at the Basel Theatre auf dem Blömlein: Traces of Transnational Circulation, Translation and Reception," 13–30, see 27–28.

[74] Carlos Maria Solare, "Meyerbeer on the Zarzuela Atage: El dúo 'La Africana' by Manuel Feernández Caballero," in *Grand Opera Outside Paris: Opera on the Move in Nineteenth-Century Europe*, ed. Jens Hesselager (New York and London: Routledge, 2018), 202.

[75] Christoforidis and Kertesz, *Carmen and the Staging of Spain*, 237–242.

the performance the Count went to meet Verônica at her dressing room and knocked at the door: "'*Go in*' she replied, '*Malheureuse. I'm malheureuse. . . .*' And [the Baron realized that] Princess Verônica spoke all European languages, in a naive and terrible confusion."[76]

While in literary realms of the status quo discussions about "proper" use of the Portuguese language started to mold associations between the language and nation-building,[77] in music halls a wide range of song styles in various languages, performed by artists from a range of nationalities, actually muddled attempts to link music and language with national identity or nationality. Furthermore, the emulation of Parisian venues was here a subterfuge, since it was common for Spanish and French singers to be fluent in both languages, as the Parisian fascination for Spain's southern culture opened up a range of jobs for these artists not only in Paris or Spain, but also in many cities across the Atlantic.[78] In music halls, performers did not only mix and match a variety of song and dance styles, but they also had to overcome language barriers to the point that fluency in several idioms became a coveted skill. The Portuguese theater director Sousa Bastos commented ironically that, considering the multilingualism in Lisbon's theaters, he could predict that one day artists would also sing "in ox tongue."[79] In 1910 Buenos Aires, 97 dramas were performed in Spanish in front of an audience of over a million, in addition to 414 performed in Italian and 119 in French to an audience of 581,000 and 328,000 respectively.[80] In this case, the idea of authenticity in style and an expected musical and textual language association with it were gimmicks used to open up job opportunities in many places to those performers who spoke several languages and performed in a variety of styles. If a large section of urban audiences attending theaters or music halls could not understand the lyrical content of all the songs they heard on a regular basis, it was the role of the performer to (re)create a song through performance, as their body movements would assist in communicating the meaning of the text and eventually shape its musical associations. A love song in any language, for example, would be understood as such, or better, heard and seen as such, provided that the performer could make it so through performance, vocal dexterity, and body movements. Artists and singers who toured constantly had to be knowledgeable in many languages and, if language was a hurdle, their gestures were

[76] João do Rio, "Gente de Music Hall," in *Cinematógrapho* (Rio de Janeiro, ABL, 2009 [1908]) 7–13.
[77] Maria Cecilia Zanon, "Fon-Fon! Um registro da vida mundana no Rio de Janeiro da Belle Époque," *Patrimônio e História* 1, no. 2 (2005): 18–30.
[78] Christoforidis and Kertesz, *Carmen and the Staging of Spain*, 237–242.
[79] Silva, *Entertaining Lisbon*, 80.
[80] Jacobo Diego, "El teatro: El gauchesco y el sainte," in *Buenos Aires: História de cuatro siglos*, ed. Luis José Romero and Luis Alberto Romero (Buenos Aires: Editorial Abril,1983), 143–153, cited in Bergero, *Intersecting Tango*, 77.

146 MUSIC AND COSMOPOLITANISM

added to experimentations with vocal quality and timbre to assist in conveying meaning to a varied audience regardless of language.[81] Evelien Jonckheere notes that in Dutch music halls the high number of foreigners in the audience favored the presentation of songs in many languages, and that it was the performer who conveyed the song's meaning. She argues that "bodies, as opposed to words, spoke a universal language," since "body language was easy to understand by many, foreigners or not." Thus, she suggests that in music halls and café-concerts a "search for [national] identities is something carried out in vain."[82] In this Babel of languages, song and dance in a myriad of styles multiplied, while their provenance and initial mode of existence, recreated in ephemeral performances, now loomed in the imaginations of audiences in cities across continents.

Rio de Janeiro's music halls were thus part of a larger trend in which many urban stories were shared through songs, regardless of style, language, and provenance of performing actors and singers. These performances were unique not because they were set in a specific place or because they aimed at or managed to consolidate feelings of locality, but because they were created at the moment and their transient natures were set to shape the ever-changing context of the cosmopolitan city's present. Referring to performances in vaudeville and musical reviews in New York City theaters, Mary Simonson reminds us to explore how performances were "flexible and circulating, less owned than enacted, existing not on paper but on stage, deeply influenced by that which came before, and that which circulated alongside." She notes that this practice was particularly noticeable among female performers, who "regularly mimicked, borrowed from, and referenced fellow performers, existing works, performance styles, and aesthetic modes across genre and medial boundaries."[83] These female performers were crucial, defining nodes in the complex cultural and musical network of the turn-of-the-century cosmopolitan city. While written chronicles, images, and buildings froze time and sociopolitical contexts and, as such, assisted in the building of history, performances and the association of musical creation with physicality were lost in the shadows of history, if alive in the reports and perception of a few. But while reconstituting performances might distance us from the historical objectivity usually assigned to written texts, these performers' activities, choices, and the contexts in which they operated can help us consider how,

---

[81] Bara, "Vedettes de la scène en tournée," 51. On the complex cultural relationship between gestures, voice, and language, see Christopher Small's *Musicking: The Meanings of Performing and Listening* (Middletown, CT: Wesleyan University Press, 1998), in particular the chapter "The Language of Gesture," 50–63.

[82] Evelien Jonckheere, "In Search of Identities: 'Foreigner' in Fin-de-Siècle Belgian Café-Concerts," *Journal of Audiences and Reception Studies* 16, no. 2 (November 2019): 394.

[83] Mary Simonson, *Body Knowledge: Performance, Intermediality, and American Entertainment at the Turn of the Twentieth Century* (New York and Oxford: Oxford University Press, 2013), 15. See also Alan Gevinson, "The Origins of Vaudeville: Aesthetic Power, Disquietude, and Cosmopolitanism in the Quest for an American Music Hall," PhD dissertation, Johns Hopkins University, 2007.

DIVERSIFYING   147

with singing and movement, they helped shape the fleeting and fragmentary nature of urban modernity, one that was local but connected to a world in constant movement.

Singing and Dancing

At the end of 1901, Artur Azevedo seems to have come to terms with the marked role that *café-cantantes* and music halls started to play in the city's culture. Rather than raging a war against the popular venues, he suggests a compromise:

> The theater today in Rio de Janeiro has a *serious enemy* [my emphasis]: the *café-cantante*. But one should not respond with aggression or falsity, but simply with work, [one needs] to offer the public good shows that also entertain them. A few nights ago, I was for the first time at the Cassino Nacional [music hall] and attested that the public is entertained there thanks to the variety of attractions offered by the company, from Parisian *cançonetas* (chansons) to gymnasts and the *cinematógrapho* (movies). Thus, one should not argue or combat this or any other establishment of this type, but work for the theater to continue alive, despite such a dangerous competitor, and this is at the mercy of the impresarios and artists. Rio de Janeiro has such a large population that it can supply audiences for all kinds of performances. The tricky thing is to know how one should attract [the audience] and, above all, not to deceive them.[84]

If Azevedo saw music halls as an adversary of the "educated theater," he also did not disagreed with Hubert Parry who, addressing the Folk Song Society in London in 1889, warned his audience that "there is an *enemy* at the door of folk music which is driving it out, namely, the common popular [music hall] songs of the day; and this enemy is one of the most repulsive and most insidious."[85] To these critics, music halls were set to derail both the traditions of the "people" and those of the "elite."

Oblivious to such enemy forces, however, Segreto and other music hall directors knew exactly how to attract to their venues varied audiences from all social standings, but they were not concerned with potential audience deception and were ready to experiment. To that end, following trends already proven successful elsewhere, they added songs and dances written and performed locally to enrich the heterogenous and cosmopolitan sonic environment of their

---

[84]   Artur Azevedo, "O Theatro," in *A Notícia*, December 26, 1901.

[85]   Cited in John Storey, *Inventing Popular Culture: From Folklore to Globalization* (Oxford: Wiley-Blackwell, 2003, Kindle).

148 MUSIC AND COSMOPOLITANISM

café-cantantes. Written in Portuguese, but sometimes also in Italian, French, Spanish, and English, these forged "local" songs and dances were performed by artists from a wide range of nationalities and abilities. Performers often appealed to the city's residents' nostalgia for an imagined, lost country life by evoking an "authentic local" in songs and dances believed to have originated in remote regions by the mythical "folk," but which were in fact written for the city's audiences, a realization that led Parry to alert his audiences. These songs helped shape stereotypical characterizations of rural "Otherness" as mythical, as well as inferior, through contrasts with the city as real, modern, and superior. Often songs suggested the countryside not only of Brazil but of other countries, which were equally effective at evoking rural nostalgia in the cosmopolitan city. Performers were at home with articulations of Otherness of many kinds, as directors quickly grasped the market value of stereotyping. In cities along the routes traveled by performers who took part in Rio de Janeiro's thriving theatrical and musical scene, caricatures and satires of non-White individuals, and mostly of females, appeared regularly alongside comic skits with musical numbers that dealt with many more Others. At a time when the world was perceived to be larger than the local and when the city provided the arena for encounters and clashes among people with a variety of histories, backgrounds, races, and genders, urban stages had unsettled and fluid internal borders, which were not delimited by familiar dualities of local versus foreign, high versus low, and so on. Rather they reflected on, overcame, or furthered amplified the anxieties generated by the porous social, gender, and racial borders of the growing turn-of-the-century city. That was particularly true in Rio de Janeiro after the abolition of slavery in 1888, when a large number of freed Blacks migrated to the city, considerably adding to its already large Black population and challenging the positivistic understanding of civilization and progress of the political status quo and their imagined White republican nation. But like many other musical trends that permeated entertainment venues in the Brazilian capital, race and gender articulations through music and performance were not formulated solely from within, nor were they solely relevant to Rio de Janeiro's context. Rather, they became a conspicuous part of the turn-of-the-20th-century cosmopolitan city and operated within urban cultural networks that looked both at the past and at the future, and that reached far and wide.

The January 19, 1900, announcement for presentations at the music hall Jardim do Guarda Velha, for example, included the usual long list of singers with Portuguese-, Italian-, French-, and Spanish-sounding names performing arias, chansons, *cançonetas*, but also *lundus*; the latter were stylized versions of African-derived song-dances for the parlor and the theater in Portuguese, mostly in duple meter (or combinations of duple/triple meters), the majority of which had lyrics dealing with romance and sex, and which in turn were presented theatrically with gender and racial innuendoes, in both text and choreography, and eventually also through musical gestures. The *lundus* in this particular 1900 music hall advertisement referred to two song-dances: "As laranjas da Sabina" (1890), with music by Francisco Carvalho and lyrics by Artur Azevedo, and "O mugunzá" (1892), music by Francisco Carvalho and lyrics by Bernardo Lisboa.[86] Described in the music score not as *lundus*, but as *fadinho* (small *fado*, a melancholic song or a dance-song from Lisbon) and *canção brasileira* (Brazilian song), respectively, both works were written for musical reviews and presented amid several burlesque numbers, in keeping with the heterogeneous and comic nature of the genre. Both were song-dance concoctions stereotypically enacting in performance Black women as both comic characters and as sexually desirable "dancing mulattas," who eventually became a recurring element within a larger set of stereotypical comic characters that routinely passed through the *fin-de-siècle* city's stages.

"As laranjas da Sabina" was first inserted in Artur Azevedo's musical review *A república* and premiered on March 26, 1890, at Theatro Variedades. As was characteristic of the musical review format, Artur Azevedo's *A república* was an assemblage of short snippets overlapping luxurious mise-en-scène, pantomime, burlesque, varied song numbers, and miscellaneous dancing and acting. The work commented on the main events of the previous year, including the proclamation of the Republic, and thus Azevedo had plenty of material to work with. He provided an allegory to the Republic as a larger political concept, as well as a satire of its implementation in Brazil. The work was divided into *quadros* (sections); each with several numbers, described as: (1) Brazil and the Republic; (2) Liberty illuminating the world; (3) Domestic scenes; (4) Alfandega (customs) Street; (5) Gold; (6) Cosmorama; (7) The Press; (8) Fire!; (9) Book-Maker Bank; (10) The Beer; (11) The Chileans; (12) Baltazar's Festim; and (13) *A república*. According to contemporary critics, *A república* had luxurious stage sets and opened with the scene "The Americas," with a large painted background as a visual allusion to places in the Americas, including an elaborate set describing the New York harbor and a scene from Santo Domingo, Haiti. The extended musical sections, compiled, arranged, and composed by Lindner, opened with a luxurious introductory number, "Grande chorus das nações americanas" (Grand Chorus of the American Nations), which Lindner set to familiar Lecocq's music; a "Choir and tango of Saint Domingo, Haiti," which Lindner set to the music by zarzuela composer Manuel Fernández Caballero (1835–1906); the scene concluded with Francisco Manuel da Silva's national anthem followed by

---

[86] *Jornal do Commercio*, January 19, 1900. For a contextual interpretation of the song "As laranjas da Sabina," see Micol Seigel and Tiago de Melo Gomes, "Sabina das Laranjas: Gênero, raça, e nação na trajetória de um símbolo popular, 1889–1930," *Revista Brasileira de História* 22, no. 43 (2002): 171–193.

150 MUSIC AND COSMOPOLITANISM

the U.S. national anthem.[87] Among the many scenes and musical numbers that followed, there was: a duet symbolizing connections between the Republic and Brazil, again set to music by Lecocq; a "tercetino dos *Chins* (Chinese)," a satire on the political discussions about Asian immigration with music by Simões Junior; a tango of the Black Guard (society), with music by Abdon Milanez (1858–1927) and commenting on the society made up by freed Blacks and abolitionists who supported Princess Isabel's work on the abolition of slavery; duets and choruses with musics by Varney, another sure hit, and by the Spanish zarzuela composers Chueca (1846–1907) and Valverde (1845–1910), most probably from *Gran via*; one aria from the opera *Lo Schiavo* (1889) by Carlos Gomes; an excerpt from an Offenbach operetta, one from zarzuela composer Francisco Asenjo Barbieri (1823–1894); and original pieces written by Lindner specifically for the review. *A república* concluded with an apotheosis to the Republic with Francisco Braga's "Anthem to the Republic" in the background, a work that had lost the competition for national anthem to Leopoldo Miguez (see Chapter 3), but which helped bring the musical status quo into the comic theater. The "Fadinho da Sabina" was thus inserted in this miscellanea of songs and dances from a variety of sources, styles, and provenances and Lindner hired an equally diverse cast to perform them: the French singer Rose Villiot (1850–1908), very popular in Rio de Janeiro's theaters in the 1880s, the actor José Gonçalves Leonardo, and the Greek-born soprano settled in Rio de Janeiro, Ana Manarezzi (1864–1903), who performed the "Fadinho da Sabina."

The lyrics for "As laranjas da Sabina" referred to a true event that took place in 1889, when a Black woman selling oranges in Rio de Janeiro's streets got caught in the middle of a political rift between White male student protesters and the government. While the song was one among several in the review's assemblage of topics, performers, composers, musical styles, and images, the "fadinho" was retained in the local repertory of *café-cantantes,* where it was repeated, rearranged, re-enacted in a myriad of performances year after year. The song was further disseminated in sheet music publications and in many recordings in the first decades of the century. In 1900, 10 years after its first performance in Azevedo's review, both lyrics and music were included in the songster *O Cancioneiro Fuminense* (1900), compiled by folklorist, poet, and historian Mello Moraes Filho (1844–1919), who understood the song as part of the local tradition of the people, as an urban folk tradition. The publication nonetheless comprised a miscellany of old and recent works, with music and poetry by various authors with different backgrounds, such as the poets Gonçalves Dias (1823–1864) and Castro Alves (1847–1871), Artur Azevedo, Xisto Bahia (1841–1894), among many others. The collection also featured a variety of musical

---

[87] *Gazeta de Notícias,* March 26, 1890.

DIVERSIFYING   151

styles appearing under a myriad of denominations, such as *modinha, canção, cançoneta, baile pastoril, lundu, balada, romanza, noturno, recitativo, serenata, scena comica, among others*. Thus, it was in a multifaceted theatrical genre like a musical review, in a musical, linguistic, and performative heterogeneous context of the music hall, and in a sundry publication like *O Cancioneiro Fuminense* that "As laranjas da Sabina" was retained in the local musical repertory, contexts that were far from uniform, stylistically, geographically, or historically.

The "Canção brasileira, O mugunzá" was written for Lisbon rather than for Rio de Janeiro as part of the music review *Tim tim por tim tim*, by the Portuguese playwright Sousa Bastos (1844–1911), and first staged in March 1889, at the Theatro da Rua dos Condes in Lisbon. "O mugunzá" was also one in a series of songs and short sections making up the usual musical review structure that included political satire and comic commentary of social situations and characters from daily life in Lisbon. *Tim tim por tim tim*'s plot opens with made-up allusions to Greek mythology, where Telêmaco escapes Calypso's seduction and leaves behind her exploits of sex, food, and her supply of "washed and ironed clothes," to arrive in Lisbon and engage in the city's daily life, walking through its real and imagined spaces. Among the review's many disparate sections, there are scenes about the changes in seasons; a scene about a female *toreadora* (bull fighter), followed by a scene about the Carnival, in which the *toreadora* dances a tango. After a "Choir of the literati," who "learned enough French to translate Dumas, Victor Hugo, and Sardou," there is a "Choir and *coplas* of food seasonings," featured as dramatic characters, olive oil, vinegar, clove, parsley, olives, pepper, salt, mustard, all with innuendos linking food to sex, since "we need to enjoy them, in the kitchen or in love." Such a miscellaneous grouping is followed by a *mandolinata* (a Portuguese string ensemble); a *canção francesa* (French song); a *canção hespanhola* (Spanish song); Portuguese *modinhas*, and the *canção brasileira* (Brazilian song) "O mungunzá," followed by a "Spanish Choir Cádiz," and a "Tango de Lola," which included a chorus in Spanish praising the Spanish woman, "Muchacha, Que viva la gracia!"[88] The scene of the food seasonings involved songs and dances performed by the review's star, the actress and singer Pepa Ruiz (Figure 6.4), who quickly changed outfits to appear on stage dressed as different foods in a fast skit, a challenging theatrical transformation that recalled Frégoli's acts and Ywonna's cabaret characters (see Chapter 5), and a trick that would become part of many musical reviews well into the first decade of the 20th century.[89] Sousa Bastos advertised that Ruiz would appear as 18 different

[88] The text here was from the 1898 publication *Tim tim por tim tim, coplas, fados, coros, e tangos* (Lisbon: Libanio & Cunha, 1898), available at the University of Pennsylvania library.
[89] The music review *Cá e lá* (1904), included three actresses constantly changing roles, Cinira Polonio, Aurélia Delorme, and Pepa Delgado.

Figure 6.4. Pepa Ruiz.
http://www.culturaniteroi.com.br/blog/municipal/2251.
Source: Cultura Niteroi, Teatro Municipal de Niteroi

characters in the review, a trick that became a performative hallmark of her career.

Tim tim por tim tim opened in Rio de Janeiro in 1892 and remained one of the city's most popular works in the genre for over a decade, helping shape Ruiz's successful career as a performer and as a powerful theatrical director in the Brazilian capital at the beginning of the new century. As was customary in musical reviews, to remain relevant over time the topics and musical numbers were changed, and new ones were added to fit new events and situations. *Tim tim por tim tim* was modified only a year after it premiered and, by the time it reached Rio de Janeiro in 1892, it had been updated a few times.[90] Thus, by the time Bastos staged *Tim tim por tim tim* in the Brazilian capital and made the "*Canção brasileira,* O mugunzá"

---

[90]. Alberto Ferreira da Rocha Junior, "Quando o cômico atravessa o oceano: o *Tim tim por tim tim* no Brasil," in *Ensaios sobre of humor Luso-Hispânico*, ed. by Laura Areias and Luís Pinheiro (Lisbon: LusoSofia Press, 2013), 353–371.

a popular "local" song, the fadinho "As laranjas da sabina" was already a local success. Bastos bet on Ruiz's reshaping her performance of "O mugunzá" enough to become a competitor to Manarezzi's performance of "As laranjas da sabina," as both actresses appeared on the stage singing and dancing in typical Bahiana outfits, with turbans, lace shirts and long rounded skirts, multicolored beaded necklaces, bracelets, and earrings (Figure 6.5).[91] Manarezzi's and Ruiz's Bahiana performances were predated in Rio de Janeiro by Aurélia Delorme's, an actress and singer born in Brazil from Spanish parents, who was well known in Rio de Janeiro's stages and had also performed with Ywonna. Delorme had appeared as a stage Bahiana, singing and dancing the *lundu* "Moqueca sinhá," in the music review *O Bendengó* (1889) by Oscar Pederneiras e Figueireido Coimbra.

On the stages of Rio de Janeiro, the Bahiana was a stereotypical impersonation of Black women who worked for a living selling food and artifacts in the street. At the same time, she was presented on the stage not as a resident of the city, but as a woman coming from the northeastern state of Bahia, where the population retained various forms of African-derived cultures after centuries of slavery. On the stage, rough and uncivilized, the Bahiana waited to be civilized in the name of urban progress, enough so to belong in the modern White city. Performed as an imagined Other woman originating "there," somewhere else, the stage Bahiana's success relied on the possession of assumed African cultures' residues, depicted in Rio de Janeiro's stages as authentic local African-ness. It was a romanticized and essentialized staged persona who was also expected to invoke cultural roots tailored for city audiences. As such, the stage Bahiana outfits for musical reviews and *café-cantantes* were entrusted to a group of Black women led by the popular Tia Ciata, who had migrated from Bahia and resided in the Rio de Janeiro neighborhood of Cidade Nova, one of several neighborhoods where Blacks, European immigrants, and rural migrants congregated in search of affordable housing. Ciata held parties with music and dancing of various styles and welcomed people of many races and social backgrounds, in addition to keeping alive in Rio de Janeiro African-derived religious and secular traditions she had learned and inherited in Bahia. As a Black woman from Bahia, Ciata's involvement in the creation of luxurious Bahiana outfits specially designed for the stage added considerable veracity to the stage Bahiana character.[92] Whether her participation in the forging of the stage Bahiana points to her empowerment or submission justified

---

[91] Bahiana literally means a woman from the state of Bahia in the northeastern coast of Brazil. In these stage performances, however, it referred specifically to Black women who dressed in attires used in African traditions retained in the state of Bahia, and who dressed in such attire to sell food in the streets in Bahia and Rio de Janeiro.

[92] Maria Clementina Pereira Cunha, *Ecos da folia: Uma história social do carnaval carioca entre 1880–1920* (São Paulo: Companhia das Letas, 2001), 217.

Figure 6.5. Cover of "O mungunzá" with photo of Pepa Ruiz.
Source: Biblioteca Nacional, Rio de Janeiro, Acervo Digital

by financial gains, her position in the forging of the stage Bahiana was certainly not a neutral one.

Despite the links between localness and African roots, the Bahiana was not presented on the stage as a Black character, but as a mulatta, a mixed-race woman whose racialized persona fit well with ideologies of a racially hybrid nation on its way to becoming White. Most importantly, the stage Bahiana was not performed by Black or mulatta women, but by White actresses whose racialized and gendered performances served to further muddle racial boundaries on stage. While Pepa Ruiz apparently used makeup to darken her face in a female version of blackface, the other performers kept their white complexion on stage. It was not until the second decade of the new century that mixed-race and Black performers, male or female, were openly accepted and ventured onto Rio de Janeiro's main stages, although, according to several local chroniclers, many performed in less prestigious theaters. Black characters in plays were not usual before World War I, and when included as part of the dramatic action as servants, slaves, or comic characters, they were played mostly by White and mixed-race actors, with or without blackface.[93] When Black and mixed-race women made it to local stages, they had to fit in with the persona of the singing and dancing mulatta already established by White actresses, and within that context there was very little that they could do, at least at first, to build their own individual creativity and performative subjectivity. As Alison Kibler has argued in regard to similar practices in U.S. vaudeville stages, "white women's increasing use of racial masquerades indicates a freedom in performance choices that black performers were often denied."[94] Ruiz thus moved seamlessly from the leading role in Paquette's *Les cloches de Corneville* to a stage Bahiana, experimenting with the character as she engaged with racial transgressions on the stage to eventually become a most successful local characterization of the stage Bahiana, one that she and other performers replicated on the stages of European cities. In addition, Black and mixed-race singers were also not the ones whose voices were heard in the first recordings of songs featuring the stage Bahiana as a mulatta. The first recording of "As laranjas da Sabina" in 1902, for example, was done by a White male singer, Cadete; in 1905, it was recorded by Pepa Delgado (1887–1945) (Figure 6.6), a White actress born in Brazil from Spanish immigrants and who also regularly performed as a stage Bahiana; in 1906, the song was recorded by the singer Baiano (Manoel Pedro dos Santos); and in 1907, the singer Maria Lino (ca. 1876–1940), who had also performed with Ywonna, provided another version. Lino became a popular Bahiana in Rio

---

[93] For discussions of the role played by race and racism in Rio de Janeiro theaters, see César Braga-Pinto, "From Abolitionism to Blackface: The Vicissitudes of Uncle Tom in Brazil," in *Uncle Tom's Cabins: The Transnational History of America's Most Mutable Book*, ed. Tracy Davis and Stefka Mihaylova (Ann Arbor: University of Michigan Press, 2018), 225–257; Antonio Herculano Lopes, "Vem cá, mulata!" *Tempo* 13, no. 26 (2009), 80–100; Paulo Roberto de Almeida, "A presença negra no Teatro de Revista dos anos 1920," Master's thesis, Universidade Federal Fluminense, 2016; Cristina Rona, *Brazilian Bodies and Their Choreographies of Identification: Swing Nation* (New York: Palgrave MacMillan, 2015); and Silvia Cristina Martins de Souza. "Que venham negros à cena com maracas e tambores: Jongo, política e teatro musicado no Rio de Janeiro nas últimas décadas do século XIX," *Afro-Ásia* 40 (2009): 145–171.

[94] Alison Kibler, *Rank Ladies: Gender and Cultural Hierarchy in American Vaudeville* (Chapel Hill: University of North Carolina Press, 1999), 118.

Figure 6.6. Photo of Pepa Delgado in a Bahiana outfit.
Source: Marcelo Bonavides archive.

de Janeiro stages in the second decade of the 20th century and her career took off when she joined the singer and dancer Duque to perform the character in Paris with great success.[95]

Since these stage Bahianas were stereotypical characterizations of a Black woman from Bahia for Rio de Janeiro's male audiences, they appeared singing and dancing, moving their hips in sexually inviting ways, in a stylized stage version of African-derived dramatic dances widely performed both in rural areas and in Rio de Janeiro's neighborhoods. However, the stage Bahiana's moving hips, displaced from their original context in the traditional folk drama as a theatrical persona, became the focal source of her desire. Delorme repeated her act over and over through the years and became famous for over-exaggerating her

---

[95] See Lisa Shaw, *Tropical Travels: Brazilian Popular Performance, Transnational Encounters, and the Construction of Race* (Austin: University of Texas Press. Kindle).

hip movements.[96] Her colleague Pepa Delgado competed as a stage Bahiana and, according to a local chronicle, Delorme and Delgado would "duel one another in their hip movements, conflating the movements with their belly dances," as they "flaunted their opulent forms."[97]

The stage Bahiana as the singing and dancing mulatta was thus created in the comic theater setting and solidified in the heterogeneous environment of music halls to become a most desired urban female persona performing on Rio de Janeiro's stages. She was also a woman in possession of an imagined sexual power and social freedom that were coveted in secret by bourgeoisie White women. As such, the stage Bahiana was a woman of many gifts, who could sing and dance, as well as cook like no one else. She walked and danced while carrying food to sell, since in the street she worked for a living. Her racialized sexualization, built in opposition to the White bourgeoisie morals and social standing, aligned sex and food, invitation and desire, the forbidden and the exotic, the faraway and the nearby, all of which was summoned in her staged image, bodily movements, singing, and dancing. Expectedly, the stage Bahianas sung mostly about food: Delorme sung, "I am the land of vatapá" ("Eu sou a terra do vatapá" [fish stew]), Menarezzi guaranteed that "[White] students could not live without my oranges," and Ruiz's song lyrics offered a whole recipe for the *mungunzá* (a coconut grit). These White artists came to represent "Black women from Bahia" on the local stages many years before Carmen Miranda (1909–1955) internationalized the character in the United States in the 1940s, dancing and moving her hips while carrying fruit on her head.[98]

More celebrated than critically appraised, White actresses singing and dancing as stage Bahianas spoke for and helped perpetuate the local system of oppression and segregation based on race. As Jayna Brown eloquently argues, rather than a disinterested gendered alliance, these performances reveal the "white women's proprietary access to the black female body," since their articulations of musical localness were "feminized racial enactment . . . shaped by notions of the black female body's abilities, availability, and utility . . . [and] as a symbol for black female

---

[96] Delorme became a most acclaimed performer and dancer in Rio de Janeiro, enough so that a group of bohemian males published a short-lived magazine, *O Delormista*, which they defined as "an organization devoted to the *fluminense* (from Rio de Janeiro) theater and to the Delormist group."

[97] *Jornal do Commercio*, October 9, 1904; cited in Marcelo Benavides's blog, "Relembrando Pepa Delgado, 134 anos," online publication, https://www.marcelobonavides.com/2020/07/relembrando-pepa-delgado-134-anos.html.

[98] For Miranda's adoption of the Bahiana stage character and the cultural and racial implications for 20th century Brazil and the United States, see Kathryn Bishop-Sanchez, *Creating Carmen Miranda: Race, Camp, and Transnational Stardom* (Nashville, TN: Vanderbilt University Press, 2016). For the construction and use of the Bahiana stage outfit, see Léa Maria Schmitt Leal and Jose Luiz Ligiéro Coelho, "A presença da baiana na cena: Indumentária e performance (1890–1938)," *Pitágoras 500* 9, no 1 (2019): 47–59, online publication, available at https://periodicos.sbu.unicamp.br/ojs/index.php/pit500/article/view/8655501/20876.

158 MUSIC AND COSMOPOLITANISM

unruliness."[99] While the stage Bahianas played with responses to a "normative model of womanhood," they also made visible and audible their "unequal politics," which were extended into the city's cultural imagination as access to "sets of (often contradictory) imagined properties associated with blackness—spiritual, sexual, obedient, rebellious, strong, weak."[100]

Some chroniclers claimed that audiences could not only delight themselves in watching the stage Bahiana dancing, but that they could also "hear her hips."[101] How did the mulatta's hips sound, as White artists resorted to gendered racialization to play with bourgeois morals? The lyrics of "As laranjas da Sabina" are set strophically and syllabically to a schematic AABBCCDD overall song structure, each section shaped squarely with the repeated 8-bar song format familiar in a multitude of contemporary songs and dances circulating across oceans, and a shorter C section, set in repeated 4-bar functions as a refrain (Musical Example 6.2). The song moves predictably from G to D major in conjunct motion and in short-range melodic contours, except at the end of sections C and D, in which an ascending leap of an octave with a fermata at the end serves as a pause to the repeated melodic movement. Manarezzi certainly used the high note as a performance gimmick to open space for imagination: "Ah!" the stage Bahiana halted to fully capture the audiences' attention, not unlike a skilled operatic prima-donna consciously leading her voice to a high note and then into silence to create suspense and prolong desire.[102] In this regard, Manarezzi used a recurrent musical cliché that could find analogs in many arias from operas, operettas, and zarzuelas also circulating in the heterogeneous musical environments of comic theaters, café-concerts, and music halls. Like in "As laranjas da Sabina," the well-known waltz-song "Valse d'oiseau" used the musical/performative device of fermatas, tempo changes, and high note stops, as did a multitude of dance/songs like habaneras, tangos, and *lundus* circulating side by side in Rio de Janeiro's stages.[103]

[99] Jayna Brown, *Babylon Girls: Black Women Performers and the Shaping of the Modern* (Durham, NC: Duke University Press, 2008), 58.

[100] Daphne Brooks, *Bodies in Dissent: Spectacular Performances of Race and Freedom.* (Durham, NC: Duke University Press, 2006), 68–70, and 100.

[101] *Gazeta de Notícias*, August 12, 1905.

[102] For a comparison of the musical structures of songs associated with "mulatta," see Leonardo de Mesquita Taveira, "A mulata e sua música no Teatro de Revista brasileiro, entre o ano de 1890 e a década de 1930: Análise de exemplos," Annals of the XVIII Congresso da Associação Nacional de Pesquisa e Pós-Graduação (ANPPOM), Salvador, BA, 2008, 108–114; and Marilda de Santana Silva, "Teatro de Revista em trânsito: Brasil e Portugal," XXXVIII Simpósio Nacional de História, Florianopolis, SC (Brazil), 2015, 1–16. The 1906 recording by Pepa Delgado is available at https://www.youtube.com/watch?v=O5IGyl1K84I.

[103] For the circulation of habaneras before the period studied here, see Joana Martins Saraiva, "Diálogos transatlânticos: A circulação da habanera nas cidades do Rio de Janeiro e Buenos Aires (1850–1880)," PhD dissertation, University of Rio de Janeiro State, 2020.

Musical Example 6.2. "O Mugunzá" sung by Pepa Ruiz in the musical review *Tim Tim por Tim tim*.
Source: Biblioteca Nacional, Rio de Janeiro, Acervo Digital

The musical structure of the song-dance "O mugunzá" (Musical Example 6.2) was also set in the established song-dance structure: three sections, each in the 32-bar popular song format, a structure that had already become a recipe for popular songs in urban stages and that had proven successful in the music printing businesses as a structural tool facilitating remembering. Thus, in terms of overall

160 MUSIC AND COSMOPOLITANISM

musical structure, harmonic, and melodic contours, the song-dances of the stage Bahiana fit well with many other established contemporary songs circulating in many cities at the turn of the century. And it would not be a stretch to see them as simplifications of operatic arias or chansons already popular and enacted on Rio de Janeiro's stages by female artists like Ywonna, if it was not for the duple-meter habanera rhythm (dotted quarter note, eighth note, and two quarter notes) and their many variations in melodic lines and/or accompaniments, such as the "tango" figure or "fork rhythm" (repeated sequences of eighth, half, eighth notes that visually suggest the shape of a fork), the *tresillo*, and the *cinquillo*, all of which show an internal kinship in musical rhythmic formulas. Within the familiar song structure, the stage Bahiana's hips moved in and sounded through a concoction of melodic and rhythmic clichés, the latter used on the stage to denote a destabilization of a "regular" rhythmic pattern, and not coincidentally associated with supposedly disruptive African-derived musical formulas. Given racial meaning on the stage by White performers' hips, such rhythmic clichés aided the White actresses' vocal skills to control their movements and to dominate their audience's response.[104] Familiar musical structures, short melodies, singable and memorable, and performance gimmicks provided visual and aural familiarity to contrast with a forged stereotypical sonic blackness rendered rhythmically on the stage as being in a "primitive" state, or as a contrast so as to be "out of time," while it acquired various meanings of alterity when rendered by gendered and racialized performances that could also be read, seen, and heard as such by cosmopolitan city's audiences.[105]

Such concoctions of visual and sonic constructions of alterity on the stage should not be taken for granted, for in the fluidity and the ethereal flow of music, White actresses performing the stage Bahiana in city theaters and music halls allowed for their parodies of female blackness to evade borders of time and space and to percolate further geographically as a dramatic cosmopolitan sounding/moving persona. At home on the stages of many cities, stage Bahianas emerged from and merged into the larger context of race and gender of the modern city and came to belong not solely to the distant Bahia, the mythical Africa, or to Rio de Janeiro's stages, but they came to be consumed as "articulations of the modern world," as part of a wider "universe of transient white mulattas, [of] shape-shifting mediums, vanishing whiteness, and hard-to-read blackness."[106] Accordingly, the sounds of the mulatta's hips and their movements heard as

---

[104] Brown, *Babylon Girls*, 86.

[105] For the stage mulattas in Havana, see Robin Moore, *Nationalizing Blackness: Afrocubanismo and Artistic Revolution in Havana: 1920–1940* (Pittsburgh, PA: University of Pittsburgh Press, 1999), 49–52.

[106] Brown, *Babylon Girls*, 20.

DIVERSIFYING   161

syncopated melodies and overstressed and recurring rhythmic accompaniments were not a particularity of songs like "As laranjas da Sabina" or "O mugunzá," but were found in a myriad of contemporary songs published and performed in theaters, music halls, and vaudevilles across the Atlantic, in Europe and the Americas, North and South. The staged Bahiana as a singing and dancing mulatta had many counterparts elsewhere.

While the deriding comic nature of the character could be traced to minstrelsy, the dramatic persona of the dark-skinned female with power to entice males through bodily movements and vocal performances could also be related to habanera songs and dances added to popular zarzuelas and musical reviews, and to excerpts from Bizet's *Carmen* and its many derivative works in the second decade of the 19th century, which were widely disseminated in the popular theater and music halls across Europe and the Americas, and further circulated in an array of sheet music publications.[107] And here the specific urban connections between Rio de Janeiro and Paris are as important as the connections among cities such as Madrid, Lisbon, New York, Buenos Aires, Montevideo, and Havana, all of which shared the craze for the music and choreography of the mulatta's hips. In all of these cities, where Black bodies were once enslaved and traded, White singers and performers continued to take the female Black body as theirs, once again taking control of their diasporic routes. Their performances surfaced with a force as turn-of-the-century cosmopolitans shared cultural products believed to have sprung from ahistorical and unspecified local contexts. As Brown noted, the racialized female body on the stage and their association with concepts of simpler times, as syncopated rhythmic formulas and bodily rhythmic pulses, were in fact "formed in a complex web of time registers . . . and [in] multi-zoned comments on geographical 'origin.'"[108]

The Rio de Janeiro stage Bahiana as a mulatta had many connections in the Americas; the most evident was in Cuba, where the mulatta also became part of a long history of literary characters, popular songs, and dances and, like elsewhere, was performed mostly by White actresses in blackface.[109] The Cuban provenance of the habanera slowly became muddled as the dance was taken back to Madrid and became a staple of zarzuelas composers before also becoming a fashion in Paris. Here, the most immediate kinship was doubtless the links to stereotyped versions of the Andalusian songs and dances available in theatrical performances, in sheet music publications, and in early recordings. Like the stage Bahiana,

---

[107] On this topic, see Christoforidis and Kertesz, *Carmen and the Staging of Spain*.

[108] Brown, *Babylon Girls*, 58–60.

[109] Susan Thomas looks at a later period in *Cuban Zarzuela*, especially in the chapter "The Mulatta Makes an Entrance," 40–80; see also see Moore, *Nationalizing Blackness*, and Lane, *Blackface Cuba*, 113–114, and 180–223. For Argentina, see Geler, *Andares negros*; and for Uruguay, see Andrews, *Blackness in the White Nation*.

162   MUSIC AND COSMOPOLITANISM

Andalusian female flamenco performers took on the roles of dark-skinned women with moving hips set to both disrupt and captivate White males through syncopations added to melodic triplets and other musical signifiers of Spanishness.[110] On Rio de Janeiro's stages, such "Spanish dancers" had been sure hits since mid-century and became more so at the beginning of the 20th, not coincidentally when their performances turned into a craze in Paris, Madrid, Lisbon, Buenos Aires, and Montevideo. But in Rio de Janeiro there was another direct connection, since large numbers of Andalusian immigrants also flaunted around the city as undesirable European Others. Mello Moraes Filho remembered well Rio de Janeiro at mid-century, where "gypsies were vagrants . . . [and] formed dangerous gangs." He describes their music and dance as prominent in the city's busy central entertaining area: "In the backyard of the houses around the Praça Tiradentes one could hear the sounds of *violas* (guitars), monotonous songs, dances with *pandeiros* (tamborins), and the sounds of finger snapping and *castañoles* . . : they were the gypsies with their *além-mar* (across the ocean) laments, and the *morena* dancers (dark-skinned women) [who would perform] lascivious dances, fandangos, and sentimental songs to lessen the harshness of their luck and life."[111] On the stages of the cosmopolitan city, these stereotypical portrayals of Andalusian women singing and dancing, now emblematic of Spain as a whole, were mixed with many staged female Others, including the stage Bahiana, and also later with cake-walk and *maxixe* dancers.[112] K. Meira Goldberg has shown how the popularity of the U.S. cake-walk in Spain led to conflations of flamencos and tangos with the cake-walk performed by women on the stage which, like the stage Bahiana, were described as "lascivious and animated by noisy confusion and ruckus (bulla and jaleo)," as they also "moved their hips provocatively as the erotic teaser."[113]

Predictably, Bastos's *Tim tim por tim tim* had a section sung in Spanish as a praise to the Spanish female in the song "La muchacha" presented before Pepa Ruiz's "O mugunzá" in seamless continuity. In Paris, Christoforis observes,

---

[110]. For considerations about the habanera in Spain see Víctor Sánchez Sánchez, "La habanera en la zarzuela española del siglo diecinueve: Idealización marinera de un mundo tropical," *Cuadernos de Música, Artes Visuales y Artes Escénicas* 3, no. 1 (October/March, 2007): 4–26. For the habanera in the transnational context see Christoforis and Kertesz, *Carmen and the Staging of Spain*, Kindle.

[111]. Mello Moraes Filho, *Factos e memórias* (Rio de Janeiro: Garnier, 1904), 122 and 134.

[112] For the cake-walk in Rio de Janeiro theaters, see Leonardo de Mesquita Taveira, "A mulata e sua música no Teatro de Revista brasileiro, entre o ano de 1890 e a década de 1930: Análise de exemplos," XVIII Congresso da Associação Nacional de Pesquisa e Pós-Graduação (ANPPOM), Salvador, 2008.

[113] K. Meira Goldberg, "Jaleo de Jerez and tumulte noir: Primitivist Modernism and Cakewalk in Flamenco, 1902–1917," in *Flamenco on the Global Stage: Historical, Critical and Theoretical Perspectives*, ed. K. Meira Goldberg, Ninotchka Devorah Bennahum, and Michelle Heffner Hayes (Jefferson, NC: McFarland, 2015), 124. See also Kibler, *Rank Ladies*, 125, and Rosa, *Brazilian Bodies* (Kindle).

musical markers of Spanish-ness were mixed with the Parisian chansons as Parisian singers and performers adopted "dance styles like the habanera or jota, with their distinctive syncopations and rhythmic patterns, triplet turns, or allusions to the Andalusian scale and cadence, always within a simple harmonic framework."[114] Such a Parisian chanson-Andalusian mix surely attracted large audiences in Rio de Janeiro already keen for chansons and Spanish songs. Ultimately, in the urban cosmopolitan context, the stage Bahiana, with its many aliases, representing both the uncivilized and the modern, or the uncivilized modern, was expected to move her hips not only with songs and dances associated with their locality, but also with habaneras, tangos, flamencos, cake-walks, *fados*, and, not to be left out, the popular *danse du ventre* which was usually included in the mix. These were linked musically through melodic and rhythmic patterns, as dance/song mostly written by men and about women, through choreographies and performances, mostly by White actresses. These song/dances circulated through a mix of labels that responded to fashion and a wide network of geographical distribution. As José Manuel Izquierdo, Jaime Cortés-Polanía, and Juan Francisco Sans have observed, a habanera "could equally have been called contradanza, danza americana, criolla, tango, danza merengue, and so on" and, by 1890, "most people in Spain could not really distinguish if a dance was a tango or a habanera, or, indeed, if they were Spanish dances or American [from the Americas]."[115] This conflation of names and styles was already evident in Rio de Janeiro at mid-century, escalating early in the 20th century as the circulation of such dances became wider and more intense. As a result, the stage Bahianas' musical and choreographic palette was fluid and adaptable, for they helped further blur the differences of individual experiences of female blackness already diluted in the modern city. In the performances of the stage Bahiana and her aliases, body language and music were especially powerful because they functioned, as Brown also pointed out, as conduits to a message not "recoverable in language," since "language affords nothing in the kind of truths, comments, impressions, and expressions only found in rituals of dance, song, and music."[116]

The Othering of Black women in Rio de Janeiro's stages, musical reviews, and café-concertos thus fit with theatrical and musical conventions of the cosmopolitan city, where the racialized female Other was contradictorily both coveted and

---

[114] Christoforidis and Kertesz, *Carmen and the Staging of Spain*,

[115] José Manuel Izquierdo, Jaime Cortés-Polanía, and Juan Francisco Sans, "The Return of the Habanera: Carmen's Early Reception in Latin America," in *Carmen Abroad: Bizet's Opera on the Global Stage*, ed. Richard Langham Smith and Clair Rowden (New York: Cambridge University Press, 2020), 173–177.

[116] Brown, *Babylon Girls*, 84.

164   MUSIC AND COSMOPOLITANISM

a constant threat to the established White patriarchy. But racialized discourses performed by White female singers and dancers served particularly well those in charge of the politics of whitening the nation, as they benefited from the stage Bahiana's power to entice male and female White bourgeoisie while diverting attention from the city's large Black population, which was racially, socially, and politically segregated. Female blackness, constructed physically and sonically and reified as White on stage, allowed for stage Bahiana's melodies, rhythms, and moving hips to captivate many through their cosmopolitan theatrical connections and musical ambiguities, including racial ambiguity. In turn, in the *fin-de-siècle* cosmopolitan theatrical culture these racialized gendered stage renditions were used as tropes of the racialized essence of an imagined *mestiço* nation not only in Brazil, but in Cuba, Spain, the United States, and so on. As Brookes argues, for such purposes "the white mulatta had the ultimate appeal," as her racial ambiguity and the heterogeneous musical styles used to activate her body language defied any "singular context and national culture."[117] The cosmopolitan stage Bahiana and her aliases were bodies "without a nation."[118] The rhythmic clichés that allowed them to act were thus shared musics rendering essentialized sonic blackness cosmopolitan.

But it was also in the cosmopolitan city that supported such "nationalism and its fictions" that a few mulatta dancers eventually came to command their own performing bodies. As they entered the small, improvised stages of small beer houses situated nearby the Praça Tiradentes, they also made a living singing and dancing, while the presence of their Black bodies further reified the stage Bahiana mythical Otherness. João do Rio fictitiously called one such performer "princess Verônica" and Edmundo recalled a "mulatta Farusca," as they detailed their performances in a quite similar manner. João do Rio noted,

"The multitudes indulged [in her dances], with their souls stuck to the vision of the perverse sylph. [Hers] was not the classic dance of the Scala or the Ópera; [hers] was not the idiot Hungarian dances, or the happy English dances; it was a new dance . . . with flowers added to her curly hair of mulatta . . . she floated like a bird or legendary serpent . . . while seeing her one is reminded of Salomé before Herodes, dancing the dance of the seven veils . . . [when she finished] the public wanted more, clapping their hands and stomping their feet, and Verônica returned [to perform] *Danses américaines*!, she explained, and following the orchestra's rhythm, her body started to disarticulate, to turn, her feet tapping on the floor, and her hips moving, her belly waving through

---

[117] Brookes, *Bodies in Dissent*, 19; Seigel and Gomes, "Sabina das Laranjas," 179.
[118] Brooks, *Bodies in Dissent*, 29.

DIVERSIFYING   165

the harmonic-rhythmic flutter; the woman disappeared in a combination of *gestured sounds* (my emphasis); she was perturbing, infernal."[119]

Edmundo's description of the "mulatta Farusca" is less Eurocentric and more focused on her blackness:

[dressed with clothes like that] of the blacks of the *Costa da Mina*,[120] with a negligée showing her naked breasts, earrings, necklaces, wristbands, she moves her hips and twists her bust, turning in the air, making everything move with her . . . [as] she recalls the drama of the nationality . . . she sings, wiggles with her hands firm on her hips . . . it's the lascivious, shameless dance of the colony . . . then with the rhythm marked by walking sticks and clapping of the syncopated *maxixe* . . . the women's body imitates a screw . . . a spiral rotating . . . with slow wiggle . . . as the room explodes in applause and screams.[121]

Such detailed descriptions of the mulatta's movements could fit many descriptions of women dancers from a number of locales. According to a Parisian chronicler, the flamenco dancer La Macarrona (Juana Vargas) "did not dance, but she twists like a snake or salamander, with a singular movement of flux and reflux, she advances and returns to place with a frenetic arm's movement."[122] To Edmundo, mulatta Farusca's body was nothing but a rotating screw, a nonhuman visualized and heard as colonial shame. To the French chronicler, the Andalusian dancer was also not a human, but an animal. Truly enough, João do Rio noted that when the mulatta eventually came to perform the Bahiana, she disappeared in "gestured sounds" already filled with meanings, a learned body movement/ music that was ready-made and difficult to be undone. But the "drama of nationality," described by Edmundo as he grappled with "mulatta Farusca's" performing body, had a clear viewpoint: the perspective of the narration was a White, male one, whose position of power gave him the license to narrate. It was such a perspective of narration of the "drama of nationality" that continued to pour into the historical memory of the city as the years passed by. And when the city eventually came to be conflated with the nation in the 1920s and 1930s, the Bahiana Black moving body was no longer imagined as a disinterested body without a nation. The stage persona and its musical clichés became mystic symbols of a nation, called on to validate a forged national consciousness, made visible/heard as homogeneous. But the nation, with its "tenuousness of nationalism and its

[119] João do Rio, "Gente de Music Hall."
[120] [Guiné coast].
[121] Edmundo, *O Rio de Janeiro do meu tempo*.
[122] Anne Décoret-Ahiha, *Les danses exotiques en France, 1880–1940* (Paris: Centre National de la Danse, 2004), 33.

166 MUSIC AND COSMOPOLITANISM

fictions,"[123] was not one, but several. As Ana López has argued, syncopated rhythms became convenient, dual foundational myths to many nations, functioning both as "markers of the instability of borders," while also "indices of the imaginary demarcations that constitute the process whereby Self/Nation defines itself and is defined in relationship to Others."[124] In the overall scheme of things, the mulatta and her gestured sounds, formed in and multiplied among cosmopolitan cities, ended up also bounding many nations struggling with the imagining of a non-White, female world.

---

[123] Brooks, *Bodies in Dissent*, 29.

[124] Ana Lópes, "Of Rhythms and Borders," in *Everynight Life: Culture and Dance in Latin/o America*, ed. Celeste Delgado and José Esteban Muñoz (Durham, NC: Duke University Press, 1997), 310; cited in Lane, *Blackface Cuba*, 149.

7

Local Cosmopolitanisms

Dandy and Quaintrelle

It was in the heterogeneous, flexible, and fleeting artistic environment of the comic theater and music halls that many local performers and composers, Brazilian or otherwise, were introduced to the city's audiences as an early generation of professional musicians, that is, artists making a living solely through the sale of their musical works and performances. As attractions at the Pavilhão Fluminense, for instance, Segreto announced the singers and performers Henriquta Gerrero, Inez Alvarez, Annie Ness, and Geraldo de Magalhães (1878-1970). The latter, known mostly by his first name, Geraldo, had migrated to Rio de Janeiro from the southern state of Rio Grande do Sul and quickly learned the benefits of being a multifaceted artist to succeed in the competitive world of entertainment. He also started singing in Rio de Janeiro's small *café-cantantes* and *choppes* (beer halls) near Praça Tiradentes, such as the Salon-Paris at the Rua do Ouvidor (street), owned by Segreto, which in the last years of the 19th century had become a gathering spot for bohemians, young artists, and politicians. The small venue, which a chronicler from *O Malho* described as "nothing but a corridor," had an improvised wooden stage of no more than 2 feet in height where Magalhães would step up to perform Italian *romanzas*, French *cançonetas*, *lundus* from the *sertão* (northeastern drylands, countryside), and several *modinhas* "updated for modernity."[1] According to the chronicler, from early in his career Magalhães showed a powerful "metallic, robust, baritone voice . . . which easily substituted for an orchestra," especially when he sang his most famous number, the *cançoneta* "North America and Spain," a song commenting on the 1898 Spain/U.S. conflict, which had made the news in Rio de Janeiro.[2] The song apparently was not published, but the title shows that music hall performers, informed and attuned to events near and far, sang the news, giving sonic life to popular topics and introducing others that otherwise would have passed unnoticed to the public. Like some bohemian chansons performed in cabarets, these songs could also be defined as "a kind of

---

[1] On April 17, 1909, the magazine *O Malho* published the artist's biography, reporting on Magalhães's path to success; several notes about the duo Os Geraldos (Magalhães and Teixeira) used in this chapter are drawn from the article.

[2] *O Malho*, April 17, 1909.

Music and Cosmopolitanism. Cristina Magaldi, Oxford University Press. © Oxford University Press 2024.
DOI: 10.1093/oso/9780199744770.003.0008

168 MUSIC AND COSMOPOLITANISM

Figure 7.1. Geraldo Magalhães.

poetical and musical journalism,"[3] but one that would reach a wider audience than both cabaret chansons and the newspaper. It is not clear how such performances would work in practice, but no doubt the artist would find ways to enliven any topic and offer his own take on the news through song. To make his *cançoneta* more appealing, Magalhães added a refrain that functioned as a sonic and performative hook, an acted laughter, "Ah, Ah, Ah!," which he had to repeat "more than one hundred times a night" and which "echoed through the streets of the Praça Tiradentes." The refrain became so popular that every singer in *café-cantantes* was asked to add a similar laughter-refrain to their songs. According to *O Malho*, French *cançonetistas* would emulate Magalhães's refrain as follows: "C'est un gaga! Ah, Ah! Qui faite comme çá! Ah! Ah! Et puis comme çá! Ah! Ah!" But no one could compete with Magalhães's voice, which "shook and vibrated all the plates and utensils on the small tables"[4] (Figure 7.1).

As a Black artist, Magalhães's laughter-refrain immediately called for comparisons with George Washington Johnson's (1846–1914) "Laughing Song"

---

[3] Hawkins, "Chanson: The French Singer songwriter," 4.
[4] *O Malho,* April 17, 1909.

LOCAL COSMOPOLITANISMS   169

(1894) recorded in the United States and available for sale in Rio de Janeiro in Fred Figner's music shop (see Chapter 8).[5] But Magalhães's laughter-refrain accompanying his singing of the news differs from Johnson's staged "funny-black performer," or the "laughing coon," which were derisive, and theatrical takes on male blackness as central attractions in and of themselves. Magalhães's laughter-refrain, added as his personal performative embellishment of the news, brought attention to the song's topic in the familiar *cançoneta* or *modinha* style. His performative addition to the topical song transformed it into a work of his own, giving durability to an otherwise topical and ephemeral *cançonetas*. Geraldo's laughing refrain shows not only a creative use of his strong baritone voice, but also his knowledge and control of similar contemporary performing strategies. Within the context of the music hall, his laughing refrain was one among many vocal-acting gimmicks used by performers from various provenances to engage with a varied audience, as they deliberately bypassed lyrics and mixed singing with laughing, screaming, and crying as extra performative attractions to songs that otherwise would not be understood, would be of no interest to the audience, or would be received as routine and monotonous. Singers would also overdo such effects when already prescribed by the composer in the score. That was the case with the laughter in the aria "C'est l'histoire amoureuse," or "L'éclat de rire" from Auber's opera *Manon Lescaut* (1856), or in "Adele's laugthing song" from Strauss Jr.'s *Die Fledermaus* (1874), or even in Varney's popular "Valse d'Oiseau," in which many performers routinely added extra vocal artifices, as can be noticed in the song's many recordings; and, of course, in Caruso's short but famous laughter in his performance of Leoncavallo's "Vesti la giubba," recorded several times at the beginning of the century, and which was no doubt available in Rio de Janeiro. Thus, Magalhães's refrain caught on when several recordings of laughter-songs were already circulating in Rio de Janeiro during the first decade of the century.

In 1902 Magalhães was one of the first artists to be recorded professionally by the Casa Edison singing *lundus*, and in 1903, at a benefit concert at the Theatro São Jose, he was already announced as the "very well-known cançonetista."[6] With the opening of the Maison Moderne, Magalhães was contracted by Segreto and established his performance routine, singing a variety of songs, from the Italian "Sole mio," translated to Portuguese by Guimarães Passos (the author of "A casa branca da serra)"[7] to *modinhas* and *cançonetas* written specifically for theatrical

---

[5] It is possible that Magalhães's song was later recorded as "A gargalhada hispano-americana" (Hispanic-American laughter); see Carlos Palombini, "Fonograma 108.077: O lundu de George W. Johnson," *Per Musi* 23 (2011): 58–70.

[6] Casa Edison catalog and Magalhães recording is announced at *O Malho*, September 1902; the performance is announced in *O Malho*, January 10, 1903.

[7] Angela Marques da Costa and Lilia Schwarcz, *Virando Séculos: 1890–1914, no tempo das certezas* (São Paulo: Companhia das Letras, 2000), 79.

170 MUSIC AND COSMOPOLITANISM

settings, to "news songs" added and modified according to current events. In 1906, Magalhães appeared regularly alongside *cançonetistas* from Spain, "the lyric singer Mizza Mavry, who performed excerpts from *Cavallaria rusticana*, the cosmopolitan dancer Sargnon, and the chanteuse Lady de Glyrres," whose performance was announced as "a model of art nouveau."[8]

In venues like the Maison Moderne, Magalhães learned well how to situate himself as an artist in a connected world, how to use the latest performing trends and techniques, how to become a cosmopolitan performer able to communicate with people from a variety of places, and how to embrace many musical styles and languages. He eventually moved to the Palace-Theater and then traveled to São Paulo, a city also emerging as a large urban center at the beginning of the century. In 1906, he partnered with the singer Nina Teixeira (ca. 1880–ca. 1940), also originally from Porto Alegre, and started the duo "Os Geraldos." Together they traveled to the south of Brazil, following the artistic route into Montevideo and Buenos Aires. The chronicler of *O Malho*, who interviewed Geraldo when the duo returned to Rio de Janeiro in 1909, asked the artists how they started as individual performers, managing their own careers in cities abroad. Geraldo explained that "we did not know anyone, we just showed our theatrical credentials and pamphlets and were hired to perform." He described their strategies to capture the audiences they encountered along the way:

> We would rent a piano and contract a maestro with a fancy name and organize a spectacular program for each place. We always announced in big letters Verdi, Ponchielli, Meyerbeer, and other popular Italians, an overture, an entrance [song], a *cançoneta*, a duet, and an extra musical number. That would always make a successful night.[9]

Having shaped their career according to their experience in Rio de Janeiro's entertainment milieu and understanding clearly the potential of their artistic skills, after their success in Buenos Aires, Os Geraldos ventured further into the cosmopolitan circuit of urban connections. They traveled to Mexico, then to Paris, and eventually settled in the French capital from where they toured other European cities.[10] In Lisbon they first performed at the Coliseu dos Recreios, and in the French capital they premiered at the Apollo Theater, also appearing at the Parisien, Théâtre Marigny, Petit Casino, and Etoile Palace.[11] Os Geraldos

---

[8] *Gazeta de Notícias*, February 8, 1906.

[9] *O Malho*, April 17, 1909.

[10] According to Alexandre Dias, they also performed in Spain and in England; see Alexandre Dias, "Os *maxixes* no exterior: O caso de "La mattchiche," online publication, https://jornalggn.com.br/musica/os-maxixes-brasileiros-no-exterior/

[11] Arthur de Faria, "Os Geraldos ou . . . Os gaúchos que levaram o *maxixe* a Paris," *Parêntesis*, April 3, 2020, online publication, https://matinal.news/arthur-de-faria-os-geraldos/. See also Ariane Witkoski, *De la matchitche a la lambada*: Presence de la Musique Populaire Brasilieenne en France,"

were then contracted to perform every night at the Parisian Restaurant Albert at l'Abbaye and continued to attend to invitations to perform at various private soirées. While Teixeira had learned French in school, Magalhães proudly remembers becoming better and better at French, which came in handy as they translated their preferred *cançonetas* into French. By 1908, Geraldo could be proud to have "conquered Montmatre," a chronicler noted, and they soon became known as cosmopolitan celebrities.[12] In Buenos Aires they performed for the grandson of the ex-emperor Pedro II, who came to congratulate them personally, and Magalhães was particularly pleased for being applauded at the Restaurant Albert in Paris by Rodrigues Alves, the Brazilian president from 1902 to 1906. The duo also did not hide their delight when Caruso heard Os Geraldos singing at the Restaurant Albert. Magalhães remembered with enthusiasm when Caruso drew his self-portrait on a napkin and gifted it to him and Teixeira in appreciation for their performances.[13]

As a Black man and a mulatta woman, Magalhães's and Teixeira's success across the Atlantic was no doubt hindered by their race, but was achieved in spite of their race. Yet the artists' many accomplishments cannot be reduced to one aspect of their personhood, at the risk of continuing one-dimensional reports of Black artists and mono-directional accounts of human beings' complex processes of self and group identities. Here, it would provide a less than adequate account of Os Geraldos' multitude of skills used to navigate the intricacies of a new globalized entertaining business and reach a wide audience. As cosmopolitan performers, Os Geraldos no doubt understood the nature of race stereotyping in the theatrical setting and how their dark skin could both hinder and boost their popularity at a time when blackness had become a source of exoticism and, as such, a coveted element both in the entertainment business and among modernist artistic circles. Their ability to navigate the mostly White cosmopolitan sonic and performative spaces of music halls and café-concerts in which they operated rested on their explorations of both their vocal abilities and performative and communicative skills on stage, as well as on their nonchalant navigating through racial stereotypes. Thus, in addition to the Italian, Spanish, Portuguese, and French songs in their repertory, Os Geraldos added several others showing their familiarity with racial profiling on the stages of the modern city. To performances of the Italian canzonetta "Sole mio," the laughter song refrain, and a Verdi aria, the duo added several *cançonetas* and *maxixes*,

---

Cahiers dú Brésil Contemporain 12 (1990); online publication, https://www.yumpu.com/fr/docum ent/read/17003900/source-maison-des-sciences-de-lhomme/2>.

[12] Ary Vasconcelos, *Panorama da música brasileira* (São Paulo: Livraria Martins, 1964), 302.
[13] *O Malho*, April 17, 1909.

the most popular being the tango-chula "Vem cá mulata" (1902), with lyrics by Bastos Tigre and music by Arquimedes de Oliveira (Musical Example 7.1).

Dedicated to the carnival group Clube dos Democratas in Rio de Janeiro in 1902, "Vem cá mulata" exploded in popularity in 1906 when it was used during the street carnival parade, after which it was published and recorded by several artists, including Os Geraldos themselves. The song's connection to Rio de Janeiro's carnival made it a staple of the duo's locality and, like many

Musical Example 7.1. "Vem cá mulata," arranged by Francis Salabert and published in Paris in 1913 as a maxixe.
Source: Bibliothèque Nacionale, France IMSLP, Petrucci Music Library, https://imslp.org/wiki/Vem_c%C3%A1_mulata_(Oliveira,_Arquimedes_de)

contemporary performers, Os Geraldos explored the racially inflected lyrics in their performances. "Vem cá mulata" (Come here mulatta) refers to the mulatta as a stage Bahiana, including the female hip-moving choreography. Like the lyrics of most songs celebrating the stage Bahiana, "Vem cá mulata" was about the carnival society's fan base invitation to dance. The first section, set syllabically, is composed of two sequences of short 3-note minor-third melodic motives, made to be performed in call and response between a male and a female talking to one another in a theatrical manner. The structure follows the typical popular song format of 8 bars in the first section and 8 bars in the second section, each repeated several times. The harmony moves straightforwardly from G to D in the first section, going to the relative E minor in the B section as a change from the repetitive opening. Although the "call," the first 3-note melodic motive, appears as a syncopation in the score, subsequent repetitions in the response by the female singer are presented without it, and in the recorded versions of the song both performers ignore the syncopations altogether, focusing instead on the conversational nature of the lyrics.[14] The accompaniment, however, is clearly set to the habanera rhythmic pattern, an expected cliché used to suggest stereotypical Black female bodily movements (see Chapter 6). The recurring cliché points to a mainstreaming of such music-rhythm-body relationships learned through performances in the many cities' stages, a characteristic that undoubtedly helped "Vem cá mulata" become a hit wherever the duo performed the song. As was customary in comic theaters and musical halls, these musical clichés needed to be at the same time evasive and malleable enough to be adaptable to varying sociopolitical and racial circumstances and to interact seamlessly with other comic acts. Titles were thus carefully added to songs as ways to entice large numbers of people in various cities. The author of "Vem cá mulata" identified the song as a *tango-chula* in the score, a musically undetermined title that nonetheless gained meaning through Os Geraldos' performances. The author may have suggested a connection to Portugal (*chula*) or to Spain (tango), a connection that could also work in Rio de Janeiro's carnival parade. Nonetheless, the song was recorded in Rio de Janeiro as a *tango brasileiro* (Brazilian tango); and in the United States in an instrumental arrangement by Francis Salabert (Musical Example 7.1), it was recorded by the Castle House Orchestra in 1914, as "Creole Girl," and was described as a *maxixe*,[15] but in the arrangement Salabert removed all bass syncopations in favor of a polka–cake-walk accompanying rhythm suitable to U.S. audiences.

The lyrics of "Vem cá mulata" call for the mulatta to act and refer clearly to the racial stereotype of the sexually inviting movement of the hip-dancing stage

[14] Two recordings of "Vem cá mulata" are available at https://www.youtube.com/watch?v=eOgy Ay4W8T0 and https://www.youtube.com/watch?v=PKUhlXk3xt8.

[15] In the 19th-century the word *maxixe* was used to refer to a Brazilian party with dance in the city's outskirts; later the word came to mean generically a syncopated dance.

174   MUSIC AND COSMOPOLITANISM

Bahiana, as the male invites her sexual advances ("come here mulatta"). And although the mulatta in the song refuses the invitation (the lyrics continues with "I'm not coming"), the song's suggestive play of words did not go unnoticed and, as such, it enjoyed popularity in Rio de Janeiro as a risqué song. But there were many detractors to the song's popularity in the Brazilian capital, and not all of them were part of a White elite interested in moving female hips, more so than in the supposedly morally uplifting music performed in the concert stage. The mulatto writer and bohemian Lima Barreto, for example, did not hide his rage when "Vem cá mulata" took over Rio de Janeiro's streets during the carnival of 1906. "The song penetrated me like an insult," he told a friend as he left the outdoor celebration in rage, "It made me remember my mother. The suggestive scoundrel invitation seemed to me to be directed to her."[16] Os Geraldos, on the other hand, did not conceal the suggestive invitation to the mulatta in their performances of the song, as Teixeira, a mulatta herself, appeared on international stages dressed in the Bahiana outfit, singing in other languages, as the duo saw it advantageous to translate the lyrics to French as "Viens çá, mullatrée, Je n'y vais pas!"[17] (Figure 7.2). In Rio de Janeiro, White performers like Ruiz and Manarezzi portrayed the mulatta, but in Parisian venues, the mulatta herself played the staged Bahiana. In this regard, Teixeira followed another performer, Plácida dos Santos (ca. 1853–1935), also a mulatta who began her career at the end of the 19th century singing *modinhas*, waltzes, chansons, arias, *lundus*, *fados*, *maxixes*, and *cançonetas*, in cabarets and *café-cantantes* in Rio de Janeiro, and then traveled to Paris in 1889 where, like Teixeira after her, she performed dressed as a stage Bahiana.[18] In the French capital, they no doubt met Black artists from many provenances and nationalities also traveling the entertainment circuits linking European capitals.[19] Together they helped shape the cosmopolitan nature of the business on a large scale, both through live performances and recordings, while ascertaining the force of a Black diaspora lodged within it.

Yet to characterize Os Geraldos' performances as "performances of race" is to ignore their many artistic abilities and to assume that Black musicians were stressing an assumed culture, delineated by race, that would separate them from White artists. That the reviews of their Rio de Janeiro performances chose

---

[16] Francisco de Assis Barbosa, *A vida de Lima Barreto* (1881–1922), 11th ed. (São Paulo and Rio de Janeiro: Autêntica Editora, 2017 [1952]). Excerpt cited in Guilherme Tauil, "O dia em que Lima Barreto 'problematizou' o carnaval," online blog, February 23, 2017, https://almanaquenilomoraes.blogspot.com/2017/04/o-dia-em-que-lima-barreto-problematizou.html

[17] *O Malho*, April 17, 1909.

[18] Lisa Shaw, *Tropical Travels*, 37.

[19] Rainer Lotz, *Black People: Entertainment of African Descent in Europe, and Germany* (Bonn: Brigit Lotz Verlag, 1997). See also Tim Brooks, *Lost Sounds: Blacks and the Birth of the Recording Industry* (Urban and Chicago: University of Illinois Press, 2004).

Figure 7.2. Nina Teixeira. *O Malho*, 1909.
Source: Biblioteca Nacional do Rio de Janeiro, Hemeroteca Digital

to focus on their bodies pejoratively rather than on the fluidity and creativity of their artistry speaks to the racialized eyes and ears of the critics and their audiences. Still, when Black artists like Magalhães and Teixeira are allowed in historical narratives of the city, their inclusion is often justified because they displayed "manifestations of Black cultural roots," as if they were not performers, but card holders of race identity. Like few artists during their time who traveled through the urban entertainment circuits, Black or not, Os Geraldos managed to enter and exit, as they saw fit, the racial stereotypes on display in theaters through music and performance. As multifaceted creative artists with wide entrepreneurial skills Os Geraldos bypassed their locality and their racial disadvantage in a predominantly White society to offer a lot to many, and in the process they played crucial roles in the shaping of the cosmopolitan and modern city. Having been in several spheres of the cosmopolitan urban network, they displayed a level of artistic freedom only bestowed to those moving through the porous borders of the entertainment circuit, especially when, to them, those borders operated at multiple extra levels. As cosmopolitan singers and performers Os Geraldos made "Vem cá mulata" and other otherwise ordinary songs into international

176   MUSIC AND COSMOPOLITANISM

successes,[20] such as Francisca Gonzaga's (1847–1935) song "Corta jaca," José Nunes's "O *maxixe* aristocrático," (1905), and Nicolino Milano's (1876–1952) "*fado* Liró."[21]

Os Geraldos also did not work as diplomats, bringing Brazilian songs to international stages in a demonstration of patriotic attachment, and less so as representatives of the *mestiço* nation. In fact, their commitment to the cosmopolitan city obliterated any assertion of the cultural nation. Their understanding of the nature of the entertainment business led them to perform songs from elsewhere and anywhere, according to the needs and vogue of city audiences where they performed. One of Os Geraldos' signature songs, for example, was the Portuguese song "Margarida vai a fonte" (Margarida goes to the spring), or simply "Margarida," with lyrics by the Portuguese João de Vasconcelos de Sá (1905?)[22] which, according to Magalhães, the duo performed every night in their shows in Portugal. For the performance of "Margarida vai a fonte," Teixeira left her Bahiana outfit and dressed instead in Portuguese traditional garb, as she dramatized the (male) story of the idyllic beautiful women from Portugal's countryside (Figure 7.2). Like "Vem cá mulata," Os Geraldos' performances of "Margarida vai a fonte" were immediate successes in Lisbon and they kept the song in their repertory, performing it in Paris, Rio de Janeiro, São Paulo, and Buenos Aires to the expected audience approval. In the same vein, their repertory also included songs from the northeast of Brazil, following the vogue for such country songs in Rio de Janeiro, as well as love songs in various languages. As a duo and in individual performances, Magalhães and Teixeira were two of the most recorded artists in the first decade of the century in Rio de Janeiro, leaving a record of their openness to engage with a variety of song styles and explore their many performing abilities. In 1910 Geraldo separated from Teixeira to marry the Portuguese artist Alda Soares. Geraldo later moved to Lisbon, where he died in 1970 at age 92.

---

[20] Os Geraldos' 1906 performance of "Vem cá mulata" by Odeon's Castle House Orchestra is available at https://playback.fm/charts/brasil/video/1906/Os-Geraldos-Vem-Ca-Mulata; the 1914 recording of "Vem Ca, Mulata" by Frank W. Mckee, the Castle House Orchestra, and Francis Salabert is available at https://www.loc.gov/item/jukebox-134576/.

[21] The *Gazeta de Notícias* (Rio de Janeiro) announced Magalhães's performances of Milano's "*fado* Liró" in Paris and Lisbon on May 26, 1909. For a 1909 recording of "*fado* Liró" by Geraldo Magalhaões, see https://www.youtube.com/watch?v=HIEvQ-DLvJY. See also Pedro Aragão, "Diálogos luso-brasileiros no Acervo José Moças da Universidade de Aveiro: Um estudo exploratório das gravações mecânicas (1902–1927)," *Opus* 22, no 2 (2016): 83–114. See also Márcia Tosta Dias, *Os donos da voz. Indústria fonográfica brasileira e mundialização da cultura*, 2nd ed. (São Paulo: Boitempo Editorial, 2008).

[22] "Margarida," recorded by Emília de Oliveira as "Margarida vai a fonte," Portuguese song by Vasconcelos e Sá and Almeida Cruz e Coro, Colúmbia Record B110 (matriz 11817-1-1); see Leonor Losa, *Machinas falantes: A música gravada em Portugal no início do século XX* (Lisboa: Tinta da China, 2014).

LOCAL COSMOPOLITANISMS 177

On May 11, 1912, at the height of Geraldo's success, João do Rio wrote an article for the *Gazeta de Notícias*, refuting an editorial published by another newspaper, *A Noite*.[23] The *A Noite* critic disparaged a European businessmen who had come to Rio de Janeiro to hire Black musicians in the hope that they could repeat the success of Os Geraldos in Paris. The critic's rationale was that Black musicians would ill-represent Brazil abroad and demean the country before Parisians, who would "applaud [Black artists] as they would applaud trained monkeys." João do Rio disagreed and reminded the critic that in Europe, "at least north of the Pyrenees, nobody was disgusted by black people," leaving it to the reader the suggestion that it was the case south of the Pyrenees, but also adding that "there are many black [performers] who represent their country better than many white [performers]." An outspoken critic of the government's early nationalist politics, João do Rio, a mulatto himself, pointed out the complexity of easy associations between race, nation, and culture, noting:

> The impresario is certainly more concerned with making money than with taking part in Brazil's propaganda. . . . All the impresario and the artists want, be them white, black, or yellow, is to have work. In addition, if Parisians would take the American clown, the black Chocolat, as the whole United States, or the Brazilian singer of *modinhas* Geraldo Magalhães as the whole Brazil, it would also be a shameful calamity for Parisians if someone would think of France as the stage of the Palace-Theatre.

The statements of both critics clearly did not fully contest each other, and there is a preoccupation between them that Black artists like Os Geraldos could and would eventually become part of their modern cosmopolitan city. However, João do Rio was ambiguous regarding race, as he (as a mulatto) had been many times before. His ambivalence was but one example in which intellectuals in Rio de Janeiro offered contrasting views about culture, *mestiçagem*, and race specifically, while not always ignoring or disavowing the achievements of Black artists, writers, and intellectuals. This was an ongoing conversation that, albeit cosmopolitan in nature, had many local specificities.[24]

Oblivious to such discussions, Os Geraldos inserted themselves in the cosmopolitan modern city nevertheless. In the mix of praise and despise, their success actually instigated in Rio de Janeiro's critics a hidden jealousy, for in reality Os Geraldos were the true cosmopolitans they aspired to be. Rather than the

---

[23] *Gazeta de Notícias*, May 11, 1912; cited in João Carlos Rodrigues, *João do Rio: Uma biografia* (Rio de Janeiro: Topbooks, 1996), 143–144.

[24] For the many views during the early Republic, see Carolina Vianna Dantas, "O Brasil café com leite: Debates intelectuais sobre mestiçagem e preconceito de cor na primeira república," *Tempo* 13, no. 26 (December 2008): 56–79.

178 MUSIC AND COSMOPOLITANISM

primitive and uneducated Blacks that local intellectuals claimed to rescue, regenerate, and bring into their civilized White city, Os Geraldos carved their social mobility and updated their artistic endeavors themselves and on their own terms. They believed in the possibilities that the city could offer them. They kept sending pictures to Rio de Janeiro's newspapers and magazines, posing in the centers of the various cities where they performed, as a way of advertisement, keeping local audiences and theater directors aware of their success abroad. In these photos they are dressed for a *flâneuristic* stroll in the modern city, as a modern Dandy and Quaintrelle, as they shaped the modern city with their performative destabilization of race as a fixed and stable identity category. Os Geraldos' performances were not a matter of political action, even if in their acts they were not liberated from the burden of race. They followed a similar path of many Black artists during the period, who provided the "real thing" to White audiences' fascination for blackness, but a blackness that was at the same time profitable and disruptive. It was a rational practice of self-insertion, of bringing themselves to belong where they were otherwise be the Other, an action made possible by artistic ingenuity and ambition, performing, and entrepreneurial skills. Their performative attitude contrasted with the majority of Rio de Janeiro's White elite notions of blackness and localness, which usually conflated blackness with submission, lack of social mobility, and which condescendingly aligned Black performance with "the popular." When these cosmopolitan artists and musicians returned home, they were no longer subjects of derision waiting to be rescued, "educated," and "civilized." As Eva Woods Peir has suggested, they returned as "exuberant bearers of modernity ... far more educated and worldly than any middle-class bourgeoisie who claimed the city for themselves."[25] If there was not a place for Os Geraldos in Rio de Janeiro, there was surely a larger cosmopolitan urban space in which they could create alternatives to the *mestiço* republican nation.

Singing Flâneurism

The cançonetista Eduardo das Neves took a different route than Geraldo Magalhães and Nina Teixeira. Also a highlight in Rio de Janeiro's entertaining venues (Figure 7.3), Neves furthered his career as an entrepreneur, poet, composer, performer, and recording artist without leaving the country. Starting as a performer in the circus and in the comic theater in the 1890s, by the beginning of the century Neves was well established in the local scene; he performed

---

[25] Eva Woods Peir, *White Gypsies: Race and Stardom in Spanish Musicals* (Minneapolis: University of Minnesota Press, 2012), 112.

Figure 7.3. Eduardo das Neves, *O Malho*, January 6, 1917.
Source: Biblioteca Nacional do Rio de Janeiro, Hemeroteca Digital.

at Segreto's *café-cantante* Parque Fluminense and, by September 1902, he was already announced as the "celebrated Brazilian cançonetista," performing at the "Festa da Moda" (fashion celebration) alongside lyric singers (singing opera excerpts) and "Spanish dancers."[26] Neves sang his own works, as well as the poetry and music of others, including the *cançoneta* "A casa branca da serra," which by the beginning of the century had left the smaller ambience of Ywonna's café-concert to become part of the repertory of several popular artists in music halls and in the recording studio.[27] Neves was admired for his ability to adapt and interpret music in many styles, but sang mostly in Portuguese, always accompanying himself with a guitar, while sometimes using the accompaniment of a piano or small ensemble in recordings. His performance style added to the eclectic mix of music halls, as his songs kept the attention of an audience also entertained by jugglers and comic acts. Neves sang about idyllic romance and exaltation of women, songs that reflected both his experience as a music-hall performer of melodramas, and as an inveterate male bohemian saddened by disillusionments of the heart believed to be caused by women. Like Magalhães, Neves also offered his audiences newspapers-in-a-song, using melodies as an aid in the narration of recent political and social events in semi-improvised lyrics sung in speech-like mode with scant guitar accompaniment. As a Black artist, Neves's experience of exclusion made him particularly cognizant of the city's hierarchical social-racial

[26] *Jornal do Commércio*, July 10, 1902; *Gazeta de Notícias*, September 11 and 20, 1902.
[27] *Kosmos*, April 4, 1904.

180   MUSIC AND COSMOPOLITANISM

makeup, and as a result his attention to the daily workings of the city was often narrated through a mix of disinterested documentary and critical sociopolitical commentary.

Martha Abreu's timely study points to Neves as an important player in the politics of race in Brazil, while placing him in a larger context of the transatlantic African diaspora, as she draws parallels between the Brazilian artist and the U.S. performer Bert Williams (1874–1922).[28] Abreu maintains that Neves's "poetic and musical trajectory represented the possibilities of participation and expression of the Black man in post-Abolition [Brazil]" and her analysis brings to the fore Neves's activism in support of full citizenship for Blacks in a racially segregated society governed by a minority White elite. Abreu points in particular to the composer's self-posturing as a Black man, as he introduced himself on the stage as "*crioulo* Dudu" (Black Dudu).[29] In Abreu's account, Neves's role in the construction of Rio de Janeiro's music and entertainment businesses rested on his Afro-diasporic connections, which she identifies in "his work, his verses, his songs, and a repertory that affirmed a valorization of the non-whites, of things black, mulatta, and *morena* (dark skinned women)."[30] To support her narrative, Abreu creates a genealogy from Neves to other luminary Black musicians of the following generation, such as Pixinguinha and Sinhô, who are today entrusted with being the definers of the local (forged as national) *choro* and *samba*, styles assumed to be the result of the country's cultural and racial *mestiçagem*.[31] In this genealogy, Neves's artistic creativity and individual subjectivity are posited as seeds in a teleological narrative that glamorizes a supposed musical essence of blackness, exoticized while reified politically as part of, and indeed a definer of, the nation, at the same time when Black citizens continued to be denied inclusion in the nation's sociopolitical institutions. Such genealogy controversially transfers to Black individuals, and specifically to Black artists, musicians, and performers, the roots of the narrative of the *mestiço* nation, presented as benign and disinterested, while obscuring the political and racial ideology of whitening in its core. This account, which has become solidified in music scholarship, bypasses Neves's individual creativity in favor of his role in a racially and

---

[28] Martha Abreu, *Da senzala ao palco: Canções e racismo nas Américas, 1870–1930* (Campinas, SP: Editora da Universidade de Campinas, 2017, Kindle), see chapter 8.

[29] The word *crioulo* had (and has) demeaning connotations, and it is possible that Neves used the word to overstress the racial stereotypes that artists like him had to overcome.

[30] Martha Abreu, "O 'Crioulo Dudu': Participação política e identidade negra has histórias de um músico cantor," *Topic* 11, no. 20 (January–June 2010): 94.

[31] Abreu, *Da senzala ao palco*, Kindle, chapter 8. For this context also see Luis Antônio Giron, "Pixinguinha, quintessência da musica popular brasileira," *Revista do Instituto de Estudos Brasileiro* 42 (1997): 43–57. For the historical context of this genealogy, see Luiza Mara Martins, "The Construction of Memory about the Oito Batutas," in *Made in Brazil*, ed. Martha Tupinambá de Ulhôa, Cláudia Azevedo, and Felipe Trotta (New York: Routledge, 2015, Kindle), 73–83.

LOCAL COSMOPOLITANISMS 181

politically constructed collectivity, one that was not of his making.[32] As a Black artist, Neves is thus expected not only to affirm but also to *embody* the idea of the *mestiço* nation. At the same time, as a Black man, he is also expected to be a "man of the people," not merely to *act* but to *be* an individual socially segregated by default, whose voice always spoke in the name of a disenfranchised minority. This aspect of the critical approach to the production of Black artists like Neves has served well to advance a range of uncritical social-racial-musical analyses that separate musical practices and tastes of the "elite" as European and White, individualistic, aesthetically superior, and universal, from "popular music" as low-class, exotic, and *mestiço*, communal, simple, redundant, and local. Ultimately, Neves's works and performances become central in a narrative in which music and music-making are believed to unproblematically display both racial and social meanings, and which are, more often than not, enforcing of each other.

The focus on Neves's political role as a Black individual fighting for equal citizenship in the *mestiço* nation, as righteous and befitting as it is, nonetheless offers a monolithic, one-dimensional account of his artistic and sociopolitical roles in the city.[33] As a result, his role in the wider context of musical transformations at the beginning of the century is reduced to a one-dimensional view, a forged lineage of blackness accepted as inherent and associated with poverty and subservience. But the multilayered aspects of Neves as a performing artist, a musician, and a businessman show a wider profile that fit well within an up-to-date cosmopolitan artistic milieu that he shared with many contemporary performers from Rio de Janeiro. Abreu also shows that Neves performed in beer houses, waiting rooms of movie theaters, music halls, and on the stages of popular theaters and circuses, places where fragmented social and heterogeneous musical contexts reflected and shaped a cosmopolitan city constantly connected to other urban entertaining circuits. Neves thus learned from and worked in an environment where artists from various provenances and with an array of backgrounds and experiences had to reinvent themselves almost daily to satisfy audiences as heterogeneous as the cast performing before them.[34] Having started his career performing in and managing his own circus, Neves had a good sense of the business, as he moved on to perform at other circuses and traveled to many cities, eventually landing important positions as a performer and producer in Rio de Janeiro's

---

[32] Among several works that abide directly or indirectly to this theology, see, for instance, Sevcenko, *Literatura como missão*; Needell, *Belle Époque tropical*; Monica Pimenta Velloso, *Tradições populares na primeira década do século 20* (Rio de Janeiro, FUNARTE, 1988); and Hermano Vianna, *O mistério do samba* (Rio de Janeiro: Zahar, 1995), among others.

[33] Several authors have challenged this approach; see for example, Maria Clementina Pereira Cunha, who notes the unilateral and univocal interpretation of samba composers early in the 20th century; see her "'Não me ponha no xadrez com esse malandrão': Conflitos e identidades entre sambistas no Rio de Janeiro do início do século XX," *Afro-Ásia* 38 (2008): 182.

[34] For this point, see Marc Herztman, *Making Samba: A New History of Race and Music in Brazil* (Durham, NC: Duke University Press, 2013), 79–85.

182 MUSIC AND COSMOPOLITANISM

music halls and in films, and also succeeding as a recording artist, published poet, and composer.

Marc Herztman has shown how Neves succeeded as a skilled entrepreneur at a time when the business of music did not yet have established legal practices, such as hiring rules or copyright laws.[35] Neves was an innovator during the very early stages of the marriage between music, commercialism, and technology, as he also kept a dominant position in the local recording business as one of the few regular performers hired by Fred Figner's pioneer recording business in the city (see Chapter 8). With the advent of the movies, Neves became involved in the new industry, participating as a performer and as a script writer. On May 23, 1909, for example, the Cine Brasil offered the premiere of his "national film performed and sung by Eduardo das Neves, who also accompanies the other movies with his magnificent guitar *choros*." Neves's short film was presented after "Gioconda, from the celebrated movie producers from Rome,"[36] while it competed with nearby theaters showing *The Merry Widow* (see Chapter 8).[37] In sum, Neves was a one-man show at a time when what constituted "the business" and "the show" were still blurry propositions. Individuals like Neves played crucial roles in bridging a myriad of musical practices, offering original solutions to a music market on the verge of becoming fully commodified. Like Magalhães, Neves's performing success and recording contracts guaranteed him financial stability and a degree of wealth, as he was an artist who fully embraced capitalism while managing his individual creativity and need for self-expression.[38] Most importantly, to achieve these goals Neves's career advances were closely tied to a musical context that was not local in its essence or in its purposes, but rather one built from and connected to an urban cultural network that also defined his time and his city. As such, his performances and his songs were the epitome of the complex sociohistorical and musical contexts of the *fin-de-siècle* city. Neves addressed an audience made up of a range of social ranks, races, and political views, and managed to navigate their diversity by offering something for all.

Unlike many of his contemporaries, at an early stage Neves became mindful about the ownership of his works. In 1903, he contracted with Pedro Quaresma, a publisher specialized in books and songsters in cheap prints that would appeal to a large sphere of Rio de Janeiro's population. The success of the Quaresma publications attests to the fact that Angel Rama's idea of the "Lettered City"

---

[35] Herztman, *Making Samba,* 68–77; see also Uliana Dias Campos Ferlim, "A polifonia as *modinhas*: Diversidade e tensões musicais no Rio de Janeiro na passagem do século XIX ao XX," Master's thesis, Universidade Estadual de Campinas, 2006, 67–96.

[36] *Gazeta de Notícias*, May 23, 1909.

[37] In January 1909, Neves had already written a short script and performed in a silent film with excerpts of the operetta.

[38] Herztman, *Making Samba*, 82.

LOCAL COSMOPOLITANISMS   183

was not circumscribed to an exclusive social and intellectual elite.[39] Rather, Quaresma's output shows that there was a market for poets and writers outside the exclusive realm of newspaper chroniclers and books published by elite intellectuals, and that ideas and ideologies were formed in practice by a large social spectrum of the city, with artists like Neves playing key roles. He managed to publish three books with Quaresma, compiling the lyrics (without the music) that were part of his performing routine, including songs authored by others: *Cantor de modinhas* (1903), *Trovador da malandragem* (1904), and *Mistérios do violão* (1905). Placing Neves's work in the context of the cosmopolitan city, in the preface of *Mistérios do Violão*, Quaresma presents the artist as follows:

> We now publish Eduardo das Neves's third book. Here we gathered the latest work of the notable author of the *cançoneta* "Homage to Santos Dumont," which is extremely popular in Brazil. Just like Aristides Bruant at the Chat Noir, like Jehan Rictus and Xavier Privas, like several artists who perform at the theaters of the *banlieue* (Paris's outskirts), at the cabarets *artistique* of Montmartre, at the scenes of the Boul'Miche (Quartier Latin in Paris), Eduardo das Neves has appeared in café-concerts, at the Parque Rio Branco, and at all the entertainment venues of this capital. His songs, *cançonetas*, poems, and *modinhas* are celebrated, memorized, and repeated at various places by singers performing with the guitar, as well as in phonographs and gramophones.[40]

Although emphasizing Neves's popularity, Quaresma's introduction also notes that Neves's poetry is not as "impeccable" as works from poets and writers like Bilac and Artur Azevedo. But at no point in the publisher's description are there any observations about Neves's race or that his poems, music, or performances exhibited essentialized characteristics of blackness, or are suggestive of localness. Instead, the publisher claims Neves's position in a wider context of cosmopolitan city connections, not coincidentally accentuating Paris's centrality by alluding to him as a cabaret cançonetista. References to Bruant's *chansons realistique*, which had become mainstays in Rio de Janeiro's cabaret scene, shaped by Mlle. Ywonna a decade earlier, indicate that Neves's work was set to appeal to the local bohemia at large. The editor's preface also suggests that those to whom the volume was addressed were knowledgeable not only of Parisian songwriters like Bruant, but of Neves's contemporary *chansonniers*, such as Jehan Rictus and Xavier Privas, who left a sizable number of songs at the Parisian *fin-de-siècle*. Yet the *Revista*

---

[39] Rama, *La ciudad letrada*.
[40] Eduardo das Neves, *Mistérios do Violão* (Rio de Janeiro: Quaresma & C, Livreiros, editores, 1905).

184 MUSIC AND COSMOPOLITANISM

Careta's chronicler, also comparing Neves with Privas, criticized the content of the local musical halls, and Neves's performances in particular, exactly for their lacking a "truthful cabaret experience":

> There are no café-concerts in Rio de Janeiro where one can . . . see the authentic *cabotine*, the feverish singer, the daring acrobat, where we can laugh without thinking. There is none because the national theater that is supposed to produce genius and semi-Gods is incapable of producing a *cançoneta*. We have, it is true, Eduardo das Neves e o Catulo da Paixão Cearence, but these are not *chansonniers* like Mayal or Xavier Privas, but poets and singers of the dissident school, one [Neves] is a follower of Casimiro de Abreu [(1839–1860)] and the other [Catulo] is perfecting himself as . . . a public employee.[41]

Attempting to distance Neves from the Parisian cabaret scene, the chronicler nonetheless links him to Rio de Janeiro's mid-century romantic poets, including Casimiro de Abreu (1839–1860), who closely followed French Romantics and Victor Hugo in particular. Despite Abreu's short life, he left several poems about love and nostalgia, loneliness, and childhood, topics which were also recurring themes in Neves's songs. Neves was also fond of Castro Alves (1847–1871), another admirer of Hugo, whose romantic poetry expresses love and suffering punctuated with exaltations of the (mother) land and support for the abolition movement.[42] Neves's *Mistérios do violão* also includes poetry by the Portuguese romantic poet and playwright Almeida Garret (1799–1854). Nonetheless, although much prone to romantic individualism, Neves's own artistic output was not a parallel to Casimiro de Abreu's or Garret's romanticism. As a man of his time, Neves's songs were to be allied to performative acts that wed sentimental romanticism and nostalgia for the countryside (mostly from the sertão region of the northeastern Brazil) with realist chronicles of urban spaces and performative narration of the city's daily life. Like Ywonna before him, Neves's songs were a kind of urban singing *flâneurism* that were to be acted, sung, and re-enacted in each individual performance, even if they were eventually printed and recorded.

João do Rio understood Neves's work in such a context, admitting that the artist was a bohemian poet and an integral part of Rio de Janeiro's soundscape. To the chronicler, Neves was in fact one of the creators of "the national cabaret" and he finds analogues to Neves not in the context of the African diaspora but, like Quaresma, in the context of the Parisian popular song. He refers to Neves

---

[41] *Careta*s, November 11, 1911.
[42] Maria Cecilia de Moraes Pinto, "Victor Hugo e a poesia brasileira," *Lettres Françaises* 5 (2003): 117–128.

as "Béranger das Neves," that is, as the Rio de Janeiro version of Pierre-Jean de Béranger (1780–1857), a well-known songwriter in mid-19th-century France.[43] To João do Rio, whose point of comparison was also Paris, the parallel was not far-fetched, despite the different time frames in which the two artists operated. Like Béranger, Neves wrote songs with social and political commentary and, like Béranger, Neves also offered contradicting and romanticized positions that both questioned the status quo and glamorized authoritarian politicians. But João do Rio is also careful to separate the two artists, noting that if in Paris one could mythicize in poetry the city's dirty streets and poverty, for "[songs are] the rhapsody of misery and the ironic [poem] of misfortune," in Rio de Janeiro, "[they are the real history of its residents,] evolving from the city's satiric, romantic, and mischievous streets."[44] To João do Rio, Béranger only imagined and expressed in poetry the gloomy life of the city's streets, while Neves was himself a product of the city's "rhapsody of misery." Ultimately, João do Rio downplays Neves's individuality as an artist, alluding to him not as a creative individual, but as a representative of a collective and the embodiment of life in the streets.

We are thus tempted to read João do Rio's and Quaresma's comparisons as an interpretation of Neves as a Black version of Béranger, Bruant, or Privas, in a conspicuously similar approach to the narrative of a Black Mozart (see Chapter 4). But unlike Nunes Garcia, whose biography, analysis, and narrative were contradictory and forged by others, Neves did not depend on João do Rio or any other critic to construct his own image and build his career. He unapologetically put into words and at the center stage what his body made obvious: he was a *criolo* in a society that valued whiteness, a demeaning word he uses consciously to dramatize his Black body as a theatrical persona, as if he were "in character," impersonating the subjects of his songs in well-known music-hall routines. With no comedic subterfuges, he also made it clear that being Black did not disavow him from furthering his career in the cosmopolitan city. Rather than being an unequivocal representative of "the people," or an unwavering fighter for social and racial equality whose individuality is expected to represent the interests of the *mestiço* nation, Neves continued to shape the growing music business of the cosmopolitan city on his own terms. Eventually dominating the local stages with an individual, marked presence that was far more porous and diversified than many contemporary artists, his "knowingness" of the city's daily life also gave him an advantageous edge, as he competed directly with a wide range of artists coming from all corners of the globe. Peter Bailey defines "knowingness" as "what everybody knows, but some know better than others . . . as a discourse

---

[43] João do Rio, "A musa urbana," in *Kosmos*, August 8, 1905. This chronicle was revised and expanded and printed as a chapter, "A musa das ruas," in his *A alma encantadora das ruas*, 173–186.

[44] João do Rio, "A musa das ruas," 177–178.

186 MUSIC AND COSMOPOLITANISM

and a practice, a spoken and unspoken language,"[45] a part of modern life in the city that was dramatized in the music hall. This knowingness was objectified and performed and thus was the domain of the artist, but was dependent on the knowingness of the audience, an interconnected, communal way of experiencing the city's everyday life.

If Neves was the creator of the "national cabaret," his work expectedly follows contemporary songs being presented in a myriad of cabarets and music halls. Accordingly, his songs eschew melodic excess, are restrained by economical harmonic progressions, and are filled with familiar musical clichés not because they lack originality or creativity, but because they were aids to poetry delivery and to individual performance and thus needed to easily fit a text and aid in its remembering. But as his recordings show, Neves's songs are filled with musical gestures and melodic hooks ready-made for improvisation during live performances, where the musical schematic is built-in to serve an artistic purpose. Neves's songs were thus set to well-defined melodic structures in sequences of 4 and 8 measures to be easily repeated and remembered, for ease of memory was a key to mass success at a time when recordings were not yet dominant. Accordingly, Neves followed the custom of cabaret and vaudeville performers, as he recycled already popular melodic lines and presented them with new poetry and in new performance contexts; in "Os estranguladores," about a crime in the city's streets, he uses the same melody as the song "O Barão do Rio Branco," an homage to a well-known diplomat, two lyrics of a totally different nature set to the same, malleable melody. Already successful tunes were also recycled in melodic variations performed with different rhythms and tempos, like in "O malandro" and "O Aquibadan," which also have melodic lines clearly derived from "Os estranguladores." Songs, like "Os reclamantes," about the sailor's rebellion in Guanabara bay, fit squarely into the music hall schemata: a familiar, memorable melody used to support the topical and local lyrics, with an added catchy refrain, which invites audience participation and propels further repetitions. Not only does the story told in the lyrics testify to his knowingness of the city, but also the recurring melodies are set to appeal to an audience's sonic knowingness. Nonetheless, some of Neves's performances went further than over-stressing the repeated chorus, as they dispensed with melody altogether and were no more than poetry recitations supported by guitar strumming without any harmonic progression. Here, Neves's performances are akin to Ywonna's as a cabaret *diseuse*, with her vocal delivery weaving speech and singing, but rather than a piano accompaniment, Neves used his guitar.

---

[45] Peter Bailey, *Popular Culture and Performance in the Victorian City* (Cambridge and New York: Cambridge University Press, 2003 [1998]), 128.

Neves's choices for rhythmic patterns, both in accompaniments and melodic lines, are varied and dependent on the nature of the lyrics, but they also follow the established marches, polkas, waltzes, and habaneras already popular in a myriad of music halls and *café-cantantes* in Rio de Janeiro and elsewhere. While in several songs Neves favors the straightforward habanera pattern, others titled *lundus* often incorporate well-defined sequences of syncopated rhythmic pattern—the fork rhythmic pattern that was also easily emulated by clapping and foot tapping—as visual imagery and performance assisted one another in propelling songs into the mainstream. However, in delivery Neves's songs are never restricted to the prescribed rhythm, but tend toward a combination or a variation of these rhythmic patterns, even if one can note a tendency toward a specific variation, the *baião* rhythm: dotted half note, eighth note, half note rest, and half note, such as in the song "Bem te vi (do sertão),"[46] his homage to "O Barão do Rio Branco,"[47] and "Bolim Bolacho," among others.[48] But most songs are plain polkas or marches, which were preferred choices for musicians like Neves and Bruant, both of whom had worked in military services. To complement the plethora of rhythmic accompaniments, Neves also embraced the recent dance craze, the cake-walk, as in the song "O caixote," which he listed in *Mistérios do violão* as set to the music of "the famous cake-walk" (see Chapter 10).

Neves's preferred topic was undoubtedly romance, as he nonchalantly played the male *conquistador* and blasted his sensuality in dance-like songs entitled *lundus*, sometimes in an all too threatening manner for the local social and moral order. Neves's was a male world in which women were idyllic parts of nature and glamorous objects to be gazed at. As a complex individual ready to succeed in a complex entertaining world, his cause for Black citizenship did not efface his womanizing songs and their support of gendered hierarchies. In "Serenata a Leonor," Neves's poem is set to the music by Aurélio Cavalcanti's popular waltz "Muchacha" (see Chapter 10), while he also dedicated poems to female artists who worked in Rio de Janeiro's music halls and circuses, like "Saudação! A' bella Ignez Cruset," who worked at the Spinelli circus with Benjamin de Oliveira (see Chapter 8). Neves had an innate ability to capture the true "love in one's heart"; his performances of romantic love, available in recordings done early in the 20th century, were among his best. Following the contemporary trend, Neves's love songs were set to waltzes, like in "O Crepúsculo," with lyrics by Casimiro de Abreu, with the typical short range, descending melodic line, but which is highly ornamented during performance and showcases Neves's vocal skills. Undoubtedly, romantic lyrical love songs were dominant in his *Mistérios*

---

[46] Recording available at https://www.youtube.com/watch?v=WZmJdYGU_XUs.
[47] Recording available at https://www.youtube.com/watch?v=HvV4AY0jtKc.
[48] Recording available at https://www.youtube.com/watch?v=u0wKZ2UaCH8.

188   MUSIC AND COSMOPOLITANISM

do violão: "Stella" (1910), with music by trombonist Abdon Lyra (1887–1962) and lyrics by romantic poet Adelmar Tavares (1888–1963), was recorded several times by other artists, but Neves's interpretation is characteristically free and shows his inclination to lyricism in an elaborate performance of wide melodic contours.[49] In the performance of the popular waltz-song "Celina" (1910), with music by Octavio Dutra (1884–1937), Neves stresses the contrast from minor in the first section to the major mode in the middle section and does not balk at the vocal skills needed for the melodic elaborations.[50] Neves closely followed Magalhães's successes, for he also performed and recorded songs with added laughter as a performative artifice, as well as the Portuguese traditional song "Margarida vai à fonte," with which Os Geraldos achieved great success in Lisbon.[51] Because some of his songs were recorded multiple times by different performers after he made them popular, one wonders if Rio de Janeiro's record-buying public at the beginning of the century already had preferences for specific performers and performances, rather than for specific songs. One can say for sure that Neves tried just about every theatrical and musical fashion and that he managed to achieve celebrity in wedding them in multiple performing media.

Since the music in these songs were used as ancillary to the delivery of lyrics, it seems insufficient to characterize artists like Neves for what, rather than how, they performed. One can conjecture that Neves's tunes, whether of his own authorship or borrowed from someone else, served well his vocal and performance improvisations in the same way that parlor melodies, dance songs, and arias from operas and operettas served as sources of instrumental improvisations for wind bands and other instrumental groups, like *choro* groups. As such, one can perhaps understand Quaresma's compilation of works composed and performed by Neves not as a way to preserve static poems and song lyrics in the canonic way, but as a way to circulate further the sources of his many performances and to help retain performances in the collective memory. That is to say that the song lyrics without the music in Quaresma's publication aided the recollection of the artist's performance, something to be recreated in one's imagination in passive engagement with the ephemeral nature of performance. Publications of works made known by Neves on the stages of Rio de Janeiro were ways of assisting in the circulation and retaining of performance at a time when recordings and films were just starting to become commonplace in the city.

Yet, as an urban singing *flanêur*, some of the topics of Neves's songs, when not blatantly womanizing, were peculiar enough to irritate most contemporary Rio de Janeiro chroniclers. Neves brought to his audiences songs that narrated

---

[49] Recording available at https://www.youtube.com/watch?v=bNvoIR3IDJM.
[50] Recording available at https://www.youtube.com/watch?v=zjWImUrxzqU.
[51] Recording available at https://www.youtube.com/watch?v=NEHJvYniMB0.

issues confronting both the city and the world: he sang about daily politics, the cost of living, neighborhood happenings, social and racial relations, and everything in between, but always in a uncompromising narrative that frustrated several chroniclers who wanted nothing but rebellious language from a popular Black artist. As Neves said himself, he remained constantly vigilant to what was going on in the city so that he could bring up-to-date stories to his performances and create meaningful communication with his audiences.[52] His songs were not political statements, since he was not a politician but an artist. In "Anglo Boer Duet," commenting on the British conflict in South Africa, his song-news delivery skills are further from Rio de Janeiro and are closely connected instead to the London music hall, where British Empire expansions were constant sources for both patriotic displays and sarcasm.

Both Neves's penchant for romance and his ambivalent political positions greatly irritated João do Rio, who set himself as a gatekeeper of the local culture within a powerful literary and intellectual elite. For João do Rio, Neves's disposition for lyrical, romantic songs was nothing but incomprehensible. "How is it possible," the chronicler asked, "that in the misery of the *urbs*, in the dust and dirt of the sordid alleys, at the dark rooms of the slums . . . [he] can echo such poetic light?"[53] The critic was also unable to recognize Neves as a part of an upper social class who flamboyantly displayed the perks of his successful career, for João do Rio saw "rich Blacks" as anomalies, as Herztman noted, while Neves continued to "crash society's gates."[54] But no other domain of the singer's output disturbed João do Rio as much as Neves's penchant for unrefined patriotism, which the critic confessed to be an "an enigma" to him.[55] While João do Rio and other bohemians and liberal republicans were brazenly critical of the repressive and corrupt republican government, Neves's political positions were rather lukewarm. If the artist played a role in the cause of Black Brazilians, he was ambiguous in relation to his individual politics, at least in the way in which he demonstrated them in his lyrical choices and performances. In his typical patronizing attitude, João do Rio saw Neves as a Black individual in need of social and political protection, as someone who did not know what was best for himself. To the chronicler's amazement, Neves's lyrics celebrated governmental authorities; he praised, for example, the military President Peixoto as a hero and was ambivalent in his report of the revolt and subsequent military massacre of Canudos in the northeast of Brazil, as his songs commend the courage of both the government soldiers

---

[52] Neves, *Mistérios do violão*, Preface.

[53] João do Rio, "A musa das ruas," 183.

[54] Hertzman, *Making Samba*, 83–84.

[55] Márcia Abreu and A. Marzano, "Entre palcos e músicas, caminhos da cidadania no Brasil dos oitocentos," in *Repensando o Brasil dos oitocentos*, ed. J. M. Carvalho and L. M. B. P. Neves (Rio de Janeiro: Civilização Brasileira, 2008), 49.

190 MUSIC AND COSMOPOLITANISM

and the insurgents. João do Rio justified Neves's positions because he sung in music halls, where one would find soldiers together with the city's populace in gleeful singalongs. But the artist's choice of topics was not merely the result of his succumbing to the needs of his audiences. After abolition, Blacks were recruited en masse to the military and other government and state institutions, which remained one of their few opportunities for work. Moreover, not unlike many music hall performers in various cities during the same period, Neves worked for the Firefighters' Corps early in the 1890s and later he attempted at working at the building of railroad tracks. Although he was dismissed for his bohemian behavior, Neves kept in constant contact with musicians who worked in the military or wind/brass bands, a connection that explains not only why the topic of some of his songs exalt the government, but also why the music used to accompany the lyrics is closely related to military marches.

Yet Neves was ambivalent. On the one hand, he did not hesitate to narrate in the song "Os reclamantes" (1910) a dramatic revolt of the naval soldiers in the Guanabara bay, most of whom were Black. On the other hand, one of Neves's most successful songs, "Oh! Minas Gerais!," celebrated the arrival at the Guanabara bay of the same ship, the Minas Gerais, which was then added to the Brazilian squadron. The song is a typical example of how Neves wedded his penchant for patriotic militarism, his experience as an up-to-date café-concert and music hall performer, and his skills as an entrepreneur in the emerging recording business. The lyrics are set to the tune of "Vieni sul mare," the traditional Italian song popularized worldwide by a recording by Caruso, and which was much in vogue among Rio de Janeiro and was later used as the anthem for the state of Minas Gerais exactly because of the popularity of Neves's song (Musical Example 7.2). To João do Rio, Neves's patriotism was "very different from *ours* [my emphasis], and indeed of the populace at large." For the chronicler, Neves's work was idiosyncratic because he was a "man of the people, in this town filled with foreigners, [who] is discursively patriotic," one who blindly "despise[s] all foreign things and always celebrated their own;" a "[man of the people who] want to dominate the foreign [and in doing so] they hide the infamy of the politicians and the weakness of the political parties." To João do Rio, Neves was like all music-hall artists, part of a group of "inebriated Jacobins." To the chronicler, the success of a Black artist like Neves only made sense if he expressed himself in opposition to the established order. Neves's patriotic displays made no sense to those who put themselves in charge of nation-building. In the end, João do Rio professed his lack of empathy for Neves because, as a "muse of the street," the artist's output was "polychrome and reflects a population that is confused and chaotic."[56]

---

[56] Joaõ do Rio, "A musa das ruas," 177.

Musical Example 7.2. "Oh! Minas Gerais!"

OH! MINAS GERAIS

Racial fraternity was not on the table from any side. João do Rio was not alone in criticizing what he saw as Neves's insular politics and questionable nationalism. Lima Barreto also desecrated Neve's achievements, noting that for "the man of the people" the main topic is "a Brazil better than any other country." Barreto saw in some of Neves's songs a "nefarious realism . . . a sterilized love for those men of the country and a virulent love for those from outside."[57] Nothing would enrage more both these critics than Neves's popular song "Santos Dumont," written in homage to Alberto Santos-Dumont (1873–1932). The son of a wealthy landowner from São Paulo, Santos-Dumont lived most of his life in Paris, where he was a pioneer in aviation and started flights with controlled, powered, and heavy-than-air aircrafts.[58] In Neves's lyrics, Dumont's achievements in Paris meant that "Europe surrendered to Brazil/And congratulated [the country] in half tone/[as] Another star emerged in the sky." It became one of Neves's most well-known song lyrics, printed and recorded numerous times. By 1911, however, when Santos-Dumont's feat was no longer news and the song's popularity waned, Barreto was quick to recall Neve's success, asking with disdain, "what happened to Santos Dumont? who after being laureated in the city through Neves's rhymes totally disappeared?" Neves's song was incorrect, Barreto argued, for what Europe did was "laugh ironically and say: you will fly, yes, but to inebriate yourselves of blue and immensity, and feel just for one second outside the misery of the country."[59] To Barreto, Neves's nationalism worked in reverse.

---

[57] Beatriz Resende, *Lima Barreto e o Rio de Janeiro em fragmentos*, 2nd ed. (Rio de Janeiro: Autêntica Editora, 2016, Kindle), 164.
[58] Brazilians contest the primacy of the Wright brothers to successfully operate a powered and controlled aircraft and continue to assert that Santo-Dumont preceded the Wright brothers.
[59] Resende, *Lima Barreto e o Rio de Janeiro em fragmentos*, 164.

192   MUSIC AND COSMOPOLITANISM

Neves was far from being insular, however. In dialogue with multiple audiences, he used appropriating tools of modern consumer economy; and his patriotic songs, controversial to João do Rio and Barreto, had clear echoes in music halls in London and elsewhere: some were indeed jingoism.[60] As Hertzman has pointedly noted, in Neves's songs and performances, he impersonated a working-class masculinity, as expressed in the life and language of the streets: it was nothing but a stage persona, one that was key to his success. Unlike Bruant in Montmatre, Neves did not occupy himself with disease, hunger, and city pimps and prostitutes, displayed as a satire of the city. Unlike Ywonna, his productions were not questionable or alternative, but rather largely conciliatory. But just like Ywonna's, his performances were not independent, but autonomous. Neves overcame the figure of the enslaved Black ethic established by the government and instead provided his own method to navigate the system, an up-do-date method resting on entrepreneurial tools he learned in the cosmopolitan business of music and performance. As such, his voice did not make sense to those in power, for it was a voice attempting to gain power and succeeding at it. If artists like Neves did not see the larger picture, which intellectuals like João do Rio thought to be entrusted only to them, Neves's output offered the *fin-de-siècle* in fragments. These fragments were not the result of clear-cut oppositional relations or simplistic essentialist ideals of both Self and Other, or of notions of authenticity or authority, but of complex and malleable dynamics of both old and new, here and there, Self and Other, all recast as fashionable, urban, and cosmopolitan.

---

[60] Music hall: David Russel, *Popular Music in England* (Manchester and New York: Manchester University Press, 1997 [1987]); and Peter Bailey, "Conspiracies of Meaning: Music-Hall and the Knowingness of Popular Culture," *Past & Present* 144, no. 1 (1994): 138–170. Penny Summerfield, "Patriotism and Empire: Music Hall Entertainment: 1870–1914," in *Imperialism and Popular Culture*, ed. John Mackenzie (Manchester: Manchester University Press, 2017 [1986]), 17–48.

8

The Widows

Many Travels

On October 1, 1908, the Italian Vergani company of operettas and comedies suspended its shows at Rio de Janeiro's Palace Theatre to make room for performances by a company from Berlin directed by L. Ferenczy. Apparently, this was the first time that an operetta group from Germany ventured to the Brazilian capital. However, coming from presentations in São Paulo, by the time it reached Rio de Janeiro the company was already in the process of disassembling. Azevedo lamented that the presentations in the Brazilian capital were done with poor scenarios, missing artists, and only eight choristers of each gender.[1] But despite the drawbacks, the company managed to present four operettas: *Wiener Blut* (1899), libretto by Victor Léon and Leo Stein and music by Johann Strauss Jr.; *Die Fledermaus* (1874), libretto by Carl Haffner and Richard Gennée and music by Johann Strauss Jr.; *Ein Walzertraum* (1907), libretto by Felix Dormann and Leopold Jacobens and music by Oscar Straus; and *Die Lustige Witwe* (1905), libretto by Victor Leon and Leo Stein and music by Franz Lehár. Because this was the first performance of *Die Lustige Witwe* in Rio de Janeiro and "because not everybody in the city speaks German," a local chronicler thought it necessary to explain the plot before the premiere so that audiences could go to the theater well-versed in the story.[2] A few months later, when Augusto Papke brought another company from Germany, plot explanations were no longer necessary, since *Die Lustige Witwe* had quickly taken the city by storm. By the beginning of 1909, Rio de Janeiro had joined a network of cities around the world that welcomed *Die Lustige Witwe* with unfettered enthusiasm.

Premiered in Vienna in December 1905, *Die Lustige Witwe* enjoyed a tremendous success in Austria and Germany in 1906;[3] translated to English and with a few plot changes, it opened in London's Daly Theater as *The Merry Widow*

---

[1] Artur Azevedo, "O Theatro," *A Notícia*, October 5, 1908. According to the *Gazeta de notícias*, September 26, 1908, before arriving in Rio de Janeiro, the German company performed at the Polytheama Theater in São Paulo.

[2] The announcement for the show claimed that the work was unknown to local audiences. The operetta was announced earlier in *O Paiz*, April 10, 1908, and in *Correio da manhã*, April 28, 1908, to be performed at the Theatro Apolo, but apparently it did not reach the stage until October.

[3] Richard Traubner, *Operetta: A Theatrical History* (London: Victor Gollancz, 1984), 234.

Music and Cosmopolitanism. Cristina Magaldi, Oxford University Press. © Oxford University Press 2024.
DOI: 10.1093/oso/9780199744770.003.0009

194   MUSIC AND COSMOPOLITANISM

in June 1907, and in October it reached New York City, only to become a craze not experienced in the city for decades.[4] An Italian company brought *La vedova alegra* to the Teatro Solis in Montevideo on July 20, 1909,[5] coming from Buenos Aires, and after performances in Rio de Janeiro. The Spanish *La viuda alegre* opened in Madrid on February 9, 1909, and arrived in Havana in October, but not before becoming popular in Rio de Janeiro. Parisians had to wait until April 28, 1909, for *La Veuve joyeuse* to be presented at the Apollo Theatre in Paris. As the operetta continued its journeys across countries and oceans, in no more than five years the work had reached all continents except Antarctica.[6] Songs and dances excerpted from the operetta circulated quickly and globally, as desirable commodities in recordings and sheet music publications, in particular "The Merry Widow Waltz" (Musical Example 8.1), which became a hit of unprecedented proportions, assisted in the making of the worldwide widow-mania.

With a story adapted from Henri Meilhac's *L'attache d'ambassade* (1861), Leon and Stein revised and updated the plot to reflect the sociocultural context of early-20th-century Vienna. Micaela Baranello argues that the success of *Die Lustige Witwe* was due to the contemporary context of its storyline, which spoke to Vienna's multi-ethnic working classes, while playing into an imaginary faraway home. Baranello further argues that *Die Lustige Witwe* presented both a "cosmopolitan vision of society" and a "socially conscious role for art," as it spoke to a city of immigrants at the cusp of urban modernization.[7] While *Die Lustige Witwe* dramatized the social fragmentation of the era and the dilemmas of urban life versus an idyllic countryside through a Paris/Austro-Hungarian binary, it also added contemporary subtopics, like international financial deeds, patriotic feelings, and the ideal modern woman. All of this was cleverly presented with rich and fashionable scenarios that dressed a love story between Hanna and Danilo, an escapist plot that could speak to even more middle-class urban residents in constant search for light entertainment.

Undoubtedly, the operetta's appeal with a large urban audience was also the result of Lehár's well-crafted, memorable, singable, and joyful melodic lines, and

---

[4] According to Derek Scott, *The Merry Widow* played for two years at Daly's Theatre in London and was seen by approximately 1,167,000 people; see his *German Operetta on Broadway and in the West End, 1900–1940* (Cambridge and New York: Cambridge University Press, 2019), 100; for the success of the operetta in London, see also John Snelson, "The Waltzing Years: British Operetta 1907–1939," in *Musical Theater in Europe 1930–1945*, ed. Michela Niccolai and Clair Rowden (Lucca, Italy: Brepols, 2017), 241–248. For the work in the United States, see Jim McPherson, "The Savages Innocents, Part II: "On the Road with Parsifal, Butterfly, the Widow, and the Girl," *The Opera Quarterly* 19, no. 1 (2003): 47–50. See also, Dizikes, *Opera in America*, 370.

[5] Susana Salgado, *The Teatro Solis: 150 years of Opera, Concert, and Ballet in Montevideo* (Middletown, CT: Wesleyan University Press, 2003), 127.

[6] Tobias Becker, "Globalizing Operetta before the First World War," *The Opera Quarterly* 33, no. 1 (2017), 12.

[7] Micaela Baranello, "*Die lustige Witwe* and the Creation of the Silver Age of Viennese Operetta," *Cambridge Opera Journal* 26, no. 2 (2014): 177–178.

Musical Example 8.1. "The Merry Widow Waltz." *Fon-Fon*, May 1, 1909.
Source: Biblioteca Nacional do Rio de Janeiro, Hemeroteca Digital

196　MUSIC AND COSMOPOLITANISM

his use of rhythmic variety of old and new dances, which were placed at crucial points in the score to entice audience participation. It was a skillful way to dramatize difference and suggest inclusion, an in-and-out of sorts, played through familiar musical clichés and stereotypes that could be easily understood both visually and musically: rhythmically driven, speech-like tunes contrasted with long lyrical melodic lines in repeated sequences, tonal and modal tunes, fast and slow passages, and so on. Tobias Becker claims that Lehár's skill as a composer was the result of his understanding of the heterogeneous sonic ambiance of the modernizing city.[8] It could also be that *The Merry Widow* summarized "the sound of an age," as Felix Salten argued, since the work traveled so widely that it came to represent "not multiple worlds but a single one," and ultimately it was able to homogenize musically a diverse and fractured world.[9] Either way, the work surely invited reflections on the contradictions and complexities of the period's cosmopolitan experiences, for *The Merry Widow* not only benefited from the globalization process, but it actually became an agent in fostering cultural connections and solidifying international trade routes for cultural goods.[10] The movements of the operetta can inform us about the cultural flows and artistic networks of the period and, most importantly, how music functioned as a conduit for the strengthening of many cultural connections and disconnections among cities.

As *The Merry Widow* marked its presence in Rio de Janeiro, satirical commentaries about the work's local success abounded in the press. On May 25, 1909, the chronicler of the *Gazeta de Notícias* offered his personal take on the extent to which the city had been seized by the operetta:

Politics continues to be the order of the day. . . . Everywhere people talk about presidential candidates, the separation of powers, a million things that bore us. . . . Now we have something else to pester our ears: *The Merry Widow*. If we manage to escape from [political] discussions, running away down the street . . . in the middle [of the street] the operetta grabs you, since the work is performed over and over by the blindman's orchestra and the German band; if we enter a coffee shop, the piano is playing "Canção do bosque" ("Vilja Lied"); in the music stores "The Merry Widow Waltz" is repeated one million times. The theaters are filled with merry widows and kids whistle the beautiful waltz in the streets. [In Rio de Janeiro] we wed politics with *The Merry Widow*: those

---

[8]　Becker, "Globalizing Operetta," 10.

[9]　Felix Salten, "Die neue operetta," *Die Zeit*, December 8, 1906, cited in Baranello, "*Die lustige Witwe*," 201–202. Hereafter, I will include the operetta's title in English, *The Merry Widow*, rather than its original title in German or its many translations, unless the translated title is necessary for a point to be made about the work presentations in Rio de Janeiro.

[10]　Becker, "Globalizing Operetta," 6.

THE WIDOWS   197

who are not into politics or don't like the theater cannot set foot outside the house.[11]

Gastão Togueiro offered a similar report about the operetta phenomenon in Rio de Janeiro:

> One would assume that there is nobody among us in this happy and entertaining city, who is relatively cognizant for social conviviality, who has five working senses, and can read a newspaper, who has not yet gone to see *The Merry Widow*, even if to satisfy their curiosity.
>
> Actually, it has been a while in the annals of our theaters since we registered such a success. . . . Everywhere one talks about *The Merry Widow*, in the street, at home, in the cable car.
>
> Kids whistle happy parts of Lehár's score in the streets; in the cafés one hears it being scratched on violin strings accompanied by the loose notes of a harp terribly performed; at the bourgeoisie's parlor the waltz is hammered from morning to night on hoarse pianos; and if this is not enough, at the street corners the German band, with its strident and out-of-tune performances and violent "trombonic" notes, has embedded in our ears all the music from *The Merry Widow*. And finally, after hearing the music so many times, we have ended up by memorizing it and, insensitively, even in the most serious moment of life, we kindle with it, whistling or singing.[12]

The success of *The Merry Widow* in the Brazilian capital was such that it overshadowed the highly anticipated inauguration of the Theatro Municipal. Opened on July 14, 1909, not coincidently on the same day as the local celebrations of the fall of the Bastille, the new theater was a crucial part of Pereira Passos's urbanization plan and epitomized the government's push for "civilization," order, and progress. The Theatro Municipal became one of the most imposing symbols of European elite culture in the city and its architectural splendor, with modern building materials and an eclectic style modeled on Garnier's Opera in Paris, was a spectacle on its own. The opening ceremony, attended by President Nilo Peçanha, Pereira Passos, government officials, and the local artistic community, was followed the next day by a performance by the French actress Gabrielle Rèjane (1856–1920), hired in Paris for the event, who appeared in several times at the new theater. All was celebration in the majestic Theatro Municipal until newspapers reported that the Parisian celebrity did not

---

[11] *Gazeta de Notícias*, May 25, 1909.

[12] Gastão Togueiro "A viúva alegre," in *Almanack dos Theatros*, ed. by Alvarenga Fonseca (Rio de Janeiro: Typ. Ao Luzeiro, 1909, Biblioteca Nacional), 13–15.

198 MUSIC AND COSMOPOLITANISM

Terceiro acto da Viuva Alegre – (Photographia do baritono E. Sachi).

Figure 8.1. Companhia de Operetas e Opera-Cômica Italiana Ernesto Lahoz, *Viúva alegre*, act III. *Careta* 59, July 15, 1909.
Source: Biblioteca Nacional do Rio de Janeiro, Hemeroteca Digital

succeed in gathering enough audience to cover the costs of the productions, a reality that generated overall disappointment. But there was one easy target to blame: *The Merry Widow*. João do Rio lamented with irony that Rèjane had been passed over for Giselda Morosini and Bertini, who played Hanna and Danilo in the Lahoz Italian company version of *The Merry Widow* (Figure 8.1) and by the many other merry widows that had overtaken the city:

> All theaters lost money [this year, 1909], [but this is only true] if we ignore the comic and vocal geniuses Giselda Morosini and the irritating Bertini, as well as the prodigies of artistic culture that are the German, Italian, Hungarian, Turkish, Swedish, Arabian, Russian, and Portuguese versions of *The Merry Widow*.[13]

João do Rio probably missed a few, since it was difficult to account for the origins of every merry widow flaunting around the city. Companies came from many places, offered various versions, and monopolized all the theaters in the

---

[13] João do Rio, "A illusão do elephante branco," *Gazeta de Notícias*, August 27, 1909.

THE WIDOWS   199

city, except for the new Theatro Municipal. The overlap created fierce competition among productions and instigated confrontations among merry widows.[14] On May 21, 1909, the newspaper *Correio da Manhã* started a plebiscite to find out which version and which artists were the preferred among its readers.[15] To choose the best widow, one had to visit various venues and attend the various versions offered by many leading actors and singers. The main female contenders were the American Virginia Foltz, who impressed with the "Apache dance," an added bonus to the U.S. version of the operetta presented by the R. H. Morgan North American operetta company; the Italian Gisela Morosini, who worked for the Ettore Vitali company from Italy and who later took the role of Hanna in the Lahoz company (and who soon became the most revered female artist in the city);[16] the Portuguese Cremilda de Oliveira (1887–1979), who starred in the Portuguese version presented by the Portuguese company Galhardo; the German Kate Hansen, who came with the Papke company; and the Spanish Luiza Vela, who performed the role of Hanna with the Sarge-Baba company coming from Madrid and Havana. These women dominated the local entertainment business for several months, captivated the chroniclers' attention, and became topics of discussion among those stopping at cafés to socialize. Their photos were stamped in major newspapers and magazines, their performances picked over in every detail, their voices criticized, compared, and emulated. These singers brought the world to the city through their performances, vocal dexterity, and displays of female celebrity (Figures 8.2a–c).

As *The Merry Widow*'s many worlds converged in the Brazilian capital, more than ever residents felt like their city was a world in miniature. To explain the importance of such a convergence, daily newspapers and magazines followed the world's travels of the operetta and regularly updated the local public about its global spread. In 1909, *Almanack dos Theatros* informed that the work was translated into 13 languages and was presented in 30 countries, including "China, Hindustan, and Siberia . . . and no fewer than 142 German and Austrian stages, 154 American, and 135 English." The *Correio da Manhã* of May 13, 1909, reported that the work saw 18,000 presentations in New York. Local newspapers also kept residents abreast of the work's financial success, claiming that "to see the operetta, New Yorkers spent a million dollars, which equal 3,300 *contos* in our coin . . . and the European editors sold 3 million copies of the operetta's libretto."[17] These numbers were updated as the operetta's appeal continued to

---

[14] "Confronto entre Viuvas Alegres," *Gazeta de Noticias*, August 28, 1909: also in *Gazeta de Noticias*, October 1, 1909.

[15] Ermínia Silva, *Circo-Teatro: Benjamim de Oliveira e a teatralidade circense no Brasil* (São Paulo: Editora Altana, 2007), 256.

[16] Morosini had traveled several times between Buenos Aires, Montevideo, São Paulo, and Rio de Janeiro in 1908 with the Ettore Vitali company and with the Lahoz company until 1911.

[17] *O Correio da Manhã*, May 13, 1909; cited in Silva, *Circo-Teatro*, 255–256.

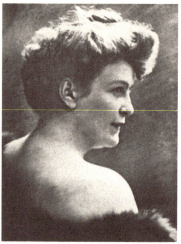

Figure 8.2 a–c. Female singers as Hanna: Kate Hansen (a). *Fon-Fon* June 26, 1909. Gisela Morosini (b). *Fon-Fon*, April, 1911. Cremilda de Oliveira (c). *O Malho*, November 6, 1909.
Source: Biblioteca Nacional do Rio de Janeiro, Hemeroteca Digital

grow, while every worldwide advance brought more local cachet to the work and, of course, fueled the arrival of more new widows.

Multilingualism

To the allure of *The Merry Widow*'s multiplicity of musical styles, multi-geographic references, heterogeneous social and ethnic contexts, and multi-Hanna celebrities, one could add another element: in Rio de Janeiro the widow spoke many languages. It took until July 9, 1909, nine months after the operetta first opened, for audiences to welcome Azevedo's Portuguese translation *A viúva alegre*, which premiered in the Theatro Apollo with the Portuguese company Galhardo and with musical direction by the composer Assis Pacheco (1865–1937). The operetta in the vernacular was undoubtedly an immediate success.[18] Nonetheless, by the time Azevedo's translation reached the stage, the city had already become a space for the nexus of widows in many languages: *Die Lustige Witwe*, *The Merry Widow*, *La vedova allegra*, *A viúva alegre*, and *La viuda alegre* were in Rio de Janeiro almost at the same time. Each language added a specific appeal to the work's production, and the concomitant staging of widows in many languages also led to a competition of idioms. A short satirical note in the magazine *O Malho* reveals the role of language in the appeal of each widow: Question, "Hey mister, have you seen *A viúva alegre*?," and the answer, "Yes, but I preferred *Die Lustige Witwe*."[19] The North American Morgan company offering Foltz's performance of the "Apache dance" also led to critics' awareness that each production in a different language had added some musical numbers and omitted others.[20] One commentator noted:

> We only talk about *The Merry Widow*. And we have many: we have it in Italian, in English, in Spanish, and we now have it in Portuguese. The public is right: *The Merry Widow* is a universal success ... [but] some people noted that the Spanish widow has fewer numbers than the Italian. But God only knows how the Italians fill in and modify the work of others just to please the audience. And the German widow had more numbers than the Italian. We now wonder how the audience will react to the Portuguese widow.[21]

---

[18] Azevedo's translation was apparently commissioned in April 1908, but it had to wait until 1909 to be performed; see Silva, *Circo-Teatro*, 58.

[19] *O Malho* 3, March 1910.

[20] The reviewer of the performance refers to the company as an "English company"; Virginia Foltz's performance was highly praised, but overall the company did not receive a good review; see *Gazeta de Notícias*, May 18, 1909.

[21] *Gazeta de Notícias*, April 21, 1909.

202   MUSIC AND COSMOPOLITANISM

In 1909, the magazine *Fon-Fon* published a satirical story about the spread of merry widows in the city, relying on easy stereotypes of both Orientalism and Eurocentrism, while describing the language-variety phenomenon caused by the operetta. The goal of the short story was to highlight the awkward circumstance created by the wide geographical circulation of the operetta in many languages which, according to the story, had dislocated a language from its country of origin. And, as the story went, within the language disconnect one would find a solution in Rio de Janeiro, where language and place of origin should not matter in the end. With the title "A sad Japanese widow who wanted to see the German merry widow," the chronicle illustrates Rio de Janeiro's public awareness of the complex linguistic scenario created by the operetta (Figure 8.3):

"[The widower] Ching-Chang-ka-tuê found out that *The Merry Widow* was performed with such great success in Berlin that he decided to go there to entertain himself and forget about the anguish caused by the loss of his wife. Ching-Chang, etc. etc., was a sad widow. He traveled to Berlin and went to the theater, but heard an Italian *Merry Widow*. He got upset because he wanted to see the original [in German]. Someone suggested that he go to Italy. He went there and saw the Portuguese *Merry Widow*. As he wanted to satisfy his curiosity, he went to Lisbon and saw the Spanish *Merry Widow*. In Spain there was one in English. He went to London and found one in French. He then gave up on his initial goal and went to Rio de Janeiro to visit his fellow Nippaku; [in Rio de Janeiro] they went to the Palace-Theater and, to their great surprise, they heard the German merry widow.[22]

As audiences reveled in the variation of languages, *The Merry Widow* prompted a unique phenomenon in the city: informal multilingualism. Togueiro noted that the many versions in different languages actually helped with the work's popularity:

The Merry Widow was already presented here [in Rio de Janeiro] last year in the anti-sonic and difficult language of Goethe. . . . At the beginning of this year, when an Italian company brought the operetta in Italian, it started a polyglot invasion that came with a flood of foreign companies offering the work, highlighting the unquestionable beauty of the score and popularizing the work, and helping to shove the entire city's population into the theater.[23]

[22] *Fon-Fon*, June 26, 1909.
[23] Gastão Togueiro, "A viúva alegre," 13–15.

Figure 8.3. "A sad Japanese widow who wanted to see the German Merry Widow." *Fon-Fon*, June 26, 1909.

Source: Biblioteca Nacional do Rio de Janeiro, Hemeroteca Digital

204   MUSIC AND COSMOPOLITANISM

In Rio de Janeiro, while each version of the operetta in a different language added more cachet or musical numbers, they also allowed for an informal engagement with and eventual learning of various languages concomitantly.

Several studies have shown music's important role in facilitating informal language learning in the 21st century, especially since, as Karen Ludke maintains (citing Weaver and Morley) "on average, we can expect to listen twice as much as we speak, four times more than we read, and five times more than we write."[24] Ludke argues that listening to songs in many languages "leads to hearing the speech sounds as they are, as opposed to mentally translating the sounds into the native language's sound system."[25] Moradewun Adejunmobi shows that the prevalence in African cities of hip-hop in English and in a multitude of other languages, and in a mix of languages, has led to an openness toward using "languages of wider communication,"[26] which he explains, "is one that enables the formation of sodalities whose members do not necessarily share the same mother tongue or primary site of belonging, and where therefore imaginations of the local are subject to reformulation."[27] Young African musicians' abilities to rap in many languages shows that African urban centers display "a significant degree of openness towards entertainment activities performed in non-native languages." Adejunmobi concludes that through hip-hop "Africans, especially in the urban areas, are on the whole polyglots" and that "the phenomenon shows the locals' informal assimilation of diverse cultural styles and trends from around the world."[28] In the context of informal communication, polyglots are actually "translanguaging," as Sarah McCarthey suggests; they are harvesting the "advantages of bilingualism for communication, cognition, and language production . . . [that] can be used as a strategy to retain and develop knowledge."[29] Significantly, translanguaging challenges ideas of "language learning as innate, monolingual, and occurring in a homogeneous environment"; rather, "bilingual learners shuttle between languages to co-construct meaning and utilize creative improvisation within social practices."[30] Translanguaging is thus not translation, but the lack thereof.

---

[24] Karen Ludke, "Songs and Music," in *The Handbook of Informal Language Learning*, ed. Mark Dressman and Randall William Sadler (New York: Wiley, 2019, online publication), 206.

[25] Ludke, "Songs and Music," 203.

[26] Moradewun Adejunmobi, "Polyglots, Vernaculars and Global Markets: Variable Trends in West Africa," *Language and Intercultural Communication* 4, no. 3 (2004): 159–174, 160. For an extended discussion of language in a globalized world of hip-hop performance, see H. Samy Alim, Awad Ibrahim, and Alastair Pennycook, eds., *Global Linguistic Flows: Hip Hop Cultures, Youth Identities, and the Politics of Language* (New York: Routledge, 2009).

[27] Adejunmobi, "Polyglots, Vernaculars and Global Markets," 173.

[28] Adejunmobi, "Polyglots, Vernaculars and Global Markets," 166–167.

[29] Sarah McCarthey, Idalia Nunez, and Chaehyn Lee, "Translanguaging across Contexts," in *The Handbook of Informal Language Learning*, ed. Mark Dressman and Randall William Sadler (New York: Wiley, 2019, online publication), 349–367.

[30] McCarthey, Nunez, and Lee, "Translanguaging across Contexts," 487.

While Rio de Janeiro audiences in café-concerts and music halls had no problems singing and listening to songs in French, Portuguese, Italian, or Spanish, whether or not they understood the meaning of the lyrics, the concurrent performances and the embrace of *The Merry Widow* in various languages call into question ideas that linguistic differentiation is to be interpreted as a main bastion of culture singularity. It also challenges associations between geography, local languages, and national cultures, and ultimately the concept of "mother tongue" and its link to "national musical styles" (i.e., the assumption that a nation is or should be made up of one language).[31] Derek Scott suggests that "rather than relating national music styles to race, it would be much more convincing to relate them to language." He brings up research by Aniruddh Patel and Wendy Berliner stating that "variations of rhythm and pitch in language could be related to the music composed by those who spoke that language," adding that research on children's musical development shows that "children pick up the *melody of language* [my emphasis] long before they recognize individual words."[32] While the sonic aspect of language, "the melody of language," can be a mode of cognition, it is questionable whether that cognition is limited to an individual's primary language. In fact, Yasemin Yildiz has shown that whereas a monolingualism paradigm has informed our "imagined collectivities such a ethnicities, cultures, and the nation-state," the phenomenon of "multilingualism . . . has been far more common worldwide than had been previously acknowledged [and] its visibility has become a remarkable new development of the globalized age."[33] The widespread of many merry widows shows that various languages' sounds, the melodies of many languages, not only made multilingualism more audible, but that they became an important part of the turn-of-the-20th-century city's sonic complex. And certainly, they added another layer of "multis" to Lehár's score and plot.

Rio de Janeiro's many widows reveal that music actually helped to overcome any linguistic shortcomings that attending the operetta in different languages could raise, if and when there were any. Scott has observed that when *The Merry Widow* traveled, necessary plot modifications were made, as was usual with many genres of musical theater, but the overall music score remained relatively untouched. Even if songs were added or left out, or the existing music was "chopped about and reorchestrated," melody, harmony, and rhythm were seldom altered, since "musical style in an operetta often appears to be independent of the setting."[34] Becker concurs, adding that "adaptations usually affected only

---

[31] Yasemin Yildiz, *Beyond the Mother Tongue: The Postmonolingual Condition* (New York: Fordham University Press, 2012), 6–7. See also Esperança Bielsa, "Cosmopolitanism beyond the Monolingual Vision," *International Political Sociology* 14 (2020): 418–430.

[32] Derek Scott, *Musical Style and Social Meaning* (Ashgate, UK: Taylor and Francis, Kindle), 89.

[33] Yildiz, *Beyond the Mother Tongue*.

[34] Scott, *German Operetta*, 59.

206 MUSIC AND COSMOPOLITANISM

the scenes and dialogues" and that audiences in different places did not exhibit "any sense of perplexity about musical style."[35] Music was thus the "language of wider communication" at the service of informal multilingualists in Rio de Janeiro. The translanguaging created by *The Merry Widow* was dependent on the repetition of the same music, however, which was the common denominator unifying the many widows. Furthermore, like the examples of hip-hop examined by Adejunmobi, in Rio de Janeiro where the level of literacy was very low,[36] the operetta's music allowed for large sectors of the population who did not have access to formal education and therefore were informal learners of the vernacular, to also become informal multilingualists—turning into, if only momentarily, informal global citizens. Music, an elusive and ephemeral expressive language, assured that meaning was not lost in translation, or, better, that meaning was carried through translanguaging.

As a sonic *flâneur*, João do Rio astutely "heard" Rio de Janeiro being transformed into a multilinguistic space, as the many languages' sounds brought a particular cosmopolitan sonic dimension to the city.[37] Describing the many *estrangeirismos* (foreign things) in the capital, he shows that "an idiom is an extensive forest with a variety of botanic species."[38] It may well be that Lehár purposely capitalized on this sonic aspect of languages and skillfully used it to bypass any cultural hurdles that specific languages could engender in the operetta's many world travels. Baranello suggests that Lehár achieved this by "musical encoding," which functioned as a means of creating meaning through common musical stereotyping and clichés learned in theatrical contexts.[39] One could add that Stein and Lehár also used both libretto and score as an exploration of language sounds, the melodies of language, to extend the work's worldwide appeal. They did so by using onomatopoeic sounds and rhythmic-music concoctions to get points across, an effect that, although not altogether innovative or new, had a tremendous impact on Rio de Janeiro's audiences.[40] Examples are plentiful in the operetta, the ensemble "Wie die Weiber" in act II (No. 9) and the "Grisetten-Lied" (No. 14) in act III, which include the percussive nonsense syllables, providing repetition of rhythmic play with the sounds (Musical Examples 8.2a and 8.2b). Baranello claims that the sounds of "chatter without meaning" and "percussive nonsense" like "trippel trippe" and "zippel zippel zapp," in the "Grisetten-Lied" numbers, functioned "as diegetic *varietés* unnecessary to the plot."[41] We

---

[35] Becker, "Globalizing Operetta," 16–17.

[36] Around 1900, the estimate is that only 33.1% of Rio de Janeiro's population was literate.

[37] Julia O'Donnell, *De olho na rua: A cidade de João do Rio* (Rio de Janeiro: Zahar, 2012, Kindle), 152–153.

[38] João do Rio, "Cinematografo," 87.

[39] Baranello, *"Die lustige Witwe,"* 178, and 184–185.

[40] Some of these solutions were used by Offenbach's scores and thus already familiar to urban audiences.

[41] Baranello, *"Die lustige Witwe,"* 195.

can extrapolate and suggest that such diegetic *variétés* actually helped audiences not familiar with foreign languages to sing along in any language and to engage with the plot through these strategies that played with language's sounds: again, music at the service of multilingualism, an strategy used well by Lehár, but which was used by opera composers before him.[42] In addition, the strategic handling of dances to invite bodily sensations, and specifically the waltz with its association of embraced lovers and deep emotions, served to further communication, showing that rhythm and melody when skillfully used together with specific dramatic purposes do not need an accompanying text in any language.

Still, when Artur Azevedo's Portuguese translation premiered at Rio de Janeiro's Theatro Apollo in July 1909, one newspaper praised the company from Lisbon for offering the operetta in the vernacular:

> We had this winter two widows in German, two Italians, one Spanish, and I don't know in how many more languages, and it is probable that the *esperantists* [my emphasis] also took them to Nitheroy [a city near Rio de Janeiro]. . . . The Portuguese translation is a true gem; the public, and I mean the wider public who, let's be frank, are not polyglots, laughed endlessly . . . since they finally understood what the plot of *The Merry Widow* was all about.[43]

Irony apart, the acknowledgment of the wider accessibility of the native language did not stop the chronicler from suggesting that the operetta had propelled the Esperanto movement in the city, the artificial language created in the 1880s to unify people beyond natural languages and bypass their association with specific places. The idea behind Esperanto was, in a sense, the opposite of multilingualism: one language for all, while keeping the "mother tongue" as a key source for nation-building. Nonetheless, Penelope Eckert suggests that the Esperanto language's goal was to create "a community of practice," which she describes as "a group of people involved in a social practice that defines their sense of belonging, regardless of their sociological traits (e.g., class, gender, ethnicity) or co-presence

---

[42] Giovanni Morelli has made a similar observation for a few operatic texts:

"Opera had a unique linguistic blend . . . that communicated to its Italian audience an equally open-minded faith in the existence, or, if not exactly the existence, at least the promise of its imminent arrival, of a language that crossed regions and classes. . . Another element that should be mentioned on the level of semi-folkloric communication is the incomprehensibility, the deliberate oddity, of certain words and phrases: examples are *Norma*'s 'sacri bronzi' Violetta's 'eggre soglie' the sarcastic Samuel and Tom's 'raggio lunar del miele' Azucena's 'perigliarti ancor languente,' . . . *Aida*'s 'fuggiam gli ardori inospiti'. . . these undecipherable expressions give the common listener the same intoxicating feeling, translated into "modern" sounds, . . . And so, once again, they provide indirect linguistic links between popularity and national communion, on the broadest scale" Giovanni Morelli, "Opera in Italian National Culture," in *Opera in Theory and Practice*, ed. Lorenzo Biaconi and Giorgio Pestelli (Chicago: University of Chicago Press, 2003), 430.

[43] *Gazeta de Notícias*, July 10, 1909.

Musical Example 8.2a. *The Merry Widow*, act II, "Wie di Weiber"

(e.g., place of living or workplace)."[44] Federico Gobho offers as an example a group of chess players:

> who define themselves by playing chess (the object level) and talking about chess and its philosophy (the meta-level) . . . a process of collective sense-making builds

---

[44] Penelope Eckert, "Communities of Practice," in *Encyclopedia of Language and Linguistics*, ed. Keith Brown, 2nd ed. (Amsterdam: Elsevier, 2006), cited in Federico Gobbo, "Beyond the Nation-State? The Ideology of the Esperanto Movement between Neutralism and Multilingualism," *Social Inclusion* 5, no. 4 (2017): 39.

Musical Example 8.2b. *The Merry Widow*, act III, "Grisetten- Lied." Franz Lehàr, *Die lustige Witwe*, complete vocal score, piano (Vienna: Doblinger, 1906)
Source: IMSLP, Petrucci Music Library, https://vmirror.imslp.org/files/imglnks/usimg/a/a7/IMSLP217044-SIBLEY1802.20825.bb74-39087011238351score.pdf

their sense of belonging, which comprises specific cultural traits, including a jargon and a distinct sense of humor, often expressed through specific metaphors.[45]

---

[45] Gobbo, "Beyond the Nation-State?", 39. For an exploration of community of practice in an online setting, see Etienne Wenger, *Communities of Practice: Learning, Meaning, and Identity* (Cambridge, UK: Cambridge University Press, 1999).

210 MUSIC AND COSMOPOLITANISM

We can thus create a parallel and suggest that *The Merry Widow* created a "community of practice" with unbounded connections, musical, linguistic, or otherwise, and that this community brought Rio de Janeiro residents close to residents in many other cities. The operetta's music, regardless of the language in which it was presented, allowed for such a collective sense-making. Listening and participating in the operetta's many productions allowed for a sonic Esperanto: Lehár's music became a language of wider communication, and the operetta allowed for the formation of a community of practice free from geographical borders.

The overcrowding of different languages in the music theater world in which the plot and music of *The Merry Widow* navigated tells us about the intricacies of the urban cultural networks at the beginning of the century. Indeed, as research starts bringing to light localized accounts of the entertainment world during the period, it becomes clear that the ability of translanguaging not only shaped the fate of works and the audiences that engaged with them,[46] but also framed the careers of artists who traveled constantly within countries and across oceans and whose success rested on their ability to constantly switch between languages. Francesca Vella suggests, for instance, that the success of Adelina Patti rested on her adaptability to changing linguistic soundscapes.[47] Carlotta Sorba offers a different view, claiming that the global diffusion of opera during the same period resulted in the dominance of a single language: Italian.[48] In practical terms, however, as with the operetta, the connections between the Italian language and the musical language of opera have been a very fluid one, in both production and reception.[49] All in all, the proliferation of *The Merry Widow* in many languages challenges such global linguistic musical monopoly on the musical theater stages, while furthering the understanding of the role of music to cross language barriers and to inspire composers, performers, and audiences to purposely and literally move with the music and beyond borders.

---

[46] For the transnational nature of the business in the Netherlands and "the untranslated" works in French and German in Amsterdam, see Annette Förster, *Women in the Silent Cinema: Histories of Fame and Fate* (Amsterdam and Chicago: Amsterdam University Press, 2017). Förster suggests that when works were presented in different languages, audiences "were presumed to understand" (p. 26).

[47] Francesca Vella, "Three Global Voices: Adelina Patti, Multilingualism, and bel canto (as) Listening," in her *Networking Operatic Italy* (Chicago: Chicago University Press, 2021), 79–108.

[48] Carlotta Sorba, "Between Cosmopolitanism and Nationhood: Italian Opera in the Early Nineteenth-Century," *Modern Italy* 19, no. 1 (2014): 54–57.

[49] Marta Mateo, "Multilingualism in Opera Production, Reception and Translation," *Themes in Translation Studies* 13 (2014): 326–354.

THE WIDOWS 211

Intermedialism

Adding to the translanguaging facilitated by *The Merry Widow*'s music, the operetta's multidimensional context could also be seen in the ease with which it flowed across media. Timing was a major catalyst, since the operetta reached Rio de Janeiro exactly during a period of extreme technological innovation and creativity resulting from the mixing of the old with the new media. Expectedly, as soon as *The Merry Widow* became a hit in theaters across cities and continents, recorded excerpts of the work performed by various artists and in many languages went on sale at Rio de Janeiro's Casa Edison, a music store owned by Frederick Figner.[50] A Czech (naturalized North American), Figner opened his shop to sell music, gramophones, and phonographs in 1900 and, in 1902, he started a new venture in the city: a recording studio.[51] Figner's Casa Edison offered printed music and recordings of various styles and artists, local and imported, "Brazilian songs, Argentine tangos, American Foxtrots, folk music from Hungary, Hebrew, Turkish, and Arab recordings, as well as recordings of the major opera stars from France or Italy." Figner lured buyers with the claim that his shop was "[a] musical Mecca [with] records in any idiom or dialect," a place where the many versions of *The Merry Widow* in various languages were incontestable bestsellers.[52]

It did not take long for the operetta to also prevail at the movies and to become a crucial part in the creative experiments with the new media. Concurrently with many contemporary cities with similar population sizes, silent movies were available in Rio de Janeiro as early as July 8, 1896, when the Lumiere Brothers' cinematograph was presented at a local theater, six months after its first commercial presentation in Paris.[53] The new Pathé Brothers' equipment arrived soon

---

[50] In addition to the 1907 full recording of the operetta by Deutch Gramophone orchestra, with Marie Ottomann and Gustav Matzner, many excerpts of the work were available through Victor's 1907 recording of the "Merry Widow Waltz," for sale in the United States. These are available through The Library of Congress website: https://www.loc.gov/item/jukebox-125264/. For "La viuda alegre vals," see *Discography of American Historical Recordings*, s.v. "Victor matrix C-4658. Merry widow waltz / Victor Dance Orchestra," https://adp.library.ucsb.edu/index.php/matrix/detail/200006407/C-4658-Merry_widow_waltz. Excerpts of the work in English were also available in 1908 in the Victor catalog. In March 1909, the Spanish baritone Emilio Sagi-Barba recorded excerpts of *La viuda alegre* (quintet) in Madrid (Victor and Gramophone). These recordings were for sale in Rio de Janeiro in 1910; see *Correio da Manhã*, April 20, 1910, cited in Silva, *Circo-Teatro*, 382.

[51] Humberto Franceschi, *A Casa Edison e seu tempo* (Rio de Janeiro: Sarapuí, 2002), 20–21.

[52] Daniela Palma, "Gramofones e gadgets para os lares do Brasil: Consumo cultural e tecnicismo na revista *Echo* (1902–1918)," *Projeto História* 43 (2011): 249 and 268. See also Maite Conde, *Foundational Films: Early Cinema and Modernity in Brazil* (Oakland: University of California Press, 2018); and Flora Süssekind, *Cinematograph of Words: Literature, Technique, and Modernization in Brazil*, trans. Paulo Henrique Brito (Stanford, CA: Stanford University Press, 1997).

[53] Conde, *Foundational Films*, 40. For Spain, see Jeanne Moisand, *Scène capitales: Madrid, Barcelona, et le monde Théâtral Fin de Siègle* (Madrid: Casa de Velásquez, 2013), 83. For Lisbon, see Silva, *Entertaining Lisbon*.

212 MUSIC AND COSMOPOLITANISM

after and, by the beginning of the new century, the new technology of moving images had become a regular part of Rio de Janeiro's entertainment life. Theaters were quickly adapted to show short moving images as an added attraction to live performances, and music halls quickly became semi-improvised movie theaters. In 1905, the opening of the grandiose Avenida Central prepared for the building of theaters solely devoted to the showing of movies, all of them still relying on music, recorded or in live performances, as attractions in waiting rooms and between short movie presentations. By 1907, Rio de Janeiro had seven such theaters, spread along the new avenue and its surroundings, in addition to the music halls; by the end of the decade, that number had grown to 17, some of which were as luxurious or more exuberant than the theaters.[54] An essential part of early 20th century urban modernity, the movies quickly took over the city and were shown in a myriad of contexts and venues.[55]

In 1904, Edouard Hervé brought to Rio de Janeiro the Lumiere Brothers' *cinématographe* and the Chronophone Gaumont, which advanced the synchronization of recorded sound with the images.[56] Hervé showed the equipment at the large Theatro Lyrico, presenting several *chanson filmées*, short songs filmed and presented with synchronized pre-recorded music, including "Berceuse vert" and "La fiacre," both with pre-recorded music sung by Yvette Guilbert and which extended the local penchant for cabaret chansons to the movie theater.[57] According to a local critic, Hervé's presentations offered an "extraordinary precision in synchronizing the talking cinematograph."[58] At the beginning, however, coordinating the phonograph with images was not entirely successful, especially considering that the recording technology was not advanced enough to offer a robust and clear enough sound to work well in large venues. If one adds the instability of electricity in these venues, the marrying of moving images with recorded music did not captivate Rio de Janeiro's audiences enough to turn a profit, and the sounding machine/image blend did not impress enough for it to compete with the singers in live theatrical performances. As an alternative, local entrepreneurs started to use artists behind the screen, who would sing while coordinating with the images, in intermedial experimentations already

---

[54] For a list of movie theaters and their locations in Rio de Janeiro see, Lima, *Arquitetura do Espetaculo*, 237–239 and 259.

[55] Conde, *Foundational Films*, 34–35.

[56] Fernando Morais da Costa, "O som no cinema Brasileiro: Revisão de uma importância indeferida," PhD dissertation, Universidade Federal Fluminense, 2006, 30; see also Vicente de Paula Araújo, *A bela época do cinema brasileiro* (São Paulo: Perspectiva, 1976), 145.

[57] Danielle Crepaldi Carvalho, "Silent Movies and Sounds in Brazil 1894–1920," *Galáxia* 34 (2017): 10. Costa, "O som no cinema Brasileiro," 26 and 32–34. See also Gilberto Ferrez, *Pathé: 80 anos na vida do Rio* (Rio de Janeiro: Ministério da Cultura, 2010).

[58] *Gazeta de Notícias*, April 28, 1908, cited in, Costa, "O som no cinema Brasileiro," 38.

THE WIDOWS 213

in progress in Italy, France, and the United States. In Rio de Janeiro these new *filmes cantantes* (singing movies) became quite popular and were considered a satisfying compromise between the familiar and the new. By the end of 1908, the synchronization of recorded music and images were all but abandoned in Rio de Janeiro in favor of *filmes cantantes* with behind-the-scenes live performances.[59]

Two local entrepreneurs invested heavily in *filmes cantantes*. In 1907, William Auler opened the Cinematógrapho Rio Branco, showing the most re-cent imported movies, as well as short scenes filmed in Rio de Janeiro and produced by his company.[60] Early in 1908, the Italian Giovanni Labanca and the Portuguese Antônio Leal opened the Cinema Palace, showing the latest movies, mostly from France and Italy, in addition to their own local productions.[61] Both imported and local movies presented by these entrepreneurs were short snippets following the typical descriptive or documentary nature of the silent films of the period, to which background music performed live on a piano or by small ensembles was often added to fill the silent presentations with sound.[62] But soon they also started to show short opera scenes in film as *filmes cantantes*, both imported and shot locally, using local artists to dub them on site. Their ventures employed instrumentalists, composers, and producers, and shaped the careers of a new breed of Rio de Janeiro singers/actors who sung "behind the scenes," such as the Italians Antonio Cataldi and Laura Grassi, and the Spaniards Claudina Montenegro, Santiago Pepe, and Ismênia Matheus, all of whom had previous careers singing and performing in café-concerts, music halls, and in the comic theater. From October to December 1908, Auler showed local productions of the aria "Vecchia Zimarra" from *La bohème*, the aria "Toreador" from *Carmen*, both sung by Cataldi; a duet from *Africana*, sung by Montenegro and Pepe; and the all-time popular "La Marseillaise," sung by Cataldi, who brought the tune into the popular domain of the movies.[63] As contradictory as it may seem, the added live voices behind the screen enhanced the "total illusion" offered by the moving

[59] The Italian Giovanni Pastrone used live performers behind the screen quite often. Between 1907 and 1908 in the United States, illustrated songs and productions by Kalem Films provided similar alternatives of singing on and behind the screen on stage; see Rick Altman, *Silent Film Sound*, 109–115 and 210–215. But the number of *filmes cantantes* in Rio de Janeiro surpassed similar enterprises in contemporary larger centers. However, after World War I, the U.S. movie industry became quite competitive and led to a rapid decrease of local productions in Brazil.

[60] William Auler was born in Rio de Janeiro, but spent his youth in the United States. When he returned to Brazil, he established himself as an entrepreneur of the new media in the city.

[61] The opening of the Cinema Palace was announced in *O Malho* 283, February 15, 1908. Labanca and Leal imported mostly from Rossi & Cia from Turim, Italy, and the Pathé Freres from Paris. The competing Cinematógrapho Parisiense, run by the Italian Staffa, also imported from Italy and France; *O Malho* 298, May 30, 1908; *Fon-Fon* 45, no. 2, February 15, 1908.

[62] A list of these films can be accessed at "Filmes estrangeiros exibidos no Brasil: 1896–1934," http://www.mnemocine.com.br/.

[63] José Inácio de Melo Souza, *Imagens do passado: São Paulo e Rio de Janeiro nos primórdios do cinema* (São Paulo: Senac, 2019 [2004]).

214 MUSIC AND COSMOPOLITANISM

images on the screen. Albeit ephemeral, *filmes cantantes* became a significant trend that boosted both the local movie and music industries.

From 1908 until 1911, an avalanche of locally produced *filmes cantantes* fueled a creative and profitable merging of the musical theater with the new technology, an appropriate wedding in a city where the theater had dominated for over a century and where the movies served to further the local drive toward a coveted urban modernity.[64] Rio de Janeiro was surely ahead of its time in this regard, as the intermedial approach propelled a craze for mélanges of sounds, images, and live performances, and brought to stardom a group of artists who otherwise would have been forgotten in the heterogeneous sphere of café-concerts and music halls. When, in January 1909, Rio de Janeiro's Theatro Lyrico welcomed *L'Assassinat du Duc de Guise* (1908, André Calmettes, Charles Le Bargy)—a production of the French Film d'Art company, which released longer movies with serious themes—the work sealed the already existing local penchant for live music synchronized with films. Premiered in the Brazilian capital only two months after its Parisian performance and one month before it was shown in New York, *L'Assassinat du Duc de Guise* was a longer film (14 minutes), included a live orchestra coordinating with the film, and had original music written by Saint-Saëns specifically for the new media. The Rio de Janeiro presentation was followed by several similar productions from Paris and inspired locally produced *films d'art* as *filmes cantantes*, which were longer and showed several connected scenes, rather than just short songs.

No other work could have served better as raw material for the experimentation afforded by the new technology and media crossing than the popular *Merry Widow*. In the second part of 1909, two local film productions of the operetta hit movie theaters, coexisting with the many theatrical versions that continued as box office successes.[65] Labanca and Leal's company was the first to release a full cinematographic *The Merry Widow* as a highlight for their movie theater.[66] The production was announced on July 22, 1909, as a *film d'art* and, according to the advertisement, it was long enough to include three acts, although surely the operetta needed to be shortened.[67] The work was filmed from the Italian Lahoz company theater production, which featured Morosini as Hanna. With scenography by Emilio Silva and cameras operated by Antônio Leal, the movie also employed a large local cast singing behind the scenes, like the Italian Elvira Benevente,

[64] Arnaldo Di Pace, "O musical antes do musical: Os filmes cantantes brasileiros, 1908–1911)," *Relici, Revista Livre de Cinema* 5, no. 1 (2018): 85.

[65] Already in April 10, 1909, the *Gazeta de Notícias* advertised a film version of *The Merry Widow*.

[66] Costa, "O som no cinema Brasileiro," 48; Vicente de Paula Araújo, *A bela época do cinema brasileiro* (São Paulo: Perspectiva, 1976), 290–291.

[67] *Gazeta de Notícias*, July 30, 1909; Silva, *Circo-Teatro*, 260; Costa, "O som no cinema Brasileiro," 49–50; Marcel Vieira Barreto Silva, "Cinema e literatura no Brasil: O caso do período silencioso," *Lumina* 5 no. 2 (2011): 4.

who dubbed Morosini's voice.[68] The production was well documented in the local press, and the photos published in magazines showed the rich scenarios of Lahoz's company.

Labanca's attempt to compete in a market already saturated with *Merry Widows* did not pan out as expected at the box office, however. Yet it took no more than two months for a new cinematographic venture to accomplish the feat of challenging the operetta's success in the theater. On September 9, 1909, Auler offered at his Cinema Rio Branco the "biggest success of our time," *The Merry Widow* as a "cinematographic operetta" (Figure 8.4).[69] His *filme cantante* used the Pathé equipment and was filmed in Rio de Janeiro by photographer Julio Ferrez (1881–1946), who became a major figure in the local movie business. The scenes were filmed with the cast of the Portuguese version of the operetta presented at the Theatro Apollo by the Galhardo company from Lisbon, with Cremilda de Oliveira as Hanna and Armando de Vasconcelos as Danilo. The production was directed by Alberto Moreira, a partner in Auler's company, who adapted Lehár's operetta for the new media and assigned the arrangement of the score for the Cinema Rio Branco's 25-member orchestra[70] to composer Costa Junior (1870–1917), who also conducted the ensemble situated in the orchestra pit. Costa Junior's score did not survive, but a local critic considered it a "delicate arrangement."[71] The image of Oliveira as Hanna was dubbed behind the scenes by the voice of Ismênia Matheus, and Vasconcelos as Danilo was dubbed by Cataldi. Announcing the work two weeks before the premiere, on August 28, 1909, the *Gazeta de Notícias* proudly showcased the cinematographic *Merry Widow* as "the first time in the world [that the work will be presented in the movies] as a complete operetta."[72] Auler's call-outs to the public in various newspapers unveiled his concerns about the production being obscured by the many competing versions of the work, and warned, "As many merry widows have sprouted from every corner of this city [we present]

---

[68] Cast included Joanita Many, Maria Mazza, Elvira Benevente, Albertina de Carvalho, Isabel Ficks, Maria da Piedade, Regina Ferreira, Antonieta de Oliveira, Mariana Ferreira, Eduardo Leite, João de Deus, Samuel Rosalvo, Américo Colombo, Joaquim de Oliveira, Luís Bastos, Tavares, J., Bastos, J. Romeu, J. Figueiredo, J. Joaquim da Silva Mendonça. Acervo cinemateca brasileira, http://cinemateca.org.br/filmografia-brasileira/. Elvira Benevente was born in Genoa, 1888; was active in São Paulo theatrical scene before being hired by Labanca and Leal's company. Early in the 1920s, she became director of a company of operettas and revistas in São Paulo; see Virginia de Almeida Bessa, "A cena musical paulistana: teatro musicado e canção popular, 1911–1934," PhD dissertation, Universidade de São Paulo, 2012, 125 and fn. 131.

[69] *Gazeta de Notícias*, September 9, 1909.

[70] Like in *café cantantes* and music halls, the number of musicians in these orchestras ranged from 8–15, being "enlarged" to 20–30 for special occasions. See, Gutsche-Miller, "Pantomime-Ballet on the Music-Hall Stage," 340.

[71] *Careta* 70, II, August 2, 1909.

[72] Altman shows one film production of *The Merry Widow* by Kalem Films, in 1908 in New York; see Altman, *Silent Film Sound*, 114 and 212.

Figure 8.4. The Merry Widow at the Cinema Rio Branco. *Careta*, October 2, 1909.

Source: Biblioteca Nacional do Rio de Janeiro, Hemeroteca Digital

THE WIDOWS 217

the only one with solos and choruses and grand orchestra." Addressing the competition, Auler pointed out that his new *filme cantante* was "just like in the theater,"[73] but also emphasized that his cinematographic *Merry Widow* offered "a new take on the popular operetta." The right combination of the familiar theatrical performance with the innovative new technology would be the recipe for the work's success.

Auler's way of driving the public's attention to his cinematographic *Merry Widow* by casting it as a better alternative to the theatrical production panned out in the end. The critic from *O Paiz* fully endorsed the production, noting that the work was "the best *Merry Widow* in Rio de Janeiro . . . with its many inventions, with sung chorus and solos, [and] with everything arranged in special tapes by Alberto Moreira's daring conception."[74] In October, Auler's Cinema Rio Branco started to sell tickets in advance to minimize the long lines at the box office that were delaying the presentation starting times, and portable chairs were added along the walls to accommodate the audience overflow.[75] In November, Auler started to show a new "Pathé Frères copy [of *The Merry Widow*] in color," which was exported for showings at theaters in Lisbon.[76] By December 17, 1909, the newspaper *O Paiz* announced that Auler's cinematographic *The Merry Widow* had been presented more than 300 times at his Cinema Rio Branco and had sold 147,612 tickets, a record for the time.[77]

The success of the production reveals both audiences' and producers' openness to the possibilities offered by the new technology and in particular to the experiments connecting sounds with images. In a 1936 interview, Francisco Serrador Carvonell (1872–1941), a Spanish entrepreneur and prominent movie producer in São Paulo and Rio de Janeiro, described the experimentations with "singing behind the scenes" in *filmes cantantes* as a long process of trial and error. He noted specifically the preoccupation with vocal projection, as he explained that several attempts were made until a satisfactory sound was achieved from behind the screen:

> The film was in reality silent. The sound was added during the projection with the presence of the orchestra and the singers at the theater. . . . We first tried to put the singers beside the stage, but it did not produce the expected result. . . . Then we changed the performers' seating in comfortable benches behind the

---

[73] *Gazeta de Notícias*, August 28, 1909.
[74] *O Paiz*, September 12, 1909.
[75] *O Paiz*, September 20, 1909.
[76] Silva, *Circo-Teatro*, 261–262.
[77] Costa, "O som no cinema Brasileiro," 47.

218   MUSIC AND COSMOPOLITANISM

screen, where they read their parts or sung the excerpts of Leoncavalo or Bizet through tubes made by wood or hard paper and positioned through the edges of screen; from there the singers would spread their chirpings through the audiences. Thus, the artists needed to be at every presentation to dub the images on the screen. The success was complete.[78]

Arnaldo Di Pace has conjectured why live voices were put behind the screen while performers in the orchestra pit were visible to the audience. The arrangement may have been the result of practical matters; if the singers were behind the scenes, they could easily be substituted without much detriment to the overall production. That was the case with Montenegro, Cataldi, and Amica Pellissier, who traveled several times between Rio de Janeiro and São Paulo to sing at movies in both cities.[79] But there were also disadvantages to the process. To achieve the desired synchronization between the live voices behind the screen, orchestra, and images, extra rehearsals were needed, and it was certainly more costly to pay the singers to be at every performance, several times a day, than to use the more up-to-date and readily available recorded synchronizing technology. Furthermore, in the interview Serrador also notes that the "behind the screen" performances put extreme strain on the artists, and he commiserated with the "poor tenor," who needed to repeat the "arias a dozen times, non-stop."[80] Considering that at the Cinema Rio Branco the cinematographic *Merry Widow* was presented four times daily, one can only fathom how the singers could cope with the strenuous physical demands of the repeated performances, not to mention the damage that such a practice would inflict on their voices.[81] Still, they continued for months, non-stop, and by mid-1910 the work showed no signs of slowing down its success at the box office.

Di Paci suggests quite pointedly that these experiments with expressive intermedialism were successful exactly because they offered sounds with novel "special marks," the new auditive experiences created by singing into tubes, which resulted in sounds that were different from the live voice performances aimed directly at the audiences without the technological mediation.[82] Di Paci assumes that the singers on the screen and the ones behind the screen were the same, as the mediation of tubes transformed the live voices, while keeping the illusion that the "real" singer on the film was

---

[78] Serrador interview, given to journalist Celestino Silveira, is cited in Arnaldo Di Paci, "O musical antes do musical," *Revista Livre de Cinema* 5, no. 1 (Jan/April, 2018): 80–82.See also, Vicente de Paula Pereira, *A bela época do cinema brasileiro* (São Paulo: Perspectiva, 1976), 44.
[79] Amica Pelisser also substituted for Hanna.
[80] Di Paci, "O musical antes do musical," 83.
[81] *Gazeta de Notícias*, September 17, 1909.
[82] Di Paci, "O musical antes do musical," 82–83.

THE WIDOWS   219

producing the sounds. That was the "fundamentàl lie" afforded by the new technology, Rick Altmanc noted, for spectators would easily believe that "the sound is produced by the image when in fact it remains independent from it."[83] In this case, the audience also did not need to be familiar with singers' voices, both on and behind the screen, since the "special mark" would be the result of the technologically mediated vocal sound offering the phantasmagoric experience expected from the new media.

But that was not the case with the cinematographic *Merry Widow*, which used the image of one well-known artist, Cremilda de Oliveira, and the voice of another, as Hanna's voice was performed behind the screen by Ismênia Matheus, who until that point had not yet performed the role in the theater. Considering that at the time of the release of the cinematographic *Merry Widow*, Oliveira's concurrent theatrical performance at the Theatro Apollo was reaching its centenary presentation, one has to assume that several in attendance at the Cinema Rio Branco would be familiar with her voice.[84] Thus, the result was both a "special mark" produced by the mediation of the tubes and a surprise "special mark" caused by the sound of Matheus's voice—a sonic/timbre mismatch between the actual voice and the expected voice to match the image. Oliveira's well-known vocal timbre was switched by an "other," strange, disembodied Matheus's voice hidden behind the screen. Thus, a new vocal timbre, as a crucial bodily site of voice, came to assume a central role to the novelty and eventual success of the cinematographic *Merry Widow*. Furthermore, Matheus, a Spanish artist who had been active in minor roles in café-concerts and comic theater prior to her movie career, provided not only an unexpected new vocal timbre to Oliveira's body image of Hanna, but also a new "language sound," since one has to assume that Oliveira's Portuguese and Matheus's Spanish accents were markedly different, even if they were both singing in Portuguese. Thus, the element of surprise was not merely in the mismatched vocal timbre/body/image, but also one allowed by the variety of "language's musicalities."[85] Audiences would then experience yet another "sonic mark" as linguistic accents also clashed with the projected body of Oliveira as Hanna. In the cinematographic *Merry Widow*, both technologically

---

[83] Rick Altman, "Introduction," *Yale French Studies* no. 60 (1980): 6. See also, Patrik Sjöberg, "The Fundamental Lie: Lip Sync, Dubbing, Ventriloquism, and the Othering of Voice in Documentary Media," in *Vocal Projections: Voice in Documentary*, ed. Annabelle Honess Roe and Maria Pramaggiore (New York: Bloomsbury Academic, 2018), 45.

[84] The operetta's centenary presentation at Theatro Apolo was announced in the *Gazeta de Notícias*, September 17, 1909, and credit was given to Matheus. See Elena Mosconi, "Silent Singers: The Legacy of Opera and Female Stars and Early Italian Cinema," in *Researching Women in Silent Cinema: New Findings and Perspectives*, ed. Monica Dall'Asta, Victoria Duckett, and Lucia Tralli (Bologna: University of Bologna and University of Melbourne, 2013), 334–352.

[85] For this topic, see Steven Feld, Aaron Fox, Thomas Porcello, and David Samuels, "Vocal Anthropology: From the Music of Language to the Language of Song," in *A Companion to Linguistic Anthropology*, ed. by Alessandro Duranti (Malden: Blackwell, 2004), 321–345..

220 MUSIC AND COSMOPOLITANISM

mediated voice and the mismatch body/sound and language/sounds became expressive tools.

Disembodied by technology, Matheus's creative agency was not lost, however, as her individuality would emerge both from the "grain of her voice," as in Barthes's reference to the bodily dimension of voice,[86] as well in a socially acquired embodied linguistic characteristic audible in her syllable and word accentuations. Substituted by Oliveira's, Matheus's absent body was part of the phantasmagoric experience of the movie, and her disembodied performance of Hanna available in the new medium added yet another *Merry Widow* version to the many available to Rio de Janeiro's audiences. At the same time, Oliveira's performances of Hanna, being presented in the theater concurrently with the cinematographic *Merry Widow*, appeared on the same night in two versions; in one, her present body matched her voice; in the other, her body as an illusion was disconnected from her voice. As a result, the cinematographic *Merry Widow* offered a new Oliveira, whose voice could be experienced through both its familiarity and its strangeness. In the end, the meshing of Oliveira with Matheus in the cinematographic sonic realm was left to multiply further in the audience's imagination. But these many juxtapositions of familiar/surprise, presence/absence, real/illusion, live performance/technology mediation, which enhanced the phantasmagoric experience of the *filmes cantantes*, were dependent on the audiences' familiarity with *The Merry Widow* in its many versions already performed and being repeated in Rio de Janeiro, without which the manipulation of "new experiences" could not have had its full effects.

Still, the voice and body relationship, and also their mismatch, was not a constant in the cinematographic *Merry Widow*. While the image of Oliveira remained, the voice behind the screen was not always that of Matheus. Artists acting and singing behind the screen could be substituted, an advantageous and flexible process for artists and directors, and one that added a floating vocal "Others" to the static body of Oliveira. If the assumption that the audience's positive interaction with the different sounds of voices coming from behind the screen was the result of hearing "surprise voices," or the strangeness of the body/voice mismatch, the element of novelty, the mismatched voice (considering that the image remained the same) could not remain constant since, as Jessica Taylor noted, "familiarity makes things natural" and thus the surprise element would vanish.[87] The "Other" voice behind the screen was thus not a constant, and the actress and singer Amica Pelisser sometimes substituted for Matheus. The possibility of yet a new voice disrupting the familiar voice/body relationship guaranteed that the audience's imagination remained fluid. In this case, the

---

[86] See Rolan Barthes, *The Grain of Voice* (New York: Random House, 2010 [1972]).
[87] Jessica Taylor, "'Speaking Shadows': A History of the Voice in the Transition from Silent to Sound Film in the United States," *Journal of Linguistic Anthropology* 19, no. 1 (2009), 1.

THE WIDOWS 221

original, the natural, the authentic was not sought after, but its opposite, the inauthentic, the artificial, the untruthful—all of which would only encounter their existence in one's imagination.

Serrador noted that in the process of singing behind the screen it was imperative that the singers not appear on the stage to receive applause, even if they were more than willing to do so. They should not disturb the experience provided by the sound experimentation in the new media; "The phantasmagory experience needed to be preserved," Serrador explained in his interview.[88] In the case of the cinematographic *Merry Widow*, the "Othering of voice" or the "Fundamental Lie" was not hidden, or merely implicit, but promoted. The vocal sound and the image needed to be totally independent from one another and the mismatch to be deliberate and perceivable enough to cause surprise and fulfill its expectation. Taylor has shown how in the early days of sound movies in the United States, the desirable result was to match body and sound perfectly to minimize the disconnect of social class, gender, language, and race.[89] In the case of the cinematographic *Merry Widow* the opposite was true, the mismatch was accepted, expected, and an essential part of the experience. The mismatch of body and voice would actually enhance each performance as an added attraction and ultimately make the vocal performance behind the screen, rather than the image on the screen, the emphasis of the show. Di Paci notes that with the choice of a live performance "behind the screen," artists could act freely, without the constraints of the body image connections visible on the stage.[90] Consequently, each time a different voice for *The Merry Widow*'s protagonists was heard behind the screen, they created further multiple relationships of body image/voice, as they benefited from the magical powers provided by the unstable nature of live performances.

The cinematographic *Merry Widow* was more than an adaptation of the theater for the movies, but another dimension of the artists' expressivity, caused by their relation with both the new technology and with the audience's new perceptions of them.[91] Before a complete separation and virtualization of both body and sound, the movie versions of *The Merry Widow* relied on their several extra lives spread throughout the globe, for the operetta's popularity became key in the experiments with the new dimensions allowed by new technology, as it asserted and challenged the fundamental attachment between the artist and the audience. This may be one of the reasons why, after the cinematographic *The*

---

[88] Cited in Di Paci, "O musical antes do musical," 84.

[89] Taylor, " 'Speaking Shadows,' " 3, 7, and 10–12. Sjöberg, "The Fundamental Lie" 59; "the voice always stands in between: body and language, biology and culture, inside and outside, between subject and other; between sound and noise. Sjöberg, *Vocal Projections*, 50.

[90] Di Paci, "O musical antes do musical," 84–85.

[91] Di Paci, "O musical antes do musical," 84–85.

Merry Widow, Auler's new productions using theatrical casts of operettas, such as Sidney Jones's *Geisha* and Straus's *Ein Walzertraum*, did not impress as much. These works achieved a relatively high success in Rio de Janeiro, but they did not entrench in the local context nearly as much as Lehár's operetta. In addition, by the time Auler presented *filmes cantantes* based on Jones's and Straus's staged works, the process was no longer new, and familiarity eventually made it natural and therefore uninteresting. *The Merry Widow* thus presented at the right time in the right place, not as a stable work, but as a work made up over and over again through its many extra lives in Rio de Janeiro, as it moved swiftly from material to virtual worlds of performative spaces.

At the Circus

After 18 months of success in Rio de Janeiro's theaters and movie theaters, on March 18, 1910, *The Merry Widow* arrived at the circus (Figure 8.5). Presented during the second part of the program as the climax of the show, the operetta followed the traditional mélange of circus attractions, including jugglers, contortionists, clowns, and comic sketches. The idea of bringing the popular operetta to the circus ring was already in the works at the end of the 1909, when the Italian entrepreneur and circus owner Afonso Spinelli saw the potential for yet another production of the operetta in the city. To win audiences all over again, he announced the circus presentation as a "thrilling novelty" and built a most luxurious performance intended to offer a new take on the already familiar work. Spinelli spared no costs and attended to every detail. He assembled a group of

Figure 8.5. Circo Spinelli, presenting A viúva alegre (1910).
A noite: Supplemento Literário, June 28, 1938.
Source: Biblioteca Nacional do Rio de Janeiro, Hemeroteca Digital

THE WIDOWS   223

designers and technicians to provide special scenarios appropriate for the circus stage and ordered the theatrical costumes directly from Europe, in accordance with the Vienna "original" first performance of the operetta.[92] He also increased the number of musicians in the circus band to take on Lehár's score and entrusted the production to his right-hand man, the veteran actor, producer, singer, writer, and "clown," Benjamin de Oliveira (1870–1954). A Black artist who was born to enslaved parents and freed at birth, Oliveira left home at age 12 to join the circus, worked with Spinelli for several years, was responsible for bringing innovative dramatic performances to the circus, transforming the arena into a circus-theater, and had a host of acting roles under his belt by the time *The Merry Widow* opened.[93]

As Oliveira took on the challenge of producing a smashing success of *The Merry Widow* at the circus, he trained the circus's acrobats, jugglers, and clowns to dance, sing, and act without prompts. He also directed the production, finding novel ways to stage the work in the circus ring. The libretto was set to a new Portuguese translation by Henrique de Carvalho, who bypassed Azevedo's version and provided his own to better fit the new venue. Paulino Sacramento (1880–1926), a Black musician familiar in bohemian circles and who worked with well-known local theater writers and directors, arranged Lehár's music for wind instruments, rehearsed, and conducted the enlarged circus wind ensemble. Hanna Glawari was performed by Lili Cardona, an English artist married to the Spanish circus artist Juan Cardona, who followed her husband's career as a juggler and acrobat.[94] Danilo was played by composer and singer Manoel Pedro de Santos, known locally as Baiano (1870–1944), who also had a successful career as a recording artist and as a singer in the city's many performing venues, and later by Eduardo das Neves. Baron Mirko was played by the comic actor Pacheco, and Oliveira himself appeared as Njegus. In an attempt to produce a work that was not merely on par with but superior to the many theatrical and movie versions of the operetta, Oliveira wrote to Lehár directly, asking for the composer's assistance with the choice of clothes and scenarios that could be appropriate to the circus setting, to which Lehár apparently replied with instructions.[95] According to Ermínia Silva, at the premiere a special libretto was distributed among the audience, so that they could follow Benjamin's setup of the operetta for the

[92] *Correio da Manhã*, March 18, 1910.
[93] Ermínia Silva has provided the most detailed investigation of the Spinelli Circus and the role of Oliveira in the operetta production; see her *Circo-Teatro*, 252–283.
[94] Lily Cardona was the daughter of Marcelino Teresa and Lizzie Stuart Teresa. Her family had moved to Spain at the beginning of the 1900s.
[95] In an interview later in life for the *Revista da Semana*, in October 1944, Benjamin told the reporter that he had corresponded with Franz Lehàr directly to clarify questions about the operetta's figurines and asserted that Lehàr provided the information; Silva, *Circo-Teatro*, 264.

224　MUSIC AND COSMOPOLITANISM

circus, an usual practice in ballets and comic theater in Europe.[96] Attentive to the movie technology available and having himself appeared in early local film productions, Oliveira was certainly familiar with the cinematographic *Merry Widows* running around the city. He thus cleverly added more novel features to the circus production, including "dances with electrical projections," most probably the last dance scene of act II, bringing to the production a desired mix of live theater, music, and new technology showing in the background.[97] As an experienced creator and performer of pantomimes, Oliveira probably heard in Lehár's *The Merry Widow* the same potential that did Felix Salten, who in 1906 noted about the operetta:

> Lehár . . . of the present moment, he gives the beat for our steps. His waltzes have pantomimic ambitions, they have dramatic points. They have seen the modern design of the Barrisons, the bravura of Saharet, the stunning gracefulness of Tortajada and the gaudier pace of variety theater. In this music, there are colors of a cake-walk atmosphere (not merely echoes), colors of Matchiche [*sic*], something of the pulsing, greedy, glowing rhythm of Matchiche. Ten thousand little authenticities of today, which would perhaps disappear together with us like bubbles without leaving a trace, bubble and sprinkle out of this music.[98]

In the city where waltzes and *maxixes* were part of daily life, when the operetta finally opened at the Spinelli Circus in March 1910, Rio de Janeiro audiences welcomed yet another *Merry Widow* with open arms. Critics raved about Henrique de Carvalho's Portuguese version of the libretto, Oliveira's success in adapting the work to the circus arena, and Sacramento's new arrangement and instrumentation of Lehár's score. The critic from *O Paiz* reported: "After wandering around the city's theaters, Hanna Glawary, the bohemian nice lady *Merry Widow*, settled at the Circo Spinelli, in San Cristóvão, from where she won't leave soon. And the beautiful lady owner of seductive millions has no reason to do so."[99] Another commentator singled out Cardona's performance: "The Spinelli company produced a luxurious *Merry Widow*. All the clothes and new scenery are beyond any critique. The artists performed brilliantly and we should highlight Lili Cardona, who was an admirable Hanna Glawary."[100] According to Cardona's biographer, "Lili Cardona entered [the ring] luxuriously dressed in a

---

[96] Silva, *Circo-Teatro*, 264. For the practice in ballets Smith, *Opera and Ballet in the Age of Giselle* (Princeton, NJ: Princeton University Press, 2000).

[97] Silva, *Circo-Teatro*, 268–269.

[98] Cited in Marion Linhardt, "Local contexts and genre construction in early continental musical theatre," in *Popular Musical Theater in London and Berlin*, ed. by Len Platt, Tobias Becker, and David Linton (Cambridge: Cambridge University Press, 2014), 57–58.

[99] *O Paiz*, Abril 7, 1910.

[100] Silva, *Circo-Teatro*, 229.

A canção montenegrina (2º acto). — A entrada de Anna Glavari, a *Viuva Alegre* (1º acto).

Figure 8.6. "The Merry Widow at the circus ring. Lili Cardona as Anna Glavari,"
Fon-Fon (March 26, 1910).
Source: Biblioteca Nacional do Rio de Janeiro, Hemeroteca Digital

toilette *gris-perle*, beautiful and very expensive . . . her voice was not too strong, but beautiful and pleasing, with excellent timbre and sufficiently in tune."[101] The critic of the *Revista da Semana* also noted that "Benjamin de Oliveira . . . [who] took on the challenge in the role of Njegus, can give lessons of sobriety, naturalness, and observation."[102] Some believed that the circus production was not only top notch, but that it had outdone the many foreign companies that had offered the work in local theaters in the previous 18 months. The *Revista da Semana* reported, "The presentation of the uncontested *Merry Widow* at the Circus Spinelli [is] as good as any other [*Merry Widow*] that had been presented here [in Rio de Janeiro], but better produced, the artists are better in tune and perform without prompts."[103] The *Fon-Fon* magazine (Figure 8.6) also provided a comparison of widows:

> It is extraordinary! Nobody can stop the unparalleled success of *The Merry Widow*. You will remember all the foreign companies that took it to the stage and that roused throngs of people to the theaters. Then the happy operetta entered the domain of the movies. It was the success that we all watched and that continues in the Cinema Rio Branco. But when we thought that all the

---

[101] Silva, *Circo-Teatro*, 233.
[102] *Revista da Semana*, April 3, 1910.
[103] *Revista da Semana*, April 3, 1910.

226 MUSIC AND COSMOPOLITANISM

sources of success for the operetta were exhausted, we now have it at the Circus Spinelli. Thus, my friends, this time the operetta was able to acquire even more success.... This popular presentation was the final thing needed for the operetta and, as a matter of fact, in no way has the performance [at the circus] left anything to be desired, or was it less attractive than the many foreign companies that were among us. Notably, in the Circus Spinelli Hanna Glawari is the [juggler] artist.[104]

Three months after the premiere, on June 19, 1910, a chronicle noted that *The Merry Widow* at the circus "still fills up." Satirizing local intellectuals who repeatedly argued for government subsidies aimed at the establishment of a national theater, a critic asked himself, referring to the operetta at the circus: "Is this [*Merry Widow*] the national theater?" But there was more to the question than its condescending tone about the circus production. It was a tacit acknowledgment that the work was not merely a fad, but that it had deeper local cultural and political significance. On July 16, 1910, four months after the premiere, the same *Fon-Fon* magazine noted: "*The Merry Widow*'s success continues at the Spinelli [circus], [a work] which everybody knows but that everybody still wants to see." On July 25, 1910, the *Gazeta de Noticias* reported that the operetta had been presented at the circus 203 times, which means that it was performed more than once a day for four months. By the second part of 1910, Cardona had become the preferred Hanna, competing with Morosini and Oliveira, a role that greatly propelled Cardona's career and allowed her to move on to new roles outside the circus (Figure 8.7). She eventually became an artist and singer in operettas and comic plays in local theaters, where she joined Ismênia Matheus, who also cashed in on her "behind the scenes" cinematographic *Merry Widow* role to play Hanna Glawari on the stage of the Chanteler Cine-theater in the second decade of the century.

In 1934, the Rio de Janeiro critic and journalist Bricio de Abreu went to Vienna to interview Lehár in the middle of Hitler's ascent to power and kept the composer abreast of the success of the operetta in the Brazilian capital. Abreu pointed out to Lehár that *The Merry Widow* was so popular in Brazil that "even a black actor" made the operetta a success.[105] Lehár did not seem surprised and reminded Abreu that "the work was performed in Addis Ababa and also in the Belgian Congo [Democratic Republic of Congo] with an all-black cast." The dates of those performances in Africa were not mentioned, so it is not clear if the primacy of a Black actor performing the operetta remained with Oliveira and with Eduardo das Neves, who had also written and performed a short-lived

[104] *Fon-Fon*, April 13, 1910.
[105] Bricio de Abreu, "A viúva alegre," *O Cruzeiro*, August 13, 1957.

Figure 8.7. Lili Cardona. *Fon-Fon*, June 8, 1912.
Source: Biblioteca Nacional do Rio de Janeiro, Hemeroteca Digital

parody of the operetta in January 1910.[106] But it may well be that a circus performance combining singing and moving images at a circus ring with a mixed-race cast was not a most common practice for the operetta's performances in 1910 in the many places where the work traveled.

If, with *The Merry Widow*'s plot and music, Lehár envisioned an appeal to Vienna's ethnic diversity, that diversity certainly did not refer to race, or touch on the racial issues that confronted Oliveira in Rio de Janeiro. While the original cast who performed the work on stages in Vienna, London, Italy, Madrid, Havana, the United States, and in many more cities, consisted of nothing but White actors, one would assume that the audiences who enjoyed the operetta's many versions in many languages in Rio de Janeiro also saw and understood Hanna and Danilo as White by default. To perform *The Merry Widow* at the Spinelli circus with Black actors in roles written and known for their original White casts,

---

[106] Silva, *Circo-Teatro*, 268–270.

228   MUSIC AND COSMOPOLITANISM

Oliveira chose to "whiten up"[107] himself as Njegus, and he also added the artifice of painting the face white later to Eduardo da Neves, who followed Bahiano as Danilo. Oliveira's choice was not lost in the *Fon-Fon* critic's response to the performance: "We applaud the performance of Lili Cardona, Pacheco, Bahiano, and Benjamin de Oliveira, a very funny Njegus and white as a Lily!"[108] To the *Fon-Fon* commentator, who was White, Oliveira's "whitening up" apparently added amusement to the role. On his part, Oliveira understood well how racial transformation of theatrical characters could be part of a facile but desired satire at the circus. That was especially true in a town like Rio de Janeiro with its large Black and mulatto population, which although in majority, occupied the lower ranks of the social and political ladder. Oliveira, who had also successfully played serious theatrical roles originally written and performed by White actors before, did not hesitate to move back and forth, from "whitening up" to perform Shakespearean characters and White clowns to back to his Black skin to perform roles he created for himself.[109] To Oliveira, race switching was a necessary and essential part of his acting tools and diverse stage personas (Figure 8.8).

Oliveira also understood that the "whitening up" in the production of *The Merry Widow* was not a comedic artifice, but a tool necessary to succeed in the creation of a version of the work that could outdo the many others available in the city. As Spinelli heavily invested in a production and impressed audiences and critics with the lavishness of the production, he envisioned the circus *Merry Widow* to be an equivalent to the Vienna "original," down to the "correct" attire design, textiles, and race of the characters. Oliveira's production thus needed to follow suit, presenting a White cast by "whitening up" the circus's actors. As such, in the circus, Black actors were taking roles as "Stage Europeans," a term used by Marvin McAllister to describe Black actors who painted their faces white to perform roles created for White characters and to assume roles never imagined, written, or intended for them.[110] As an actor, Oliveira understood the character as White and, perhaps from an uncritical perspective, he did not feel compelled to mess with *The Merry Widow*'s whiteness. As a result, no critic in the city disparaged his acting capabilities in the operetta; on the contrary, he was the one who received the most acclaim for the presentation, both as a producer and as an actor. Still, as a well-known popular actor and playwright in Rio de Janeiro, everyone in the audience knew that Oliveira was not White. His stage whiteness

[107] This is a term used by Marvin McAllister in *Whiting Up: Whiteface Minstrels and Stage Europeans in African American Performance* (Chapel Hill: University of North Carolina Press, 2011).
[108] *Fon-Fon*, April 13, 1910.
[109] Silva, *Circo-Teatro*.
[110] McAllister, *Whiting Up*, 51. See also Richard Deyer, "The Matter of Whiteness," in *Theories of Race and Racism: A Reader*, ed. John Solomons and Les Back (New York: Routledge, 2000), 539–548.

THE WIDOWS 229

Figure 8.8. Benjamin de Oliveira and his various theatrical characters. Postcard, 1909.

was devised to keep the "original" operetta in view and, in a sense, whiteness was to be accepted like European props and garments that circulated with the idea of the "original" operetta.

230 MUSIC AND COSMOPOLITANISM

While modifications were often deemed necessary to adjust the plot to local sociocultural contexts as the work traveled around the globe, Lehár's operetta achievement in disseminating and welcoming diversity also contradictorily contributed to make whiteness cosmopolitan and natural. Nonetheless, while it was probably not Oliveira's intention to directly question his own city's racial and sociopolitical hierarchies, he was not afraid to confront them either. More than any other dimension of the operetta's many versions, in the skin of Black actors artificially hidden by white makeup, the characters of the circus *The Merry Widow* made the cosmopolitan whiteness visible. Oliveira's *The Merry Widow* allowed a shared experience of whiteness to be confronted by the non-whiteness of the larger world. In Oliveira's production, whiteness is dislodged, leaving the status of "default and natural" to become raced. In the circus, Oliveira identifies racial difference by "making visible what is rendered invisible," the whiteness of the supposedly all-inclusive and flexible *Merry Widow*'s plot.[111]

Not everything in the circus *Merry Widow* was kept as the imagined original, however, for Oliveira did not refrain from messing with the operetta's original sound in his choice of instrumentation. Rather than hiring string performers to reproduce Lehár's score as faithfully as possible, Oliveira chose to keep the circus wind band, departing from the "original timbre" of the orchestral sounds, which Rio de Janeiro's audiences had learned to appreciate in *The Merry Widow*. If one had to "see" the work like the original, in dress, scenography, and whiteness, in the circus the operetta's familiar melodies sounded different. Sacramento's score did not survive, thus we do not know for sure if he kept all the music numbers according to Lehár's original, although one has to assume that the full operetta would not fit in a third section of a nightly circus program and thus modifications needed to happen. Yet there was no mention in the press of any additions or cuts, as it was customary when the work traveled in different languages. But whether or not the music numbers did not change, the timbre certainly did. The score adapted to wind band was in fact one of the elements in the production that Oliveira praised the most. In the announcement for the work's premiere at the circus, he stressed that Sacramento's score "is an utter miracle" as he lured audiences to go to the circus specifically to hear the familiar music to the sound of a wind band.

By the time Sacramento was charged with arranging Léhar's music to the Spinelli's circus band, he already had an extensive experience in many entertainment venues of the city. He had been a colleague of the composer Francisco Braga, the trombonists Albertino Pimental, and Candinho Trombone while they were student performers at the band of the Asilo dos Meninos Desvalidos,

---

[111] Hazel Carby, "Imagining Black Men: The Politics of Cultural Identity," *Yale Review* 80, no. 3 (1992): 186–197, see 193.

THE WIDOWS   231

a governmental institution that educated orphans. Both Sacramento and Braga eventually became directors of the ensembles, although their career followed different paths afterward. Braga, a White man devoted to the concert music scene, received a governmental fellowship to study in Europe and returned as a celebrity with a role to play at the local musical establishment, although he did not eschew from conducting wind bands and worked with musicians not belonging to the Instituto Nacional de Música. Sacramento, a Black musician, continued in the business of popular entertainment, as a prolific composer, arranger, conductor, pianist, and a gifted trumpet player, a skill that gave him a privileged role at the prestigious Banda do Corpo de Bombeiros (Fire Department band). Like many military or social bands in the city, independent wind bands employed the middle-sector of the city's social fabric, who in turn played key roles in music education by using portable instruments, and in particular brass instruments that were easier to play than strings or the piano.[112] Wind band musicians were also very active in smaller instrumental ensembles that performed informally in social gatherings and in bars, improvising over well-known tunes, groups that were known as *chorões* in Rio de Janeiro, but that also followed a trend in many similar instrumental ensembles performing in other cities.[113] Therefore, Sacramento transited easily within the heterogeneous social and racial fabric of the city's entertainment venues, which was well represented in the Spinelli's circus audiences, if segregated by seating assignments. Listening to *The Merry Widow* through the circus band made sense to various sectors of the city's sociocultural context, including middle-level government employees, lower-ranking working classes, and small business owners—mostly Portuguese and Italian immigrants.[114] These were city residents already familiar with well-known operatic tunes and dances performed in public squares by such wind bands (see Chapter 9).[115]

---

[112] Trevor Herbert has showed how wind bands were adaptable to widely different performing contexts; see his "Nineteenth-Century Bands: Making a Movement," in *The British Brass Band: A Musical and Social History*, ed. Trevor Herbert (Oxford and New York: Oxford University Press, 2000), 10–60. Regarding the sound of the military band as music of "the crowd," see his "The Band Is the Instrument: The Crowd and the Legacy of the Long Nineteenth Century," in *Our Music/ Our World: Wind Bands and Local Social Life*, ed. Maria do Rosário Pestana et al. (Lisbon: Edições Colibri, 2020). 17; for general considerations about the importance of brass bands in various social contexts, see Suzel Ana Reily, "The Power of the Brass Band," in *Our Music/Our World: Wind Bands and Local Social Life*, ed. Maria do Rosário Pestana, André Granjo, Damien François Sagrillo, and Gloria Rodriguez Lorenzo (Lisbon: Edições Colibri, 2020), 27–40.

[113] For the increasing presence of brass instruments and military band performers in similar instrumental groups in other parts of the Americas see Ruth "Sunni" Witmer, "Cuban *Charanga*: Class, Popular Music, and the Creation of National Identity" PhD dissertation, University of Florida, 2011, 72–95.

[114] Silva, *Circo-Teatro*, 265.

[115] For England see, Dave Russel, *Popular Music in England:1840–1914* (Manchester and New York: Manchester University Press, 1997), 228–239. For operatic arrangements for bands in Italy, see Leydi, "The Dissemination and Popularization of Opera," 325–329.

232 MUSIC AND COSMOPOLITANISM

Rio de Janeiro's critics commented on Sacramento's score for *The Merry Widow* only in passing, however. Yet in the next presentation at the circus of Oliveira's own play, *Os Pescadores*, there was a laudatory note about the actor's successful play and performance in the newspapers, but a harsh criticism about how music was used in the productions at the circus, which the commentator faulted exactly because it lacked an orchestra with string instruments.[116] If, to most music critics, a complete symphonic orchestra with strings was necessary for the production of *The Merry Widow* to be faithful to the work's original, one would assume that timbre had also become part of the shared experience of the operetta. But while Oliveira's production goal was to keep with the "original" as much as possible to attract audiences willing to pay for the show, he nonetheless was proud of Sacramento's score that was unfaithful to the "original" sound and offered instead Lehár's popular melodies in an alternative sonic dimension. This is not to highlight a cross-cultural experience, since the wind band, like the full orchestra with strings, was nothing but European and as such it fit well in the overall nature of popular entertainment circulating in many cities. But while Oliveira's "whitening up" made whiteness visible, the listening experience of the circus *Merry Widow* provided yet another way to engage with the familiar operetta. For well-known music performed in new ways put the focus of novelty on the performance and on the overall sound, rather than on the music itself, as Spinelli's circus band pointed to a novelty specifically associated with timbre, or how to sound the same music differently. Musicians like Sacramento played key roles in bridging such a heterogeneous context, not by developing new, unique participation channels unconnected from the established mediums of the status quo, as some have claimed.[117] Artists like Oliveira and Sacramento took an active part in molding a coexistence of the many realms of the social and racial city through music, performance, and sound explorations. That Oliveira could reach a wide spectrum of the city's socially and racially diverse population with his *Merry Widow* production is a case in point. And he chose to do so by changing only one aspect of the operetta: its overall sound.

---

[116] *O Malho*, April 1910.

[117] Monica Velloso, for example, explored what she calls a "parallel citizenship" formed by non-elite sectors of Rio de Janeiro society; see her, *Modernismo no Rio de Janeiro: Turunas e Quixotes* (Rio de Janeiro: KBR, 2015), 28.

9

Cosmopolitan Traditions

An Unexplainable Tradition

At the time of Verdi's death in 1901, Artur Azevedo wrote in his weekly chronicle that "here [in Rio de Janeiro] we heard all of his operas, which are exceptionally popular; [the operas were also] spread in places without a theater, around the country, through the piano, or more precisely, through the *realejo*."[1] Azevedo's observation about the local pervasiveness of Verdi's music was corroborated in 1903, when a critic, distraught by the endless repetition of *Aïda* (1871) in the city's theaters, noted in a rather disappointing tone that the music "is [here] an unexplainable, if acceptable, tradition."[2] Although from different perspectives, both writers acknowledge Verdi's music as an integral part of Rio de Janeiro's musical life, both in and outside the theater. But Azevedo was not concerned with the repetition of popular operas. If in 1901 he cheered that "the lyric company will not open with *Aïda* [but] . . . with *La bohemia* [1896], which is much desired, appreciated, and beloved by our public,"[3] later in 1907 he also admitted, "Yesterday I went to *Ballo in maschera*, one of the operas by the divine Verdi that most appeals to my musical eclecticism. It is *a profusion of melodies* [my emphasis] that the great composer spread in that score with a liberty of a crazy nabob."[4] *Un ballo in maschera* (1859) was a fifty-year-old opera when Azevedo wrote this comment without a hint of frustration about the work being old-fashioned or of audiences being tired of it: novelty was not a concern, for the opera's "profusion of melodies" were still moving him. Azevedo's embrace of a core operatic repertory was not shared by all, however. João do Rio, for instance, was less accepting of the repetition of the same works every year. In 1904, he commiserate about an even longer list of unexplained traditions: "The impresarios don't risk bringing a new repertory [to Rio de Janeiro], offering invariably [Amilcare Ponchielli's] *Gioconda* [1876], *Aïda*, *Il Trovatore* [1853], *Un*

---

[1] Artur Azevedo, "O Theatro," in *A Notícia*, January 31, 1901. Azevedo's theatrical chronicles were reprinted as *O Theatro: crônicas de Artur Azevedo*, ed. Larissa de Oliveira Neves and Orna Messer Levin (Campinas: Editora de Unicamp, 2009).

[2] *Gazeta de Notícias*, October 16, 1903; quoted in Ferreira, "Cenários da ópera na imprensa carioca," 61.

[3] Azevedo, *A Notícia*, January 31, 1901.

[4] Artur Azevedo, "O Theatro," *A Notícia*, October 10, 1907.

Music and Cosmopolitanism. Cristina Magaldi, Oxford University Press. © Oxford University Press 2024.
DOI: 10.1093/oso/9780199744770.003.0010

234   MUSIC AND COSMOPOLITANISM

ballo in maschera [1859], the three most acclaimed operas by Puccini, *Manon Lescaut* (1893); *La bohemia; Tosca* (1900), as well as [Mascagni's] *Cavalleria rusticana* (1890), [Leoncavallo's] *Il Pagliacci* (1892) . . . and [Carlos Gomes's] *Il Guarany* (1871). And they stay there."[5] João do Rio's complaint referred not to the works' origins or styles, nor to issues of politics, cultural geography, or aesthetics, but to the fact that the operas were not new, i.e., they had been repeated in local theaters for several years. To both chroniclers, *Un ballo in maschera*, a mid-century opera in which Verdi experiments with a mix of styles thus fulfilling Azevedo's eclectic preferences, and *Aïda*, a grand opera that had premiered in Rio de Janeiro back in 1876, were understood not as fashions or as canonic works, but as part of a local tradition together with more recent works more in line with *verismo*, such as *Cavalleria rusticana*, *La bohemia*, and *Tosca*. But in the end João do Rio was not too concerned about these unexplainable traditions, for he also believed that ultimately these works would not remain in the local repertory for long. In 1907, he noted that "[t]he *cariocas* (residents of Rio de Janeiro) are variable like the weather, the problem is to discover their barometer . . . beyond the *maxixe* [dance] and 'Vissi d'arte' [aria from *Tosca*], there is nothing in this country that has resisted five years of life."[6] To the chronicler's disappointment, however, in the following years the same operas continued to be staged multiple times every season in several theaters, and their tunes further repeated in musical excerpts circulating outside theaters in various formats, in several media, and disconnected from the original plots that had rendered their initial dramatic character. By the end of the first decade of the 20th century, Rio de Janeiro's audiences had not yet moved on from *Aïda*s, nor from *Rigoletto*s and *Traviata*s, while the "Puccini invasion" had taken the hearts and ears of the city's residents to also become a part of local unexplainable traditions.[7]

These chroniclers' observations show that at the dawn of the new century, the city's theatrical audiences were familiar with and expected to hear again and again an established operatic repertory made up of mostly Italian and a few French operas. Ferreira's thorough study shows that the majority of opera companies that operated in Rio de Janeiro in the two decades after the proclamation of the Republic were Italian and, expectedly, 74 percent of the operas presented were by Italian composers, mostly from an established and well accepted repertory in Italy, Europe, and elsewhere. The choices were predictable since Italian directors and artists were fully aware of opera's overseas commercial potential, and understandably would not risk long trips across the ocean without

---

[5] João do Rio, "O mez no theatro," *Kosmos* 1, no. 9, September 1904.
[6] João do Rio, under the pseudonym "Joe," *Gazeta de Notícias*, June 10, 1907.
[7] "Invasão Pucciniana," *O Paiz*, May 15, 1914, cited in Ferreira, "Cenários da ópera," 73.

the certainty of financial returns. Their choices thus attest to both the works' profitability and their wide acceptance in the city. According to Ferreira, during the two decades after the proclamation of the Republic the most performed operas in Rio de Janeiro were Pucinni's *La bohème* (147 times) and *Tosca* (137), Verdi's *Aïda* (131), Ponchielli's *La Gioconda* (118), and Leoncavallo's *Pagliacci* (98). Verdi's earlier works also dominated with *Rigoletto* (90) and *La Traviata* (64). Boito's *Mefistofele* (1868) (57) competed with a few French works, such as Bizet's *Carmen* (1875) (72), Gounod's *Faust* (1859) (60), Meyerbeer's *Les Huguenots* (1836) (43) and *L'Africaine* (1865) (21), Saint-Säens's *Samson et Dalila* (1877) (15), and Massenet's *Werther* (7) (1887). The Brazilian opera composer Carlos Gomes (1836–1896), who had his *Il Guarany* performed 85 times, was the only local composer to achieve such a prominent place. Although a widely performed composer in the early and mid-19th century, the popularity of Rossini had certainly decreased by the end of the century. Still, *Il barbiere di Siviglia* (1816) was staged 52 times during the two decades studied here, while Donizetti's *bel canto* opera *Lucia di Lammermoor* (1835) was performed no fewer than 84 times, both works competing in popularity with more recent works by Verdi and Puccini and surpassing operas by French composers such as Bizet's *Carmen* and Gounod's *Faust*.[8] All in all, works that may be seen today as distinct from one another, geographically, stylistically, and historically, made up the core of the repertory regularly offered at local theaters in the early 20th-century city, for here tradition and modernity were flexible notions rarely set against each other.

The case of Rio de Janeiro's operatic core contradicts Charle's assertion that at the turn of the century there was an "empire of [operatic] French works . . . that equaled that of Italian opera and [that was] bigger than the one before 1870,"[9] at least not outside Europe and the French colonies. The few French operas that made it to Rio de Janeiro at the turn of the 20th century also challenge the idea that French music and culture were the only dominating trends in the city. True, the connection to the Parisian world was inescapable in the Brazilian capital since mid-century, from architecture and fashion to the dominance of French novels in the city's bookstores, in French or in translation, and to the influence of French politics and ideologies among the local intelligentsia. In Rio de Janeiro's theaters, French plays and operettas remained in fashion, French artists who visited, such as Sarah Bernhardt, were guaranteed successes, and they were surely

---

[8] Ferreira, "Cenários da ópera," 48, and "Anexo II," 512–517.

[9] Christophe Charle, "Opera in France, 1870–1914: Between Nationalism and Foreign Imports," in *Opera and Society in Italy and France From Monteverdi to Bourdieu*, ed. Victoria Johnson, Jane F. Fulcher, and Thomas Ertman (Cambridge, UK: Cambridge University Press, 2007); 262; see also Christophe Charle, "La circulation des opéras en Europe au XIXe siècle," *Relations internationales* 155, no 3 (2013): 11–31.

236 MUSIC AND COSMOPOLITANISM

competitors to the prima donnas specialized in operatic works.[10] That was also true in regard to musical trends in the concert hall, and one should not be surprised to find instrumental works by Massenet and Saint-Säens as regulars in concert programming at the beginning of the 20th century, Aware of the popularity of his music, Saint-Säens visited the country twice, in 1899 and in 1905.[11] However, as the 19th century progressed and the circulation of ideas, literature, goods, and musical offerings diversified, the preferences for French operas and operettas were diluted within a multitude of newer fashions from Paris and elsewhere, while the penchant for a number of well-known Italian operas remained relatively constant, attesting to their durability among local audiences.

If one is to use the available statistical data, it is reasonable to say that Italian opera prevailed in Rio de Janeiro despite claims of Gallicism in the theater and, as Ferreira also concluded, it most certainly defied all attempts at Germanism supported by the musical establishment.[12] The data provided by Ferreira should also serve as suggestions to our investigative eyes and ears for an exploration into more complex sociocultural and musical systems at play historically, geographically, and aesthetically when considering the implications of the spread of opera in the city. Already in 1889, the critic from the newspaper O Paiz admitted that in Rio de Janeiro, "We lie, we lie scandalously, with the ease that a politician lies, or a boyfriend, every time we point to our zeal towards the cult of sounds. Music for the Fluminense [from the state of Rio de Janeiro] is summed up in the lyric opera."[13] Yet Ferreira shows an operatic picture in Rio de Janeiro that seems incredibly static and limited at a time of intense diversification and heterogeneity, a reality that did not escape local chroniclers who regularly acknowledged the music's inescapable presence while making a habit of complaining about it. Critics were not shy to repeat year after year the reasons why the city's stages were at such a standstill. Disillusionment with the new government made it an easy target, since it did not supply the necessary subsidies expected by the musical establishment to build an adequate opera hall, or to hire large companies, skilled orchestra performers, and famous singers to perform a more varied and newer repertory. Critics, in consonance with critics from many other cities, were also quick to assign fault to the audience, a large undefined group whose musical tastes they believed were beyond dubious, a public satisfied with the same old facile tunes sung over old plots, which aroused immediate bodily pleasures that did not require the challenging of their minds or further refining their auditory

---

[10] See, for example, Orna Messer Levin, "Theatrical Culture and Global Audience," in The Cultural Revolution of the Nineteenth-Century: Theater, the Book-Trade, and Reading in the Transatlantic World, eds. Márcia Abreu and Ana Cláudia Suriani da Silva, (London: Bloomsbury, 2016), 234–251.

[11] Carol Hess, "Saint-Saëns and Latin America," in Saint-Saëns and His World, ed. Jann Pasler (Princeton, NJ: Princeton University Press, 2012), 201–209.

[12] Ferreira. "A ópera no Rio de Janeiro," 1–12.

[13] França Junior, O Paiz, October 1, 1889.

skills in accordance with their expectations of a new urban bourgeoisie. And as the old and limited operatic repertory was eventually deemed not only unexplainable but unavoidable, critics abandoned the aesthetic and resorted to a political argument, blaming those who lingered in the theater to listen over and over to old-fashioned music inherited from the monarchical years. Giovanni Morelli has shown that in mid-century Italian cities, critics were eager for "political modernization to be translated into cultural experiences," but were frustrated that it did not materialize as expected.[14] The same can be said for the turn-of-the-century Brazilian capital, where critics and the musical establishment, the "Musical Republic," never lost hope that in the new republican city opera would eventually disappear and make room for the appreciation of instrumental works by the Austro-German "classics" and 19th-century romantic composers. Their hopes also failed to materialize: Rio de Janeiro was indeed "the city of opera."[15]

But if the limited operatic repertory presented in Rio de Janeiro theaters was perceived by some as a dubious local tradition, it was surely not an unexplainable one. In fact, the operas presented in the Brazilian capital were much in sync with the emergence in several contemporary cities of a core operatic repertory resting mostly on a limited number of Italian works and a few French ones. One could thus tell similar stories of "unexplainable" local traditions from the perspective of many cities across continents, from large and powerful operatic centers like Paris and Milan to other metropolises such as London and New York, from middle-sized cities like Madrid, Lisbon, Mexico City, Havana, Buenos Aires, and Montevideo to cities further away from the Atlantic routes such as Cairo, Hanoi, Manilla, and many more.[16] In the second half of the 19th century, Verdi's mid-century works, and *Aïda* in particular, were undoubtedly the most performed, with Puccini's competing for the top position at the beginning of the new century, while Gounod's *Faust* and Bizet's *Carmen* were the most popular operas of French provenance, followed by Meyerbeer's *Les Huguenots* and *L'Africaine*. Enrique Río Prado claims that Cubans had such a passion for Verdi to the point of fanaticism.[17] The Havana Opera Company, consisting mostly

---

[14] Morelli, "Opera in Italian Nacional Culture," 384.

[15] This term is used as title of Vanda Freire's *Rio de Janeiro, sec. XIX: A cidade da ópera* (Rio de Janeiro: Editora Garamond, 2013).

[16] See MeLê Yamomo, "Global Currents, Musical Streams: European Opera in Colonial Southeast Asia," *Nineteenth Century Theatre and Film* 44, no. 1 (2017): 54–74; also Jutta Toelle, "Der Duft der großen weiten Welt: Ideen zum weltweiten Siegeszug der italienischen Oper im 19. Jahrhundert," in *Die Oper im Wandel der Gesellschaft. Kulturtransfers und Netzwerke des Musiktheaters in Europa*, ed. Sven Oliver Müller, Philipp Ther, Jutta Toelle, and Gesa zur Nieden (Wien: Böhlau, 2010), 251–261.

[17] Enrique Río Prado, *Pasión cubana por Giuseppe Verdi: La obra y los intérpretes verdianos en La Habana colonial* (Havana: Ed. Unión 2001), 10. Irina Bajini, "Traviatas que cantan habaneras y Faustos que tocan tambor: Parodias operísticas en la Cuba Decimonónica," *Gramma* 22, no. 48 (2011): 63–74;

238　MUSIC AND COSMOPOLITANISM

of Italian musicians and singers, offered first-rate operatic seasons in Havana with plenty of Verdi, and they also offered plenty of Italian operas to audiences in the United States as they toured north several times, reaching New Orleans, Cincinnati, Pittsburgh, Philadelphia, Baltimore, New York, and Washington.[18] Italian opera companies, coming from Italy or assembled in the Americas, did not need a lot of assistance to succeed in the U.S. major opera houses, for the music was among the most widely accepted in U.S. cities.[19] Mexico City's audience had favored Italian operas since early in the century, a preference that only increased as more companies arrived in the city as the century progressed; some even suggested that Mexico City would eventually become the "Italy of the New World."[20] In fact, the data compiled by Ferreira for operas presented in Rio de Janeiro correlates with the operas presented in Mexico City compiled by José Octavio Sosa,[21] as well as with Karen Ahlquist's operatic repertory list presented at New York's Metropolitan Opera House from 1883 on.[22] Ahlquist claims that regardless of the increase in German opera production supported by the high number of German immigrants in the United States, in the second half of the century Italian opera remained the most available foreign-language tradition among English-speaking New Yorkers,[23] even if the constant repetition of Gounod's *Faust* was such that at one point the Metropolitan Opera House was satirically portrayed as a "Faustspielhaus."[24] Italian immigrants in Buenos Aires and Montevideo guaranteed the success of Italian operas since the early 1800s,[25]

[18] The U.S. itineraries of the Havana Opera Company are described in Katherine K. Preston, *Opera on the Road: Traveling Opera Troupes in the United States, 1825–60* (Urbana: University of Illinois Press, 1993); see also Dizikes, *Opera in America*; and Roberto Ignacio Diaz, "Transatlantic Deficits; or, Alberto Vilar at the Royal Opera House," *Bulletin of Latin American Research* 30 (2011): 128–140.

[19] Karen Ahlquist, "International Opera in Nineteenth-Century New York: Core Repertories and Canonic Values," in *The Oxford Handbook of the Operatic Canon*, ed. Cormac Newark and William Weber (Oxford: Oxford University Press, 2018, online publication), 244–245.

[20] Ignacio Altamirano, "Mexico es la Italia del Nuevo Mundo," Crónica de la Semana, *El Renacimiento,* May 23, 1869, cited in Anna Agranoff Ochs, "Opera in Contention: Social Conflict in Late Nineteenth-century Mexico City," PhD dissertation, University of North Carolina at Chapel Hill, 2011, 43; see also Ricardo Miranda, "El espejo idealizado: Un siglo de opera en México (1810–1910)," in *Opera en España y Hispanoamerica: Una creación propia*, Actas del Congreso Internacional La Ópera en España e Hispanoamérica, ed. Alvaro Torrente Sánchez-Guisande and Emilio Francisco Casares Rodicio vol. 2 (Madrid, Universidad Complutense de Madrid, 2001), 155.

[21] José Octavio Sosa, *La ópera en México, de la independencia al inicio de la revolución (1821–1910)* (México City: Instituto Nacional de Bellas Artes y Literatura, 2010).

[22] Ahlquist, "International Opera in Nineteenth-Century New York," 244–245.

[23] Ahlquist, "International Opera in Nineteenth-Century New York," 252.

[24] Daniel Snowman, *The Gilded Stage: A Social History of Opera* (New York: Atlantic Books, 2010, Kindle). The satire was in the comparison of the Met with Wagner's "Festspielhaus" at Bayreuth. For the dissemination of Verdi's operas in the United States, see Martin George, *Verdi at the Golden Gate: Opera in San Francisco in the Gold Rush Years* (Berkeley: University of California Press, 1993), and *Verdi in America: Ogberto through Rigoletto* (Rochester, NY: University of Rochester Press, 2011).

[25] Benjamin Walton, "Canons of Real and Imagined Opera: Buenos Aires and Montevideo, 1810–1860," in *The Oxford Handbook of the Operatic Canon*, ed. Cormac Newark and William Weber (Oxford: Oxford University Press, 2018, online publication), 270–292; see also Claudio Benzecry, "An Opera House for the "Paris of South America:" Pathways to the Institutionalization of High Culture," *Theory and Society* 43, no. 2 (March 2014): 169–196.

COSMOPOLITAN TRADITIONS 239

a taste that was further ingrained in the local culture later in the century as opera served to unite a large number of newly arrived Italian workers, who formed a large diasporic group and who were prone to repeated listening of their preferred works to feed the nostalgia for their homeland, while socializing with their fellow citizens and building local sociopolitical power.[26]

Across the Atlantic, the pattern was the same. Charle notes the dominant presence of a core operatic repertory in Paris late in the 19th century, which was made up of an overwhelming number of works from the Italian core repertory that included *bel canto* old-timers, a limited number of Verdi works, the expected duo Mascagni's *Cavalleria rusticana* and Leoncavallo's *Pagliacci*, and the up-and-coming Puccini. Charle points out that the clinging to an established group of Italian works was because "few impresarios and directors would venture the staging of new works [in Paris]—with new sets, more rehearsals, etc.—without having the returns already secured by consecrated, old works." Like in Rio de Janeiro, after 1870 "musicians and critics [in Paris] complained bitterly about the never ending revivals of repertory works" mostly from Italy, although by the end of the century French works were prioritized over foreign ones.[27] Lisbon's critics added to the complaints: "Always *Trovador*, always *Rigoletto*, always *Traviata*," they proclaimed in the 1870s as the core repertory dominated in Lisbon's prestigious Teatro S. Carlos, a trend that intensified as *Aïda* prevailed in the 1890s.[28] In Spanish cities, the dominance of the *bel canto* at mid-century also led critics to go against audiences' favorable responses to it. But Verdi's connection to Spain went beyond audience support at the operatic theater, for the composer's interest in Spanish plays as sources for his librettos fueled intense local debates among critics and supporters. The debate only intensified when Verdi traveled to Spain in 1863, as his following grew exponentially.[29] That was the case especially in

---

[26] Aníbal Cetrangolo, "*Aïda* Times Two: How Italian Veterans of Two Historic '*Aïda*' Productions Shaped Argentina's Music History," *Cambridge Opera Journal* 28, no. 1 (2016): 79–105. For the operas presented in Buenos Aires, see Alfredo Kelly, *Cronologia de las operas: Dramas liricos, oratorios, himnos, etc. cantados en Buenos Aires* (Buenos Aires: Riera & Cia., 1934). For Montevideo, see Susana Salgado, *Teatro Solis: 150 Years of Opera, Concert, and Ballet in Montevideo* (Middletown, CT: Wesleyan University Press, 2003); also John Rosselli, "The Opera Business and the Italian Immigrant Community in Latin America 1820–1930: The Example of Buenos Aires," *Past & Present* 127 (May,1990): 155–182.

[27] Charle, "Opera in France, 1870–1914," 245.

[28] Luísa Cymbron, "A produção e recepção das óperas de Verdi em Portugal no século XIX", in *Verdi em Portugal (1843–2001)*, Catálogo da Exposição comemorativa do centenário da morte do compositor (Lisbon: Biblioteca Nacional, Teatro Nacional de São Carlos, 2001), 21 and 39. See also Maria José Borges, "Verdi e o gosto pela opera italiana em Portugal no século XIX," *Estudos Italianos em Portugal* 8 (2013): 11–28; Paulo Ferreira de Castro, "Visto de Portugal: Verdi, Wagner e o teatro das nações," in *Alemanha/Portugal: Aspectos e momentos em revista*, ed. F. Ribeiro (Lisbon: Húmus, 2015), 157–173; Gabriela Cruz, "Sr. José, the Worker *mélomane*, or Opera and Democracy in Lisbon ca. 1850," *19th Century Music* 40, no. 2 (2016): 81–105.

[29] Víctor Sánchez Sánchez, "Verdi ante el espejo de España," in *Verdi Reception in Europe and the United States*, ed. Lorenzo Frassa and Michela Niccolai (Lucca: Brepol, 2013), 3–32.

240 MUSIC AND COSMOPOLITANISM

Madrid, where *Aïda* eventually became the most performed opera at the Teatro Real from its premiere there in December 1874 until 1925.[30] Gounod's *Faust* and Bizet's *Carmen* were sure hits in London's Convent Garden heterogeneous artistic environment until the beginning of the 20th century, while the core repertory from Italy remained much alive, regardless of the familiar critical debasement, in particular Verdi's works and his *Aída*.[31] Ingeborg Zechner has observed that London was at the crossroads of the Italian opera industry, serving as a gateway to Italian opera venues and traveling operatic troupes in North America.[32] Yet, at the time of Verdi's death in 1901, London's critics still resisted the composer's success with local audiences, noting with contempt, "If popularity were a sure test of merit, Verdi would indisputably be the greatest operatic composer of the second half of the last century."[33] Gundula Kreuzer has shown the same pattern in Germany, where critics, imbued with music idealism to assert the political dominance of the German culture, attempted to distance themselves from the popular appeal of Italian opera, and Verdi in particular. But that was an unsuccessful attempt, Kreuzer notes, since "Italian music was a quantitative menace to the claim of German [musical] hegemony."[34]

One could certainly extend the net of supporters, and of detractors, for a core Italian operatic repertory to an even larger audience spread over larger geographical areas to evince the fact that, as the 19th century came to a close, a limited number of operatic works created unrivaled sociocultural-aesthetic-musical links among large numbers of people scattered in many cities across a large geographical area. This core operatic repertory went through a long process of "mainstreaming" similar to popular musics in the 20th century, such as rock and roll and rap, which Toybee defines as "a formation that brings together large numbers of people from diverse social groups and across large geographical areas in common affiliation to a musical style."[35] The parallel between operatic

---

[30] Víctor Sánchez Sánchez, *Verdi y España* (Madrid: Akal, 2014), 305–309.

[31] Paul Rodmell, *French Music in Britain 1830-1914* (New York: Routledge, 2020), 72 and 92. For the success of *Aída* in London, see Roberta Montemorra Marvin, "Selling a 'False Verdi' in Victorian London," in *The Idea of Art Music in a Commercial World, 1800-1930*, ed. Christina Bashford and Roberta Montemorra Marvin (Woodbridge, Suffolk, UK: Boydell Press, 2016), 223–249. For a list of performances worldwide, see *Aïda: Verdi* (Paris: L'Avant-Scène, 1974), 109–125. For the vogue for Italian opera in England in the first years of the 20th century, see Paul Rodmell, *Opera in the British Isles, 1875-1918* (London and New York: Ashgate, 2013), 81–84.

[32] Ingeborg Zechner, "Cosmopolitanism in Nineteenth-Century Opera Management," in *Music History and Cosmopolitanism*, ed. Anastasia Belina, Kaarina Kilpiö, and Derek B. Scott (New York: Routledge, Kindle), 43.

[33] "Verdi," *The Athenaeum*, February 2, 1901, 153, cited in Massimo Zicari, *Verdi in Victorian London* (Cambridge: Open Books, 2016), 255.

[34] Gundula Kreuzer, *Verdi and the Germans: From Unification to the Third Reich* (Cambridge, UK: Cambridge University Press, 2010), 13.

[35] Jason Toynbee, "Mainstreaming, from Hegemonic Centre to Global Networks," in *Popular Music Studies*, ed. David Hesmondhalgh and Keith Negus (London: Arnold, (2002 [1992]), 150. For an updated research on this topic see, Bernhard Steinbrecher, "Mainstream Popular Music research: A Musical Update," *Popular Music* 40, no. 3-4 (Dec 2021): 406–427.

COSMOPOLITAN TRADITIONS   241

music at the turn of the 20th century and rock and roll later in the century may seem far-fetched to those who are used to sheltering some European musics of the past from an audience not restricted to exclusive performing spaces, or from critical aesthetic judgments not anchored on unrepeatable models or cultural authenticity. Nonetheless, while this short overview does not offer precise statistics and a clear-cut cartography, it shows that by the time Rio de Janeiro chroniclers and critics were reckoning with an Italian operatic core repertory and a handful of French works as an unexplainable local tradition, the music had actually become part of an unprecedented complex urban cultural network in which the Brazilian capital was but a module. It became a local tradition tied to the commercial possibilities of the emerging entertaining business and new technologies and, at the same time, a tradition that comfortably merged the old and the new or, as Morelli put it, the "quasi-old" with the "quasi-new."[36] It was a tradition built upon and characterized by a city's connection to other cities, where one would also find these unexplainable traditions. In fact, as a tradition, few would spend time speculating on where the music came from or how it came to be. It was indeed a local tradition entangled with European imperialism and unfettered capitalism, but it was also a tradition built with and dependent on the subjectivity of a broad spectrum of cities' residents. If some in Rio de Janeiro understood themselves as nothing but European and, as such, claimed to be holders of such a tradition, the majority of those who, willing or not, engaged with opera and operatic music never participated in operatic performances, never left the city, and were unconcerned with the outcomes of globalization or the enthrallments of other metropolises. It was a tradition that had a long history, since it was planted in the city during the colonial and monarchical years, but also a tradition that helped define Rio de Janeiro's turn-of-the-20th-century present.

It was also a tradition that would be discreetly overlooked, if not ignored, in official historical and critical accounts of the period and therefore destined to disappear from the official narratives by those in charge of safeguarding local traditions, and who were often engaged with forging African-derived musics as "pure," "authentic," and national, or with claiming concert musics of Austro-German provenances as their opposite and universal. At the dawn of the new century, few were able, or willing, to fully grasp the historical, aesthetic, and political implications of operatic music as part of a local tradition, nor its role in propelling the early mass dissemination of musics. This is a reality that Rio de Janeiro's music critics and historians also share with those in other cities, such as Buenos Aires, Montevideo, Cuba, Lisbon, Madrid, and others, where Italian opera was also a trend eagerly embraced by a broad spectrum of local audiences and equally derided by music critics. As Aníbal Cetrangolo pointedly shows,

[36] Morelli, "Opera in Italian National Culture," 417.

242 MUSIC AND COSMOPOLITANISM

that continues to be the case to this day in preferences for performances and scholarly explorations.[37] But the critical and scholarly disregard for opera's wide acceptance was not solely the result of aesthetic hierarchies entrenched in musical idealism. For throughout the 19th and 20th centuries a local cultural tradition, imagined or not, was understood as the autochthonous, or the "folk," or something that could pass as such in the service of nation-building. And while intellectuals, anthropologists, and music historians were attempting to understand and define autochthonous traditions having the nation as a framework, none of them brought opera into consideration, at least no work not written by a local composer, and even so with many reservations, as I will discuss below. In turn-of-the-century Rio de Janeiro, operatic music was an unexplainable tradition because it could not be traceable to a mystic, imagined, and ahistorical tradition to support unique national cultural roots, nor could it seemingly be entangled with African-derived musical cultures to support the ideological narrative of *mestiçagem*, although, like in many other cities, it eventually and expectedly happened in practice.[38]

Operatic music was thus not an "invented tradition" in Hobsbawm's sense of being forged by and for political purposes to symbolically portray a sense of the national.[39] On the contrary, opera was a local tradition that contradicted and complicated such attempts, for it exposed the grim realization that such a tradition, one dependent on the participation of groups of people not united by a nation, actually circumvented the power of government institutions, the music establishment, and academics as gatekeepers of local musical tastes. But while this unexplainable local tradition was not prone to being used as an "invented tradition," it eventually did inculcate "values and norms of behavior by repetition."[40] The dissemination of opera and operatic music helped create a "network of conventions," as Hobsbawm put it, but one that did not assist in nation-building, but rather helped foster an urban network of musical conventions, aesthetics, and performance practices that evaded nationalisms; a network that delineated shared sociocultural practices and musical aesthetic experiences across borders. As recent studies have started to offer more data in this regard, it has become clear operatic music became part of local urban traditions through

---

[37] Aníbal Cetrangolo, "*Aida* Times Two: How Italian Veterans of Two Historic *Aida* Productions Shaped Argentina's Music History," *Cambridge Opera Journal* 28, no. 1 (2016): 81.

[38] For the conflation of operatic music and Black and mixed-race audiences ,see Larry Hamberlin, *Tin Pan Opera: Operatic Novelty Songs in the Ragtime Era* (Oxford and New York: Oxford University Press, 2011); see also Renne Lap Norris, "Opera and the Mainstreaming of Blackface Minstrelsy," *Journal of the Society for American Music* 1, no. 3 (2007): 341–365; Stephanie Elaine Dunson, "The Minstrel in the Parlor: Nineteenth-Century Sheet Music and the Domestication of Blackface Minstrelsy," PhD dissertation, University of Massachusetts, Amherst, 2004.

[39] E. J. Hobsbawm, "Introduction," in *The Invention of Tradition*, ed, Terence Ranger and E. J. Hobsbawm (Cambridge: Cambridge University Press, 2012 [1983]), 4.

[40] Hobsbawm, "Introduction," 4.

COSMOPOLITAN TRADITIONS   243

a socially mediated process that was not solely of local making. Opera eventually became a tradition neither from here nor from there, but one that could be from many places at the same time: it became a cosmopolitan tradition. Moretti followed the dissemination of the novel through the long 19th century in Europe and claims that where exactly the genre began is of little importance, but "where it managed to survive and grow, [that] is relevant . . . [as] to allow the simultaneous explorations of widely different paths."[41] One can choose the same investigative route for operatic music and explore how it mattered to large numbers of people and how it managed to survive and grow through its many paths.

To be sure, opera and operetta were nomadic, commercial genres at their inception and started as global phenomena in a much earlier period than the one covered here. The stories of the dissemination of works by Rossini and Offenbach, for example, are now being retold by considering the context of the global dynamics of which they were a part and which they helped fuel.[42] But as the 19th century progressed, technology developed, capitalism extended its tentacles, and communication and the circulation of people and goods across long distances increased to unprecedented levels, opera's border crossings became more a rule than an exception. In addition, agency in the process widened and functioned within more complex sociopolitical and cultural dynamics. From a historical perspective, it can be said that in the long 19th century no other musical repertory circulated beyond borders as much as opera, and Italian opera in particular. And I would dare to say, comparatively, that it is so even if one considers today's mobile-friendly and technologically advanced music-sharing cultures, which help music to circulate widely but which also fuel a level of musical heterogeneity that has diluted the power of specific repertories to be shared by large

---

[41] Moretti, *Distant Reading*, 27.

[42] José Manuel Izquierdo had argued that in the 1820s and 1830s, "The arrival of printing presses, immigrants, ideas and revolutions was increasingly accompanied by the sound of Rossini"; see his "Rossini's Reception in Latin America: Scarcity and Imagination in Two Early Chilean Sources," in *Gioachino Rossini 1868–2018: La musica e il mondo*, ed. Ilaria Narici, Emilio Sala, and Emanuele Senici (Pesaro, Italy: Fondazione Rossini Pesaro, 2018), 413. For an overview of the spread of Italian opera in Latin America in the 19th century, see Aníbal Cetrangolo, "L'opera nei paesi Latino-americani nell'eta moderna e contemporanea, here" in *Musica in scena: Storia dello spettacolo musicale*, ed. A. Basso (Turin: UTET, 1996), 654–691.

For an exploration of the cosmopolitan nature of Offenbach's works, see Laurence Senelick, *Jacques Offenbach and the Making of Modern Culture* (Cambridge, UK: Cambridge University Press, 2017); see also Mark Everist, "Jacques Offenbach: The Music of the Past and the Image of the Present," in *Music, Theater, and Cultural Transfer: Paris, 1830–1914*, ed. Annegret Fauser and Mark Everist (Chicago: University of Chicago Press, 2009), 74–98; Anaïs Fléchet, " Offenbach à Rio: La fièvre de l'opérette dans le Brésil du Segundo Reinado," in *La circulation transatlantique des imprimés—connexions*, ed. Márcia Abreu and Marisa Midori Deacto (Campinas: UNICAMP/IEL/Secteurs des publications, 2014), 321; Orna Messer Levin, "Offenbach et le public brésilien (1840–1870)," in *La circulation transatlantique des imprimés—connexions*, ed. Márcia Abreu and Marisa Midori Deacto (Campinas: UNICAMP/IEL/Secteurs des publications, 2014), 307. Walton Benjamin locates the beginnings of operatic globalization in the years around 1830; see his "Italian Operatic Fantasies in Latin America, *Journal of Modern Italian Studies* 17, no. 4 (September 2012): 460–471.

244   MUSIC AND COSMOPOLITANISM

numbers of people. The music deriving from the 19th-century theater, although extremely varied, had more musical kinship holding it together than differences separating it, even when dispersed through geographical borders in a myriad of media. The outcome of this, from the perspective of Rio de Janeiro, thus opens a window into the extent to which opera became meaningful concomitantly to people scattered in cities across oceans and continents. It also shows that, while opera originated in specific cities, it was also through many cities that the operatic repertory started to lose its geographical origins to become a cosmopolitan tradition shared by many.

Much has been written about opera's role in building communal alliances at the service of a unified nation in Italy, but Michela Ronzani notes that as one starts grappling with the international circulation of opera, it becomes clearer how the telling of opera's history is misled by ideologies of national construction, an argument that supports Anselm Gerard's earlier study concerning grand opera.[43] John Davis argues that to those who claim that in Italy "opera was important because of its association with nationalism [got] the formula the wrong way around. The reason why the nationalists wanted to harness opera to their cause was because opera mattered."[44] And while Ronzani and Davis are addressing Italian audiences and the political context in mid-century Risorgimento Italy, one could extrapolate and ask how and why, as the century progressed, opera and operatic music continued to matter, and increasingly so, to large numbers of people living near and far from one another. Statistics of commercial and business practices and performances of particular works offer a supporting general picture, but they do not tell us what it meant at the turn of the 20th century to have opera as part of one's culture, of one's culture that is also part of someone else's culture, of someone else who lives far away and is estranged geographically and historically. The available data should nonetheless open our investigative eyes and ears to the fact that there is something about opera as a dramatic genre, and something specifically about operatic music, that enticed people across continents, something beyond acclaims or disdains by music critics, beyond the social capital claimed by bourgeoise audiences, beyond business gimmicks, and beyond the powerful voices and performances of star singers.

The social context of opera houses has nonetheless generated a rich literature, albeit one focused almost entirely on the elite status of (White) audiences, their power to delineate social and political barriers, and to evade musical standardization while supporting canonization of specific works and authors. Those social barriers became a topic of enduring interest to explorations of music as

---

[43] Michela Ronzani, "'Melodramma,' Market, and Modernity: Opera in Late Nineteenth-Century Italy," PhD dissertation, Brown University, 2015, 3; Gerhard, *The Urbanization of Opera*.

[44] John Davis, "Opera and Absolutism in Restoration Italy, 1815–1860," *Journal of Interdisciplinary History* 36, no. 4 (Spring, 2006): 569–594.

COSMOPOLITAN TRADITIONS   245

a part of an imperialistic project, in particular in places outside the European operatic centers, and in places like Rio de Janeiro where social and racial segregation were tangible realities and where therefore those barriers were brazenly clear.[45] Roberto Leydi notes that originally Italian opera did not concern the lower classes and was not produced and created by "the people," although operatic music eventually filtered away from the closed circles of the opera house to take a hold among "the popular" or rural classes to become a "folk" cultural product of sorts.[46] Leydi maintains that it was exactly the genre's association with luxurious opera houses and fashionable bourgeoisie habits that instilled a prestige and social cachet to the music, and that it was this cachet that was carried into the streets, music halls, and early recordings at the beginning of the 20th century, moving from "elite" circles to eventually become "popularized." This was also true in many cities outside Italy. In Rio de Janeiro, when presented in the Theatro Lyrico and later at the majestic Theatro Municipal by foreign operatic troupes with famous singers, operatic music was supported mostly by elite patrons, broadly defined, and those willing to pay for expensive tickets to see and hear the same operas over and over again, sometimes alongside governmental authorities or the president of the new republic. Even local music critics who, in concert with critics in Europe and the Americas, openly disparaged operatic music did not stop regularly attending the operatic theater, if only to comment on the music's superficiality, the less than perfect traveling groups, out-of-tune orchestras, and singers' lack of vocal skills.[47] To some scholars, these critics eventually played key roles in shaping audience's tastes, while others assert that a few music publishers who assumed central roles in the business of opera became "the mediators between the creation of music and its production and use," as they heavily profited from opera as an international commodity.[48]

Yet these various foci rest on opera's potential for delimiting social borders. Ronzani claims, for instance, that around the turn of the 20th century the cultural and social status of opera "developed along two opposing trajectories: on the one hand, the newly acquired commercial potential of a wider popular audience; on

---

[45] For the characterization of "elite" culture at the Theatro Lyrico, in Rio de Janeiro, see Needell, *A Tropical Belle Epoque*.

[46] Leydi, "The Dissemination and Popularization of Opera," 314–342.

[47] Karen Ahlquist argues that "[i]dealized attitudes toward classical [German] music influenced ideas about artistic value in opera; in "International Opera in Nineteenth-Centtury New York," 246. For a critique of musical value and its association with social class see her "Balance of Power: Music as Art and Social Class in Late Nineteenth Century," in *Rethinking American Music*, ed. Tara Browner and Thomas Riis (Chicago: University of Illinois Press, 2019), 7–33.

[48] Michela Ronzani, "'Melodramma,' Market, and, 24. For the role of critics, see Alessandra Campana, *Opera and Modern Spectatorship in Late Nineteenth-Century Italy* (Cambridge, UK: Cambridge University Press, 2015).

246 MUSIC AND COSMOPOLITANISM

the other hand, an elitist redefinition of opera as an artistic and cultural product for the intellectual enjoyment of the cultural urban elites."[49] To many historians, this social divide of opera became clearer in the second part of the 19th century, when opera moved from popular entertainment to sacralized art to be enjoyed in the opera house.[50] But such a focus on opera's high-brow/low-brow duality hardly describes the reality it encountered in large urban areas, where as the century came to a close the social composition of audiences became extremely fluid and complex, and the city's social dynamics made it difficult to define "middle class," or the "elite," as well as the most encompassing "bourgeoisie." Karen Ahlquist maintains that, "[t]he binary distinction [high-brow/low-brow] is inadequate . . . in part because it conflates the purported aesthetic position of an artistic genre with the purported social position of its devotees,"[51] and she also pointedly notes that in the case of opera it is "only the high-brow aspect [that] has interested scholars."[52] It seems that in terms of social class fluidity, audiences of opera halls and audiences of music halls were equally undefinable under the high-brow/low-brow musical taste duality, unless under the strictest rules of critics and intellectuals who worked as history's gatekeepers. Even Roberto Leydi's exploration of opera's "growing diffusion downward" comes with a warning: "to follow the various paths taken by Italian opera when it left behind the environment for which it was created [operatic theater] is fraught with difficulties, if not a hopeless undertaking."[53] Still, such an undertaking, difficult as it may be, is the only way to start grappling with how and why certain musical genres and styles circulated among a wide crowd and mattered to large numbers of people. One should start by taking "audiences" as a large and socially complex entity, one that ultimately had the power to shape markets, rather than the other way around, one that could actually be seen as a force of "anti-[economic] market," as Moretti puts it, with a subjectivity that asserts or rejects novelties and fashions and that ultimately guides businesspeople, theater managers, and eventually composers.[54] Leydi suggests that was the case in Italy at the end of the 19th century, and I believe that was also the case in Rio de Janeiro.

---

[49] Ronzani, "'Melodramma,' Market, and Modernity," 15.
[50] Robert Levine uses the term "sacralization of art" to describe the process in the later part of the 19th century in the United States; see his *Highbrow/Lowbrow: The Emergence of Cultural Hierarchy in America* (Cambridge, MA: Harvard University Press, 1988).
[51] Karen Ahlquist, "Balance of Power: 12–15. In this respect, for a shift in taste and social class distinctions at the turn of the 20th century in the music hall, see Barry Faulk, *Music Hall and Modernity* (Athens: Ohio University Press, 2004), 189–196.
[52] Karen Ahlquist, *Democracy at the Opera: Music, Theater, and Culture in New York City, 1815–60* (Urbana: University of Illinois Press, 1997), 266.
[53] Leydi, "The Dissemination and Popularization of Opera," 314.
[54] Moretti, *Distant Reading*, 39.

COSMOPOLITAN TRADITIONS   247

Some scholars assign importance to operatic plots as main elements in opera that enticed many in Europe, in particular the use of well-known novels adapted in flexible, re-adaptable librettos.[55] Others have pointed to the mass printing of excerpts from operas that "domesticated the music . . . keeping alive the memory of what they heard and saw [in the theater],"[56] or have argued that singers were the main culprits in the dissemination and eventual popularization of opera, since as "stars" their individual choices and vocal skills determined the popularity of specific works or brought them into the canon.[57] A case in point is Caruso, not coincidentally an Italian singer, whose voice helped further disseminate arias from already well-known operas in newly available recordings. Others have moved beyond the social dynamics of markets to argue that the widespread popularity of opera in the long 19th century was related to its musical structure, since opera was never a "musical work" in the sense of an immutable work to be preserved in its original form, at least not in the same way that the canon of instrumental music to be performed in concert halls is preserved and studied today.[58] And yet the operas mentioned as part of a local tradition in Rio de Janeiro at the turn of the 20th century are alive and well today as "musical works" in opera halls all over the world, and they have been incorporated in canon-making publications, such as textbooks used in academic courses in universities in Europe and the Americas.

What seems to be at stake is the dislodged place of operatic music as an object of study when its existence lies outside its dramatic function and away from elite opera houses.[59] One can study rock, rap, k-pop, or EDM outside their places of origin as musics of the many, since they are understood as belonging to "the people" by definition, as "popular" culture, rather than as culture, as John Storey has noted, even if the term "popular" added to "culture" seems to draw a line as to what deserves to be studied musically.[60] These musics were never entangled with monarchies, aristocracies, elite theaters, and issues of social and aesthetic distinction that are unquestionably integral parts of opera's history and which

[55] James Parakilas, "The Operatic Canon," in *The Oxford Handbook of Opera*, ed. Helen Greenwalk (Oxford: Oxford University Press, 2014), 864–865.

[56] Parakilas, "The Operatic Canon," 866.

[57] See, for instance, Hilary Poriss, *Changing the Score: Arias, Prima Donnas, and the Authority of Performance* (Oxford: Oxford University Press, 2009).

[58] Sorba, "Between Cosmopolitanism and Nationhood," 54–57; see also Axel Körner, "Music of the Future: Italian Theaters and the European Experience of Modernity between Unification and World War One," *European History Quarterly* 41, no. 2 (2011): 189–212.

[59] Franco Fabbri, "An 'Intricate Fabric of Influences and Coincidences in the History of Popular Music:' Reflections on the Challenging Work of Popular Music Historians," in *Music History and Cosmopolitanism*, ed. Anastasia Belina, Kaarina Kilpiö, and Derek Scott (New York: Routledge, 2019, Kindle), 77.

[60] John Storey, *From Popular Culture to Everyday* Life (London and New York: Routledge, 2014), 9. For an extended discussion, see also Simon Frith, *Performing Rites: On the Value of Popular Music* (Cambridge, MA: Harvard University Press, 1996).

248   MUSIC AND COSMOPOLITANISM

have served to justify the study of opera as part of a European music canon. Yet even when one moves away from staged presentations of specific operas toward their reception in alternate modes of music-making and practices, in the direction of the "growing diffusion downward," to recall Leydi's term, one still feels compelled to hold on to origins in elite, aristocratic, European (Italian, French, German, and White) culture as a justification for its study. "Within which theoretical framework can they be studied?" Franco Fabbri has asked, referring to some repertories circulating in late-19th-century Italian cities, as he notes that popular music studies have no theoretical framework to approach such musics.[61]

I thus suggest that rather than defining operatic music as a delimiter of social and national boundaries, one should explore opera, and operatic music in particular, as the quintessential border breaker at the dawn of the 20th century. On the one hand, operatic music crossed geographical, social, artistic, generational, and media boundaries, among others. On the other hand, it wedded the old and the new, connected audiences, and served, contradictorily, as a centralizing force for the heterogeneous musical repertories and practices of the cosmopolitan city. Ultimately, the widespread of operatic music in various spaces, formats, and media made concrete for the first time the anonymous masses. Leydi's note about the difficulties in the study of opera's diffusion outside large opera houses is fortunately counteracted by Larry Hamberlin's exploration of the crucial and multiple roles played by operatic music in shaping Tin Pan Alley's songs early in the 20th century in New York City, where one sees both the "admiration for opera as cultural legacy and disdain for opera going as social spectacle."[62] Hamberlin maintains that, as a cultural legacy, the many musical domains of opera were characterized not by social separation but by a coexistence that complicated understandings of not only high and low cultures, but also of social and racial boundaries, all believed to live apart from one another. He notes that in the Tin Pan Alley golden era, "the notion of opera as the exclusive property of the social and economic elite was hotly contested," and that "whether or not audiences were enjoined to view the opera-loving African, Irish, Italian, and Jewish American protagonists of these songs as outsiders, those characters do not see themselves that way: they simply love opera."[63] Why? As a dramatic form opera depended not only on plots, singers, and stage effects, but also on songs that were songful

---

[61] "An Intricate Fabric," 74. For another approach to the topic of popular music in the 19th-century focusing on France, see Jann Pasler, *Writing Through Music: Essays on Music, Culture, and Politics* (New York and London: Oxford University Press, 2007), in particular the chapter "Material Culture and Potsmodern Positivism: Rethinking the "Popular" in Lat Nineteenth-Century French Music," 417–449.
[62] Hamberlin, *Tin Pan Opera*, 9.
[63] Hamberlin, *Tin Pan Opera*, 7.

COSMOPOLITAN TRADITIONS   249

and memorable, as Grétry suggested a song should be (see Chapter 3), enough so to sustain extra lives that moved beyond origins, staged performances, plots, and written scores. As songful and memorable, they melded oral and written traditions, live and recorded practices, and in the process they helped shape an early globalized music scenario that depended on the coexistence of many socio-political actors and factors and performance geographies, a coexistence that, for the most part, has defied music history documentary methodologies and critical apparatus.

A Profusion of Melodies

How can we address operatic music originating in specific cities in Europe and then further multiplied across continents through a myriad of live performances and new technologies, such as mass printing, recordings, and movies, to become widespread enough as to challenge Europe as a unified center and evade its borders, and eventually emerge as part of urban traditions elsewhere? What can we infer from João do Rio's ease in pairing Puccini's "Vissi d'arte" with the Rio de Janeiro local dance craze *maxixe* as local traditions, when the former is all but excluded from local historical narratives and the latter has been touted as the main bastion in nationalistic discourses about the specificities, or the "Brazilian-ness," of local, popular culture?

Azevedo's reason for repeatedly going back to the Rio de Janeiro theater to hear Verdi's *Un ballo in maschera* was not to see a new staging of the old work by a specific opera company, nor the attractiveness of the plot, the orchestra's performance, or a specific performer's vocal abilities: his reason was the opera's "profusion of melodies." We can thus follow Azevedo's clue and start grappling with the fact that while opera crossed many geographical and cultural borders, while it was presented concomitantly in a myriad of ways, by various artists, in a range of theatrical settings across continents, while it permeated opera houses, music halls, and the streets to eventually become a city tradition in multiple places, its coexistence in many places, venues, and practices was marked by the endurance of one element which was invariably the same: the melody. Thus, we may conjecture that one of the reasons why operatic music traveled so far, so intensely, and for so long may lie in the music, and in the song more precisely.[64] Whatever imperialistic impulses drove operas to all corners of the globe, whatever stories they were set up to tell, whatever business tools were developed to explore them, and whatever theatrical engines and skilled voices delivered them, the potential

---

[64] This suggestion goes against Parakilas's claim that "music itself was rarely the main reason why opera succeed or failed when it travelled"; see his "The Operatic Canon," 858.

250   MUSIC AND COSMOPOLITANISM

of their melodies to survive long-distance travels seems to have equaled, or perhaps surpassed, the cultural capital operas acquired from monarchs, aristocrats, and the urban bourgeoisie, or the financial gains the works promised from the box office. Michal Grover-Friedlander asserts that it was the "Italian notion of song" that prevailed, for opera "engenders a state in which one is always listening in anticipation of, or listening toward . . . beautiful moments of singing." Dizikes describes these elements as "contagious singableness" that were associated with vocality and thus ephemeral, but were also intertwined with and dependent on songful and memorable tunes, "attractive melodies" that endured many travels through time.[65]

On the one hand, the operatic developments during the long 19th century were characterized by the establishment of a limited repertory of static musical-dramatic works presented at large opera houses to become part of a canon celebrated by urban bourgeoisies in many cities and further solidified by music scholarship in the 20th century. On the other hand, the same operatic developments were marked by the genre's intense dissemination in a fragmented format, as its structured parts were disassembled and redistributed in a myriad of different formats and contexts. Thus, one could explore opera not merely as an assemblage of musical sections and storytelling presented in a stable social setting, but also consider its disassemblage as a process with powerful cultural and historical relevance.[66] These processes were undoubtedly intertwined and dependent on each other, but there is much to be explored about opera as a multilayered genre that played a central role in the fragmentation of the "musical work," understood as a large, stable, unified, organic whole, sewing together various musical structures through harmonic progressions, which in turn was claimed to be endowed with superior, abstract aesthetic qualities.[67] When opera was disassembled, in most cases at the same time or immediately after it came into being as a music-dramatic work, its music problematized such organicism. It was "an art existing in pieces," Dizikes suggests,[68] dismantled into songful and memorable melodies that few city residents could claim to be oblivious to, and

[65] Michal Grover-Friedlander, *Vocal Apparitions: The Attraction of Cinema to Opera* (Princeton, NJ: Princeton University Press, 2005), 3. Dizikes, *Opera in America*, 95.

[66] I have read with interest the many uses in the academia of the theory of "assemblage theory" as outlined by Guattary and Deleuze (1988), the complex process of non-hierarchical interactions of parts to whole. It is tempting at this point to engage with such theories, but here I will only describe one of its practical outcomes, and one which has received less attention, the process of disassemblage. For a nuanced description and critical analysis of assemblage theory, see Manuel DeLanda, *Assemblage Theory* (Edinburgh: Edinburgh University Press, 2016).

[67] For the standard critique on the idea of "the musical work," see Lydia Goehr, *The Imaginary Museum of Musical Works: An Essay in the Philosophy of Music* (Oxford and New York: Oxford University Press, 1992). For the idea of a musical work as an assemblage, see Giorgina Born, "Mediation Theory," in *The Routledge Reader on the Sociology of Music*, ed. J. Shepherd and K. Devine (New York: Routledge, 2015), 359–368.

[68] Dizikes, *Opera in America*, 95.

COSMOPOLITAN TRADITIONS 251

then further fragmented into even smaller parts, as sonic incipits still holding meaning and power to represent, entertain, and embody. Operatic melodies became the common denominator when commercial enterprises invested in the genre's potential to produce profits across cities, countries, and continents. It was operatic melodies that enthralled people to engage with new ways of listening through new technological devices and to cross the divide between the old and the new.[69] It was operatic arias that were highlighted in ornate instrumental arrangements made so as to further spotlight melodies above the musical rest. When disassembled into smaller units and further separated from a unified work, it was the melodies that assisted someone's lonely but unencumbered vocal expression to sound above the intimate silence of one's home, or that propelled the street organ performer to use them in repetitive mechanisms to sound with and above the noise of the modern city. Without losing their meaning, appeal, and relevance in the city, operatic melodies could be amplified through instrumental arrangements aimed at reaching people listening together in large outdoor public concerts; or, fragmented as needed, they prompted groups to sing together and, when supported by rhythmic accompaniments, they inspired people to dance together and at the same time, even when estranged from one another by geographical distances. Melodies were the expressive texts that survived through the disassemblage of operas, and in their constant movements across borders of many kinds they remain a remarkable phenomenon in the history of musics' travels.

That music travels needs no spelling out, and one also does not need to point out that operatic melodies were not the only ones to have long geographical and historical traveling trajectories; the story of "La Marseillaise" is a case in point (see Chapter 3). Still, one can easily assert that while all musics traveled, some travel more than others. Thus, it would be hard to deny that before Rossini and Offenbach, music traveled at a much slower pace, reached a narrower geographical area, and had fewer extra lives. Improvement in technology and modes of transportation and the forces of capitalism surely had a lot to do with music's faster and further travels as the century unfolded. Nonetheless, when one considers the long and persisting process of operas' disassemblage during the long 19th century, one aspect becomes conspicuously clear: that it was the melodies that made possible their long-distance travels.

The literature on 20th-century popular music suggests that in a "song," as a combination of lyrics and melody, it is the melody that is retained first, rather

---

[69] For a list of opera recording in Italy at the beginning of the 20th century Italy, see Leydi, "The Dissemination and Popularization of Opera," 362–365. For the dissemination of operatic melodies in Italy through wind bands, choral societies, and in the church, see Alan Mallach, *The Autumn of Italian Opera* (Lebanon, NH: Northeastern University Press, 2007), 175–180.

252 MUSIC AND COSMOPOLITANISM

than the words.[70] Eighteenth-century composition treatises emphasized melodic construction before other parameters, and mid-19th-century orchestration companions warned that the potent sound of new instruments should not obliterate the melodic line.[71] Yet in musicological literature melodies are not usually considered musical parameters with historical meaning and aesthetic force by themselves and even less as musical parameters that helped define the period in its widest Western European contexts. Rather, melodies are usually understood as glues that tie together larger harmonic structures holding the "organic (instrumental) work" as an abstract "art" devoid of social engagements. In the operatic realm, melodies are tools at the service of the drama, and it is in that capacity that they have occupied the attention of critics and philosophers as musical parameters with aesthetic significance. If taken without words, melodies are the undesirable elements in the simplistic but all too common formalistic musical dualism of melody versus harmony that has well served musical ideological national cleaving, as well as in the art versus popular and the high versus low divides that still feed aesthetic hierarchies. Saint-Saëns articulated such hierarchies quite clearly, in a most Eurocentric and racist way:

> People who only like melodies are unconsciously confessing that they are unwilling to take the trouble to appreciate and coordinate the different elements of a complete work so as to understand it as a whole . . . such people, together with Orientals and savages, make up the public whose inertia blocks the course of art across the world.[72]

Historical revisionist narratives continue to reduce melodies to idiosyncratic happenstances, while some have felt compelled to justify, condescendingly, their undeniable widespread presence. Benjamin Walton argues, compellingly, that Rossini's operas were popularized across borders not because they included

---

[70] Ruth Finnegan, "O que vem primeiro: o texto, a música, ou a performance?," in *Palavra cantada: Ensaios sobre poesia, música, e voz*, ed. Cláudia Matos, Elizabeth Travassos, and Fernanda de Medeiros (Rio de Janeiro: 7Letras, 2008), 32–33. See also Simon Frith, "Why Do Songs Have Words?," in *Popular Music: Critical Concepts in Media and Cultural Studies*, ed. Simon Frith (New York: Routledge, 2004), 186–212.

[71] Heinrich Christoph Koch, "Introductory Essay on Composition: The Mechanical Rules of Melody," Sections 3 and 4, *Versuch einer Anleitung zur Composition*, 1782–1793, translated by Nancy Kovaleff Bake (New Haven: Yale University Press, c1983); see Elaine Sisman's review of this publication in *Journal of Music Theory* 29, no. 2 (Fall 1985): 341–347. For the observance of mid-19th-century orchestration companions, Berlioz's in particular, in Gomes's operatic language, see Isaac William Kerr, "Instrumentação e orquestração em Antônio Carlos Gomes: Um estudo em seus prelúdios e sinfonias," Master's thesis, Universidade Estadual de Campinas, SP, 2016.

[72] Camille Saint-Saëns, *On Music and Musicians*, trans. and ed. Roger Nichols (London and New York: Oxford University Press), 21.

"pretty melodies," but because they were a part of something much larger, as part of an operatic whole that became an "audible symbol of romantic modernism."[73]

Dispossessed of musical aesthetic force as "pretty melodies," like rhythm as "catchy rhythms," melodies by themselves were understood as suggestive of a regress toward music's elementary aesthetic state, one believed to exist in a remote past re-emerging in romantic imaginary tales. In such a state, melodies were related to the "folk," something that is lost in the communal and the unnamed, and divested of individual artistic creativity. Indeed, the fragrant reappearances of operatic tunes as folk music in Italy has been the main focus of scholarly studies following the extra lives of a few arias, but seldom as part of a larger urban context, and only so when destitute of expressive and social meaning as victims of unscrupulous marketing strategies. Conversely, the power of a single melody to entice large numbers of people across borders became a burden to those attempting to associate music as the essence of a nation and to articulate musical nationality. As Trippett has argued, melody had the power "to express what language could not" and as such it was "dauntingly undefinable." As a result, melodies' intangible power to connect people across borders generated large anxieties, especially at a time when linguistic unity became a main focus for forging national unity, and when a parallel search for a national musical language rested on the operatic logic of music at the service of language.[74] Still, the ease with which melodies traveled on their own, regardless of language, origins, or large sociopolitical apparatus, did not escape mid-century theorist William Tappert, who in his 1866 study about the practice of melodic borrowing argued that "there are no music police who ask for birth certificates [of melodies] and certificates of conduct.... Melodies roam.... They are the most tireless tourists on earth! They cross raging rivers, pass the Alpine mountains, emerge beyond the ocean, and nomadize in the desert."[75]

Operatic melodies fulfilled, at the same time, both the movement toward European opera canonization and social distinction and the trend toward the popularization of music, that is, of music increasingly becoming a part of "the culture of everyday lives"[76] of many peoples, of the invisible masses who made the city their home. Gino Stefani maintains that:

---

[73] Benjamin Walton, *Rossini in Restoration Paris: The Sound of Modern Life* (Cambridge, UK: Cambridge University Press, 2011), 5.

[74] David Trippett, *Wagner's Melodies: Aesthetics and Materialism in German Musical Identity* (Cambridge, UK: Cambridge University Press, 2013), 3 and 7.

[75] Wilhalm Tappert, *Wandernde Melodien: eine musikalische Studie* (Berlin: Brachvogel & Ranft, 1889 [1868]), cited in Trippett, *Wagner's Melodies*, 141.

[76] This process is discussed at length by Certeau, *The Practice of Everyday Life*. See also Storey, *From Popular Culture to Everyday Life*, and Shirley Fedorak, "What Is Popular Culture?," in *The Routledge Handbook of Popular Culture and Tourism*, ed. Christine Lundberg and Vassilios Ziakas (New York: Routledge, 2018), 9–18.

254 MUSIC AND COSMOPOLITANISM

melody is a notion belonging to everyday culture, [it is the part of] music [that is] close at hand; it is that dimension of music which everyone can easily appropriate in many ways: with the voice by singing, whistling or putting words to it; with the body by dancing, marching, etc. . . . [melody] is something familiar, the friendly face of music, involving and gratifying, obsessive and liberating.[77]

Outside the stage, without a connection to a place, a plot, a composer, or a specific singer, operatic melodies became autonomous musical entities that retained meaning through a familiarity acquired in the process of performance and aural repetition in which music kept relating back to itself in spiraling, continuous movements.

Exploring the cultural and psychological outcomes of music repetition through performance and listening, Elizabeth Margulis has observed that melodies play a crucial role in the process of musical retention, since "timbres and chords aren't 'catchy' in the way a tune can be."[78] Significantly, Margulis also maintains that in the process of melodic repetition, one's attention moves toward "a goal-demotion from the syntax function towards the very surface of the materiality of the tune." Melodies are the easiest to remember, since "the sounds that people can vividly remember and repeat are the sounds that they can actually produce, i.e., sing."[79] Most importantly, Margulis claims that the resulting "melodic knowingness" through repetition assists in the process of shaping collective memory, as in "the feeling that a specific tune was there forever," as it instills "a shared recognition [that] connects audiences as insiders." When melodies are executed and repeated without much conscious attention, they carry "an actual or virtual invitation to participate": actual by performance and listening and virtual by remembering.[80] Melodies play a role in experiences of collective participation through repeated performance and listening and then by unconscious repetition and recognition.

We can thus suggest that the wide availability of operatic melodies in many cities concomitantly underlines a performing and listening collective behavior resulting from their sheer presence and their ease of being repeated and remembered. At a time when emerging technologies of sound reproduction fostered repetition and became a kind of social behavior and cultural experience,[81] melodies, and operatic melodies in particular with their long history of widespread travel, also had a special role in fostering shared collective

---

[77] Gino Stefani, "Melody: A Popular Perspective," *Popular Music* 6, no. 1 (1987): 21.

[78] Elizabeth Margulis, *On Repeat: How Music Plays the Mind* (Oxford and New York: Oxford University Press, 2013), 66–67.

[79] Margulis, *On Repeat*, 82–83.

[80] Margulis, *On Repeat*, 143–144, and 150.

[81] Emanuele Senici, *Music in the Present Tense: Rossini's Italian Operas in Their Time* (Chicago: University of Chicago Press, 2019), 53.

engagements within the modernizing city. They became evocative of the *fin-de-siècle* urban experience of participation through repetition and its consequent pleasure in collective recognition. While technology allowed for "concrete precise repetition," Margulis further notes, melodic repetition by performing and listening offered an experience of a different kind, one that was sometimes involuntary and sometimes imaginative.[82] Why some melodies ultimately prevailed over others continues to be an enigma that some have tried, unsuccessfully, to decode, even if some established composers of melodies believed to have a formula for successful hits (see Chapter 3). Yet wide public acceptance should not be taken as mere happenstance; rather, it could be considered the result of melodies' aesthetic power to serve as markers of specific time and place: the cosmopolitan city at the turn of the 20th century.

The making of operatic music into a city tradition rested on both aesthetic and social aspects: on the one hand, on the musical qualities of its most well-designed tunes, which allowed for repetition to be possible by performing and listening and pleasurable by recognition; on the other, these musical qualities also served as an invitation to collective actual, virtual, and imaginative participation, within and beyond luxurious theaters. Operatic melodies retained signification through appropriation and repetition even when they were broken into smaller units and undressed from their music-dramatic coherence, language, or musical-structural continuity. Because they allowed for and encouraged repetition, melodies not only endured time, but also filled many spaces. To paraphrase Moretti, melodies are like many other artistic endeavors, which "need not only time to grow and diversify but [also space]; . . . and when it does, like the economy, they take off."[83] Aural familiarity through repetition of operatic melodies filled many spaces, a process that was not solely the result of fortune, but one that was facilitated by both its initial sociopolitical power and then by musical craftsmanship, which ultimately created the necessary music-contextual space for operatic melodies to take off. Most importantly, when that process was well on its way, operatic melodies displaced opera's visibility, its dominant place as one of the century's most enduring visual spectacles, to gain force exactly in its invisibility. In its sonic ethereal qualities fed by repetition, aural familiarity, and pleasurable recognition, operatic melodies connected people aurally to become one of the most ubiquitous cultural experiences of the turn-of-the-century city.

When one considers their nomadic paths, a few operatic melodies stood for entire works, as sonic incipits not to be written down and preserved in catalogs, but to be performed and heard by many and preserved in their memories as

---

[82] Margulis, *On Repeat*, 81–83.
[83] Moretti, *Distant Reading*, 19.

256 MUSIC AND COSMOPOLITANISM

local traditions, wherever they happen to be.[84] As melodic fragments were further repeated, rearranged, parodied, and inserted in new comedies, reviews, vaudevilles, and music halls, they were caught in a spiraling musical recycling movement that is hard to grasp intellectually and to study methodologically, exactly as Leydi warned us it would be. Yet as soon as the business of music started to acquire characteristics of mass production and began the shaping of an emergent popular entertainment of mass culture, it became clear that operatic melodies were among the main engines propelling their force. In catalogs of 19th-century publications of piano works in reduction or arrangements, operatic tunes prevailed.[85] Operatic melodies permeated the new sound-producing mechanical devices, from the musical box, barrel organs, and stroll pianos, to the new gramophone and early films, competing equally in the emerging mass market with local tunes that had more long-standing local histories. And as more audiences grew familiar with opera's most attractive tunes in the city's streets coming from bars, *realejos*, wind bands, children singing them while playing, people whistling as they waited for the cable car, or at home in piano renditions, in recordings, in new media such as film, operatic melodies and their fragments—now even more undefinable, as Tippet asserted, but still memorable and songful, as Grétry thought a melody should be—melodies were not only repeated and heard ad libitum, but were remembered ad libitum in a process of musical-human engagement that in the end also confronted impersonal new technologies of sound repetition and multiplication. Operatic melodies allowed for an overlap of oral, aural, written, audible, and recorded modes of learning and remembering, in an unprecedented, large-scale, circular motion of music transmission through communal participation that eventually came to characterize an epoch. Most of these melodies were not new, and certainly needed not be. In fact, it was their long history, lost in spiraling movements of repetition and fragmentation that no longer recognized origins, social status, or models, that sustained their social and cultural significance. In their fully disassembled state, operatic melodies were eventually embraced as cosmopolitan sonic aesthetic experiences that formed the core of music transmission in turn-of-the-20th-century cities.

---

[84] Several examples of arias that traveled long distances are compiled in the 2016 issue "Remaking the Aria," in *Cambridge Opera Journal* 28, no. 2 (2016); see especially James Davies, "The Progress of an Aria Bellini, 'Ah! non pensar che pieno,' Beatrice di Tenda, Act I," 155–159; and Jonathan Hicks, "Should Manrico Escape? Verdi, 'Miserere . . . Ah, che la morte ognora' (Leonora, Manrico), *Il trovatore*, Act IV," 187–190; and Andy Fry, "The 'Caruso of Jazz' and a 'Creole Benvenuto Cellini' Verdi, 'Miserere . . . Ah, che la morte ognora' (Leonora, Manrico), *Il trovatore*, Act IV," 183–186.

[85] William Lockhart examined the Friedrick Hofmeister catalog of 19th-century publications, and shows that 30 percent of unaccompanied piano pieces were arrangements, a vast majority of operatic tunes; see his "Listening to the Domestic Music Machine: Keyboard Arrangements in the Nineteenth-Century," PhD dissertation, Humboldt-Universität zu Berlin, 2012, 910.

COSMOPOLITAN TRADITIONS   257

Is there something suggestive in a melody apart from its undefinable songful and memorable characteristics? Charle observed that the audience's taste late in the 19th century had a "limit range," and even when audiences preferred new works for the operatic stages, managers still relied on "simple patterns and formulas that could recall 'old memories' and attenuate their novelty."[86] Of course, musical patterns are socially and culturally learned, and many non-musical factors are at play in the process of recognition. But formulas are also ways for one to become cognizant of how and why things need to be repeated to be understood and then remembered, regardless of cultural context. Melodic formulas made remembering music easier in a time when acute feelings of time and space compression became part of the city's daily complex routine, and when the city's heterogeneous and varied musics available concomitantly were mostly transmitted through the ephemeral nature of live performances. Senici notes that in Rossini's operas the most venerable tunes were formulaic and most repeatable by singing, which in turn were also repeated by others, and then by mechanical devices, and learned by repeated hearing, thus activating memory, through actual and virtual participation.[87] Melodic formulas also served well the function of distribution and further dissemination of music by stimulating sonic remembrance, a strategy found in many musical practices and cultures, but which was especially fragrant at the beginning of the mass consumption of music. When Ronzani explores the commercial practices and Ricordi's publicity campaigns for Pucinni's *La bohème*, the focus is on the images used in advertisement of music, but not on the melodies as a force to advertise music.[88] And yet, while audience approval of and engagement with certain melodic patterns or a specific melody can be a disputable criteria in commercial practices, businesspeople depended on musical formulas that were sanctioned at the performance level by audiences across many borders. This reminds us that locality, or exceptionalism of specific cultural contexts, is not the only, and certainly not the main, aspect to consider when exploring audience response and the eventual success of a musical work; rather, audience responses are sometimes similar in many different places. They are linked to the contours and effectiveness of specific melodies that allow for easy recognition and further repetition. Stefani suggests that melodies defy local contextualization and that their inherent power of widespread appropriation

---

[86] Charle, "Opera in France, 1870–1914," 249–250, and 259. For the standardization of the repertory, see Jutta Toelle, "Operatic Canons and Repertories in Italy c. 1900," in *The Oxford Handbook of the Operatic Canon*, ed. Cormac Newark and William Weber (Oxford: Oxford University Press, 2018, online publication), 226–241.

[87] Senici, *Music in the Present Tense*, 15.

[88] Michela Ronzani, "Creating Success and Forging Imaginaries: The Innovative Publicity Campaign for Puccini's *La bohème*," in *The Idea of Art Music in a Commercial World, 1800–1930*, ed. Christina Bashford and Roberta Montemorra Marwin (Suffolk, UK: Boydell & Brewer Press, 2016), 39–59.

258   MUSIC AND COSMOPOLITANISM

"cannot but concern a relatively autonomous part of a musical piece: a part which people recognize as being the same melody in different arrangements and contexts . . . it is a part endowed with a quality—precisely 'melodicity.' "[89]

Roger Parker has considered the separation of operatic music from its larger operatic-dramatic context to foreground "music's contribution to the operatic work." He reminds us of:

> sound's unruly elective affinities—the way it can attach itself happily to what might at first seem the most unlikely text or plot or character; the flamboyantly multiple interpretive possibilities it can provide . . . the sheer slipperiness of music's signifying field ensures that the operatic "work" can survive startling transformations and still remain coherent.[90]

With a similar argument, Philip Gossett points to Verdi's compositional method as an example, since the composer's sketches show that he wrote melodies with a bass as parts of an opera's "skeleton score" and only later did he add parts and orchestration. Gossett notes that with Verdi's most popular opera, *La traviata*, the composer "began contemplating the melodic substance before having received the libretto, before having decided on the names of the characters."[91] Parker further contends that "orchestral thought," in the sense implied by Theodor Adorno in connection with "advanced" 20th-century music, rarely occurs in Verdi." But Parker also suggests that as the composer continued his lifelong compositional practice of isolating the various creative phases, he ultimately allowed for the "sound" to achieve "independence."[92]

The conscious use of melodic formulas is not the same as lack of ingenuity, social agency, or aesthetic signification, and, of course, musical formulas are integral parts of any composer's *métier*. Therefore, opera composers' attention to crafting melodies so that they could exist on their own, be easily retained, and then travel swiftly, cannot be taken for granted; in other words, the craftsmanship of creating the non-unique yet appealing. One can say that the understanding of both melody's aesthetic power and its commercial force became commonplace for composers in the emerging music business as the 19th century unfolded. Senici shows that Rossini's and Verdi's melodic craftsmanship were formulaic but notable elements in their compositional process. In this sense, the specific shape of a few tunes aided the memory of the auditory and furthered its power

---

[89] Stefani, "Melody," 22.

[90] Roger Parker, *Remaking the Song: Operatic Visions and Revisions from Handel to Berio* (Berkeley: University of California Press, 2006), 11.

[91] Philip Gossett, "Verdi the Craftsman," *Revista Portuguesa de Musicologia* 11 (2001): 93–95; Parker, *Remaking the Song*, 6.

[92] Parker, *Remaking the Song*, 76.

COSMOPOLITAN TRADITIONS   259

to be shared as a cosmopolitan musical experience, but this does not necessarily imply an unattractive, non-crafted melody. After decades of studying Italian opera, Gossett professed that:

> what first drew me to this repertory [Verdi's operas] . . . is a series of extraordinary melodies, often over simple orchestral accompaniments. . . . There are other aspects of the sketches . . . contrapuntal passages, recitative, ensembles. But it is to Verdi's melodic ideas we constantly return.[93]

Gossett was taken aback not only because "[Verdi's] tunes play a significant dramatic and musical role in Italian opera," but also because many "emerge unscathed from a hurdy gurdy, an organ grinder, or a juke box." Significantly, he wondered if it makes sense to argue for the role played by the composer's craftsmanship, since "[s]ome [melodies] seem to spring directly from the head of their creator. . . . Once heard [the melodies] seem always to have existed."[94] But craftsmanship did play a key role, Gossett concludes, as sketches also show that composers such as Verdi, Rossini, and Bellini polished their initial melodic ideas; they controlled "its peaks and troughs, [toyed] with its harmonic structure [to forge] an extraordinary melody."[95] Senici also argues that one needs to focus on "the melody as a cultural mode of cognition, maybe of alienation, that relied on the composer's knowingness [as well as on] audience selection."[96] In other words, both the composer and the audience were implicated in the creation and melodic recognition, and I would also add the performer, in a process that was not as random as it may seem.

Yet there are many ways to strip operatic melodies of aesthetic force. Studying arrangements of opera during the 19th century, William Lockhart claims that "popular transcription may well have changed the nature of what opera meant to many listeners." Lockhart cites Roger Chartier (1995), who suggested that:

> [w]hen the same text is apprehended through very different mechanisms of representation, it is no longer the same. Each of its forms obeys specific conventions that mold and shape the work according to the laws of that form and connect it, in differing ways, with other arts, other genres, and other texts.[97]

In this interpretation, when removed from the operatic stage, Verdi's craftsmanship is no longer under consideration, as his tunes supposedly mean

---

[93] Gossett, "Verdi the Craftsman," 81 and 111; see also Antonio Rostagno, "L'Invenzione melodica di Verdi: costruzione e ispirazione," *Revista Portuguesa de Musicologia*, 11 (2001): 113–137.

[94] Gossett, "Verdi the Craftsman," 81.

[95] Gossett, "Verdi the Craftsman," 81.

[96] Senici, *Music in the Present Tense*, 15.

[97] Lockhart, "Listening to the Domestic Music Machine," 913.

260   MUSIC AND COSMOPOLITANISM

something other than opera, and eventually other than music. In the end, one is led to believe that, depending on whose ears are activated in the social process of listening, with which practices or performance media they are delivered, the music is no longer the same music. When estranged from the operatic stage, the music ceases to be Verdi-crafted tunes to become "deformations of the original," through "mass commodification of the aesthetic experience (of opera)," although Lockhart emphasizes that "it did offer a musical experience *of sorts* [my emphasis]."[98] Parakilas puts forward a similar argument, that "[o]pera transcriptions offer a radically different aesthetic frame for opera,"[99] while Thomas Christensen is less dismissive, claiming that if one does not include arrangements in the history of opera, then one leaves large amounts of musics "without history."[100] And we are thus left with an array of operatic melodies circulating in many cities at the same time, but which are devoid of any aesthetic, social, or historical force.

In Rio de Janeiro, the popularity and communal recognition of Verdi's tunes confirmed not only the composer's melodic craftsmanship, but also their crucial place in the history of the *fin-de-siècle* city. After being repeated over and over in full and partial staged versions, few in Rio de Janeiro could escape a handful of Verdi's most songful and memorable melodies. Performed and heard in the city's streets over several decades and by musicians and audiences of all sorts, it was through the *realejo* that one could best engage with Verdi's melodies as sonic incipits, through the mechanical process of sonic repetition, listening, and memorizing passively. Throughout the city's streets, the *realejo* repeated Verdi's melodies non-stop, they became not merely "deformations of the original," but non-music. The very same melodies that enthralled the ears of audiences in opera houses and were perpetrators of social prestige and part of history became a city nuisance and turned into a threat to social distinction as non-music, and as such they were disavowed from history. In fact, street barrel performers turned into scapegoats for encouraging street noise and became a matter for law enforcement in many cities on both sides of the Atlantic.[101] But they performed

---

[98] Lockhart, "Listening to the Domestic Music Machine," 913.

[99] Parakilas, "The Operatic Canon," 862–880; see also Jutta Toelle, "Opera as Business? From Impresario to the Publishing Industry," *Journal of Modern Italian Studies*, 448–459, 17 (July 2012): 455.

[100] Thomas Christensen, "Sounding Offstage," in *The Oxford Handbook of Opera*, ed. Helen Greenwald (Oxford: Oxford University Press, 2014, online publication), 900.

[101] For a study of the role of *realejos* in the oral transmission of music in Rio de Janeiro early in the 19th century, see Martha Ulhôa, "Cosmoramas, realejos e cobras ferozes: A transmissão musical no Rio de Janeiro oitocentista," in *Visões da América, sonoridades da América*, Annals of the XII Congress of the IASPM-Latin America (São Paulo: Letra e Voz, 2017), 550–554. For discussions about music, sound, and noise in the city involving street organs and similar instruments, see Samuel Llano, "Street Music, Honour and Degeneration: The Case of Organilleros," in *Writing Wrongdoing in Spain, 1800–1936: Realities, Representations, Reactions*, edited by Alison Sinclair and Samuel Llano (Suffolk, UK: Boydell & Brewer, 2017), 197–215. For London, see John Picker, *Victorian Soundscapes*

COSMOPOLITAN TRADITIONS 261

the very same melodies heard in the opera houses, easily recognizable and understood as "already being there," but which were assigned aesthetic force only if performed at one place, but not the other, considered as suitable for the history of one audience, but not for another, those who threatened to transform the music into "something else." Some places, some people, and some performance mediums supposedly pushed the music to nonexistence just by being part of it and by engaging with it. It is in this regard that operatic melodies' routes through history differ greatly from other contemporary popular melodies, which were kept apart from claims of social distinction and rarely were considered (mistakenly) as having aesthetic force in the first place. Operatic melodies blurred social capital, musical aesthetics, and mass appeal, complicating social/musical associations and making conspicuous the segregation tactics of music criticism and questionable historical musical analysis.

Meanwhile, Verdi's tunes continued to travel to even more places and reach even more audiences. In the opinion of a Rio de Janeiro critic, melodies repeated over and over by the *realejos* were the embodiment of "eternal music,"[102] but not because they were associated with humanism, but because they were a part of the city, as if they were always there. The critic noted that *realejos* performing Verdi's "'Misereri' from *Il trovatore* turned the melody into a ritual of the city," not a ritual that defined local uniqueness, but one of the cosmopolitan city created through actual and virtual participation via a most well-crafted tune. From all of Verdi's operas, *Il trovatore* was the most performed in Rio de Janeiro, both on stages and in the streets, where it mingled easily with Emile Waldeteufeul's "Skaters Waltz," Planquette's "Les cloches de Corneville," and later also with Lehár's "Merry Widow Waltz." In 1910, a critic from the magazine *Fon-Fon* wrote, "For me, in terms of music, the *realejo* represents the supreme term of the popular consecration . . . [and the] popularization of 'Misereri' from *Il trovatore* is due emphatically to the *realejo*"[103](Figure 9.1). The *realejo* played the tune "in inverse mode," another chronicler argued, "as if un-swallowing the music we already heard, only to play it again, and bore us again by our ears."[104] And just like that, the *realejo* made the music eternal, and the eternal music was ingrained in the cosmopolitan city's present. At the same time, an advertisement in the *Gazeta de Noticias* just a year earlier had claimed that the theater still had a "full house" to watch and hear the 56-year-old *Il trovatore*.[105] If this overlap of social existences made a few operatic melodies historically significant, it was not only

(Oxford: Oxford University Press, 2013), and Patricia Pye, *Sound and Modernity in the Literature of London, 1880–1918* (London: Palgrave Macmillan, 2017), 73–96.

[102] *O Malho* 5, no. 205, August 18, 1906.
[103] *Fon-Fon* 4, no. 42, October 15, 1910.
[104] *Fon-Fon* 3, no. 13, March 27, 1909.
[105] *Gazeta de Noticias*, September 14, 1909.

Figure 9.1. "The old *realejo* performer who only plays "Miserere" from *Il trovatore*." *O Malho*, June 4, 1904.
Source: Biblioteca Nacional do Rio de Janeiro, Hemeroteca Digital

because of the mechanics of sound reproduction that made them into an "object like" music, as Jonathan Hicks suggests, again taking the music out of the melody.[106] Their historical relevance was marked by actual musical factors and authorial craftsmanship, as well as by the people who engaged with them, who heard them and repeated them. These operatic melodies did not have merely "alternative sorts of presence: street versus stage; stage versus record; then versus now," but simultaneous presence and extra lives across spaces, regardless of the many borders they crossed. They indeed allowed for "redistribution of agency," as Hicks also suggests, but one that still remains to be fully accounted for.

The Guaranis

On September 14, 1908, the Cinema-Palace in Rio de Janeiro announced the film *Os Guaranis* as one attraction in a four-part program of short films that made

---

[106] Hicks, "Should Manrico Escape?," 189–190.

Figure 9.2. Carlos Gomes (photo ca. 1886–1991).
Source: Archive of the Museu Carlos Gomes.

the nightly entertainment.[107] *Os Guaranis* was filmed in the circus from a pantomime production with the same title, presented by the Spinelli's troupe and directed and acted by Benjamin de Oliveira, who had been staging the show in the circus around the city since 1903. Inspired by José de Alencar's (1829–1877) romantic novel *O Guarany* (1857), by Carlos Gomes's opera *Il Guarany* (1870), and by the melodrama *O Guarany* (1874), *Os Guaranis* was such a hit that it prompted no fewer than 11 other films on the same topic throughout the 20th century, becoming the most adapted work in the history of Brazilian cinema (Figure 9.2).[108] But before the pantomime and film became a success in the circus and movie theaters, both the novel *O Guarany* and the opera *Il Guarany* had wide traveling paths within and beyond Rio de Janeiro, travels that furthered the roles that the works played in shaping the cosmopolitan city and, eventually, also the republican nation. It was a process spanning over five decades—and that continued to reverberate through the 20th century—that involved complex

---

[107] *Gazeta de Notícias*, September 14, 1908. *Os Guaranis*. Production by Labanca, Leal e Cia Companhia Produtora.
[108] Iañez Gonçalves da Silva, "O Guarany no cinema brasileiro: Visão da imprensa entre 1908 e 1926," *Anagrama* 7, no. 1 (2013), 1–14. Benjamin presented the pantomime in São Paulo in 1902, then in Rio in 1903; see Silva, *Circo-Teatro*, 210–211. For a list of silent movies based on Alencar's novel, see Jurandyr Noronha, "No tempo dos 'falantes e cantantes': Literatura no cinema mudo," *Revista do Livro* 49 (September 2007): 23–40.

264   MUSIC AND COSMOPOLITANISM

sociopolitical dynamics and cultural engagements with the works, individually and collectively, and that depended on music's potential to travel across borders.

The plot of the novel *O Guarany* takes place in the 17th century in outskirts of Rio de Janeiro and tells a love story between the daughter of a Portuguese settler and landowner, Ceci, and a Guarany indian, Peri, who saves her from several competitors and from abduction by warriors from the Aymoré tribe. The result is a story filled with pacts and conflicts among Indigenous groups and Europeans, on top of a daring love story that created suspense and offered many entertaining thrills to a city readership eager for the excitement of mid-century romantic novels, serialized publications, and melodramas. Thus, *O Guarany* appropriately first came out as a *folhetim*, a serialized publication appearing in *Diario do Rio de Janeiro* newspaper over four months, from January to April 1857, before being published as a book later in the year. The work first galvanized Rio de Janeiro's literate audience (no more than 20% of the population at mid-century), who became fascinated by a love story involving Indigenous characters and created not in Paris or London, but by a Rio de Janeiro novelist writing in a newspaper office located amid the city's familiar streets. Readers were also enticed by a story taking place in romanticized remote days of the country's Portuguese colonization, in a fictional account of Europeans confronting and interacting with Indigenous peoples, and by Alencar's descriptions of untarnished nature, delivered piecemeal as entertainment in a newspaper and in an accessible language to the city's readers. The success of the *folhetim* was such that as soon as a new issue of *Diario do Rio de Janeiro* would come out, it prompted group readings among family members, in salons, and in discussions in cafés: for four months the novel became part of the daily life of the city. By all accounts, *O Guarany* was a bestseller in Rio de Janeiro at mid-century according to the period's notion of a hit (i.e. a book selling over 1,000 copies in the city before a new edition was issued).[109]

Published anonymously and quickly to make the newspaper's deadline, the bestseller was not shaped by Alencar alone, however. The *folhetim* had the help of the audience, who would write to the author with suggestions and sometimes with passionate pleas for how they believed the story should proceed, an interaction that defined the novel's presentness. He would then use those ideas to build, modify, and extend the plot, a strategy that helped sell more newspapers and that, in turn, prompted more audiences to engage with the work. Alencar also used a narrator who responds directly to the reader as if the author and audience were intimate, one and the same. These were unmistakably commercial moves. The success of Alencar's *folhetins*, including *O Guarany*, was thus due in part to the author's skill in writing a novel as a commercialized product from the start.

---

[109] Andreia Carneiro, "Nascimento de um índio na rua do ouvidor: José de Alencar Best-seller," Master's thesis, Universidade Estadual de Feira de Santana, 2012.

COSMOPOLITAN TRADITIONS 265

Ignoring critics' disdains, Alencar worked for and with a reading public and was involved in many strategies for distributing his own works, including door-to-door book sales, a task usually done by enslaved Blacks. Taunay remembered clearly the impact that the novel had in the city:

> Rio de Janeiro read *O Guarany en mass* and would follow the *folhetins* moved by Ceci and Peri's pure and discreet love; they engaged [with the story] with sympathy, amid dangers and the sagacity of the savages, and the various dangers and fates of the main characters of the captivating novel, penned in the "indianist" mold of Chateaubriand and Feminore Cooper, but with an individual style that was opulent, unique, as if [the novel] was itself derived from exotic flowers from our virgin and lush forests.[110]

The convenient confluence of forged reality and imaginary ideals involving romanticized Indigenous groups in a historically remote locale presented in *O Guarany* clearly followed contemporary romantic literary trends, as Alencar himself professed his knowledge, admiration for, and inspiration in Byron, Hugo, Dumas, and Cooper, among others.[111] Nonetheless, taking place around Rio de Janeiro, the story was aimed directly at the city's audiences: Alencar describes, for example, one of the main characters, the Portuguese settler D. Antônio Mariz's, as "a Portuguese nobleman and one of the founders of the city of Rio de Janeiro."[112] *O Guarany's* subtitle, "A National Novel," also appealed because it referred mostly to the locale, characters, and subject matter involving the country's early colonial history, rather than the story of kings and queens in remote lands that was commonplace in the romantic literature also sold concurrently and profusely in the city's bookstores. But *O Guarany* was not purposely nationalistic in a politico-ideological sense; one may call it nativist, although its success aided in fortifying the myth of national foundation involving Indigenous groups, one that eventually crystallized during the early days of the republican government.

An outspoken critic against the abolition of slavery, Alencar favored the idea of gradual, "harmonious integration" of both the Indigenous and the enslaved Blacks into Brazilian society through their submission to the European "civilized" culture, a seamless integration that only over time, he believed, could serve well to support a new Brazilian nation.[113] The idea was explored in the novel on

---

[110] Alfredo d'Escragnolle Taunay, *Reminiscências* (São Paulo: Companhia Melhoramentos, 1923), 85.

[111] José de Alencar, *Como e porque sou romancista* (Campinas, SP: Pontes, 1990).

[112] *O Guarany*, "Um antigo fidalgo," chapter 2, 11 (Rio de Janeiro: Empreza Nacional do Diario, 1857). The citation is from the 1857 edition of the novel, available at the Biblioteca Nacional do Rio de Janeiro, http://objdigital.bn.br/objdigital2/acervo_digital/div_obrasraras/or18418/or18418.pdf.

[113] Joyce Nathália de Souza Trindade, "José de Alencar e a escravidão: necessidade nacional e benfeitoria senhorial," Master's thesis, Universidade Federal dee São Paulo, 2014.

266 MUSIC AND COSMOPOLITANISM

several levels, where cordial relations among Indigenous groups and Europeans are fantasized enough to conceal the systems of oppression and avoid the topic of slavery. A resident of Rio de Janeiro, Alencar was also an avid reader of travelers' chroniclers and ethnographic studies about Indigenous groups and descriptions of landscapes in remote locations by both local and foreign writers. He used the information to write a novel that includes footnotes with explanations and lists of sources, several of which are in French, in an attempt to offer a "truthful history." As a result, *O Guarany* narrated a love story in a journalistic vein, while appealing to urban contemporary readers' appetites for scientific knowledge about what they believed to be the "roots of civilization."

Alencar's novel nonetheless clashed with some critics in Rio de Janeiro, in particular with José Gonçalves de Magalhães, the author of the Indianist epic poem by *A Confederação dos Tamoios* (1856), who claimed that Alencar discarded realistic portrayals of Indigenous lives, traditions, and their fights for their land. Yet these two authors summarize well the overall imagination about the Indigenous in the cosmopolitan city during the mid- and late 19th century: on one hand, the Tupis (of which the Guaranys are a part) are portrayed as docile, willing to form alliances, the "noble savage" who could be easily integrated; on the other hand, the Tapuias (of which the Aymorés are a part) are depicted as the fighters who disrupted the European civilizing mission. Central to this imaginary is a Darwinist system of natural selection, in which the Indigenous would either integrate with Europeans or eventually disappear in the face of "civilization."[114] The novel clearly highlights this duality: while the Aymorés are feared warriors, the Guarany character avoids conflict and is portrayed as a heroic "gentlemen with noble feelings," and as a selfless individual communing with nature, but also ready for integration with Catholicism and the cultures of the European.[115] Alencar's view of the noble savage, in accordance with many contemporary romantic authors, eventually prevailed as part of the myth of the nation's foundation, based on a fictitious and self-serving integration of Europeans and the

---

[114] John Manuel Monteiro, "As 'raças' indígenas no pensamento brasileiro do império," in *Raça, ciência e sociedade*, ed. Marcos Maio and Ricardo Ventura Santos (Rio de Janeiro: Ed. Fiocruz, 1996), 15; and Antonio Cavalcanti de Almeida, "Aspectos das políticas indigenistas no Brasil," *Interações* 19, no. 3 (July–September 2018), 611–626, online publication https://www.scielo.br/j/inter/a/rQk3vztR BF6WNbwCdwPTPFQ/?lang=pt.

See also Maria Regina Celestino de Almeida, "A atuação dos indígenas na História do Brasil: Revisões historiográficas," *Revista Brasileira de História* 37, no. 75 (May–August 2017), 17–38, online publication, https://www.scielo.br/j/rbh/a/b7Z47VbMMmvPQwWhbHfdkpr/?lang=pt#B26.

[115] For an analysis of Alencar's sources and a comparison between Alencar's novel and the epic poem by José Gonçalves de Magalhães, *A Confederação dos Tamoios* (1856), see Cristina Ferreira and Thiago Lenz, "Duas narrativas para o lugar dos indígenas nas origens da nação: A história ficcional de Magalhães e Alencar," *Almanack* 23 (September–December 2019): 202–238. See also David Treece, *Exiles, Allies, Rebels: Brazil's Indianist Movement, Indigenist Politics, and the Imperial Nation-State* (London: Greenwood Press, 2000).

Indigenous. The myth served well not only monarchists but also republicans, as they started to forge the country's history according to their own precepts. The new government not only left unchanged such romanticized monarchical foundational myths, but also made wide use of them. For example, the new constitution of 1891 did not address the Indigenous peoples' rights for the land and in turn left unchanged monarchical laws that empowered European landowners over the Indigenous, while endowing European immigrants with Brazilian citizenship.

Alencar's approach also helped propel the novel through wider traveling routes. To follow the story of *O Guarany*, readers outside the capital would have to wait eagerly for several days for mailed copies of *O Diário do Rio de Janeiro* to arrive, prompting the appearance of various pirate publications while furthering the popular appeal of *O Guarany* as a national bestseller. Taunay recalled groups of students in São Paulo gathering around those who were fortunate enough to get hold of the newest *Diário do Rio de Janeiro* with a new chapter of the story, and who would read aloud in communal areas to others in a kind of improvised reading/theatrical show.[116] The story of *O Guarany*, constructed with the city's readership in mind, was thus further shared by word of mouth in a "performance of orality," in a coexistence of modes of transmission that involved the writer, readers, and listeners scattered in cities throughout the country, now intimately dependent on one another, a coexistence that eventually blurred social boundaries shaped by literacy.[117] As the work's popularity grew over the years, commercial exploits prompted the naming of locales and things as "Guarany" throughout the country, from bars, cafés, shops, to miscellaneous products for sale, while the Indigenous characters of the novel slowly became a part of Rio de Janeiro's daily life. This is a process that is all too familiar today in cities where Hollywood movies have turned fictional characters into icons who, for good or for bad, have become a living presence in the lives of many around the world.

Meanwhile, *O Guarany* also broke away from the city to cross the Atlantic. As early as 1864, seven years after the novel's publication in a Rio de Janeiro newspaper and eight years before Gomes's opera, Milanese had available to them two translations of the work. Giovanni Fico, the Italian translator, added a preface to his publication noting that the story should appeal to the Italian public because it came from "beyond the equator" and included abundant "exotic nature, landscape, and history," while reminding the Italian reader that they should also be interested because the novel's focus was on "the people's passion, which is the same everywhere, with rivalry, disdain, revenge" (Figure 9.3).[118] Similarities between

---

[116] Taunay, *Reminiscências*, 8.

[117] Souza, *Carpinteiros teatrais*, 28.

[118] Valéria Cristina Bezerra, "*Il Guarany* e *Ubiraiara*: Os romances de José de Alencar na Itália," *FronteiraZ* 19 (December 2017): 53–64.

Figure 9.3. Cover page of the Italian translation of *O Guarany*.
Source: Archive of the University of Illinois, Urbana-Champain

Alencar's works and [James Fenimore] Cooper's frontier novels in the United States, their use of raw nature and Native American protagonists to convey a mythical origin of a nation, have not escaped critics over the years.[119] The novel's translator in the United States, James William Hawes, for instance, noted that the work was "full with a noble red man, gallants, and villains, fair damsels, and fierce beasts, [which is] curiously suggestive of our own early fiction, Cooper's

---

[119] See, for instance, Renata Wasserman, "Re-inventing the New World: Cooper and Alencar," *Comparative Literature* 36, no. 2 (1984): 130–145.

in special."[120] However, *O Guarany* started like many contemporary novels, as a malleable artistic, commercial, and traveling work, offering excitement, variety, and familiarity, and feeding into the imagination of various audiences in many cities across continents, who became well accustomed to, and exited by, a peculiar love story set in exotic locales.

When Gomes's opera *Il Guarany* opened in 1870, *O Guarany* already had a large audience on both sides of the Atlantic. With an Italian libretto by Antonio Scalvini, with whom Gomes had worked earlier in the comic theater, and revised and completed by Carlo D'Ormeville, the opera nonetheless offered a modified version of the novel, further patronizing the Indigenous as a noble savage hero and diluting the racial tensions in the original story through the elimination of several characters in the novel. In the opera, Isabel, the *mestiça* half-sister of the heroine, is left out and Ceci is the only female character, her *coloratura* soprano voice strategically set up against basses, baritones, and tenors throughout the opera.[121] The librettists then substituted the Italian priest in the novel with the character of a Spanish adventurer, who also competes for Ceci's love, a strategic move since the opera was to be first presented to Milanese audiences. One of *Il Guarany*'s most memorable moments, the love duet of Ceci and Peri at the end of the first act, was absent in the novel, as the opera highlights the subjective and complex nature of individual relationships, on top of the exotic story of Europeans winning over the Indigenous. Scalvini and D'Ormeville also bypassed the novel's grandiose ending, where Alencar's penchant for visual imagery and suggestion of national foundation are most prominent, with Ceci and Peri floating together on a palm tree leaf through the flooding Paquequer river. Instead, the librettists opt for a scene in which the lovers flee the burning castle and together contemplate the destruction from afar and suggest a new future together. Sections with appeal for visual displays were not absent in the opera, however. The scene in the Aymorés' quarters in act III asks for various artists on stage to perform "ritual dances" and "indigenous prayers," with the visual effects expected from successful contemporary grand operas. The libretto also explores multi-partite pacts and competitions not only between Europeans and Indigenous groups, but between Portuguese and Spanish and between Aymorés and Guaranys, while the only female character becomes central to all conflicts and interactions. The enticing pretense of conquest and submission told through a love story continued to be presented in the remote past, now earlier in the 16th

---

[120] Valéria Cristina Bezerra, "The Honey-Lips e The Guarany: Os Romances de José De Alencar em língua inglesa no final do século XIX," *Signo* 41, no. 72 (2016): 24.

[121] For a larger study of gender in the opera, see Anne Meyer, "A construção musical da feminilidade na ópera *Il Guarany* (Carlos Gomes)," in *Annals of the VI Brazilian Simposium of Graduates in Music* (SIMPOM 2020) (Rio de Janeiro: Universidade Federal do Estado do Rio de Janeiro), 475–486. For the adaptations of the novel in the libretto, see Maria Alice Volpe, "Carlos Gomes: A persistência de um paradigma em época de crepúsculo," *Brasiliana* 17 (2004): 2–11.

270   MUSIC AND COSMOPOLITANISM

century, a familiar subterfuge in 19th-century novels, operas, and melodramas, alongside dazzling stage constructions of tropical forests that offered a visual spectacle for those eager for the exotic in the many cities in which the opera circulated, including Rio de Janeiro.

The changes to Alencar's novel in the opera also reflected the source used to build the libretto. At the time, Gomes was looking to write an opera on a "Brazilian topic" in Milan to satisfy a condition of the scholarship he had received from the Opera Nacional in Rio de Janeiro, Alencar's novel was conveniently available to Scalvini in Italian translations. The Italian publication of the novel may in fact have laid the groundwork and created expectations for the opera's premiere in Milan, while later translations of the novel in German, English, and French may also have helped propel *Il Guarany*'s success beyond Italy, fulfilling identifications with both the novel and the opera at multiple levels in the many places to which the work traveled.[122] Thus, the opera's initial appeal also rested on the popularity of the novel. Gomes's strategy of using a novel with an established audience to further the chances for his opera's success was one used by many opera composers during his lifetime, including Verdi, who favored French novels with an already guaranteed audience across Europe.[123] Premiered at La Scala in Milan in September and in Rio de Janeiro in December 1870 with a gala presentation honored by the presence of Emperor Pedro II, *Il Guarany* not only relied on the prestige of Alencar's story, but it considerably widened the novel's traveling paths. It opened successfully in various cities in Italy and in London in 1872, in Santiago do Chile in 1873, in Buenos Aires in 1874, in Vienna and Stockholm in 1875, in Montevideo, Brussels, Barcelona, and Warsaw in 1876, in Corfú in 1877, in Havana, St. Petersburg, and Moscow in 1879, in Nice in 1880, and in New York in 1884, with presentations in the larger operatic circuit continuing well into the late 1890s.[124] *Il Guarany* remains one of the few operas

---

[122] For French translations see, Valéria Cristina Bezerra, "A recepcão crítica de José de Alencar em Língua Francesa (1858-1902)," *Recorte* 13, no. 2 (July–December, 2016): 1–14; For English translations see Valéria Cristina Bezerra, "The Honey-Lips e The Guarany"; and Ilana Heineberg, "Peri com sotaque francês: Um estudo preliminar de três traduções de O Guarani no século XIX," in *José de Alencar: Século XXI*, ed. Marcelo Peloggio, Arlene Fernandes, and Valéria Cristina Bezerra (Fortaleza: Brazil Edições UFC, 2015), 241–265; For German translation see, Wiebke Roben de Alencar Xavier, "O encontro do Ubirajara Alencariano com a sua primeira tradução alemã de 1886," in *José de Alencar: Século XXI*, ed. Marcelo Peloggio, Arlene Fernandes, and Valéria Cristina Bezerra (Fortaleza: Edições UFC, 2015), 267–286.

[123] Sorba, "Between Cosmopolitanism and Nationhood," 56–59.

[124] For a full list of performances of *Il Guarany* in Europe and the Americas, see Marcello Conati, "Fortuna e aspetti del 'Guarany' di Gomes," *Revista de Musicología* 16, no. 1 (1993): 71–264. Olga Freitas, "Il Guarany de Antônio Carlos Gomes: A história de uma ópera nacional," Master's thesis, Universidade Federal do Paraná, 2011, 140. Also Dimitiros Kiousopoulos, "L'opera lirica nazionale in prospettiva internazionale: I casi della Grecia e del Brasile nel XIX secolo," *Memoria e Ricerca* 29 (2008): 47.

COSMOPOLITAN TRADITIONS   271

by a non-European composer to achieve such a large recognition abroad in its heyday, an honor that has guaranteed him a stable place in the operatic canon.

The use of excerpts from *Il Guarany*'s music in the melodrama *O Guarany* was nonetheless one of the earliest attempts to expand the opera's appeal into the popular theater and to widen its social relevance and the impact of its forged history among Rio de Janeiro's audiences. With Portuguese text by de Visconti Coroacy and Pereira da Silva, and directed by Francisco Corrêia Vasques, the melodrama opened on May 9, 1874, at the Theatro Ginásio Dramático, four years after the opera's premiere. Albeit presented only a few times in the city because of disagreements with Alencar about the production, Vasques not only offered a theatrical version of the romantic epic story, but expanded the visual elements of the novel's ending to the level of the spectacular through the use of elaborate stage machinery and mise-en-scène.[125] In doing so, Vasques opened the romantic novel's allure to those who had never read Cooper, Byron, Hugo, Schiller, Dumas, and others from whom Alencar had found inspiration for his novel, while also introducing Gomes's music to those whose limited financial resources initially prevented them from attending the opera hall.[126] The staging of the melodrama's four acts was also tied directly to the opera in that it included the extended section on the Aymorés with elaborate costumes and ballets that called for no fewer than 250 dancers and actors on stage. The amplification of visual effects in the melodrama was then achieved through skillful use of Gomes's music, adapted, rehearsed, and conducted by Henrique Alves de Mesquita (1830–1906). A prolific composer of operettas, short pieces for intermezzi, and dances, Mesquita had wide experience in making music enhance the dramatic action. A contemporary of Gomes, Mesquita was also graced with a fellowship to study abroad and graduated from the Paris conservatory. In Rio de Janeiro, Mesquita taught at the conservatory and later in the Instituto Nacional de Música and made a successful career conducting, arranging, and writing music for comic theater, reviews, and *féeries*. Mesquita's arrangement of *Il Guarany* unfortunately did not survive, and Vasques's production remained the only stage version of Alencar's novel until Oliveira put on his pantomime in Spinelli's circus 30 years later. But one of Mesquita's published works did use excerpts from *Il Guarany*, the polka

---

[125] Crepaldi Carvalho, "D'O Guarani de José de Alencar e Carlos Gomes aos Guaranis do clown Benjamin: Diálogos entre literatura, cinema,circo e música1," *Aniki* 5, no. 1 (2018): 92–93; see also João Roberto de Faria, "José de Alencar: A polêmica em torno da adaptação teatral de O Guarani," *Letras* 31 (1982): 59–101.

[126] The libretto for *Il Guarany* was translated into Portuguese only in the 1930s; see Alberto Pacheco, Adriana Kayama, Lúcia de Fátima Vasconcelos, "Era uma vez um príncipe: Uma versão brasileira e ópera *Il Guarany* de Carlos Gomes," in *Anais do Terceiro Simpósio Internacional de Musicologia da Universidade Federal do Rio de Janeiro* (Rio de Janeiro: Universidade Federal do Rio de Janeiro, 2013), 97–108.

272 MUSIC AND COSMOPOLITANISM

"Carlos Gomes" (188?), a piece that shows how a composer for the theater may have used the opera's tunes to enhance the drama and aid in its durability.[127]

The success with *Il Guarany* came to Gomes at a young age, and immediately after he had conquered Italian audiences as a composer for the comic theater, with two successful *rivista musicali*: *Se sa minga, rivista de 1866* (1867) with libretto by Scalvini, and *Nella luna, rivista del 1868* (1869), with libretto by Eugenio Torelli Viollier.[128] After *Il Guarany*, Gomes continued his career focusing mostly on operas, with the production of *Fosca* (1873), *Salvator Rosa* (1874), *Maria Tudor* (1879), *Lo Schiavo* (1889), and *Condor* (1891), which were also performed in Europe and the Americas but with variable degrees of success.[129] At the time of the proclamation of the Republic in 1889, Gomes was 54 and at the height of his career. If there was a composer in both the local and the transoceanic operatic scenes who could boast the credentials to be a representative of musical Brazil, Gomes was it. Nonetheless, not everyone in Rio de Janeiro's musical establishment embraced Gomes, and his music continued to hold an uncertain place within the historiography, even after the Indigenous and the "tropical land" became crystallized as tropes of a new nation.[130] The ostracizing of the composer by the intellectual status quo became particularly evident in the second decade of the 20th century, when nationalistic prescriptions of what constituted a local (and national) musical heritage conflicted with understandings of opera's role in it. Touted as foreign, as an outdated genre, and as a European-dominating force, opera was assumed to be against the nation, not a part of it.[131]

Local politics, of course, played a role in the "Musical Republic's" avoidance of the composer during the early days of the new regime: like Alencar, Gomes was a monarchist, and *Il Guarany* was dedicated to Emperor Pedro II, who provided monetary assistance for the opera's production in Milan. Unlike other artists who quickly and conveniently changed sides during the early years of the new government or managed to bypass antagonizing politics, Gomes refused to openly

---

[127] The score with the piano performance of this work by pianist Roberto Szidon is available at https://www.youtube.com/watch?v=pDU5CqIsL9Q.

[128] Alexandre Bispo, "Teatro de revista em processos político-culturais italianos o conservadorismo moderado, a crítica ao volúvel e o apelo ao bom senso 'Nella Luna'—rivista del 1868—de E. Torelli Viollier (1842–1900) e A. Carlos Gomes (1836–1896)," *Revista Brasil-Europa: Correspondência Euro-Brasileira* 162, no. 6 (2016), online publication http://revista.brasil-europa.eu/162/Nella_Luna_de_Carlos_Gomes.html.

[129] José Maurício Brandão, "Carlos Gomes: Um ilustre desconhecido," *Revista Modus* 7, no. 11 (2012): 17–26, 20; see also Lenita Nogueira, "Música e política: O caso de Carlos Gomes," in *ANPPOM (Annals of the XV Congress*, 2005), coord. Marcelo Verzoni, (Rio de Janeiro: Universidade Federal do Rio de Janeiro, 2006), 249.

[130] Volpe, "Carlos Gomes," 6.

[131] During the 1920s, modernist Oswald de Andrade defined Gomes's music as "inexpressive, artificial, and disgraceful"; see José Miguel Wisnik, *O Coro dos Contrários: a music em torno da semana de 22*, 2nd ed. (São Paulo: Livraria Duas Cidades, 1983), 81. Mário de Andrade dismisses the 19th-century Italian bel canto as "exterior" and a "gigantic banality"; see his *Pequena história da música* (Belo Horizonte: Editora Itatiaia Limitada, 1987 [1942]), 134–135.

support the republican government. Gomes claimed not to be an individual with deep political convictions or specific intellectual affiliations,[132] although he left a fair number of anthems dedicated to national movements in Italy, and his works for the comic theater make direct references to the *Risorgimento*.[133] Gomes professed his right, as a "Brazilian patriot," to disagree with some republican intellectuals and to criticize those who, in his opinion, were nothing but "politicians and music dilettanti."[134] These criticisms, undoubtedly directed at Miguez, now the director of the Instituto Nacional de Música, did not help Gomes advance his own cause with Rio de Janeiro's musical establishment. The composer was left with no options but to remain in Italy, but now without any financial perks, and his efforts to further his professional career outside Brazil did not achieve much monetary success. Gomes's inability to deal with the business side of his career just made his financial situation worse, as he allowed himself to be manipulated by impresarios and publishers within an environment of steep competition that was the Milan operatic scene. With deteriorated health and constant financial difficulties, he returned to Brazil in 1895 when he was offered the chairmanship of the conservatory in the state of Pará. Gomes died in 1896, far from the Brazilian capital and leaving behind few material rewards to show for his work.

The story of *Il Guarany* has often been linked to the narrative of Gomes's fall from grace during the early years of the republican government and to the critical appraisal of his works as passé, artificial, "easy," and foreign.[135] Such a demise, of course, was not solely an issue pertaining to local music critics. The Mexican composer Melesio Morales, an outsider to Brazilian internal politics but a contemporary and competitor of Gomes in the operatic world, for example, suspiciously saw in *Il Guarany* an artificial display of visual and musical effects, claiming that the opera was written not for Italian audiences, nor for Rio de Janeiro's opera houses, but for the "yankees," a work written for audiences in

---

[132] Marcus Góes, *A força indômita* (Pará, Brazil: Secult, 1996); see also Marcos Virmond, "Algumas reflexões em torno de Antônio Carlos Gomes," *Mimesis* 23, no. 1 (2002): 47–48.

[133] Alexandre Bispo, "O canto popular veneziano e o ressurgimento nacional italiano: A Canzonetta veneziana "Lisa me vostu ben?" de A. Carlos Gomes (1836–1896) dedicada a Antonio Pavan (1823–1898) no decanto do amor de Piero Foscari (1865–1923) e Elisabetta Widmann Rezzonico (1878–1953)," *Revista Brasil-Europa: Correspondência Euro-Brasileira* 163, no. 6 (2016), online publication, http://revista.brasil-europa.eu/163/Lisa_me_vostu_ben.html.

[134] Carta a Theodoro Teixeira Gomes, Milão, 04 de janeiro de 1894.

[135] This is an issue still pervading scholarship. In terms of Gomes's familiar operatic structures and melodies working against him, see Durval Cesetti's observation that "it is at least ironic that . . . one of the elements that made him [Gomes] so popular in Brazil and so accessible to European audiences at the time was [what] made him so irrelevant"; see "*Il Guarany* for Foreigners: Colonialist Racism, Naïve Utopia, or Pleasant Entertainment?," *Latin American Music Review* 31 (2010): 102. For the contemporary critical discussions about Gomes's music and its association with Verdi and Meyerbeer, see Lutero Rodrigues, *Carlos Gomes, um tema em questão: A ótica modernista e a visão de Mário de Andrade* (São Paulo: Editora Unesp, 2011).

274 MUSIC AND COSMOPOLITANISM

New York City, who were also eager to exploit the Indigenous as exotic.[136] In some accounts, if there was an eventual acceptance of Gomes's operas during the early days of the new regime, it was less the endorsement of his music than the result of timing. When the composer died in 1896, the political disruptions of the new government were starting to wane and the country had elected Prudente de Moraes (1841–1902) in 1894, the first civilian president. With a promise of political stability came the realization of the loss of a composer who had brought attention to and elevated the name of the country abroad. According to a prevailing narrative, Gomes's death led to a sense of collective mourning and contributed to the awareness among local politicians and critics that the country had lost an accomplished musician with an international career who was, after all, a son of the Brazilian nation.[137] Be it as it may, the position in which Gomes found himself within a *fin-de-siècle* operatic world has analogies in the careers of many contemporary opera composers, who were caught within the growing political forces of the nation-state. They felt the need to negotiate their individual artistic expressions through many social and cultural binaries that supported imaginaries of the nation, such as "pure" artistic endeavors versus commercialized work, live performances versus new media technologies of recordings and film, original and copy, "elite" versus "popular" culture, among many others.

Yet it was exactly the "in-between-ness" of works like *Il Guarany*, that is, their power to move effortlessly within the porous political, sociocultural, and musical spheres of complex urban networks, that eventually propelled the opera to become a powerful agent in the shaping of the cosmopolitan city. If one moves beyond the idea of the unique and the authentic as sine qua non conditions for understanding the success with the public and interest of critics, or for the inclusion of a work in a canon, and focuses instead on the composer's choice of topics and skill in manipulating musical gestures in the theatrical domain to reach wide urban audiences eager for visual-sonic-sensorial experiences, one can start to grasp how the music from *Il Guarany* ended up permeating multiple spaces and places over several decades. One of the reasons was the composer's skillful use of music to enhance the melodrama's power and to explore the complex subjectivities of individual characters, their deep passions, and psychological conflicts, tools which, as Crepaldi notes, eventually became an access

---

[136] Verónica Zárate Toscano and Serge Gruzinsk, "Ópera, imaginación y Sociedad: México y Brasil, siglo XIX: Histórias conectadas: *Ildegonda* de Melesio Morales e *Il Guarany* de Carlos Gomes," *Historia Mexicana* 58, no. 2 (2008): 807.

[137] For accounts of the coverage of Gomes's death, see Geraldo Coelho, *O brilho da supernova: A morte bela de Carlos Gomes* (Rio de Janeiro: Agir, 1995); Emerson Dionisio de Oliveira, "Últimos dias de Carlos Gomes": Do mito 'gomesiano' ao 'nascimento' de um acervo," *Revista CPC* 4 (May–October 2007): 87–113; and Mônica Vermes, "A recepção de Carlos Gomes na Primeira República: Entre os vínculos imperiais e o panteão musical nacional," *Annals of the XXVI Congress of the Associação Nacional de Pesquisa e Pós-Graduação em Música* (Belo Horizonte, 2016), 1–8.

to a collectivity who could easily identify with the opera's characters.[138] In this regard, Gomes's skill in writing songful and memorable melodies to highlight a love story through the sufferings of a female character and the physical and moral strength of male warriors found fertile grounds for dissemination among city audiences, who were already enthralled by well-known complex characters delivered through tunes from operas by Rossini, Donizetti, Bellini, and Verdi. But in *Il Guarany*'s most famous duet between the two main characters, Ceci and Peri, Gomes intersperses continuous singing with clear-cut melodic passages, making use of the schematic operatic *forma solita* with ample liberty. This fragmentation served to highlight different aspects of the love story, Peri's love declaration in "Sento un forza indomita," (Musical Example 9.1a) contrasted with Ceci's response "Qualunque via dischiuderti," (Musical Example 9.1b) male and female, the Indigenous and the European, separated by different melodic constructions, each section of the duet free to follow different extra lives outside the stage, as I will show below (Musical Example 9.1a and 9.1b).

Like many composers of opera and ballet of his generation, in *Il Guarany* Gomes explores the mimetic effectiveness of music to propel an imaginary world, both near and far from the city, and to magnify music's power to enhance and forge the fantastic and cinematic aspects of the overall plot. The score had plenty to offer in that regard. The work's initial appeal lay in its grand opera style, contemporary with Meyerbeer's *L'Africaine* (1865) and Verdi's *Aïda* (1871), two works that also circulated greatly alongside *Il Guarany* among audiences in cities across the Atlantic.[139] Published by Riccordi as *Opera-ballo in quattro atti*, Gomes's *Il Guarany* included several dances and choruses and the expected stage grandeur of grand operas. The work also benefited from Gomes's ingenious handling of palatable musical voyeurisms to assist the dramatic action and help portray exotic locales sonically through musical clichés already familiar to opera goers, ballet, and comic theater audiences for well over 50 years.[140] The chorus "Aspra, crudel, terribile," for example, is one of several instances where Gomes uses fast, repeating, syllabic text settings, here by stressing the word "Portoghese" ("Ma per l'empio Portoghese"), unmistakably recalling Rossinian sonic effects for expressing confusion and speeding action, which Gomes adds to bring attention to a drama dealing simultaneously with warriors, conquest, and love. In the second act, the song for Gonzales, a baritone and the villain of the opera, "Senza teto, senza cuna" (known in Portuguese as "A canção do aventureiro")

---

[138] Crepaldi Carvalho, "D'O Guarani," 90.

[139] Although focusing solely on Europe, Hesselager studied grand opera as a transnational genre, in *Grand Opera Outside Paris.*

[140] For a discussion of these musical techniques, see Smith, *Opera and Ballet in the Age of "Giselle."* For the use of music to "speak" what was implied in theatrical contexts later in the century, see Sarah Gutsche-Mille, "Pantomime-Ballet on the Music-Hall Stage: The Popularisation of Classical Ballet in Fin-de-Siècle Paris," PhD dissertation, McGil University, 2010.

Musical Example 9.1a. *Il Guarany*, act I, duet Pery, "Sento una forza indomita."
Source: Milan: Ricordi, 1889. IMSLP, Petrucci Music Library, https://vmirror.imslp.org/files/imglnks/usimg/5/56/IMSLP92176-PMLP67581-Gomes_-_Il_Guarany_VS_UNC.pdf

Musical Example 9.1b. *Il Guarany*, act I, duet Ceci ,"Qualunque via dischiuderti."
Source: Milan: Ricordi, 1889. IMSLP, Petrucci Music Library, https://vmirror.imslp.org/files/imglnks/usimg/5/56/IMSLP92176-PMLP67581-Gomes_-_Il_Guarany_VS_UNC.pdf

Musical Example 9.1b. (Continued)

shows Gomes's explorations of musical Spanish-ness on the stage, with the expected clichés of melodic/rhythmic features—melodic triplets and hemiolas—easily recognizable in stages across the Atlantic (Musical Example 9.2). Peri's "Son giunto in tempo!" in act II is another instance of the musical familiar, with the suggestion of danger and the unknown in the forest through use of music to mimic nature sounds such as the dense orchestral textures in the low register with oscillating and repeating short chromatic lines. With the marked repeated notes in the low strings without harmonic support to introduce the "primitive" in the Aymorés' quarters in act III, Gomes uses the expected to create suspense, a technique used by numerous composers before him, and which Stravinsky also used quite effectively as late as 1913. In act III, Gomes also uses music as both insider and outsider of the drama's imagery, as he introduces an ensemble on the stage suggesting movie-like diegetic elements in accord with a vogue in the operatic stage, ballets, and pantomimes. These familiar musical clichés to imitate things, sounds, animals, movements, and recreating and suggesting feelings through musical imagery, were thus used generously by those composers conversant with the theatrical métier operating for centuries, and that continues alive and well today in films and TV. They were also learned and easily identified by city audiences in many places where such clichés were heard and recognized as "always being there." These clichés were added to a musical score to communicate the familiar through music to large groups in many cities, to tell a story that could be recreated in the imagination of many through visual/sound/repetitions.

The opera's famous Aymoré-call motive in act III, "O Dio degli aimoré" (Musical Example 9.3) is a concise sequence of five notes, in duple-meter

Musical Example 9.2. *Il Guarany*, "Senza tetto, senza cuna."
Source: Milan: Ricordi, 1889. IMSLP, Petrucci Music Library, https://vmirror.imslp.org/files/imglnks/usimg/5/56/IMSLP92176-PMLP67581-Gomes_-_Il_Guarany_VS_UNC.pdf

tune, an ascending fourth followed by a downward line with accented notes constructed over A♭ major and F minor alternating chords in parallel motion, sounding through trombones and trumpets in a military and triumphant style. The tune is another familiar operatic and musical cliché of introducing strong

Musical Example 9.3. *Il Guarany*, act III, "O Dio degli aimoré."

Source: Milan: Ricordi, 1889. IMSLP, Petrucci Music Library, https://vmirror.imslp.org/files/imglnks/usimg/5/56/IMSLP92176-PMLP67581-Gomes_-_Il_Guarany_VS_UNC.pdf

male figures through horns' call and to refer to a warrior's courage and military bravery in marching rhythms. This short motive, easy to remember and repeat, appears fragmented throughout the opera at key points of encounters between Europeans and Indigenous; the tune is plain enough to easily "fit in" in various spots, and Gomes strategically uses "O Dio degli aimoré" to frame the beginning and the end of the opera. Displacing one's attention from the central characters and their music, from the lovers Ceci and Peri, to the Aymoré, the warrior/villain, in "O Dio degli aimoré," Gomes adds variety, not novelty, as it unseats the main love storyline through music. Act III's congruence of disparate elements culminates in the *ballabile* as it was expected from the work's grand opera style.

But it is the *ballabile* in act III that has received the most conflicting reviews from both Rio de Janeiro's critics and those in the many cities where the opera circulated: for some, it was the worst part of the work, while for others it was exactly the section that enticed the most.[141] Here, as the musical familiar is used to further the scene's sonic/visual appeal, Gomes shows his skill not only in offering variety, but in handling musical heterogeneity and discontinuity. In the *ballabile* it becomes clear that one cannot disassociate *Il Guarany* from Gomes's previous experience in entertaining mass audiences: like Alencar's *O Guarany*, *Il Guarany* was composed with the audience in mind. Gomes's two successful *rivista musicali* written for the Italian public show his ease in stitching together musical variety to enhance theatrical action and create comic energy. To that end, his *rivistas* are filled with melodic-rhythmic clichés used widely in Rossini's, Auber's, and Offenbach's comic operas, such as the incorporation of choruses interspersing, responding and commenting on characters' dialogues, and use of repetition of short motives and quick single notes, the use of register changes to anticipate and create mystery, and the inclusion of a variety of popular dances that pulled the audiences into the story by appealing to sonic familiarity, audiovisual memory, and sensory responses.[142] Alexandre Bispo has noted the association of Gomes's songs in his *rivista musicali* with the widespread of *canzonas* in Italian popular musical theater, and that the composer was aware of the power of familiar music to entice Milanese audiences. In the song "Il Fuccille ad ago" in *Se sa minga*, Gomes uses music to satirically comment on the new *fuccille* (rifle), easier to reload, that gave Prussians and Italians advantage in the 1866 war

---

[141] For a full transcription of *Il Guarany*'s critic in Italian press, see Gaspare Vetro and Marcello Conati, *Antônio Carlos Gomes–correspondências Italianas* (Rio de Janeiro: Livraria editora Cátedra–Instituto Nacional do Livro, 1982).

[142] Alexandre Bispo, "150 anos: 'Se sa minga:' Rivista di 1866 de Antonio Scalvini (1835–1881) e A. Carlos Gomes (1836–1896), *Rivista* do ano de guerra nacional italiana contra a Áustria pelo Vêneto nos seus elos com a Alemanha," online publication at http://revista.brasil-europa.eu/163/Se_sa_minga.html.

282 MUSIC AND COSMOPOLITANISM

against Austria.[143] Gomes's repetitive melodic-rhythmic motives squarely structured in 4 or 8 measures, use of staccatos, and a march/polka rhythmic accompaniment, a potpourri of theatrically informed clichés through musical gestures, were set smoothly to the subject matter and forecast musical-cinematic effects that resurfaced with great force in the early years of the film industry. No wonder that the work was printed and sold well in Italy during his residency there. Such uses of music to create extra-musical effects were not Gomes's unique creation, of course. Rather, they abound in mid-century ballets, operettas, comic theater, and operas, as well as in purely instrumental musics written by composers of all walks of life.[144] But when one is not looking for the musical exception but rather trying to grasp commonalities that endured time and place, one can say with a degree of certainty that the exploration and expectation of music's programmatic effects, both in the theater and the concert hall, became a most significant staple of music making during the long 19th century, more so than the idealisms associated with formalistic concepts of "absolute music." And in this regard, Gomes's early works triumphed among the many.

Se sa minga's overture, with a typical mélange of tunes heard later in the work, included marches, waltzes, polkas, and popular songs, which the composer ties together economically in quick succession, making them flow from one rhythm to another, and one tune to the next, in a musical conglomerate that not only makes musical sense when together they propel the drama in the theater, but that are also set to be easily disassembled and, in fragments, to be heard, sung, danced, and heard in various performing/listening contexts.[145] *Se sa minga*'s overture provides a most direct link to *Il Guarany*'s *ballabile*, a piece that has often been touted as being out of place in the opera for being disjointed and incoherent. Bruno Kiefer observed the section's kinship with circus music, a comment that was meant to demean the work but which fully grasped the nature of the music. And this was one of the aspects of the work that may have enticed Benjamin to explore it further in his circus pantomime.[146] But Gomes's *ballabile* also shows a composer exploring instrumentation and orchestral texture to the limits, the lower brass alternating with piccolos, homophonic

---

[143] For the piano score and piano performance of "Il Fuccille ad ago," see the site of the Instituto Piano Brasileiro, André Pédico at the piano. https://www.youtube.com/watch?v=zuo-FZ-rnek.

[144] Smith, *Opera and Ballet in the Age of "Giselle,"* and Gutsche-Mille, "Pantomime-Ballet on the Music-Hall Stage," summarize these clichés.

[145] For information on *Se sa minga* see Marcos Virmond, Lucas D' Alessandro Ribeiro, Rosa Maria Tolon, and Lenita Waldige Mendes Nogueira, "*Se sa minga* de Antonio Carlos Gomes: Contextualização histórica," *Mimesis* 35, no. 1 (2014): 25–48, 201. For a recording of the Prelude of act II, listen to https://soundcloud.com/jorge-coli/antonio-carlos-gomes-prelude-act-2-from-se-sa-minga-live-aylton-escobar-2001.

[146] Bruno Kiefer, *História da música brasileira, dos primórdios ao início do séc. XX* (Porto Alegre: Movimento, 1977), 95, cited in Carvalho, D'O Guarani de José de Alencar e Carlos Gomes aos Guaranis do clown Benjamin," 94.

COSMOPOLITAN TRADITIONS   283

textures contrasting with antiphonal instrument groupings, themes presented on trumpets and punctuated by strings, sometimes sharing the melody among soloist instruments, such as clarinets, flutes, and violins, and especially the use of tutti at the end, overpowered by lower brass and full-percussion session. At the same time, with a mass of sound obtained by full use of the large orchestra at his disposal at La Scala, Gomes's orchestration never dares to overpower the melodies, for he follows closely mid-century orchestration treatises, including Berlioz's, and stresses instrument-doubling melodic lines, and opposing timbres to create contrasts and further emphasize the melody.[147]

Gomes's shrewd use of musical clichés to advance dramatic action and to suggest feelings learned in the comic theater endowed *Il Guarany* with its most memorable moments, while the songful and memorable quality of his melodies, made of the usual sequences of 4 or 8 bars that could easily fit various texts, allowed the work to travel freely through the city's many borders. Such a conglomerate of familiar elements within one opera points to Gomes's youthful explorations of musics that worked to propel the story on the stage, but it also shows that the fragmentation within *Il Guarany* made it easy for the work to be disassembled, to pervade many realms of the city's sociocultural fabric, and to ensure the work's long durability. While the idea of unity in musical works has served as a baseline for 20th-century music criticism, the display of an "aesthetic of discontinuity"[148] revealed in works like *Il Guarany* points to a realm of musical expression and interpretation that still needs further attention, specifically their potential for disassemblage at a historical point of music dissemination to a wide audience through a myriad of media.

By the time of the proclamation of the republic, *Il Guarany*'s most memorable excerpts had already been repeated enough inside and outside the opera house to become, alongside tunes from Italian operas and French operettas, a part of the city's local tradition: few could claim to be oblivious to them, as if "they were always there." Since its early running in Rio de Janeiro, *Il Guarany*'s sinfonia (1871)—a compilation of the works' most memorable tunes—was regularly included in concerts celebrating national occasions in the city, usually performed alongside the national anthem and confirming the work's role in asserting the country's position vis-à-vis Europe. That was the case during the monarchy, continued to be so after the regime change, and remained so through the 20th century. The work was chosen, for example, to be performed at the celebrations of the first year of the new republican government, on November 16, 1890, in the pompous concert organized in Rio de Janeiro by Miguez, in the program that

---

[147] For a study of Carlos Gomes's orchestration, see Kerr, "Instrumentação e orquestração em Antônio Carlos Gomes.

[148] Altman, *Silent Film Sound*, 51.

284 MUSIC AND COSMOPOLITANISM

also included Wagner's *Rienzi* overture and Miguez's own symphonic poem *Ave Libertas* (see Chapter 11). It was also included in the concert conducted by Assis Pacheco to celebrate the fourth centenary of the "discovery" of Brazil on January 1, 1900, alongside the national anthems of Brazil and Portugal.[149] To the leaders of the "Musical Republic," *Il Guarany*, a work dedicated to Emperor Pedro II, seemed to fit well among works judiciously chosen to glorify the new regime. Moreover, by the time of Gomes's death in 1896, *Il Guarany* was already a part of the established repertory of operatic companies traveling to Rio de Janeiro and was the opera of choice among foreign directors in need of a work that would serve as a kind of greeting card to local audiences. During the first two decades of the new republican government, *Il Guarany* was performed every season, in various theaters, and, in fact, the work was among the most performed operas in Rio de Janeiro, being fully staged at least 85 times, behind only Verdi's *Aïda* and Pucinni's *Tosca*.[150]

Like with Verdi's operas, excerpts from *Il Guarany* acquired many extra lives, serving the construction of the nation when the sinfonia began to be performed as a secondary national anthem in official celebrations, while also helping shape the cosmopolitan city's heterogeneous social sonic context when it was performed in the music hall, in the streets, and eventually in the movie theater. Excerpts from *Il Guarany* served well, for example, as a musical opening to Artur Azevedo's 1901 musical review, *A capital federal*, fitting nicely within its assorted musical offerings put together by the musical director Nicolino Milano (1876–1962) at the Theatro Recreio Dramático, in a show directed by Pepa Ruiz.[151] In the same year, the opera's sinfonia was also heard in the music hall Polytheama Fluminense, opening a show alongside "many attractions, including zarzuelas,"[152] while Sousa Bastos concurrently offered *Il Guarany*'s sinfonia at the Theatro Apollo, followed by excerpts from comic operas, vaudevilles, comedy skits, and musical reviews. In 1904, the Theatro Recreio Dramatico opened the review *Cá e lá* (Here and There), with text by Tito Martins e Bandeira de Gouvêa, as a "review of national and foreign costumes and news" that also included an homage to the Portuguese writer Eça de Queiroz (1845–1900). With the participation of actresses/singers/dancers Cinira Polonio, Aurélia Delorme, and Pepa Delgado, the review included 50 musical numbers by Chiquinha Gonzaga, João Nunes, Luiz Moreira, and Carlos Gomes, in addition to many "foreign composers."[153]

---

[149] *Gazeta de Notícias*, December 20, 1999.
[150] Ferreira, "Opera in Rio de Janeiro," v.
[151] *O Paiz*, February 15, 1901.
[152] *Gazeta de Notícias*, September 2, 1901.
[153] *Jornal do Brasil*, March 16, 1904.

COSMOPOLITAN TRADITIONS · 285

Among the earliest recordings done in the city by Casa Édson in 1902 included the Banda of the Firefighter Corps conducted by Anacleto de Medeiros, who chose to include the national anthem and *Il Guarany*'s "Protofonia" (Overture). Not surprisingly, when Paschoal Segreto bought the old Theatro Santanna in 1904 and invested in its remodeling and updating, he opened the new venue in January 1905 as Theatro Carlos Gomes, a venue in which plays, operettas, reviews, and a miscellanea of popular entertainment were linked to the name of a composer of operas. The theater remains to this day the only in Rio de Janeiro named after a local composer.[154]

Il Guarany's songful and memorable melodies supported the plot's main narrative, that is, the misadventures and fortunes of love told through historicized cultural/racial encounters, and the "powerful savage" warrior. But in their many extra lives outside the opera hall, these tunes competed on equal grounds with the most popular melodies of the day, helping power the dissemination of music as a cosmopolitan cultural product of Rio de Janeiro's present. The popularity of *Il Guarany*'s melodies, for example, did not fade even when competing with popular tunes of the first decade of the 20th century, including Planquette's "Sinos de Corneville Waltz" (see Chapter 6), Verdi's "Miserere," Puccini's "Vissi d'arte," and the "Merry Widow's Waltz" (see Chapter 8). In fact, over the years *Il Guarany*'s melodies remained among the most notable elements of the opera, perhaps more so than the encounter with the "noble savage," or the tropical mise-en-scène that enticed opera goers. Commenting on the 1996 Plácido Domingo performance of the opera with the Baltimore Symphony, for example, Stephen Wigler claimed,

> The more important things to note about '*Il Guarany*' [are] that its tunes are memorable; that its use of the soprano voice, whether by itself or in duet with those of the tenor, baritone or basso, is absolutely terrific; that its orchestration is intriguing; that its use of the concertato—in which a melody is shared by several voices (whether individual soloists or deployed in groups)—shows a command of vocal texture almost Verdian in its mastery; and that its composer knew how to use music to tell a compelling story.[155]

The musicologist Gerard Béhague also starts his critique with the opera's melodies, stating, "The triumph of *Il Guarany*, which remains [Gomes's] most important work, was due to its effective melodies, its dramatic construction, and not least its libretto."[156] The historian Jorge Coli also points exactly to Gomes's "fecund

---

[154] The announcement of the deal appeared in the *Gazeta de Notícias*, September 25, 1904.

[155] Stephen Wigler, "'Il Guarany' is a dramatic directing debut for Domingo," *Baltimore Sun*, November 12, 1996.

[156] Gerárd Behague, "Carlos Gomes," in *Grove Music online*, https://doi-org.proxy-tu.researchp ort.umd.edu/10.1093/gmo/9781561592630.article.11423.

286 MUSIC AND COSMOPOLITANISM

and spontaneous inspiration and extraordinary talent to invent melodies and combine timbres."[157]

Like the melodies from the most popular operas of the 19th century, the contours of *Il Guarany*'s tunes were not always concise but were formulaic and well-crafted enough to allow for easy remembering and repeating, and thus were essential to support the pervasiveness and durability of the plot's narrative, ultimately standing in for the plot itself solely through the power of music to evoke and suggest, rather than to particularize and represent. And when fragmented into sonic incipits they invited endless actual and virtual collective participation by singing and listening, as well as through recreations in a myriad of instrumental elaborations. Like tunes from Verdi's operas, *Il Guarany*'s melodies were set in, dependent on, and grew within a complex urban cosmopolitan cultural network that gave them meaning. Thus, to view Gomes's opera as an essential part of turn-of-the-century Rio de Janeiro's sonic realm, one needs to start from the premise that, alongside exotic tales and locales, the grand opera style appealing with visuals, choruses, and dances, and the plot's call for the nation's foundational imaginaries, melodies from *Il Guarany* traveled and flourished among many to eventually become a part of the local tradition of the cosmopolitan city's present.

Outside Rio de Janeiro, excerpts from *Il Guarany* flowed easily from Ricordi and Lucca's publishing houses[158] to be figured prominently in early recordings made to fit no more than a few minutes, but which resonated through the voices of the most well-known opera singers of the early 20th century. The famous love duet, "Sento una forza indomita," for example, was recorded by the tenor Francesco Marconi and soprano Bice Mililotti in 1907, by soprano Agnes Hannick and tenor Alberto Amadi in 1913, and by Enrico Caruso and Emmy Destinn in 1914. The soprano Roxy King preferred the Ceci's *balattta* "C'era una volta un principe," which she recorded in 1908, with Agnes Hannick following in 1913, as well as Pasquale Amato's 1909 recording of "Senza tetto, senza cuna," the Gonzalez's "Spanish Song," with orchestra and chorus, and with added castanets, and Mattias Battistini in 1912, among others. The Aymoré warrior call, "O Dio degli aimoré," has served well as a call for patriotic displays outside the opera hall, as in the concert organized by Miguez to celebrate the new republic in

---

[157] Jorge Coli, "Carlos Gomes: A grande travessia," *Revista do Instituto de Estudos Brasileiros* 26 (1986): 107.

[158] Alexandre Bispo, "Verona: Processos de difusão cultural no presente e no passado. Da ópera à música para banda, canto e piano no século XIX. Reduções e transcrições no comércio, na criação e na vida musical. Carlos Gomes (1836–1896) e Nicolò Celega (1844–1906)," *Revista Brasil-Europa: Correspondência Euro-Brasileira* 162, no. 8 (2016), online publication, http://revista.brasil-europa.eu/162/Nicolo_Celega_e_Carlos_Gomes.html. See also Alexandre Bispo, "Brasil e Itália na música para piano do século XIX: Fantasias de óperas e sentimentos identitários: A homenagem a Carlos Gomes (1836–1896) de Paolo Canonica (1846–1902)," *Revista Brasil-Europa: Correspondência Euro-Brasileira* 162, no. 7 (2016), online publication, http://revista.brasil-europa.eu/162/Paolo_Canonica_e_Carlos_Gomes.html.

COSMOPOLITAN TRADITIONS   287

1890 mentioned above. The short five-note motive exemplifies Gomes's skillful use of timbre, melodic, harmonic, and rhythmic simplicity so to be easily absorbed at first hearing and repeated ad libitum by many in several circumstances, mostly in association with community participation, from recordings in the United States by John Philip Sousa's band (1903) and Arthur Pryer's band (1904) to renditions in carnival marches, with large groups parading through Rio de Janeiro's streets: the short tune became *Il Guarany*, and through the tune *O Guarany* became the nation.

The opera's famous melodies, which João Itiberê da Cunha refers to as "leitmotifs,"[159] were also a significant part of Rio de Janeiro's emergent recording industry, as Figner and his Casa Edison bet on local talents to increase profits. And here, *Il Guarany*'s most enduring tunes were further fragmented to tell many more stories. As early as 1904, two of the opera's most well-known tunes appeared side by side as "A canção do Indio" (The Indian song) in a recording by the singer Mário Pinheiro (1883–1923). A baritone who sang with guitar accompaniment in the city's various entertainment venues, Pinheiro's career as a recording artist took him to the United States to work for Columbia and Victor, and to Milan, where he was sent by Victor to perfect his singing and where he ventured into the world of opera.[160] Pinheiro's many recordings reflect both his personal experiences and the musical context of his time, when artists needed to excel in various styles and build careers around musics that could entice large audiences, and when operatic music mingled easily with non-operatic works. One of Pinheiro's earlier recordings, "A canção do Indio," shows this versatility in terms of his performing choices, as well as the flexibility that musical arrangements of *Il Guarany* entailed. The piano introduction is a fragment of the Aymoré-call, "O Dio degli aimoré." However, after the piano introduction, "A canção do Indio" does not continue with one of the melodies from act III, but with the melody that brought fame to Ceci's love story, an excerpt from the final love duet of act I, Ceci's "Qualunque via dischiuderti." The stepwise melodic line covering an interval of a fifth, easily singable and memorable, repeated in a modified melodic sequence, is another staple of Gomes's musical economy. The tune is self-contained and suitable for Pinheiro's baritone voice, while fitting well with the new Portuguese lyrics provided by Catulo da Paixão Cearense (1863–1946).[161] When João Barros (ca. 1888–??) recorded the same song in 1907, he abbreviated the introduction to just

---

[159] João Itiberê da Cunha, "Il Guarany (1870): Algumas palavras sobre a ópera," in *Carlos Gomes: Uma obra em foco* (Rio de Janeiro: FUNART, 1987), 137.

[160] "Mário Pinheiro," *Dicionário Cravo Albin da Música Popular Brasileira*, online publication, available at https://dicionariompb.com.br/artista/mario-pinheiro/

[161] For more on Cearense, see Uliana Dias Campos Ferlim, "Catulo da Paixão Cearense e os embates cancioneiros na virada do século XIX ao XX no Rio de Janeiro," *Revista Brasileira da Música* 24, no. 1 (January–June 2011): 171–192.

288   MUSIC AND COSMOPOLITANISM

a few chords, a short fragment to recall the "*índio*," but his rendition of "canção do Indio" focuses solely on Ceci's melody, the opera's only female character, now also standing for the "*índio*." Later in 1910, Mário Pinheiro recorded the song again and, like Barros, he chose to skip the introduction, accompanying himself on the guitar instead, to sing just Ceci's tune.[162]

By the beginning of the second decade of the 20th century, "A canção do Indio" no longer had sonic remembrances from the Indigenous warrior's call, the sound of "*índio*" was all but implicit, only to reappear regularly as a substitute for the national anthem in contexts of official nature to convene national pride. But in "A canção do Indio," Ceci's tune stood for the whole opera, ultimately fulfilling a gendered sonic display of the nation as a parallel musical account of national belonging. Not coincidentally, Cearense's Portuguese lyrics to Ceci's "Qualunque via dischiuderti" had clear-cut nationalistic overtones. The verses are reminiscent of Gonçalves Dias's (1823–1864) romantic poem "Canção do Exilio" (1843), with references to nature and birds of the Brazilian northeastern region standing for the whole country, to suggestions of the missing of "the land where I was born" and the "margins of the Paraiba River," and "the brave companions of Peri's tribe." To Cearense, the land of the Indigenous is "my land," in another romantic nationalist twist that came to characterize several popular songs during the period. Here, Ceci's "Qualunque via dischiuderti" is no longer the tune of her love for Peri in an Italianate opera, but for the love of lost countryside that disappeared in the modern city, one that nonetheless was dependent on the cosmopolitan city to emerge. These two tunes from a four-act opera, traveling through the disconnected sociohistorical contexts of the city, now re-emerge as two separate versions of the nation, while the foundation myth that started with Alencar five decades earlier was now linked to the opera's music, more so than with the novel.[163]

In 1903, Benjamin de Oliveira bet on both the story and the music to still fully resonate among a young crowd now historically removed both from Alencar's incipient marketing techniques and from opera halls' selective audiences. Understanding both *O Guarany* and *Il Guarany* as a unified entity that was part of the written, visual, oral, and aural traditions of the modern city, Oliveira opened his pantomime *Os Guaranis* at the circus, expecting Alencar's story and Gomes's musical variety to easily fit within the circus's program.[164] On July 24, 1903, when

---

[162] See Martha Ulhôa, *A música popular gravada—modinhas e lundus, 4*; recordings of Gomes's "Canção do Indio," https://discografiabrasileira.com.br/en/artist/3973/joao-barros for João Barros, and https://www.discografiabrasileira.com.br/fonograma/rel_content_id/820/p/71 for Mário Pinheiro.

[163] Carvalho, "D'O Guarani," 78–104; see also Crepaldi Carvalho, "O cinema silencioso e o som no Brasil (1894–1920)," 85–97.

[164] Silva, *Circo-Teatro*, 210–211.

COSMOPOLITAN TRADITIONS   289

the Circo Spinelli was touring in the city of Niteroi (a city in the state of Rio de Janeiro), a newspaper advertised that, on regular nights "when we do not offer the pantomime *A feira em Seville* (The market in Seville), with two or more bulls, we present *Os Guaranis*, extracted from the novel by José de Alencar."[165] Here, the Spanish, the Italian, and the Brazilian elements lose their referents to locality and overlap as equal attractions to the city audience. In March 1904, Oliveira presented *Os Guaranis* in the circus in the neighborhood of Cascadura in Rio de Janeiro, then continued to offer the work at the Spinelli circus's final setting in the São Cristóvão neighborhood.

The pantomime had spoken sections, with a script written in Portuguese especially for the Spinelli company by Manoel Braga, the second such Portuguese text paraphrasing the novel. Offered as a "pantomime of indigenous customs,"[166] Benjamin took the role of Peri, while Ceci was performed by Ignez Cruzette, an Argentinian circus juggler, actress, and singer, who added Spanish to the Portuguese spoken sections of the work. *Os Guaranis*, presented with a cast of 70 artists, was also advertised as including "22 musical numbers extracted from the beautiful score of *O Guarany* . . . [and] ending with an apotheosis 'A fuga de Ceci e Peri' (The scape of Ceci and Peri)."[167] Gomes's music was arranged for the circus band by composer and trombonist Irineu de Almeida (1863–1914), a very active performer in instrumental groups and well-known in the city's bars and cafés. While Portuguese and Spanish were used in spoken dialogues, it is not clear if the actors would sing in Italian, or if the musical numbers were also set to Portuguese lyrics, but the announcement says that "the artists will sing in Portuguese and Spanish."[168] If that's the case, then this would be an instance of *Il Guarany*'s music being sung in Portuguese well before the "official" Portuguese libretto was published in 1938.

But the move from the pantomime to the film involved something more. Although announced as a *film d'art*, presented with the accompaniment of an "enlarged orchestra," the film *Os Guaranis* lasted only approximately 9–12 minutes; thus the 22 numbers of music selected to be performed in the pantomime needed to be reduced to three or four in the film. Although we do not know which excerpts Oliveira chose to be included in the film, pictures made for advertisement of the film show the scene with Peri and Ceci and one with Benjamin as Peri alone, thus one can infer that the famous duet in act I was included (Figure 9.4). We can also guess that the Spanish song "Senza, senza cuna"

---

[165] *Gazeta de Notícias*, July 24, 1903. *Os Guaranys* continued in the repertory of the circus, presented again in August 26, 1904 (*Paiz*, August 26, 1904); and in January 3, 1905, in Petrópolis (*Gazeta de Notícias*, January 3, 1905).

[166] *O Paiz*, March 5, 1907; *Gazeta de Notícias*, June 12, 1907.

[167] *Gazeta de Notícias*, September 10, 1907; also in *O Paiz*, March 5, 1907.

[168] Carvalho, "D'O Guarani," 17.

Figure 9.4. Benjamin de Oliveira and Cruzet as Peri and Ceci.
A noite: Supplemento Literário, 28 de Junho, 1938.
Source: Biblioteca Nacional do Rio de Janeiro, Hemeroteca Digital

was also included, since in 1908, William Auler also produced the short *filme cantante* titled "A canção do aventureiro."[169] Whatever the musical choices for the film, these shows serve as examples of the ease with which *Il Guarany* was disassembled into a myriad of scattered parts suitable for a variety of venues, media, and occasions that eventually turned the opera into one of the most well-known musical works in Rio de Janeiro, a dynamic process that involved many actors nearby and faraway, historically and geographically, time and space shaping the work's association with the cosmopolitan imagination.

But in *Os Guaranis* Oliveira adds his own perspective to the already complex nature of the nation's foundational myths through the impersonating of the Indigenous character, for which he chose not to paint his face for the role as he did for *The Merry Widow*. Instead, he decided to act and sing the *"índio"*

---

[169] In a 1911 film production of *Il Guarany*, the advertisement explicitly noted, "The company of S. Lazzaro produced a film from Il Guarany, Carlos Gomes's most popular opera... the score needed to have a few cuts, only those necessary to organize the film, which could not have the same duration of the opera. The artists who sing behind the white screen, did not sacrifice Gomes's music, and the audience showed their liking with enthusiastic applause. The company is now working on the production of Cavalleria and other operas"; see Freire, *Rio de Janeiro, cidade da ópera*, 97.

character as a Black man in love with a White woman as Ceci, complicating easy associations of nation with the mythical Indigenous, while asserting the possibility of *mestiçagem*. In Oliveira's *Os Guaranys*, the myth of national foundation including a Black individual co-opted the official historiography in alternative ways and highlighting not the homogeneous nation, but the complex socioethnical culture of the modern city.[170] Yet, by the time Benjamin appeared on stage as an Indigenous character, his perspective should not have been taken as an oddity, since for several decades during Rio de Janeiro carnival, groups of Blacks and mulattos had already fully appropriated the "Indigenous" character, as they paraded through the city's streets, in the *cordões*, dressed in "costumes" as noble savages, as well as in noble Venetian garbs and blond wigs. Here the foundational myth of the nation was both asserted and questioned as it was presented in a myriad of alternative versions. As Maria Clementina Cunha has pointedly observed, these stagings reveal worlds of traditions presented together as if without time and space, as they constantly revolved around a variety of social and racial contexts to tell stories of physical suffering and cultural renewal.[171] And while the stylized "Indigenous" was taken by the new Republic as a myth of national foundation through the sound of Gomes's "O Dio degli aimoré," those in the city who were not recognized as integral parts of such a Republic also engaged with the myth, claiming their part in the nation's history as noble Europeans, as well as "*índios*"; it was a performance recalling "those who are no more and yet are living forever,"[172] a performance that paralleled and counteracted the story of *Il Guarany*. Cunha points to those parading in the *cordões* as having a "globalizing identity," one that reveals more refined and complex subjectivities than usual excluding denominations as "the popular" or that of a "Black Brazil." Rather, it is a performance of the history of "individuals who lived in the same place and time."[173] Joseph Roach has explored such concatenation of histories in New Orleans where, like in Rio de Janeiro, during carnival African Americans also parade as Native Americans, keeping alive through performance the complex intersection of histories that have more than local relevance: they are, as Roach points out, global performances of incomplete forgetting.[174]

The contradiction between narratives about the building of music canons during the early days of the Republic excluding Gomes's music on the one hand, and the pervasiveness of *Il Guarany*'s music in the city on the other, lies in the assumption that opera's aesthetic and social relevance rested solely within the

---

[170] Capaldi Carvalho, "D'O Guarani," 85.

[171] Cunha, *Ecos da folia*, 300.

[172] Joseph Roach, *Cities of the Death: Circum-Atlantic Performance* (New York: Columbia University Press, 1996), 189.

[173] Cunha, *Ecos da folia*, 300.

[174] Roach, *Cities of the Death*, 7; see also the chapter "One Blood," 179–237.

292 MUSIC AND COSMOPOLITANISM

realm of opera houses. Writing about "Brazilian culture" in 1982, Enio Squeff and José Miguel Wisnik claimed categorically that "[i]n Brazil, as in other countries, the operatic genre does not identify with the world where it is cultivated."[175] And yet *Il Guarany* flowed intensely and freely throughout diverse sections of the city, resulting in a local phenomenon that one could call "Guaranism," the multiplication of many "Guaranis," in a complex cultural and musical context captured in the title of Benjamin's pantomime. The story and the enactment of Guaranisms dislocate the historiography of the opera *Il Guarany*, focusing on its appropriateness, or lack thereof, as a source for nation-building and, as such, as the reason for its retention or denial in the local canon. Instead, Guaranisms point to alternative ways of telling the opera's story, resting on the perspective of audiences in interconnected cosmopolitan cities, on the successful marriage of the visual with the musical, on the role of melodies to traverse the porous city, and on the participation of large sectors of the city's population in building myths of national foundation.

These stories also invite us to explore the making and sustaining of music canons through those who produced the works alongside those who engaged with them nearby and faraway, rather than solely as a result of commercial enterprises, consumer fetishisms, music critics, or governmental policies. Moretti argues that, in the case of the 19th-century novel, readers and subsequently markets made canons, not academics, and that the latter rely sooner or later on the former.[176] The same can be assumed to be the case with the novel *O Guarany* which, published in serialized, journalistic fashion to create expectations and gather wider interest, eventually circulated through a wide readership in Europe and the Americas. But the process is more multilayered and complex in the case of music, and even more so in the case of *Il Guarany*. Unlike the novel, which requires a level of literacy to circulate in its frozen state on the written page, only then to move into the realm of the oral transmission as it was recreated in the imagination of individual readers, music's ephemeral and aural nature relies less on formal education and fixed images rendered by a few, and more on communal participation by way of performances and listening, allowing for fluid and flowing imaginaries of belonging. Together with composers and critics, those engaging with the works as arrangers, performers, and listeners were also canon-makers of *Il Guarany*, and no less than businesspeople in charge of printing and recording music, or *realejos* prompting the involuntary listening and remembering of the opera's most memorable tunes until they became eternal in the city. When looked at from the perspective of one work, these

---

[175] Enio Squeff and José Miguel Wisnik, *O nacional e o popular na cultural brasileira* (São Paulo: Editora Brasiliense, 1983 [1982]), 25.

[176] Moretti, *Distant Reading*, 76.

COSMOPOLITAN TRADITIONS 293

multilayered processes make tangible the complex, communal, and fluid sonic and aural realms that entail the making of music traditions in the city. They also show that canon-making is not the exclusive domain of a few, and that canons are not always set in abstract value-laden analysis or concrete sales numbers, but rather are solidified within the realm of the practical, experiential, and collective aesthetic engagements with the music by a large spectrum of the city's audiences. Most importantly, the multilayered paths which *Il Guarany* traveled within Rio de Janeiro to eventually become part of the local tradition are not different from the paths traveled by Verdi's operas and many other works not tied to a local, or "national," story. But the focus on "Guaranisms" eventually shows that official accounts of the relevance, or lack thereof, of *Il Guarany* to the city and the nation coexisted with many alternative proposals that are too often left unaccounted for. Jorge Coli noted that "one of the enthralling aspects of [these coexistences] lie exactly in the strangeness that is the product of complicated cultural relationships and the fascinating richness of its ramifications."[177]

Benjamin's alternative rendition of the myth of the nation's foundation, then, puts into a clear view the ways in which Gomes's opera, fragmented multiple times and recreated multiple times, came to belong to many, to the point of being invoked as one of the nation's all-encompassing symbols: as a substitute for the national anthem. Therefore, what many self-proclaimed modernist critics of the 1920s wanted to dismiss in *Il Guarany*, and to "leave outside history," was not merely the outdatedness and foreignness in Gomes's operatic language, but the multiple everyday local *Guaranis* that contradicted such assertions. In an article about the need to reform the National Institute of Music written in 1907, two years before the film *Os Guaranis* came out, a journalist concerned with the level of musical education in the city noted: "Just imagine Benjamin de Oliveira or Eduardo das Neves singing in *Aída*, even in translation [to Portuguese], and you will have an approximate idea of the impression artists with imperfect diction and tottering gesticulation would create in such a serious work."[178] The critic was probably one of the few who needed to imagine such a situation, for Oliveira and Neves had been doing just that for several years with wide public acclaim, while *Aída* was also sung in the streets during carnival.

Yet Gomes's place in the local music canon continues unresolved, even if his career and the nature of his music have recently received a more judicious scholarly scrutiny.[179] Understood as "a man of his time" writing opera in innovative

---

[177] Coli, "Carlos Gomes," 112.

[178] *A Noticia*, September 10, 1907; cited in Shaw, *Tropical Travels*, 65.

[179] Lenita Nogueira has summarized the main publications on the composer in "Carlos Gomes e a musicologia no Brasil: Novas perspectivas," in *Actas do VI Simpósio Internacional de Musicologia*, Goiânia, GO (2016): 100–111. For a study tracing intellectuals' view on Carlos Gomes, see Lutero Rodrigues, *Carlos Gomes*.

294 MUSIC AND COSMOPOLITANISM

ways, historical studies also evoke his music as an antecedent to the modernist *antropofagista* movement due to the heterogeneous musical languages and effects that the composer managed to mingle in his opera.[180] This aspect of the work has proved useful to propel its travels, not because the composer was an adept of the modernist movement at an early date. Rather, when Gomes wrote *Il Guarany* he was a young composer looking for ways to capture the attention of the Milanese audiences in the prominent language of opera, one that was also an intrinsic part of Rio de Janeiro's tradition.

---

[180] Sebastián Figueroa, "Carlos Gomes: opera, nación y antropofagia," in *Imaginarios nacionales: Viajes, territorios e identidades*, ed. Ana Traverso and Andrea Kottow (Valdivia-Santiago, Austral University, Chile: RIL edition, 2016), 108.

10

Sounds of Urban Worlds

Composing and Performing Places

Aurélio Cavalcanti (1874–1915) was a pianist, composer, and a prominent figure in Rio de Janeiro nightlife in the first decade of the 20th century (Figure 10.1). He performed at café-concerts and in music halls, movie theaters, dance halls, the private salons of middle-class families, the beer houses in the city's entertainment area near the Praça Tiradentes, and many other venues along the new Avenue Rio Branco. Local chroniclers describe Cavalcanti with an enthusiasm usually reserved today for pop stars; he was a "showman," self-confident of his virtuoso abilities, and was known for showing off by playing with his back to the piano. He was also a savvy businessman who used up-to-date commercial practices to distribute his music and schedule his performances, and his successful career as a composer of instrumental music distinguished him from many during his time.[1] Cognizant of the musical spaces of the city, João do Rio observed that while ladies in the Laranjeiras neighborhood preferred to dance waltzes by the Strausses and by (Rodolphe) Berger (1864–1916), those in the balls of the middle-class neighborhood of Catumbi only knew Cavalcanti's "new" music.[2] Cavalcanti wrote mostly for piano solo while, like Berger, he also followed the connections with the musical theater. Already in 1900, Cavalcanti's works appeared in the catalog of the Vieira Machado publishers, and they continued to be issued well into the second decade of the century. In 1903 alone, for example, Cavalcanti published the waltz "La bohemia," with tunes from Puccini's *La bohème*, in addition to the polka "Frenética" and the schottische "Zinha."[3] On March 17, 1905, one of his waltzes was performed at the Theatro São Pedro alongside a potpourri of excerpts from operas and operettas, suggesting that they were proper for listening,[4] and by 1908 his renown was such that he was hired as director and conductor of the orchestra of the Cinematographo Parisiense, one of the city's most coveted movie theaters.

Inside the movie theater, Cavalcanti provided music for several silent "moving scenes," ranging from "dramatic scenes of incomparable beauty from the frontiers

---

[1] For biographical information on Cavalcanti, see Robervaldo Rosa, *Como é bom poder tocar um instrumento: Pianeiros na cena urbana brasileira* (Goiânia, Brazil: Cânone Editorial, 2014), 108–118.

[2] João do Rio, *A alma encantadora das ruas*, 12.

[3] *Jornal do Commercio*, January 25, 1903.

[4] *Jornal do Commercio*, March 17, 1905.

Music and Cosmopolitanism. Cristina Magaldi, Oxford University Press. © Oxford University Press 2024.
DOI: 10.1093/oso/9780199744770.003.0011

Figure 10.1. Aurélio Cavalcanti.

of Italy and France" to the film *Gli ultimi giorni di Pompeii* (1908) (The last days of Pompeii), produced in Turin and directed by Arturo Ambrosio and Luigi Maggi, a film that circulated widely within and beyond Italy.[5] Like many composers and pianists during his time, Cavalcanti's job was to "accompany the scenes" by providing the proper sonic ambience that would aid the audience attending silent films to fully enter the many landscapes, places, objects, and situations that appeared as visual magic before their eyes. In *Gli ultimi giorni di Pompeii*, Cavalcanti's performances were supposed to enhance a state-of-the-art cinematic epic of the ancient world with elaborate scenarios, visual effects, and crowd scenes, including an unprecedented number of extras on the set. Although we do not know which music Cavalcanti chose to sonically enrich the Italian superproduction that recalls the tradition of grand opera, it would be safe to assume that one of his many lyrical waltzes could accompany the love story of Glaucus and Jone at the time of the destruction of Pompeii. And considering that the

---

[5] *Jornal do Commercio*, March 7, 1909. *Gli ultimi giorni di Pompeii* was a film by Ambrosio Films production in Turin, directed by Arturo Ambrosio and Luigi Maggi; see Gian Piero Brunetta, *The History of Italian Cinema: A Guide to Italian Film from Its Origins to the Twenty-First Century* (Princeton, NJ: Princeton University Press, 2009).

musical resources available to the composer were immense, Cavalcanti surely would not have problems finding popular love arias to add sound accompaniment to the film, as well as other musics that would appropriately add sounds to the epic story. But the same night that Cavalcanti worked with *Gli ultimi giorni di Pompeii*, he also provided music to a comic scene, a film titled "Politics," which was advertised as a success because of "its originality and actuality [with many] moments of laughter for the audience."[6] Whether using his own compositions or other well-known and appropriate works, Cavalcanti used music to facilitate the move from one geographical scene to the next, from a story about the past to one about the present, from a comic scene to an action scene, or to a love story, filling silent images with visual/musical connections of his own choosing, while adding extra effects through his individual choices as a performer at the piano and as a conductor of the theater's ensemble. Before the widespread publication of scores with compilations of works specifically aimed at aiding performers in early movie theaters, which included suggestions on how and where to play specific musics in the silent film, these visual/musical connections were part of an unwritten routine for performers who created the associations themselves. It was an artistic skill that required simultaneous expertise in viewing, composing, performing, acting, and improvising, all of which were also dependent on the audience's previous knowledge and easy recognition of a vast array of sonic and visual connections.

As a skilled musician, Cavalcanti was particularly attuned to the many ways in which music and sounds could enhance the visual, a skill that he honed from experiences with music halls and pantomimes, from operatic music, and from improvising in performances. But Cavalcanti did not offer a story through music as operetta and opera composers did, for the latter created the dramatic aspects of a story together with and through the use of music, even if they relied on previously accepted musical clichés or well-known stories. Cavalcanti's work was to disassemble such works and their ready-made, music/story links and offer new connections that enhanced his audiences' visual imagination through the sonic. By doing so, Cavalcanti offered individualized ways of telling stories through music and performance, exploring multilevel relationships, old and new. He connected both original and pre-composed musics to imaginary people and places both nearby and faraway, presented in short silent movies, furthering the sound/image intermedial experiences that characterized his time. Musicians like Cavalcanti were crucial to the process of expanding the possibilities of music cognition during a period of intense visual stimulation, allowing the abstract, fleeing nature of sound and music to turn into concrete living experiences.

Like Strauss and Berger, Cavalcanti was particularly well-known for his instrumental dances, mostly waltzes and polkas, an output estimated to have

---

[6] *Jornal do Commercio*, March 7, 1909.

298   MUSIC AND COSMOPOLITANISM

reached over 300 pieces and which followed dance structures and rhythmic/melodic freshness familiar to the city's growing audiences. Cavalcanti's "Bregeira, polka francesa" (French polka) (1900), for example, is written in the expected dance format of three self-contained sections that repeat, AABBAACCAA, and melodies constructed with regular pairs of 8-bar melodic phrases. Following the familiar structure, descending melodic lines followed by sudden leaps of up to an octave (G to G), "Bregeira" had the unmistakable melodic gist of operatic tunes devised for trained voices, but their endings on the accented note also demonstrate the composer's use of the yodeling motives used in Strauss's and Waldelfeul's dances, in which the confluence of melodic lines and rhythmic movement, enhanced through performance and bodily engagements, helped define the musical 19th century.[7] Cavalcanti's "Bregeira" thus makes use of the characteristic polka melodic rhythm, a combination of quarter, eighth, and two sixteenth notes, to oppose the steady um-pah, march-like rhythmic figure in the bass, and which allowed for the adding of the lively "swing" realized in performance both by performers and dancers. His "Bregeira" also reveals an awareness of predictable harmonic movements with frequently added sixth and ninth and non-tonal notes that made composers of dance music successful, and which had become a cliché for writing dance music during Cavalcanti's time: the added sixth note in the melody in the second measure creates melodic interest to the expected move from B♭ to E♭ and F (Musical Example 10.1). In sum, "Bregeira" shows Cavalcanti as a composer of polka at his best, fulfilling perfectly the expectations of dancers and listeners. But Cavalcanti called his "Bregeira" a "French" polka, a title that also shows his awareness and intentional use of distinctions of tempo in polka performances favored in specific cities. "French" here most probably meant that his "Bregeira" should be performed in a slower tempo than was customary in a Viennese ballroom.

Referred to by some of his contemporaries as the "king of the waltz," Cavalcanti penned hundreds of them, some of which reveal a breadth of melodic/rhythm invention hard to find in the works of the most well-known composers of his day. His waltz "Buenos dias, valsa espanhola" (Spanish waltz), offers another facet of the composer's ability to write music suggestive of places. Like in many contemporary cities, Cavalcanti's audiences in Rio de Janeiro were enthralled by musical clichés of Spanish-ness to evoke a European internal Other,[8] conveniently also explored as Rio de Janeiro's local Other: Pepa Ruiz danced to it, Carlos Gomes recreated it in his *Il Guarany* (see Chapters 6 and 9). "Buenos dias" was but one of several of Cavalcanti's *valsas espanholas* and serves as a conspicuous example of musical exoticism recycled as part of the cosmopolitan urban

---

[7] Scott, *Sounds of the Metropolis*, 3–12.
[8] Derek Scott, "Orientalism and Musical Style," *Musical Quarterly* 88, no. 2 (1998): 309–335.

Musical Example 10.1. Aurélio Cavalcanti, *Brejeira*, Polka Francesa (1900).
Jornal das Modas (Rio de Janeiro: A. Lavignasse Fillho & Cia.).
Source: Biblioteca Nacional, Rio de Janeiro, Acervo Digital

Musical Example 10.1. Continued

network. The waltz includes all the required elements marking the music's difference from his "French" polka "Bregeira": the rhythmic displacements of the melody accentuating the second beat in the first section, the use of the triplets and suggestions of Phrygian mode in the melody in the third section, while at the same time with a harmonic progression that helps reiterate the dance's prototypical structure.[9] However, Cavalcanti's use of the syntax of Spanish-ness à la Chaminade, Waldeuteufel, and many contemporary composers of opera, concert hall, and music hall, shows him exploring such musical gestures as fashionable sonic trends, rather than as a conscious way of "Othering." Cavalcanti's "Valsa espanhola" is also an evocation of place with its suggestive title, a gimmick used by composers and publishers to sell music, but which was also the result of the composer's conscious use of musical gestures of Spanish-ness that depended on his and his audiences' familiarity with ready-made models. Similarly, his "Valsa sertaneja" (from *sertão*, the countryside in the Brazilian northeast), in which he suggests a regional style through melodic/rhythmic concoctions, can be interpreted in the same way as his polka "Bregeira" and his waltz "Buenos dias," as explorations of a cosmopolitan culture passed to him through ready-made imaginaries of places and peoples; in the case of the *sertaneja*, the place was located within Brazil. As a composer and performer, Cavalcanti was able to offer his audiences an imagined sonic world as broad as possible, and that wide palette included nearby regionalisms made for the city.

Away from the movie theater, Cavalcanti's piano works were made to evoke places and to create an experience through music "without the distraction of the visual." Musicians like Cavalcanti wrote instrumental works with suggestive titles to provide an experience of imaginary places, objects, or a person. These were musicians riding the period's "descriptive wave," Rick Altman observed, a process that involved both the composer's musical evocations and the listener's imagination.[10] A large number of late 19th-century dances and songs were linked to specific localities, people, or things, if not by musical codes, then solely by suggestive titles such as "Polka Madrid," "La Parisienne," "The Yankee," or "Valsa sertaneja."[11] "Places," near and far, used in these titles were surely marketing tools to widen the interest of a cosmopolitan buying public and functioned as a kind of "fancy dress" that brought more interest to the works by suggesting geographical locations, state of mind, and individuals' physical characteristics, mostly women in the eyes and ears of male performers/composers. Often, when musical clichés were added, they rested on music-place-object-feeling relations learned through social interaction and theatrical performances. Nonetheless,

---

[9] For melodic-rhythmic structures of the 19th-century waltzes, see Eric McKee, *Decorum of the Minuet, Delirium of the Waltz: A Study of Dance-Music Relations in 3/4 Time Waltzing* (Bloomington: Indiana University Press, 2012), 90–128.

[10] Altman, *Silent Film Sound*, 50. See also Rick Altman, "The Living Nickelodeon," in *The Sounds of Early Cinema*, ed. Richard Abel and Rick Altman (Bloomington: Indiana University Press, 2001), 232–240.

[11] For Lydia Goehr's discussion of G. E. Lessing's and later Theodor Adorno's views on easy and uncritical associations between title and content, see her "From Opera to Music Drama: Nominal Loss, Titular Gain," in *Richard Wagner and His World*, ed. Thomas Grey, 65–86 (Princeton, NJ: Princeton University Press, 2009); see particularly pages 83–84.

they were not necessarily tied to a specific musical style or local musical element of the geographical place described in the title. They were also not merely essentialized displays of learned musical codes of Otherness; an "African polka," written within or outside an African locale, did not necessarily include anything deemed "African" in the eyes and ears of composers or audiences, in Africa or elsewhere. Altman has argued that sometimes a song was chosen to fit a specific spot in a silent movie "not because of musical characteristics, but because its title provides an ironic or comic match to the events it accompanies."[12] Thus, title words themselves could create the match as a verbal cue to later musical/image association. But for these works to "fit" they needed to fulfill an expectation of a common, shared style and musical praxis; they needed first to follow a common language recognized as part of a cosmopolitan continuum—they needed to be easily recognizable as waltzes and polkas, for example—and only then could they work as musical markers of geographical origins or exoticism. Thus a "French" polka needed first to be a polka. Cavalcanti's skill in writing dances highlights his position as a creative contributor in an urban musical sonic network of musical imaginations that intertwined image and music, as well as words.

When Saint-Saëns wrote original music for the film *Assassinat du duc de Guise* in 1906, a French critic suggested that such music was an aesthetic break from previous works, for it was "programmatic music, that is, music whose character is purely instrumental and has as its origin a clearly defined literary tone as artistic themes." It was not merely accompaniment music for film, but programmatic music that "not only moves us through sounds, but also awakens other feelings in us, through the spontaneous conjuring-up of images, of scenes involving well-defined mood and actions." The music is "capable of creating images in the spectator's mind," the reviewer continues, it is a "musical composition [that is] not necessarily abstract . . . [but] the listener attentive enough, even without musical knowledge, eventually discovers the scenes it contains."[13] This virtual image/musical synesthesia, which the reviewer believed Saint-Saëns achieved quite well, was a skill that many composers perfected throughout the long 19th century and that had been put to use in music in the theater, pantomimes, and ballets, and also in purely instrumental pieces, from Liszt and Berlioz to Verdi, Wagner, Saint-Saëns, and Puccini, and many others in between. Instrumental dances with specific titles and musical gestures re-created such images in the listener's mind, who could in turn express them through listening and/or dancing, using their bodies to further engage with the sound of places.

[12] Altman, *Silent Film Sound*, 221.
[13] *Ciné-Journal*, December 3, 1908; cited in François Jost, "The Voices of Silence," in *The Sounds of Early Cinema*, ed. Richard Abel and Rick Altman (Bloomington: Indiana University Press, 2001), 48–56.

What Cavalcanti provided was the instrumental equivalent to the *flâneuristic* songs that made Eduardo das Neves's work so relevant to the city, or to the written chronicles provided by João do Rio. And like Neves and João do Rio, Cavalcanti's musical *flâneurisms* were not solely about Rio de Janeiro. His pieces sounded in the Brazilian capital but were about many places, both within and beyond the city's borders. Cavalcanti's sonic *flâneurism* enlivened the soundscape of Rio de Janeiro's nightlife and the many worlds that it embraced: they were both collective and individualized musical resonances of the turn-of-the-century city. Most importantly, his musical *flâneurisms*, his music/image connections, were not mere "sounding souvenirs," a practice quite common among 19th-century composers, usually compared to traveling postcards, and which Alexander Rehding describes as "materialities of tourism, anthropological cultural reveries, and sonic remembrances recreating something one has experienced in the past, a sounding miniature that stayed as a representative of the whole . . . written by a composer as a remembrance of a place visited or a specific person one misses or admires."[14] Rather, Cavalcanti's compositions were the sonic equivalent to the images displayed in travel brochures with images and texts that help people anticipate and decide where they would like to go: suggestions for the imagination to create desire. Cavalcanti's pieces evoke and forge a place that one has not yet been to or a person one may not know. They were made to suggest travels and encountering people while staying put. He created ready-made sonic travels, musical experiences as imagination of places, even if he had never traveled to those places himself or met the people his music was supposed to portray. Cavalcanti's music reflected the world's soundscape that he encountered in cosmopolitan Rio de Janeiro.

One can say that the success of Cavalcanti's work as a composer of polkas and waltzes lies in his ability to cater to the needs of the city's audiences to locate themselves in a generic and somewhat abstract growing city at the turn of the 20th century. It may also be postulated that engaging with his works allowed for a wide spectrum of the worldly feel, as they encapsulated a myriad of places rendered through the composer's imagination to audiences who also had never left Rio de Janeiro and for whom those experiences were easily malleable. These musical portraits of places are a mix of the imaginary and the actual sound. The composer is the one creating the imaginary, but his imagination is not all his; it is a complex concatenation of sonic imaginaries circulating as a form of sonic cultural tourism.[15] In Cavalcanti's touristic music, people do not travel to places;

---

[14] Alexander Rehding, *Music and Monumentality* (London and New York: Oxford University Press, 2009), 93–94.

[15] See John Urry and Jonas Larsen, *The Tourist Gaze 3.0* (London: Sage, 2011 [1990]); see also Tim Edensor, "The More-Than-Visual Experiences of Tourism," *Tourism Geographies* 20, no. 5 (2018): 913–991.

304 MUSIC AND COSMOPOLITANISM

rather, places come to the people who hear them, a place that is first heard then imagined, but not actually traveled. Cavalcanti's pieces are sounding metaphors of places and peoples rendered through the expressive, discursive but fleeting logics of musical experiences.

Geographically far from the centers of music production and from the geographical references posed in his works, Cavalcanti was a cosmopolitan without constraints who created a multitude of sounding imaginary places not confined to a static setting, but which nonetheless depended on the city's experience. He was one among several artists at the turn of the century whose "fictional constructs" cannot be understood outside "a wider context of urban cultural politics."[16] Marcy Schwartz points to Pedro Balmaceda Toro, a chronicler who covered current Parisian salons, personalities, fashions, cafés, and receptions for the Chilean daily *La epoca* late in the 19th century, but who had never been to Paris. His column was a way of inhabiting "Paris as both a poetic and politicized space for the cultural imaginary."[17] They become "poetic geographies," to use Michael Certeau's term, liberated spaces that can be occupied.[18] The Nicaraguan writer, poet, novelist, and critic Rubén Dario (1867–1916) also saw some travel writings as belonging to the realm of poetry, not of journalism, and so should be Cavalcanti's instrumental renditions of places.

No work among Cavalcanti's compositions was as successful as his waltz "Muchacha" (Musical Example 10.2). With a title in Spanish as a reference to a woman from Spain, "Muchacha" was heard in the city for over a decade. While the composer shows his understanding and creative stylization of musical clichés of Spanish-ness, he moves beyond the immediate musical/image association and raises his waltz to the level of musical abstraction, a work that is more suitable for listening and imagining than for dancing. Despite the waltz's suggestion of national origins and evocation of a woman in the score cover sheet, for which one could find many aliases elsewhere, Cavalcanti's waltz was nothing but the resoundings of his own local experiences with Spanish-ness in Rio de Janeiro. Here, triplets suggesting Spanish-ness in *jota* style are integrated with the long melodic line that flows lyrically and seamlessly with the piano's timbre and the overstressed two quarter notes in the accompaniment. The connection of the *muchacha*'s image and sounds are displayed in multiple ways, but he escapes the objective and concrete innuendos by rarifying them enough so as to facilitate perceptive abstraction through listening, even if such musical transcendence is still dependent on already existing clichés. Cavalcanti thus follows the conventional dance structure AABBACCA organized in 8-bar sequences, but adds new

---

[16] Schwartz, *Writing Paris*, 2.
[17] Schwartz, *Writing Paris*, 1.
[18] Certeau, *The Practice of Everyday Life*, 105.

Musical Example 10.2. Aurélio Cavalcanti, *Muchacha*, Valsa Hespanhola (c.1903). (Rio de Janeiro: André da Costa e Co.).
Source: Biblioteca Nacional, Rio de Janeiro, Acervo Digital

Musical Example 10.2. Continued

interest in every section by moving through tonal centers and building a melodic line that is both familiar and unique. "Muchacha" is a well-balanced work as an invitation for cosmopolitan listeners to imagine a person, in this case a man imagining a woman. Like several male composers during his time, Cavalcanti offered his listeners a woman through his own musical imagination: his was not a male "gaze," but a male's sonic creation of his imagined sounding woman. And Cavalcanti's imagined sounding woman was a *muchacha*.[19]

One can offer, as Beatriz Jaguaribe has argued, that the "creation of uniqueness is oftentimes unintentional and arises from an assemblage of urban factors," a claim that while true at some level, may suggest that Cavalcanti's "Muchacha" stemmed less from his own skill and creativity than from serendipity of the communal and as an expression of the collective. But subjective/artistic imagination and craftsmanship and embracing the cliché are not exclusionary attributes to the cosmopolitan composer. Cavalcanti's works indeed follow ready-made musical structures, respond to the communal and the commercial, and the standardized dance form, attributes that allowed many to engage with them through performing and listening. But the success of "Muchacha" in the cosmopolitan city shows a composer expanding the familiar through his individual take; it is his own individual "subjective/artistic imaginations [that endowed] the everyday with meaning and memory."[20] That's the role of the cosmopolitan artist: to submit oneself to the collectivity through one's individuality and to allow the imaginary and the ephemeral to acquire historical meaning.

Cake-Walking

In February 1903, the first page of a Rio de Janeiro newspaper featured an article about the cake-walk craze in Europe and anticipated its local success. The author explains that the cakewalk "[o]riginated among the blacks from the U.S., [who] get together in bars, form a ring, and with the sound of the banjo, perform the most eccentric jumps and leg movements around a cake; [the cakewalk then spread] to café-concerts . . . and ended up becoming universal, thanks to what one calls the Americanization of the World."[21] The commentator was not exaggerating, since the cake-walk spread easily via the urban musical circuit from New York to Paris, London, Paris, Rio de Janeiro, and many other cities in Europe and Latin America. At a time when the economic and political power of the United States was growing at a fast pace, the spread of the cake-walk and other similar dances and songs derived from African-American musical

---

[19] The score and a performance of the waltz is available at https://www.youtube.com/watch?v=ccpj5eNtBzc. Eduardo das Neves was aware of the work's popularity and set "La Muchacha" as a song, furthering a labyrinth of musical stereotypes and intermedial connections. Neves's lyrics are published in Violão with a note: "set to the music of La Muchacha by Cavalcanti"—apparently without the consent of the author, for which Neves apologized.

[20] Beatriz Jaguaribe, *Rio de Janeiro: Urban Life through the Eyes of the City* (New York: Routledge, 2014, Kindle), 4.

[21] "*The* Cake Walk," *Correio da Manhã*, February 19, 1903. See also the article "Americanização do mundo" (The Americanization of the World) in the same newspaper on May 8, 1903.

308 MUSIC AND COSMOPOLITANISM

expressions helped expand the urban cultural circuits to also include cities like New York and Chicago. As a result, Rio de Janeiro's chronicler highlighted the dance's connection with African Americans while pointing to the dance's "universal appeal" and, in the process, also revealing his awareness of the wide circulation of cultural products from the United States in an anticipation to the "McDonaldizaion of the world" that preoccupied intellectuals at the close of the 20th century.

In February 1903, Rubén Dario also wrote about the widespread popularity of the dance. Dario traveled numerous times throughout the Americas and Europe, lived in Chile and Buenos Aires, then in Madrid and Paris, from where he wrote "Cake-walk. El baile de moda" (Cake-walk: The fashionable dance) and sent it to newspapers in Buenos Aires and Mexico City. Dario talks about the cake-walk overtaking many other popular dances in Parisian salons and music halls, but he also stresses the diasporic African-derived kinship of the dance with a myriad of others in Latin America:

> The cake-walk moves the world; the cake-walk [is like] the craze *danzón* of African origin; [it is a] yanqui *candombe*; the *bábula* [*sic*] from Virginia; a relative of the *timbirimbas* and *mozamalas* of blacks from Lima; and the steps of the blacks in Cuban plantations, of the *boritos* [*sic*] and *cumbiambas* of blacks from Panama; the *toumblacke* [*sic*] from the blacks of Guadaloupe, and the ingenious and extraordinary choreographies of blacks from all places.... No one can dance the cake-walk like the blacks; the admirer of the cake-walk ... has to admire ... the black [dancer].[22]

Despite the genealogy of African heritage that Dario assigns to the dance and, in that regard, his position as an outsider, as *baile da moda* one should not be surprised that the cake-walk started to appear in carnival parties, music halls, and theaters in the Brazilian capital immediately after the U.S. group Les Elkes performed the cake-walk in the revue *Les joyeux nègres* at Nouveau Cirque de Paris between November 1902 and January 1903, and the African-American women's group "Florida Creole Girls" performed the cake-walk at the Casino de Paris.[23] The show inspired the Parisian composer Berger to write his cake-walk "Joyeux nègres" (1903), a work dedicated to John Phillip de Sousa, who had included band arrangements of ragtimes and cake-walks in his many European tours in the early 1900s. In 1903 Rio de Janeiro, the

---

[22] Ruben Dario, "Cake-walk. El baile de moda," *Revista Moderna de México*, February 1903; also published in *La Nacion* in Buenos Aires, on March 19, 1903.
[23] Rio de Janeiro's article echoed the reviews of the presentation of the Les Elkes performance of the dance at the Nouveau Cirque in Paris, in October 1902.

SOUNDS OF URBAN WORLDS 309

cake-walk was one more cosmopolitan product with urban appeal, as the dance appeared in the theater and music halls alongside French chansons, operatic arias, and excerpts from the popular Sidney Jones's operetta *San Toy* (1899). Presented at the Casino Nacional music hall in May 1903, a cake-walk by Luis Moreira was already for sale in music stores in June.[24] On July 2, 1903, the music-hall Theatro Casino announced an "Italian duet singers, [and] an Italian cantatrice," but the show was especially appealing because it featured "the celebrated American cake-walk danced by the troupe from Nouveau Cirque de Paris."[25] On September 21, 1903, Segreto included the dance in the miscellaneous program of his Parque Fluminense music hall, when "the *cançonetista* from Paris, Marie Dalberg" joined Jenny Cook and Juanita Many to dance the "famous cake-walk with the accompaniment of an orchestra of 15 musicians under the conductor Costa Junior."[26] On July 7, 1903, Segreto also presented in Rio de Janeiro the French short film *Le cake-walk infernal* (1903) by Georges Méliès (1868–1938), shortly after it was shown at Théâtre Robert-Houdin in Paris and in the United States on June 13, 1903.[27] The five-minute film included actors/dancers in blackface recreating a scene from "the devil in hell" and featuring the cake-walk dance. By August 1904, Eduardo das Neves had already caught up with the trend, as he appeared singing the cake-walk, accompanying himself on the guitar at Sociedade Phonographica Brasileira;[28] and he included in his *Mistérios do violão* the song "O caixote," which he suggests should be performed with music from "the famous" cake-walk, although he does not specify which (most probably Berger's). By December 1904, the cake-walk was an expected part of Segreto's venues, including the Maison Moderne, where the dance appeared in the program of a matineé open "to families."[29] In 1905, Berger's "Joyeux Nègres, Cake-Walk" was for sale in Rio de Janeiro at Arthur Napoleão's musical shop alongside Berger's waltzes "Petite Annonce," "Etoile d'Amour," and "Amour que passe,"[30] and by then the cake-walk was an expected dance in carnival parades.

Sometimes referred to as "American dance," sometimes as part of some unspecified Black culture, and sometimes directly connected to well-known

---

[24] *O Fluminense*, June 7, 1903.

[25] *Jornal do Commercio*, July 2, 1903.

[26] *Correio da Manhã*, September 21, 1903.

[27] The work is listed in the database "Filmes estrangeiros exibidos no Brasil: 1896–1934," and can be accessed at http://www.mnemocine.com.br/; for the cake-walk from the U.S. in 1903, see The Library of Congress at https://loc.gov/item/96520361/. Other 1903 films showing the cake-walk from the Pathé production were *Le célèbre cake-walk par les Elks*, and *Le cake-walk des nains*.

[28] *O Malho* 3, no. 99, August 6, 1904.

[29] *Correio da Manhã*, December 27, 1903.

[30] *Jornal do Commercio*, February 5, 1905.

310 MUSIC AND COSMOPOLITANISM

Parisian music halls, the cake-walk easily flowed into Rio de Janeiro's hetero-geneous musical worlds. To intellectuals and chroniclers of the city, the cake-walk was a dance among many, but its popularity in the city, if ephemeral, overcame all others, and its overwhelming presence led to vast analyses and interpretations of its role the city, and of its many travels beyond the city. In 1906, Bilac wrote an article to the magazine *Kosmos* sketching the social geography of Rio de Janeiro using as examples the many dances available. According to him, in Rio de Janeiro "dance is more than entertainment: it is a passion, a mania, a fever," and he notes with sarcasm that knowing each dance could point to "which *country* I am in the *urbs*." To Bilac, the waltz was from Catumbi, the *maxixe* from the Cidade Nova, the *pas-de-quatre* from Botafogo, and the "military polka" from Engenho Velho. Bilac also stresses that not all dances were uplifting, for there was also the "dance macabre" of death to which we are all destined, and he concludes arguing, without naming specific neighborhoods, that everyone should dance the cake-walk because it "is a precious dance with an exceptional virtue of lowering man to the level of the kangaroo and elevating the kangaroo to the level of man."[31] Bilac's human/animal connection and racial overtones are not difficult to unpack, since he was notorious for supporting those "civilizing" the city with modernization projects à la Europe, while dehumanizing specific areas where large numbers of Blacks and immigrants lived in substandard housing complexes. But his reference to the cake-walk as a dance without a specific location brings to the fore many other complex political and socio-racial connections and disconnection shaping the city through music-making.

In a 1904 chronicle, the Rio de Janeiro novelist, playwright, journalist, and public servant Lima Campos (1872–1929) uncompromisingly associated the cake-walk with the idea of *mestiçagem,* while at the same time assigning to the dance wider cultural-racial-geographical paths than Dario had done one year earlier:

The cake-walk is a caricature of a dance in movement, as in a [Paul] Gavarni [drawing][32] . . . where clear lines mix the morbid [hip] swaying of the African *jongo* with the celebre tapping of Scottish solos, voluptuous Aragonese *jotas*, and the disarticulations of the can-can. . . . It was born in the taciturn life of the *senzalas*—the monasteries of slavery . . . then it crossed with the white and

---

[31] Bilac (under pseudonym Fantasio), *Kosmos* III, no. 5 (May 1906).
[32] Paul Gavarni (Sulpice Guillaume Chevalier, Paris, 1804–1866) was an illustrator who provided caricatures for the French magazine *Le Charivari*.

turned *mestiço*, who gave [the dance] its swaying of the Britanic graceful steps, *"can-caned"* the music, modernized the movements and the [dance] figures, and the delirious march began: the cake-walk moved through the countryside, was successful in small cities, walked through the *Far-West*, passed the great central rivers, the Mississipi, the Ohio, the Mackenzie, the Tennessee and penetrated towards the north; then crossed the Appalachia and dominated Washington, Philadelphia, New York, Boston, and on the other side of the rockies, arrived in Oregon and San Francisco; and from the enchanting cosmopolitanism of California it moved through the Pacific and the Atlantic aboard' in the *steamers* and the mercantile sails, it traversed the high waters and was spilled through the world, to the orient, to the occident, to the north, and to the south, to insinuate the yellow lasciviousness, the Latin sensuality, the hypocrite luxury from Germania and Scandinavia. And this is the cake-walk that we see today, stomped in the small stages of the café-concerts, before foreign audiences of hot blood, performed by women of light, English skin, straight teeth, and brown eyes, whom Uncle Sam also exports and all the capitals welcome.[33]

Like habaneras before them, cake-walks came to represent and propel complex ideas of racialized cultures in movement, first as deviant through performative satire and eccentric choreographic moves, but also through sounds and specifically through rhythmic patterns performed in lively tempos, syncopations in particular, learned through theatrical performances as rhythms deviant from the "regular" pattern of duple meter polkas, a connection to which the cake-walk was dependent to signify. While European essentialist understandings of "Black culture" connections with dancing and rhythm appear in theaters going back to the 18th century, the appeal of the (supposedly) "African" or "Black element" in music and music-making through rhythmic patterns took a wider cosmopolitan turn in the mid-19th century with the popularity of minstrel theatrical shows, with either Black casts or White casts in blackface, performing in the Americas, Europe, and several African countries.[34] When the cake-walk started to circulate in many cities concomitantly at the beginning of the 20th century, the theatrical association with minstrelsy was still implicit but, outside the theater, like all dances, the cake-walk was intrinsically linked to bodily responses to music

---

[33] Lima Campos, "Cake walk," *Kosmos* I, no. 8 (August 1904): 52.
[34] Few minstrel groups made it to Rio de Janeiro. On June 6, 1887, a minstrel group was presented at the Theatro Sant'Anna which, according to the critic, was "a cheerful entertainment according to English tastes," *Jornal do Commercio*, June 6, 1887.

312   MUSIC AND COSMOPOLITANISM

and rhythm in particular and, as such, could serve an array of sociopolitical purposes.[35]

That a specific rhythmic pattern came to have social or racial connotations points to how the travels of music helped communicate shared understandings of race, of blackness and whiteness, at a moment of global shifts in power relations. And the cake-walk association with repeated rhythm patterns, emphasizing an opposition to the "regular" beat, helped the dance resonate in the urban network of connections and disconnections at an unprecedented pace. Rae Beth Gordon has argued that the popularity of the cake-walk in large cities converged contemporary social Darwinian ideas of primitivism with nervous pathology. In the music-hall it turned into an expression of the *fin-de-siècle* modernity, one that also added race to the European search for boundaries between body and mind, the conscious and the unconscious.[36] Here music is again disassembled into one parameter, rhythm, and then is further fragmented into one rhythmic combination, syncopation, to serve explorations of bodily responses to a mind out of control. But the human body is also disassembled into one as a prototype for this "out of control" mind, the Black body, one understood as a "out of time," always in a primitive state, and one that White bourgeoisies clung to as a return to the natural state of being, and as an antithesis to the civilized city marked by a convoluted uncivilized modernity. Thus, when the dance was announced at the Nouveau Cirque de Paris, Les Elkes were accompanied on stage by two "Négrillons," whose Black bodies attracted considerable attention in the press, and "Les Joyeux Nègres" provided Paris's residents with what a reviewer described as *"une danse de sauvages."*[37]

As Derek Scott has noted, these elements combined to allow for the development of a musical syntax of blackness, a racialized musical syntax, a rhythmic pattern usually set alongside call and response in idiomatic instrumental music and suggestions of bare pentatonic melodies.[38] This musical syntax of blackness was usually presented against a set of unassembled, though unmarked, musical whiteness: harmonic progressions as abstract music of the mind and the spirit of the civilized European, and melodies from the operatic stage, understood as pleasurable for the eyes and ears of many. These disassembling of musical parameters into implied racialized discourses paralleled the disassembling of musical parameters to imply the nation: German harmony and Italian melody,

---

[35] See, in this regard, Catherine Cole, "American Ghetto and Ghanaian Concert Parties: A Transnational Perspective on Blackface," in *Burnt Cork: Traditions and Legacies of Blackface Minstrelsy* (Amherst and Boston: University of Massachusetts Press, 2012), 238.

[36] Rae Beth Gordon, *Dances with Darwin, 1875–1910: Vernacular Modernity in France* (London and New York: Routledge, 2016 [2009]), Kindle.

[37] Rae Beth Gordon, "Les rythmes contagieux d'une danse noire: Le cake-walk," *Intermédialités* 16 (Fall 2010): 64

[38] Scott, *Sounds of the Metropolis*, 154, 149–157.

for example. Together, these processes of disassembling became hallmarks of the social, cultural, racial, gender, and political fragmentation of the *fin-de-siècle* city.

While the participation of Black musicians in the production and performance of cake-walks and similar dances gave them some authority over a booming business, their presence added the "authenticity" needed for the music to be displaced, again, as the Other. The Black body, parodied or not, was thus a coveted element in performance. At the same time, such performances were but performances; they were critical engagements, not displays of racial identities. While Black musicians and performers on both sides of the Atlantic were disposed of political power within a capitalistic, growing music industry, they were not disposed of artistic authority and individual subjectivity. The production, performance, and consumption of cake-walks in the city operated within larger complex systems of social, ethnic, and racial exchanges and moving political dynamics of representations on both sides of the Atlantic, exchanges in which the lines between Self and Other were not clear-cut or inflexible. And as cake-walks started to make their way to Rio de Janeiro, their status as fashionable dances made to represent Black musical practices was filtered through a predominantly White music business that helped it acquire many extra lives.

Expectedly, the cake-walk also occupied Cavalcanti as a composer, who saw in the music/dance another way to appeal to his Rio de Janeiro audiences. His "Cake-walk," most probably composed at the end of the first decade of the 20th century, is a march with the same dance structure as his polkas, three sections that repeat. The work, which shows an unequivocal resemblance to Berger's "Joyeux nègres," includes the already established trait of non-stop melodic syncopations that emphasize the first beat of the march, rather than the syncopated note, with the added suggestion of pentatonic construction in the melody; at the same time, the composer makes use of the added sixth in the melody in the second measure, recalling his fashionable waltzes. Cavalcanti's use of accentuated, syncopated chords in the second section recalls his use of the accented chords in the second section of his *Valsa espanhola*, both of which served to highlight his middle section's element of surprise (Musical Example 10.3). Thus, in his "Cake-Walk," Cavalcanti was fully aware that syncopation was necessary to define the piece's exotic element, but he was also quick to combine it with other Others, such as his French polkas or his Spanish waltzes. Cavalcanti's use of "musical Africanisms,"[39] translated into syncopations, were musical elements added to his tools of worldliness and otherwordliness to recreate an urban sonic world familiar to him, one

---

[39] Kofi Agawu argues that the idea of Orientalisms as musical constructs can parallel that of Africanisms; see his *Representing African Music: Postcolonial Notes, Queries, Positions* (New York: Routledge, 2003), 95.

Musical Example 10.3. Cavalcanti "Cake-walk" (c. 1903) (Rio de Janeiro: Editor Manoel Antonio Guimarães).
Source: Biblioteca Nacional, Rio de Janeiro, Acervo Digital

Musical Example 10.3. Continued

Musical Example 10.3. Continued

that situated his music and his audiences as part of a large urban soundscape of *fin-de-siècle* cities.

While the appeal of the cakewalk in Rio de Janeiro sheds light on a cosmopolitan culture at the beginning of the 20th century in which disassembled musical elements traveled as racial signifiers, it also points to cosmopolitanism à la Europe in a city that had been dominated by African-derived cultures and musical traditions since colonial days: a context that Ruben Dario, who visited the city only in 1906, would not have missed in his earlier article. The spread of musical Africanisms as fashionable rhythms was thus particularly significant in Rio de Janeiro as both an engagement with and an escape from the ongoing discussion of Blacks' role in the construction of Brazilian nationality. Perceived both as an eccentric dance of U.S. Blacks and a worldly dance fashionable in Paris, the cake-walk became a most desirable addition to Rio de Janeiro's urban soundscape, where it shared the space with waltzes, polkas, and marches, but also with a local dance called *maxixe* which, like the cake-walk, was a variant of the European polka and march, no less conspicuously ornamented with syncopations in both melodic line and accompaniment as a musical cliché.

In the carnival season of 1909, for example, Paschoal Segreto offered in his music hall a lively "Yankee ball with the delicious cake-walk and the not less delicious *maxixe*."[40] The inclusion of both the *maxixe* and the cake-walk was one more pairing of cosmopolitanisms with locality, marked by exoticism. By locating the *maxixe* as local and exotic, the dance could be celebrated the moment it became part of a local imaginary of a global urban modernity.[41] The *maxixe* in this context could lose its potential for self-exoticism and instead become a convenient tool for business explorations, as well as for larger politics of race representation through music. Micol Seigel has offered a most compelling analysis of the appearance and disappearance of the *maxixe* in the United States, focusing on the dance's relation to other Afro-diasporic cultural exchanges in the second decade of the 20th century.[42] The story of this exchange from the viewpoint of the emergent music business in Rio de Janeiro offers similar examples, but can also provide another layer to the already complex cosmopolitan interactions: it highlights not only Afro-diasporic musical expressions as cosmopolitan, but also shows their relocation in a local racial-social context. On the one hand, rhythmic patterns in cake-walks, disguised as the exotic Other, served as a strong marketing tool for fashionable dances coming from overseas. On the other hand, cake-walk dances and songs were particularly useful in validating the local *maxixe* production by also highlighting local "blackness" as both fashionable and desirable by all.

---

[40] *Jornal do Commercio*, February 19, 1909.

[41] See my discussion of the *maxixe* in this context in "Before and after Samba: Modernity, Cosmopolitanism, and Popular Music in Rio de Janeiro at the Beginning and End of the Twentieth Century," in *Postnational Musical Identities: Cultural Production, Distribution, and Consumption in Globalized Scenario*, ed. Ignacio Corona and Alejandro L. Madrid (Lanham, MD: Lexington Books, 2008): 173–184.

[42] Micol Siegel, "The Disappearing Dance: *Maxixe's* Imperial Erasure," *Black Music Research Journal* 25, no. 1–2 (Spring–Fall 2005): 93–117.

318   MUSIC AND COSMOPOLITANISM

Yet, viewed first as one more element in the wide array of possibilities offered by the international circulation of music and widespread cultural cosmopolitanism, the popularity of songs and dances saturated with syncopations acquired a life of their own in the Brazilian capital. While part of a larger discourse of African-derived expressions that had emerged as representations of Otherness set primarily (but not exclusively) by White audiences and businesspeople on both sides of the Atlantic, they became celebrated signifiers of Rio de Janeiro's music, signifiers that effectively and conveniently blurred concepts of race, cosmopolitanism, and local uniqueness into a singular discourse. In the 1930s, during the height of a dictatorship and within discourses of ideological nationalisms in Brazil, syncopations in popular songs and dances were no longer celebrated as representations of "Black culture," or Otherness, but as a symbol of local authenticity and of national belonging. Desperately sought after by most (White) musicologists within Brazil and abroad as an aesthetical validation of the local musical production, syncopations were in fact a shared experience and musical practice of the modern city, but one that also ultimately locked the musical expressions of Black Brazilians in an essentialist box marked by disassembled rhythms as race and difference, a box from which there was no escape—for it became the ultimate sonic symbol, one forged to represent not only imaginaries of musical expressions by Black people, but also of Brazilian-ness at large, an unquestionable icon, for which authenticity was undeniable and history played no role. In this way, Brazilian popular music became historically inseparable from made-up representations of African-derived musical expressions, which were actually created in the cosmopolitan continuum of racialized discourses and recreated as a myth of Brazilian singularity that continues to this day.[43] Still, one wonders how a society ruled by a minority White elite whose take on race was modeled on racist European theories, and who invested in the "whitening" of the population as a just cause for self-serving debates of identity and representation, could see in these forgings of blackness a potential for local constructions of national identity; put simply, how could those in charge of "whitening" the population favor "blackening" the music?

Beyond the celebration of *maxixes* and cake-walks as fashionable and desirable, music-making in the Brazilian capital was dominated by large numbers of Blacks and mulattos who sought and found work in Rio de Janeiro's emergent music industry. They understood well and made use of Orientalisms, Africanisms, and various Europeanisms, while positioning themselves as true cosmopolitans. Like Eduardo das Neves and Os Geraldos, Cavalcanti was a Black artist whose success

---

[43] For a study of the role of Black musicians in Brazilian popular music, see Darién Davis, *White Face, Black Mask: Africaneity and the Early Social History of Popular Music in Brazil* (East Lansing: Michigan State University Press, 2009).

as a composer and performer in music halls, café concerts, and movie theaters did not escape contemporary chroniclers. After "a French chanson, a Japanese song, and a Spanish dance," Edmundo recalls that Cavalcanti could satisfy the audiences with polkas and waltzes of many types, and also with cosmopolitan musics that included cakewalks and ragtimes, habaneras, tangos, and *maxixes*. Edmundo did not exalt the lyrical melody of Cavalcanti's "La Muchacha," but he was quick to praise his performances for their "syncopated cadences of the African batuque," a characteristic that the chronicler claimed "*they* [my emphasis] added to all musics," and that showed them as "barbarians . . . so much so that one could not accept any other *type* [my emphasis] of performer during carnival."[44] To him, the Black body was crucial to add local "authenticity" to the cosmopolitan music, an authenticity that could then be presented and represented as parody in carnival parades for the enjoyment of many.

This political play with music, fragmented into rhythmic cells and bodies in movement, was not a unique case of the cake-walk, however. The emergence of the waltz a century earlier also invited a host of discussions about music's power over the body, and of rhythm in particular, and its role in moving groups across borders.[45] What made the cake-walk rage significant within the turn-of-the-century city was its entanglement with racialized Black bodies, while the waltz flowed easily within a racially unmarked White crowd, although it quickly acquired gendered and generational associations. While in Rio de Janeiro the engagement of Black musicians and performers with the cake-walk and the *maxixe* served well to lend the musics "Black authenticity," these dances proved especially malleable when used politically by a few White groups who were in charge of populist nationalizing strategies,[46] as they claimed them not as an integral part of the cosmopolitan city, but of a nation with a majority Black population.

[44] Edmundo, *O Rio de Janeiro do meu tempo*, 179.
[45] In this regard, see McKee, *Decorum of the Minuet, Delirium of the Waltz*.
[46] For this argument, see Tiago de Melo Gomes, "Para além da casa da Tia Ciata: Outras experiencias no universo musical carioca, 1830–1930," *Afro-Ásia* 20, no. 30 (2003): 175–198.

11

A World of Many Musics

One Thread in the World of Musics

In the introduction of his 1976 book, *Wagner e o Brazil* (Wagner and Brazil), Chaves Junior wrote: "This book was written with the love of those who follow Richard Wagner's cult as something very important for humanity. In truth, the art and culture of this planet would be strongly lessened if Wagner had not existed."[1] In a more recent account and addressing specifically Western music, Richard Taruskin makes a similar assertion, claiming that Wagner's musical technique was "so novel and so impressive that neither the music of his own day nor that of succeeding generations is conceivable without him."[2] And in the opening to their book *Wagnerism in European Politics*, David Large, Willian Weber, and Anne Sesssa go further, claiming Wagnerism to be one of the "main cultural and intellectual movements of the 19th century," comparable in scale and significance to Darwinism and positivism.[3] These authors' conjectures are rather commonplace among music historians of the West, and they should not be taken for granted since deterministic claims about Wagner's ideas and his music as representatives of an all-encompassing culture of the West have a long history and wide geographical reach. Starting in the mid-19th century with the composer's advocacy for his ideologies and as a spokesperson for his works while enjoying the support of a moneyed aristocracy, the controversial nature of Wagner's claims and the idiosyncrasies of his operas have been inflated by intellectuals, writers, musicians, and music critics from across Europe, the Americas, and beyond, who have generated a literature of gigantic proportions that few dare to confront. To be sure, the wide dissemination of Wagner's music and ideals certainly shows that they touched a nerve among some of those trying to understand and manage the role of music as art in a period of constant political, economic, and social changes. Vazsonyi argues that the impact of Wagner's music went beyond

---

[1] Edgard de Brito Chaves Junior, *Wagner e o Brasil* (Rio de Janeiro: Emebê, 1976), ix.

[2] Richard Taruskin, *Music in the Nineteenth Century: The Oxford History of Western Music* (Oxford and New York: Oxford University Press), 508–509.

[3] David Large and Willian Weber, and Anne Sesssa eds., *Wagnerism in European Culture and Politics* (New York: Cornell University Press, 1984), 7. Emma Sutton suggests that "Wagnerism was not exclusively or even primarily a musical trend"; see her "Karlowicz and fin-de-siècle Wagnerism," in *European fin de siècle and Polish Modernism: The Music of Mieczyslaw Karlowicz*, ed. Luca Sala (Bologna, Italy: Ut Orpheus Edizioni, 2010), 121.

Music and Cosmopolitanism. Cristina Magaldi, Oxford University Press. © Oxford University Press 2024.
DOI: 10.1093/oso/9780199744770.003.0012

its role in the process of nation-building in Germany and in Europe, and that his music was spread widely with the "comforting claim that it contained universal truths and timeless values . . . [claims] that came accompanied by notions of high art and quasi-religious experience, as opposed to entertainment."[4] As the 20th century unfolded, the understanding of the dominant position of Wagner's music in the context of supposedly all-encompassing Western European music as art with universal appeal, its role in the forging of cultural representations of nation-states, and in shaping a "musical modernity," gradually became commonplace to the point that assertions like the ones made by Chaves and Taruskin have been taken at face value. In the end, the nature of the literature about Wagner and his works led to a parade of ideologies and aesthetic hierarchies that have muddled the historical contexts in which the composer's music emerged, was disseminated, and endured to this day.[5]

Hector Berlioz argued that the "music of the future" that Wagner professed was not his alone, but the music of their present: "we are of that school, belong to it heart and soul, with profound conviction and the warmest sympathy."[6] Full manipulation of orchestration to aid in storytelling, the use of melodic recurrences to substitute for or to "speak" for characters, and the amplification of the harmonic language for the sake of the drama were tools all too familiar to Wagner's contemporaries and became nothing but musical clichés after him. But, unlike most of his contemporaries, Wagner did theorize about musical aesthetic and ethical roles in society, using his own work to support his ideas and, with the aid of aristocrats and other moneyed individuals, he also put into practice some of his ideas, including the building of a massive performing center that has served as model to many entertaining enterprises throughout the 20th century. Ultimately, however, Wagner's future was not solely about musical elaborations or techniques still to come, but about his understanding of music's sociopolitical force and how it could be used at the service of xenophobic nationalism—as indeed it was. The historical survival and canonizing of Wagner's music rest on such ideological claims, as well as on a singular, deterministic idea of progress that has his own present as its utmost pinnacle. If everything after that was left "to be determined," it fit conveniently an all-too-familiar deterministic account of "the future," "the modern," and their connections to "the end of tonality" that pervaded modernistic narratives in the first part of the 20th century. Yet those claiming that Wagner's music endured beyond his time through "Wagnerisms"

---

[4] Nicholas Vazsonyi, *Richard Wagner: Self-Promotion and the Making of a Brand* (Cambridge, UK: Cambridge University Press, 2010), 170.

[5] For this topic, see Emma Sutton, *Aubrey Beardsley and British Wagnerism in the 1890s* (New York: Oxford University Press, 2002), 2.

[6] Hector Berlioz, *À travers chants* (Paris, 1981), 321; cited in Peter Vergo, *The Music of Painting: Music, Modernism, and the Visual Arts from the Romantics to John Cage* (London and New York: Phaidon Press, 2010), 17.

rest on political aesthetic stances that correlate the work of one composer with overall historical musical categories identified as Wagnerian, Wagnerism, and post-Wagnerism. Peter Virgo notes how intriguing it is that Wagnerism exists at all, considering that we do not have such a thing as "Mozartism," or "Beethovenism."[7]

Chaves Junior's and Taruskin's assumption that had Richard Wagner not existed the musical world would be entirely different may be true, of course. It is not my intention to dwell on hypothetical historical scenarios, nor to deny the importance of Wagner's ideas and music in the overall context of Western Europe. The sheer fact that this section is focused on the dissemination of his music attests to the extent to which narratives about his works and ideas can be overbearing. I suggest, nonetheless, that if one considers the overall musical worlds of turn-of-the-20th century emerging cities like Rio de Janeiro, Wagner's music was but one thread in a plethora of musics available to local audiences and musicians, that it became a topic of interest among a very limited number of musicians and critics, and that its relevance was asserted for a very short period, in limited ways, well beyond the composer's own time, and at a time when understandings and experiences of "modernity" were vast and heterogeneous. Within the specific scenario of the urban cultural network of the turn of the century, Wagner's ideas and music changed things to a much lesser degree than Chaves and Taruskin claim. In fact, Wagner's music traveled alongside a torrent of other musics, was distributed through a gamut of performing venues and in a range of formats, and was experienced in different performance contexts. Despite the composer's claims about the power that his musical dramas could have as a media spectacle for political, ideological, and aesthetic purposes, as a union of the arts, his efforts to publicize and disseminate his work as such, "to create a niche [and] impose a brand," and to become a "global industry," did not always succeed as Vazsonyi suggests.[8] If one is to claim that Wagner and Wagnerism did dominate the musical world and the world of music ideas, one should concede to the fact that his was a small and very limited world. And yet, during the first decades of the new republican government in Brazil, a few composers and critics did not eschew from using Wagner as an example of musical goodness, and as an example to be blindly followed by musicians and performers. As this group, the "Musical Republic" eventually became gatekeepers of the "official" musical scene in Rio de Janeiro; they also came to serve as a focal point guiding historians of music-making in the city.

---

[7] Vergo, *The Music of Painting*, 17.

[8] Vazsonyi claims that Wagner's techniques to publicize his works were creative and partially adopted by publishers and other sections of the entertainment industry; see his *Richard Wagner*, 7, 202, and 207.

Wagner's music was not completely unknown in turn-of-the-20th-century Rio de Janeiro, of course. Nonetheless, in a city with one of the most enduring operatic traditions in the Southern Hemisphere, it took almost 30 years after the premiere of *Lohengrin* (1855) for an Italian company to offer Rio de Janeiro audiences the first fully staged Wagner opera. The work, which by 1883 had premiered in several European centers and in the United States but with a high degree of suspicion, was performed in the Brazilian capital without success. Performed in Italian, a language familiar to most opera goers in the city, one contemporary commentator nonetheless noted specifically that "as a musical conception, *Lohengrin* is deplorable."[9] Local residents and opera aficionados had to wait nine more years to attend another fully staged Wagner opera, *Tannhäuser* (1845), also in Italian and by an Italian company, which was presented in the Theatro Lyrico on September 30, 1892, 47 years after its premiere in Germany. After being postponed twice due to inclement weather and political unrest in the early years of the Republic, the work finally made it to the Rio de Janeiro stage, but the public was unconvinced by both the music and the performance. The novelist and critic Machado de Assis did not eschew from observing, jokingly, that the presentation of Wagner's music was a fad, one among many novelties that arrived in the city:

> *Tannhäuser* and electric cable cars (*bondes*): We have finally in the land these great novelties. The manager of the Teatro Lírico did us a favor by offering the famous Wagner's opera, while the electric company had the courage to transport us more quickly [in electric *bondes*]. Is this the fall of the donkey's cars and Verdi? It all depends on the circumstances.[10]

Chaves Junior minimized the poor reception of *Tannhäuser*, arguing that the presentation was just "the introduction to Wagnerian music,"[11] and that with time and more performances, audiences would eventually appreciate the work, an argument that was commonplace in the writings of many turn-of-the-century critics in Rio de Janeiro and elsewhere and that remains familiar among music students and the general public to this day. Some critics attempted to ignore the public's negative response altogether, claiming that the performance was both "an important event in the music world . . . and a path to further performances of Wagnerian music in Rio de Janeiro," and that the music is "*for some* [my emphasis], the most beautiful."[12] Time, however, did not improve the perception of Wagner's music. *Lohengrin* was presented again in 1893 after *Tannhäuser*

---

[9] This author, *Music in Imperial Rio de Janeiro* (Lanham, MD: Scarecrow Press, 2004), 50.
[10] *Gazeta de Notícias*, October 2, 1892.
[11] Chaves Junior, *Wagner e o Brasil*, 20.
[12] Chaves Junior, *Wagner e o Brasil*, 20.

324   MUSIC AND COSMOPOLITANISM

but again with similar response, even if, according to Chaves, the work had good chances of succeeding in Rio de Janeiro, since it "is the most accessible of Wagner's works to the ears of those used to the 19th-century Italian opera,"[13] another argument, ironically drawn with its association with Italian opera, used elsewhere and over time to introduce Wagner's music. The mixed reviews of the performance, however, did not point to Wagner as a challenger to Verdi, the most performed operatic composer in Rio de Janeiro in the last decade of the century, or as a competitor to the operas and operettas of many other provenances, which were guaranteed box-office successes (see Chapters 8 and 9).

In fact, *Lohengrin* and *Tannhäuser* remained the only fully staged works by Wagner performed in Rio de Janeiro until 1905, when *Meistersinger* (1868) was premiered with a "cold atmosphere [and] without enthusiasm." *Tristan and Isolde* (1865) had to wait until 1910, and critics continued to decry the "terrible performance," even if, apparently, "the public respected the author of the tetralogy."[14] *Parsifal* (1882) and *Die Walkirie* (1870) premiered in 1913, but still did not change the grim reception for Wagner's music by Rio de Janeiro's audiences. Altogether, during the first two decades of the Republic, audiences in the Brazilian capital heard 37 fully staged performances of six of Wagner's operas, all of them in Italian, with *Lohengrin* (performed 17 times) and *Tannhäuser* (11 times) being repeated considerably more than the other four works. Considering that, according to Ferreira, Verdi's *Aída* alone was performed 131 times during the same period, Pucinni's *La Bohème* 147 times, *Tosca* 137, and Ponchielli's *La Gioconda* 118 times,[15] one can say that Wagner's operas did not square well with the competition. In Rio de Janeiro, only a sample of Wagner's fully staged operas was heard and even so very sparingly and in Italian, with *Lohengrin* and *Tannhäuser* leading the list.

Comparatively in Berlin, from 1859 to 1906 there were 500 staged presentations of *Lohengrin* alone, a number that could lead us to conclude that the Brazilian capital was an exception in the spread of the so-called Wagnermania.[16] Nonetheless, despite the whole debacle about Wagner and his music's love-hate reception within Parisian circles, performances of his works at Opéra and the Opéra-Comique were on par with or behind those of Gounod, Massenet, and

---

[13] Chaves Junior, *Wagner e o Brasil*, 20.
[14] Chave Junior, *Wagner e o Brasil*, 23
[15] Ferreira, "Opera in Rio de Janeiro," 507–517.
[16] Emma Sutton, "Karlowicz and *fin-de-siècle* Wagnerism," 121. *Lohengrin* had already reached Vienna in 1858, Berlin in 1859, Rotterdam in 1862, St. Petersburg in 1868, Brussels in 1870, New York and Bologna in 1871, London in 1875, Rome in 1878, Nice (its first performance in France) and Madrid in 1881, and Lisbon, Buenos Aires, and Rio de Janeiro in 1883. Other works by Wagner, such as *Tristan* and *Die Meistersinger*, present a similar history. By comparison, *Lohengrin* took 37 years to reach Paris, at which time it was given at a lesser theater (the Eden), taking another four years for the work to reach the Opéra.

Puccini.[17] Christopher Charles has analyzed the repertory of operas in Parisian theaters and concluded that "[t]he lasting success of Italian composers and their French counterparts, along with [a policy] of translation [into Italian or French], underscores the resistance of the international public's taste, and not just France's, to the innovations identified with Wagner." Charle also reminds us that "[i]n the aftermath of defeat in 1871, not only was Wagner banned from French stages, but no French composer could allow himself to be suspected of importing elements of Wagner's work under a native guise."[18] Unlike Verdi's, or later Puccini's operas, Wagner's full-scale music dramas took a long time to be performed outside Germany and European main theaters, and they were not repeated enough to make an impact beyond very closed circles. In Buenos Aires, another major operatic center in the Americas, for example, the dates for premieres of fully staged Wagner operas replicated the presentations in Rio de Janeiro and, similarly, they were always presented in Italian by Italian companies.[19] John Koegel and Hanna Chan have shown that in the United States, groups of German immigrants were for the most part those who supported the performances of Wagner's music.[20] Chan notes the limited extent to which U.S. audiences facilitated—and themselves engaged with—the Wagner transatlantic connection, and that "the nineteenth-century mania for Wagner [in the U.S.] . . . was primarily led by the middle and upper-middle classes (encompassing of Anglo- and German-Americans) who were guided by the notion that cultivating an appreciation of his music enabled their social mobility."[21] Social mobility, rather than musical taste, was behind these presentations. In European cities it was no different. In Madrid, not until the last years of the 19th century did local audiences see and hear staged performances of works other than *Lohengrin*, *Rienzi* (1842), and *Tannhäuser*.[22] In Lisbon, as in Rio de Janeiro and Buenos Aires, it took until 1883

---

[17] See Thomas Kaufman's review of Huebner's *French Opera at the Fin de Siecle: Wagnerism, Nationalism, and Style* (Oxford: Oxford University Press, 1999) in *The Opera Quarterly* 18, no. 2 (2002): 265, where he contests Huebner's assertion that Wagner was by far the most frequently performed composer in the Opera in the 1890s. The first complete Wagner production at the Opéra (Paris) after *Tannhäuser* did not take place until 1891 (*Lohengrin*), with all of the composer's operas appearing in the following two decades.

[18] Charle, "Opera in France and Italy," 257.

[19] Donald Dolkart, "The Bayreuth of South America: Wagnerian Opera in Buenos Aires," *The Opera Quarterly* 1, no. 3 (1983): 84–100.

[20] Hanna Chan, "Der Ring des Nibelungen in the New World: The American Performance and Reception of Wagner's Cycle, 1850–1903," PhD dissertation, University of Illinois at Urbana-Champaign, 2014; John Koegel, *Music in German Immigrant Theater: New York City 1840–1940* (Rochester, NY: University of Rochester Press, 2009). See also Joseph Horowitz, *Wagner Nights: An American History* (Berkeley: University of California Press, 1994).

[21] Chan, "Der Ring des Nibelungen," 3.

[22] *Rienzi* premiered in Madrid in 1876; *Lohengrin* in 1881, *Tannhäuser* in 1890, *Meistersinger* in 1893, and *Die Walküre* in 1899. In 1901, the whole Tetralogy was presented; in 1909, *Siegfried* and *Götterdämmerung*, in 1910 *Das Rheingold*, and *Tristan und Isolde* in 1911; see Palona Ortiz-de-Urbina Sobrino, "Primera reecepción de Richard Wagner en Madrid," in *The Legacy of Richard*

326 MUSIC AND COSMOPOLITANISM

for *Lohengrin* to be presented, again in Italian and, like in Rio de Janeiro, it was ill-received by audiences and critics. When, in 1893, *Lohengrin* was repeated and *Der Fligender Hollander* arrived, the reception was no different; *Tristan* and *The Ring* had to wait until the 1908/1909 season.[23] In Poland and other European cities outside the major operatic theatrical hubs in Germany and England, the staging of Wagner's works followed the same pattern as in Rio de Janeiro.[24]

If one is to forgo the limited number of musical centers that have served to assert Wagner's dominant role in the music of the long 19th century, and instead focus on the many places where Wagner's operas were performed a meager number of times, several decades after their premieres, and mostly subsidized by a limited number of individuals and governmental institutions, a different picture than the one painted by Taruskin and Chaves emerges. In most cases, fully staged works reached people some 30–50 years after they were written. To claim Wagner's role in the turn-of-the-20th-century musical world, one could suggest that Wagner's works were ahead of their time, or that they endured over time, or one could follow the modernist dogma and claim that success with the public is oppositional to musical value. Yet, at the end of the century, audiences and critics were not always in disagreement regarding Wagner's music. If his works were a novelty in the middle and second parts of the 19th century, they hardly spoke to the context of the growing and fragmented urban audiences at the beginning of the 20th century, even among those whose social standing allowed them to regularly attend the opera house and to use such access to impose their social status. In this context, claims about the pursuit of the new and a break with the past that support claims about Wagner's music become very deceiving, especially when, as John Deathridge argues, they rely on assumptions that the "newness" which

---

Wagner: Convergences and Dissonances in Aesthetics and Reception, ed. Luca Sala (Turnhalt, Belgium: Brepols, 2012), 399–416.

[23] See Maria José Artiaga, "Continuity and Change in Three Decades of Portuguese Musical Life," PhD dissertation, Royal Holloway, University of London, 2007, 98–107; Paulo de Castro, "Wagnerism at the Edge: Some Aspects of Richard's Wager's Impact on Portuguese Fin-de-Siècle Culture," in *The Legacy of Richard Wagner: Convergences and Dissonances in Aesthetics and Reception*, ed. Luca Sala (Turnhalt, Belgium: Brepols, 2012), 417–432; Maria João Rodrigues de Araújo, *The Reception of Wagner in Portugal: From the Dawn of Wagnerism to Its Apogee (1880–1930)* (London: Lambert Academic Publishing, 2010); and Silva, *Entertaining Lisbon*, 91–92.

[24] See Rosamund Bartlett, *Wagner and Russia* (Cambridge, UK: Cambridge University Press, 1995); Hannu Salmi, *Wagner and Wagnerism in Nineteenth-Century Sweden, Finland, and the Baltic Provinces: Reception, Enthusiasm, Cult* (Rochester, NY: University of Rochester Press, 2005): for the late performances of Wagner's works and the dominance of French opera in the Baltic countries, see 124–125; for the late arrival of Wagner's opera in Sweden, see 227–228; and for the prevalence of *Tannhäuser*, 229–231. See also Stephen Muir and Anastasia Belina-Johnson, eds., *Wagner in Russia, Poland and the Czech Lands: Musical, Literary, and Cultural Perspectives* (Farnham, UK: Ashgate, 2013); for the competition of Puccini and Wagner, see Alexandra Wilson, *The Puccini Problem: Opera, Nationalism, and Modernity* (Cambridge, UK: Cambridge University Press, 2007), in particular, 40–68.

rested in his works, according to some critics, could continue to be so 50 plus years after the works' premieres. The premise that "the pursuit of the new can only achieve its aim through rupture and discontinuity," Deathridge notes, "is a burden the moment it embraces the possibility of failing to break with the past,"[25] or to endure in the future. Most importantly, the historical determinism of the overall literature on Wagner's music is thus confronted by its limited globalizing force and is suggestive of critical and scholarly hegemonic stances. Mark Evarisk has argued that overall, German theater music played a much smaller role on the European stage than is claimed in modern histories of music if compared with "Franco-Italian" works. He calls it a "mismatch" between the narrative of Teutonic Universalism and "the reality of the cosmopolitan basis for almost everything that underpinned quotidian musical life."[26]

Studying the use of Wagner's operatic music in the publications of excerpts and arrangements in the United States as the 19th century came to a close, Matthew Blackmar highlights a "disconnect between historiography and historical reality." Blackmar points out that if Wagner's innovations were achieved through the Musikdrama, that achievement paled in comparison to the high number of arrangements of excerpts of his early operas *Tannhäuser* and *Lohengrin*. He points to a "false theology [that] conflated historical economic realities with Wagner's artistic development from opera to Musikdrama," and claims that "however important *Der Ring des Nibelungen* came to be perceived in the history of art music, at no point during the nineteenth century did any of its attendant music dramas eclipse *Tannhäuser* as a source of sheet music sales . . . [as well as] orchestral concert excerpts, and band transcriptions," which were also regularly performed in German popular music theaters in New York.[27] That assertion would also be correct if one considers the stagings of Wagner's operas elsewhere in the Americas.

It may well be, as Hannus Salmi suggests, that with the 1876 opening of Bayreuth, Wagner's focus changed away from promoting an outward, border-crossing dimension for his works and instead moved toward a centripetal approach, to a centralized worldview of Wagnerism.[28] Furthermore, even if a few of Wagner's works did circulate beyond Europe, in practical terms the sheer size and economic investments needed to fully stage Wagner's later music dramas as the composer envisioned them made them much less portable than other competing forms of musical theater that dominated the emerging music business. When

---

[25] John Deathridge, *Wagner beyond Good and Evil* (Berkeley and Los Angeles: University of California Press, 2008, Kindle), especially the section "Configurations of the New."

[26] Evarisk, *Music History and Cosmopolitanism*, 13 and 27.

[27] Matthew Blackmar, "Wagner Domesticated, Wagner Democratized: The Parlor Reception of *Musikdrama*," Master's thesis, California State University, Long Beach, 2012, 78, and 97–98.

[28] Salmi, *Wagner and Wagnerism*, 225.

328   MUSIC AND COSMOPOLITANISM

a few works finally branched outside a couple of Europe's main theaters, they were not only passé, but they had competitors of many ilk, works that together could better express the multiplicity of tastes, technological advances, and the heterogeneous nature of the new times, in the opera house and in many other sociocultural contexts. In fact, the unequivocal association of Wagner's operas with an exclusive elite and institutionalizing agents at a time of extreme social fragmentation points to the reactionary and selective, rather than the revolutionary and universal, contexts in which Wagner's music and ideas flourished. In addition, when performed under less-than-ideal conditions, the ideology and claimed novelty behind Wagner's musical dramas and their dependence on visual and sonic spectacles to affect the audience were mostly lost. Yet the composer's not-so-new and not-so-unique ideas of how music could propel the drama, and his harmonic and orchestral techniques to make that happen in practice, have served well to support the myth of origins in the teleological narrative of Wagner's relevance in an age dominated by the circulation of images and new technologies such as film and recording. Marcia Citron and Anthony Sheppard have rightly asked "Why Wagner?" since many other opera composers, Puccini in particular, have provided far more up-to-date creative connections between music, technology, and visual effects at the service of storytelling.[29] In practice, Wagner's musical ideals and their impacts on the turn-of-the-century cosmopolitan network of musical sharing were seldom realized, especially in a time when musicians and performers were experimenting with alternative ways of performing and conceiving music and venturing into larger cultural markets requiring adaptability and flexibility of techniques and styles.

In turn-of-the-century Rio de Janeiro, and in many cities of similar sizes, the success of Wagner's music and its supposed aesthetic supremacy were imagined and reshaped by a very small group of intellectuals, composers, and critics who were sometimes not themselves fully convinced by the controversies that the music provoked. In Rio de Janeiro, a small group of Wagner devotees, congregated in and around the Instituto Nacional de Música, bolstered their political and authoritative power by supporting Wagner's ideas, and suggesting that Wagner's work was the realization of a musical modernity that the new nation should embrace. Nonetheless, if a few works composed by Brazilian composers as symphonic poems and short operas reveal links to Wagnerisms in terms of orchestration and overall harmonic devices, they were composed with and performed amid many musical grammars that also betray links to Schumann, Mendelson, Liszt, Berlioz, Fauré, Debussy, and many others. In the

---

[29] Marcia Citron, "Visual Media," in *The Oxford Handbook of Opera*, ed. Helen Greenwald (Oxford: Oxford University Press, 2014), 927. The citation is from Anthony Sheppard, "Review of *Wagner and Cinema*, ed. Jeongwon Joe and Sander Gilman," *Journal of the American Musicological Society* 64, no. 2 (2011): 444–455.

cosmopolitan city, there was no such a thing as purist Wagnerism. In the 1920s and 1930s, when a nationalistic political narrative started to dominate intellectual discourses in Brazil, the pseudo power of Wagner's European-ness and modernity were rarified in critics' rhetoric, becoming but an idiosyncratic venture of a few aficionados like Chaves.

Yet during the first two decades of the Republic, critics regularly published in daily newspapers and magazines translations of articles about Wagner excerpted from Parisian outlets in an attempt to ignite local musical partisanship that equaled the Parian controversies. It was also not unusual for them to articulate those ideas themselves, especially as a means of comparison with and praise of a local composers' work: the more they could point to some kind of Wagnerism, the better the work, in their view. In 1905, playing the sick and suffering bohemian, Duque ventured into music criticism to comment on the premiere of *The Meistersingers* in Rio de Janeiro. His narrative is a testament to the social segregationist and aesthetic reactionary views postulated by powerful individuals under the guise of Wagnerism. In an article Duque praises the work and the composer while scorning the local elite's pretentious engagement with it. Rio de Janeiro's audiences were pseudo-Wagnerians, Duque suggested, they were not good enough to engage with the "Master" composer:

> An ugly theater with an ugly room, where [Rio de Janeiro] hosted the society with its entertaining [and] twinkling precious metals, which rubbed against the white epidermis that emerged from soft luxurious fabrics, and the severe negritude of the smoking [jackets] of the well-groomed men. . . . *Wagnolatria* also reached us Brazilians but in a very strange way, since some imprudent Wagnerians . . . are of a fragrant incoherence with the artistic ideal of the great master. Captivated by leitmotivs and touched by the vibrations of the instrumental grandeur of the Pilgrims' Chorus [from *Tannhäuser*], they contradict themselves in their enthusiasm and love . . . for one would expect that the admiration or, better, the cult of the art . . . should impede the same level of admiration for opposing [aesthetic] productions. But this is precisely what happens with the Wagnerians of my acquaintance. . . . The master's aesthetic, founded on the principle of an idealist art, profoundly humanist, and in a new form that orients other artistic manifestations, should be followed in all of its precepts and not utilized to suit other purposes . . . [in Rio de Janeiro] [the master's] art is trivialized by these beautiful men, well-groomed and dressed, and who claim to know the musical transcendentalism of *Parsifal* and *Tristan*; [what they] show is that all human culture is subject to trivialization and hypocrisy.[30]

---

[30] Gonzaga Duque, "Três imagens de Wagner," in *Graves & Frivolos* (Lisbon: Livraria Classica, 1910), 89–96.

330   MUSIC AND COSMOPOLITANISM

Duque's scoffing at the local audience's engagement with Wagner's drama is symptomatic of the bohemian scorn for the status quo, but his critique is not directed at the music itself, to which he does not devote a single word, but at those who attempt and never reach the necessary aesthetic purity and uncontested loyalty he believed the composer deserved. For Duque, Rio de Janeiro's opera goers were not "perfect Wagnerites,"[31] for they attended Wagner's opera one night, just to flock to the nearest theaters to hear operettas and Italian operas the next day. The heterogeneity and fragmentation of music repertories characteristic of the period, the audience's eclectic musical tastes, and "admiration of opposing [aesthetic] productions" tainted the Master's ideal: in Duque's view, Rio de Janeiro's audiences did not deserve Wagner.

Wagner's music did find fertile grounds in which to grow in the city, however, if in alternative formats and performance venues. Following contemporary practice, his music was heard mostly outside the theatrical and dramatic context, presented in excerpts and, alongside a myriad of musics from other composers, it was reworked to fit various performance media. Excerpts reduced for soloist with accompaniment, or orchestral excerpts with and without chorus, mainly from popular early works like *Lohengrin* and especially from *Tannhäuser,* were regularly included in concerts, while they also circulated in sheet music publications for domestic consumption. In this case, Wagner's works were an attraction not for his attempts to associate music, drama, and various media, but possibly for some specific harmonic and timbre combinations, and mostly for his exceptional moments of melodic creation, which are abundant in his overtures, orchestral interludes, choral passages, or excerpted vocal lines replicated in various formats and performance media. If one is to look at the many sounds and musics that made up the cosmopolitan city, one needs to consider the potential of Wagner's melodies to make him into "a drawing room composer," as Salmi has suggested.[32] In fact, it was in this context that Wagner's music became a part of the turn-of-the-century urban cultural network. Like the musics of operettas and Italian opera, the wider reception of Wagner's works rested on their fragments, for excerpts with songful and memorable melodies were scattered in concerts and performed by many wind bands in arranged versions. Wagner himself first shunned arrangements of his work but slowly gave in, first by authorizing a few arrangements by Liszt and then by using excerpts to create anticipation for his upcoming works, as in a sneak-preview, and "leaving the staging to the imagination," a clever marketing move that shows his engagements with early capitalist

---

[31] A reference to George Bernard Shaw, *The Perfect Wagnerite: A Commentary on the Ring of the Niblungs* [*sic*] (London: G. Richards, 1898).

[32] Salmi, *Wagner and Wagnerism*, 31–55; for the popularity of *Tannhäuser* and *Lohengrin* over other works, see 38–39.

practices.[33] But, above all, Liszt also engaged with fragments of Wagner's work, a different musical aesthetic and practice than Wagner's impetus for a total interconnection of the many elements of his operas.[34]

Most importantly, the mode of reception of Wagner's music was not separated from the modes of reception of arias from Italian and French operas: they were listened to as melodies, ones that are easily remembered and repeated. Books of compilation of the so-called leitmotifs with melodies from Wagner's operas propelled the works' many extra lives. These books became the means by which audiences who were not familiar with Wagner's work could grasp the idea of a "total artwork," contradictorily, by engaging with their fragmented melodies. By the turn of the 20th century, these books were circulating independently from staged presentations alongside reductions and arrangements of the tunes. Wagner's conception of "melodic moments" as nonverbal artistic expression was easily detached from the whole, the music drama, to circulate with titles that could bring meaning to a melodic line confronting Wagner's own distrust in adding titles to music.[35]

Blackmar also claims that Wagner's works traveled in excerpted print materials to become a part of the "culture of print media," as his music was stripped from their operatic and dramatic context, their timbre coloristic, sonic depth (no orchestra), harmonic, and scenic experimentation, a path traveled by the works of many other opera composers.[36] And since excerpts were printed as potpourris and arrangements for specific instrumental groups, it was common practice that the author be listed alongside the arranger and the title of the work, and sometimes the author was ignored altogether, only the title and the arranger remaining. As the work was diluted further and further in rearrangements and reworkings, it eventually lost its relation to an author and an original altogether.[37] If print culture played a role in the dissemination of Wagner's music, it may also, contradictorily, have played a role in effacing his authorial role. The grandeur and ideological and political roles in which the narratives of Wagner's music's all-encompassing uniqueness and universality rested have been slowly diluted through its extra-lives to become part of everyday urban experiences of many.[38] In Rio de Janeiro, excerpts of Wagner's works started to become more evident in

---

[33] Salmi, *Wagner and Wagnerism*, 38, and Vassonyi, *Richard Wagner*, 191. See also Kenneth Hamilton, "Wagner and Liszt: Elective Affinities," in *Richard Wagner and His World*, ed. Thomas Grey (Princeton, NJ: Princeton University Press, 2009), 33–43; and Thomas Christensen, "Sounding Offstage," in *The Oxford Handbook of Opera*, ed. Helen Greenwald (Oxford: Oxford University Press, 2014), 900.

[34] Hamilton, "Wagner and Liszt," 59.

[35] Christian Thorau, "Guides for Wagnerites: Leitmotifs and Wagnerian Listening," in *Wagner and His World*, ed. Thomas Grey (Princeton, NJ: Princeton University Press, 2009), 138.

[36] Blackmar, "Wagner Domesticated," 24–25.

[37] Blackmar, "Wagner Domesticated," 97–98.

[38] Blackmar, "Wagner Domesticated," 83 and 99.

332 MUSIC AND COSMOPOLITANISM

the first decade of the 20th century as a part of a wide palette of options available as models for young composers, as offerings to concert and movie audiences, as alternatives to those making music at home, and to those who preferred to enjoy them at the music hall. It is in these environments that Wagner's works found their most enduring social, cultural, and political relevance, as part of urban heterogeneous settings where his expressive melodies, which if not altogether singable were undoubtedly memorable, traveled easily to become an important part of the 20th-century cosmopolitan city.

The Concert Hall and the Music Hall

It was thus in an instrumental excerpt that Wagner's music appeared during the Rio de Janeiro concert to celebrate the first anniversary of the proclamation of the Republic, on November 16, 1890. Organized and conducted by Miguez, now the director of the Instituto Nacional de Música, the concert was offered as a matinée at 1:00 p.m. at the Theatro Lyrico. It was featured as part of a two-day event that included various civic celebrations, when ships at the port and military quarters were illuminated, military bands performed through the streets, and a brigade of 7,000 men marched toward the Praça da República.[39] Miguez's choice for the program was supposed to entice an audience consisting of distinguished government officials and diplomatic corps, with many authorities supportive of the new regime and with the president in attendance. The concert opened with Miguez's own anthem to the Republic, with its reminiscences of "La Marseillaise" (see Chapter 3), followed by: Wagner's *Rienzi* overture; a "French song" "Prúre de soir" by C. Reinecke; a "Swedish song" by J. S. Swendsen; Berlioz's "Hungarian march"; Miguez's symphonic poem *Ave Libertas!*; "Samba" from *Scenas brasileiras* (1890) by Alexandre Levy (1864–1892); and an "Intermezzo Symphonico" by Carlos Gomes. The concert closed with Silva's national anthem. Miguez was entrusted with the difficult task of organizing a concert that helped conjure up civic feelings and much-needed public support during a very unstable political period, thus his inclusion of two patriotic anthems that had recently been the subject of passionate discussions in the press (see Chapter 3). The inclusion of Alexandre Levy's "Samba," written as an homage to the 1888 abolition of slavery, another recent event that galvanized the entire country, also shows Miguéz's use of music at the service of politics. Most of all, Miguez's own *Ave Libertas!* was written especially for the event and was dedicated to President

---

[39] *O Paiz*, November 11, 1890, describes the celebrations; *O Paiz*, November 17, 1890, includes a review of the concert by Oscar Guanabarino.

A WORLD OF MANY MUSICS   333

Deodoro da Fonseca, placing him at the musical center within the new military regime's motto of "order and progress."

Blatant call for patriotism notwithstanding, the concert also exhibited a distinctively eclectic grouping of pieces and composers, works that can be seen today as accounts of the period's diverse musical worlds. In fact, the program shows a side of Miguez's ideas for the Musical Republic that conflicts with the common narrative of his utter devotion to Wagner and Wagnerism. Miguez's choice of musical numbers for such a high-profile event shows the cosmopolitan context of his aspirations and foreshadows the nature of his 12-year leadership at the government-subsidized Instituto Nacional de Música. Wagner's overture to *Rienzi* (1842), performed during the celebratory concert outside its dramatic context was nonetheless well placed here, for this early work is packed with memorable melodic lines surrounded by horn calls and a concluding military march made to fit the occasion. Berlioz's Hungarian march from *La damnation of Faust* (1846), which by 1890 was a favorite in concert halls throughout Europe, also fit the program well with its opening military call, engaging tunes, and its many brass outbursts toward the end. Miguez's own *Ave Libertas!* in the form of a symphonic poem and set in a schematic sonata form, also includes a section with a military march that fits well as a companion to Wagner's and Berlioz's works.[40] Still, Miguez's choice of musical numbers was not totally devoted to national militarism to accord with the political moment. On the contrary, the composer assumed that government officials, local personalities, and the select audience in attendance would also welcome songs in many languages and styles by composers of many nationalities. In fact, rather than highlighting Miguez's Wagnerian inclination, the program exemplifies Duque's concern about the local bourgeoisie's heterogeneous tastes and their lack of unconditional reverence for Wagner.

Miguez supported the use of music for education as a tool for aesthetic discernment following ideals of musical progress envisioned by republican officials, ideas that were also widespread in many places in Europe and the Americas, promulgated by those in charge of the politics of culture. These goals were compatible with many European "schools," past and present, rather than an acquiescence to a specific musical style. When in 1896 Miguez extended his pre-planned trip to Europe in search of music schools that could serve as models for Rio de Janeiro's Instituto Nacional de Música, he visited an assortment of music schools in Paris, Vienna, Prague, Brussels, Dresden, Leipzig, Cologne, Berlin, Munich, Rome, Naples, Milan, Florence, Genoa, Bologna, and Turin.[41] Overall,

---

[40] For an analysis of the work, see Norton Dudeque, "Ave, Libertas!, Op. 18 de Leopoldo Miguéz, considerações sobre a estrutura musical," *OPUS* 27, no. 1 (January–April 2021): 1–23.

[41] Monica Vermes, "Por uma renovação do ambiente musical brasileiro: O relatório de Leopoldo Miguez sobre os conservatórios europeus," *Revista eletrônica de musicologia* 8 (December 2004). The report is reproduced in Renato Carlos Nogueira Figueiredo, "O piano de Miguez: subsídios para um

334 MUSIC AND COSMOPOLITANISM

German schools leveled better in his view than the Italian ones because, according to his report, the latter lacked discipline and used outmoded methods, while the German schools showed better organization and disciplined teachers and students. There were, however, good things and bad things about each school he visited, according to his report, even if he downgraded Italian music for being in a "state of decadence." Yet Miguez did not list a specific repertory that students at Instituto Nacional de Música should pursue or avoid. He notes that the majority of the Institute's students were female pianists and singers who were restricted to a repertory suitable to their performing media, rather than to a specific composer. Furthermore, throughout Miguez's tenure he could not secure a stable orchestra with students and teachers of the institution without hiring musicians from outside, mostly musicians from opera companies on tour in the city, a reality that further restricted the knowledge of and engagement with orchestral music and "classical" composers of Austro-German provenance. Thus, the concerts organized by the institution he led were varied in terms of styles, provenances, composers, historical period, and performing media. While Miguez believed that a full orchestra was needed to communicate social and aesthetic values, the nature of the music presented at the institution was nothing but an eclectic grouping of pieces. This was a reality in turn-of-the-century Rio de Janeiro, as well as in other contemporary cities, where devotion to a particular composer, or group of composers from a particular country, time period, or musical style, was not the rule. A list of "great composers" was wide and their "musical works" were presented according to the available resources. William Weber observed that in the first decade of the 20th century in Europe, the miscellanea of orchestral and vocal pieces of the early 1800s diminished but still persisted, even when presented in more socially exclusive venues. Weber argues that social and cultural institutions established in musical life in 1850 remained in place until the onset of the Great War and the predominance of composers of one or two generations earlier became commonplace, while new works, unfamiliar to audiences, became more difficult to program.[42]

In Rio de Janeiro, the programs of the "Concertos populares" (Popular concerts) organized by Carlos de Mesquita (1870–1916) can serve as examples of Weber's claims. In a concert on April 29, 1890, Mesquita offered: Beethoven's 4th Symphony; Massenet's "Le dernier sommeil de la vierge"; Saint-Saëns's symphonic poem *Phaeton*, and the ballet from *Henry the VIII*; Tchaikosvisky's

---

resgate interpretativo," Master's thesis, Universidade de São Paulo, USP, 2003. See also Maria Alice Volpe, "Compositores românticos brasileiros: estudos na Europa," *Revista Brasileira de Música* 21/51–76 (1994–1995): 60.

[42] Weber, *The Great Transformation of Musical Taste* (Cambridge, UK: Cambridge University Press, 2008), 305 and 312.

Capriccio italiano; Gounod's march from *La reine de Saba*; and a Gavotte by the local Delgado de Carvalho (1884–1980).[43] On May 19, 1891, in addition to his own compositions, Mesquita's program included works by Beethoven, Massenet's "Sènes Pittoresques," excerpts from his *Le roi de Lahore*, alongside works by Vieuxtemps, Charpentier, Guiraud, Gounod, Delibes, Moskowski, Rossini, and excerpts from Wagner's operas.[44] A pianist, composer, and a student of Massenet, Mesquita's endeavor to present orchestral concerts with a mission of "educating" Rio de Janeiro's audiences was in sync with Pasdeloup's Paris concerts at mid-century and later with the Colonne et Lamoureux concerts.[45] His choices were veered toward his experiences in Paris and show his bias toward his teachers at the Conservatoire. Nonetheless, a local critic noted that Mesquita's concerts were successful exactly because he knew how to put together "music that is good and varied, to please the public who is not made up of professionals." The critic also pointed out that;

[i]f [Mesquita] gave us just the grave and profound German classics, it is most likely that it would chill the audience's ears and put to sleep the neophytes. Instead, he gives us the incomparable Beethoven alongside the brilliant Massenet and the most original Saint-Saëns, and many others representatives of the modern school. The program of the concert was conciliating and very adequate to its goals.[46]

In June 1896, Artur Azevedo wrote in his weekly chronicle about the difficulty in forming a stable audience in Rio de Janeiro for the concert hall, suggesting that musical variety could be a worthy strategy:

The first focus of our artists and dilettantes, with the noble goal of developing our musical taste, is to conquer the public through a well-devised catechism. Residents of Rio de Janeiro are eclectic in terms of musical taste and have prejudice against concerts; it is necessary to persuade them that this generous attempt is done with the goal of offering them a few hours of delight and not of imposing them with a program that they will take because *noblesse oblige*.[47]

That was the idea in the Symphonic Concerts put together in 1901 by Francisco Braga, who had recently arrived from his studies in Paris. In addition

---

[43] *Gazeta de Notícias*, April 29, 1890.

[44] These programs were advertised in newspapers; I also used the programs themselves, held at the Divisão de Música, National Library at Rio de Janeiro.

[45] Yannick Simon, *Jules Pasdeloup et les origines du concert populaire* (Lyon: Symétrie, 2011).

[46] *Gazeta de Notícias*, May 20, 1901.

[47] *A Notícia*, May 4, 1896; cited in Ferreira, "Cenários da ópera," 48.

336 MUSIC AND COSMOPOLITANISM

to his own works, the program included music by Tchaikovsky, Saint-Saëns, Carlos Gomes, H. Vieuxtemps, Mozart, Wagner, Gounod, Schubert, Carl Weber, Van Westerhout, and A. Levy. Six years later, Nepomuceno continued Mesquita's Concertos Populares at the Theatro Lyrico with programs that featured excerpts from a few of Wagner's operas, works by Saint-Saëns, Luigi Mancinelli, Wieniawsky, Carlos Gomes, Carl Weber, Donizetti, Glinka, Beethoven, Gounod, E. Oswald, Miguez, Schumann, and Berlioz. In 1898, the Italian Vicenzo Cernicchiaro managed to put together an orchestra of 80 musicians for a "Grand Symphonic Concert" in Rio de Janeiro that included Liszt, Chopin, Chaminade, Grieg, Wagner, J. S. Bach, Chopin, and Andersen. The programs of concerts held at the Instituto Nacional de Música's concert hall highlighted an even larger variety of pieces, for here there was a predominance of solo and chamber pieces performed by students and teachers. The concert organized by Ignácio Porto Alegre on May 5, 1895, for example, included works by Chopin, Haendel, Vieuxtemps, Wieniawsky, Verdi, D. Popper, Schumann, Liszt, Palestrina, and Massenet.[48] This miscellanea of authors, styles, and periods was the result of the availability of instruments and performers, rather than devotion to a specific composer, style, or genre, while the music's European provenance is evident. Overall, in all of these concerts one can observe a clear predominance of short works, programmatic works, excerpts from operatic music, and of soloists with orchestral accompaniment.

When Mesquita established himself in Paris for good later in the 1890s, several individuals attempted similar educational projects to continue to shape the audience's taste as they saw appropriate. The formation of a Sociedade de Concertos Populares in 1897 is a case in point. The society started with a meeting that took place at the music store owned by Portuguese pianist Arthur Napoleão and included the following individuals who supported the Instituto Nacional de Música: Ferreira de Araújo as president, Harold Hime as vice president (substituting for Delgado de Carvalho), Luiz Castro as secretary, Arthur Napoleão as treasurer, and Nepomuceno as artistic director. The group recruited teachers from the Instituto Nacional de Música to form the orchestra, but also needed musicians from the Italian opera company directed by the Italian Sansone, who was invited to be part of the group. In the end, they managed to assemble an orchestra of 60 musicians to perform four concerts at the Theatro Lyrico between June and August 1897. According to the resolution taken at the meeting, the programs should include orchestral pieces and works for solo voice, piano, violin, and cello, by the following composers: Beethoven, Mozart, Berlioz, Bizet, Schumann, Glinka, Pierné, Mancinelli, Godard, Massenet, Saint-Saëns, Vianna da Motta, Wagner, and Widor. The organizers promised first

---

[48] *Gazeta de Notícias*, May 5, 1895.

A WORLD OF MANY MUSICS   337

auditions of Glinka's *Kamarinskaya*, Bizet's *Petit suite d'orchestre*, Piernier's *First suite d'orchestre*, Vianna da Motta's Symphony *Pátria*, excerpts from Wagner's *Die Walküre, Parsifal, Das Rheingold*, and Widor's *Korrigana*. Schumann's piano concerto in A minor (1845) and Saint-Saëns's 5th piano concerto (1896) were also promised in first performances, in addition to auditions of works by local composers, such as Nepomuceno's *Suite Brazileira*, H. Oswald's *Suite d'orchestre*, Francisco Valle's *Poema Symphonico*, and Miguez's orchestration of A. Levy's "Variaçoes sobre o Bitu."[49] Forwarding almost 10 years to the concerts organized by Alberto Nepomuceno for the 1908 celebration of the opening of the ports in Rio de Janeiro, all the composers above are still featured, with the addition of a few orchestral works by Debussy, performed for the first time in Rio de Janeiro. Yet there is still no predominance of a composer or a musical style: the unifying feature continues being the media in which the music was delivered, orchestral music, with and without a soloist, and the way in which the music was presented, with elaborate programs and explicative notes that translated to the audiences the history and significance of the works.

That such a heterogeneity was expected in the concert hall, and not only in the music hall, is a reality that confronts the narrative about the dominance of a particular repertory within the institutionalized realms of the city. Instead, what these Concertos Populares show is a variety of old and new works by many composers of many provenances presented in a variety of instrumentations. As Rick Altman has noted,

> Though each late-nineteenth century musical domain provides a character-istic model, different in important ways from all others, we may identify three common strategies bridging several contemporary musical contexts. The broadest tendency involves what I have called the "aesthetic of discontinuity," whereby divergent sound experiences alternated within a single program. . . . Today's assumptions about the importance of clearly integrating all elements of a performance were not operative at this time.[50]

Altman is referencing the music performed in movie theaters, music halls, and vaudeville shows at the beginning of the 20th century, but the discontinuity, already pointed out by Weber, was a reality of the many musical contexts of the turn-of-the-20th-century modern city. In addition, while heterogeneous programs continued to be the rule rather than the exception, the vast majority of their musical content was also regularly performed as preludes to film, and

---

[49] An article with the details about the Sociedade de Concertos Populares appeared in *Gazeta de Notícias*, June 2, 1897.
[50] Altman, *Silent Film Sound*, 51.

338 MUSIC AND COSMOPOLITANISM

excerpts of songs and short instrumental pieces, such as marches, polkas, and waltzes, were also heard at the music hall and other informal musical gatherings, and were not an exclusive domain of the concert hall.[51] Yet it is the search for one performance of works of one composer, Wagner, that have occupied most narratives of music-making in the domains of Rio de Janeiro's concert halls.

No Extra-Lives

No composer's story in Rio de Janeiro was dictated by the Wagner spell as much as that of Miguez, to the point that it has become almost impossible to view the composer in any other light. In fact, to composers of Miguez's generation, in Europe and elsewhere, Wagner's shadow became more overbearing than inspirational or visionary. Miguez was educated in Porto, Portugal, as a violinist, and his early musical career in Rio de Janeiro was set not in an environment where works by Wagner had any significance. Although a businessman early in his career, Miguez managed to perform regularly at local concerts as an amateur violinist and wrote a few short pieces for orchestra, for piano, voice, and anthems much in vogue. In 1880, he decided to quit the music business and devote himself to performing and composing full-time. His first positions as a conductor and his early compositions show that he was exposed to many musics, in particular those trending in Paris, Brussels, Lisbon, and Porto, places where he had kept connections since his childhood, and suggests that his musical output and his career as a conductor and composer could easily be retold from this viewpoint. His many works written for the piano show his attention to works by Schumann and Liszt, among many others; they were short pieces, with straightforward melodies and accompaniments appropriate for a salon concert, and his harmonic language looms beyond anything strictly "Wagnerian."[52] These works are nonetheless usually bypassed in favor of his orchestral works, which clearly tend more toward Liszt's and Berlioz's symphonic poems, connecting to Wagner but in indirect ways.

In December 1882, Miguez left Brazil to study in Europe and pursue an international career as a composer.[53] With a subsidy from the imperial government, Miguez arrived in Paris with a letter from Pedro II introducing him to Ambroise Thomas, the director of the Paris Conservatoire and an influential figure within the European musical world. Miguez's stay in Europe was short, however. He

---

[51] James Sanders, "The Vanguard of the Atlantic World: Contesting Modernity in Nineteenth-Century Latin America," *Latin American Research Review* 46, no. 2 (2011): 104–127.

[52] Victor Cayres de Mendonca, "The Piano Works of Leopoldo Miguéz (1850–1902)," DMA dissertation (Boston University, 2014), 101.

[53] *Jornal do Commercio*, December 9, 1882.

had a few composition classes while in Paris and attempted to have his works performed in local venues but was not successful. In August 1883, Taunay, the monarchist supporter of the arts, asked the parliament for financial assistance in support of Miguez's attempts to present his work at the prestigious Concerts Colonne at the Théâtre du Châtelet in Paris, but his motion was denied.[54] Frustrated by the failed attempts to launch a career in Paris, Miguez left France and traveled to other European musical centers with open curiosity and in search of artistic direction. In the process he was exposed to a variety of contemporary styles and techniques, fashions, ideas, experiences, and ideologies. In October 1883, Miguez returned to Rio de Janeiro, where he concentrated on writing new works and attempted to gain local recognition as a composer. With the advent of the Republic, he was appointed director of the Instituto Nacional the Música, the state-sponsored school of music, and continued to play a key role in the establishing official standards and guidelines for formal music education in the city. Unfortunately, Miguez died in 1902 at the early age of 52, at the height of his career and as Brazil's most powerful musician; he came to represent the musical status quo and the country's musical path toward a desired "musical progress."

A few years before his death, Miguez wrote an opera, *Il Saldunes* (1897–1898), with Portuguese libretto by Coelho Netto, and had it translated into Italian by H. Malaguti. The work was presented first as an oratorio on the stage of the Instituto Nacional de Música in 1900 and was staged no more than three times in 1901 at the Theatro Lyrico by an Italian opera company led by Sanzone, with an orchestra of only 62 musicians and 55 singers in the chorus, with the second concert having the Brazilian president in attendance.[55] The work was dedicated to his friend Luis Castro, a local critic and an inveterate Wagner devotee, who guided Miguez toward a Wagnerian musical language and helped delineate the narrative of the composer's Wagnerian drive. The libretto, published in Lisbon in 1900, nonetheless includes Netto's preface acknowledging the germ of the work as the French author Eugene Seu's (1804–1857) "Les mistères du Peupleu." Nevertheless, that one would translate the work based on a French tale and from Portuguese into Italian shows that, at the beginning of the century, inspiration came from a variety of sources and that Italian was still the preferred language in Rio de Janeiro's opera halls. Yet the work's Wagnerian traits are the ones that sealed Miguez's reputation as a follower of Wagner. This is evident in the article written by Artur Azevedo at the time of the premiere of *Il Saldunes*, in which the

---

[54] *Gazeta de Noticias*, August 22, 1883. *Jornal do Commercio*, August 24, 1883, includes the news about Taunay's speech in the parliament. According to the *Jornal do Commercio*, August 21, 1883, Miguez also connected with Mesquita in Paris, who was also a student at the Paris Conservatoire under Cesar Frank, Émile Durand, and Jules Massenet.

[55] *Gazeta de Notícias*, September 11 and 17, 1901.

340 MUSIC AND COSMOPOLITANISM

critic describes the opera as the summation of the composer's life's output.[56] The article describes a meeting Azevedo had with Miguez in Paris 18 years before (in 1883),[57] when Miguez was still an amateur violinist and an apprentice composer, but suggests that Miguez was already the utmost follower of Wagner's credo, which colored the understanding and critical judgment of the composer's entire output.[58] The article also shows that Azevedo—a well-read, highly educated music dilettante, and an influential individual in Rio de Janeiro's intellectual and musical circles—was oblivious to Wagner's music, and put into clear perspective the varied musical worlds that came to define European-ness from outside European centers:

> When, 18 years ago (1883), Richard Wagner died in Venice, I was in Paris, and had the pleasure of having every day the companionship of Leopoldo Miguez. . . . One night we went to the Opéra to see *Coppelia* by Léo Delibes, but the performance also included Rossini's *Le comte Ory*. I would never forget the violent and sincere indignation that (Rossini's) opera caused in Miguez. "That is not music!" he said . . . "[and] It surprises me that in Paris, the capital of the world, this kind of music is part of the repertory of the Music Academia!" I [Azevedo], who always heard Rossini with admiration and with a deference devoted to a semi-God, I who still [in 1901] admire the composer of *The Barber of Seville* and *William Tell*, was surprised when confronted with Miguez's explosion.

Azevedo continues by describing Miguez's interest in going out to hear Wagner's music instead:

> Lamoureux, who at that time offered excellent concerts at the Chateau-d'Eau every Sunday with a magnificent orchestra, [after the news of Wagner's death] immediately announced a series of Wagnerian concerts. Miguez's enthusiasm led him immediately to ask me to accompany him to the first concert. "You!," he shouted at me, "made me listen to all the music from the Excelsior and the Eden-Théatre; you, who impinged on me the operettas at the Nouveautés; you, who took me for a night at the cafés-concerts! Now as a noble vengeance, I ask you to come with me to the Chateau-d'Eau and listen to one act of the *Lohengrin* and one of the *Parsifal*!"

[56] Artur Azevedo, "O Theatro," in *A Notícia*, September 19, 1901. *Il Salduni* premiered on September 20, 1901.
[57] Artur Azevedo, "O Theatro," in *A Notícia*, September 26, 1901.
[58] Artur Azevedo, "O Theatro," in *A Notícia* September 26, 1901.

But Azevedo's reaction to the concert summed up not merely the young Miguez's interest in Wagner's music, but also his own reaction to the concert as a visual/musical spectacle:

> We heard and enjoyed the beautiful spectacle that offered a large orchestra on the stage of an amphitheater, the violin bows moved up down and the flutes moved back and forth to the performer's mouths with a symmetry and geometric precision that made me remember the choreographies of the Excelsior.... I was listening to Wagner for the first time ... and I still had in my ears the operetta's tra-la-la of the night before. But that music took me by surprise, I say it sincerely.... [Still] the spectacle that most diverted me was not the music of Wagner, but Miguez's ecstasy ... watching him enchanted by the sounds of that nebulous and fantastic music, I had the dreadful feeling of envy for not being able to understand what he understood, to hear what he was hearing, and to revel in what he was experiencing. After this memorable concert, I started to look at Miguez as a man as laudable as an eminent astronomer, who goes high into the sky through ladders made of algorithms, to borrow an expression of Michelet, and who, up from the heights, discovers the secrets of the universe.

Il Saldunes failed in Rio de Janeiro. Azevedo blamed the uneducated audience, the usual argument, and lamented that the work was "a plant born in bad soil."[59] He also resorted again to the 1883 concert in Paris he had attended with Miguez: "The audience at the [Theatro] Lyrico, hearing Miguez's music, found themselves, with rare exceptions, in the same spirits that I had found myself at the Chateau-d'Eau listening to the music of Wagner." But Azevedo also predicted that *Il Saldunes* would not die like mere humans do, but would instead survive for posterity. His prognosis did not materialize, however, for *Il Saldunes*, much unlike *Il Guarany*, did not travel beyond strictest circles or the narrative of a few critics; revivals and publications still await scholarly interest. *Il Saldunes* had no extra-lives and its relevance in the story of music is but a footnote.

Yet, while Azevedo's chronicle shows an apprentice composer fascinated by Wagner's music, it also illustrates his own contrasting position. His story tells us that the Musical Republic was not one musical world or two musical worlds contrasting each other—German versus Italian versus French—but several worlds coexisting and offering an array of possibilities to city audiences. In turn-of-the-century Rio de Janeiro, Europe was a Babel of places.[60] From the concert hall to the music hall, many worlds dispersed and were pasted together in

---

[59] Artur Azevedo, "O caso dos Saldunes," *A Notícia*, December 19, 1901.
[60] For a similar suggestion regarding the European novel, see Moretti, *Distant Reading*, 46.

new alternative musical possibilities that do not make sense to the eyes and ears of those looking for musical coherence. We might be tempted to keep looking for Wagnerisms in Miguez's music after Azevedo's passionate chronicle and, as many scholars have shown, we would find plenty. But while Miguez's symphonic poems *Ave Libertas!* and *Prometeus!* show that, like many composers of his generation, he was attentive to how orchestration and harmonic blocks could enhance the musical experience, he was also a composer, like many others of his generation, who navigated the business of music at a time of constant sociopolitical changes, when the relevance of music as an individual expression was confronted by the listenings and expressions of many.

Assembling Music

Alberto Nepomuceno lived through the trenches of a complex *fin-de-siècle* musical world of the concert hall within its predominantly European-centered music environment (Figure 11.1). The composer lived in Germany, Italy, and France, and studied with well-known European teachers in prestigious musical institutions. In Rome, he learned from Giovanni Sgambatti at the Liceo Musicale Santa, and then traveled to Berlin, where he enrolled at the Königliche Akademie der Künste (1891–1892) under the compositional guidance of

Figure 11.1. Alberto Nepomuceno.

Heinrich von Herzogenberg. Later, Nepomuceno transferred to the Etern'sches Komservatorium der Musik, where he had composition lessons with Arno Kleffel and connected as a student and as a colleague with figures like Brahms, Max Bruch, and Schoenberg. Nepomuceno then moved to Paris, where he attended the Schola Cantorum, studied organ with Alexandre Gilmant, and interacted with well-known figures such as Saint-Saëns, Fauré, Massenet, Vincent d'Indy, and Debussy. His personal and professional life also led to connections with Edward Grieg and Gustav Mahler. Altogether, Nepomuceno's biography intersects with an array of late-19th-century Europe's prestigious music circles, names, and places.[61] Like many of his contemporaries, Nepomuceno had aspirations to write music for large audiences, both local and faraway, and to belong to a modern musical world as he perceived it: one that was shaped in Europe and that, he believed, had the potential to be timeless and universal. But Nepomuceno was not a citizen of, nor had political commitments to, any of the European countries in which he lived and traveled. At 30 years of age, he crossed the Atlantic to settle back in Rio de Janeiro and spent his life far from European concert and opera halls and the scrutiny of powerful publishers, audiences, and critics. The publications of his music during his lifetime seldom made it to the coveted venues in Europe or were heard in major cities, although some were performed in Rio de Janeiro, mostly as part of his own attempts to build his career among the local musical status quo. Within a European musical context in which he was immersed, Nepomuceno's works were out of "sight-and-ears and out of mind," a state that attests to the domain of centers of music power during his time and the predictable directions of musical flows.

At the same time, Nepomuceno's life was set in a hub of 19th-century urban cultural connections, and within this context he became an accomplished composer who acquired a solid position as the leader of Rio de Janeiro musical establishment. He was nominated director of the Instituto Nacional de Música from 1902 to 1903, and again from 1906 to 1916, and later he managed to secure government subsidies for the creation of a state orchestra. On the one hand, Nepomuceno remained imbued with core Enlightenment ideals, faithful to notions of progress and human freedom that he believed the new Republic provided: "It is through working together with intelligence that one has formed the patrimony of humanity," he noted.[62] On the other hand, the constant political and social transitions during his life left a strong mark on his understanding of the larger world around him. In this regard, Nepomuceno experienced, with

---

[61] Sérgio Alvin Correa, *Alberto Nepomuceno: Catálogo Geral* (FUNARTE/Instituto Nacional de Música, 1985).

[62] *Jornal do Comercio*, July 15, 1913; cited in Flavio Cardoso de Carvalho, "A Ópera *Abul* de Alberto Nepomuceno e sua contribuição para o patrimônio musical brasileiro da primeira república," PhD dissertation, Universidade Estadual de Campinas, 2005, 11.

344 MUSIC AND COSMOPOLITANISM

many others, the promises and disillusionments of a modernity that were inescapable to his generation, from the rise of public entertainment to the angst caused by the globalizing effects of a bloating capitalism, from the need to safeguard European masterworks, to the powerlessness of the individual within the rapidly growing political nationalism.

Recently there has been a boom in scholarly explorations of Nepomuceno's work. Wide-ranging in their methodologies and foci, these studies bring to light one major common thread: the composer's large and varied music output does not fit within the historically linear flow of developments of European musics during the period, nor does his work satisfy the scrutiny of nationalists gaining power within the government. The composer's works do not exhibit the clear-cut musical markers of locality and nationality expected to emerge from a composer of music of European derivation active outside Europe.[63] He created a campaign toward using Portuguese in songs for the concert hall after having written songs in a myriad of languages, and his crusade served well nationalist scholars in the following generation to justify his name in the pantheon of national composers.[64] At the same time, Nepomuceno's complex output shows a composer experimenting with several major trends and "isms" fashionable during his lifetime. His ability in melodic development and his fondness for classic formal structures in instrumental works have earned him the stature of a neo-Brahmsian. His exploration of ambivalent tonal centers and his regular use of altered chords have led some to align his music with contemporary Wagnerians, while pentatonicism and whole-tone scales used in many of his works put him

---

[63] Recent scholarship on the composer is mostly in Portuguese, and suggests the heterogeneous nature of his output. A selective list includes: Carvalho, "A Ópera *Abul* de Alberto Nepomuceno"; Luiz Guilherme Goldberg, *Um Guaratuja entre Wotan e o Fauno: Alberto Nepomuceno e o modernismo musical brasileiro* (Porto Alegre, Brazil: Movimento, 2011); Goldberg, "Alberto Nepomuceno: Vínculos modernistas no Trio em Fá sustenido menor (1916)," *Música em perspectiva* 3, no. 1 (2010): 1–24, online source available at https://www.researchgate.net/publicat ion/273170570_Alberto_Nepomuceno_vinculos_modernistas_no_Trio_em_Fa_sustenido_ menor_1916; João Vidal, "Formação germânica de Alberto Nepomuceno: estudos sobre recepção e intertextualidade," PhD dissertation, Universidade de São Paulo, 2011; Vidal, "Nepomuceno e Max Bruch: Análise de uma (recém-descoberta) conexão," *Revista Brasileira de Música* 24, no. 1 (2011): 129–153; Vidal, "Nepomuceno e Brahms: A questão da influência revisitada," *Música em Perspectiva* 3, no. 1 (2010): 88–135; Norton Dudeque, "Aspectos do academicismo germânico no primeiro movimento do Quarteto nº 3 de Alberto Nepomuceno," *Ictus* 6 (2005): 211–232; Dudeque, "Realismo musical no primeiro movimento da Série Brasileira de Alberto Nepomuceno," *Anais do XX Congresso da ANPPOM* (2010): 1042–1047; Rodolfo Coelho de Sousa, "Aspectos de modernidade na música de Alberto Nepomuceno relacionados ao projeto de tradução do *Harmonielehre* de Schoenberg," *Em Pauta* 17, no. 29 (2006): 63–81; Sousa, "Influencia e intertextualidade na Suite Antiga de Nepomuceno," *Música em Perspectiva* 1–2 (2008): 53–82; Sousa, "A 'Bar form' nas canções de Nepomuceno," *Revista Eletrônica de Musicologia* 11 (2007): 7–17; Souza, "A influência do simbolismo nas obras de Nepomuceno," in *Atualidade da ópera,* Annals of the International Symposium of Musicology, Universidade Federal do Rio de Janeiro, org. by Maria Alice Volpe (Rio de Janeiro: UFRJ, 2012), 223–232.

[64] See Dante Pignatari, "Canto da língua: Alberto Nepomuceno e invenção da canção Brasileira," PhD dissertation, São Paulo University, 2009.

side by side with Wagnerian opponents. As a composer dwelling with his own modernity, Nepomuceno explored the limits of tonality, experimented with the contingencies of musical form, toyed with various exoticisms, and made incursions into popular music styles, sometimes congruently and sometimes disjunctively. He penned large and small orchestral pieces and smaller instrumental works in various timbristic combinations. Nepomuceno wrote a long list of exquisite songs in a variety of languages, exploring the musical potential of poetry in German, French, Italian, and Norwegian, as well as in Portuguese. Nepomuceno was a music chameleon, Dante Pignatari asserts, able to move among and make use of all styles, genres, formal, and technical possibilities available to him.[65]

When scholars delve into Nepomuceno's works, they are confronted with the lack of a unique individual style, or one that could distinguish his music from that of his contemporaries. They also cannot establish a homogeneous musical style that could identify Nepomuceno's geographical presence and musical political agency within his nation. Scholars are nonetheless successful in pointing out Nepomceno's expertise in many musical languages considered to be the defining properties of people living faraway. Within a lack of uniformity, scholars have explored the many similarities that Nepomuceno's music shares with works by specific European composers considered to be the originators and owners of musical techniques, some of whom were Nepomuceno's contemporaries in Europe, while others were considered passé during his time. A list of such composers identified in the various analyses of his music include Bach, Chopin, Beethoven, Schubert, Mendelssohn, Brahms, Max Bruch, Liszt, Strauss, Wagner, Massenet, Saint-Saëns, Debussy, d'Indy, Cesar Frank, Chabrier, Dupark, Grieg, Albéniz, Schoenberg, Satie, Honegger, and Hugo Wolf—and this is surely not a comprehensive list. In Ulf Hannerz's definition, Nepomuceno's[66] array of "musical competencies" clearly defines him as a cosmopolitan composer, one who is comfortable in various musical and cultural contexts, a composer that, in Taruskin's view, could unite "the best of the West."[67]

One could suggest that Nepomuceno was, like his predecessor Mendelssohn, a composer skilled in "code switching," in moving between various musical languages that are assumed to identify and belong to someone else, to those who ultimately became the holders not merely of a style or technique, but of a culture. As such, Nepomuceno's works have served well music analysts as examples of "musical intertextuality," understood as a natural process, albeit ahistorical and socially decontextualized, one that presupposes that creative texts "talk" to one

---

[65] Pignatari, "Canto da língua," 43.
[66] Hannerz, *Transnational Connections*, 151.
[67] Taruskin, *Nineteenth-Century Music*, 239.

346 MUSIC AND COSMOPOLITANISM

another through their inherent stylistic common features.[68] Be that as it may, Nepomuceno's varied and non-historically linear output disrupts attempts to depict his music either as compellingly nationalistic or as original works that can be separated from other "original masterworks." To the music analyst, his output is entrapped by its lack of originality.

Still, the nature of Nepomuceno's music continues to puzzle scholars. Goldberg and Vidal have pointed out that the composer was particularly successful in conjuring up techniques usually understood as disparate, a juxtaposition that does not reveal a synthesis, but a collage of apparently discordant modes of expressions.[69] Here, one will find parallels to the eclectic literary approaches of Rushdie, Sebald, and Jorge Luis Borges (see Introduction). Examples of this collage are noticeable throughout Nepomuceno's output, but the usual prototype of these compositional "discordances" has been his "Variations Sur un thème original," op. 29 for piano (1902?) (Musical Example 11.1). The "original" in the title refers to the "theme," as opposed to Suite Brasileira, where he uses a "Brazilian theme" as a referent to a supposedly local, collective, traditional tune. But in his Variations, "theme" is illusory in itself, since a long line first presented in the canon only makes sense in its dependency of a chordal support of ever-changing harmonic centers. As the theme is repeated in variations over the work, it becomes harder, not easier, for it to be remembered, as if the theme is original but not the central idea. This may be understood as part of the work's complexity, but it also speaks to the difficulty in grasping a tune not well defined at the start, purposely or not. As the theme is presented in many disguises, as was customary with similar pieces, Nepomuceno moves to the lower register of the piano just to prepare for a long stretch of thematic forgetting through undetermined, parallel chords, resulting in a cluster or musical fog that came to be associated with Debussy. At the end, Nepomuceno's "original" theme is hardly identifiable; rather than remembered, it is forgotten; as the work arrives at end, the tune is not only not singable and memorable, but becomes a sound experiment resting on chordal textures and varied timbers: a conglomerate of sounds and disorganized music. The theme is just a passing thread in a work that is made to be forgotten; it is a piece of a musical collage displaying various techniques and modes of musical expressions available to the composer at the end of the 19th century, as it moves through diatonicism, chromaticism, bitonality, modal harmonies, suspended cadences, polytonality, harmonic clusters, pentatonicism,

[68] Vidal offers an excellent summary of the uses of the concept of intertextuality in musicology and its usefulness in the study of Nepomuceno's music; see "Formação germânica de Alberto Nepomuceno," 61–71.

[69] Goldberg, *Um Guarataja*, 128; Vidal, "Nepomuceno e Brahms," 108. For a recording of the piece, listen to Miguel Proença, *Alberto Nepomuceno: Obra integral para piano*, available at https://discografia.discosdobrasil.com.br/discos/coletanea-piano-brasileiro-alberto-nepomucemo-obra-integral-para-piano

Musical Example 11.1a. Alberto Nepomuceno, "Variations sur un thème original," op. 29, opening theme.

and whole-tone scale without the need for bridges or hybridization. Goldberg has argued that the work is a summary of Nepomuceno's ambiguous modernities and sees in it a reflection of the composer's historical position.[70]

Although it is easy to read in this collage a celebration of Nepomuceno's eclecticism that exposes the originality and ownership of others, the resulting stylistic

---

[70] Goldberg, *Um Guaratuja*, 114–130.

Musical Example 11.1b. Nepomuceno, Variations sur un thème original op. 29, final variation (XI). (Rio de Janeiro: Editora Arthur Napoleão, 1902).
Source: IMSLP, Petrucci Music Library, https://imslp.org/wiki/Variations_sur_un_th%C3%A8me_original,_Op.29_(Nepomuceno,_Alberto)

ambivalence of works like this allows for an alternate reading: rather than an "object in the background," to use Adorno's expression, placed in relation to the authority of the original, Nepomuceno's music can be revealed as a "source of knowledge or experience," as musical experiments that both reflects on, and helps build a *fin-de-siècle* cosmopolitan consciousness, one in which the present is but a passing, unstable conglomerate of past experiences.[71] If one abandons the usual methodological nationalism that requires the identification of an unique, new, and individual approach to music, and instead addresses the composer's work as the result of a shared cosmopolitan experience, one is confronted with an output bounded by an aesthetic stance that relies not only on techniques of the fragmentary, but also on the artistry of assembly: a process that is not entirely decontextualized from social relations or traditions and works that identify the period's "kaleidoscope of sounds," rather than the "kaleidoscope of visions (see Chapter one)." As a cosmopolitan composer, Nepomuceno's agency becomes visible as he provides an individual take on a collection of possibilities that were available to several—nonetheless, an individual take that could have resonances within and beyond his locality; his works can be read as a "self-reflexive repositioning of the self in the global sphere."[72]

Nepomuceno's cosmopolitanism involves reflecting and expanding on something assumed to be complete and opening it up again to further creative possibilities, a method of coming to terms with the fact that the new is never dissociated from the not-new and that uniqueness is but a political ideal that often conflicts with individual creativity. Nepomuceno's cosmopolitanism also involves demystifying and problematizing pre-established imagined identities, collective and individual, and their safeguarded borders by rethinking and recontextualizing origins. His approach was nothing but unique. Along with several composers of his generation, he was not bounded by centeredness as he transforms and recontextualizes the supposed models of establishment. His eclecticism can serve literally to hinder the models' claims of distinctiveness by offering open-ended alternative interpretations as he assembles them according to his own perspective. While Nepomuceno's music reveals similarities with many in the European music status quo, his works are more than acts of deliberate imitation or parody. His stance was different from, for example, from Charles Ives in the United States, but the impetus was similar.[73] One can thus easily find many

---

[71] Theodor Adorno, "Music in the Background," in *Essays on Music*, ed. Richard Leppert, trans. Susan Gillespie (Los Angeles and Berkeley: University of California Press, 2002), 506–509; see also Jonathan Wipplinger, "The Aural Shock of Modernity: Weimar's Experience of Jazz," *The Germanic Review: Literature, Culture, Theory* 82, no. 4 (2007): 304.

[72] Melba Cuddy-Keane, "Modernism, Geopolitics, Globalization," *Modernism/Modernity* 10, no. 3 (2003): 546, cited in Walkowitz, *Cosmopolitan Style*, 2.

[73] Nepumuceno also provided music as parody in his Prelude to *Guaratuja* (1904), an incomplete comic opera with a libretto based on José de Alencar.

350   MUSIC AND COSMOPOLITANISM

"Nepomucenos" in many contemporary cities, composers who were consciously reflecting on the period's kaleidoscope of sounds. Taken together, each output was not the same, while individually they were not unique. Their works defy specific models as they have been defined in scholastic works, while they do not suggest innovative ones that could be frozen as representatives of one technique, genre, or style of a specific period that could then be understood as canonic works to be. They produced music that was heterogeneous enough to suggest that at the turn of the 20th century composers were actually moving past canonicity and beyond place and time to invest in music as an individual reflective act of the present.

Nepomuceno's compositional tools are part of the period's modes of musical critique, not merely because he transforms or amends various models as they flow in his direction, but because he highlights invisible connections. His works are indeed part of an "identity matrix" centered in Europe as the 19th century came to a close, but his musical assemblages allowed him to break the usual associations with places and names to make previous narratives of homogeneous cultural attachments and cultural ownership, national or otherwise, irrelevant: the moving parts of his musical assemblages are independent from one another and without hierarchical connections. His works offer ubiquitous cosmopolitan aesthetic stances that de-nationalize, de-Europeanize, and ultimately de-essentialize the musics being produced in Europe, while at the same time rendering possible their universalizing force.[74] As such, his cosmopolitan aesthetics problematizes boundaries between the specific and the universal, between originals and copies, between margins and centers, and, ultimately, between the European and the non-European. Composers like Nepomuceno allow us to see how cosmopolitan musicians resisted geographical, cultural, and political constraints, and how they reflected on and challenged the limits of the European imagination and authority (and the French, the German, the English, etc.) by expanding on the musics' many aesthetic possibilities. One can say that the condition of marginality becomes an asset for Nepomuceno, for it offers him the flexibility of locating himself within several realms of the cosmopolitan scape, to invest in the possibilities of large patterns of cultural and musical connections, and to act on the implications of this cosmopolitanism by negotiating a view of the world through participation. These cosmopolitan stances are artistic takes that reflect on modernity's lack of unity. Nepomuceno's subjectivity becomes particularly significant because it is through his output, and the output of many composers like him, that global networks become apparent; it is through his

---

[74] Here I also share Walkowitz's claim that these "extra connections" or "entanglements" serve "not simply [to] offer alternatives to national affiliation [. . .] they attempt to make national cultures less homogeneous"; Walkowitz, *Cosmopolitan Style*, 24–25.

output that one can see that cosmopolitan networks not only touch and define local experiences, but also make possible aspirations for universality.

Rodolfo Coelho de Sousa points to a challenging question in this regard. Through a careful analysis of Nepomuceno's music, Coelho notes that Nepomuceno's harmonic structures and formal choices in his songs were concurrent, or antecede, the choices by composers in large cities in Europe. Sousa points to particularities in Nepomuceno's songs in French of the early 1890s, for instance, that reveal chord progressions and musical syntaxes that are considered to be hallmarks, if not the property of, Debussy and Schoenberg.[75] Without suggesting that Nepomuceno guided Debussy's or Schoenberg's musical choices, or wondering innocuously who did it for the first time, one can suggest that a shared cosmopolitan experience allowed various composers in various places to arrive at similar solutions to similar problems within their individual global imaginaries.[76] Thus, the exploration of Nepomuceno's music as a cosmopolitan experience casts new light on ideals of universality commonly granted to the music production of Europe, and particularly accorded to narratives of a specific music canon. A cosmopolitan aesthetic allows for the universality of models within a canonic narrative to become visible, not through the recalling of their homogeneous narratives, but through the revelation of their fragmentary and "uncertain surfaces," to use Adorno's expression again, ones that is revealed as the music travels in many unpredictable directions.[77] And if the cosmopolitan aesthetics reveals untapped universal possibilities, it does so from a position of aesthetic openness that problematizes the idea of cultural identity as a marker of distinctiveness at the service of the nation. At the same time, explorations through a cosmopolitan lens reveal the limits of the cosmopolitan experience as it encounters the forces of sociopolitical-economic agents. That Nepomuceno's music did not circulate much outside its place of origin and his cosmopolitan output did not help him transcend his locality speaks to the politics of the cosmopolitan aesthetic soundscape and to the exclusionary outcomes of a turn-of-the century modernity.

---

[75] Rodolfo Coelho de Sousa, "Nepomuceno e a gênese da canção de camera brasileira," *Música em perspectiva* 3, no. 1 (2010): 38; for a relationship between Nepomuceno and Schoenberg, see Sousa's "Aspectos de modernidade na música de Alberto Nepomuceno," 73.

[76] In this regard, see Jadwiga Paja-Stach, "The Contribution of Mieczyslaw Karlowicz to European Musical Culture," in *European Fin-de-Siècle and Polish Modernism: The Music of Mieczyslaw Karlowicz*, ed. Luca Sala (Bologna: Ut Orpheus Edizioni, 2010), 95–105; and Peter Franklin, "Shared Stories?: Karlowicz and the Fin-de-Siècle Musical Narrative," in *European Fin-de-Siècle and Polish Modernism: The Music of Mieczyslaw Karlowicz*, ed. Luca Sala (Bologna: Ut Orpheus Edizioni, 2010), 107–118.

[77] Adorno, *Essays*, 509; Adorno, *Jazz in Germany*, 305.

Conclusion

Arriving at the Future

In 1890s, Artur Azevedo started a campaign to build in Rio de Janeiro a large theater subsidized by the Republican government, a place where he envisioned a national theatrical company producing works by local playwrights, and where the city's residents would have the opportunity to see and hear spectacles of "high standing." The results were not immediate, but the author's pleas in his weekly writings continued until the government set up plans to build the Theatro Municipal, a saga with many twists and turns. Early in the new century, Pereira Passos received governmental money and political support to include the building of the theater in the city's reformation plans as part of a conglomerate of buildings devoted to the arts and "cultivated knowledge." Together with the building of the National School of Arts and the National Library, the buildings were spaces aimed at offering "civilization and culture for the people."[1] The work for the theater began in 1905 and was concluded four years later, with a project led by the engineer Francisco Oliveira Passos (son of Rio de Janeiro's mayor), who graduated from the Dresden school of engineering, and by his French assistant René Badra. Passos's model looked to the impetuous Paris Opéra, which provided inspiration for shape, structure, material, and overall internal structure of the new theater. The Municipal theater of Rio de Janeiro was thus part of a series of constructions that followed Garnier's Opéra, with its architectural eclecticism reshaping traditional models with state-of-the-art materials. The achievement of unity through variety characterized the overall aesthetic of the building and symbolized the idea of civilization, order, and progress (Figure C.1).

While Passos received his share of criticism, the outcome of the project was considered a success. The Theatro Municipal of Rio de Janeiro opened on July 14, 1909, with the performance of Silva's national anthem, a long speech by Bilac, and with a concert featuring works by local composers, including the symphonic poem *Insônia* (1908) by Francisco Braga and excerpts from the opera *Condor* by Carlos Gomes, sung by Mário Pinheiro. Although Azevedo died eight months before the theater's opening, a new company named "Compania Artur Azevedo" presented the play *Bonanza* (1909) by Coelho Netto, and the

---

[1] Lima, *Arquitetura do espetáculo*, 208.

Music and Cosmopolitanism. Cristina Magaldi, Oxford University Press. © Oxford University Press 2024.
DOI: 10.1093/oso/9780199744770.003.0013

Figure C.1. Theatro Municipal, Rio de Janeiro, 1908. Fichel David Chargel Collection.
Source: Enciclopédia Itaú Cultural de Arte e Cultura Brasileira. São Paulo: Itaú Cultural, 2022. "https://enciclopedia.itaucultural.org.br/obra25924/o-teatro-municipal-rio-de-janeiro-rj"

night concluded with the performance of the one-act opera *Moema* (1894) by Delgado de Carvalho. The artists featured in the festivities thus came to represent the Republican government's aesthetic ideals of modernity.

In 1913, João do Rio was entrusted with writing a book describing the theater for the government's advertisement purposes. Published in Portuguese and in French, the work served as a documentary history of the project. Starting with a critical note, however, the chronicler notes that the theater "is a monument like other monuments, [like] the Pantheon in Athens, the Santa Maria dei Fiori in Florence, the Duomo in Milan . . . just like an avenue is just like another avenue, and the squares in any latitude cannot express more than the mold of a square"; João do Rio concludes his opening saying that "[c]osmopolitanism [has given] away the originality under the discipline of the equal."[2] If his opening suggested ambivalence toward the theater, João do Rio's typical understanding of local issues through a European lens makes it difficult to uncover his true opinion about the project. Nonetheless, the chronicler proceeds with a long, detailed history

---

[2] João do Rio, *Theatro Municipal do Rio de Janeiro* (Rio de Janeiro: n.p., 1913), 9.

354 CONCLUSION

of the project, the artists involved, and the architectural and artistic elements of the building, descriptions that come with luxurious illustrations. The book, now held at the National Library in Rio de Janeiro, thus sealed the idea that the future as envisaged by Azevedo had arrived.

But, of course, the future is but a floating goal. Despite all its grandiosity, the theater's stage was found to be faulty for theatrical and musical presentations not long after its inauguration. Its large, monumental rooms began to serve as a space for conferences, political banquets, official celebrations, and gala presentations. Plays staged in French by companies and artists hired abroad predominated, as well as Italian operatic companies offering the same repertory that critics were complaining about 20 years earlier, regardless of the complaints about the stage's improper acoustics. In 1913, Nepomuceno organized a Wagner festival, with orchestral excerpts of several operas and vocal excerpts performed by tenor Karl Jorn, from the Metropolitan Opera in New York, who was hired for the occasion with government funds, but the concert did not echo much beyond local circles.[3] In the end, in the Theatro Municipal, architecture, art, plays, and music were symbols of a past that overburdened the present without suggesting a new future. Rather than a new beginning, music here was frozen, like the architecture.

Significantly, the artists who provided sculptures and paintings for decorating the new theater chose to include just a few local composers in their works, none of whom belonged to the Musical Republic. In addition to Francisco Manuel da Silva, the author of the National Anthem, it was Carlos Gomes who represented the musical city in the new theater. His portrait was included in a grandiose painting by Italian Eliseu Visconti (1866–1944), displayed in the front stage curtain of the new theater. Gomes's portrait was a significant part of an impressionist work done as an allegory to writers, philosophers, playwrights, and composers considered to be part of the "civilized" country and of "humanity's" intellectual and artistic history, and also included: Palestrina, Mozart, Beethoven, Rossini, Berlioz, Liszt, Verdi, Meyerbeer, and Wagner, with Gomes occupying a prominent position in the whole painting, as the image of Peri in his operatic garb is featured under the title, *Guarani*. After Visconti elevated *Il Guarany* to the pantheon of frozen symbols, statues of Gomes were erected throughout the country and placed in front of important, majestical buildings suggestive of power.[4] But that symbolism was most effective when presented aurally. During the first radio transmission in Brazil, as part of the celebrations of the Centenary

[3] *O Paiz*, June 20, 1913.

[4] See Fanny Lopes, "Dois monumentos a Carlos Gomes na Primeira República," in *Atas do XIV Encontro de História da Arte: Histórias do Olhar* (Campinas, SP: Universidade de Campinas, 2020), 757–771. The composer's status as a national icon was confirmed in 1936, during one of the country's most nationalist governments, when his face was chosen to be featured in the $300 réis coin, and in 1990 his picture was printed in the $5,000 cruzeiros bill.

CONCLUSION   355

of Independence in 1922, listeners heard excerpts from *Il Guarany* immediately after the discourse by President Epitácio Pessoa.[5] From there, *Il Guarany*'s music continued to be used politically as a connection between the audiences' musical memory and the nation's populist government that followed.

Lima Barreto understood the building of the Theatro Municipal quite differently, however. As a critic of the project from its inception, he wrote in 1910:

> The re-ordering of the city by mayor Pereira Passos, like it had happened with Haussmmn's Paris, did not follow aesthetic options or urbanization, but political decisions, imposing control in a world out of control, avoiding, by the separation of spaces, movements of the masses, and the conflicts that occurred earlier at the city's center; he attempted to reorganize the population sociality.

Barreto saw in Pereira Passos:

> a businessman, son of a landowner, educated at the time of the slavery regime, [who] never showed any interest in this city. What he wanted was a sumptuous edifice [the theater], where the political magnates, the owners of the commerce, and the farming and industry could hear operas without the fleas of the old [Teatro] Pedro II.

To Barreto:

> The theater has no use for the people, since it is too luxurious; for the national dramatic arts it is useless, since it is too big and there are few who enjoy it; but it cost twelve thousand contos, not counting the price of the necessary fixings. A lot of people got rich with it . . . and it has been used by a rich bourgeoisie, or those who pretend to be one, who exhibit their wives and daughters with their jewels and dresses in spectacles by foreign companies, lyric or not; [and it is] the mulato, poor who gather bananas in Guaratiba (bay) to sell, who contribute to these companies through the many government subsidies.[6]

To Barreto, the future had indeed arrived, one in which separation, rather than porosity, defined the city.

But the city did not succumb to the sounds and silences emanating from the new theater. A city soundscape, like all cultural expressions, does not appear and

---

[5] Marc Hertzman, *Making Samba: A New History of Race and Music in Brazil* (Durham, NC: Duke University Press), 327–328.

[6] Lima Barreto, "O Conselho Municipal e a Arte," in *Vida urbana, artigos e crônicas* (São Paulo: Editora Brasiliense, 1956), 109–111. See also Fábio José da Silva, *O Dândi e o boêmio: João do Rio e Lima Barreto no mundo literário da primeira república* (São Paulo: Giostri, 2015).

356   CONCLUSION

disappear in well-defined waves. Despite all the governmental money invested in the Theatro Municipal and the audience's frustrated expectations, which João do Rio defined with his characteristic irony as the "illusion of the White Elephant,"[7] music-making in the city continued its heterogeneous soundings and inevitable connections to many places. Meanwhile, in 1910 Benjamin de Oliveira was presenting his own works at the Spinelli circus with great success and the local mulattas started to dominate in vaudeville shows, leaving behind their foreign competitors. Cremilda Oliveira left the circus and was now at the Theatro Apollo performing the role of Hanna in another sold-out presentation of *The Merry Widow* that easily overshadowed the most prestigious artists featured at the monumental Theatro Municipal.

---

[7] João do Rio, "A ilusão do Elephante Branco," *Gazeta de Notícias*, August 27, 1909.

Bibliography

Abbas, Ackbar. "Cosmopolitan De-scriptions: Shanghai and Hong Kong." In *Cosmopolitanism*, edited by Carol Brenckenridge, Sheldon Pollock, Homi K. Bhabha, and Dipesh Chakrabarty 209–228. Durham, NC: Duke University Press, 2002.

Abbate, Carolyn. *In Search of Opera*. Princeton, NJ: Princeton University Press, 2001.

Abreu, Martha. *Da senzala ao palco: Canções e racismo nas Américas, 1870–1930*. Campinas, SP: Editora da Universidade de Campinas, 2017.

Abreu, Martha. "Histórias musicais na Primeira República." *ArtCultura* 13, no. 22 (2011): 71–83.

Abreu, Martha. "O 'Crioulo Dudu': Participação política e identidade negra has histórias de um músico cantor." *Topic* 11, no. 20 (January–June 2010): 92–113.

Acerbi, Patricia. "A Long Poem of Walking": Flâneurs, Vendors, and Chronicles of Post-abolition Rio de Janeiro." *Journal of Urban History* 40, no. 1 (2014): 97–115.

Adorno, Theodor. *Essays on Music*, edited by Richard Leppert. Berkeley and Los Angeles: University of California Press, 2002.

Agathocleous, Tanya. *Urban Realism and the Cosmopolitan Imagination in the Nineteenth Century: Visible City, Invisible World*. Cambridge, UK: Cambridge University Press, 2010.

Agawu, Kofi. *Representing African Music: Postcolonial Notes, Queries, Positions*. New York: Routledge, 2003.

Aguilar, Gonzalo. "The National Opera: A Migrant Genre of Imperial Expansion." *Journal of Latin American Studies* 2, no. 1 (March 2003): 83–94.

Agulhon, Maurice. *Marianne Au pouvoir: L'imagerie et la symbolique républicaines de 1880 à 1914*. Paris: Flammarion, 1989.

Ahlquist, Karen. "Balance of Power: Music as Art and Social Class in Late Nineteenth Century." In *Rethinking American Music*, edited by Tara Browner and Thomas Riis, 7–33. Chicago: University of Illinois Press, 2019.

Ahlquist, Karen. "International Opera in Nineteenth-Century New York: Core Repertories and Canonic Values." In *The Oxford Handbook of the Operatic Canon*, edited by Cormac Newark and William Weber, 244–245. Oxford: Oxford University Press, 2018.

Alberto, Paulina. *Terms of Inclusion: Black Intellectuals in 20th-Century Brazil*. Chapel Hill: University of North Carolina Press, 2011.

Albuquerque, Wlamyra. "A vala comum da 'raça emancipada': Abolição e racialização no Brasil, breve comentário." *História Social* 19 (2010): 92–108.

Alencar, José de. *Como e porque sou romancista*. Campinas, SP: Pontes, 1990.

Alim, H. Samy, Awad Ibrahim, and Alastair Pennycook, eds. *Global Linguistic Flows: Hip Hop Cultures, Youth Identities, and the Politics of Language*. New York: Routledge, 2009.

Almeida, Antonio Cavalcanti de. "Aspectos das políticas indigenistas no Brasil." *Interações* 19, no. 3 (July–September 2018), online publication. https://www.researchgate.net/publication/326268004_Aspectos_das_politicas_indigenistas_no_Brasil#fullTextFile Content

358 BIBLIOGRAPHY

Almeida, Maria Regina Celestino de. "A atuação dos indígenas na História do Brasil: Revisões historiográficas." *Revista Brasileira de História* 37, no. 75 (May–August 2017): 17–38.

Almandoz, Arturo. "Introduction." In *Planning Latin Ameria's Capital Cities, 1850–1950*, edited by Arturo Almandoz, 1–12. New York: Routledge, 2010.

Almeida, Antonio Cavalcanti de. "Aspectos das políticas indigenistas no Brasil." *Interações* 19, no. 3 (July–September 2018): 611–626. online publication.

Almeida, Flávia Ferreira de. "O mercado de trabalho dos espetáculos: Atrizes das companhias Portuguesas nos palcos do teatro musicado Carioca." *Transversos: Revista de História* 9 (2017): 222–246.

Almeida, Paulo Roberto de. "A presença negra no Teatro de Revista dos anos 1920." Master's thesis, Universidade Federal Fluminense, 2016.

Almeida, Renato. *História Da Música Brasileira*. Rio de Janeiro: F. Briguiet, 1942 [1926].

Alonso, Ângela. "Arrivistas e decadentes: O debate político-intelectual Brasileiro na primeira década republicana." *Novos Estudos* 85 (2009): 131–148.

Alonso, Ângela. "De positivismos e de positivistas: Interpretações do positivismo brasileiro." *Revista Dados* 42 (1996): 109–134.

Alonso, Ângela. "A teatralização da política: A propaganda abolicionistta." *Tempo Social* 24, no. 2 (2012): 101–112.

Altman, Rick. "The Living Nickelodeon." In *The Sounds of Early Cinema*, edited by Richard Abel and Rick Altman, 232–240. Bloomington: Indiana University Press, 2001.

Altman, Rick. *Silent Film Sound*. New York: Columbia University Press, 2004.

Altman, Rick. "Introduction." *Yale French Studies* no. 60, (1980): 3–15.

Anderson, Amanda. *The Powers of Distance: Cosmopolitanism and the Cultivation of Detachment*. Princeton, NJ, and Oxford: Princeton University Press, 2001.

Anderson, Benedict. *The Age of Globalization: Anarchists and the Anticolonial Imagination*. London: Verso, 2005.

Anderson, Benedict. *Imagined Communities*, rev. ed. London and New York: Verso, 2006 [1983].

Andrade, Clarissa Lapolla Bomfim de. *A Gazeta Musical: Positivismo e missão civilizadora nos primeiros anos da república no Brasil*. São Paulo: Editora Unesp, 2013.

Andrade, Debora. "A árvore e o fruto: A promoção dos intelectuais no século XIX." PhD dissertation, Universidade Federal Fluminense, 2008.

Andrews, George Reid. *Blackness in the White Nation: A History of Afro-Uruguay*. Chapel Hill: University of North Carolina Press, 2010.

Appadurai, Arjun. *Modernity at Large: Cultural Dimensions of Globalization*. Minneapolis: University of Minnesota Press, 1996.

Appignanesi, Lisa. *The Cabaret*. New York: Universe Books, 1976.

Applegate, Celia. "How German Is It? Nationalism and the Idea of Serious Music in the Early Nineteenth Century." *19th-Century Music* 21, no. 3 (1998): 274–296.

Aragão, Pedro. "Diálogos luso-brasileiros no Acervo José Moças da Universidade de Aveiro: Um estudo exploratório das gravações mecânicas (1902–1927)." *Opus* 22, no. 2 (December 2016): 83–114.

Araújo, Vicente de Paula. *A bela época do cinema brasileiro*. São Paulo: Perspectiva, 1976.

Azevedo, Andre Nunes. *A grande reforma urbana do Rio de Janeiro: Pereira Passos, Rodrigues Alves e as idéias de civilização*. Rio de Janeiro: PUC, 2016.

Azevedo, Artur. "O Mambembe." In *Artur Azevedo: Obras*. Rio de Janeiro: Biblioteca Digital, 2013 [1904]. Kindle.

BIBLIOGRAPHY 359

Azevedo, Luis Heitor Correa de. *100 anos de música no Brasil*. Rio de Janeiro: José Olympio, 1956.

Bachmann-Medick, Doris, ed. *The Trans/National Study of Culture: A Translational Perspective*. Berlin and Boston, MA: De Gruyter, 2016.

Bailey, Peter. "Conspiracies of Meaning: Music-Hall and the Knowingness of Popular Culture." *Past & Present* 144, no. 1 (1994): 138–170.

Bajini, Irina. "Traviatas que cantan habaneras y Faustos que tocan tambor: Parodias operísticas en la Cuba decimonónica." *Gramma* 22, no. 48 (2011): 63–74.

Baker, Jeffrey. *Music and Urban Society in Colonial Latin America*. Cambridge, UK: Cambridge University Press, 2011.

Balme, Christopher. "Theater and Globalization, the Cairo Opera house." In *Syncretic Arenas: Essays on Postcolonial African Drama and Theatre for Esiaba Irobi*, edited by Isidore Diala, 133–157. Amsterdam: Brill, 2014.

Balme, Christopher, and Nic Leonhardt. "Introduction: Theatrical Trader Routes." *Journal of Global Theatre History* 1, no. 1 (2016): 1–9.

Ballarotti, Carlos Roberto. "A Construção do mito de Tiradentes: De mártir republicano a herói cívico na atualidade." *Antíteses* 2, no. 3 (2009): 201–225.

Bara, Olivier. "Vedettes de la scène en tournée: Première mondialisation culturelle au XIXe siècle?" *Romantisme* 163, no. 1 (2014): 41–52.

Baranello, Micaela. "*Die lustige Witwe* and the Creation of the Silver Age of Viennese Operetta." *Cambridge Opera Journal* 26, no. 2 (2014): 175–202.

Barbosa, Francisco de Assis. *A vida de Lima Barreto (1881–1922)*, 11th ed. São Paulo and Rio de Janeiro: Autêntica Editora, 2017 [1952].

Barbuy, Heloísa. *A Cidade-Exposição: Comercio e cosmopolitismo em São Paulo, 1860–1914*. São Paulo: Edusp, 2006.

Bardet, Jean-Pierre, and Jacques Dupâquier. *Histoire des populations de l'Europe*. Paris: Fayard, 1997.

Barreto, Lima. *Recordações do escrivão Isaías Caminha*. Rio de Janeiro: Obliq, 2018 [1909], Kindle.

Barroso, Maria Aida. "Ornamentação e improvisação no método de pianoforte de José Maurício Nunes Garcia." Master's thesis, Universidade Federal do Rio de Janeiro, 2005.

Barthes, Rolan. *The Grain of Voice*. New York: Random House, 2010 (1972).

Bastos, Antonio Sousa. *Carteira do artista: Apontamentos para a história do theatro portuguez* Lisbon: J. Bastos, 1899.

Bastos, Maria Helena Camara de. "A educação dos escravos e libertos no Brasil: Vestígios esparsos do domínio do ler, escrever e contar (Séculos XVI a XIX)." *Cadernos de História da Educação* 15, no. 2 (May–August 2016): 743–768.

Bayly, Christopher. "The Great Acceleration." In *The Birth of the Modern World*, 451–487. Oxford: Blackwell, 2004.

Beck, Ulrich. *Cosmopolitan Vision*. Cambridge, UK: Polity Press, 2006.

Becker, Tobias. "Globalizing Operetta before the First World War." *The Opera Quarterly* 33, no. 1 (2017): 7–27.

Benchimol, Jaime. *Pereira Passos: Um Haussmann tropical. A renovação urbana do Rio de Janeiro no início do século XX*. Rio de Janeiro: Departamento Geral de Documentação e Informação, 1992.

Benjamin, Walter. *The Arcades Project*, edited by Rolf Tiedemann, translated by Howard Eiland and Kevin McLaughlin. Cambridge, MA: Harvard University Press, 2002.

360 BIBLIOGRAPHY

Benjamin, Walter. "Paris: The Capital of the Nineteenth Century." In *The Work of Art in the Age of Its Technological Reproducibility and Other Writings on Media*, edited by Michael Jennings, Brigit Doherty, and Thomas Levin, 96–115. Cambridge, MA: Harvard University Press, 2008.

Benzecry, Claudio. "An Opera House for the 'Paris of South America': Pathways to the Institutionalization of High Culture." *Theory and Society* 43, no. 2 (March 2014): 169–196.

Bergero, Adriana. *Intersecting Tango: Cultural Geographies of Buenos Aires*, translated by Richard Young. Pittsburgh, PA: University of Pittsburgh Press, 2008.

Bethell, Leslie. *Brazil: Empire and Republic, 1822–1930*. Cambridge, UK: Cambridge University Press, 1989.

Bezerra, Valéria Cristina. "*Il Guarany* e *Ubiraiara*: Os romances de José de Alencar na Itália." *FronteiraZ* 19 (December 2017): 53–64.

Bezerra, Valéria Cristina. "The Honey-Lips e The Guarany: Os Romances de José De Alencar em língua inglesa no final do século XIX." *Signo* 41, no. 72 (2016): 16–26.

Bezerra, Valéria Cristina. "Recepção crítica de José de Alencar em língua francesa (1858–1902)." *Recorte* 13, no. 2 (July–December, 2016): 1–16.

Bielsa, Esperança. "Cosmopolitanism beyond the Monolingual Vision." *International Political Sociology* 14 (2020): 418–430.

Bilac, Olavo (under the pseudonym Fantasio). "O gato Preto." *Gazeta de Notícias*, June 7, 1896.

Bilac, Olavo. "Chronica." *Gazeta de Notícias*, November 3, 1907.

Bilac, Olavo (under the pseudonym Fantasio). "A dansa no Rio de Janeiro." *Kosmos* 5, May, 1906.

Bishop-Sanchez, Kathryn. *Creating Carmen Miranda: Race, Camp, and Transnational Stardom*. Nashville, TN: Vanderbilt University Press, 2016.

Bispo, Alexandre. "Verona: Processos de difusão cultural no presente e no passado. Da ópera à música para banda, canto e piano no século XIX. Reduções e transcrições no comércio, na criação e na vida musical. Carlos Gomes (1836–1896) e Nicolò Celega (1844–1906)," *Revista Brasil-Europa: Correspondência Euro-Brasileira* 162, no. 8 (2016), online publication. http://revista.brasil-europa.eu/162/Nicolo_Celega_e_Carlos_Gomes.html.

Bispo, Alexandre. "Brasil e Itália na música para piano do século XIX: Fantasias de óperas e sentimentos identitários. A homenagem a Carlos Gomes (1836–1896) de Paolo Canonica (1846–1902)," *Revista Brasil-Europa: Correspondência Euro-Brasileira* 162, no. 7 (2016), online publication.

Blake, J. "Taking the Cake: The First Steps of Primitivism in Modernist Art." In *Le Tumulte Noir: Modernist Art and Popular Entertainment in Jazz-Age Paris, 1900–1930*. University Park: Pennsylvania State University Press, 1999.

Bloechl, Olivia, Melanie Lowe, and Jeffrey Kallberg, eds. *Rethinking Difference in Music Scholarship*. Cambridge, UK: Cambridge University Press, 2015, Kindle.

Boehrer, George. *Da Monarquia à República: História do epubli epublican no Brasil*. Belo Horizonte: Editora Itatiaia, 2000.

Bohlman, Phillip. "Prologue: Again Herder." In *Song Loves the Masses: Herder on Music and Nationalism*, edited and translated by Phillip Bohlman, 1–20. Los Angeles: University of California Press, 2017.

Bolon-Reichert, Christine. *The Age of Eclecticism: Literature and Culture in Britain 1815–1885*. Columbus: Ohio State University Press, 2009.

BIBLIOGRAPHY 361

Bonavides, Marcelo. "Estrelas que nunca se apagam" (online publication). https://www. marcelobonavides.com/.

Borges, Maria José. "Verdi e o gosto pela opera italiana em Portugal no século XIX." *Estudos Italianos em Portugal* 8 (2013): 11–28.

Bourdieu, Pierre. "The Forms of Capital." In *Handbook of Theory and Research for the Sociology of Education*, edited by John Richardson, 241–258. New York: Greenwood Press, 1986.

Born, Giorgina. "Mediation theory." In *The Routledge Reader on the Sociology of Music*, edited by J. Shepherd and K. Devine, 359–368. New York: Routledge, 2015.

Born, Giorgina. "For a Relational Musicology: Music and Interdisciplinarity, Beyond the Practice Turn." *Journal of the Royal Music Association* 135, no. 2 (November 2010): 205–242.

Born, Georgina, and David Hesmondhalgh, eds. *Western Music and Its Others: Difference, Representation, and Appropriation in Music*. Los Angeles: University of California Press, 2000.

Borucki, Alex. *From Shipmates to Soldiers: Emerging Black Identities in the Río de la Plata*. Albuquerque: University of New Mexico Press, 2015.

Bosi, Alfredo. *Literatura e Resistência*. São Paulo: Companhia das Letras, 2002.

Boutin, Aimée. *City of Noise: Sound and Nineteenth-Century Paris*. Urbana and Chicago: University of Illinois Press, 2015.

Bowan, Kate. "Friendship, Cosmopolitan Connections and Late Victorian Socialist Songbook Culture." In *Cheap Print and Popular Song in the Nineteenth Century: A Cultural History of the Songster*, edited by Paul Watt, Derek Scott, and Patrick Spedding, 91–111. Cambridge, UK: Cambridge University Press, 2017.

Braga, Flávia da Silva. "Para além do bestializado: diferentes interpretações da (não) participação popular." *Revista Hydra* 1, no. 1 (2019): 167–194.

Braga-Pinto, César. "From Abolitionism to Blackface: The Vicissitudes of Uncle Tom in Brazil." In *Uncle Tom's Cabins: The Transnational History of America's Most Mutable Book*, edited by Tracy Davis and Stefka Mihaylova, 225–257. Ann Arbor: University of Michigan Press, 2018.

Brandão, José Maurício. "Carlos Gomes: Um ilustre desconhecido." *Revista Modus* 7, no. 11 (2012): 17–26.

Brigstocke, Julian. *The Life of the City: Space, Humour, and the Experience of Truth in Fin-de- Siècle Montmartre*. New York: Routledge, 2014.

Broadberry, Stephen, and Kevin O'Rourke. *The Cambridge Economic History of Modern Europe*, Vol. 2: *1870 to the Present*. Cambridge, UK: Cambridge University Press, 2010.

Brooks, Daphne. *Bodies in Dissent: Spectacular Performances of Race and Freedom*. Durham, NC: Duke University Press, 2006.

Brooks, Tim. *Lost Sounds: Blacks and the Birth of the Recording Industry*. Urbana and Chicago: University of Illinois Press, 2004.

Brown, Jayna. *Babylon Girls: Black Women Performers and the Shaping of the Modern*. Durham, NC: Duke University Press, 2008.

Brown, Matthew, and Gabriel Paquette. "Between the Age of Atlantic Revolutions and the Age of Empire: Europe and Latin America in the Axial Decade of the 1820s." In *Connections after Colonialism: Europe and Latin America in the 1820s*, edited by Matthew Brown and Gabriel Paquette, 1–28. Tuscaloosa: University of Alabama Press, 2013.

362 BIBLIOGRAPHY

Brunetta, Gian Piero. *The History of Italian Cinema: A Guide to Italian Film from Its Origins to the Twenty-First Century*. Princeton, NJ: Princeton University Press, 2009.

Budasz, Rogério. "New Sources for the Study of Early Opera and Musical Theater in Brazil." In *Annals of the Conference Music and Culture in the Imperial Court of João VI in Rio de Janeiro*. Austin: University of Texas, 2005, online publication.

Budasz, Rogério. *Teatro e música na América Portuguesa, conversões, repertório, raça, gênero*. Curitiba, Brazil: DeArtes, 2008.

Burton, Antoinette. *After the Imperial Turn: Thinking with and through the Nation*. Durham, NC: Duke University Press, 2003.

Caballero, Carlo. "Patriotism or Nationalism? Fauré at the Great War." *Journal of the American Musicological Society* 52, no. 3 (1999): 593–625.

Caddy, Davinia. "Parisian Cake Walks." *19th-Century Music* 30, no. 3 (2007): 288–317.

Calhoun, Craig J. "The Class Consciousness of Frequent Travelers: Towards a Critique of Actually Existing Cosmopolitanisms." *The South Atlantic Quarterly* 101, no. 4 (2002): 869–897.

Callari, Cláudia Regina. "Os Institutos Históricos: Do patronato de D. Pedro II à construção do Tiradentes." *Revista Brasileira de História* 21, no. 40 (2001): 59–83.

Callipo, Daniela Mantarro. "De vedette a poeta: A trajetória de Rose Mérys." *Miscelânea* 24 (July–December 2018): 145–163.

Campana, Alessandra. *Opera and Modern Spectatorship in Late Nineteenth-Century Italy*. Cambridge, UK: Cambridge University Press, 2015.

Campello, André Emmanuel. "A escravidão no império do Brasil: Perspectives jurídicas." In *Brazil: Sindicato nacional dos procuradores da fazenda nacional*. Sinprofaz, 2013, online publication. https://www.sinprofaz.org.br/artigos/a-escravidao-no-imperio-do-brasil-perspectivas-juridicas/

Campos, Lima. "Cake-walk." *Kosmos* I, no. 8 (August 1904).

Canclini, Nestor Garcia. *Culturas híbridas: Estrategias para entrar y salir de la modernidad*. México City: Grijalbo, 1990.

Candido, Antonio. *O método crítico de Silvio Romero*. São Paulo: Editora Edusp, 1988.

Carballo, Borja, Fernando Vicente, and Rubén Pallol. *El ensanche de Madrid: Historia de una capital*. Madrid: Catarata, 2013.

Cardoso, Lino de Almeida. "O som e o soberano: Uma história da depressão musical carioca pós- Abdicação (1831–1843) e de seus antecedentes." PhD dissertation, Universidade de São Paulo, 2006.

Carneiro, Andreia. "Nascimento de um índio na rua do ouvidor: José de Alencar Bestseller." Master's thesis, Universidade Estarual de Feira de Santana, 2012.

Carter, Tim. "The Sound of Silence: Models for an Urban Musicology." *Urban History* 29, no. 1 (May 2002): 8–18.

Carvalho, Bruno. *Porous City: A Cultural History of Rio de Janeiro*. Liverpool, UK: Liverpool University Press, 2013.

Carvalho, Danielle Crepaldi. "D'O Guarani de José de Alencar e Carlos Gomes aos Guaranis do 'clown' Benjamin: diálogos entre literatura, cinema, circo, e música." *Aniki, Portuguese Journal of the Moving Image* 5, no. 1 (2018): 78–104.

Carvalho, Danielle Crepaldi. "O cinema silencioso e o som no Brasil (1894–1920)." *Galaxia* 34 (2017): 85–97.

Carvalho, Flavio Cardoso de. "A ópera *Abul* de Alberto Nepomuceno e sua contribuição para o patrimônio musical Brasileiro da Primeira República." PhD dissertation, Universidade Estadual de Campinas, 2005.

BIBLIOGRAPHY   363

Carvalho, José Murilo de. *A formação das almas*. São Paulo: Companhia das Letras, 2005 [1990].

Carvalho, José Murilo de. "O Rio de Janeiro e a República." *Revista Brasileira de História 5*, no. 8–9 (1985): 117–138.

Carvalho, José Murilo de. *Os Bestializados*. São Paulo: Companhia das Letras, 1987.

Carvalho, José Murilo de. "Radicalismo e republicanismo." In *Repensando o Brasil do oitocentos: Cidadania, política e liberdade*, edited by José Murilo de Carvalho and Lúcia Maria Bastos Pereira das Neves, 19–48. Rio de Janeiro: Civilização Brasileira, 2009.

Carvalho, José Murilo de. "República, democracia, e federalismo no Brasil, 1870–1991." *Vária História 27*, no. 45 (2011): 141–157.

Carvalho, Lia de Aquino. *Habitações populares: Rio de Janeiro: 1866–1906*. Rio de Janeiro: Secretaria Municipal de Cultura, 1995.

Carvalho, Reis. "O Feriado Brazileiro de 14 de Julho." *Kosmos*, 5 no. 7 (July 1908).

Castagna, Paulo. "A produção musical carioca entre c. 1780–1831." In *Apostila do curso de história da música Brasileira 8*. São Paulo: Instituto de Artes da UNESP, n.d.

Castro, Paulo Ferreira de. "Visto de Portugal: Verdi, Wagner e o teatro das nações." In *Alemanha Portugal: Aspectos e momentos em revista*, edited by F. Ribeiro, 157–173. Lisbon: Húmus, 2015.

Castro, Paulo Ferreira de. "Wagnerism at the Edge: Some Aspects of Richard's Wager's Impact on Portuguese Fin-de-Siècle Culture." In *The Legacy of Richard Wagner: Convergences and Dissonances in Aesthetics and Reception*, edited by Luca Sala, 417–432. Turnhalt, Belgium: Brepols, 2012.

Cavalcanti, Ana Maria Tavares. "Os embates no meio artístico carioca em 1890: Antecedentes da reforma da Academia das Belas Artes." *19&20 2*, no. 2 (2007), online publication. http://www.dezenovevinte.net/criticas/embate_1890.htm

Certeau, Michael de. *The Practice of Everyday Life*, translated by Steven Randall. Berkley and Los Angeles: California University Press, 1984.

Cetrangolo, Aníbal Enrique. "*Aida* Times Two: How Italian Veterans of Two Historic *Aida* Productions Shaped Argentina's Music History." *Cambridge Opera Journal 28*, no. 1 (2016): 79–105.

Cetrangolo, Aníbal Enrique. "L'opera nei paesi Latino-americani nell'età moderna e contemporanea." *In Musica in scena. Storia dello spettacolo musicale*, edited by A. Basso, 654–691. Turin: UTET, 1996.

Cesetti, Durval. "*Il Guarany* for Foreigners: Colonialist Racism, Naïve Utopia, or Pleasant Entertainment?" *Latin American Music Review 31* (2010): 101–121.

Chalhoub, Sidney. *Cidade febril. Cortiços e epidemias na corte imperial*. São Paulo: Cia. das Letras, 1999.

Chalhoub, Sidney. "The Politics of Silence: Race and Citizenship in Nineteenth-Century Brazil." *Slavery & Abolition 27*, no. 1 (2006): 73–87.

Chan, Hanna. "Der Ring des Nibelungen in the New World: The American Performance and Reception of Wagner's Cycle, 1850–1903." PhD dissertation, University of Illinois at Urbana-Champaign, 2014.

Chanda, Nayan. *Bound Together: How Traders, Preachers, Adventurers, and Warriors Shaped Globalization*. New Haven, CT: Yale University Press, 2007.

Charle, Christophe. "La circulation des opéras en Europe au XIXe siècle." *Relations internationales 155*, no. 3 (2013): 11–31.

Charle, Christophe. *Thèâtres en capitales: Naissance de la société du spectacle à Paris, Berlin, Londres, et Vienne*. Paris: Albin Michael, 2008.

364 BIBLIOGRAPHY

Charle, Christophe. "Opera in France, 1870–1914: Between Nationalism and Foreign Imports." In *Opera and Society in Italy and France: From Monteverdi to Bourdieu*, edited by Victoria Johnson, Jane F. Fulcher, and Thomas Ertman, 243–266. Cambridge, UK: Cambridge University Press, 2007.

Chaves Junior, Edgard de Brito. *Wagner e o Brasil*. Rio de Janeiro: Emebê Editora, 1976.

Cheah, Pheng. "The Cosmopolitical—Today." In *Cosmopolitics: Thinking and Feeling beyond the Nation*, edited by Pheng Cheah and Bruce Robbins, 22–30. Minneapolis: University of Minnesota Press, 1998.

Cheah, Pheng, and Jonathan Culler, eds. *Grounds of Comparison: Around the Work of Benedict Anderson*. New York: Routledge, 2003.

Chernavsky, Analía. *A construção dos mitos e heróis do Brasil nos hinos esquecidos da Biblioteca Nacional*. Rio de Janeiro: Fundação Biblioteca Nacional, 2009.

Christensen, Thomas. "Sounding Offstage." In *The Oxford Handbook of Opera*, edited by Helen Greenwald, 899–920. Oxford, UK: Oxford University Press, 2014.

Christo, Maraliz de Castro Vieira. "Pintura, história e heróis no século XIX: Pedro Americo e 'Tiradentes Esquartejado.'" PhD dissertation, Universidade Estadual de Campinas, 2005.

Christoforidis, Michael, and Elizabeth Kertesz. *Carmen and the Staging of Spain: Recasting Bizet's Opera in the Belle Epoque*. Oxford and New York: Oxford University Press, 2019.

Cicchelli, Vincenzo, and Sylvie Octobre. *Aesthetico-Cultural Cosmopolitanism and French Youth: The Taste of the World*. New York: Palgrave Macmillan, 2018.

Citron, Marcia. "Visual Media." In *The Oxford Handbook of Opera*, edited by Helen Greenwald, 921–940. Oxford, UK: Oxford University Press, 2014.

Clifford, James. *Routes: Travel and Translation in the Late Twentieth Century*. Cambridge, MA: Harvard University Press, 1997.

Coelho, Geraldo M. *O brilho de supernova: A morte bela de Carlos Gomes*. Rio de Janeiro: Agir, 1995.

Cohen, Brigid. "Diasporic Dialogues in Mid-Century New York: Stefen Wolpe, George Russel, and Hannah Arendt, and the Historiography of Displacement." *Journal of the Society for American Music* 6, no. 2 (2012): 143–173.

Cole, Catherine M. "American Ghetto and Ghanaian Concert Parties: A Transnational Perspective on Blackface." In *Burnt Cork: Traditions and Legacies of Blackface Minstrelsy*, edited by Stephen Johnson, 223–258. Amherst and Boston: University of Massachusetts Press, 2012.

Coli, Jorge. *Música Final: Mário de Andrade e sua coluna jornalística mundo musical*. Campinas: Editora da Unicamp, 1998.

Coli, Jorge. "Carlos Gomes: A grande travessia." *Revista do Instituto de Estudos Brasileiros* 26 (1986): 106–114.

Conati, Marcello. "Fortuna e aspetti del 'Guarany' di Gomes." *Revista de Musicología* 16, no. 1 (1993): 71–264.

Connelly, Owen. *Blundering to Glory: Napoleon's Military Campaigns*, 3rd ed. Lanham, MD: Rowan and Littlefield, 2006.

Conde, Maite. *Consuming Visions: Cinema, Writing, and Modernity in Rio De Janeiro*. Charlottesville: University of Virginia Press, 2011.

Conde, Maite. "Film and the Crônicas: Documenting the New Urban Spaces in Turn-of-the-Century Rio De Janeiro." *Luso-Brazilian Review* 42, no. 2 (2005): 66–88.

Conde, Maite. *Foundational Films: Early Cinema and Modernity in Brazil*. Oakland: University of California Press, 2018.

BIBLIOGRAPHY   365

Conway, Kelley. *Chanteuse in the City: The Realist Singer in French Film*. Berkeley: University of California Press, 2004.

Cook, Nicholas. "Anatomy of the Encounter: Intercultural Analysis as Relational Musicology." In *Critical Musicological Reflections: Essays in Honor of Derek B. Scott*, edited by Stan Hawkins, 193–208. Aldershot, UK: Ashgate, 2012.

Cook, Nicholas. "Music as Performance." In *The Cultural Study of Music: A Critical Introduction*, edited by Martin Clayton, Trevor Herbert, and Richard Middleton, 184–194. London: Taylor & Francis Group, 2011.

Cook, Nicholas. "Western Music as World Music." In *The Cambridge History of World Music*, edited by Philip Bohlman, 75–100. Cambridge, UK: Cambridge University Press, 2013.

Cooper, Fredrick. "What Is the Concept of Globalization Good for? An African Historian's Perspective." *African Affairs* 100, no. 399 (April 2001): 189–213.

Corrêa, Mariza. *As ilusões da liberdade: A escola Nina Rodrigues e a antropologia no Brasil*, 2nd ed. Bragança Paulista: Editora da Universidade de São Francisco, 2001, Kindle.

Correa, Sérgio Alvin. *Alberto Nepomuceno: Catálogo Geral*. Rio de Janeiro: FUNARTE, 1985.

Costa, Angela Marques da, and Lilia Schwarcz. *Virando Séculos: 1890–1914, no tempo das certezas*. São Paulo: Companhia das Letras, 2000.

Costa, Fernando Morais da. *O som no cinema Brasileiro: Revisão de uma importância indeferida*. PhD dissertation, Universidade Federal Fluminense, 2006.

Costa Junior, Alberto Ferreira da. "Quando o cômico atravessa o oceano: O Tim tim por tim tim no Brasil." In *Ensaios sobre o humor Luso-Hispânico*, edited by Laura Areias and Luís Pinheiro, 353–371. Lisbon: LusoSofia Press, 2013.

Cruz, Gabriela. "Sr. José, the Worker *mélomane*, or Opera and Democracy in Lisbon ca. 1850." *19th Century Music* 40, no. 2 (2016): 81–105.

Cunha, João Itiberê da. "Il Guarany (1870): Algumas palavras sobre a ópera." In *Carlos Gomes: Uma obra em foco*, 137–142. Rio de Janeiro: FUNART, 1987.

Cunha, Maria Clementina Pereira. *Ecos da folia: Uma história social do carnaval carioca entre 1880–1920*. São Paulo: Companhia das Letras, 2001.

Cunha, Maria Clementina Pereira. "'Não me ponha no xadrez com esse malandrão': Conflitos e identidades entre sambistas no Rio de Janeiro do início do século XX." *Afro-Ásia* 38 (2008): 179–210.

Cymbron, Luísa. "A produção e recepção das óperas de Verdi em Portugal no século XIX." In *Verdi em Portugal (1843–2001)*, 21–39. Lisbon: Biblioteca Nacional, Teatro Nacional de São Carlos, 2001.

Cymbron, Luísa. "Camões in Brazil: Operetta and Portuguese Culture in Rio de Janeiro, circa 1880." *The Opera Quarterly* 30, no. 4 (2014): 330–361.

D'Acol, Mítia Ganade. "Decoro musical e esquemas galantes: Um estudo de caso das seções de canto solo das Missas de Requiem de José Maurício Nunes Garcia e Marcos Portugal." Masters' thesis, Universidade de São Paulo, 2015.

Dantas, Carolina Vianna. "O Brasil café com leite: Debates intelectuais sobre mestiçagem e preconceito de cor na primeira república." *Tempo* 13, no. 26 (December 2008): 56–79.

Davies, James. "'Ah! non pensar che pieno': The Progress of an Aria." *Cambridge Opera Journal* 28, no. 2 (2016): 155–159.

Davies, James. "A Musical Souvenir: London in 1829." PhD dissertation, Cambridge University, 2005.

366 BIBLIOGRAPHY

Davis, John. "Opera and Absolutism in Restoration Italy, 1815–1860." *Journal of Interdisciplinary History* 36, no. 4 (Spring 2006): 569–594.

Dahlhaus, Carl. *Nineteenth-Century Music.* Berkeley and Los Angeles: California University Press, 1989.

Deaville, James. "Cakewalk in Waltz Time? African-American Music in Jahrhundertwende Vienna." In *Reverberations. Representations of Modernity, Tradition and Cultural Value in/between Central Europe and North America*, edited by Susan Ingram, Markus Reisenleitner, and Cornelia Szabó-Knotik, 17–39. Frankfurt am Main: Peter Lang, 2002.

Deaville, James. "Debussy's Cakewalk. Race, Modernism and Music in Early Twentieth-Century Paris." *Revue musicale* 2, no. 1 (2014): 20–39.

Deaville, James. "Music and Cultures of Racial Representation in the Nineteenth Century." *Nineteenth-Century Music Review* 3, no. 1 (2006): ix–xiii.

Décoret-Ahiha, Anne. *Les danses exotiques en France, 1880–1940.* Paris: Centre National de la Danse, 2004.

DeLanda, Manuel. *Assemblage Theory.* Edinburgh: Edinburgh University Press, 2016.

Delanty, Gerard. "Cosmopolitanism and Violence: The Limits of Global Civil Society." *European Journal of Social Theory* 4, no. 1 (2001): 41–52.

Delanty, Gerard. "The Cosmopolitan Imagination: Critical Cosmopolitanism and Social Theory." *The British Journal of Sociology* 57, no. 1 (2006): 25–47.

Delanty, Gerard. "Nationalism and Cosmopolitanism: The Paradox of Modernity." In *The SAGE Handbook of Nations and Nationalism*, edited by Gerard Delante and Krishan Kumar, 357–368. London: Sage, 2006.

Delanty, Gerard, ed. *Routledge International Handbook of Cosmopolitan Studies.* New York: Routledge, 2012.

Delanty, Gerard, and B. He. "Cosmopolitan Perspectives on European and Asian Transnationalism." *International Sociology* 23, no. 3 (2008): 323–344.

De Mello Kujawski, G. *Idéia do Brasil: A arquitetura imperfeita.* Rio de Janeiro: Senac, 2001.

DeNora, Tia. *After Adorno: Rethinking Music Sociology.* Cambridge, UK, and New York: Cambridge University Press, 2003.

Desan, Suzanne, Lynn Hunt, and William Nelson, eds. *French Revolution in a Global Perspective.* Ithaca, NY: Cornell University Press, 2013.

De Sapio, Joseph Jeffrey. *Modernity and Meaning in Victorian London: Tourist Views of the Imperial Capital.* New York and London: Palgrave Macmillan, 2014.

Deyer, Richard. "The Matter of Whiteness." In *Theories of Race and Racism: A Reader*, edited by John Solomons and Les Back, 539–548. New York: Routledge, 2000.

Dhanvantari, Sujaya. "French Revolutionary Song in the Haitian Revolution 1789–1804." In *African Diasporas in the New and Old Worlds: Consciousness and Imagination*, edited by Geneiève Fabre and Klaus Benesch, 101–119. Amsterdam and New York: Rodopi, 2004.

Dias, Alexandre. "Os *maxixes* no exterior: O caso de "La mattchiche." In *Acervo Ernesto Nazareth: 150 Anos.* Rio de Janeiro: Instituto Moreira Salles, online publication. https://blogdoims.com.br/os-maxixes-no-exterior-parte-i-o-caso-de-la-mattchiche/

Dias, Márcia Tosta. *Os donos da voz. Indústria fonográfica brasileira e mundialização da cultura*, 2nd ed. São Paulo: Boitempo Editorial, 2008.

Diaz, Roberto Ignacio. "Transatlantic Deficits; or, Alberto Vilar at the Royal Opera House." *Bulletin of Latin American Research* 30 (2011): 128–140.

DiMaggio, Paul. "Cultural Boundaries and Structural Change: The Extension of the High Culture Model to Theater, Opera, and Dance, 1900–1940." In *Cultivating Differences*, edited by M. Lamont and M. Fournier, 21–57. Chicago: University of Chicago Press, 1992.

Di Pace, Arnaldo. "O musical antes do musical: Os filmes cantantes brasileiros, 1908–1911." *Relici, Revista Livre de Cinema* 5, no. 1 (2018): 73–93.

Dizikes, John. *Opera in America: A Cultural History*. New Haven, CT: Yale University Press, 1993.

Dolan, Therese. *Manet, Wagner, and the Musical Culture of Their Time*. Surrey, UK: Ashgate, 2013.

Dominguez, Beatriz Helena. "Cidades como pessoas: uma genealogia das formulações de Richard Morse sobre as cidades na América Latina." *Intellectus* 15, no. 2 (2016): 1–24.

Dominguez, Beatriz Helena. "Do 'Fausto' de Goethe ao 'Fausto' de Estanislao del Campo: Cidades e identidades em arenas 'periféricas' da Europa e da America Latina em fins do século XIX." In *História da América: Historiografia e interpretações*, edited by Luis Estevão de Oliveira Fernandes, 306–319. Rio Preto, Brazil: Editora Universidade Federal de Ouro Preto, 2012.

Donald, James, *Imagining the Modern City*. Minneapolis: University of Minnesota Press, 1999.

Dostoevsky, Fyodor. *The Brothers Karamazov: A Novel in Four Parts with Epilogue*, translated and annotated by Richard Pevear and Larissa Volokbonsky. New York: Farrar, Straus, and Giroux, 2002 [1880].

Dottori, Mauricio. *The Church Music of Davide Perez and Niccolò Jommelli with Special Emphasis on Funeral Music*. Curitiba, Brazil: Editora Universidade Federal do Paraná, 2008.

Doughty, Karolina. "Rethinking Musical Cosmopolitanism as a Visceral Politics of Sound." In *Sounding Places: More-than-Representational Geographies of Sound and Music*, edited by Karolina Doughty, Michelle Duffy, and Theresa Harada, 189–201. Northampton, UK: Edward Elgar, 2019.

Driessen, Henk. "Mediterranean Port Cities: Cosmopolitanism Reconsidered." *History and Anthropology* 16, no. 1 (2005): 129–141.

Dudeque, Norton. "Aspectos do academicismo germânico no primeiro movimento do quarteto nᵒ 3 de Alberto Nepomuceno." *Ictus* 6 (2005): 211–232.

Dudeque, Norton. "*Ave, Libertas!* Op. 18 de Leopoldo Miguéz, considerações sobre a estrutura musical." *Opus* 27, no. 1 (2021): 1–23.

Dudeque, Norton. "*Prométhée, op. 21 de Leopoldo Miguez*: Considerações sobre o poema sinfônico, seu programa e a forma sonata." *Opus* 22, no. 1 (2016): 9–34.

Dudeque, Norton. "Realismo musical, nacionalismo e a Série Brasileira de Nepomuceno." *Música em Perspectiva* 3, no. 1 (2010): 136–166.

Dunson, Stephanie Elaine. "The Minstrel in the Parlor: Nineteenth-Century Sheet Music and the Domestication of Blackface Minstrelsy." PhD dissertation, University of Massachusetts, Amherst, 2004.

Duprat, Régis, and Nise Obino. "O estanco da música no Brasil colonial," *Anuário Interamericano de Investigacion Musical* 4 (1968): 98–XX

Duque Estrada, Luis Gonzaga. "O cabaret da Ivonne." *Kosmos* 5, no. 11 (November 1908).

Duque Estrada, Luis Gonzaga. "Princezes e Pierrots." In *Graves & Frivolos*, 113–123. Lisbon: Livraria Classica, 1910.

368 BIBLIOGRAPHY

Durval, Cesetti. "*Il Guarany* for Foreigners: Colonialist Racism, Naïve Utopia, or Pleasant Entertainment?" *Latin American Music Review* 31 (2010): 101–121.

Eckert, Penelope. "Communities of Practice." In *Encyclopedia of Language and Linguistics*, edited by Keith Brown, 2nd ed, 109–112. Amsterdam: Elsevier, 2006.

Edensor, Tim. "The More-Than-Visual Experiences of Tourism." *Tourism Geographies* 20, no. 5 (2018): 913–991.

Edmundo, Luis. *O Rio de Janeiro do meu tempo*, vol. 1. Brasília, Brazil: Senado Federal, 2003 [1938].

Erlmann, Veit. "The Aesthetics of the Global Imagination." *Public Culture* 8, no. 3 (1996): 467–487.

Erlmann, Veit. *Music, Modernity, and the Global Imagination: South Africa and the West.* New York: Oxford University Press, 1999.

Espagne, Michel. "Comparison and Transfer: A Question of Method." In *Transnational Challenges to National History Writing*, edited by Matthias Midddell and Lluis Roura, 54–139. New York and London: Palgrave Macmillan, 2013.

Everist, Mark. "Cosmopolitanism and Music for the Theater: Europe and Beyond, 1800–1870." In *Music and Cosmopolitanism*, edited by Anastasia Belinda, Kaarina Kilpiö, and Derek Scott, 12–31. New York: Routledge, 2019.

Everist, Mark. *Mozart's Ghosts: Haunting the Halls of Musical Culture.* New York: Oxford University Press, 2012.

Everist, Mark. "Reception Theories: Canonic Discourses, and Musical Value." In *Rethinking Music*, edited by Nicholas Cook and Mark Everist, 378–402. Oxford and New York: Oxford University Press, 1999.

Fabbri, Franco. "An 'Intricate Fabric of Influences and Coincidences in the History of Popular Music': Reflections on the Challenging Work of Popular Music Historians." In *Music History and Cosmopolitanism*, edited by Anastasia Belina, Kaarina Kilpiö, and Derek Scott, 74–77. New York: Routledge, 2019, Kindle.

Fagundes, Luciana Pessanha, "Música e guerra: Impactos da Primeira Guerra Mundial no cenário musical carioca." *Revista Brasileira de História* 37, no. 76 (2017): 23–44.

Faria, Arthur de. "Os Geraldos ou . . . Os gaúchos que levaram o *maxixe* a Paris." Online publication. https://www.academia.edu/10001957/Porto_Alegre_Uma_Biogra fia_Musical_Cap%C3%ADtulo_II_Os_Geraldos

Faria, Gentil de. "Comparative Literature below the Equator: The Cultural Dilemma of Choosing the Best Colonizer." In *Literature as Cultural Memory: Colonizer and Colonized*, edited by Theo D'Haens and Patricia Krüs, 259–267. Proceedings of the XVth Congress of the International Comparative Literature Association. Amsterdam and Atlanta, GA: Rodopi, 2000.

Fauser, Annegret. *Musical Encounters at the 1889 Paris World's Fair.* Rochester, NY: University of Rochester Press, 2005.

Fauser, Annegret, and Mark Everist. "Introduction." In *Music, Theater and Cultural Transfer: Paris, 1830-1914*, edited by Mark Everist and Annegret Fauser, 1–8. Chicago: Chicago University Press, 2009.

Fedorak, Shirley. "What is Popular Culture?" In *The Routledge Handbook of Popular Culture and Tourism*, edited by Christine Lundberg and Vassilios Ziakas, 9–18. New York: Routledge, 2018.

Feld, Steven. *Jazz Cosmopolitanims in Accra: Five Musical Years in Accra.* Durham, NC: Duke University Press, 2012.

BIBLIOGRAPHY 369

Feld, Steven, Aaron Fox, Thomas Porcello, and Davis Samuels. "Vocal Anthropology: From the Music of Language to the Language of Song." In *A Companion to Linguistic Anthropology*, edited by Alessandro Duranti, 321–345. Malden: Blackwell, 2004.

Ferlim, Uliana Dias Campos. "A polifonia das *modinhas*: Diversidade e tensões musicais no Rio de Janeiro na passagem do século XIX ao XX." Master's thesis, Universidade Estadual de Campinas, 2006.

Fernández, María. *Cosmopolitanism in Mexican Visual Culture*. Austin: University of Texas Press, 2013.

Ferreira, Aléxia Lorrana Silva. "Jacinto Heller: Repertório de um empresário teatral (1875–1885)." *Cadernos Letra e Ato* 6, no. 6 (2016): 28–41.

Ferreira, Cristina, and Thiago Lenz. "Duas narrativas para o lugar dos indígenas nas origens da nação: A história ficcional de Magalhães e Alencar." *Almanack* 23 (September–December 2019): 202–238.

Ferreira, Liliane Carneiro dos Santos. "Cenários da ópera na imprensa Carioca: Cultura, processo civilizador e sociedade na belle èpoque (1889–1914)." PhD dissertation, Universidade de Brasília, 2017.

Ferreira, Liliane Carneiro dos Santos. "A imprensa e a ópera italiana nos primeiros anos da república (Rio de Janeiro, 1889–1898)." *Anais do VII Simpósio Nacional de História Cultural*. São Paulo: Universidade de São Paulo, 2015. https://gthistoriacultural.com. br/VIIsimposio/Anais/Liliane%20Carneiro%20dos%20Santos%20Ferreira.pdf

Ferreira, Liliane Carneiro dos Santos. "A ópera no Rio de Janeiro do início da República: Reflexões sobre seus múltiplos significados e possibilidades de abordagem histórica." In *XXVII Simpósio Nacional de História*. Florianópolis, Brazil, 2015. https://www.academia.edu/40547535/A_%C3%B3pera_no_Rio_de_Janeiro_no_ in%C3%ADcio_da_Rep%C3%BAblica

Ferrez, Gilberto. *Pathé: 80 anos na vida do Rio*. Rio de Janeiro: Ministério da Cultura, 2010.

Figueiredo, Carlos Alberto. "Análise da edição de Luiz Heitor Correia de Azevedo da Missa de Defuntos (CPM 184), de José Maurício Nunes Garcia (1767–1830)." In *Patrimônio musical na atualidade: Tradição, memória, discurso, e poder*, edited by Maria Alice Volpe, 83–96. Rio de Janeiro: University of Rio de Janeiro Press, 2013.

Figueroa, Sebastián. "Carlos Gomes: Opera, nación y antropofagia." In *Imaginarios nacionales: Viajes, territorios e identidades*, edited by Ana Traverso and Andrea Kottow, 93–110. Valdivia-Santiago, Austral University, Chile: RIL edition, 2016.

Fine, Robert. "Cosmopolitanism and Violence: Difficulties of Judgment." *British Journal of Sociology* 57, no. 1 (2006): 49–67.

Finnegan, Ruth. "Music, Experience, and the Anthropology of Emotion." In *The Cultural Study of Music: A Critical Introduction*, edited by Martin Clayton, Trevor Herbert, and Richard Middleton, 352–353. London: Taylor & Francis Group, 2011.

Fléchet, Anaïs. "Offenbach à Rio: La fièvre de l ' opérette dans le Brésil du Segundo Reinado. " In *La circulation transatlantique des imprimés: Connexions*, edited by Márcia Abreu and Marisa Midori Deacto, 321–.341 Campinas: UNICAMP/IEL/Secteurs des publications, 2014.

Fojas, Camilla. *Cosmopolitanism in the Americas*. West Lafayette, IN: Purdue University Press, 2005.

Fonseca, Thais Nívia de Lima. "Da infâmia ao altar da pátria: Memória e representações da inconfidência mineira e de Tiradentes." PhD dissertation, Universidade de São Paulo, 2001.

370 BIBLIOGRAPHY

Fonseca, Thais Nívia de Lima."A Inconfidência Mineira e Tiradentes vistos pela Imprensa: A vitalização dos mitos (1930–1960)." *Revista Brasileira de História* 22, no. 44 (2002): 439–462.

Franceschi, Humberto. *A Casa Edison e seu tempo*. Rio de Janeiro: Sarapuí, 2002.

Franklin, Peter. "Shared Stories? Karlowicz and the Fin-de-Siècle Musical Narrative." In *European Fin-de-Siècle and Polish Modernism: The Music of Mieczylaw Karlowicz*, edited by Luca Scala, 107–118. Bologna, Italy: UT Orpheus Edizioni, 2010.

Fraser, Robert. *Literature, Music, and Cosmopolitanism: Culture as Migration*. London: Palgrave Macmillan, 2018.

Fry, Andy. "The 'Caruso of Jazz' and a 'Creole Benvenuto Cellini' Verdi, 'Miserere . . . Ah, che la morte ognora' (Leonora, Manrico), Il trovatore, Act IV." *Cambridge Opera Journal* 28, no. 2 (2016): 183–186.

Freire, Vanda. "As Mágicas e a Circularidade de Gêneros Musicais no Século XIX." In *Música e história no longo século XIX*, edited by Antonio Herculano, Martha Ulhôa, and Mônica Pimenta Velloso, 209–235. Rio de Janeiro: Fundação Casa de Rui Barbosa, 2011.

Freire, Vanda. *Rio de Janeiro, séc. XIX: A cidade da ópera*. Rio de Janeiro: Editora Garamond, 2013.

Freitas, Eduardo da Silva. "A ideologia nacionalista republicana na história da literatura brasileira de Silvio Romero." *Matraga* 24, no. 40 (2017): 207–224.

Freitas, Olga. "*Il Guarany* de Antônio Carlos Gomes: A história de uma ópera nacional." Master's thesis, Universidade Federal do Paraná, 2011.

Fridman, Fania, and Mauricio Abreu. *Cidades latino-americanas: Um debate sobre a formação de núcleos urbanos*. Rio de Janeiro: Casa da Palavra, 2010.

Frijhoff, Willem, Yann Bank, and Maarteen van Buuren. *Dutch Culture in a European Perspective. 1900: The Age of Bourgeoisie Culture*. London: Palgrave Macmillan, 2004.

Fritzsche, Peter. "The City and Urban Life." In *The Fin-de-Siècle World*, edited by Michael Saler, 29–44. New York: Routledge, 2015.

Frith, Simon. "Music and Identity." In *Questions of Cultural Identity*, edited by Stuart Hall and Paul Du Gay, 108–127. London: SAGE Publications, 1996.

Frith, Simon. *Performing Rites: On the Value of Popular Music*. Cambridge, MA: Harvard University Press, 1996.

Frith, Simon. "Why Do Songs Have Words?" In *Popular Music: Critical Concepts in Media and Cultural Studies*, edited by Simon Frith, 186–212. New York: Routledge, 2004.

Frost, Mark. "Maritime Networks and the Colonial Public Sphere, 1840–1920." *New Zealand Journal of Asian Studies* 6, no. 2 (2004): 63–94.

Gafijczuk, Dariusz. *Identity, Aesthetics and Sound in the Fin de Siècle: Redesigning Perception*. New York: Routledge, 2014.

Gagnier, Regenia. *Individualism, Decadence, and Globalization: On the Relationship of Part to Whole, 1859–1920*. New York: Palgrave Macmillan, 2010.

Gay, Peter. *Schnitzler's Century: The Making of Middle-Class Culture, 1815–1914*. New York: W. W. Norton, 2002.

Gebhardt, Nicholas. *Vaudeville Melodies: Popular Musicians and Mass Entertainment in American Culture, 1870–1929*. Chicago: Chicago University Press, 2017.

Geler, Lea. *Andares negros, caminos blancos: Afroporteños, estado y nación Argentina a fines del siglo XIX*. Rosario, Argentina: Prohistoria Ediciones, Universidad de Barcelona, 2010.

BIBLIOGRAPHY   371

Gerhard, Anselm. *The Urbanization of Opera: Music in Paris in the Nineteenth Century*, translated by Mary Whitall. Chicago: University of Chicago Press, 1998.

Gevinson, Alan. "The Origins of Vaudeville: Aesthetic Power, Disquietude, and Cosmopolitanism in the Quest for an American Music Hall." PhD dissertation, Johns Hopkins University, 2007.

Geyer, Michael. "Review of *Transnationale Geschichte: Themen, Tendenzen und Theorien*, edited by Gunilla Budde, Sebastian Conrad, and Janz, Oliver (Göttingen, Germany: Vanden-hoeck & Ruprecht, 2006). *H-soz-kult* (October 11, 2006), online publication, www.hsozkult.de/publicationreview/id/reb-9016.

Geyer, Michael, and Charles Bright. "World History in a Global Age." *American Historical Review* 100, no. 4 (1995): 1034–1060.

Gienow-Hecht, J. C. E. *Sound Diplomacy: Music and Emotions in Transatlantic Relations, 1850–1920*. Chicago: University of Chicago Press, 2009.

Giles, Paul. "Transnationalism and American Literature." *PMLA* 118, no. 1 (2003): 62–77.

Gilroy, Paul. *Against Race: Imagining Political Culture Beyond the Color Line*. Cambridge, MA: Harvard University Press, 2000.

Gilroy, Paul. *The Black Atlantic: Modernity and Double Consciousness*. London: Verso, 1993.

Ginger, Andrew. "Cultural Modernity and Atlantic Perspectives." *Atlantic Studies* 4, no. 1 (2007): 27–36.

Giron, Luis Antônio. "Pixinguinha, quintessência da musica popular brasileira." *Revista do Instituto de Estudos Brasileiro* 42 (1997): 43–57.

Gobbo, Federico. "Beyond the Nation-State? The Ideology of the Esperanto Movement between Neutralism and Multilingualism." *Social Inclusion* 5, no. 4 (2017): 38–47.

Goehr, Lydia. *The Imaginary Museum of Musical Works: An Essay in the Philosophy of Music*. Oxford and New York: Oxford University Press, 1992.

Góes, Marcos. *Carlos Gomes: Uma força indômita*. Belém: Secult, 1996.

Goldberg, K. Meira. "Jaleo de Jerez and tumulte noir: Primitivist Modernism and Cakewalk in Flamenco, 1902–1917." In *Flamenco on the Global Stage: Historical, Critical and Theoretical Perspectives*, edited by K. Meira Goldberg, Ninotchka Devorah Bennahum, and Michelle Heffner Hayes, 124–142. Jefferson, NC: McFarland, 2015.

Goldberg, Guilherme. *Transcrições Guanabarinas: Antologia crítica*, vols. 1–4, edited by Amanda Oliveira, and Patrick Menuzzi. Porto Alegre: LiquidBook, 2019, online publication.

Goldberg, Luis Guilherme. "Alberto Nepomuceno e a Missa de Santa Cecília de José Maurício." In *Anais do VI Encontro de Musicologia Histórica*, 138–172. Juiz de Fora: Centro Cultural Pró-Música, 2006.

Goldberg, Luis Guilherme. "Alberto Nepomuceno: Vínculos modernistas no Trio em fá sustenido menor (1916)." *Música em Perspectiva* 3, no. 1 (2010): 54–87.

Goldberg, Luis Guilherme. "José Maurício Nunes Garcia: Um mulato civilizado na Primeira República." *Per Musi* 39 (2019): 1–18.

Goldberg, Luis Guilherme. *Um Guaratuja entre Wotan e o Fauno: Alberto Nepomuceno e o modernismo musical brasileiro*. Porto Alegre, Brazil: Movimento, 2011.

Goltz, Jennifer. "Pierrot le diseur." *The Musical Times* 147, no. 1894 (2006): 59–72.

Gomes, Tiago de Melo. "Para além da casá da Tia Ciata: Outras experiencias no universe musical carioca, 1830–1930." *Afro-Asia* 20, no. 30 (2003): 175–198.

Gonçalves, Rafael. *Favelas do Rio de Janeiro: História e direito*. Rio de Janeiro: Editora da Pontifícia Universidade Católica do Rio de Janeiro, PUC, 2013.

372 BIBLIOGRAPHY

González, Juan Pablo, and C. Rolle. *Historia social de la música popular en Chile, 1890–1950*. Santiago, Chile: Ediciones Universidad Católica de Chile, Santiago, 2005.

Gooley, Dana. "Cosmopolitanism in the Age of Nationalism: 1848–1914." *Journal of the American Musicological Society* 66, no. 2 (2013): 523–549.

Gooley, Dana. "Meyerbeer, Eclecticism, and Operatic Cosmopolitanism." *The Musical Quarterly* 99, no. 2 (Summer 2016): 166–200.

Gordon, Rae Beth. *Dances with Darwin, 1875–1910: Vernacular Modernity in France*. London and New York: Routledge, 2016 [2009].

Gordon, Rae Beth. "Les rythmes contagieux d'une danse noire: Le cake-walk." *Intermédialités* 16 (Fall 2010): 57–81.

Gossett, Philip. "Verdi the Craftsman." *Revista Portuguesa de Musicologia* 11 (2001): 81–111.

Greenblatt, Stephen. *Cultural Mobility: A Manifesto*. Cambridge, UK: Cambridge University Press, 2010.

Grimley, Daniel. *Grig: Music, Landscape and Norwegian Identity*. Suffolk, UK: Boydell Press, 2006.

Grimley, Daniel. "Hearing Landscape Critically: Prospects and Reflections." *Studien Zur Wertungsforschung* 62 (2019): 89–101.

Grimley, Daniel "Music, Landscape, Attunement: Listening to Sibelius's Tapiola." *Journal of the American Musicological Society* 64, no. 2 (2011): 394–398.

Grinberg, Keila. "Slavery, Liberalism, and Civil Law: Definitions of Status and Citizenship in the Elaboration of the Brazilian Civil Code (1855–1916)." In *Honor, Status, and Law in Modern Latin America*, edited by Suseann Caulfield, Sarah C. Chambers, and Lara Putnam, 109–127. Durham, NC: Duke University Press, 2005.

Grover-Friedlander, Michal. *Vocal Apparitions: The Attraction of Cinema to Opera*. Princeton, NJ: Princeton University Press, 2005.

Gutsche-Miller, Sarah. "Pantomime-Ballet on the Music-Hall Stage: The Popularisation of Classical Ballet in Fin-de-Siècle Paris." PhD dissertation, McGill University, 2010.

Hagemeyer, Rafael Rosa. "Levando ao longe o canto da pátria: Gravações em disco e difusões no rádio do Hino Nacional (1900–1945)." *Revista de História e Estudos Culturais* 8, no. 3 (2008): 1–22.

Hamberlin, Larry. *Tin Pan Opera: Operatic Novelty Songs in the Ragtime Era*. Oxford and New York: Oxford University Press, 2011.

Hamilton, Kenneth. "Wagner and Liszt: Elective Affinities." In *Richard Wagner and His World*, edited by Thomas Grey, 27–63. Princeton, NJ: Princeton University Press, 2009.

Hanley, Keith, and Greg Kucich. "Introduction: Global Formations and Recalcitrances." In *Nineteenth-Century Worlds, Global Formations Past and Present*, edited by Keith Hanley and Greg Kucic, 1–8. New York: Routledge, 2013.

Hannerz, Ulf. *Transnational Connections: Culture, People, Places*. London: Routledge, 1999.

Hansen, David. "Chasing Butterflies Without a Net: Interpreting Cosmopolitanism." *Studies in Philosophy and Education* 29, no. 2 (2010): 151–166.

Hanson, Helen, and Catherine O'Rawe, ed. *The Femme Fatale: Images, Histories, Contexts*. New York and London: Palgrave Macmillan, 2010.

Harvey, David. *The Condition of Postmodernity: An Enquiry into the Origins of Cultural Change*. Cambridge, MA: Blackwell, 1989.

Harvey, David. *Paris: Capital of Modernity*. Oxford and New York: Routledge. 2003.

Hawkins, Peter. *Chanson: The French Singer-Songwriter from Aristide Bruant to the Present Day*. New York: Ashgate, 2000, Kindle.

Hazan, Marcelo Campos. "José Maurício, Marcos Portugal e a sonata de Haydn: desconstruindo of mito." *Brasiliana* 28 (December 2008): 2–11.

Hazan, Marcelo Campos. "Raça, Nação e José Maurício Nunes Garcia." *Ressonâncias* 13, no. 24 (2009): 23–40.

Heffernan, Michael. "Fin de Siècle, Fin du Monde? On the Origins of European Geopolitics: 1890–1920." In *Geopolitical Traditions: A Century of Geopolitical Thought*, edited by Klaus Dodds and David A. Atkinson, 27–51. London and New York: Routledge, 2000.

Heineberg, Ilana. "Peri com sotaque francês: Um estudo preliminar de três traduções de O Guarani no século XIX." In *José de Alencar: século XXI*, edited by Marcelo Peloggio, Arlene Fernandes, and Valéria Cristina Bezerra, 241–265. Fortaleza: Brazil Edições UFC, 2015.

Helmers, Rutger. "The Traveling Musician as Cosmopolitan: Western Performers and Composers in Mid-Nineteen-Century St. Peterburg and Moscow." In *Confronting the National in the Musical Past*, edited by Elaine Kelly, Markus Mantere, and Derek Scott, 64–77. London and New York: Routledge, 2018.

Henkin, David. *The Postal Age: The Emergence of Modern Communications in Nineteenth Century America*. University of Chicago Press, 2007.

Henson, Karen. *Opera Acts: Singers and Performance in the Late Nineteenth Century*. Cambridge, UK: Cambridge University Press, 2015.

Hertzman, Marc A. *Making Samba: A New History of Race and Music in Brazil*. Durham, NC: Duke University Press, 2013.

Hesmondhalgh, David. "Towards a Political Aesthetics of Music." In *The Cultural Study of Music: A Critical Introduction*, edited by Martin Clayton, Martin Clayton, Trevor Herbert, and Richard Middleton, 364–374. London: Taylor & Francis Group, 2011.

Hess, Carol. "Saint-Saëns and Latin America." In *Saint-Saëns and His World*, edited by Jann Pasler, 201–209. Princeton, NJ: Princeton University Press, 2012.

Hesselager, Jens. "Introduction." In *Grand Opera Outside Paris: Opera on the Move in Nineteenth-Century Europe*, edited by Jens Hesselager, 16–25. New York and London: Routledge, 2018.

Hicks, Jonathan. "Should Manrico Escape? Verdi, 'Miserere . . . Ah, che la morte ognora' (Leonora, Manrico), Il trovatore, Act IV." *Cambridge Opera Journal* 28, no. 2 (2016): 187–190.

Hindson, Catherine. *Female Performance Practice on the Fin-de-Siecle Popular Stage of London and Paris*. Manchester, UK: Machester University Press, 2007.

Hobsbawm, Eric John. *Age of Empire 1875–1914*. New York: Vintage Books, 1989.

Hobsbawm, Eric John. *Echoes of the Marseillaise: Two Centuries Look Back on the French Revolution*. London and New York: Verso, 1990.

Hoganson, Kristin. "Cosmopolitan Domesticity: Importing the American Dream, 1865–1920." *The American Historical Review* 107 (2002): 55–83.

Holloway, Thomas. *Policing Rio de Janeiro: Repression and Resistance in a Nineteenth-Century City*. Stanford, CA: Stanford University Press, 1993.

Holton, Robert. *Cosmopolitanisms: New Thinking and New Directions*. New York: Palgrave Macmillan, 2009.

Holton, Robert. "Some Coments on Cosmopolitanism and Europe." In *European Cosmopolitanism in Question*, edited by R. Robertson and A. Krossa, 25–43. London and New York: Palgrave MacMillan, 2012.

Hopper, Paul. *Understanding Cultural Globalization*. Cambridge, UK: Polity, 2007.

374 BIBLIOGRAPHY

Horowitz, Joseph. *Wagner Nights: An American History*. Berkeley: University of California Press, 1994.

Howard, Michael. "The Down of the Century." In *The Oxford History of the Twentieth Century*, edited by Michael Howard and Roger Louis, 3–9. New York and Oxford: Oxford University Press, 2000.

Huyssen, Andreas. "Introduction: World Cultures, World Cities." In *Other Cities, Other Worlds: Urban Imaginaries in a Globalizing Age*, edited by Andreas Huyssen, 1–23. Durham, NC: Duke University Press, 2008.

Izquierdo, José Manuel. "The Cosmopolitan Muse: Searching for a Musical Style in Early Nineteenth-Century Latin America." In *Music History and Cosmopolitanism*, edited by Anastasia Belina, Kaarina Kilpiö, and Derek Scott, 58–72. New York: Routledge, 2019, Kindle.

Izquierdo, José Manuel. "Rossini's Reception in Latin America: Scarcity and Imagination in Two Early Chilean Sources." In *Gioachino Rossini 1868-2018: La musica e il mondo*, edited by Ilaria Narici, Emilio Sala, and Emanuele Senici, 413–436. Pesaro, Italy: Fondazione Rossini Pesaro, 2018.

Izquierdo, José Manuel, Jaime Cortés-Polanía, and Juan Francisco Sans. "The Return of the Habanera: Carmen's Early Reception in Latin America." In *Carmen Abroad: Bizet's Opera on the Global Stage*, edited by Richard Langham Smith and Clair Rowden, 164–178. New York: Cambridge University Press, 2020.

Jackson, Lee. *Palaces of Pleasure: From Music Halls to the Seaside to Football, How the Victorians Invented Mass Entertainment*. New Haven, CT: Yale University Press, 2019.

Jaguaribe, Beatriz. *Rio de Janeiro: Urban Life through the Eyes of the City*. London and New York: Routledge, 2014.

Johnson, J. H. *Listening in Paris: A Cultural History*. Berkeley and Los Angeles: University of California Press, 1996.

Jonckheere, Evelien. "In Search of Identities: 'Foreigner' in Fin-de-Siècle Belgian Café-Concerts." *Journal of Audiences and Reception Studies* 16, no. 2 (November 2019): 384–403.

Jordan, Matthew. *Le Jazz: Jazz and the French Cultural Identity*. Urbana: University of Illinois Press, 2010.

Jost, Francois. "The Voices of Silence." In *The Sounds of Early Cinema*, edited by Richard Abel and Rick Altman, 48–56. Bloomington: Indiana University Press, 2001.

Keefe, Simon. *Mozart's Requiem: Reception, Work, Completion*. Cambridge, UK: Cambridge University Press, 2012.

Keightley, Keir. "Un voyage via barquinho . . . Global Circulation, Musical Hybridization, and Adult Modernity, 1961-9." In *Migrating Music*, edited by Jason Toynbee and Byron Dueck, 112–126. New York: Routledge, 2012.

Kelly, Elaine, Markus Mantere, and Derek Scott, eds. *Confronting the National in the Musical Past*. London and New York; Routledge, 2018.

Kenrick, John. "The Merry Widow 101: History of a Hit," online publication.

Kern, Stephen. *Culture of Time and Space, 1880-1918*. Cambridge, MA, and London: Harvard University Press, 1983.

Kerr, Isaac William. "Instrumentação e orquestração em Antônio Carlos Gomes: Um estudo em seus prelúdios e sinfonias." Master's thesis, Universidade Estadual de Campinas, SP, 2016.

Kibler, M. Alison. *Rank Ladies: Gender and Cultural Hierarchy in American Vaudeville*. Chapel Hill: University of North Carolina Press, 1999.

BIBLIOGRAPHY 375

Kiousopoulos, Dimitrios. "L'opera lirica nazionale in prospettiva internazionale: I casi della Grecia e del Brasile nel XIX secolo." *Memoria e Ricerca* 29 (2008): 47–62.

Kirkland, Stephanie. *Paris Reborn: Napoléon III, Baron Haussmann, and the Quest to Build a Modern City*. New York: St. Martin Press, 2013.

Kleingeld, Pauline. "Six Varieties of Cosmopolitanism in Late Eighteenth-Century Germany." *Journal of the History of Ideas* 60, no. 3 (1999): 505–524.

Koegel, John. *Music in German Immigrant Theater: New York City 1840–1940*. Rochester, NY: University of Rochester Press, 2009.

Kok, Glória. *Rio de Janeiro na época da Av. Central*. São Paulo: Bei Comunicação, 2005.

Körner, Axel. "From Transnational History to Transnational Opera: Questioning National Categories of Analysis," University College, London, 2015, online publication.

Körner, Axel. "Music of the Future: Italian Theaters and the European Experience of Modernity between Unification and World War One." *European History Quarterly* 41, no. 2 (2011): 189–212.

Kreuzer, Gundula. *Verdi and the Germans: From Unification to the Third Reich*. Cambridge, UK: Cambridge University Press, 2010.

Krims, A. *Music and Urban Geography*. New York: Routledge, 2007.

Landers, Jane. *Atlantic Creoles in the Age of Revolutions*. Cambridge, MA: Harvard University Press, 2011.

Lane, Jill. *Blackface Cuba, 1840–1895*. Philadelphia: University of Pennsylvania Press, 2005.

Large, David, and Willian Weber, eds. *Wagnerism in European Culture and Politics*. New York: Cornell University Press, 1984.

Larsen, Juliane Cristina. "Republicana, moderna, e cosmopolita: A música de concerto no Rio de Janeiro entre 1889 e 1914." PhD dissertation, Universidade de São Paulo, 2018.

Lavan, Myles, Richard E. Payne, and John Weisweiler. *Cosmopolitanism and Empire: Universal Rules, Local Elites, and Cultural Integration in the Ancient Near East and Mediterranean*. New York: Oxford University Press, 2016.

Lawson, S. "Cosmopolitan Pluralism: Beyond the Cultural Turn." *Cosmopolitan Civil Societies: An Interdisciplinary Journal* 3, no. 3 (2011): 27–46.

Ledford, Julian A. "Joseph Boulogne, the Chevalier de Saint-George and the Problem with Black Mozart." *Journal of Black Studies* 51, no. 1 (2020): 60–82.

Ledger, Sally, and Roger Luckhurst. *The Fin de Siecle: A Reader in Cultural History, c. 1880–1900*. New York: Oxford University Press, 2000.

Leme, Monica. "Cancioneiros populares para Ioiôs e Iaiás: O mercado editorial para a 'música ligeira' no Rio de Janeiro (1870–1920)." In *Vida divertida: Histórias do lazer no Rio de Janeiro (1830–1930)*, edited by Andrea Marzano and Victor Andrade de Melo, 179–209. Rio de Janeiro: Apicuri, 2010.

Lenz, Cristina Ferreira, and Thiago Lenz. "Duas narrativas para o lugar dos indígenas nas origens da nação: a história ficcional de Magalhães e Alencar." *Almanack* 23 (September–December 2019): 202–238.

Lessa, Carlos. "Nação e nacionalismo a partir da experiência brasileira." *Estudos Avançados* 22, no. 62 (2008): 237–256.

Levin, Orna Messer. "Offenbach et le public brésilien (1840–1870)." In *La circulation transatlantique des imprimés: Connexions*, edited by Márcia Abreu and Marisa Midori Deacto, 299–310. Campinas: UNICAMP/IEL/Secteurs des publications, 2014.

Levin, Orna Messer. "Theatrical Culture and Global Audience: French Repertory in Rio de Janeiro." In *The Cultural Revolution of the Nineteenth-Century: Theater, the*

376 BIBLIOGRAPHY

Book-Trade, and Reading in the Transatlantic World, edited by Márcia Abreu and Ana Cláudia Suriani da Silva, 234–251. London: Bloomsbury, 2016.

Leydi, Roberto. "The Dissemination and Popularization of Opera." In *Opera in Theory and Practice*, edited by Lorenzo Bianconi and Giorgio Pestelli, 314–342. Chicago: University of Chicago Press, 2003.

Lima, Evelyn Furquim Werneck. *Arquitetura do espetáculo: Teatros e cinemas na formação da Praça Tiradentse e da Cinelândia*. Rio de Janeiro: Editora da UFRJ, 2000.

Linhardt, Marion. "Local Contexts and Genre Construction in Early Continental Musical Theater." In *Popular Musical Theater in London and Berlin*, edited by Len Platt, Tobias Becker, and David Linton, 57–74. Cambridge, UK: Cambridge University Press, 2014.

Lins, Vera. "Em revistas, o simbolismo e a virada de século." In *O moderno em revistas: Representações do Rio de Janeiro de 1890–1930*, edited by Mônica Pimenta, Vera Lins, and Cláudia de Oliveira, 15–42. Rio de Janeiro: Garamon, 2010.

Lins, Vera. "O moderno em revista." In *O moderno em revistas: Representações do Rio de Janeiro de 1890–1930*, edited by Mônica Pimenta, Vera Lins, and Cláudia de Oliveira, 1–14. Rio de Janeiro: Garamon, 2010.

Llano, Samuel. "Street Music, Honour and Degeneration: The Case of Organilleros." In *Writing Wrongdoing in Spain, 1800–1936: Realities, Representations, Reactions*, edited by Alison Sinclair and Samuel Llano, 197–215. Martlesham, UK: Boydell & Brewer, 2017.

Lobo, Helio. *Manuel de Araújo Porto Alegre*. Rio de Janeiro: ABC, 1938.

Locke, Ralph. *Musical Exoticism: Images and Reflections*. Cambridge, UK, and New York: Cambridge University Press, 2009.

Locke, Ralph. "Nineteenth-Century Musics: Quantity, Quality, Qualities." *Nineteenth-Century Music Review* 1, no. 1 (2004): 3–41.

Lockhart, William. "Listening to the Domestic Music Machine: Keyboard Arrangements in the Nineteenth-Century." PhD dissertation, Humboldt-Universität, Berlin, 2012.

Lopes, Antonio Herculano. "Vem cá, mulata!" *Tempo* 13, no. 26 (2009): 80–100.

López, A. M. "Early Cinema and Modernity in Latin America." *Cinema Journal* 40, no.1 (2000): 48–78.

Losa, Leonor. *Machinas falantes: A música gravada em Portugal no início do século XX*. Lisboa: Tinta da China, 2014.

Loss, Jaqueline. *Cosmopolitanisms and Latin America: Against the Destiny of Place*. New York and London: Palgrave Macmillan, 2005.

Lotz, Rainer. *Black People: Entertainers of African Descent in Europe, and Germany*. Bonn: Brigit Lotz Verlag, 1997.

Love, Joseph. "The Brazilian Federal State in the Old Republic: Did Regime Change Make a Difference?" In *State and Nation Making in Latin America and Spain: Republics of the Possible*, edited by Miguel Centeno and Agustin Ferrano, 100–115. Cambridge, UK, and New York: Cambridge University Press, 2013.

Lowerson, John. *Amateur Operatics: A Social and Cultural History*. Manchester, UK: Manchester University Press, 2005.

Ludke, Karen. "Songs and Music." In *The Handbook of Informal Language Learning*, edited by Mark Dressman and Randall William Sadler, 203–213. New York: Wiley 2018, online publication.

MacClary, Susan. *Conventional Wisdom: The Content of Musical Form*. Berkeley and Los Angeles: University of California Press, 2001.

BIBLIOGRAPHY   377

Magaldi, Cristina. "Before and after Samba: Modernity, Cosmopolitanism, and Popular Music in Rio de Janeiro at the Beginning and End of the Twentieth Century." In *Postnational Musical Identities: Cultural Production, Distribution, and Consumption in Globalized Scenario*, edited by Ignacio Corona and Alejandro Madrid, 173–184. Lanham, MD: Lexington Books, 2008.

Magaldi, Cristina. "Cosmopolitanism and Music in the Nineteenth Century." In *Oxford Handbooks Online: Music: Scholarly Research Review*. Oxford: Oxford University Press, 2016, online source. https://academic.oup.com/edited-volume/42059

Magaldi, Cristina. "Music and Cosmopolitanism in Rio de Janeiro." *Musical Quarterly* 92, no. 3 (2009): 329–364.

Magaldi, Cristina. *Music in Imperial Rio De Janeiro: European Culture in a Tropical Milieu*. Lanham, MD: Scarecrow Press, 2004.

Magaldi, Cristina."Sonatas, Kyries, and Arias: Reassessing the Reception of European Music in Imperial Rio de Janeiro." In *Music and Culture in the Imperial Court of João VI in Rio de Janeiro*. Austin: University of Texas, 2005, online publication. http://www.lanic.utexas.edu/project/etext/llilas/cpa/spring05/missa/magaldi-1.pdf

Mainente, Renato Aurélio. "O período joanino e as transformações no cenário musical no Rio de Janeiro." *Revista história e cultura* 2, no. 1 (2013): 132–145.

Malcomson, Scott. "The Varieties of Cosmopolitan Experiences." In *Cosmopolitics: Thinking and Feeling beyond the Nation*, edited by Pheng Cheah and Bruce Robbins, 238–240. Minneapolis: University of Minnesota Press, 1998.

Mallach, Alan. *The Autumn of Italian Opera*. Lebanon, NH: Northeastern University Press, 2007.

Mammi, Lorenzo. *Carlos Gomes*. São Paulo, Brazil: Publifolha, 2001.

Manfredonia, Gaetano. "De l'usage de la chanson politique: La production anarchiste d'avant 1914," *Cités* 19 (Paris, 2004): 43–53.

Margulis, Elizabeth. *On Repeat: How Music Plays the Mind*. Oxford and New York: Oxford University Press, 2013.

Marshall, Alex. "The Twists and Turns of 'La Marseillaise.'" *New York Times*, December 13, 2016.

Martin, George. *Verdi at the Golden Gate: Opera in San Francisco in the Gold Rush Years*. Berkeley: University of California Press, 1993.

Martin, George. *Verdi in America: Ogberto through Rigoletto*. Rochester, NY: University of Rochester Press, 2011.

Martins, Camila Pereira. *Republicanismo no Rio de Janeiro e em Lisboa: 1870–1891*. PhD dissertation, Universidade de Juiz de Fora, 2015.

Martins, Luiza Mara. "The Construction of Memory about the Oito Batutas." In *Made in Brazil*, edited by Martha Tupinambá de Ulhôa Cláudia Azevedo and Felipe Trotta, 73–83. New York: Routledge, 2015, Kindle.

Martins, William de Souza Nunes. "Paschoal Segreto: 'Ministro das diversões' do Rio de Janeiro (1883–1920)." PhD dissertation, Universidade Federal do Rio de Janeiro, 2004.

Marvin, Roberta Montemorra. "Selling a 'False Verdi' in Victorian London." In *The Idea of Art Music in a Commercial World* 1800–1930, edited by Christina Bashford and Roberta Montemorra Marvin, 223–249. Woodbridge, Suffolk, UK: Boydell Press, 2016.

Mateo, Marta. "Multilingualism in Opera Production, Reception and Translation." *Themes in Translation Studies* 13 (2014): 326–354.

Matsuda, Matt. *The Memory of the Modern*. New York: Oxford University Press, 1996.

378 BIBLIOGRAPHY

Matsumoto, Naomi. "Giovanni Vittorio Rosi's Musical Theater: Opera, Operetta and the Westernisation of Modern Japan." In *Musical Theater in Europe, 1830–1934*, edited by Michela Niccolai and Clair Rowden, 351–385. Lucca, Italy: Brepolss, 2017.

Mattos, Cleofe Person de. *José Maurício Nunes Garcia: Biografia.* Rio de Janeiro: Ministério da Cultura, 1997.

McAllister, Marvin Edward. *Whiting Up: Whiteface Minstrels and Stage Europeans in African American Performance.* Chapel Hill: University of North Carolina Press, 2011.

McCann, Bryan. *Hello, Hello Brazil: Popular Music in the Making of Modern Brazil.* Durham, NC: Duke University Press, 2014.

McCarthey, Sarah, Idalia Nunez, and Chaehyn Lee. "Translanguaging Across Contexts." In *The Handbook of Informal Language Learning*, edited by Mark Dressman and Randall William Sadler, 349–367. New York: Wiley, 2019, online publication.

McKee, Eric. *Decorum of the Minuet, Delirium of the Waltz: A Study of Dance-Music Relations in 3/4 Time.* Bloomington: Indiana University Press, 2012.

McKinley, Alexander. "Anarchists and the Music of the French Revolution." *Journal for the Study of Radicalism* 1, no. 2 (2007): 1–33.

McPhee, Kit. "'Immigrants with Money Are No Use to Us': Race and Ethnicity in the Zona Portuária of Rio de Janeiro, 1903–1912." *The Americas* 62, no. 4 (April 2006): 623–650.

McPherson, Jim. "The Savages Innocents, Part II: On the Road with *Parsifal, Butterfly*, the *Widow*, and the *Girl.*" *The Opera Quarterly* 19, no. 1 (2003): 28–63.

Meade, Teresa. *Civilizing Rio: Reform and Resistance in a Brazilian City, 1889–1930.* University Park: Pennsylvania State University Press, 1997.

Meade, Teresa. "Living Worse and Costing More: Resistance and Riot in Rio de Janeiro, 1890–1917." *Journal of Latin American Studies* 21, no. 2 (May, 1989): 241–266.

Meinecke, Friedrich. *Cosmopolitanism and the Nation State*, translated by Robert B. Kimber. Princeton, NJ: Princeton University Press, 1970.

Mello, Guilherme de. *A música no Brasil.* Rio de Janeiro: Imprensa Nacional, 1947 [1908].

Mello, Maria Teresa Chavez de. "A modernidade Republicana." *Tempo* 13, no. 26 (2009): 15–31.

Mello, Maria Teresa Chavez de. *A república consentida: Cultura democrática e científica do final do Império.* Rio de Janeiro: Editora FGV/UFRJ, 2011.

Mello, Maria Teresa Chavez de. "A republica e o sonho." *Varia História* 27, no. 45 (Belo Horizonte, 2011): 121–139.

Mello, Ricardo Marques de. "Hino Nacional Brasileiro: Entre espaços de experiências e horizontes de expectativas." *Revista Múltipla* 18, no. 24 (June, 2008): 77–93.

Mencarelli, Fernando Antonio. "A voz e a partitura: Teatro musical, indústria, e diversidade cultural no Rio de Janeiro (1868–1908)." PhD dissertation, Universidade de Campinas, 2003.

Menezes, Lená Medeiros de. "Ventos Franceses nas noites cariocas: A 'cocotte comedienne' e o Alcazar Lyrique no Rio de Janeiro Imperial." *Revista do Instituto Histórico e Geográfico do Rio de Janeiro* 24, no. 24 (2017): 99–120.

Meyer, Anne. "A construção musical da feminilidade na ópera *Il Guarany* (Carlos Gomes)." In *Annals of the VI Brazilian Simposium of Graduates in Music* (SIMPOM 2020), 475–486.

Middel, Matthias, and Lluís Roura. "The Various Forms of Transcending the Horizon of National History Writing." In *Transnational Challenges to National History*

Writing, edited by Matthias Middel and Lluís Roura, 1–35. New York: Palgrave Macmillan, 2013.

Middel, Matthias, and Lluís Roura. "The Writing of World History in Europe from the Middle of the Nineteenth Century to the Present: Conceptual Renewal and Challenge to National Histories." In *Transnational Challenges to National History Writing*, edited by Matthias Midddell and Lluis Roura, 54–139. New York: Palgrave Macmillan, 2013.

Mignolo, Walter. "The Many Faces of Cosmo-Polis: Border Thinking and Critical Cosmopolitanism." *Public Culture* 12, no. 3 (2000): 721–748.

Miller, Nicole. *Reinventing Modernity in Latin America: Intellectuals Imagine the Future, 1900–1930*. New York: Palgrave Macmillan, 2008.

Minor, Ryan. "Beyond Heroism: Music, Ethics, and Everyday Cosmopolitanism." *Journal of the American Musicological Society* 66, no. 2 (2013): 533–534.

Mishkin, Frederic S. *The Next Great Globalization: How Disadvantaged Nations Can Harness Their Financial Systems to Get Rich*. Princeton, NJ: Princeton University Press, 2006.

Moechli, Laura. "Parisian Grand Opera at the Basel Theatre auf dem Blömlein: Traces of Transnational Circulation, Translation and Reception." In *Grand Opera Outside Paris: Opera on the Move in Nineteenth-Century Europe*, edited by Jens Hesselager, 13–30. New York and London: Routledge, 2018.

Moisand, Jeanne. *Scènes capitales: Madrid, Barcelona et le monde théâtral fin de siècle*. Madrid: Casa de Velázqvez, 2013.

Molz, Jeannie Germann. "Cosmopolitanism and Consumption." In *The Ashgate Research Companion to Cosmopolitanism*, edited by Maria Rovisco and Magdalena Nowika, 33–35. Surrey, UK: Ashgate, 2011.

Mondelli, Peter. "Phonocentric Revolution." *Acta Musicologica* 88, no. 2 (2016): 154.

Monteiro, Antonio. "Marcos Portugal x Padre José Maurício: A rivalidade cordial," online publication, https://padrejosemauricio.wordpress.com/author/monteirocampos antonio/

Monteiro, Antonio. "Marcos Portugal x José Maurício: O autodidata, o clássico alemão," online publication, https://padrejosemauricio.wordpress.com/author/monteiroca mposantonio/

Monteiro, John Manuel. "As 'raças' indígenas no pensamento brasileiro do império." In *Raça, ciência e sociedade*, edited by Marcos Maio and Ricardo Ventura Santos, 15–22. Rio de Janeiro: Ed. Fiocruz, 1996.

Moore, Robin. *Nationalizing Blackness: Afrocubanismo ad Artistic Revolution in Havana: 1920–1940*. Pittsburgh, PA: University of Pittsburgh Press, 1999.

Mora, Kiko. "Carmencita on the Road: Baile español y vaudeville en los Estados Unidos de América (1889–1895)." *Lumière* (2011), online publication, https://www.academia.edu/2452568/Carmencita_on_the_Road_Baile_espa%C3%B1ol_y_vaudeville_en_l os_Estados_Unidos_de_Am%C3%A9rica_1889_1895_

Moraes Filho, Mello. *Factos e memórias*. Rio de Janeiro: Garnier, 1904.

Moreiras, Alberto. *The Exhaustion of Difference: The Politics of Latin American Cultural Studies*. Durham, NC: Duke University Press, 2001.

Morelli, Giovanni. "Opera in Italian National Culture." In *Opera in Theory and Practice, Image and Myth*, edited by Lorenzo Bianconi and Giorgio Pestelli, 377–435. Chicago: University of Chicago Press, 2003.

Moretti, Franco. *Distant Reading*. London: Verso Books, 2013.

380 BIBLIOGRAPHY

Morse, Richard. "'Peripheral' Cities as Cultural Arenas (Russia, Austria, Latin America)." *Journal of Urban History* 10, no.4 (1984): 423–462.

Mullen, John. "Patriotic Palaces of Pleasure? The Popular Music Industry in 1900." *Civilisations* 13 (2014): 179–200.

Munholland, John Kim. "Republican Order and Republican Tolerance in Fin-de-Siècle France: Montmartre as a Delinquent Community." In *Montmartre and the Making of Mass Culture*, edited by Gabriel Welsberg, 15–36. New Brunswick, NJ: Rutgers University Press, 2001.

Nabuco, Joaquim. *Minha Formação*. Rio de Janeiro: Garnier, 1900.

Nasaw, David. *Going Out: The Rise and Fall of Public Amusements*. Cambridge, MA: Harvard University Press, 1993.

Needell, Jeffrey. "Rio De Janeiro and Buenos Aires: Public Space and Public Consciousness in Fin-de-Siècle Latin America." *Comparative Studies in Society and History* 37, no. 3 (1995): 519–540.

Needell, Jeffrey. *A Tropical Belle Epoque: The Elite Culture of Turn-of-the-century Rio de Janeiro*. New York: Cambridge University Press, 1987.

Nettl, Bruno. "On World Music as a Concept in the History of Music Scholarship." In *The Cambridge History of World Music*, edited by Philip V. Bohlman, 23–54. Cambridge, UK: Cambridge University Press, 2013.

Neves, Larissa de Oliveira, and Orna Messer Levin, eds. *O Theatro: Crônicas de Arthur Azevedo*. Campinas: Editora de Unicamp, 2009.

Nieden, Geza Zur. "The Internationalization of Musical Life at the End of the Nineteenth Century in Modernized Paris and Rome." *Urban History* 40, no. 4 (November 2013): 663–680.

Nogueira, Lenita. "Carlos Gomes e a musicologia no Brasil: Novas perspectivas." In *Annals do VI Simposio Internacional de Musicologia*, 100–111. Goiânia, Brazil: Universidade Federal de Goiás, 2016. Online source https://www.scribd.com/document/360191014/ANAIS-2016-musicologia-pdf

Nogueira, Lenita. "Música e política: O caso de Carlos Gomes." *ANPPOM, Annals of the XV Congress* (2005): 243–249. Online source https://www.academia.edu/es/703744/M%C3%BAsica_e_Pol%C3%ADtica_o_caso_de_Carlos_Gomes

Nogueira, Marcos Pupo. *Muito além do melodrama: Os prelúdios e sinfonias das óperas de Carlos Gomes*. São Paulo: Editora Unesp, 2006.

Noronha, Jurandyr. "No tempo dos 'falantes e cantantes': Literatura no cinema mudo." *Revista do Livro* 49 (September 2007): 23–40.

Norris, Renne Lap. "Opera and the Mainstreaming of Blackface Minstrelsy." *Journal of the Society for American Music* 1, no. 3 (2007): 341–365.

Ochs, Anna Agranoff. "Opera in Contention: Social Conflict in Late Nineteenth-Century Mexico City." PhD dissertation, University of North Carolina at Chapel Hill, 2011.

O'Donnell, Julia. *De olho na rua: A cidade de João do Rio*. Rio de Janeiro: Zahar, 2008.

Oliveira, Anderson de. "Padre José Maurício: "Dispensa da cor," mobilidade social e recriação de hierarquias na América Portuguesa." In *Dinâmica imperial no antigo regime Português: Escravidão, governos, fronteiras, poderes, legados, séc. XVII a XIX*, edited by Roberto Guedes, 51–66. Rio de Janeiro: Mauad, 2011.

Oliveira, Cláudia. "A representação da grande Avenida e o sublime dos 'melhoramentos urbanos' nas ilustradas *Fon-Fon!* e *Para Todos*." *Escritos: Revista da Casa Rui Barbosa* 1, no. 1 (2007): 93–109.

BIBLIOGRAPHY 381

Oliveira, Cláudia. "Arqueologia: Viagens ao passado da cidade." In *Fon-Fon: Buzinando a modernidade*, Annals of the Conference Celebrating 100 Years of the Publication, 45–58. Rio de Janeiro: Secretaria Especial de Comunicação Social, 2008. https://www.rio.rj.gov.br/dlstatic/10112/4204434/4101430/memoria22.pdf

Oliveira, Diogo de Castro. *Onosarquistas e patafísicos: A boemia literária no Rio de Janeiro find-de-siècle*. Rio de Janeiro: Letras, 2008.

Oliveira, Emerson Dionísio de. "Últimos dias de Carlos Gomes: Do mito 'gomesiano' ao 'nascimento' de um acervo." *Revista CPC* 4 (May–October, 2007): 87–113.

Oliveira, Jetro Meira de. "Structural Issues in the Three Requiem Masses of Padre José Maurício Nunes Garcia (1767–1830), and the Requiem Mass CT 190 by Damião Barbosa de Araújo, with Editions of CT 182 and CT 184." PhD dissertation, University of Illinois at Urbana-Champaign, 2002.

O'Rourke, Kevin, and Jeffrey Williamson. *Globalization and History: The Evolution of a Nineteenth-Century Atlantic Economy*. Boston, MA: MIT Press, 2001.

Ortiz, Renato. *Cultura brasileira e identidade nacional*, 2nd ed. São Paulo: Brasiliense, 1986.

Osterhammel, Jürgen. *The Transformation of the World: A Global History of the Nineteenth Century*, translated by Patrick Camiller. Princeton, NJ: Princeton University Press, 2014 [2009].

Oxfeldt, Elisabeth. *Nordic Orientalism: Paris and the Cosmopolitan Imagination 1800–1900*. Copenhagen: Museum Tusculanum Press, 2005.

Pacheco, Alberto. "As *modinhas* do Padre José Maurício Nunes Garcia: Fontes, edição e prática." *Per Musi* 39 (2019): 1–5.

Pacheco, Alberto, Adriana Kayama, and Lúcia de Fátima Vasconcelos. "Era uma vez um príncipe: Uma versão brasileira e ópera *Il Guarany* de Carlos Gomes." In *Anais do Terceiro Simpósio Internacional de Musicologia da Universidade Federal do Rio de Janeiro*, 97–108. Rio de Janeiro: Universidade Federal do Rio de Janeiro, 2013. Online source https://www.researchgate.net/publication/263504076_VOLPE_Maria_Alice_org_Anais_do_III_Simposio_Internacional_de_Musicologia_da_UFRJ_Patrimonio_Musical_na_Atualidade_Tradicao_Memoria_Discurso_e_Poder_Rio_de_Janeiro_Universidade_Federal_do_Rio_de_Janeiro

Paja-Stach, Jadwiga. "The Contribution of Mieczyslaw Karlowicz to European Musical Culture." In *European Fin-de-Siècle and Polish Modernism: The Music of Mieczyslaw Karlowicz*, edited by Luca Sala, 95–105. Bologna: Ut Orpheus Edizione, 2010.

Pallol, Rubén. *El ensanche de Madrid: Historia de una capital*. Madrid: Catarata, 2013.

Palma, Daniella. "Gramofones e gadgets para os lares do Brasil: Consumo, cultura e tecnicismo na revista *Echo* (1902–1918)." *Projeto História* 43 (2011): 249–272.

Papastergiadis, Nikos. *Cosmopolitanism and Culture*. Cambridge, UK: Polity Press, 2013.

Parakilas, James. "The Operatic Canon." In *The Oxford Handbook of Opera*, edited by Helen Greenwalk, 862–880. Oxford: Oxford University Press, 2014.

Parker, Roger. *Remaking the Song: Operatic Visions and Revisions from Handel to Berio*. Berkeley: University of California Press, 2006.

Parsons, Deborah. *A Cultural History of Madrid: Modernity and the Urban Spectacle*. New York: Berg, 2003.

Pasler, Jann. *Composing the Citizen: Music as Public Utility in Third Republic France*. Berkeley and Los Angeles: University of California Press, 2009.

Pasler, Jann. "Contingencies of Meaning in Transcriptions and Excerpts: Popularizing 'Samson et Dalila.'" In *Approaches to Meaning in Music*, edited by Byron Almén and Edward Pearsall, 170–213. Bloomington: Indiana University Press, 2006.

382 BIBLIOGRAPHY

Pasler, Jann. "Musical Scores in French Magazines and Newspapers." In *The Idea of Art Music in a Commercial World, 1800–1930*, edited by Christina Bashford and Roberta Montemorra Marvin, 297–325. Suffolk, UK: Boydell & Brewer, 2016.

Pasler, Jann. *Writing Through Music: Essays on Music, Culture, and Politics*. New York and London: Oxford University Press, 2007.

Peir, Eva Woods. *White Gypsies: Race and Stardom in Spanish Musicals*. Minneapolis: University of Minnesota Press, 2012.

Pereira, Avelino. "Hino Nacional brasileiro: Que história é esta?" *Revista do Instituto de Estudos Brasileiros* 38 (1995): 21–42.

Pereira, Avelino. *Música, sociedade e política: Alberto Nepomuceno e a república musical*. Rio de Janeiro: Universidade Federal do Rio de Janeiro Press, 2007.

Pereira, Avelino. "Uma República Musical: música, política e sociabilidade no Rio de Janeiro oitocentista (1882–1899)," XXVII Simpósio Nacional de História, 22–26 July, 2013.

Perpetuo, Irineu Franco. "João e José: Visões de um monarca e seu mestre de capela." Austin: LLILAS at University of Texas, 2005, online publication.

Picker, John. *Victorian Soundscapes*. Oxford: Oxford University Press, 2013.

Pignatari, Dante. "Canto da língua: Alberto Nepomuceno e invenção da canção Brasileira," PhD dissertation, São Paulo University, 2009.

Pinto, Maria Cecilia de Moraes. "Victor Hugo e a poesia brasileira." *Lettres Françaises* 5 (2003): 117–128.

Platt, Len, and Tobias Becker. "Berlin/London; London/Berlin: Cultural Transfer, Musical Theater and 'the Cosmopolitan' 1870–1914." *Nineteenth-Century Theater and Film* 40, no. 1 (2013): 1–14.

Poole, Mary Ellen. "Chansonnier and Chanson in Parisian 'Cabarets Artistiques,' 1881–1914." PhD dissertation, University of Illinois at Urbana-Champaign, 1994.

Porto Alegre, Manuel de Araújo. "Apontamentos sobre a vida e as obras do Padre José Maurício Nunes Garcia." *Revista do Instituto Histórico e Geográfico Brasileiro* 19, no. 3 (1856): 354–369.

Porto Alegre, Manuel de Araújo. "Iconographia brazileira." *Revista do Instituto Historico e Geographico do Brazil* 19, no. 34 (1856): 349–378.

Porto Alegre, Manuel de Araújo. "Sobre a música no Brasil." In *Nitheroy: Revista Brasiliense*, edited by Domingos José de Magalhães, Francisco de Sales Torres Homem, and Manuel de Araújo Porto Alegre, vol 1, 173–183. Paris: Dauvin et Fontaine Libraries, 1836.

Preston, Katherine K. *Opera on the Road: Traveling Opera Troupes in the United States, 1825– 60*. Urbana: University of Illinois Press 1993.

Preuss, Ori. "Discovering 'os ianques do sul': Towards an Entangled Luso-Hispanic History of Latin America." *Revista Brasil Política Internacional* 56, no. 2 (2013): 157–176.

Preuss, Ori. *Transnational South America: Experiences, Idea, and Identities, 1860s–1900s*. New York: Routledge, 2016.

Prokopovych, Markian. "Introduction: Music, the City and the Modern Experience." *Urban History* 40, no. 4 (November 2013): 597–605.

Pye, Patricia. *Sound and Modernity in the Literature of London, 1880–1918*. New York and London: Palgrave Macmillan, 2017.

Radano, Ronald. *Lying Up a Nation: Race and Black Music*. Chicago: Chicago University Press, 2003.

Rama, Angel. *La Ciudad Letrada*. Hanover, NH: Ediciones del Norte Hanover, 1984.

BIBLIOGRAPHY 383

Rearick, Charles. *The Pleasures of the Belle Époque: Entertainment and Festivity in Turn-of-the- Century France.* New Haven, CT: Yale University Press, 1985.

Rebouças, André. "O D. João de Mozart no Rio de Janeiro." *Revista musical e de bellas artes* 2/16 (July 10, 1880): 121–122.

Reeds, K. "Urban Pessimism and the Optimism between the Lines: Literary Latin American Cities and Roberto Bolaño's 2666." *Hipertexto* 14 (2011): 139–147.

Regev, Motti. "Cultural Uniqueness and Aesthetic Cosmopolitanism." *European Journal of Social Theory* 10, no. 1 (2007): 123–138.

Regev, Motti. "Musical Cosmopolitanism, Bodies, and Aesthetic Cultures." In *Roads to Music Sociology,* edited by Alfred Smudits, 79–93. Wiesbaden, Germany: Springer, 2019.

Rehding, Alexander. *Music and Monumentality.* London and New York: Oxford University Press, 2009.

Rempe, Martin, and Claudius Torpe. "Cultural Brokers and the Making of Glocal Soundscapes." *Itinerario* 41, no. 2 (2017): 223–233.

Resende, Beatriz. *Lima Barreto e o Rio de Janeiro em fragmentos.* Rio de Janeiro: Autêntica, 2016.

Resende, Maria Efigênia Lage de. "O processo político na Primeira República e o liberalismo oligárquico." In *O Brasil Republicano: O tempo do liberalismo excludente,* edited by Jorge Luis Ferreira and Lucília de Almeida Delgado, 91–120. Rio de Janeiro: Civilização Brasileira, 2003.

Richard, Nelly. "Cultural Peripheries: Latin America and Postmodernist De-Centering." *Boundary* 20, no. 3 (1993): 156–161.

Rinehart, Nicholas T. "Black Beethoven and the Racial Politics of Music History." *Transition* 112 (2013): 117–130.

Rio, João do. *A alma encantadora das ruas.* Rio de Janeiro: Prefeitura do Rio de Janeiro, 1995 [1908]. Companhia das Letras, 2008 [1908].

Rio, João do. "A decadência dos Chopps." In *Cinematógrafo, crônicas cariocas,* 92–97. Rio de Janeiro: ABL, 2009 [1908].

Rio, João do. "A musa urbana." *Kosmos* 2/8 (August 8, 1905).

Rio, João do. "Gente de Music Hall." In *Cinematógrafo, crônicas cariocas,* 7–13. Rio de Janeiro: ABL, 2009 [1908].

Roach, Joseph. *Cities of the Death: Circum-Atlantic Performance.* New York: Columbia University Press, 1996.

Robbins, Bruce. "Introduction Part I: Actually Existing Cosmopolitanism." In *Cosmopolitics: Thinking and Feeling beyond the Nation,* edited by Pheng Cheah and Bruce Robbins, 1–19. Minneapolis: University of Minnesota Press, 1998.

Robbins, Bruce, and Paulo Lemos, eds. *Cosmopolitanisms.* New York: New York University Press, 2017.

Rocha, Osvaldo. *A era das demolições: Cidade do Rio de Janeiro, 1870–1920.* Rio de Janeiro: Prefeitura do Rio de Janeiro, 1995.

Rocha Junior, Alberto Ferreira da. "Quando o cômico atravessa o oceano: O *Tim tim por tim tim* no Brazil." In *Ensaios sobre o humor Luso-Hispânico,* edited by Laura Areias and Luís Pinheiro, 353–371. Lisbon: LusoSofia Press, 2013.

Rodger, Gillian. "Female Hamlets and Romeos: Cross-Dressing Actresses in Nineteenth Century." In *Just One of the Boys: Female-to-Male Cross-Dressing on American Variety Stage,* 17–27. Urbana: University of Illinois Press, 2018.

Rodmell, Paul. *French Music in Britain 1830–1914.* New York: Routledge, 2020.

Rodmell, Paul. *Opera in the British Isles, 1875–1918.* London and New York: Ashgate, 2013.

384 BIBLIOGRAPHY

Rodrigues, João Carlos. *João do Rio: Uma biografia*. Rio de Janeiro: Topbooks, 1996.

Rodrigues, Lutero. *Carlos Gomes, um tema em questão: A ótica modernista e a visão de Mário de Andrade*. São Paulo: Editora Unesp, 2011.

Romero, José Luis. *Latinoamérica: Las Ciudades y las ideas*, 2nd ed. Buenos Aires: Siglo XXI Editores, 2007.

Rona, Cristina. *Brazilian Bodies and Their Choreographies of Identification: Swing Nation*. New York and London: Palgrave MacMillan, 2015.

Ronzani, Michela. "Creating Success and Forging Imaginaries: the Innovative Publicity Campaign for Puccini's *La bohème*." In *The Idea of Art Music in a Commercial World, 1800–1930*, edited by Christina Bashford and Roberta Montemorra Marwin, 39–59. Suffolk, UK: Boydell & Brewer Press, 2016.

Ronzani, Michela. "'Melodramma,' Market, and Modernity: Opera in Late Nineteenth-Century Italy." PhD Dissertation, Brown University, 2015.

Rosa, Robervaldo. *Como é bom poder tocar um instrumento: Pianeiros na cena urbana brasileira*. Goiânia, Brazil: Cânone Editorial, 2014.

Rosselli, John. "The Opera Business and the Italian Immigrant Community in Latin America 1820–1930: The Example of Buenos Aires." *Past & Present* 127 (May, 1990): 155–182.

Rostagno, Antonio. "L'Invenzione melodica di Verdi: costruzione e ispirazione." *Revista Portuguesa de Musicologia* 11 (2001): 113–137.

Roth-Gordon, Jennifer. *Race and the Brazilian Body: Blackness, Whiteness, and Everyday Language*. Oakland: University of California Press, 2017.

Rothstein, William. "Common-Tone Tonality in Italian Romantic Opera: An Introduction," *Music Theory Online* 14 (March 2008), online publication. https://www.mtosmt.org/issues/mto.08.14.1/mto.08.14.1.rothstein.html

Russel, Dave. *Popular Music in England: 1840–1914*. Manchester and New York: Manchester University Press, 1997.

Saint-Saëns, Camille. *On Music and Musicians*, translated and edited by Roger Nichols. London and New York: Oxford University Press, 2008.

Saler, Michael, ed. *The Fin-de-Siècle World*. New York: Routledge, 2015.

Salgado, Susana. *The Teatro Solis: 150 years of Opera, Concert, and Ballet in Montevideo*. Middletown, CT: Wesleyan University Press, 2003.

Salmi, Hannu. *Wagner and Wagnerism in Nineteenth-Century Sweden, Finland, and the Baltic Provinces: Reception, Enthusiasm, Cult*. Rochester, NY: University of Rochester Press, 2005.

Samson, Jim, ed. *The Cambridge History of Nineteenth-Century Music*. Cambridge, UK: Cambridge University Press, 2008.

Sánchez, Víctor Sánchez. "La habanera en la zarzuela española del siglo diecinueve: Idealización marinera de un mundo tropical." *Cuadernos de Música, Artes Visuales y Artes Escénicas* 3, no. 1 (October–March 2006-2007): 4–26.

Sánchez, Víctor Sánchez. "La revista *La Gran Via*: Representaciones sociales en a través de la música en el género chico." In *La zarzuela e sus caminos: Del siglo VII a la actualidad* edited by Tobias Brandenberger and Antje Dreyer, 137–159. Berlin: Lit Verlag, 2016.

Sánchez, Víctor Sánchez. "Verdi ante el espejo de España." In *Verdi Reception in Europe and the United States*, edited by Lorenzo Frassa and Michela Niccolai, 3–32. Lucca: Brepol, 2013.

Sánchez, Víctor Sánchez. *Verdi y España*. Madrid: Akal, 2014.

BIBLIOGRAPHY   385

Santiago, Silviano. "Worldly Appeal: Local and Global Politics in the Shaping of Brazilian Culture." In *The Space In-Between: Essays on Latin American Culture*, 147–174. Durham, NC: Duke University Press, 2001.

Santos, Jocélio. "De pardos disfarçados a brancos pouco claros: Classificações raciais no Brasil dos Séculos XVIII–XIX." *Afro-Ásia* 32 (2005): 115–137.

Saraiva, Joana Martins. "Diálogos transatlânticos: A circulação da habanera nas cidades do Rio de Janeiro e Buenos Aires (1850–1880)." PhD dissertation, UNIRIO, Universidade Federal do Estado do Rio de Janeiro, 2020.

Senelick, Laurence. *Jacques Offenbach and the Making of Modern Culture*. Cambridge, UK: Cambridge University Press, 2017.

Sevcenko, Nicolau. "A capital irradiante: técnica, ritmos, e ritos do Rio." In *História da vida privada no Brasil República: Da Belle Époque à era do rádio*, edited by Fernando Novais and Nicolau Sevcenko, 513–580. São Paulo: Companhia da Letras, 1998.

Sevcenko, Nicolau. *Literatura como missão: Tensões sociais e criação cultural na Primeira República*. São Paulo: Companhia das Letras, 2003.

Schneider, Alberto Luis. *Silvio Romero: hermeneuta do Brasil*. São Paulo: Annablume, 2005.

Schvarzman, Sheila, and Mirrah Iañez. "O Guarani no cinema brasileiro: O olhar imigrante." *Galaxia* 24 (2012): 153–165, online publication.

Schwarctz, Lilia. *1890–1914: No tempo das certezas*. São Paulo: Companhia das Letras, 2007.

Schwarctz, Lilia. *A abertura para o mundo: 1889–1930, História do Brasil Nação*, vol. 3, edited by Lilia Schwarctz. Rio de Janeiro: Objetiva, 2012.

Schwarctz, Lilia. *O espetáculo das raças. Cientistas, instituições e questão racial no Brasil, 1870–1930*. São Paulo: Companhia das Letras, 1993.

Schwartz, M. E. *Writing Paris: Urban Topographies of Desire in Contemporary Latin American Fiction*. Albany: State University of New York Press, 1999.

Schwartz, Vanessa. *Spectacular Realities: Early Mass Culture in Fin-de-Siècle Paris*. Los Angeles and Berkeley: University of California Press, 1999.

Schwartz, Vanessa, and Jeannene Przyblyski. "Introduction." In *The Nineteenth-Century Visual Culture Reader*, edited by Vanessa Schwartz and Jeannene Przyblyski, 3–12. New York: Routledge, 2004.

Schweitzer, Marlis. "'Darn That Merry Widow Hat': The On- and Offstage Life of a Theatrical Commodity, Circa 1907–1908." *Theatre Survey* 50, no. 2 (2009): 189–221.

Scott, Derek. "British Musical Comedy in the 1890s: Modernity without Modernism," Keynote paper presented at the biennial Music in Nineteenth-Century Britain conference, University of Birmingham, 28–30 June 2017, online publication.

Scott, Derek. "In Search of Genetically Modified Music: Race and Musical Style in the Nineteenth Century." In *Musical Style and Social Meaning*. New York: Routledge, 2016, Kindle.

Scott, Derek. "Introduction." In *Music, Culture, and Society: A Reader*, edited by Derek Scott, 1–15. London and New York: Oxford University Press, 2002 [2000].

Scott, Derek. "The Music-Mall Cockney: Flesh and Blood, or Replicant?" *Music and Letters* 83, no. 2 (2002): 237–259.

Scott, Derek. *The Singing Bourgeois: Songs of the Victorian of the Victorian Drawing Room and Parlor*, 2nd ed. New York: Routledge, 2001 [1989].

Scott, Derek. *Sounds of the Metropolis: The 19th Century Popular Music Revolution in London, New York, Paris and Vienna*. New York and Oxford: Oxford University Press, 2008.

386 BIBLIOGRAPHY

Seigel, Micol. "The Disappearing Dance: *Maxixe's* Imperial Erasure." *Black Music Research Journal* 25, no. 1–2 (Spring–Fall, 2005): 93–117.

Seigel, Micol, and Tiago de Melo Gomes. "Sabina's Oranges: The Colors of Cultural Politics in Rio de Janeiro, 1889–1930." *Journal of Latin American Cultural Studies* 11, no 1 (2002): 5–28.

Sennett, Richard. "Capitalism and the City: Globalization, Flexibility and Indifference." In *Cities of Europe: Changing Contexts, Local Arrangements, and the Challenge to Urban Cohesion*, edited by Yuri Kazepov, 109–122. New York: Blackwell, 2008.

Sennett, Richard. "Cosmopolitanism and the Social Experience of Cities." In *Conceiving Cosmopolitanism: Theory, Context and Practice*, edited by Steven Vertovec and Robin Cohen, 42–47. Oxford: Oxford University Press, 2002.

Sennett, Richard. "The Public Realm." In *The Blackwell City Reader*, edited by Gary Bridge and Sophie Watson, 261–272. Malden, MA: Blackwell Publishing, 2010.

Sevcenko, Nicolau. "A capital irradiante: técnica, ritmos, e ritos do Rio." In *História da vida privada no Brasil República: Da Belle Époque à era do rádio*, edited by Fernando Novais and Nicolau Sevcenko, 513–580. São Paulo: Companhia das Letras, 1998.

Sevcenko, Nicolau. *Literatura como missão: Tensões sociais e criação cultural na Primeira República*. São Paulo: Companhia das Letras, 2003.

Shaw, Lisa. *Tropical Travels: Brazilian Popular Performance, Transnational Encounters, and the Construction of Race*. Austin: University of Texas Press, 2018.

Sikka, Sonia. *Herder on Humanity and Cultural Difference: Enlightened Relativism*. Cambridge, UK: Cambridge University Press, 2011.

Silva, Iañez Gonçalves da. "O Guarany no cinema brasileiro: Visão da imprensa entre 1908 e 1926." *Anagrama* 7, no. 1 (2013), 1–14.

Silva, João. *Entertaining Lisbon: Music, Theater, and Modern Life in the Late 19th Century*. Oxford and New York: Oxford University Press, 2016.

Silva, Maurício. *A hélade e o subúrbio: Confrontos literários na belle époque carioca*. São Paulo: Editora Universidade de São Paulo, 2006.

Simões Junior, Alvaro Santos. *A Sátira do Parnaso: Estudo da poesia satírica de Olavo Bilac de 1894 a 1904*. São Paulo: Editora Unesp, 2007.

Simonson, Mary. *Body Knowledge: Performance, Intermediality, and American Entertainment at the Turn of the Twentieth Century*. New York and Oxford: Oxford University Press, 2013.

Siskind, Mariano. *Cosmopolitan Desires: Global Modernity and World Literature in Latin America*. Evanston, IL: Northwestern University Press, 2014.

Sisman, Elaine. "Review of Heinrich Christoph Koch, *Introductory Essay on Composition: The Mechanical Rules of Melody*, Sections 3 and 4 (From Versuch einer Anleitung zur Composition, 1782–1793), translated by Nancy Kovaleff Bake." *Journal of Music Theory* 29, no. 2 (Fall 1985): 341–347.

Sjöberg. Patrik. "The Fundamental Lie: Lip Sync, Dubbing, Ventriloquism, and the Othering of Voice in Documentary Media." In *Vocal Projections: Voice in Documentary*, edited by Annabelle Honess Roe and Maria Pramaggiore, 45–62. New York: Bloomsbury Academic, 2018.

Small, Christopher. *Musicking: The Meanings of Performing and Listening*. Middletown, CT: Wesleyan University Press, 1998.

Smil, Vaclav. *Creating the Twentieth Century: Technical Innovations of 1867–1914 and Their Lasting Impact*. New York: Oxford University Press, 2005.

BIBLIOGRAPHY 387

Smith, Marian. *Opera and Ballet in the Age of Giselle*. Princeton, NJ: Princeton University Press, 2000.

Smith, Maya Ramos. *Teatro Musical y Danza en el México de la Belle Epoque* (1867–1910). Mexico City: Universidad Autónoma Metropolitana y Grupo Editorial Gaceta, 1995.

Snelson, John. "The Waltzing Years: British Operetta 1907–1939." In *Musical Theater in Europe 1930–1945*, edited by Michela Niccolai and Clair Rowden, 241–266. Lucca, Italy: Brepols, 2017.

Snowman, Daniel. *The Gilded Stage: A Social History of Opera*. New York: Atlantic Books, 2010, Kindle.

Sobrino, Palona Ortiz-de-Urbina. "Primera recepción de Richard Wagner en Madrid." In *The Legacy of Richard Wagner: Convergences and Dissonances in Aesthetics and Reception*, edited by Luca Sala, 399–416. Turnhalt, Belgium: Brepols, 2012.

Solare, Carlos Maria. "Meyerbeer on the zarzuela stage: El dúo 'La Africana' by Manuel Fernández Caballero." In *Grand Opera Outside Paris: Opera on the Move in Nineteenth- Century Europe*, edited by Jens Hesselager, 199–212. New York and London: Routledge, 2018.

Sorba, Carlotta. "Between Cosmopolitanism and Nationhood: Italian Opera in the Early Nineteenth-Century." *Modern Italy* 19, no. 1 (2014): 53–67.

Sorba, Carlotta. "The Origins of the Entertainment Industry: The Operetta in Late Nineteenth-Century Italy." *Journal of Modern Italian Studies* 11, no. 2 (2006): 282–302.

Sorba, Carlotta. "To Please the Public: Composers and Audiences in Nineteenth-Century Italy." *The Journal of Interdisciplinary History* 36, no. 4 (2006): 595–614.

Sosa, José Octavio. *La ópera en México, de la independencia al inicio de la revolución (1821–1910)*. México City: Instituto Nacional de Bellas Artes y Literatura, 2010.

Souza, Fernando de, and Priscila de Lima. "Músicos negros no Brasil colonial: Trajetórias individuais e ascensão social (segunda metade do século VIII e início do XIX)." *Revista Vernáculo* 19/20 (2007): 30–66, online publication. https://revistas.ufpr.br/vernaculo/article/view/20544/13729

Souza, José Inácio de Melo. *Imagens do passado: São Paulo e Rio de Janeiro nos primórdios do cinema*. São Paulo: Senac, 2019 [2004].

Souza, Silvia Cristina Martins de. *Carpinteiros teatrais: Cenas cômicas e diversidade cultural no Rio de Janeiro oitocentista*. Londrina, Brazil: Eduel, 2017.

Souza, Silvia Cristina Martins de. "Dos jornais ao palco: Romances, folhetins, e textos teatrais no Rio de Janeiro da segunda metade do século XIX." *Tempo* 18, no. 32 (2012): 193–221.

Souza, Silvia Cristina Martins de. "Que venham negros à cena com maracas e tambores: Jongo, política e teatro musicado no Rio de Janeiro nas últimas décadas do século XIX." *Afro-Ásia* 40 (2009): 145–171.

Spohr, Arne. "'Mohr und Trompeter': Blackness and Social Status in Early Modern Germany." *Journal of the American Musicological Society* 72, no. 3 (2019): 613–663.

Squeff, Enio, and José Miguel Wisnik. *O nacional e o popular na cultural brasileira*. São Paulo: Editora Brasiliense, 1983 [1982].

Stefani, Gino. "Melody: A Popular Perspective." *Popular Music* 6, no.1 (1987): 21–35.

Sterne, Jonathan. *Audible Past*. Durham, NC, and London: Duke University Press, 2003.

Sterne, Jonathan. "Sonic Imaginations." In *The Sound Studies Reader*, edited by Jonathan Sterne, 1–17. New York: Routledge, 2012.

Stevenson, Robert. "Wagner's Latin American Outreach (to 1900)." *Inter-American Music Review* 9, no. 2 (1983): 63–83.

388 BIBLIOGRAPHY

Stokes, Martin. "On Musical Cosmopolitanism." *Macalester International* 21 (2008): 3–26. Online publication. https://digitalcommons.macalester.edu/cgi/viewcontent.cgi?arti cle=1463&context=macintl

Storey, John. *Culture and Power in Cultural Studies: The Politics of Signification.* Edinburgh: Edinburgh University Press, 2010.

Storey, John. *Inventing Popular Culture: From Folklore to Globalization.* Oxford: Wiley-Blackwell, 2003, Kindle.

Strohm, Reinhard. *Studies on a Global History of Music: A Balzan Musicology Project.* New York: Routledge, 2018.

Summerfield, Penny. "Patriotism and Empire: Music Hall Entertainment: 1870–1914." In *Imperialism and Popular Culture*, edited by John Mackenzie, 17–48. Manchester, UK: Manchester University Press, 2017 [1986].

Süssekind, Flora. *Cinematograph of Words: Literature, Technique, and Modernization in Brazil*, translated by Paulo Henrique Brito. Stanford, CA: Stanford University Press, 1997.

Sutton, Emma. *Aubrey Beardsley and British Wagnerism in the 1890s.* New York: Oxford University Press, 2002.

Sutton, Emma. "Karlowicz and *Fin-de-Siècle* Wagnerism." In *European Fin de Siècle and Polish Modernism: The Music of Mieczyslaw Karlowicz*, edited by L. Sala, 119–146. Bologna, Italy: Orpheus Edizioni, 2010.

Sweeney, Regina M. *Singing Our Way to Victory: French Cultural Politics and Music during the Great War.* Middletown, CT: Wesleyan University Press, 2001.

Tabak, F. "Imperial Rivalry and Port-Cities: A View from Above." *Mediterranean Historical Review* 24, no. 2 (2009): 79–94.

Tacucchian, Ricardo. "O Réquiem Mozartiano de José Maurício." *Revista brasileira de música* 19 (1991): 33–52.

Taruskin, Richard. "Nationalism." In *The Revised New Grove Dictionary of Music and Musicians*, edited by Stanley Sadie and John Tyrrel, 687–906. Basingstoke, UK: Macmillan, 2001.

Taruskin, Richard. *Nineteenth-Century Music.* New York: Oxford University Press, 2010.

Tauil, Guilherme. "O dia em que Lima Barreto 'problematizou' o carnaval," April 6, 2017. online publication, https://almanaquenilomoraes.blogspot.com/2017/04/o-dia-em-que-lima-barreto-problematizou.html

Taunay, Afonso. *Dous artistas máximos: José Maurício e Carlos Gomes.* São Paulo: Melhoramentos, 1930.

Taunay, Afonso. *Uma grande glória brasileira: José Maurício Nunes Garcia.* São Paulo: Melhoramentos, 1930.

Taunay, Alfredo d'Escragnolle. "D. Juan de Mozart no Rio de Janeiro." *Revista musical e de bellas artes* (July 1880): 122–123.

Taunay, Alfredo d'Escragnolle. *Reminiscências.* São Paulo: Companhia Melhoramentos, 1923 [1908].

Taveira, Leonardo de Mesquita. "A mulata e sua música no Teatro de Revista brasileiro, entre o ano de 1890 e a década de 1930: Análise de exemplos." In *XVIII Congresso da Associação Nacional de Pesquisa e Pós-Graduação (ANPPOM)*, Salvador, 2008. Online publication https://www.anppom.org.br/anais/anaiscongresso_anppom_2008/comunicas/COM349%20-%20Taveira.pdf

Taylor, Jessica. "'Speaking Shadows': A History of the Voice in the Transition from Silent to Sound Film in the United States." *Journal of Linguistic Anthropology* 19, no. 1 (2009): 1–20.

BIBLIOGRAPHY   389

Taylor, Timothy. *Beyond Exoticism: Western Music and the World*. Durham, NC: Duke University Press, 2007.

Taylor, Timothy. *Strange Sounds: Music, Technology, and Culture*. New York: Routledge, 2001.

Tenorio-Trillos, Mauricio. *I Speak of the City: Mexico City at the Turn of the Twentieth Century*. Chicago: University of Chicago Press, 2012.

Thomas, Susan. *Cuban Zarzuela: Performing Race and Gender on Havana's Lyric Stage*. Urbana: University of Illinois Press, 2009.

Thorau, Christian. "Guides for Wagnerites: Leitmotifs and Wagnerian Listening." In *Wagner and His World*, edited by Thomas Grey, 133–150. Princeton, NJ: Princeton University Press, 2009.

Thurman, Kira. *Singing like Germans: Black Musicians in the Land of Bach, Beethoven, and Brahms*. Ithaca, NY: Cornell University Press, 2021.

Tippet, David. *Wagner's Melodies: Aesthetics and Materialism in German Musical Identity*. Cambridge, UK: Cambridge University Press, 2013.

Toelle, Jutta. "Der Duft der großen weiten Welt. Ideen zum weltweiten Siegeszug der italienischen Oper im 19. Jahrhundert." In *Die Oper im Wandel der Gesellschaft. Kulturtransfers und Netzwerke des Musiktheaters in Europa*, edited by Sven Oliver Müller, Philipp Ther, Jutta Toelle, and Gesa zur Nieden, 251–261. Wien: Böhlau, 2010.

Toelle, Jutta. "Opera as Business? From Impresario to the Publishing Industry." *Journal of Modern Italian Studies* 17 (July 2012): 448–459.

Toelle, Jutta. "Operatic Canons and Repertories in Italy c. 1900." In *The Oxford Handbook of the Operatic Canon*, edited by Cormac Newark and William Weber, 227–244. Oxford: Oxford University Press, 2018, online publication.

Togueiro, Gastão. "A viúva alegre." In *Almanack dos Theatros*, edited by Alfarenga Fonseca, 13–15. Rio de Janeiro: Typ. Ao Luzeiro, 1909.

Toscano, Verónica Zárate, and Serfe Gruzinski. "Ópera, imaginación y sociedad: México y Brasil, siglo xix: historias conectadas: *Ildegonda* de Melesio Morales e *Il Guarany* de Carlos Gomes." *Historia Mexicana* 58, no. 2 (October–December 2008): 803–860.

Toynbee, Jason. "Mainstreaming, from Hegemonic Centers to Global Networks." In *Popular Music Studies*, edited by David Hesmondhalgh and Keith Negus, 149–163. London: Arnold, 2002 [1992]).

Toynbee, Jason, and Byron Dueck. *Migrating Music*. New York: Routledge, 2011.

Tralongo, Stéphane. "Des passages aux cinemas: Le music-hall comme espace de mobilité." *Études théâtrales* 2, no. 65 (2016): 28–40.

Traubner, Richard. *Operetta: A Theatrical History*. London: Victor Gollancz, 1984.

Treece, David. *Exiles, Allies, Rebels: Brazil's Indianist Movement, Indigenist Politics, and the Imperial Nation-State*. London: Greenwood Press, 2000.

Trentmann, Frank. "Crossing Divides: Consumption and Globalization in History." *Journal of Consumer Culture* 9, no. 2 (2009): 187–220.

Trindade, Joyce Nathália de Souza. "José de Alencar e a escravidão: Necessidade nacional e benfeitoria senhorial." Master's thesis, Universidade Federal de São Paulo, 2014.

Trippett, David. *Wagner's Melodies: Aesthetics and Materialism in German Musical Identity*. Cambridge, UK: Cambridge University Press, 2013.

Tsing, Anna. *Friction*. Princeton, NJ: University Press, 2004. Kindle.

Tuchman, Barbara. *The Proud Tower: A Portrait of the World before the War, 1890-1914*. New York: Random House, 2011 [1963].

390 BIBLIOGRAPHY

Turino, Thomas. *Nationalists, Cosmopolitans, and Popular Music in Zimbabwe*. Chicago: University of Chicago Press, 2000.

Ulhôa, Martha. "Cosmoramas, realejos e cobras ferozes: A transmissao musical no Rio de Janeiro oitocentista." In *Visoes da America, sonoridades da America, Annals of the XII Congress of the IASPM-Latin America*, 550–554. Sao Paulo: Letra e Voz, 2017

Ulhôa, Martha. "Discografia de Mário Pinheiro, 1904–1013" and "Discografia do Bahiano, 1902–1915," online publication, 2010. https://www.academia.edu/39535663/DISCOGRAFIA_DO_BAHIANO_1902_1915; https://www.academia.edu/39535697/DISCOGRAFIA_DE_MARIO_PINHEIRO_1904_1913.

Ulhôa, Martha. "'Perdão Emília!' Transmissão oral e aural na canção popular." In *Palavra cantada: Ensaios sobre poesia, música, e voz*, edited by Cláudia Matos, Elizabeth Travassos, and Fernande de Medeiros, 249–267. Rio de Janeiro: 7 Letras, 2008.

Urry, John. *Consuming Places*. New York: Routledge, 1995.

Urry, John, and Jonas Larsen. *The Tourist Gaze 3.0*. London: Sage, 2011 (1990).

Vaccari, Pedro Razzante. "O Padre José Maurício Nunes Garcia e o mulatismo musical: Embranquecimento histórico?" *Revista Música* 18, no. 1 (2018): 170–185.

Valle, Arthur. "Sociabilidade, boêmia e carnaval em ateliês de artistas brasileiros em fins do século XIX e início do XX." *Oitocento* 4 (2017): 43–55.

Vasconcelos, Ary. *Panorama da música brasileira*. São Paulo: Livraria Martins, 1964.

Vazsonyi, Nicholas. *Richard Wagner: Self-Promotion and the Making of a Brand*. Cambridge, UK: Cambridge University Press, 2010.

Velloso, Monica. *Modernismo no Rio de Janeiro: Turunas e Quixotes*. Rio de Janeiro: KBR, 2015.

Vergo, Peter. *The Music of Painting: Music, Modernism, and the Visual Arts from the Romantics to John Cage*. London and New York: Phaidon Press, 2010.

Vermes, Mônica. "A Cena Musical no Rio de Janeiro: 1890–1920." In *Anais do XXVI Simpósio Nacional de História*, 1–12. São Paulo, 2011. Online publication. https://www.academia.edu/1351185/A_Cena_Musical_do_Rio_de_Janeiro_1890_1920

Vermes, Mônica. "A recepção de Carlos Gomes na Primeira República." In *Annals of the XXVI Congress of the Associação Nacional de Pesquisa e Pós-Graduação em Música (ANPPOM)*, 1–8. Belo Horizonte, 2016. Online publication. https://anppom.org.br/anais/anaiscongresso_anppom_2016/4220/public/4220-14109-1-PB.pdf

Vermes, Mônica. "Por uma renovação do ambiente musical brasileiro: O relatório de Leopoldo Miguez e os conservatórios europeus." *Revista Eletrônica de Musicologia* 8 (December 2004), online publication. http://www.rem.ufpr.br/_REM/REMv8/miguez.html

Vertovec, S., and R. Cohen. *Conceiving Cosmopolitanism: Theory, Context and Practice*. Oxford: Oxford University Press, 2002.

Verzosa, Noel Orillo. "The Absolute Limits: Debussy, Satie, and the Culture of French Modernism." PhD dissertation, University of California, Berkeley, 2008.

Vianna, Joaquim. "A Reação contra a influencia intellectual Franceza." *Kosmos* 5, no. 12 (December 1908): .

Vidal, João Vidal. "Formação germânica de Alberto Nepomuceno: Estudos sobre recepção e intertextualidade." Universidade de São Paulo, USP, 2011.

Vidal, João Vidal. "Nepomuceno e Brahms: A Questão da Influência Revisitada." *Música em Perspectiva* 3, no. 1 (2010): 88–135.

Vidal, João Vidal. "Nepomuceno e Max Bruch: Análise de Uma (Recém-Descoberta) Conexão." *Revista Brasileira de Música* 24, no. 1 (2011): 129–153.

BIBLIOGRAPHY   391

Vieira, Carolina. "Música popular carioca, afro-religiosidades e o mundo da fonografia no pós-abolição (1902–1927)." In *Annais do 28th Symposium de História, July 2015*, 1–18. Florianopolis, SC, Brazil. Online publication. https://www.snh2015.anpuh.org/resources/anais/39/1428361698_ARQUIVO_Textoco mpletoanpuh2015.pdf

Vieira, Carolina. "Ninguém escapa do feitiço: Música popular carioca, afro-religiosidades e mundo da fonográfica, 1902–1927." Master's thesis, Universidade Estadual do Rio de Janeiro, UERJ, São Gonçalo, 2010.

Virmond, Marcos. "Algumas reflexões em torno de Antônio Carlos Gomes." *Mimesis* 23, no. 1 (2002): 47–48.

Virmond, Marcos, and Irandi Daroz. "Orientalismo e discurso dramático-musical no 'Notturno' de Condor de Carlos Gomes." *Revista Brasileira de Música* 24, no. 1 (2011): 61–70.

Virmond, Marcos, Rosa Maria Tolon Marin, and Edu Toledo Correio. "Destruindo o mito e construindo o homem: Revendo Antônio Carlos Gomes." *ICTUS* 9 (2008): 57–71.

Virmond, Marcos, Rosa Maria Tolon Marin, and Lenita Waldige Mendes Nogueira. "Uma ária para Virginia Damerini: A última *Fosca* de Carlos Gomes." *Opus* 19 (2013): 111–140.

Vizcaya, Benita Sampedro. "Engaging the Atlantic: New Routes, New Responsibilities." *Bulletin of Hispanic Studies* 89, no. 8 (December 2012): 905–922.

Volpe, Maria Alice. "Carlos Gomes: A persistência de um paradigma em época de crepúsculo." *Brasiliana* 17 (2004): 2–11.

Volpe, Maria Alice. "Compositores românticos brasileiros: estudos na Europa." *Revista Brasileira de Música* 21, no. 51–76 (1994–1995): 51–76.

Volpe, Maria Alice. "Traços Romerianos no mapa musical do Brasil." In *Música e História no longo século XIX*, edited by Antônio Herculano Lopes, 15–35. Rio de Janeiro: Casa Rui Barbosa, 2011.

Waeber, Jacqueline. "Yvette Guilbert and the Reevaluation of the Chanson Populaire and Chanson Ancienne during the Third Republic, 1889–1914." In *The Oxford Handbook of the New Cultural History of Music*, edited by Jane F. Fulcher, 264–306. New York: Oxford University Press, 2011.

Waldron, Jeremy. "What Is Cosmopolitan?" *The Journal of Political Philosophy* 8, no. 2 (2000): 227–243.

Walkowitz, Judith. *Night Out: Life in Cosmopolitan London*. New Haven, CT: Yale University Press, 2012.

Walkowitz, Rebecca. *Cosmopolitan Style: Modernism beyond the Nation*. New York: Columbia University Press, 2006.

Walton, Benjamin. "Canons of Real and Imagined Opera: Buenos Aires and Montevideo, 1810 1860." In *The Oxford Handbook of the Operatic Canon*, edited by Cormac Newark and William Weber, 270–292. Oxford: Oxford University Press, 2020, online publication.

Walton, Benjamin. "Italian Operatic Fantasies in Latin America." *Journal of Modern Italian Studies* 17, no. 4 (2012): 460–471.

Walton, Benjamin. *Rossini in Restoration Paris: The Sound of Modern Life*. Cambridge, UK: Cambridge University Press, 2011.

Wasserman, Renata. "Re-inventing the New World: Cooper and Alencar." *Comparative Literature* 36, no. 2 (1984): 130–145.

Weber, Eugen. *Fin de Siècle*. Cambridge, MA: Belknap Press, 1986.

BIBLIOGRAPHY

Weber, Ryan. *Cosmopolitanism and Transatlantic Circles in Music and Literature.* London: Palgrave Macmillan, 2018.

Weber, William. "Canonicity and Collegiality: 'Other' Composers, 1790–1850." *Common Knowledge* 14, no. 1 (2008): 105–123.

Weber, William. "Cosmopolitan, National, and Regional Identities in Eighteenth Century European Musical Life." In *Oxford Handbook of the New Cultural History of Music*, edited by J. Fulcher, 209–227. New York: Oxford University Press, 2011.

Weber, William. *The Great Transformation of Musical Taste.* Cambridge, UK: Cambridge University Press, 2008.

Weber, William. *The Musician as Entrepreneur, 1700–1914: Managers, Charlatans, and Idealists.* Bloomington: Indiana University Press, 2004.

Weisethaunet, Hans. "Historiography and Complexities: Why Is Music 'National'?" *Popular Music History* 2, no. 2 (2007): 169–199.

Wenger, Etienne. *Communities of Practice: Learning, Meaning, and Identity.* Cambridge, UK: Cambridge University Press, 1999.

Werbner, Pnina. "Introduction: Towards a New Cosmopolitan Anthropology." In *Anthropology and the New Cosmopolitanism: Rooted, Feminist, and Vernacular Perspectives*, edited by Pnina Werbner, 1–30. London: Bloomsbury Academic, 2008.

White, Harry, and Michael Murphy. "Introduction." In *Musical Constructions of Nationalism*, edited by Harry White and Michael Murphy, 1–15. Cork, Ireland: Cork University Press, 2001.

White, Jerry. *London in the Nineteenth Century: 'A Human Awful Wonder of God.'* London: Vintage, 2011, Kindle.

Whiting, Steven. *Satie the Bohemian: From Cabaret to Concert Hall.* New York: Oxford University Press, 1999.

Wigler, Stephen. " 'Il Guarany' is a dramatic directing debut for Domingo." *Baltimore Sun*, November 12, 1996.

Williams, D. *Culture Wars in Brazil: The First Vargas Regime, 1930–1945.* Durham, NC: Duke University Press Books, 2001.

Wilson, Alexandra. "Music, Letters and National Identity: Reading the 1890s' Italian Music Press." *Nineteenth-Century Music Review* 7, no. 2 (2010): 101–118.

Wilson, Elizabeth. *Bohemians: The Glamorous Outcasts.* New Brunswick, NJ: Rutgers University Press, 2000.

Wipplinger, Jonathan. "The Aural Shock of Modernity: Weimar's Experience of Jazz." *The Germanic Review: Literature, Culture, Theory* 82, no. 4 (2007): 299–320.

Wise, Jennifer. "L'Enfant et le tyran: 'La Marseillaise' and the Birth of Melodrama." *Theatre Survey* 53, no. 1 (April 2012): 29–57.

Wisnik, José Miguel. *O coro dos contrários: A música em torno da semana de 22.* São Paulo: Livraria Duas Cidades, 1983.

Witkoski, Ariane. "*De La Matchitche a La Lambada*: Presence de la Musique Populaire Bresilienne en France." *Cahiers dú Brésil Contemporain* 12 (1990), online publication, https://www.yumpu.com/fr/document/read/17003900/source-maison-des-sciences-de-lhomme/2

Wohlgemut, Esther. *Romantic Cosmopolitanism.* New York: Palgrave Macmillan, 2009.

Wolf, Eri. *Europe and the People without History.* Los Angeles and Berkeley: California University Press, 1982.

Yamomo, meLê. "Global Currents, Musical Streams: European Opera in Colonial Southeast Asia." *Nineteenth Century Theatre and Film* 44, no. 1 (2017): 54–74.

Yildiz, Yasemin. *Beyond the Mother Tongue: The Postmonolingual Condition.* New York: Fordham University Press, 2012.

Xavier, Wiebke Roben de Alencar "O encontro do Ubirajara Alencariano com a sua primeira tradução alemã de 1886." In *José de Alencar: Século XXI,* edited by Marcelo Peloggio, Arlene Fernandes, and Valéria Cristina Bezerra, 267–286. Fortaleza: Edições UFC, 2015.

Zanon, Maria Cecilia. "Fon-Fon! Um registro da vida mundana no Rio de Janeiro da Belle Époque." *Patrimônio e História* 1, no. 2 (2005): 18–30.

Zárate Toscano, Verónica, and Serge Gruzinsk. "Ópera, imaginación y Sociedad: México y Brasil, siglo XIX. Histórias conectadas: Ildegonda de Melesio Morales e Il Guarany de Carlos Gomes." *Historia Mexicana* 58, no. 2 (2008): 803–860.

Zechner, Ingeborg. "Cosmopolitanism in Nineteenth-Century Opera Management." In *Music History and Cosmopolitanism,* edited by Anastasia Belina, Kaarina Kilpiö, and Derek B. Scott, 32–45. New York: Routledge, 2019. Kindle.

Zephyr, Frank. *Reading Rio de Janeiro: Literature and Society in the Nineteenth Century.* Stanford, CA: Stanford University Press, 2016.

Zicari, Massimo. *Verdi in Victorian London.* Cambridge: Open Books, 2016.

Zohn, Steven. *Music for a Mixed Taste: Style, Genre, and Meaning in Telemann's Instrumental Works.* New York: Oxford University Press, 2008.

Index

For the benefit of digital users, indexed terms that span two pages (e.g., 52–53) may, on occasion, appear on only one of those pages.

Figures are indicated by *f* following the page number

"A canção do aventureiro," 275–78
"A canção do Indio," 287–88
"A casa branca da serra," 131–34
A Confederação dos Tamoios, 266–67
A república, 149–50
Abreu, Casimiro de, 184, 187–88
acculturation, 12–13
aesthetic of discontinuity, 140, 283, 337
Africa, 2–3, 23–24, 30–31, 51–52, 96–97, 102, 160–61, 188–89, 226–27
African-derived cultures, 19, 153–54, 316–17
African-derived dramatic dances, 156–57
African-derived musical formulas, 159–60
African-derived song-dances, 148–49
African-ness, 153–54
Africanisms, 313–17, 318–19
Aïda, 233–35, 237–40, 275–78, 283–84
Albéniz, Isaac, 345
Albuquerque, Medeiros de, 61–63
Alcazar Parque, 141–42
Alencar, José de, 262–67, 269–73, 281–82, 288–89
Algiers, 35–37
Alhambra, 48, 121–23
Almeida, Irineu de, 289
Alves, Castro, 150–51, 184
Amadi, Alberto, 286–87
Amato, Pasquale, 286–87
Americas, 2–3, 39–40, 41–42, 48–51, 69–70, 82–83, 89–90, 97–98, 127, 129, 140–41, 149–50, 160–63, 237–39, 244–45, 247, 272, 292–93, 308, 311–12, 320–21, 324–26, 327, 333–34
anarchist, 31, 71–72, 73, 103–4
Andalusian, 161–63, 165–66
Anderson, Benedict, 26–27, 63–64
Andrade, Mario de, 96
anthems, 63–64, 66, 67, 283–84, 332–33, 338
Arabian Peninsula, 48
Araújo Porto-Alegre, Manuel de, 88

aria, 87–88, 131–33, 148–50, 158–60, 168–69, 171–72, 173–74, 188, 213–14, 218, 233–34, 247, 250–51, 253, 295–97, 308–9, 331
arrangement, 58, 77–78, 121–23, 127, 172–73, 215–17, 218, 224–25, 250–51, 255–58, 259–60, 271–72, 287–88, 308–9, 327, 330–32
"As laranjas da Sabina," 148–51, 154–56, 158, 160–61
Assassinat du duc de Guise, 302
assemblage, 14–15, 19, 149–51, 250–51, 307, 350–51
Assis, Machado de, 29, 295, 323
Auber, Daniel, 81–82, 168–69, 281–82
aural flâneur, 53–54
Austria, 71–72, 97–98, 121–23, 193–94, 281–82
Austro-German, 82–85, 94–96, 236–37, 241–42, 333–34
Austro-Germanic musics, 17
Ave Libertas, 283–84, 332–33, 341–42
Avenida Central, 49*f*, 121–23, 211–12
Avenida Rio Branco, 121–23
Azevedo, Artur, 8–9, 46, 46*f*, 47, 104–5, 123–24, 125–26, 129, 137–38, 139–40, 147, 148–51, 183–84, 193, 201, 207, 223–24, 233–34, 249–50, 284–85, 335, 339–40, 341–42, 352–54
Azevedo, Luis Heitor Correa de, 88

Babel, 140–41, 142–46, 341–42
Bach, J. S., 335–36
Bahia, 102, 150–51, 153–54, 156–57, 160–61
Bahia, Xisto, 150–51
Bahiana, 152–66, 156*f*, 172–74, 175*f*, 176
baião, 187
Ballo in maschera, 233–34
Baltimore, 237–39, 285
banjo, 307–8
Barbieri, Francisco Asenjo, 149–50
Barbosa, Januário da Cunha, 91–92

396 INDEX

barcarolle, 131–33
Barcelona, 121–23, 270–71
barrel organ (see also realejo), 53–55, 126–28, 255–56
Barreto, Lima, 8–9, 44, 74–75, 173–74, 191–92, 355
Barreto, Paulo (see Rio, João do), 8–9
Barros, Amelia, 108, 123–24, 134–35
Barros, João, 133–34, 287–88
Barroso, Inezita, 133–34
Bastos, Sousa, 145–46, 151–53, 162–63, 171–72, 284–85
Battistini, Mattias, 286–87
Baudelaire, Charles, 112–13
Baudelairian, 4–5
Bayreuth, 327–28
Beethoven, Ludwig van, 54–55, 69–70, 78, 81–82, 93–94, 334–37, 345, 354–55
"bel canto," 234–35, 239–40
belle époque, 35–37, 40
Béranger, Pierre-Jean de, 184–85
"berceuse bleue," 115–17, 116*f*, 129, 131–33
Berlin, 35–38, 42, 48, 114, 121–23, 193, 202, 324–26, 333–34, 342–43
Berlioz, Hector, 55–56, 69–70, 78, 81–82, 282–83, 302, 321–22, 328–29, 332–33, 335–37, 338, 354–55
Bernhardt, Sarah, 235–36
Bilac, Olavo, 8–9, 27–29, 48, 53–54, 100–2, 104–5, 105*f*, 106–8, 109–10, 111–12, 131, 183–84, 309–10, 352–53
Bizet, Georges, 161, 217–18, 234–35, 237–40, 336–37
blackface, 154–56, 161–62, 308–9, 311–12
blackness, 93–94, 95–96, 97–98, 157–58, 159–61, 162–64, 168–69, 171–72, 177–78, 180–82, 183–84, 312–13, 317–18
Blairat, Eugene, 102
bohemian, 8–9, 17, 31, 72–73, 100–2, 104–8, 111, 115–17, 118, 121, 130–31, 167–68, 173–74, 178–80, 184–85, 189–90, 223–25, 329, 330
Bonaparte, Princess Mathilde, 106–8
borders, 5–6, 11–13, 15, 17–18, 21, 23, 27–29, 32–33, 38, 39–40, 44–45, 70–71, 72–73, 118–19, 133–34, 147–48, 160–61, 165–66, 174–76, 210, 242–44, 245–46, 249–51, 252–53, 257–58, 261–64, 283, 303, 319, 349–50
Borges, Jorge Luis, 13, 346–47
Borja Reis, Eduardo de, 66
Bosc, Auguste, 102
bossa nova, 23–24

Braga, Francisco, 149–50, 230–31, 335–36, 352–53
Braga, Manoel, 289
Brazil, 1–3, 4, 25–26, 38–39, 42–43, 47–48, 57, 58, 61–63, 64, 67, 68–69, 74, 81, 82–83, 84–85, 96–97, 98–99, 108–9, 130–31, 147–48, 149–50, 152–53, 154–56, 163–64, 170, 176–77, 180–81, 183, 184, 189–90, 191, 226–27, 272–73, 283–84, 290–92, 298–301, 318, 320–21, 322, 328–29, 338–39, 354–55
Brazilian-ness, 81, 249, 318
"Bregeira, polka francesa," 299*f*
Bridgetower, George, 93–95
Bruant, Aristide, 7–8, 100–2, 108–13, 109*f*, 114–18, 131–33, 183–84, 185–86, 187, 192
Bruch, Max, 342–43, 345
Buenos Aires, 2–3, 4–5, 35–37, 41–42, 108, 121–24, 131, 141–46, 161–62, 170–71, 176, 193–94, 237–39, 241–42, 270–71, 308, 324–26
"Buenos dias, valsa espanhola," 298–301
Byron, George, 23–24, 265, 271–72

"Caballero de Gracia," 127–28
Caballero, Manuel Fernández, 69–70, 149–50
cabaret, 17, 33–34, 55–56, 69–70, 72, 100–10, 101*f*, 111–13, 114–20, 121, 123–25, 130–33, 151–52, 167–68, 173–74, 183–85, 186, 212–13
cabaret songs, 33–34
cable cars, 48–51, 53–54, 118, 323
Cadete, 154–56
café-cantante, 135–36, 141–42, 147–48, 150–51, 153–54, 167–68, 173–74, 178–80, 187
café concerts, 17–18, 138–39, 318–19
cafés, 47, 54–55, 128, 197, 198–99, 264, 267, 289, 304, 340
Cairo, 237–39
cake-walk, 19, 33–34, 161–63, 172–73, 187, 224, 307–12, 313–17, 318–19
Calcutta, 35–37
Campos, Lima, 310
canção brasileira, 148–49, 151–53
cançoneta, 54–56, 130–33, 134–35, 141–44, 147, 148–49, 150–51, 167–72, 173–74, 178–80, 183, 184
cançonetistas, 141–42, 167–68, 169–70
"Canção do Exilio," 288
canonic, 6–8, 33–34, 55–56, 93–95, 188, 233–34, 349–50, 351
Canudos, 102, 189–90
canzonettas, 55–56

INDEX 397

capitalism, 2–3, 21–22, 27, 31–32, 35–37, 40, 58, 82–83, 105–6, 120, 182, 240–41, 243–44, 251, 343–44

Cardona, Lili, 7–8, 223–25, 226, 227–28, 227*f*

cariocas, 137–38, 233–34

Carlota Joaquina, D., 76–77

Carmen, 141–42, 157, 161, 213–14, 234–35, 237–40

Caruso, Enrico, 54–55, 168–69, 170–71, 190, 247, 286–87

Carvalho, Delgado de, 334–35, 336–37, 352–53

Carvalho, Francisco, 148–49

Carvalho, Norberto Amancio de, 76–77

Casa Edison, 54–55, 126–27, 169–70, 211, 287–88

Casino de Paris, 308–9

Casino Nacional, 137–38, 147, 308–9

castañoles, 161–62

Castro, Luis de, 83–84

Cataldi, Antonio, 72, 213–14, 215–17, 218

Cavalcanti, Aurélio, 7–8, 19, 187–88, 295–302, 296*f*, 299*f*, 303–7, 305*f*, 313–16, 314*f*, 318–19

Cavalleria rusticana, 233–34, 239–40

Cernicchiaro, Vincenzo, 83–84

chanson realistique, 114, 115–17

chansons, 17, 55–56, 114–15, 117–19, 131–33, 134–35, 147, 148–49, 159–60, 162–63, 167–68, 173–74, 183–84, 212–13, 308–9

"Chant du Départ," 61–63

chanteuse-barytone, 112–13

chanteuses, 141–42

Charpentier, Gustave 334–35

Chat Noir, 72, 100–2, 108–9, 113, 115, 121, 134–35, 183

Chauvim, Eugènie, 123–24

Cheret, Jules, 108–9

Chile, 270–71, 308

Chopin, Frédéric, 335–36, 345

choppes, 167–68

choro, 180–81, 182

Chueca, Frederico, 127–28, 149–50

Cidade Nova, 153–54, 309–10

Cincinnati, 237–39

Cinema-Palace, 262–64

cinquillo, 159–60

clichés, 16, 159–60, 163–64, 165–66, 172–73, 186, 194–96, 206–7, 275–78, 281–82, 283, 297, 298–302, 304–7, 321–22

Coliseu dos Recreios, 170–71

colonialism, 30–31, 44–45, 95

Colonne et Lamoureux, 334–35

communal performance, 63–64, 67, 68–69, 70–71, 72

Comte, 44, 58, 106–8

concert hall, 4, 32–34, 55–56, 138–39, 142–44, 235–36, 247, 281–82, 298–301, 333, 335–36, 337–38, 341–43, 344–45

Concertos populares, 334–35

Concerts Colonne, 338–39

Condor, 272, 352–53

Convent Garden, 239–40

Cook, Jenny, 308–9

Coroacy, Visconti, 271–72

Corrêia Vasques, Francisco, 271–72

cosmopolitan city, 4, 7–9, 17–18, 74–75, 118, 130, 146–48, 159–60, 161–62, 163–64, 176, 177, 181–84, 185–86, 248–49, 254–55, 261–64, 266–67, 274–75, 284–85, 286, 288, 291–92, 307, 319, 328–29, 330–32

cosmopolitanism, 1, 9–10, 11–12, 13–14, 16–17, 18, 19, 21–29, 30–32, 34–35, 39–40, 56, 255–56, 310–11, 316–18, 349–51

Cruzette, Ignez, 289

Cuba, 123–24, 161–62, 163–64, 241–42

cultural brokers, 32–33

cultural network, 35–38, 40–41, 56, 67, 70–72, 130–31, 147–48, 182, 210, 240–41, 286, 322, 330–31

cultural transfer, 12–13

Cunha, João Itiberê da, 287–88

D. Maria Amelia, Princess, 76–77

dancing mulatta, 17–18, 148–49, 154–56, 157, 160–61

danse du ventre, 162–63

Dans la Rue, 111

Darbilly, Cavalier, 134–35

Dario, Rubén, 304, 308–9, 310, 316–17

Debussy, Claude, 69–70, 328–29, 336–37, 342–43, 345, 346–47, 351

decadents, 104–5, 112–13

Delgado, Pepa, 154–57, 156*f*, 284–85

Delmet, Paul, 115

Delorme, Aurélia, 123–24, 152–53, 156–57, 284–85

Der Fligender Hollander, 324–26

Destinn, Emmy, 286–87

Dias, Gonçalves, 150–51, 288

Die Walkirie, 324

d'Indy, Vincent, 342–43, 345

disassemblage, 14–15, 18–19, 250–51, 283

diseuse, 110–11, 112, 113, 114, 118, 119–20, 186

distant reading, 3–4

Divan Japonaise, 113

Domingo, Plácido, 285

Donizetti, Gaetano, 234–35, 274–75, 335–36

398 INDEX

D'Ormeville, Carlo, 269–70
Dostoevsky, Fyodor, 27–29
Duque, Gonzaga, 8–9, 102–5, 103f, 108, 109–10, 111, 114–15, 119, 131, 154–56, 329, 330, 333
Dutra, Octavio, 187–88

Echo du cabaré, 124–25
eclectic, 13–15, 19, 53–55, 56, 85, 115, 141–42, 178–80, 197–98, 233–34, 330, 333–34, 335, 346–47
eclecticism, 13–14, 233–34, 347–50, 352
Editora Quaresma, 133–34
Edmundo, Luis, 8–9, 48, 54–55, 106–8, 164–66, 318–19
Eldorado, 108, 113, 121, 134–35
England, 47–48, 71–72, 113, 121–24, 129, 324–26
Enlightenment, 21–22, 25, 26–29, 30–31, 44, 57, 70, 73–74, 81–82, 84–85, 343–44
Etern'sches Komservatorium der Musik, 342–43
ethnomusicological, 25
Etoile Palace, 170–71
Eurocentric, 30–31, 33–34, 38, 42–43, 48, 93–94, 95, 164, 251–52
Europe, 2–3, 17–18, 25–26, 27–29, 31–32, 35–38, 39–42, 43–44, 48, 51–52, 57–58, 69–70, 71–72, 81–83, 97–98, 121–24, 127, 129, 134–35, 140–41, 142–44, 160–61, 177, 191, 222–24, 230–31, 234–36, 242–43, 244–45, 247, 249, 270–71, 272, 283–84, 292–93, 307–8, 309–10, 311–12, 316–17, 320–21, 322, 327–28, 333–34, 338–39, 341–43, 344–45, 350–51
European, 2–4, 6–8, 19, 21, 26–29, 30–31, 39–41, 42–43, 44–45, 47, 55–56, 70–71, 78, 80–89, 92–96, 97–99, 121, 140, 141–44, 153–56, 161–62, 170–71, 173–74, 177, 180–81, 197–98, 199–201, 228–29, 232, 240–41, 244–45, 247–48, 251–52, 253, 264, 265–67, 269–71, 272, 274–75, 278–81, 290–91, 298–301, 308–9, 311–13, 316–17, 318, 320–21, 323, 324–27, 328–29, 333–34, 335–36, 338–40, 342–45, 349–51, 353–54
European Enlightenment, 21
European imperialism, 2–3, 44–45, 240–41
European-ness, 26–27, 38, 81–82, 88–89, 328–29, 339–40
extra lives, 15, 128, 221–22, 248–49, 251, 253, 274–75, 284–85, 313

fado, 47–48, 148–51, 152–53, 162–63, 173–74
Faust, 234–35, 237–40, 333

favela, 51–52
Fico, Giovanni, 267–69
film d'art, 214–15, 289–90
filme cantante, 72, 215–17, 289–90
fin-de-siècle, 1–3, 8–9, 35–37, 39–40, 55–56, 105–6, 110, 111, 115, 118, 119–20, 124–25, 148–49, 163–64, 182, 183–84, 192, 254–55, 260–61, 273–74, 312–16, 342–43, 347–49
flamenco, 161–63, 165–66
flâneur, 8–9, 17–18, 52, 53–54, 114, 206–7
flâneurism, sonic, 303
flanueristic, 8–9
Florence, 2–3, 51–52, 333–34, 353–54
folk traditions, 81
Fon-Fon, 54–55, 142–44, 193–94, 195f, 202, 203f, 224–26, 225f–27f, 227–28, 261–62
Fonseca, Marechal Deodoro da, 57–59, 64, 76, 332–33
fork rhythm, 159–60, 187
forma solita, 274–75
Fosca, 272
fragments, 192, 255–56, 282–83, 330–31
Franco-Prussian War, 39–40
Frègoli, Leopoldo, 111–12, 114
French revolution, 69–71, 73–74

Gabriel Montoya, 114, 116f
Gangloff, Lèopold, 114, 115
Garcia, José Maurício Nunes, 7–8, 17, 76–80, 77f–86f, 83–96, 97–99, 185–86
Garret, Almeida, 184
Garrido, Eduardo, 125–26
German band, 54–55, 196–97
Germany, 47–48, 71–72, 78, 81–82, 92–93, 97–98, 108, 113, 121–24, 141–42, 193–94, 239–40, 320–21, 323, 324–26, 342–43
Gilbert, Yvette, 7–8, 113, 114–15, 117
Gil Blas Illustré, 115
Gilmant, Alexandre, 342–43
Gioconda, 182, 233–35, 324
Glinka, Mijaíl, 13–14, 335–37
global history, 10
globalization, 11, 18–19, 23–24, 27–29, 30–31, 39–41, 44–45, 70–71, 194–96, 240–41
global music history, 10–11
Goiás, 48
Gomes, Antônio Carlos, 7–8, 18–19, 137, 149–50, 233–35, 262–64, 263f, 267–89, 290–92, 293–94, 298–301, 332–33, 335–36, 352–53, 354–55
Gonzaga, Francisca (Chiquina), 174–76, 284–85

Gossec, François-Joseph, 69–70
gramophone, 53–55, 183, 211, 255–56
Gran Opera, 142–44
Grétry, André, 68–69, 248–49, 255–56
Grieg, Edvard, 54–55, 335–36, 342–43, 345
Guanabarino, Oscar, 83–84, 87–88
guitars, 54–55, 161–62

habanera, 128, 158–60, 161–63, 172–73, 187,
    311–12, 318–19
Hannick, Agnes, 286–87
Hanoi, 237–39
Haussman, Georges-Eugène, 48–51
Havana, 2–3, 37–38, 42–43, 121–23, 161, 193–
    94, 198–99, 227–28, 237–39, 270–71
Haydn, Joseph, 78, 81–82, 84–85, 92–93
Henry the VIII, 334–35
Herder, Johann Gottfried, 21
heterogeneous, 1–2, 17–18, 55–56, 71–72,
    73–74, 121, 138–39, 142–44, 148–49,
    150–51, 157, 158, 163–64, 167–68, 181–
    82, 194–96, 201, 214, 230–32, 239–40,
    248–49, 257–58, 284–85, 293–94, 309–10,
    322, 327–28, 331–32, 333, 337–38, 349–
    50, 355–56
hip-hop, 23–24, 204, 205–6
Hugo, Victor, 151–52, 184, 265, 271–72
hybridity, 1–2, 12–13

Il barbiere di Siviglia, 234–35
Il Guarany (see also O Guarany), 18–19, 33–34,
    233–35, 262–64, 269–94, 276*f*–80*f*, 298–
    301, 341, 354–55
Il Pagliacci, 233–34
Il Saldunes, 339–40, 341
Il Trovatore, 33–34, 233–34
imperialism, 2–3, 21–22, 27–32, 40, 44–45, 73,
    95–96, 240–41
Instituto Nacional de Música, 87–88, 134–35,
    230–31, 271–73, 328–29, 332–34, 335–37,
    339–40, 343–44
intermedialism, 218–19
Isabel, Princess, 58, 61–63, 149–50
Italian opera, 18–19, 83–84, 235–40, 241–42,
    243–46, 258–59, 283–84, 323–24, 330–31,
    336–37, 339–40
Italy, 47–48, 81–82, 92, 97–98, 108, 123–24,
    198–99, 202, 211, 212–14, 227–28, 234–35,
    237–40, 244–46, 253, 270–71, 272–73,
    281–82, 295–97, 342–43

jaleo, 161–62
Jardim do Guarda Velha, 148–49

jazz, 23–24
Jommelli, Niccolò, 85
Jones, Sidney, 221–22, 308–9
jongo, 310–11
jota, 128, 162–63, 304–7, 310–11
Junior, Costa, 215–17, 308–9

K-pop, 23–24
Kabbalah, 106–8
Kant, Immanuel, 21
Kardec, Allan, 106–8
Karr, Alphonse, 104–5
King, Roxy, 286–87
Kleffel, Arno, 342–43
Königliche Akademie der Künste, 342–43

"La Batingnolles," 118
La Bohème, 233–34, 295, 324
La damnation of Faust, 333
L'Africaine, 234–35, 237–39, 275–78
La Gioconda, 234–35, 324
La Gran Via, 127–28
L'Ambassadeur, 141–42
La Macarrona, 165–66
"La Marseillaise," 17, 33–34, 61–64, 62*f*, 66–75,
    102, 213–14, 251, 332–33
L'amor mouillé, 127
La Scala, 47–48, 270–71, 282–83
language, 1–20, 23, 26–27, 38–39, 47, 89–90,
    125–26, 129, 131–33, 141–47, 162–64, 170,
    173–74, 176, 185–86, 188–89, 192, 199–
    201, 202–8, 210–11, 219–20, 221, 227–28,
    230, 237–39, 253, 255, 264, 293–94, 301–2,
    321–22, 323, 333, 338, 339–40, 344–46
Latin America, 12–14, 37–38, 121–24, 134–35,
    307–8
Leccocq, Charles, 7–8, 55–56, 149–50
Lehár, Franz, 4, 7–8, 18, 33–34, 53–54, 55–56,
    121, 129, 193, 194–96, 197, 205, 206–7,
    210, 215–17, 221–25, 226–28, 230, 232,
    261–62
Le Mareille, Xavier, 115
Le roi de Lahore, 334–35
Les cloches de Corneville, 121, 154–56
Les Elkes, 312
Les Huguenots, 234–35, 237–39
"Les joyeux nègres," 308–9, 313–16
Lettered city, 141
Levy, Alexandre, 61–63, 332–33, 335–37
Liceo Musicale Santa, 342–43
Lindner, Adolpho, 123–24, 139–40, 149–50
Lino, Maria, 123–24, 154–56
Lisboa, Bernardo, 148–49

400 INDEX

Lisbon, 2–3, 4–5, 37–38, 47–48, 82–83, 109–10, 121–24, 141–46, 148–49, 151–52, 161–62, 170–71, 176, 187–88, 202, 207, 215–17, 237–40, 241–42, 324–26, 338, 339–40
Lisle, Claude Joseph Rouget de, 61–63, 62f, 66–67
Lohengrin, 323–26, 327, 330–31, 340
London, 2–3, 35–38, 42, 47–48, 111–12, 121–23, 127, 138–39, 147, 188–89, 192, 193–94, 202, 227–28, 237–40, 264, 270–71, 307–8, 354
Lo Schiavo, 149–50, 272
Lucca's publishing, 286–87
Lucia di Lammermoor, 234–35
lundu, 54–55, 148–49, 150–51, 152–53, 158, 167–68, 169–70, 173–74, 187–88
Lyra, Abdon, 187–88

Madrid, 2–3, 4–5, 35–38, 42, 121–24, 127–28, 141–44, 161–62, 193–94, 198–99, 227–28, 237–40, 241–42, 301–2, 308, 324–26
Magalhães, Geraldo, 7–8, 17–18, 167–72, 168f, 174–76, 177, 178–80, 182, 187–88, 266–67
Magalhães, José Gonçalves de, 266–67
Mahabarata, 106–8
Mahler, Gustav, 342–43
Maison Moderne, 135–36, 137–39, 137f, 169–70, 308–9
Mallarmé, Stéphane, 104–5
Manarezzi, Ana, 149–50
Manilla, 237–39
Many, Juanita, 142–44, 308–9
march, 61–63, 75, 102, 281–82, 297–98, 310–11, 313–17, 332–33, 334–35
Marconi, Francesco, 286–87
"Margarida vai a fonte," 176
Maria I, Queen, 76–77
Maria Tudor, 272
Marseille, 68, 73–74
Massenet, Jules, 55–56, 234–36, 324–26, 334–37, 342–43, 345
Matheus, Ismênia, 7–8, 213–14, 215–17, 219–21, 226
maxixe, 33–34, 130–31, 161–62, 164, 171–76, 172f, 224–25, 233–34, 249, 309–10, 316–17, 318–19
mechanical pianos, 53
Mello, Guilherme de, 88
Mello, Valentim de, 61–63
melodic knowingness, 254
melody, 16, 53–54, 83–84, 93–94, 118, 121–23, 127, 129, 131–34, 159–61, 163–64, 178–80, 186, 188, 205–7, 230, 232, 233–34,

249–59, 261–62, 274–75, 282–83, 285–86, 287–88, 291–92, 297–301, 312–16, 318–19, 330–32, 338
memorable (melody), 63–64, 68–71, 127, 128, 129, 133–34, 159–60, 186, 194–96, 248–51, 255–58, 260–61, 269–70, 274–75, 283–84, 285, 287–88, 292–93, 330–32, 333, 341, 346–47
Menezes, Cardoso de, 61–63
Méryss, Rose, 123–25
Mesquita, Carlos de, 334–35
Mesquita, Henrique Alves de, 271–72
mestiçagem, 177, 180–81, 241–42, 290–91, 310
mestiço, 80, 91, 93, 97, 163–64, 176, 177–78, 180–82, 185–86, 310–11
methodological cosmopolitanism, 25–26
methodological nationalism, 25–26, 347–49
Metropolitan Opera House, 237–39
Mexico City, 2–3, 4–5, 237–39, 308
Meyerbeer, 13–14, 55–56, 170, 234–35, 237–39, 275–78, 354–55
Miguez, Leopoldo, 7–8, 19, 64–67, 65f, 69, 83–84, 87–88, 142–44, 149–50, 272–73, 283–84, 286–87, 332–34, 335–37, 338–42
Milan, 37–38, 48, 237–39, 270–71, 272–73, 287–88, 333–34, 353–54
Milanez, Abdon, 149–50
Milano, Nicolino, 174–76, 284–85
Mililotti, Bice, 286–87
Minas Gerais, 190, 191f
Mirliton, 108–9
Mistérios do violão, 182–83, 184, 187–88, 308–9
modernista, 13–14
modernity, 1–2, 4–5, 17, 21–22, 27–31, 32–33, 34–38, 40, 44–45, 48–51, 52–53, 55–56, 58, 104–5, 114, 118, 119–20, 130, 139–40, 141, 146–47, 167–68, 177–78, 211–12, 214, 234–35, 312, 317, 320–21, 322, 328–29, 343–45, 350–51, 352–53
modinhas, 54–56, 85, 134–35, 151–52, 167–68, 169–70, 173–74, 177, 182–83
Moema, 352–53
Montevideo, 37–38, 41–43, 108, 123–24, 141–44, 161–62, 170, 193–94, 237–39, 241–42, 270–71
Montmartre, 17, 72, 100–2, 103–4, 108–9, 111, 113, 115–17, 119, 121, 183
Montmartre cabaret, 113
Montmartre chansons, 17
Montoya, Gabriel, 114, 115–17, 116f
Moraes, Mello Filho, 150–51, 161–62
Moraes, Prudente de, 103–4, 273–74
Morales, Melesio, 273–74

INDEX 401

Moreira, Luiz, 139–40, 284–85, 308–9
Moreno, Carmen Dauset (Carmensita), 141–42, 143*f*
Moretti, Franco, 3–4, 38, 129, 242–43, 245–46, 255, 292–93
Morosini, Giselda, 7–8, 197–99, 200*f*, 214–15, 226
Morris, William, 104–5
Motta, Vianna da, 336–37
Moulin Rouge, 48, 135–36, 136*f*, 137, 138–40, 141–42
movies, 4, 19, 39–40, 48–51, 52, 72, 114, 139–40, 147, 182, 211–14, 215–17, 218, 221–22, 225–26, 249, 267, 297
movies, silent, 19, 211–12, 297
movie theater, 4, 19, 48, 121–23, 126–27, 181–82, 211–13, 214–15, 222–23, 262–64, 284–85, 295–97, 301–2, 318–19, 337–38
moving scenes, 19, 295–97
Mozart Fluminense, 92–94
Mozart, Wolfgang Amadeus, 7–8, 33–34, 55–56, 78, 81–82, 84–85, 92–95, 185–86, 335–37, 354–55
"Muchacha," 151–52, 187–88, 304–7, 305*f*, 318–19
mulata, 164, 171–76, 172*f*
mulataria, 96–97
mulatismo, 93
mulatto, 8–9, 44, 53–54, 74–75, 89–91, 92–93, 94–95, 173–74, 177, 227–28, 290–91, 318–19
multilingualism, 18, 145–46, 202, 205, 206–8
Murat, Luis, 131
music business, 17–18, 32–33, 35–37, 55–56, 120, 185–86, 258–59, 313, 317, 327–28, 338
music of the future, 19, 321–22
musical circuit, 307–8
musical clichés, 16, 165–66, 172–73, 186, 194–96, 275–78, 283, 297, 298–302, 304–7, 321–22
musical familiar, 16, 275–78, 281–82
Musical Republic, 19, 64, 83–84, 236–37, 272–73, 283–84, 322, 333, 341–42, 354–55
musical work, 1, 4, 5–7, 13–14, 15–16, 18–19, 31–32, 33–34, 139–40, 141, 167–68, 247, 250–51, 257–58, 283, 289–90, 333–34
music hall, 4, 32–33, 48, 55–56, 69–70, 72, 111–12, 121–23, 135–36, 137–49, 150–51, 157, 158, 160–61, 167–69, 171–72, 178–80, 181–82, 185–90, 192, 205, 211–12, 213–14, 244–46, 249–50, 255–56, 284–85, 295, 297, 298–301, 308–10, 317, 318–19, 331–32, 337–38, 341–42
music historiography, 6–7, 25

Nabuco, Joaquim, 27–29

Naples, 51–52, 76–77, 333–34
Napoleão, Arthur, 308–9, 336–37
National Anthem, 60*f*, 354–55
nationalism, 1–2, 21, 25–29, 38–39, 44–45, 70–71, 98, 164–66, 191, 242–43, 244, 318, 321–22, 343–44, 347–49
nation-state, 10, 21, 22–23, 25–26, 30–31, 34–37, 205, 273–74, 320–21
naturalists, 104–5
Nella luna, 272
Nepomuceno, Alberto, 7–8, 13–14, 19, 68–69, 83–84, 87–88, 142–44, 335–37, 342–51, 342*f*–48*f*, 354
Neto, Coelho, 131
Neukomm, Sigismund, 78, 87–88, 92–93
Neves, Eduardo das, 7–8, 17–18, 178–80, 179*f*, 182, 183, 184–85, 191, 223–24, 226–27, 293, 303, 308–9, 318–19
New Orleans, 237–39, 290–91
New York, 2–3, 5–6, 35–38, 41–42, 48, 121–23, 141–42, 143*f*, 146–47, 149–50, 161, 193–94, 199–201, 214, 237–39, 248–49, 270–71, 273–74, 307–8, 310–11, 327
Ney, Paula, 131
Niteroi, 288–89
noble savage, 266–67, 269–70, 285, 290–91
Nouveau Cirque de Paris, 308–9, 312
Nunes, José, 174–76
Nunes, João, 284–85

Odeon, 54–55
Offenbach, Jacques, 69–70, 81–82, 149–50, 243–44, 251, 281–82
O Guarany (see also Il Guarany), 262–66, 267–70, 268*f*, 271–72, 281–82, 286–87, 288–89, 292–93
Oliveira, Benjamin de, 7–8, 187–88, 222–23, 224–25, 227–28, 229*f*, 262–64, 288–90, 290*f*, 293, 355–56
Oliveira, Cremilda de, 7–8, 198–99, 200*f*, 215–17, 219–20, 355–56
Oliveira, J. C. de, 131
"O mugunzá," 148–49, 151–53, 159–61, 162–63
opera, 13–14, 18–19, 54–56, 81–84, 85, 121, 129, 137–38, 121–23, 141–44, 149–50, 158, 168–69, 178–80, 188, 206–7, 210–11, 213–14, 233–51, 252–53, 255–64, 267–90, 291–94, 295–97, 298–301, 320–21, 323–29, 330–32, 333–37, 339–40, 342–43, 352–53, 354, 355
Opéra, 324–26, 340, 352
opera-comique, 81–82, 121–23

402 INDEX

operettas, 81–82, 83–84, 121, 123–24, 127, 129, 131, 140, 142–44, 158, 188, 193, 221–22, 226, 235–36, 271–72, 281–82, 283–85, 295, 323–24, 330–31, 340
Order and Progress, 43, 79–80, 84–85
Os Geraldos, 170–78, 187–88, 318–19
Os Guaranis, 262–64, 288–91, 293
Oswald, H., 335–37

Pacheco, Assis, 46, 201, 223–24, 227–28, 283–84
Paixão Cearense, Catulo da, 287–88
Palace Théatre, 137
Palestrina, Givanni Pierluigi, 335–36, 354–55
pandeiros, 161–62
pantomime, 109–10, 121, 129, 135–36, 149–50, 223–24, 262–64, 271–72, 275–78, 282–83, 288–90, 291–92, 297, 302
Paris, 2–3, 4–6, 35–38, 42, 47–51, 87–88, 92–93, 108, 111, 113, 115–17, 118, 121, 123–24, 134–35, 141–46, 154–56, 161–63, 167–68, 170–71, 172*f*, 173–74, 176–77, 183–85, 191, 193–94, 197–98, 211–12, 214, 235–36, 237–40, 264, 271–72, 304, 307–9, 312, 316–17, 333–37, 338–40, 341, 342–43, 352, 354, 355
Pão, pão, queijo, queijo, 130–31
Parisien (the), 170–71
Parque Fluminense, 141–42, 178–80, 308–9
Parque Rio Branco, 183
Parsifal, 324, 329, 336–37, 340
Passos, Francisco Oliveira, 352
Passos, Francisco Pereira, 48–51, 197–98, 352, 355
Passos, Guimarães, 131, 169–70
Passos, Pereira, 48–51, 197–98, 352, 355
Patrocínio, José do, 58, 131
Pavilhão Fluminense, 167–68
Pederneiras, Oscar, 152–53
Pedro I, D., 59–61, 76–77
Pedro II, D., 57–58, 59–61, 76–77, 170–71, 270–71, 272–73, 283–84, 338–39, 355
Peixoto, Marechal Floriano, 76–78, 79, 87–88, 189–90
Peladan, Sar, 106–8
Perez, Davide, 85
performance, 1–5, 6–7, 9–10, 12–14, 16–18, 26–27, 33–34, 37–38, 54–55, 59–64, 67, 68–74, 75, 76–78, 79–80, 83–85, 87–88, 93–94, 100–2, 108, 109–10, 111, 112–13, 114, 115–20, 121–24, 128–29, 130–33, 137, 138–49, 150–51, 152–53, 154–56, 157–60, 161–63, 164, 167–76, 177–81, 182, 183–84, 186–90, 192, 193–94,

197–99, 201, 205, 211–13, 214, 215–17, 218–20, 221, 222–23, 224–28, 232, 240–43, 244, 248–50, 254, 257–58, 259–61, 267, 273–74, 285, 290–91, 292–93, 295–98, 301–2, 311–12, 313, 318–19, 322–26, 330–31, 336–38, 340, 352–53
performance practices, 1–2, 3–4, 6–7, 9–10, 16, 17–18, 242–43
Petit Casino, 170–71
Phaeton, 334–35
Philadelphia, 42, 237–39, 310–11
phonograph, 39–40, 48–51, 53–55, 183, 211, 212–13
Pinheiro, Mário, 126–27, 287–88, 352–53
Pittsburgh, 237–39
Plaquette, Robert, 7–8, 55–56, 121–23, 129, 131–33
polka, 19, 33–34, 54–55, 128, 172–73, 187, 271–72, 281–83, 295, 297–302, 303–4, 309–10, 311–12, 313–17, 318–19, 337–38
Polonio, Cinira, 284–85
Porto Alegre, 89–90, 92–93, 170, 335–36
Portugal, 47–48, 51–52, 57, 76–77, 89–90, 92, 97–98, 108, 172–73, 176, 283–84, 338
Portugal, Marcos, 89–90
Praça da República, 121–23, 332–33
Praça Tiradentes, 100–2, 121, 161–62, 164, 167–68, 295
Privas, Xavier, 183–84, 185–86
progress, 16, 31, 40, 80, 104–5, 119–20, 140–41, 147–48, 153–54, 197–98, 321–22, 332–34, 338–39, 343–44, 352
Prometeus, 341–42
Puccini, Giacomo, 53–54, 55–56, 233–35, 237–40, 249, 285, 295, 302, 324–26, 327–28

Quaresma, Pedro, 133–34, 182–86, 188
Queiroz, Eça de, 284–85

race, 2–3, 6–7, 8–9, 27–29, 42–43, 44, 57, 74–75, 80, 83–84, 89–96, 97–99, 114, 119, 147–48, 153–56, 157–58, 160–61, 171–72, 174–76, 177–78, 180–81, 183–84, 221, 226–30, 271–72, 312, 317–18
racialized discourses, 91, 93–94, 163–64, 312–13, 318
racism, 30–31, 95–96
ragtimes, 308–9, 318–19
Ramas, Angel, 53
Ramayana, 106–8
realejo (see also barrel organ), 54–55, 233–34, 255–56, 260–62, 262*f*, 292–93
realists, 44, 104–5

INDEX 403

recording industry, 32–33, 287–88
Recreio Dramático, 108, 142–44, 284–85
Republic, 19, 43, 57–59, 59f, 61–63, 64–67,
  65f, 74, 76–77, 79, 80–81, 83–84, 91,
  93, 95, 103–4, 149–50, 226–27, 234–35,
  236–37, 272–73, 283–84, 290–92, 322–
  23, 324, 329, 332–33, 338–39, 341–42,
  343–44, 354–55
Republic of Letter, 64, 83–84
República Musical, 64, 83–84
republicanism, 17, 43, 57, 58, 59–64, 67, 70–71,
  73–75, 79–80, 83–85, 103–4
Requiem, 33–34, 76–78, 79–80, 85–88, 86f
revistas, 48–51, 56
rhythm, 16, 66, 93–94, 128, 130–31, 159–60,
  164–66, 172–73, 186–87, 205–7, 224, 253,
  278–81, 282–83, 297–301, 311–12, 316–17,
  318, 319
Ricordi, 257–58, 286–87
Rictus, Jehan, 183–84
Rienzi, 283–84, 324–26, 332–33
Rio de Janeiro, 1–3, 4–9, 14–15, 17–18, 19,
  27–29, 30–31, 37–42, 43–45, 46, 47–56,
  49f–51f, 58–59, 59f, 61–64, 67, 70, 72,
  73–75, 76, 79–80, 81–88, 89–91, 92–93,
  94–95, 100–4, 101f, 106–8, 107f, 110–13,
  114–19, 120, 121–24, 125–28, 129, 130–
  35, 137, 140–44, 146–48, 149–57, 158–66,
  167–69, 170–71, 172–92, 179f, 193–94,
  196–99, 201, 202–4, 205–7, 210, 211–14,
  215–17, 216f, 218, 219–20, 221–23,
  224–29, 230–32, 233–42, 243–47, 249–50,
  260–64, 265–74, 281–82, 283–85, 286–91,
  292–94, 295, 298–301, 299f–314f, 303–10,
  313–19, 322–26, 328–30, 331–40, 341–44,
  352–54
Rio, João do, 2–3, 8–9, 51–52, 54–55, 83–84,
  106–8, 107f, 112–13, 121–23, 126–28, 142–
  44, 164–66, 177, 184–86, 189–92, 197–99,
  206–7, 233–34, 249, 295, 303, 353–54
Risorgimento, 244, 272–73
rivista musicali, 272, 281–82
rock 'n' roll, 23–24
Rodrigues Barbosa, José, 77–78, 83–84
Rollinat, Maurice, 112–13
romantics, 44, 104–5
Rome, 2–3, 48, 121–23, 182, 333–34, 342–43
Romero, Sílvio, 80–81
"Ronda Infernale, Titania," 134–35
Rossini, Gioachino, 69–70, 81–82, 234–35,
  243–44, 251, 252–53, 257–59, 274–75,
  281–82, 334–35, 340, 354–55
Rousseau, Jean-Jacques, 58

Roydel, L., 115
Rua do Ouvidor, 53–54, 167–68
Ruiz, Pepa, 7–8, 108, 123–24, 125–26, 134–35,
  151–53, 152f, 154–56, 154f, 157, 162–63,
  173–74, 284–85, 298–301
Rushdie, Salman, 13, 346–47
Ruskin, John, 104–5
Russia, 48–51, 69–70, 123–24

Saint-George, Chevalier de, 93–95
Saint-Saëns, Camille, 55–56, 87–88, 214, 251–
  52, 302, 334–37, 342–43, 345
Salis, Rodolphe, 72, 108–9
Salvator Rosa, 272
samba, 180–81
Sampaio, Moreira, 127
Samson et Dalila, 234–35
Santos, Manoel Pedro dos, 154–56, 223–24
Santos-Dumont, Alberto, 191
San Toy, 308–9
Satie, Eric, 345
Scalvini, Antonio, 269–71, 272
Schiller, Friedrich, 271–72
Schoenberg, Arnold, 112, 342–43, 345, 351
Schola Cantorum, 342–43
Schubert, Franz, 335–36, 345
Schumann, Robert, 328–29, 335–37, 338
Second Empire, 48–51
Segreto, Paschoal, 135–36, 139–40, 141–42,
  147–48, 167–68, 169–70, 178–80, 284–85,
  308–9, 317
Se sa minga, 272, 281–83
Sgambatti, Giovanni, 342–43
shared experience, 18, 118–19, 138–39, 230,
  232, 318
shared urban experiences, 56
Silva Xavier, Joaquim José da, 57, 115, 183–84
Silva, Francisco Manuel da, 17, 57, 58–61, 60f,
  87–88, 149–50, 271–72, 354–55
Silva, Pereira da, 17, 271–72
singable, 159–60, 194–96, 287–88, 331–32,
  346–47
Sitte, Camillo, 104–5
slavery, 1–3, 17, 29, 30–31, 42–45, 58, 61–63,
  70–71, 73, 74–75, 80, 88–91, 95–96, 97–98,
  147–48, 149–50, 153–54, 265–66, 310–11,
  332–33, 355
social Darwinism, 44, 58, 80
Sociedade de Concertos Populare, 336–37
songful and memorable, 68–71, 127, 128, 129,
  133–34, 248–51, 257–58, 260–61, 274–75,
  283, 285, 330–31
songfulness, 68, 69, 75

404 INDEX

sonic ethos, 53–54
sonic flânerie, 114
Sousa, Ernesto de, 61–63
Sousa, John Phillip de, 308–9
South Africa, 23–24, 188–89
Spanish-ness, 141–42, 161–63, 275–78, 298–301, 304–7
Spencer, Herbert, 58
stage Bahiana, 152–64, 172–74
Steilen, Théophile, 108–9
Stravinsky, Igor, 275–78
Swedenborg, Emanuel, 106–8
Switzerland, 71–72
symbolism, 67, 68–69, 79–80, 115–17, 219–20, 354–55
symbolists, 44, 104–5, 112–13
syncopations, 130–31, 161–63, 172–73, 311–12, 313–17, 318
São Paulo, 123–24, 141–42, 170, 176, 191, 193, 217, 218, 267
São Pedro de Alcantara, 137

tango, 54–55, 149–50, 151–52, 158–60, 161–63, 171–73, 211, 318–19
tango brasileiro, 172–73
tango-chula, 171–73
Tannhäuser, 33–34, 323–26, 327, 329, 330–31
Taunay, Visconde Alfredo d'Escragnolle, 78, 84–85, 87–88, 91, 92–93, 264–65, 267, 338–39
Tavares, Adelmar, 187–88
technology, 1, 2–5, 18, 27–30, 39–40, 117–18, 182, 211–13, 214–17, 218–19, 220, 221–22, 223–24, 240–41, 243–44, 249, 251, 254–56, 273–74, 327–28
Teixeira, Nina, 170–72, 173–76, 175*f*, 178–80
Teixeira, Orlando, 130–31
telephone, 39–40, 48–51
Teutonic universalism, 82–83, 93
Théâtre Marigny, 170–71
Theatro Apollo, 46, 125–26, 137, 201, 207, 215–17, 219–20, 284–85, 355–56
Theatro Carlos Gomes, 137, 284–85
Theatro Eudorado, 134–35
Theatro Ginásio Dramático, 271–72
Theatro Lucinda, 134–35, 137
Theatro Lyrico, 64, 111–12, 137, 212–13, 214, 244–45, 323, 332–33, 335–37, 339–40
Theatro Municipal, 4, 19–20, 197–99, 244–45, 352–53, 353*f*, 354, 355–56
Theatro Recreio Dramatico, 108, 123–24, 125–26, 284–85
Theatro Santanna, 284–85

Theatro São José, 137
Theatro São Pedro, 295
Theatro Variedades, 123–24, 135–36, 149–50
Thèbes, Madame de, 106–8
Thereza Christina Maria, D., 76–77
Third Republic, 57–58
Thomas, Ambroise, 338–39
The Meistersingers, 329
The Merry Widow, 4, 18, 33–34, 53–55, 121–23, 182, 193–98, 195*f*–208*f*, 199–201, 202, 205–7, 210–11, 214–17, 216*f*, 218, 219–32, 225*f*, 261–62, 285, 290–91, 355–56
Tia Ciata, 153–54
Tim tim por tim tim, 151–53, 162–63
Tin Pan Alley, 248–49
Tiradentes, 57, 79, 95, 100–2, 121, 161–62, 164, 167–68, 295
Toledo, Demetrio de, 102, 130–31
Tosca, 53–54, 233–35, 283–84, 324
Toulouse-Lautrec, Henri de, 108–9
transcription, 259–60, 327
transcultural, 12–13, 70–71
transnational, 11–12, 70–71
tresillo, 128, 159–60
Tristan and Isolde, 324
Turkey, 48–51
typewriter, 53–54

Un ballo in maschera, 233–34, 249–50
unisonance, 63–64
United States, 31–32, 35–38, 39–41, 42, 48–51, 57, 58, 113, 121–24, 134–35, 141–42, 149–50, 154–56, 157, 161–62, 163–64, 167–69, 172–73, 177, 180–81, 198–99, 212–13, 221, 227–28, 237–39, 267–69, 286–88, 307–9, 316–17, 323, 324–26, 327, 349–50
universalism, 30–31, 33–34, 44, 57, 67, 70, 73–74, 82–83, 93
urban bourgeoisie, 31, 48–51, 236–37, 249–51
urban experience, 34–35, 52–53, 56, 118–19, 254–55, 331–32
urban landscape, 51–52
urban modernity, 1, 17, 34–37, 48–51, 52, 56, 146–47, 211–12, 214, 317
urban network, 14–15, 17, 19, 33–39, 44–45, 147–48, 174–76, 210, 242–43, 274–75, 298–301, 312
urbanscape, 27–29
urban sonic cosmopolitanism, 56

Valle, M. del, 123–24
Valsa espanhola, 298–301, 313–16

INDEX   405

Valsa sertaneja, 298–301
"Valse des cloches de Corneville," 121–23, 127–28
"Valse d'Ousieux," 127–28
Varney, Louis, 7–8, 55–56, 127, 129, 131, 149–50, 168–69
Vaucaire, Maurice, 115
Vedha, 106–8
"Vem cá mulata," 171–76, 172*f*
Verdi, Giuseppe, 7–8, 33–34, 53–54, 55–56, 81–82, 170, 171–72, 233–35, 237–40, 249–50, 258–62, 270–71, 274–78, 283–85, 286, 292–93, 302, 323–26, 335–36, 354–55
Verlaine, Paul, 104–5
Verne, Jules, 47
Vicenzo, Cernicchiaro, 83–84, 335–36
Victor, 54–55, 127, 151–52, 184, 193, 287–88
"Vieni sul mare," 190
Vienna, 2–3, 193–94, 121–23, 222–23, 226–29, 270–71, 333–34
Villiot, Rose, 149–50
viola, 161–62
violin, 53–55, 96–97, 123–24, 127–28, 197, 282–83, 336–37, 341
"Vissi d'arte, 233–34, 249, 285
Voltaire, François-Marie, 58

Wagner, Richard, 7–8, 19, 33–34, 35–37, 55–56, 78, 81–82, 283–84, 302, 320–29, 330–33, 334–38, 339–42, 345, 354–55

Waldteufe, Émile, 297–301
waltz, 54–55, 115, 121–23, 126–28, 129, 131–33, 158, 187–88, 196–97, 206–7, 295, 298–301, 304–7, 309–10, 319
Waltzertraum, 54–55
Waltz-songs, 129
Weber, Carl, 13–14, 334–36, 337–38
Werther, 234–35
whiteness, 91, 93–94, 95–96, 98, 160–61, 185–86, 228–30, 232, 312–13
Wilde, Oscar, 104–5
Willette, Adolphe, 108–9
Williams, Bert, 180–81
wind band, 53–54, 188, 230–32, 255–56, 330–31
Winter Garden, 48
world literature, 10
World War I, 39–40, 154–56, 333–34

Xanrof, Léon, 114, 117

Yann-Nibor, 115
Ywonna, Mlle., 7–8, 17–18, 72, 100–13, 101*f*, 114–20, 121–28, 129, 130–33, 134–35, 139–40, 151–53, 154–56, 159–60, 178–80, 183–84, 186, 192

zarzuela, 69–70, 123–24, 127–28, 129, 149–50, 158, 161–62, 284–85
Zola, Émile, 104–5